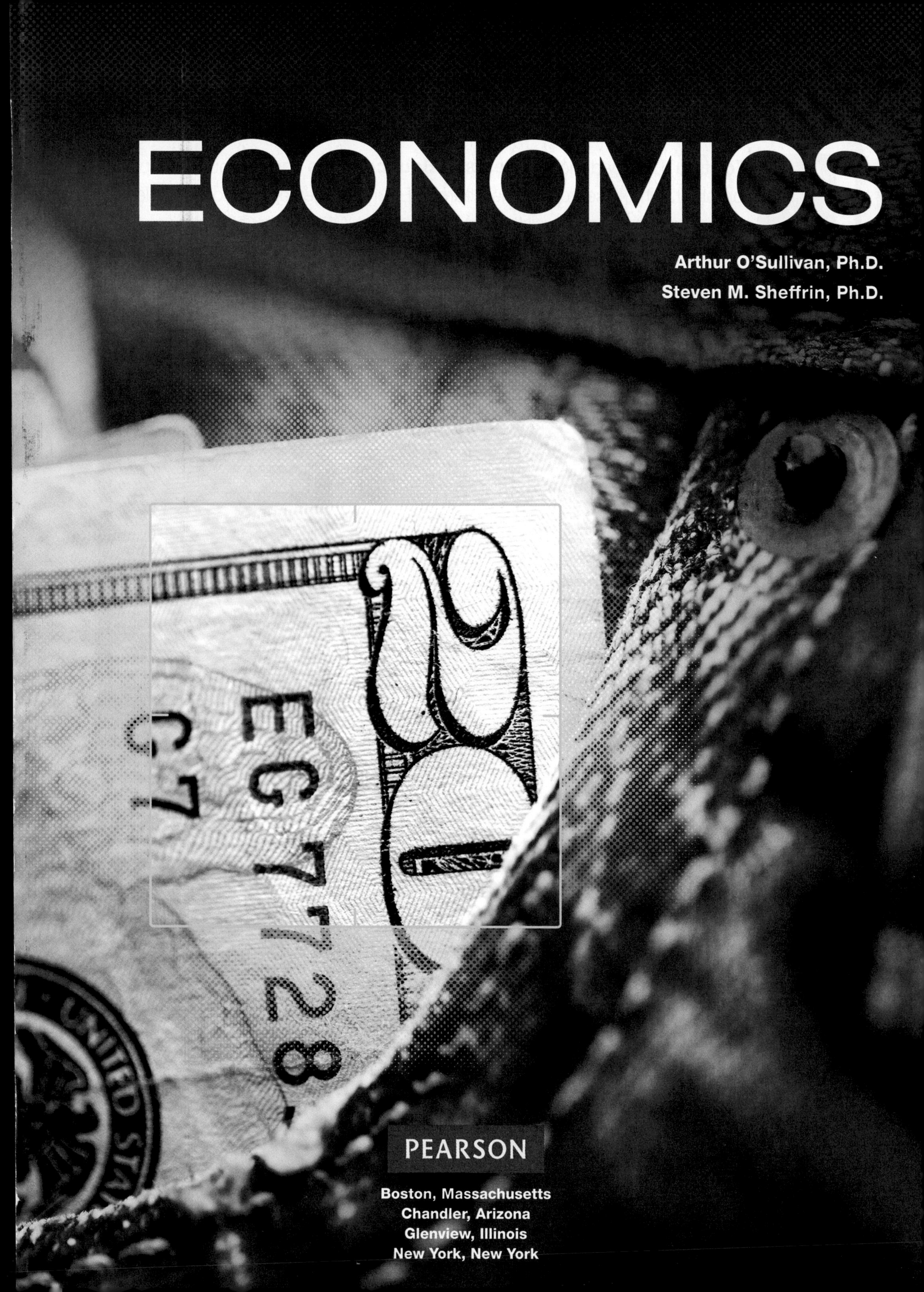

ECONOMICS

Arthur O'Sullivan, Ph.D.

Steven M. Sheffrin, Ph.D.

PEARSON

Boston, Massachusetts
Chandler, Arizona
Glenview, Illinois
New York, New York

Social Studies Reimagined

To start, download the free **Pearson BouncePages** app on your smartphone or tablet. Simply search for the Pearson BouncePages app in your mobile app store. The app is available for Android and IOS (iPhone®/iPad®).

Make your book come alive!

Activate your digital course interactivities directly from the page.

To launch the myStory video look for this icon.

To activate more interactivities look for this icon. ▶ **Interactive**

1. **AIM** the camera over the image so it is easily viewable on your screen.

2. **TAP** the screen to scan the page.

3. **BOUNCE** the page to life by clicking the icon.

tap screen to scan

Cover Image: Money in pocket. Oxford/Getty Images

Acknowledgments appear at the end of the book, which constitute an extension of this copyright page.

ISBN-13: 978-0-13-330693-4
ISBN-10:   0-13-330693-3

[Authors]

Arthur O'Sullivan, Ph.D.

Arthur O'Sullivan is a Professor of Economics at Lewis and Clark College in Portland, Oregon, where he teaches microeconomics and urban economics. After receiving his B.S. degree in economics at the University of Oregon, he spent two years in the Peace Corps, working with city planners in the Philippines. He received his Ph.D. degree in economics from Princeton University in 1981 and has taught at the University of California, Davis, and Oregon State University. Professor O'Sullivan's research explores economic issues concerning urban land use, environmental protection, and public policy. His articles appear in many economics journals, including the *Journal of Urban Economics*, the *Journal of Environmental Economics and Management*, the *National Tax Journal*, the *Journal of Public Economics*, and the *Journal of Law and Economics*.

Steven M. Sheffrin, Ph.D.

Steven M. Sheffrin is Professor of Economics and Director of the Murphy Institute at Tulane University in New Orleans. Previously, he was Dean of the Division of Social Sciences and Professor of Economics at the University of California, Davis. He has been a visiting professor at Nuffield College, University of Oxford; the London School of Economics and Political Science; Princeton University; and Nanyang Technological University, Singapore. He holds a BA from the College of Social Sciences, Wesleyan University, and a Ph.D. in economics from Massachusetts Institute of Technology. Professor Sheffrin is the author of numerous books and articles in the fields of macroeconomics, public finance, and international economics.

[Program Consultant]

Dr. Kathy Swan is an Associate Professor of Curriculum and Instruction at the University of Kentucky. Her research focuses on standards-based technology integration, authentic intellectual work, and documentary-making in the social studies classroom. Swan has been a four-time recipient of the National Technology Leadership Award in Social Studies Education. She is also the advisor for the Social Studies Assessment, Curriculum, and Instruction Collaborative (SSACI) at CCSSO.

[Program Partners]

NBC Learn, the educational arm of NBC News, develops original stories for use in the classroom and makes archival NBC News stories, images, and primary source documents available on demand to teachers, students, and parents. NBC Learn partnered with Pearson to produce the myStory videos that support this program.

Constitutional Rights Foundation is a nonprofit, nonpartisan organization focused on educating students about the importance of civic participation in a democratic society. Constitutional Rights Foundation is the lead contributor to the development of the Civic Discussion Topic Inquiries for this program. Constitutional Rights Foundation is also the provider of the Civic Action Project (CAP) for the *Economics* and *Magruder's American Government* programs. CAP is a project-based learning model for civics, government, and economics courses.

Pearson Economics was developed especially for you and your students. The story of its creation began with a three-day Innovation Lab in which teachers, historians, students, and authors came together to imagine our ideal Social Studies teaching and learning experiences. We refined the plan with a series of teacher roundtables that shaped this new approach to ensure your students' mastery of content and skills. A dedicated team, made up of Pearson authors, content experts, and social studies teachers, worked to bring our collective vision into reality. Kathy Swan, Professor of Education and architect of the new College, Career, and Civic Life (C3) Framework, served as our expert advisor on curriculum and instruction.

Pearson would like to extend a special thank you to all of the teachers who helped guide the development of this program. We gratefully acknowledge your efforts to realize Next Generation Social Studies teaching and learning that will prepare American students for college, careers, and active citizenship.

[Program Advisors]

Campaign for the Civic Mission of Schools is a coalition of over 70 national civic learning, education, civic engagement, and business groups committed to improving the quality and quantity of civic learning in American schools. The Campaign served as an advisor on this program.

Buck Institute for Education is a nonprofit organization dedicated to helping teachers implement the effective use of Project-Based Learning in their classrooms. Buck Institute staff consulted on the Project-Based Learning Topic Inquiries for this program.

[Program Academic Consultants]

Barbara Brown
Director of Outreach
College of Arts and Sciences
African Studies Center
Boston University
Boston, Massachusetts

William Childs
Professor of History Emeritus
The Ohio State University
Columbus, Ohio

Jennifer Giglielmo
Associate Professor of History
Smith College
Northhampton, Massachusetts

Joanne Connor Green
Professor, Department Chair
Political Science
Texas Christian University
Fort Worth, Texas

Ramdas Lamb, Ph.D.
Associate Professor of Religion
University of Hawaii at Manoa
Honolulu, Hawaii

Huping Ling
Changjiang Scholar Chair Professor
Professor of History
Truman State University
Kirksville, Missouri

Jeffery Long, Ph.D.
Professor of Religion and Asian Studies
Elizabethtown College
Elizabethtown, Pennsylvania

Gordon Newby
Professor of Islamic, Jewish and
   Comparative Studies
Department of Middle Eastern and
   South Asian Studies
Emory University
Atlanta, Georgia

Mark Peterson
Associate Professor
Department of Asian and Near Eastern
   Languages
Brigham Young University
Provo, Utah

William Pitts
Professor, Department of Religion
Baylor University
Waco, Texas

Benjamin Ravid
Professor Emeritus of Jewish History
Department of Near Eastern and
   Judaic Studies
Brandeis University
Waltham, Massachusetts

Harpreet Singh
College Fellow
Department of South Asian Studies
Harvard University
Cambridge, Massachusetts

Christopher E. Smith, J.D., Ph.D.
Professor
Michigan State University
MSU School of Criminal Justice
East Lansing, Michigan

John Voll
Professor of Islamic History
Georgetown University
Washington, D.C.

Michael R. Wolf
Associate Professor
Department of Political Science
Indiana University-Purdue University
   Fort Wayne
Fort Wayne, Indiana

Social studies is more than dots on a map or dates on a timeline. It's where we've been and where we're going. It's stories from the past and our stories today. And in today's fast-paced, interconnected world, it's essential.

Welcome to the next generation of social studies!

Pearson's new social studies program was created in collaboration with educators, social studies experts, and students. The program is based on Pearson's Mastery System. The System uses tested best practices, content expectations, technology, and a four-part framework—Connect, Investigate, Synthesize, and Demonstrate—to prepare students to be college-and-career ready.

The System includes:

- Higher-level content that gives support to access complex text, acquire core content knowledge, and tackle rigorous questions.
- Inquiry-focused Projects, Civic Discussions, and Document Analysis activities that develop content and skills mastery in preparation for real-world challenges;
- Digital content on Pearson Realize that is dynamic, flexible, and uses the power of technology to bring social studies to life.
- The program uses essential questions and stories to increase long-term understanding and retention of learning.

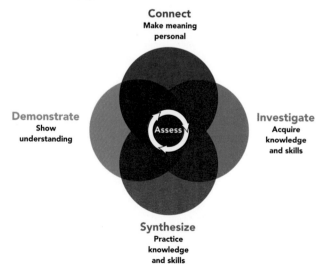

Connect
Make meaning personal

Demonstrate
Show understanding

Assess

Investigate
Acquire knowledge and skills

Synthesize
Practice knowledge and skills

» **Go online to learn more and see the program overview video.**

PEARSON
realize™

The digital course on Realize!

The program's digital course on Realize puts rich and engaging content, embedded assessments with instant data, and flexible tools at your fingertips.

CONNECT! Begin the Pearson Mastery System by engaging in the topic story and connecting it to your own lives.

Preview—Each Topic opens with the Enduring Understandings section, allowing you to preview expected learning outcomes.

>> Instruction begins with an **Essential Question**. These thought-provoking questions engage students and introduce the Topic.

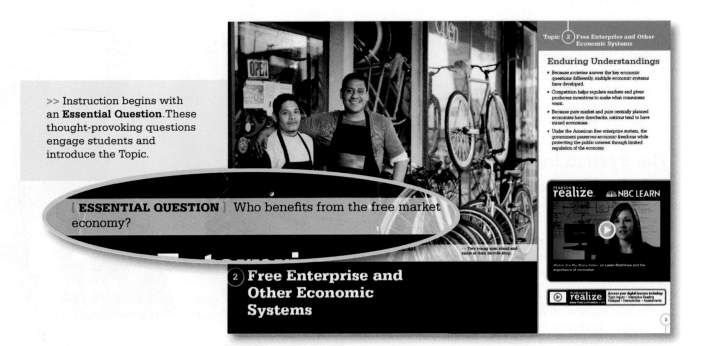

Topic 2 Free Enterprise and Other Economic Systems

Enduring Understandings

- Because societies answer the key economic questions differently, multiple economic systems have developed.
- Competition helps regulate markets and gives producers incentives to make what consumers want.
- Because pure market and pure centrally planned economies have drawbacks, nations tend to have mixed economies.
- Under the American free enterprise system, the government preserves economic freedom while protecting the public interest through limited regulation of the economy.

[**ESSENTIAL QUESTION**] Who benefits from the free market economy?

2 **Free Enterprise and Other Economic Systems**

Watch the My Story Video on Leslie Bradshaw and the importance of innovation.

Watch the My Story Video on Leslie Bradshaw and the importance of innovation.

Developed in partnership with NBCLearn, the **My Story** videos help students connect to the Topic content by hearing the personal story of an individual whose life is related to the content students are about to learn.

INVESTIGATE! Step two of the Mastery System allows you to investigate the topic story through a number of engaging features as you learn the content.

>> **Active Classroom Strategies** integrated in the daily lesson plans help to increase in-class participation, raise energy levels and attentiveness, all while engaging in the story. These 5-15 minute activities have you use what you have learned to draw, write, speak, and decide.

>> **Interactive Primary Source Galleries:** Use primary source image galleries throughout the lesson to see, analyze, and interact with images that tie to the topic story content.

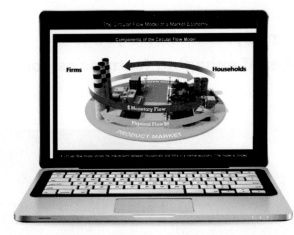

>> Feel like you are a part of the story with **interactive 3-D models**.

>> Continue to investigate the topic story through **dynamic interactive charts, graphs, and illustrations**. Build skills while covering the essential standards.

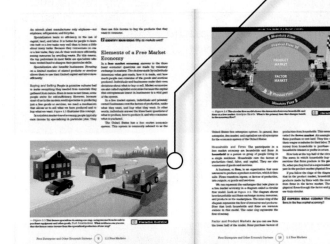

>> Learn content by reading narrative text online or in a printed Student Edition.

Synthesize: Practice Knowledge and Skills

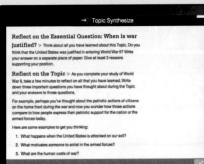

SYNTHESIZE!

In step three of the Mastery System, pause to reflect on what you learn and revisit an essential question.

DEMONSTRATE! The final step of the Mastery System is to demonstrate understanding of the text.

PEARSON realize™

>> The digital course on Realize! The program's digital course on Realize puts engaging content, embedded assessments, instant data, and flexible tools at your fingertips.

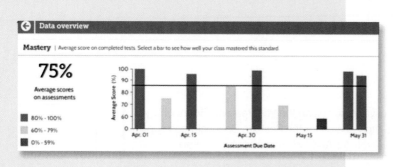

>> Assessment. At the end of each lesson and topic, demonstrate understanding through Lesson Quizzes, Topic Tests, and Topic Inquiry performance assessments. The System provides remediation and enrichment recommendations based on your individual performance towards mastery.

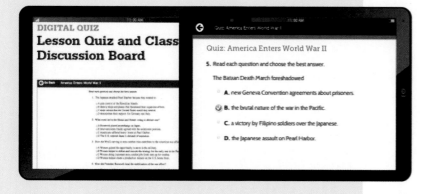

>> Class and Data features on Realize make it easy to see your mastery data.

 To activate your digital course interactivities download the free **Pearson BouncePages** app on your smartphone or tablet. Simply search for the Pearson BouncePages app in your mobile app store. The app is available for Android and IOS (iPhone®/iPad®).

TOPIC **4**   Competition and Market Structures   126

TOPIC 10   Trade, Development, and Globalization   388

Many types of digital resources help you investigate the topics in this course. You'll find biographies, primary sources, maps, and more. These resources will help bring the topics to life.

Core Concepts

 ## Culture

- What Is Culture?
- Families and Societies
- Language
- Religion
- The Arts
- Cultural Diffusion and Change
- Science and Technology

 ## Economics

- Economics Basics
- Economic Process
- Economic Systems
- Economic Development
- Trade
- Money Management

 ## Geography

- The Study of Earth
- Geography's Five Themes
- Ways to Show Earth's Surface
- Understanding Maps

- Earth in Space
- Time and Earth's Rotation
- Forces on Earth's Surface
- Forces Inside Earth
- Climate and Weather
- Temperature
- Water and Climate
- Air Circulation and Precipitation
- Types of Climate
- Ecosystems
- Environment and Resources
- Land Use
- People's Impact on the Environment
- Population
- Migration
- Urbanization

 ## Government and Civics

- Foundations of Government
- Political Systems
- Political Structures
- Conflict and Cooperation
- Citizenship

History

- How Do Historians Study History?
- Measuring Time
- Historical Sources
- Archaeology and Other Sources
- Historical Maps

Personal Finance

- Your Fiscal Fitness: An Introduction
- Budgeting
- Checking
- Investments
- Savings and Retirement
- Credit and Debt
- Risk Management
- Consumer Smarts
- After High School
- Taxes and Income

Landmark Supreme Court Cases

- *Korematsu* v. *United States*
- *Marbury* v. *Madison*
- *McCulloch* v. *Maryland*
- *Gibbons* v. *Ogden*
- *Worcester* v. *Georgia*
- *Dred Scott* v. *Sandford*
- *Plessy* v. *Ferguson*
- *Schenck* v. *United States*
- *Brown* v. *Board of Education*
- *Engel* v. *Vitale*

- *Sweatt* v. *Painter*
- *Mapp* v. *Ohio*
- *Hernandez* v. *Texas*
- *Gideon* v. *Wainright*
- *Wisconsin* v. *Yoder*
- *Miranda* v. *Arizona*
- *White* v. *Regester*
- *Tinker* v. *Des Moines School District*
- *Roe* v. *Wade*

- *Baker* v. *Carr*
- *Grutter* v. *Bollinger*
- *Edgewood* v. *Kirby*
- *Texas* v. *Johnson*
- *National Federation of Independent Businesses et al.* v. *Sebelius et al.*
- *Mendez* v. *Westminster* and *Delgado* v. *Bastrop*

Interactive Primary Sources

- Code of Hammurabi
- Psalm 23
- The Republic, Plato
- Politics, Aristotle
- Edicts, Asoka
- Analects, Confucius
- First Letter to the Corinthians, Paul
- The Quran
- The Magna Carta
- Travels, Ibn Battuta
- The Destruction of the Indies, Bartolomé de Las Casas
- Mayflower Compact
- English Petition of Right
- English Bill of Rights
- Two Treatises of Government, John Locke
- The Spirit of Laws, Baron de Montesquieu
- The Social Contract, Jean-Jacques Rousseau
- The Interesting Narrative of the Life of Olaudah Equiano
- "Give Me Liberty or Give Me Death," Patrick Henry
- "Remember the Ladies," Abigail Adams
- Common Sense, Thomas Paine
- Declaration of Independence
- Virginia Declaration of Rights
- Virginia Statute for Religious Freedom, Thomas Jefferson
- "To His Excellency, General Washington," Phillis Wheatley
- Articles of Confederation
- Anti-Federalist Papers
- The Federalist No. 10, James Madison
- The Federalist No. 39, James Madison
- The Federalist No. 51
- The Federalist No. 78, Alexander Hamilton
- Northwest Ordinance
- Iroquois Constitution
- Declaration of the Rights of Man and the Citizen
- Farewell Address, George Washington
- Mexican Federal Constitution of 1824
- State Colonization Law of 1825

- Law of April 6, 1830
- Debate Over Nullification, Webster and Calhoun
- Turtle Bayou Resolutions
- Democracy in America, Alexis de Tocqueville
- 1836 Victory or Death Letter from the Alamo, Travis
- Texas Declaration of Independence
- Declaration of Sentiments and Resolutions
- "Ain't I a Woman?," Sojourner Truth
- Uncle Tom's Cabin, Harriet Beecher Stowe
- "A House Divided," Abraham Lincoln
- First Inaugural Address, Abraham Lincoln
- Declaration of Causes: February 2, 1861
- Emancipation Proclamation, Abraham Lincoln
- Gettysburg Address, Abraham Lincoln
- Second Inaugural Address, Abraham Lincoln
- "I Will Fight No More Forever," Chief Joseph
- How the Other Half Lives, Jacob Riis
- The Pledge of Allegiance
- Preamble to the Platform of the Populist Party
- Atlanta Exposition Address, Booker T. Washington
- The Jungle, Upton Sinclair
- Hind Swaraj, Mohandas Gandhi
- The Fourteen Points, Woodrow Wilson
- Two Poems, Langston Hughes
- Four Freedoms, Franklin D. Roosevelt
- Anne Frank: The Diary of a Young Girl, Anne Frank
- Charter of the United Nations
- Universal Declaration of Human Rights
- Autobiography, Kwame Nkrumah
- Inaugural Address, John F. Kennedy
- Silent Spring, Rachel Carson
- "I Have a Dream," Martin Luther King, Jr.
- "Letter From Birmingham Jail," Martin Luther King, Jr.
- "Tear Down This Wall," Ronald Reagan
- "Freedom From Fear," Aung San Suu Kyi
- "Glory and Hope," Nelson Mandela

Biographies

- Abigail Adams
- John Adams
- John Quincy Adams
- Samuel Adams
- James Armistead
- Crispus Attucks
- Moses Austin
- Stephen F. Austin
- James A. Baker III
- William Blackstone
- Simón Bolívar
- Napoleon Bonaparte
- Chief Bowles
- Omar Bradley
- John C. Calhoun
- César Chávez
- Wentworth Cheswell
- George Childress
- Winston Churchill
- Henry Clay
- Bill Clinton
- Jefferson Davis
- Martin De León
- Green DeWitt
- Dwight Eisenhower
- James Fannin
- James L. Farmer, Jr.
- Benjamin Franklin
- Milton Friedman
- Betty Friedan
- Bernardo de Gálvez
- Hector P. Garcia
- John Nance Garner
- King George III
- Henry B. González
- Raul A. Gonzalez, Jr.
- Mikhail Gorbachev
- William Goyens

- Ulysses S. Grant
- José Gutiérrez de Lara
- Alexander Hamilton
- Hammurabi
- Warren Harding
- Friedrich Hayek
- Jack Coffee Hays
- Patrick Henry
- Adolf Hitler
- Oveta Culp Hobby
- James Hogg
- Sam Houston
- Kay Bailey Hutchison
- Andrew Jackson
- John Jay
- Thomas Jefferson
- Lyndon B. Johnson
- Anson Jones
- Barbara Jordan
- Justinian
- John F. Kennedy
- John Maynard Keynes
- Martin Luther King, Jr.
- Marquis de Lafayette
- Mirabeau B. Lamar
- Robert E. Lee
- Abraham Lincoln
- John Locke
- James Madison
- John Marshall
- George Marshall
- Karl Marx
- George Mason
- Mary Maverick
- Jane McCallum
- Joseph McCarthy
- James Monroe
- Charles de

- Montesquieu
- Edwin W. Moore
- Moses
- Benito Mussolini
- José Antonio Navarro
- Chester A. Nimitz
- Richard M. Nixon
- Barack Obama
- Sandra Day O'Connor
- Thomas Paine
- Quanah Parker
- Rosa Parks
- George Patton
- John J. Pershing
- John Paul II
- Sam Rayburn
- Ronald Reagan
- Hiram Rhodes Revels
- Franklin D. Roosevelt
- Theodore Roosevelt
- Lawrence Sullivan Ross
- Haym Soloman
- Antonio Lopez de Santa Anna
- Phyllis Schlafly
- Erasmo Seguín
- Juan N. Seguín
- Roger Sherman
- Adam Smith
- Joseph Stalin
- Raymond L. Telles
- Alexis de Tocqueville
- Hideki Tojo
- William B. Travis
- Harry Truman
- Lech Walesa
- Mercy Otis Warren
- George Washington

- Daniel Webster
- Lulu Belle Madison White
- William Wilberforce
- James Wilson
- Woodrow Wilson
- Lorenzo de Zavala
- Mao Zedong

21st Century Skills

- Identify Main Ideas and Details
- Set a Purpose for Reading
- Use Context Clues
- Analyze Cause and Effect
- Categorize
- Compare and Contrast
- Draw Conclusions
- Draw Inferences
- Generalize
- Make Decisions
- Make Predictions
- Sequence
- Solve Problems
- Summarize
- Analyze Media Content
- Analyze Primary and Secondary Sources
- Compare Viewpoints
- Distinguish Between Fact and Opinion
- Identify Bias
- Analyze Data and Models

- Analyze Images
- Analyze Political Cartoons
- Create Charts and Maps
- Create Databases
- Read Charts, Graphs, and Tables
- Read Physical Maps
- Read Political Maps
- Read Special-Purpose Maps
- Use Parts of a Map
- Ask Questions
- Avoid Plagiarism
- Create a Research Hypothesis
- Evaluate Web Sites
- Identify Evidence
- Identify Trends
- Interpret Sources
- Search for Information on the Internet
- Synthesize
- Take Effective Notes
- Develop a Clear Thesis
- Organize Your Ideas

- Support Ideas With Evidence
- Evaluate Existing Arguments
- Consider & Counter Opposing Arguments
- Give an Effective Presentation
- Participate in a Discussion or Debate
- Publish Your Work
- Write a Journal Entry
- Write an Essay
- Share Responsibility
- Compromise
- Develop Cultural Awareness
- Generate New Ideas
- Innovate
- Make a Difference
- Work in Teams
- Being an Informed Citizen
- Paying Taxes
- Political Participation
- Serving on a Jury
- Voting

Atlas

- United States: Political
- United States: Physical
- World Political
- World Physical
- World Climate
- World Ecosystems
- World Population Density
- World Land Use
- North Africa and Southwest Asia: Political
- North Africa and Southwest Asia: Physical
- Sub-Saharan Africa: Political
- Sub-Saharan Africa: Physical
- South Asia: Political
- South Asia: Physical
- East Asia: Political

- East Asia: Physical
- Southeast Asia: Political
- Southeast Asia: Physical
- Europe: Political
- Europe: Physical
- Russia, Central Asia, and the Caucasus: Political
- Russia, Central Asia, and the Caucasus: Physical
- North America: Political
- North America: Physical
- Central America and the Caribbean: Political
- Central America and the Caribbean: Physical
- South America: Political
- South America: Physical
- Australia and the Pacific: Political
- Australia and the Pacific: Physical

> "We hold these Truths to be self-evident, that all Men are created equal, that they are endowed by their Creator with certain unalienable Rights, that among these are Life, Liberty and the Pursuit of Happiness. That to secure these Rights, Governments are instituted among Men, deriving their just Powers from the Consent of the Governed."
>
> — Declaration of Independance

Declaration of Independence

When the Continental Congress issued the Declaration of Independence in 1776, they did more than announce their separation from Great Britain. They also summed up the most basic principles that came to underlie American government. This section is sometimes called the "social contract" section. You can read the words at left.

These ideas have had significant effect on later developments in American history. You will notice the relationship of the ideas behind the Declaration of Independence to the American Revolution, the writing of the U.S. Constitution, including the Bill of Rights, and the movements to end slavery and to give women the right to vote. You'll see how the United States became a nation of immigrants, with its rich diversity of people, and the ways this development relates to the ideas of the Declaration of Independence.

Read the first three paragraphs of the Declaration of Independence. Then recite words from the Declaration of Independence quoted at left. Consider their meaning and then answer these questions.

ASSESSMENT

1. **Identify Central Idea** This part of the Declaration is sometimes called the "social contract" section. Based on these statements, what is a social contract? Who benefits from it?
2. **Contrast** How does the idea of government based on a "social contract" differ from the idea behind a monarchy? A dictatorship?
3. **Apply Information** Identify two ways that your federal, state, or local government protect the rights to life, liberty, or the pursuit of happiness.

Constitution Day Assembly

September 17 is Constitution Day, and your school may hold an assembly or other celebration in honor of the day. As part of this celebration, your teacher may ask you to participate in planning and holding a Constitution Day assembly.

Organize As a class, create the basic plan for your assembly. Discuss the following:

1. When and where should the assembly take place?

2. How long should it take? Should you plan on a short program taking a single class period, or a longer program?

3. Who should be involved? Will other classes or other grades take part? Will you invite outsiders, such as parents or people from the community?

4. What activities might be included?

Plan After your discussion, divide the class into committees to complete jobs such as getting permission from the school administration, preparing a program, inviting any guests, advertising the plan beforehand, and blogging about it afterward.

Give thought to the types of activities that might be included in the assembly. You might invite a guest speaker from your community. You might run an essay contest among students and have the winners read their essays during the assembly. Some students might prepare a video presentation about the Bill of Rights. Others might write and perform a skit about what the Declaration of Independence or U.S. Constitution mean to them.

You might start your assembly by asking everyone to rise to say the Pledge of Allegiance to the United States flag. One student might give a brief speech about how the pledge reflects the ideas of the Declaration of Independence and the U.S. Constitution.

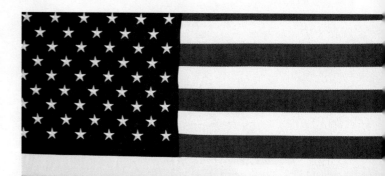

>> Your school may hold a Constitution Day assembly like the one shown here.

Communicate Present your Constitution Day assembly. After the assembly is over, discuss the event with the class. Ask yourselves questions such as these:

1. How well was the assembly planned and organized? What imporvements could we have made?

2. How would you rate each of the presentations or other activities of the assembly?

3. Was the audience engaged?

4. How effectively did the class work together?

[ESSENTIAL QUESTION] How does economics affect everyone?

① Fundamentals of Economics

Enduring Understandings

- Economics is the study of how people seek to satisfy their needs and wants by making choices among scarce resources.

- Every economic decision involves trade-offs; the most desirable choice given up is the opportunity cost.

- Production possibilities curves show how efficiently an economy uses its resources.

>> A customer at a cafe pays with a credit card.

Watch the My Story Video on the fundamentals of economics.

Access your digital lessons including:
Topic Inquiry • Interactive Reading
Notepad • Interactivities • Assessments

www.PearsonRealize.com

1.1 You have so many different ways you can spend your money. You really want that new video game. You also want to upgrade to the newest smartphone model. At the same time, you need to pay your car insurance. With limited funds, you can't have it all. How will you choose?

>> Even in an affluent society like the United States, everyone must make economic choices.

▶ **Interactive Flipped Video**

>> Objectives

Explain why scarcity and choice are the basis of economics in every society.

Summarize how entrepreneurs fuel economic growth.

Describe the three economic factors of production and the differences between physical and human capital.

Explain how scarcity affects the factors of production.

>> Key Terms

need
want
goods
services
scarcity
economics
shortage
entrepreneur
factors of production
land
labor
capital
physical capital
human capital

Scarcity

Scarcity Means Making Choices

What's true for you is also true for your neighbors, your school, the gas station on the corner, a major television network, and the U.S. Congress. That's what economics is all about. Economics is the study of how individuals, businesses, and governments make choices when faced with a limited supply of resources.

Scarcity forces us all to make choices by making us decide which options are most important to us. In this section, you will examine the problem of scarcity as it relates to such varied resources as water and the ingredients needed to make a ham and cheese sandwich.

Unlimited Wants, Limited Resources The study of economics begins with the fact that people cannot have everything they need and want. A **need** is something essential for survival, such as food or medical care. A **want** is something that we desire but that is not necessary for survival, such as video games or stylish haircuts.

People satisfy their needs and wants with goods and services. **Goods** are physical objects that someone produces, such as food, clothing, or video games. **Services** are actions or activities that one person performs for another. Medical care and haircuts are services.

People's needs and wants are unlimited. When one want is satisfied, others arise. After eating lunch, you might want to go to a movie or buy some clothes. Goods and services, however, are limited.

No one can have an endless supply of anything. Sooner or later, a limit is always reached. The fact that limited amounts of goods and services are available to meet unlimited wants is called **scarcity**.

At many different levels, scarcity forces people to make choices. For example, you have to decide how to spend your time. If you decide to study for a test, you cannot go to the mall or do volunteer work at the same time. A store must choose between hiring ten new workers or paying for more advertising to attract new customers. A city council debates whether to use its money to fix an aging school building or to hire more firefighters.

Economics is the study of how people seek to satisfy their needs and wants by making choices. Because people act individually, in groups (such as businesses), and through governments, economists study all three of these arenas for economic decision-making.

Scarcity Does Not Mean Shortage Scarcity is not the same thing as shortage. A **shortage** occurs when consumers want more of a good or service than producers are willing to make available at a particular price. Fans of a top singer will find a shortage of $25 seats at one of his or her concerts. Performers and promoters are simply not willing to provide many seats at that price. Shortages may be temporary or long-term.

Unlike shortages, scarcity always exists and is a problem faced by all societies. There simply are not enough goods and services to supply all of society's needs and wants. Each of that singer's fans not only wants to go to the concert, but also wants to download the singer's songs, have dinner, buy a new top, and purchase other goods and services. Scarcity is unavoidable, because the resources that go into making goods and services are themselves scarce.

? **SYNTHESIZE** What is the main focus of economics?

Entrepreneurs Use Factors of Production

How are scarce resources turned into goods and services? Entrepreneurs play a key role. **Entrepreneurs** are people who decide how to combine resources to create new goods and services. Anyone who opens a business, large or small, is an entrepreneur. To make a profit, entrepreneurs are willing to take risks. They develop new ideas, start businesses, and, if they are successful, even create new industries. By producing new goods and services and hiring workers, they fuel economic growth.

The first task facing an entrepreneur is to assemble **factors of production**, or the resources used to

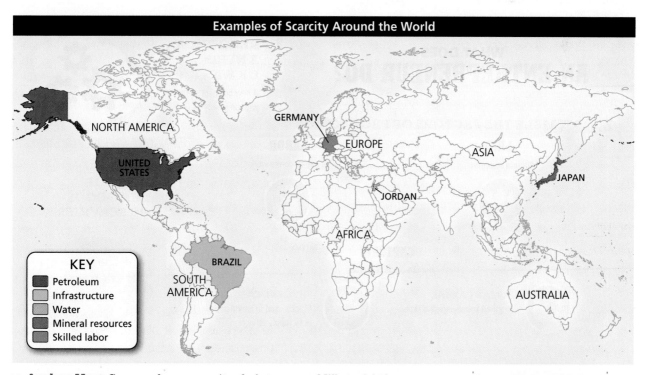

Examples of Scarcity Around the World

KEY
- Petroleum
- Infrastructure
- Water
- Mineral resources
- Skilled labor

>> **Analyze Maps** Germany faces a scarcity of what resource? What might be a possible cause of that scarcity?

▶ Interactive Map

make all goods and services. The three main factors of production are land, labor, and capital. Jean-Baptiste Say, an eighteenth-century French economist, thought the risk-taking entrepreneur so important that he should be considered a fourth factor of production.

Land Economists use the term **land** to refer to all natural resources used to produce goods and services. Natural resources are any materials found in nature that people use to make things or to provide services. These resources include fertile land for farming, as well as resources found in or on the land such as oil, iron, coal, water, and forests.

Labor The second factor of production is labor. **Labor** is the effort people devote to tasks for which they are paid. Labor includes the medical care provided by a doctor, the classroom instruction provided by a teacher, and the tightening of a bolt by an assembly-line worker. Labor is also an artist's creation of a painting or a technician's repair of a television.

Capital The term **capital** refers to any human-made resource that is used to produce other goods and services. Economists divide capital into two types—physical capital and human capital.

Human-made objects used to create other goods and services are **physical capital**. (Sometimes economists use the term *capital goods* for physical capital.) The buildings that house a computer manufacturing company are physical capital, as are all the equipment and tools needed to make those computers.

In addition to producing physical capital, people can also invest in themselves. The knowledge and skills a worker gains through education and experience are **human capital**. Computer designers go to college to study engineering, electronics, and computers. They increase their human capital, making it possible for them to design and build faster and more powerful computers. Auto mechanics also increase their human capital through schooling and experience. This knowledge gives them the skills to diagnose and fix an engine that is not running properly.

An economy requires both physical and human capital to produce goods and services. Doctors need both stethoscopes and schooling to provide healthcare. Carpenters require both tools and the skills they gain through training and practice.

The Effectiveness of Capital Capital is a key factor of production because people and companies can use it to save a great deal of time and money. Physical capital such as machines and tools helps workers produce goods and services more easily and at less cost. Businesses that buy and use these kinds of business property usually become more productive. Human capital such

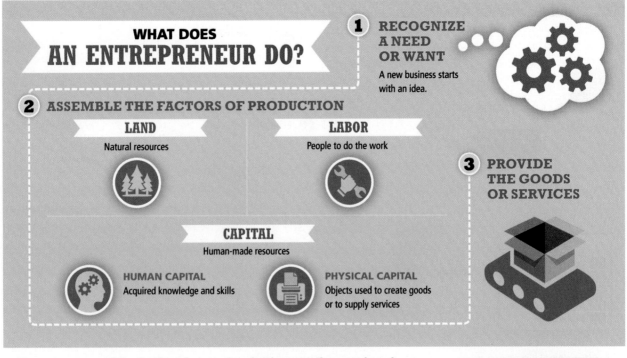

>> Entrepreneurs combine the three factors of production to produce goods and services.

▶ **Interactive Chart**

Machinery Improves Productivity

Dish Washing Over Time	Time Washing by Hand	Time Using Dishwasher	Time Saved
1 Day	3 hours	1 hour	2 hours
1 Week	21 hours	7 hours	14 hours
1 Month	84 hours	28 hours	56 hours
6 Months	546 hours	182 hours	364 hours
1 Year	1,092 hours	364 hours	728 hours

>> **Analyze Charts** What resource becomes less scarce as a result of using a dishwasher to wash dishes every day?

as technical knowledge has the same result. The more skills a worker gains, the more productive he or she becomes. Many businesses provide training for their employees for this reason.

To understand the benefit of purchasing capital, consider the following example: A family washes dishes by hand after every meal—breakfast, lunch, and dinner. That is a total of 21 meals per week. It takes 30 minutes per meal for two family members working together to scrape, stack, wash, rinse, dry, and put away the dishes. As a result, the family spends 21 hours a week cleaning dishes—time that could have been spent on other, more productive activities.

Now, suppose that the family saves up and spends $400 on a piece of physical capital—a dishwasher. Using the dishwasher, it takes only one family member a mere 15 minutes after each meal to stack the dishwasher and another family member just 15 minutes at the end of the day to empty the machine and put the dishes away, for a total of 1 hour a day. A chore that used to require 21 hours a week to complete now takes only 7 hours a week. This example shows the typical benefits of using capital:

1. *Extra time* The family saves 14 hours a week. This is time that can be used for other activities.

2. *More knowledge* By learning how to use the dishwasher, family members learn more about using household appliances in general. They can apply that knowledge to using washing machines, dryers, and other appliances.

In the same way that a family benefits from investing in a piece of physical capital like a dishwasher, a business usually benefits from purchasing and using business property. When a business invests in technology, such as new machinery, it often benefits by saving time. In addition, workers are likely to gain new types of knowledge.

3. *More productivity* With extra time and more knowledge, family members can use their resources and labor to do other chores, to learn other skills, or simply to enjoy themselves. Every member of the family benefits.

?IDENTIFY A plow used to prepare soil for planting is an example of what factor of production?

All Resources Are Scarce

All goods and services are scarce because the resources used to produce them are scarce. Consider a fresh sandwich made at a restaurant. The sandwich roll might have started as wheat in a field in Kansas and then been milled into flour and later baked in an oven. The cheese might have been made from milk from Wisconsin cows, and the chicken may have been raised in Arkansas. The lettuce and tomatoes may have been grown in California. All of these ingredients may have been shipped to a restaurant in Seattle, where a chef made the sandwich and served it to a hungry customer.

All the factors of production used to produce the sandwich are scarce. First, the amount of land and water available for growing crops and raising livestock is limited. Second, the labor available to grow the crops, mill the flour, bake the rolls, and serve the food is limited by the size, time, age, and energy of the population. Finally, the amount of physical capital

>> Even though this woman has an abundance of sandwich ingredients, scarcity still exists here. The land, labor, and capital resources used to produce these ingredients are all scarce.

The same principles apply to a pair of blue jeans, a tablet computer, or a space shuttle. No matter what good or service we look at, the supplies of land, labor, and capital used to produce it are scarce.

We also notice another fact about those resources—each one has many alternative uses. The land could have been used to grow yams or parsnips. The farm workers could have chosen to work in the timber industry. Physical capital could have been put to other uses as well. Individuals, businesses, and governments have to choose which alternative they most want.

❓ IDENTIFY MAIN IDEAS Why are goods and services scarce?

ASSESSMENT

1. **Apply Concepts** Give two examples of needs and two examples of wants.

2. **Distinguish** What is the difference between scarcity and a shortage?

3. **Identify** Why do entrepreneurs take the risk to start or expand a business?

4. **Categorize** What are the factors of production?

5. **Infer** If increasing physical capital increases productivity, why would a company not buy newer, faster computers for all its workers every year?

available to produce the sandwich, such as farm machines or baking equipment, is also limited.

You are cleaning your bedroom. Boxes, clothes, and other items cover your bed, the floor, the entire room. Suddenly, your phone rings, and a friend invites you to a party. You consider your options and quickly decide that going to the party will be more fun than cleaning your room.

>> When business owners decide what goods to sell in their store, they give up the profits they might have made if they had decided to sell other items.

▶ **Interactive Flipped Video**

Opportunity Cost and Trade-Offs

Making Decisions

Later, tired but happy, you enter your bedroom and realize that you now have to clear off your bed when all you want to do is sleep. Your decision to go to the party cost you the time you needed to clean up your room. Was the benefit of your choice worth the cost?

Every time we choose to do something, we give up the opportunity to do something else. As you will see, even such a simple decision as how late to sleep in the morning involves weighing costs and benefits. Scarcity forces us to make choices among limited resources.

Economists point out that all individuals, businesses, and large groups of people—even governments—make decisions that involve trade-offs. A **trade-off** is the act of giving up one benefit in order to gain another, greater benefit. Trade-offs often involve things that can be easily measured, such as money, property, or time. But trade-offs may also involve values that are not so easy to measure. Such intangibles include enjoyment, job satisfaction, or the feeling of well-being that comes from helping somebody.

Individual Decisions At every stage of life, you have to make trade-offs. Taking a part in the school play prevents you from playing soccer

>> Objectives

Identify why every decision involves trade-offs.

Explain the concept of opportunity cost.

Describe how people make decisions by thinking at the margin.

>> Key Terms

trade-off
guns or butter
opportunity cost
thinking at the
 margin
cost/benefit analysis
marginal cost
marginal benefit

or getting a part-time job. A few years from now, you might decide to turn down an exciting but low-paying job in favor of a less interesting job that pays better. Still later, you may choose to give up a vacation in order to put more money away for your retirement.

Business Decisions The decisions that businesses make about how to use their factor resources—land, labor, and capital—also involve trade-offs. A farmer who plants broccoli cannot at the same time use the same area of land to grow squash. A furniture company that decides to use all of its equipment to make chairs eliminates the possibility of using the same equipment to build tables or desks.

Government Decisions National, state, and local governments also make decisions that involve trade-offs. Economists and politicians use the term "**guns or butter**" to describe one of the common choices facing governments: the choice between spending money on military or domestic needs. A country that decides to produce more military goods ("guns") has fewer resources to devote to consumer goods ("butter") and vice versa. The steel needed to produce a tank cannot then be used to produce a tractor.

For example, as the war in Afghanistan began drawing to a close in 2013, the United States began debating how to rein in military spending and government spending in general.

One commentator described this debate:

> "Guns versus butter" has come back in vogue politically. "Guns" basically means spending on security concerns (military defense needs) as opposed to welfare pursuits or "butter" (education, hospitals, housing, schools, etc.). The choice for nations isn't usually either "guns" or "butter" but rather how many guns and how much butter . . . . But the question remains: How many guns are necessary to maintain a high level of security for the U.S., and how much butter can the nation afford without hurting guns and vice versa?
>
> —David Briceno, "'Guns vs. Butter,' America's Political Dilemma," *The Union*

In the end, the reason for the "guns or butter" trade-off is the same as the reason for any other trade-off: scarcity. Goods and services are limited, but our needs and wants are unlimited.

? DEFINE What are trade-offs?

Opportunity Cost

In most trade-off situations, one of the rejected alternatives is more desirable than the rest. The most desirable alternative somebody gives up as the result of a decision is the **opportunity cost**. Take the farmer in the example above. If squash is the most profitable alternative to broccoli, then the opportunity cost of deciding to plant broccoli is the chance to plant squash.

Even simple decisions carry opportunity costs. Consider the following choices:

Sleep late or wake up early to study for a test?

Sleep late or wake up early to eat breakfast?

Sleep late or wake up early to go on a ski trip?

Most likely, you did not choose "sleep late" for all three decisions. Your decision depended on the specific opportunity cost—the value to you of what you were willing to sacrifice.

Using a Decision-Making Grid At times, the opportunity cost of a decision may be unclear or complicated. Using a decision-making grid can help

>> The phrase "guns or butter" refers to the trade-off that governments make between military and domestic spending.

▶ **Interactive Gallery**

Karen's Decision-Making Grid

	ALTERNATIVES	
	SLEEP LATE	**WAKE UP EARLY TO STUDY**
BENEFITS	• Enjoy more sleep • Have more energy during the day	• Better grade on test • Teacher and parental approval • Personal satisfaction
BENEFITS FORGONE	• Better grade on test • Teacher and parental approval • Personal satisfaction	• Enjoy more sleep • Have more energy during the day
OPPORTUNITY COST	Extra study time	Extra sleep time

>> **Figure 1.1 Analyze Charts** What would you do if you were Karen? Why?

▶ **Interactive Chart**

you determine whether you are willing to accept the opportunity cost of a choice you are about to make.

In **Figure 1.1**, a high school student named Karen is trying to decide whether to sleep late or get up early to study for a test. Because of the scarcity of time, she cannot do both.

To help her make her decision, Karen lists the benefits of each alternative on the grid. Waking up early to study will probably result in her receiving a better grade. She will also receive teacher and parental approval and experience a sense of personal satisfaction.

On the other hand, Karen enjoys sleeping. In addition, the extra sleep would give her more energy during the day. She would have to give up these benefits if she decided to get up earlier.

Making the Decision Karen is a practical person. After considering the opportunity cost of each alternative, she decides that waking up early to study offers her the most desirable benefits. She knows that she is giving up the pleasure of more sleep and the extra energy it would provide. But she is willing to accept this opportunity cost.

If Karen faced other decisions with other opportunity costs, she might choose differently. What if the choice were between sleeping late and getting up early to have breakfast? What if her decision to sleep late or study were on a Saturday rather than on a school day? With each different set of alternatives, the possible benefits and opportunity costs change as well.

One thing does not change, though. We always face an opportunity cost. As economists say, "Choosing is refusing." When we select one alternative, we must sacrifice at least one other alternative and its benefits.

? IDENTIFY MAIN IDEAS Why does every choice involve an opportunity cost?

Thinking at the Margin

When economists look at decisions, they point out one more characteristic in addition to opportunity cost. Many decisions involve adding or subtracting one unit, such as one hour or one dollar. From an economist's point of view, when you decide how much more or less to do, you are **thinking at the margin**.

To understand what it means to think at the margin, think about folding a piece of paper with important notes on it to put in your pocket. If you fold the paper in half and then in half again, it can just squeeze into your pocket and will lay fairly flat. If you continued folding it in half two or three more times, it would fit more easily in your pocket. But the paper would also become more bulky with each additional fold. The question is, how many folds is the best number for fitting easily into your pocket and laying flat once inside?

Analyzing Costs and Benefits Deciding by thinking at the margin is just like making any other decision. Decision makers have to compare the opportunity costs and the benefits—what they will sacrifice and what they will gain. This decision-making process is sometimes called **cost/benefit analysis**.

To make rational, or sensible, decisions at the margin, you must weigh marginal costs against marginal benefits. The **marginal cost** is the extra

Decision Making at the Margin

OPTIONS	BENEFIT	OPPORTUNITY COST
1st hour of extra study time	Grade of C on test	1 hour of sleep
2nd hour of extra study time	Grade of B on test	2 hours of sleep
3rd hour of extra study time	Grade of B+ on test	3 hours of sleep

>> **Figure 1.2** Karen decides to wake up two hours earlier to study with the expectation of raising her grade to a B. **Analyze Charts** Do you agree with that decision? Why or why not?

cost of adding one unit, whether it be sleeping one extra hour or building one extra house. The **marginal benefit** is the extra benefit of adding the same unit. As long as the marginal benefits exceed the marginal costs, it pays to add more units.

Making Decisions at the Margin Look again at the example of Karen's decision on how late to sleep. The decision-making grid used an "all or nothing" approach. Either Karen was going to wake up early to study, or she was going to sleep late and not study at all that morning.

In reality, Karen could have decided from among several options rather than just two. She could have decided to get up one, two, or three hours earlier. Making a decision about each extra hour would involve thinking at the margin.

To make a decision at the margin, Karen should look at the marginal cost of each extra hour of studying and compare it to the marginal benefit. In **Figure 1.2**, we can see that one hour of studying means an opportunity cost of an hour of sleep, while the probable benefit would be passing the test with a C. Two hours of

studying means losing two hours of sleep and perhaps getting a B. When Karen gives up three hours of sleep, however, the probable benefit rises only slightly, to a grade of B+.

Karen concludes that the marginal cost of losing three hours of sleep is no longer worth the marginal benefit because her grade will improve only slightly. Based on her cost/benefit analysis, Karen decides to awaken two hours earlier.

Like opportunity cost, thinking at the margin applies not just to individuals, but to businesses and governments as well. Employers think at the margin when they decide how many extra workers to hire. Legislators think at the margin when deciding how much to increase spending on a government program.

? **CHECK UNDERSTANDING** How can a cost/benefit analysis help people make decisions?

ASSESSMENT

1. **Express Problems Clearly** Give an example of a "guns or butter" trade-off your school or local government might have to make. Describe the issues on each side of the debate.

2. **Apply Concepts** Suppose a friend is trying to decide whether to purchase a car. Use what you know about opportunity cost to help your friend arrive at a wise decision.

3. **Support Ideas With Examples** Can all opportunity costs be evaluated using a cost/benefit analysis? Use an example to explain your answer.

4. **Analyze Information** Think of a recent decision you made. Review your decision in terms of opportunity cost. Do you think you made a wise decision?

5. **Apply Concepts** What marginal costs and benefits might a retail business owner have to consider when trying to decide whether to stay open an additional hour?

Your class decides to sponsor a community breakfast as a fundraiser. Can you make more money by serving eggs or pancakes? Should you offer both? To decide, you'll have to look at the cost of ingredients, the number of workers you have, and the size of the kitchen. Also, does it take more time to scramble eggs or to flip pancakes? What you decide will affect how much money you raise.

>> New technology, such as these robots, can increase the efficiency of a nation's production and lead to economic growth.

▶ **Interactive Flipped Video**

Production Possibilities

Production Possibilities

Nations face similar decisions about what to produce. For nations, however, the consequences of these decisions can be far more serious.

To decide what and how much to produce, economists use a tool known as a production possibilities curve. You will see how an imaginary country uses this tool to decide between producing two very different products: shoes and watermelons.

Economists often use graphs to analyze the choices and trade-offs that people make. Why? Because graphs help us see how one value relates to another value. A **production possibilities curve** is a graph that shows alternative ways to use an economy's productive resources. The axes of the graph can show categories of goods and services, such as farm goods and factory goods or capital goods and consumer goods. The axes can also display any pair of specific goods or services, such as hats on one axis and shoes on the other.

Drawing a Production Possibilities Curve To draw a production possibilities curve, an economist begins by deciding which goods or services to examine. In this example, we will look at a fictional country called Capeland. Government economists in Capeland must

>> **Objectives**

Interpret a production possibilities curve.

Explain how production possibilities curves show efficiency, growth, and opportunity cost.

Explain why a country's production possibilities depend on its resources and technology.

>> **Key Terms**

production possibilities curve
production possibilities frontier
efficiency
underutilization
law of increasing costs

PEARSON **realize**™ www.PearsonRealize.com Access your Digital Lesson.

decide whether to use the nation's scarce resources to manufacture shoes or to grow watermelons. The economists determine that, if Capeland used all of its resources to produce only shoes, it could produce 15 million pairs of shoes. At the other extreme, if Capeland used all of its resources to produce only watermelons, it could produce 21 million tons of watermelons.

The Capeland economists use this information to create a production possibilities curve (**Figure 1.3**). The vertical axis of the graph represents how many millions of pairs of shoes Capeland's factories can produce. The horizontal axis shows how many millions of tons of watermelons Capeland's farmers can grow. At point a, Capeland is producing 15 million pairs of shoes but no watermelons. At point c, Capeland is producing 21 million tons of watermelons but no shoes.

There is a third, more likely alternative. The citizens of Capeland can use their resources to produce *both* shoes and watermelons. The table shows four different ways that Capelanders could use their resources to produce both shoes and watermelons. Using the made-up data from the table, we can plot points on the graph.

This line, called the **production possibilities frontier**, shows combinations of the production of both shoes and watermelons. Any spot on that line represents a point at which Capeland is using all of its resources to produce a maximum combination of those two products.

Trade-Offs Along the Production Possibilities Frontier Each point on the production possibilities frontier reflects a trade-off. Near the top of the curve, factories produce more shoes, but farms grow fewer watermelons. Farther down the curve, farms grow more watermelons, but factories make fewer pairs of shoes.

These trade-offs are necessary because factors of production are scarce. Using land, labor, and capital to make one product means that fewer resources are left to make something else.

? DEFINE Why is a production possibilities curve helpful to economists?

Changing Production Possibilities

Production possibilities curves give useful information. They can show how efficient an economy is, whether an economy is growing, and the opportunity cost of producing more of one good or service.

Efficiency A production possibilities frontier represents an economy working at its most efficient level. **Efficiency** is the use of resources in such a way as to maximize the output of goods and services. However, sometimes economies operate inefficiently. For example, suppose some workers were laid off. The farms or factories where they worked would produce fewer goods. The economic policies that a nation enacts can also affect efficiency. For example, if laws that lowered manufacturing costs were passed, the businesses might hire back those laid-off workers. In

Production Possibilities Curve

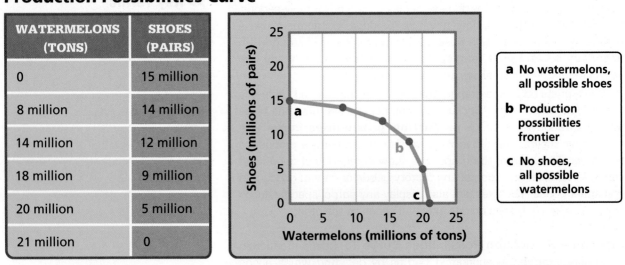

WATERMELONS (TONS)	SHOES (PAIRS)
0	15 million
8 million	14 million
14 million	12 million
18 million	9 million
20 million	5 million
21 million	0

a No watermelons, all possible shoes

b Production possibilities frontier

c No shoes, all possible watermelons

>> **Figure 1.3 Analyze Graphs** Is it more efficient to produce 8 million tons of watermelons and 14 million pairs of shoes or 21 million tons of watermelons and no shoes? Explain your answer.

▶ Interactive Chart

Economic Growth

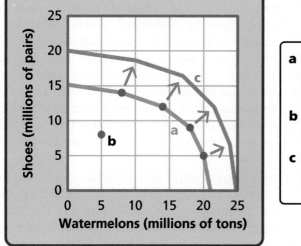

a **Production possibilities frontier before economic growth**

b **Point of underutilization**

c **Production possibilities frontier after economic growth**

>> **Figure 1.4 Analyze Graphs** Based on this curve, how would you describe a situation in which Capeland produces 10 million tons of watermelons and 10 million pairs of shoes?

Interactive 3-D Model

that case, the economy could become more efficient and return to the production possibilities frontier.

Any point inside the production possibilities frontier indicates **underutilization**, or the use of fewer resources than the economy is capable of using. At point b in **Figure 1.4**, Capeland is growing 5 million tons of watermelons and making 8 million pairs of shoes. This is inefficient because it is less than the maximum possible production.

Growth A production possibilities curve is a snapshot. It reflects current production possibilities as if a country's resources were frozen in time. In the real world, however, available resources are constantly changing. If the quantity or quality of land, labor, or capital changes, then the curve will move. For example, a wave of immigration may increase a nation's labor supply. This rise in a factor of production increases the maximum amount of goods the nation can produce.

When an economy grows, economists say that the production possibilities frontier has "shifted to the right." To see such a shift, look at line c in **Figure 1.4**. Notice that the possible output of both shoes and watermelons has increased at each point along the line.

However, when a country's production capacity decreases, the curve shifts to the left. A decrease could occur, for example, when a country goes to war and loses part of its land as a result.

Opportunity Cost We can also use production possibilities graphs to determine the cost involved in

a decision. Remember that cost does not necessarily mean money. To an economist, cost nearly always means opportunity cost.

Looking at the production possibilities table for Capeland, we can see that the opportunity cost of moving from producing no watermelons to producing 8 million tons of watermelons is 1 million pairs of shoes. In other words, in order to produce 8 million tons of watermelons, Capeland had to sacrifice the opportunity to produce 1 million pairs of shoes. In the same way, if Capeland later decides to increase watermelon production from 8 million tons to 14 million tons—an increase of only 6 million tons—it costs 2 million pairs of shoes.

In the first step, those 8 million tons of watermelons cost 1 million pairs of shoes. In the second step, an increase of only 6 million tons of watermelons costs an additional 2 million pairs of shoes. This amounts to 3 million pairs of shoes for 14 million tons of watermelons.

Every additional step of switching from shoes to watermelons has an increasing cost. Each time Capeland grows more watermelons, the sacrifice in terms of shoes increases. Eventually, it costs Capeland an additional 5 million pairs of shoes to increase watermelon production by only 1 million tons.

Economists explain these increasingly expensive trade-offs through the **law of increasing costs**. This principle states that as production shifts from making one item to another, more and more resources are necessary to increase production of the second item. Therefore, the opportunity cost increases.

"Now that we're completely automated, there's no one to yell at."

>> Automation, the use of equipment that runs largely on its own, increases efficiency. **Analyze Political Cartoons** What concern might the cartoonist be expressing about this technology?

Why does the cost increase? The reason is that some resources are better suited for use in farming while others are more appropriate for manufacturing. Moving resources from factory to farm production means that farmers must use resources that are not as suitable for farming. For example, when deciding to produce 8 million tons of watermelons, Capeland devoted its most fertile land to this crop. That shift used up the country's best land, so with each additional step, farmers had to use poorer land that produced less per acre than the fertile land could. To increase output on the poorer land, farmers had to use more land and other resources. This left even fewer resources for producing shoes.

The law of increasing costs explains why production possibilities curve. As we move along the curve, we trade off more and more for less and less added output.

Technology and Training When economists collect data to create production possibilities curves, they must first determine which goods and services a country can produce with its current resources. A country's resources include its land and natural resources, its workforce, and its physical and human capital.

Both human and physical capital reflect a vital ingredient of economic growth—technology. Technology is the process used to create goods and services. At any time, countries have used different forms of technology to produce shoes or watermelons or any of the thousands of products that are made. So economists must assess each country's level of technological know-how. Do workers in Capeland pick watermelons by hand? Do they use assembly lines to make shoes?

Technology is one of the factors that can increase a nation's efficiency. Therefore, many governments spend money investing in new technology. For the same reason, they may also invest in education and training so that people can develop and use new technologies. Highly skilled workers can increase efficiency and lead to economic growth.

? CHECK UNDERSTANDING Why is it important to pair advances in technology with education and training?

ASSESSMENT

1. **Generate Explanations** How does a production possibilities frontier show efficient uses of a country's resources?

2. **Express Problems Clearly** Suppose that a country has the resources to produce 3 million cars and 100 million tons of iron ore every year. Why is it a problem if the country produces 2 million cars and 75 million tons of iron ore one year?

3. **Apply Concepts** Explain how the law of increasing costs would apply in Capeland if the country decided to direct more resources into making shoes than into growing watermelons.

4. **Predict Consequences** How would the widespread use of a new type of chemical fertilizer affect a nation's production possibilities frontier? Why?

5. **Determine Relevance** Why is there so much emphasis on education in the modern world?

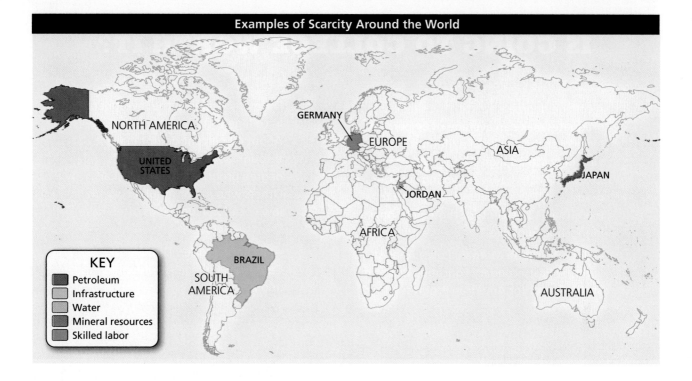

Examples of Scarcity Around the World

KEY
- Petroleum
- Infrastructure
- Water
- Mineral resources
- Skilled labor

1. **Explain Basic Economic Problems** Using the map above, answer the following questions: Which country on the map is an example of the scarcity of mineral resources? According to the map, what is a scarcity the United States faces? In what ways can a country still face a scarcity even if the particular resource is plentiful within its borders?

2. **Explain Scarcity** What is scarcity, as the term is used in economics? What is an everyday example of scarcity that demonstrates why scarcity is a basic economic problem that faces every society?

3. **Explain Basic Economic Problems** Write a paragraph that explains why choice is a basic economic problem faced by every society. Answer the following questions: How does the text define economics using the idea of making choices? In what ways does scarcity make the problem of choice inevitable in all societies?

4. **Explain Economic Concepts** Write a paragraph that explains the concept of opportunity costs by restating the main idea of the concept in your own words.

5. **Interpret Curves** Review the tables and charts in Lesson 3 that illustrate Capeland's production possibilities regarding shoes and watermelons. Based on that example, create a production possibilities curve graph, using economic data of your own creation. Include one curve that you interpret as an efficient use of resources and one that is inefficient. First create a table and then a graph based on the information in the table.

6. **Explain a Concept and Create a Written Presentations** Create a written presentation that explains the concept of scarcity and why it is a basic economic problem faced by every society. Be sure to explain the difference between scarcity and a shortage. Make an outline of your main points before you begin to write and include examples as supporting evidence for your presentation.

IS GOING TO COLLEGE WORTH IT?

"A college degree is **worth it**. College graduates make an average of 84 percent more over the course of a lifetime than those who only attend high school. **The unemployment rate** for young college grads **is under 5 percent** compared to more than 13 percent for those with only a high school diploma.

— Julie Margetta Morgan, Policy Analyst with the Postsecondary Education Program at the Center for American Progress

"For many students, the investment in college is **not profitable**. About 40 percent do not make it through a four-year bachelor's degree program in even six years. Others who major in subjects with low vocational demands often have **trouble getting jobs**.

— Richard Vedder, Director of Center for College Affordability and Productivity

7. **Explain Economic Concepts** Using the quotations above, describe the decision-making process you would use to decide whether going to college is worth it, making reference to specific opportunity costs. Write a paragraph summarizing your decision-making process that includes gathering information, identifying options, predicting consequences, and taking actions to implement the decision.

8. **Explain Basic Economic Problems** Create an oral presentation in which you explain the trade-offs that are involved in making personal economic choices and decisions. Define terms as you present them and tailor your presentation to your audience, pausing for questions and refocusing your points as necessary.

9. **Describe Economic Factors** Write a paragraph that describes aspects of the economic factors of production. In your paragraph, describe physical and human capital, making the difference between the two clear.

10. **Explain Economic Concepts** Write a paragraph in which you explain the term "guns or butter" in the context of economic trade-offs and opportunity costs. Is "guns or butter" an inevitable choice? Explain you answer using real-life examples.

11. **Explain Scarcity** Write a paragraph in which you answer the following questions related to the concept of scarcity: Are resources limited or unlimited? What does it mean that the things people want are unlimited? How does scarcity relate to resources and the wants of people?

12. **Describe Economic Factors** Write a paragraph that describes the economic factors of production. Consider the following questions: What are the three economic factors of production? Which factor of production would the effort of an assembly-line worker be an example of? Coal is an example of which factor of production? A bank of computers is an example of which factor of production?

13. **Write About the Essential Question** **Write an essay on the Essential Question: How does economics affect everyone?** Use evidence from your study of this Topic to support your answer.

Go online to PearsonRealize.com and use the texts, quizzes, interactivities, Interactive Reading Notepads, Flipped Videos, and other resources from this Topic to prepare for the Topic Test.

Texts

Quizzes

Interactivities

Interactive Reading Notepads

Flipped Videos

While online you can also check the progress you've made learning the topic and course content by viewing your grades, test scores, and assignment status.

[ESSENTIAL QUESTION] Who benefits from the free market economy?

2 Free Enterprise and Other Economic Systems

>> Two young men stand and smile at their bicycle shop.

Enduring Understandings

- Because societies answer the key economic questions differently, multiple economic systems have developed.

- Competition helps regulate markets and gives producers incentives to make what consumers want.

- Because pure market and pure centrally planned economies have drawbacks, nations tend to have mixed economies.

- Under the American free enterprise system, the government preserves economic freedoms while protecting the public interest through limited regulation of the economy.

PEARSON realize ™ **NBC LEARN**

guide

Watch the My Story Video on Leslie Bradshaw and the importance of innovation.

▶ **PEARSON realize** ™
www.PearsonRealize.com

Access your digital lessons including:
Topic Inquiry • Interactive Reading
Notepad • Interactivities • Assessments

>> In the United States, we have chosen to make a public education available to all young people.

Interactive Flipped Video

When you go to a supermarket, you see rows of shelves stacked with a variety of foods and products. But suppose the government limited your choice to just one brand of cereal and one brand of soap. Or what if the only goods available to you were what you and your neighbors could grow or make yourselves? All of these examples represent ways different societies have dealt with the challenge of meeting people's needs and wants.

>> **Objectives**

Identify the three basic economic questions that all societies must answer.

Describe the economic goals that determine how a society answers the three economic questions.

Define the characteristics of a traditional economy.

>> **Key Terms**

economic system
factor payments
profit
safety net
standard of living
innovation
traditional economy

The Three Basic Economic Questions

Three Basic Economic Questions

In fact, every society faces three basic questions about the production and consumption of goods and services. How people answer these questions shapes our freedom of choice—and what we have to choose from.

Resources are scarce everywhere. As a result, every society must answer three basic economic questions:

- What goods and services should be produced?
- How should these goods and services be produced?
- Who consumes these goods and services?

The way a society answers these questions defines its economic system. An **economic system** is the structure of methods and principles a society uses to produce and distribute goods and services.

What Goods and Services Should Be Produced? Every society must decide what to produce in order to satisfy society's needs and wants. While all people need food and shelter, societies face additional considerations. Which consumer goods should we produce? How much of our resources should we devote to national defense, education, or consumer goods? Because resources are limited, each decision comes with an opportunity cost.

How Should Goods and Services Be Produced?

A society must also decide how to produce goods and services. Is education best delivered through public schools or private schools? What fuel should we use to generate electricity—oil, solar power, or nuclear power?

Although there are many ways to produce goods and services, all require land, labor, and capital. These factors of production can be combined in different ways. For example, look at **Figure 2.1**. Before the introduction of modern farming equipment, producing 15 bushels of wheat may have required 56 hours of labor, 1 acre of land, and simple hand tools. Today, mechanical equipment and other technologies make farming more efficient. Farmers can use just 2.9 hours of labor to produce 40 bushels of wheat on that same acre of land. While the amount of land used remains the same, labor has gone down, and the amount of capital needed has gone up.

These decisions involve trade-offs, too. What else could the society produce with those 56 hours of work in the time of hand tools? What could today's society make if the capital employed as mechanized farm equipment were used in some other way?

Who Consumes the Goods and Services That Are Produced? Societies also make decisions that determine how goods and services are consumed. How can people meet their needs for food and medical care? Who gets to drive a new luxury car and who can only afford bus fare? Who gets access to a college education?

The answers to such questions are largely determined by how societies distribute income. **Factor payments** are the income people receive in return for supplying factors of production—land, labor, or capital. Landowners collect rent, workers earn wages, and those who lend money receive payments called interest. Factor payments also include the profits that entrepreneurs earn if their enterprises succeed. **Profit** is the amount of money a business receives in excess of its expenses. Profits are the rewards entrepreneurs receive for taking the risk of starting a business.

How much should we pay the owners of the factors of production? How do we decide how much teachers should earn versus how much doctors should earn? The answers to such questions tell us a great deal about a society's values.

? **IDENTIFY MAIN IDEAS** What are the three basic economic questions?

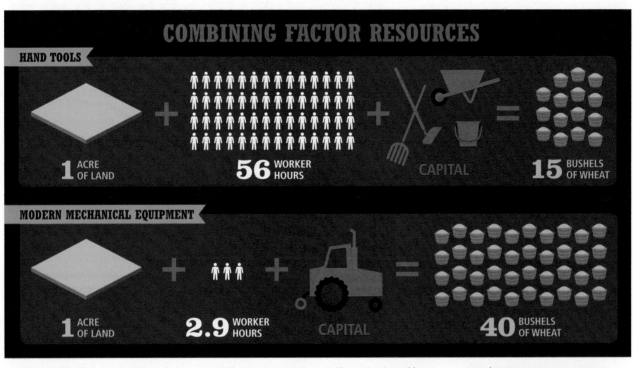

>> **Figure 2.1** This illustration shows two different approaches to the question of how to combine the factors of production. **Analyze Information** Which approach is most efficient? Explain your answer.

▶ Interactive Chart

Economic Goals of Society

Different societies answer the three economic questions based on the importance they attach to various economic goals. These goals include efficiency, freedom, security, equity, and growth. All societies pursue each of these goals to some degree.

Efficiency Because resources are always scarce, societies try to maximize what they can produce using the resources they have. If a society can accurately assess what its people need and want, it increases its economic efficiency. A manufacturer would be wasting resources producing desktop computers if people prefer laptops.

The goal of reducing waste also involves the second and third economic questions. Producers seek better ways to create goods and to make them available to consumers. An economy that cannot deliver the right goods in the right quantity to the right people at the right price is not efficient.

Freedom Most people value the opportunity to make their own choices. Still, people all over the world face limits to their economic freedom.

Americans face limits as well. But in general, individual freedom is a key cultural value for Americans. We prize the freedom to buy what we can pay for, to seek work where we want, to own property, and to become entrepreneurs. In order to obtain these benefits, we accept the costs that come with freedom—for example, the potential of failure. Not everyone is able to prosper, and some people experience poverty.

Security Most people do not like uncertainty. We want to know we can get milk or bread every time we go to the store. We want the security of knowing we will get our paychecks every payday. Ideally, economic systems seek to reassure people that goods and services will be available when needed and that expected payments will arrive on time.

We also want the security of knowing that help is available if we are in need. Many governments provide a **safety net**, or set of programs to protect people who face unfavorable economic conditions such as layoffs, injuries, or natural disasters. Many countries also provide some sort of base income for retired persons to ensure that they can support themselves in retirement.

Equity Equity, or fairness, is another economic goal that is defined differently in different societies. (See **Figure 2.2** for information about one measure of equity in the United States in recent years.) Each society must decide how to divide its economic pie. Should everyone get the same share of the goods and services a nation produces? Or should one's consumption depend on how much one produces? How much should society provide

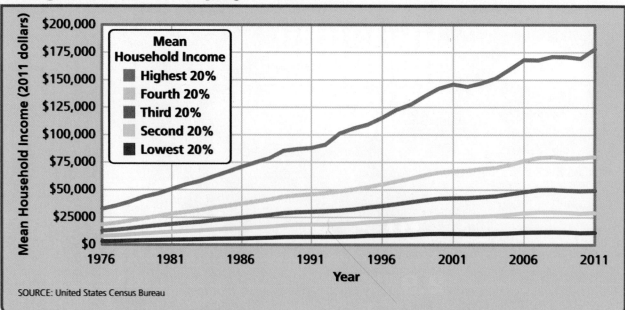

Changes in Economic Equity, 1976–2011

Mean Household Income
- Highest 20%
- Fourth 20%
- Third 20%
- Second 20%
- Lowest 20%

Mean Household Income (2011 dollars): $0, $25000, $50,000, $75,000, $100,000, $125,000, $150,000, $175,000, $200,000

Year: 1976, 1981, 1986, 1991, 1996, 2001, 2006, 2011

SOURCE: United States Census Bureau

>> **Figure 2.2** Household income rose between 1976 and 2011 at all five income levels—but not at equal rates. **Analyze Graphs** Which income group saw the greatest change?

for those who are unable or unwilling to produce? How are the benefits of economic freedom compromised by the goal of economic equity—or is inequity possibly a cost of freedom?

Growth A nation's economy must grow with its population so it can provide jobs for the new people joining the workforce. A nation's economy must grow if people are going to have more income. When that occurs, the nation improves its **standard of living**, or level of economic prosperity.

Innovation plays a huge role in economic growth. **Innovation** is the process of bringing new methods, products, or ideas into use. During the Industrial Revolution of the 1700s and 1800s, innovations in technology increased the efficiency of production and introduced new goods and services. Many problems arose, such as harsh conditions in factories and crowded cities, as well as increased pollution of air and water. Yet, the Industrial Revolution also sparked economic growth and led to an overall rise in standards of living. Today, innovations in computer and networking technology are changing how people work, do business, find information, and communicate.

Conflicting Economic Goals A society may value goals other than these. Environmental protection, full employment, or protecting national industries may be among a nation's chief economic goals.

Sometimes, economic goals conflict with one another. For example, when a society provides a safety net for all citizens, the added cost may slow economic growth. To protect the environment, a government may impose regulations on manufacturers that curb economic freedom. Thus, all nations must prioritize their economic goals, or arrange them in order of importance. Each choice comes with some kind of trade-off. Choosing among conflicting economic goals is a basic economic problem that every society must face.

Traditional Economies Societies have developed four different economic systems to address the three basic economic questions. Each system reflects a different prioritization of economic goals. It also reflects the values of the societies in which these systems are found.

The oldest and simplest of economic systems is the traditional economy. A **traditional economy** relies on habit, custom, or ritual to answer the three basic economic questions. There is little room for innovation or change.

The traditional economic system revolves around the family unit—often an extended family made up

>> This U.S. National Guard soldier is helping to deliver aid to victims of a storm. This is one way government helps maintain people's economic security in times of need.

>> Traditional economies still exist in many parts of the world. This Inuit man lives in North America and depends on hunting and fishing, much as his ancestors did hundreds of years ago.

of several generations. Work tends to be divided along gender lines. Boys tend to take up the occupations of their fathers, while girls follow those of their mothers.

Traditional economies are usually found in communities that tend to stay relatively small and close. Often people in these societies work to support the entire community, rather than just themselves or their immediate families. In these societies, agricultural and hunting practices usually lie at the center of people's lives, laws, and religious beliefs.

Societies with traditional economies are economically successful if they meet their own needs. But they have few mechanisms to deal effectively with the effects of environmental disaster, such as a flood or drought. They also tend to be slow to adopt new ideas or technology. They may not have access to a wide range of goods. In most cases, these communities lack modern conveniences and have a relatively low standard of living.

? IDENTIFY What are two examples of economic goals?

1. **Apply Concepts** A clothing company produces a new line of inexpensive jeans using a special process that is environmentally friendly. In this example, how has society answered the three basic economic questions?

2. **Analyze Information** (a) Why would it be inefficient today for a manufacturer to produce music CDs instead of digital MP3 music files? (b) What role does scarcity play in a manufacturer's decision to produce MP3 files and not CDs?

3. **Generate Explanations** (a) What are some examples of types of investments on the part of manufacturers that result in growth? (b) How does this help improve a nation's standard of living?

4. **Draw Conclusions** What economic goals might come into conflict if a factory polluted a local water supply?

5. **Apply Concepts** Which basic economic goals can be achieved easily in a traditional economy? Which cannot? Explain.

Do you value freedom? If you thought about this question in terms of freedom of speech or freedom of religion, you probably said yes. What about the freedom to own property, to get a job, or to spend your money the way you want? To Americans, economic freedom is also highly valued. It has shaped the system under which we live.

>> Specialized skill and knowledge enables this man to fix complex refrigeration equipment—and to earn a living. Draw Conclusions How does this worker benefit from having specialized skill and knowledge?

▶ **Interactive Flipped Video**

Free Markets

Why Do Markets Exist?

Indeed, economic freedom is the chief characteristic of a free market economy. You will soon see how the free market affects every household and community in the United States, including yours.

Markets Defined What do a farmer's market, a sporting goods store, the New York Stock Exchange, and a community bulletin board where you posted a sign advertising baby-sitting services have in common? All are examples of markets. A **market** is any arrangement that allows buyers and sellers to exchange things.

Markets eliminate the need for any one person to be self-sufficient. None of us produces all we require to satisfy our needs and wants. You probably did not grow cotton plants, process that cotton into cloth, or weave that cloth into the shirt you are wearing. Instead, you purchased your shirt at a store. Markets allow us to exchange the things we have for the things we want.

The Role of Specialization Instead of being self-sufficient, each of us specializes in a few products or services. **Specialization** is the concentration of the productive efforts of individuals and businesses on a limited number of activities. A baker specializes in making breads, cakes, and cookies. A nurse specializes in caring for the sick.

>> **Objectives**

Explain why markets exist.

Explain a circular flow model of a free market economy.

Describe how self-interest and competition lead to the self-regulating nature of the marketplace.

Identify the advantages of a free market economy.

>> **Key Terms**

market
specialization
free market
   economy
household
firm
factor market
product market
Adam Smith
   (1723–1790)
self-interest
incentive
competition
consumer
   sovereignty

An aircraft plant manufactures only airplanes—not airplanes, refrigerators, and bicycles.

Specialization leads to efficiency in the use of capital, land, and labor. It is better for people to learn one task or a few tasks very well than to learn a little about many tasks. Because they concentrate on one or a few tasks, they can do their work more efficiently, saving resources by avoiding waste. For this reason, the top performers in most fields are specialists who have worked hard to sharpen their particular skills.

Specialization also benefits businesses. Focusing on a limited number of related products or services allows them to use their limited capital and labor more efficiently.

Buying and Selling People in primitive cultures had to make everything they needed from materials they gathered from nature. Even in more recent times, some people strive for self-sufficiency. However, because most of us in the modern world specialize in producing just a few goods or services, we need a mechanism that allows us to sell what we have produced and to buy what we want. **Figure 2.3** illustrates this concept.

In a modern market-based economy, people typically earn income by specializing in particular jobs. They then use this income to buy the products that they want to consume.

? IDENTIFY MAIN IDEAS Why do markets exist?

Elements of a Free Market Economy

In a **free market economy**, answers to the three basic economic questions are made by voluntary exchange in markets. The choices made by individuals determine what gets made, how it is made, and how much people can consume of the goods and services produced. Individuals and businesses make their own decisions about what to buy or sell. Market economies are also called capitalist economies because the capital that entrepreneurs invest in businesses is a vital part of the system.

In a free market system, individuals and privately owned businesses own the factors of production, make what they want, and buy what they want. In other words, individuals answer the three basic questions of what to produce, how to produce it, and who consumes what is produced.

The United States has a free market economic system. This system is commonly referred to as the

>> **Figure 2.3** This farmer specializes in raising one crop, using income from its sale to purchase equipment and other goods. **Test Conclusions** What evidence can you see that the farmer earns income from the specialized production of one crop?

▶ **Interactive Illustration**

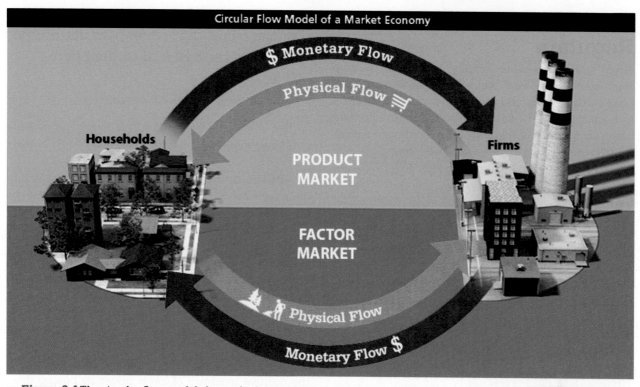

Circular Flow Model of a Market Economy

$ Monetary Flow

Physical Flow

Households

PRODUCT
MARKET

Firms

FACTOR
MARKET

Physical Flow

Monetary Flow $

>> **Figure 2.4** The circular flow model shows the interaction between households and firms in a free market. **Analyze Charts** What is the primary item that changes hands in the monetary flow?

▶ **Interactive 3-D Model**

United States free enterprise system. In general, *free enterprise, free market,* and *capitalism* are all synonyms for the economic system of the United States.

Households and Firms The participants in a free market economy are households and firms. A **household** is a person or group of people living in a single residence. Households own the factors of production—land, labor, and capital. They are also consumers of goods and services.

A business, or **firm**, is an organization that uses resources to produce a product or service, which it then sells. Firms transform inputs, or factors of production, into outputs, or goods and services.

We can represent the exchanges that take place in a free market economy in a diagram called a circular flow model. Look at **Figure 2.4**. The diagram shows how households and firms exchange money, resources, and products in the marketplace. The inner ring of the diagram represents the flow of resources and products. Note that both households and firms are resource owners in this model. The outer ring represents the flow of money.

Factor and Product Markets As you can see from the lower half of the model, firms purchase factors of

production from households. This arena of exchange is called the **factor market**. An example of this is when firms purchase or rent land. They hire workers, paying them wages or salaries for their labor. They also borrow money from households to purchase capital, paying households interest or profits in return.

Now look at the top half of the circular flow model. The arena in which households buy the goods and services that firms produce is the **product market**. So, when you buy food at a supermarket, you are taking part in the product market physical flow.

If you follow the rings of the diagram, you will see that in the product market, households purchase the products made by firms with the money they receive from firms in the factor market. The monetary and physical flows through the factor and product markets are truly circular.

❓ **EXPRESS IDEAS CLEARLY** What is the role of firms in the free market economy?

How Markets Self-Regulate

Firms and households usually cooperate to give each other what they want—factor resources from households to firms, and goods and services from firms to households. Why should they cooperate when we live in such a competitive society? According to **Adam Smith**, competition and our own self-interest actually help to keep the marketplace functioning.

Self-Interest Adam Smith was a Scottish social philosopher. In 1776, he published a book titled *The Wealth of Nations* that described how markets function. Smith observed that an economy is made up of countless individual transactions. In each of these exchanges, the buyer and seller consider only their own **self-interest**, that is, their own personal gain.

Smith observed:

> Give me that which I want, and you shall have this which you want . . . and it is in this manner that we obtain from one another the far greater part of those good [services] which we stand in need of. It is not from the benevolence of the butcher, the brewer, or the baker that we expect our dinner, but from their regard to their own interest.

—Adam Smith, *The Wealth of Nations*

Self-interest, in other words, is the motivating force in the free market—the push that leads people to act.

Incentives and Competition Consumers, pursuing their self-interest, have the incentive to look for lower prices. Look at **Figure 2.5**. An **incentive** is the hope of reward or fear of penalty that encourages a person to behave in a certain way. Many incentives are monetary, or based on money, such as the promise of higher wages or profits. Others are nonmonetary, such as the prestige and personal satisfaction one gets from running a successful business.

Adam Smith observed that people respond in a predictable way to both positive and negative incentives. Consumers, for instance, will respond to the positive incentive of lower prices by buying more goods, because spending less money on a good lowers the opportunity cost of the purchase.

Firms, meanwhile, seek to make higher profits by increasing sales. Let's take, for example, a shirt

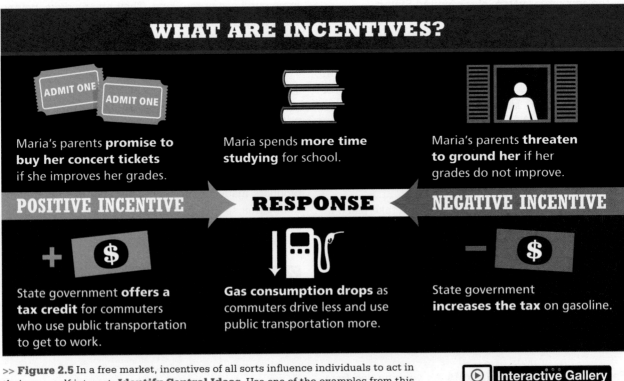

WHAT ARE INCENTIVES?

Maria's parents **promise to buy her concert tickets** if she improves her grades.

Maria spends **more time studying** for school.

Maria's parents **threaten to ground her** if her grades do not improve.

POSITIVE INCENTIVE → **RESPONSE** ← **NEGATIVE INCENTIVE**

State government **offers a tax credit** for commuters who use public transportation to get to work.

Gas consumption drops as commuters drive less and use public transportation more.

State government **increases the tax** on gasoline.

>> **Figure 2.5** In a free market, incentives of all sorts influence individuals to act in their own self-interest. **Identify Central Ideas** Use one of the examples from this diagram to explain how the incentive given leads to the response indicated.

▶ **Interactive Gallery**

>> **Figure 2.6** The free market system offers many benefits to producers and consumers. **Analyze Charts** Which of the advantages of the free market do you think is most important to producers? Explain your answer.

manufacturer. The manufacturer finds that striped shirts are far outselling polka-dotted shirts. The manufacturer has the incentive—from more potential sales and profits—to produce more striped shirts. Other manufacturers, seeing consumers' desire for striped shirts, also have the incentive to make those shirts.

Now consumers can get all the striped shirts they want—but what will it cost them? What if all these producers charged high prices for those shirts so they could maximize their profits? The fact that there are so many producers helps to discourage that.

Suppose most manufacturers charge $30.00 for a striped shirt, while one decides to sell them for $25.00. Consumers, pursuing their self-interest, will buy the lower-priced shirt. If the other manufacturers want to sell more striped shirts, they will have to drop the price.

Economists call this struggle among producers for the dollars of consumers **competition**. While self-interest is the motivating force behind the free market, competition is the regulating force.

The Invisible Hand Self-interest and competition tend to work together to keep the marketplace fair and its prices responsive. Self-interest spurs consumers to purchase certain goods and services and firms to produce them. Competition causes firms to produce more and moderates their desire to raise prices. As a result, consumers usually get the products they want at prices that more closely reflect the cost of producing them. That is, prices are responsive to market forces rather than to the choices of individual producers.

All of this happens without any central planning or direction. No consumer or producer has made decisions based on what's good for the marketplace, yet the end result is a marketplace that operates efficiently. Adam Smith called this self-regulating mechanism the "invisible hand" of the marketplace.

? **DRAW CONCLUSIONS** What does competition among producers in a free market accomplish for consumers?

Advantages of a Free Market

As you saw, each society tries to achieve a variety of economic goals. Under ideal conditions, the free market meets many of these goals—summarized in **Figure 2.6**—on its own.

1. *Economic efficiency* Because it is self-regulating, a free market economy such as the U.S. free enterprise system can respond efficiently to rapidly changing conditions. Producers attempt to provide only the goods and services that consumers want, and at prices consumers are willing to pay.

2. *Economic freedom* Free market economies have the highest degree of economic freedom of any system. For example, in the U.S. free enterprise system, workers work where they want, firms produce what they want, and individuals consume what they want.

3. *Economic growth* Because competition encourages innovation, free markets encourage growth. Entrepreneurs in the U.S. free enterprise system are always seeking profitable opportunities, contributing new ideas and innovations.

4. *Additional goals* Free markets, such as the U.S. free enterprise system, offer a wider variety of goods and services than any other system, because producers have incentives to meet consumers' desires. Consumers, in essence, have the power to decide what gets produced. This is called **consumer sovereignty**.

The free enterprise system of the United States illustrates the many advantages of a free market system. Despite the advantages, however, no country today operates under a pure, unregulated free market system. There are several reasons for this. For example, some societies have goals that are not always easy to achieve in a pure market system, such as economic equity or security. Later you will read about how countries modify the free market system in order to better meet the entire array of economic goals.

? GENERATE EXPLANATIONS Why does a free market economy result in the availability of a wide variety of goods and services?

ASSESSMENT

1. **Analyze Information** How does specialization make an economy more efficient?

2. **Compare** How do self-interest and competition affect the free market?

3. **Interpret** Explain what Adam Smith meant by the "invisible hand" of the marketplace.

4. **Infer** How can specialization benefit both producers and consumers in a free market economy?

5. **Connect** In a free market system, how are incentives related to the principle of consumer sovereignty?

Suppose you lived in Cuba. Each month, the government would give you cards entitling you to buy a set amount of food at low prices. However, this amount often will not last the entire month. To buy enough food for the rest of the month, you would need to pay much higher prices. If you are like most Cubans, this is difficult because your salary is low. Even if you had money, you might not be able to buy the food you want because shortages are common.

>> Customers at a Cuban bakery receive their daily ration of bread allowed by the Cuban government. **Express Problems Clearly** In this situation, who is deciding how much bread is produced by this bakery?

▶ **Interactive Flipped Video**

Centrally Planned Economies

The Features of Central Planning

Why is the situation in Cuba so different from that in the United States? One reason is that the two countries have different economic systems. Cuba does not have a market economy, but a centrally planned one.

Societies that rely on central planning answer the basic economic questions differently from those that depend on market principles. In a **centrally planned economy**, the government, rather than individual producers and consumers, answers the three basic questions; a central bureaucracy decides what items to produce, how to produce them, and who gets them. The government owns both land and capital. In a sense it owns labor, too, because it controls where people work and what they are paid. The government directs workers to produce a certain number of trucks, so many yards of cotton fabric, and so on. Farmers are told what to plant and where to send their crops.

Centrally planned economies, also known as **command economies**, operate in direct contrast to free market systems. Command economies oppose private property, free market pricing, competition, and consumer choice. Free market forces of self-interest, incentives, and competition are absent. As you will read shortly,

>> **Objectives**

Describe how a centrally planned economy is organized.

Distinguish between socialism and communism.

Analyze the use of central planning in the Soviet Union and China.

Identify the disadvantages of a centrally planned economy.

>> **Key Terms**

centrally planned economy
command economy
socialism
communism
authoritarian

communism and socialism are two examples of economic systems that feature central planning.

To see how such an economy works, we will follow the decision-making process for the production of uniforms for members of the military and the production of sweaters for consumers.

1. The top planners decide that more military uniforms than sweaters will be made. They send this decision to the materials committee.

2. Knowing how much cotton is available, the materials committee decides how many uniforms and sweaters to produce. They send their decision to the makers of cotton, buttons, and elastic.

3. The cotton, the buttons, and the elastic arrive at factories, where they are used to make uniforms and sweaters.

Clearly, there is no consumer sovereignty under centrally planned economies. Many people might need new sweaters but be unable to buy them because the sweaters were not produced.

? IDENTIFY CENTRAL IDEAS What is the process by which basic economic decisions are made in a centrally planned economy?

How Socialism and Communism Differ

The terms most often linked to central planning are socialism and communism. Though often used interchangeably, the terms actually describe different systems, as described in **Figure 2.7**.

Socialism Socialism is not a single economic system. Rather, the term describes a range of economic and political systems based on the belief that wealth should be evenly distributed throughout society. Economic equity, socialists argue, can exist only if the centers of economic power are controlled by the government or by the public as a whole, rather than by individuals or corporations.

In some nations, such as Sweden, socialism coexists with free market practices. Under this "market socialism," the government uses its powers of taxation to redistribute wealth and provide extensive services. Other socialists stress government ownership of the means of production. They consider socialism to be an intermediate stage between capitalism and communism.

Communism In the 1800s, socialism gave rise to communism. Under **communism**, the central government owns and controls all resources and means of production and makes all economic decisions.

COMPARING AND CONTRASTING SOCIALISM AND COMMUNISM

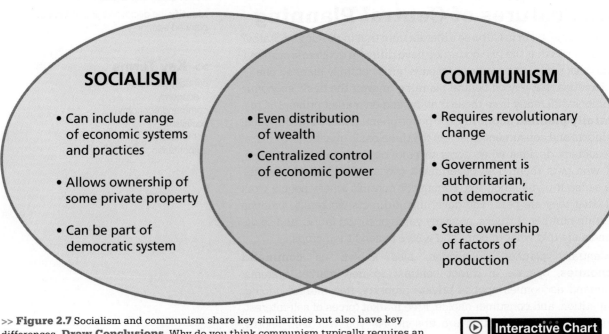

SOCIALISM
- Can include range of economic systems and practices
- Allows ownership of some private property
- Can be part of democratic system

- Even distribution of wealth
- Centralized control of economic power

COMMUNISM
- Requires revolutionary change
- Government is authoritarian, not democratic
- State ownership of factors of production

>> **Figure 2.7** Socialism and communism share key similarities but also have key differences. **Draw Conclusions** Why do you think communism typically requires an authoritarian government while socialism does not?

▶ **Interactive Chart**

Production Goals of First Five Year Plan, 1928–1933

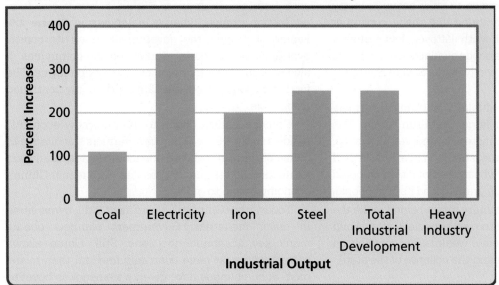

>> **Figure 2.8** Under Stalin, the communist Soviet government set ambitious production goals. **Identify Central Issues** How does this graph represent the concept of central planning?

Communism derived largely from the writings of German philosopher Karl Marx. Unlike Adam Smith, who stressed mutually beneficial relations between producers and consumers, Marx stressed the conflict between labor and capital. He believed that labor was the source of all value. But under capitalism, he said, all the profit created by the labor of workers ended up in the hands of capitalists, such as factory owners:

> Capitalist production . . . develops technology and the combining together of various processes . . . only by sapping the original sources of all wealth—the soil and the laborer.

—Karl Marx, *The Communist Manifesto*

The inevitable result of capitalism, Marx argued, was the exploitation of workers and an unfair distribution of wealth.

Marx and later communists believed that a socialist society could only result from a violent revolution. While countries with socialist economies can be democratic, communist governments have always been authoritarian. **Authoritarian** governments limit individual freedoms and require strict obedience from their citizens. Every communist nation has been dominated by a single dictator or political party.

? IDENTIFY MAIN IDEAS What beliefs did Karl Marx hold about capitalism?

Two Communist Economies

During the twentieth century, communist revolutions occurred in several countries. The histories of two of these nations, the Soviet Union and China, reveal key features of centrally planned economies.

The Soviet Union In 1917, revolutionaries toppled the Russian government. Once in power, they renamed themselves communists, instituted a reign of terror, and murdered the former czar and his family. They also initiated a radical economic program. This marked the beginning of what became the Soviet Union, the world's first communist state. In 1928, Soviet leader Joseph Stalin imposed the first in a series of strict five-year plans to boost industrial and agricultural production. (See **Figure 2.8**.) Until it broke up in 1991, the Soviet Union continued to operate as a command economy.

Soviet economic planners sought to build national power and prestige. They allocated the best land, labor, and capital to the armed forces and to heavy industry. Heavy industry requires large capital investment and produces goods, such as chemicals or steel, used in other industries. The decision to favor heavy industry had a harsh effect on factories that made consumer goods. They were stuck with leftover, lower-quality resources. As a result, the goods available to consumers were few in number and poorly made. Severe shortages were common.

Agriculture faced similar problems. Farmers were forced to work on large, state-run farms. The government supplied all materials and set all wages. The results were often disastrous. While Russia had been a major exporter of wheat, the Soviet Union could not always produce enough grain to feed its own people.

Heavy industry and military might helped make the Soviet Union a world superpower, especially after World War II. But in time, economic weaknesses contributed to the fall of communism and the collapse of the state.

China Like Russia, China adopted central planning as the result of a communist revolution. From 1949 to the late 1970s, government planners controlled every aspect of the Chinese economy.

At first, the communist government allowed some farmland to remain in private hands while it focused on building industry. The government tried to build small factories to produce goods to be sold in nearby areas. But these goods were expensive to make and of very poor quality.

In the 1950s, the government forced many peasants onto farming communes. Within a few years, farm production dropped sharply, as shown in **Figure 2.9**. Facing shortages, the government eased its control over decisions made by workers on the communes. It also sent many factory workers to work on farms. The food crisis was solved, but China's economy continued to stumble.

Chinese leaders began to institute new economic policies in the 1970s. They gave farmers the chance to own more land and offered bonuses to factory managers for making better quality products. As a result, China's economy began to grow.

Today, the Chinese government still owns firms in major industries. Government planners control many key economic decisions. Still, China allows entrepreneurs far more economic freedom than in the past. Such changes have given a tremendous boost to China's economy.

? IDENTIFY What changes led to economic growth in China starting in the 1970s?

China's Grain Output, 1956–1963

		Years affected by Great Leap Forward
1956	193 million metric tons	
1957	195 million metric tons	
1958	200 million metric tons	
1959	170 million metric tons	
1960	143 million metric tons	
1961	148 million metric tons	
1962	160 million metric tons	
1963	170 million metric tons	

SOURCE: "The Great Leap Forward: Anatomy of a Central Planning Disaster," study by Wei Li (University of Virginia) and Dennis Tao Yang (Virginia Polytechnic Institute and State University)

>> **Figure 2.9** China's grain output fell sharply after the start of the Great Leap Forward. **Draw Conclusions** Based on this evidence, how would you characterize the success of central planning during the Great Leap Forward?

Disadvantages of Central Planning

Despite the differences between centrally planned and free market economies, the two systems share many of the same basic goals. However, nations with centrally planned economies have often had trouble meeting these goals in practice.

1. *Economic efficiency* In a centrally planned economy, the government owns all production factors. Since the government fixes wages, workers lack the incentive to work faster or produce more. The large, complex bureaucracy needed to make thousands of economic decisions hurts efficiency as well. It is expensive to run and lacks the flexibility to adjust quickly to consumer demands and changing economic conditions.

2. *Economic freedom* Traditionally, command economies sacrifice individual freedoms in order to pursue societal goals. Sometimes, the results have been brutal; millions of peasants were killed in Stalin's drive to reform Soviet agriculture. But even in better circumstances, central planning discourages competition and takes most or all economic choices away from producers and consumers.

3. *Economic growth* Innovation is a key to economic growth. Command economies, however, do not tend to reward innovation—in fact, they discourage change. Managers must follow an approved government plan. There is no profit incentive to encourage entrepreneurship.

4. *Economic equity* In theory, a major goal of communism is to increase equity by distributing goods and services fairly. Such equity has proven rare, though. Government officials and people in favored careers enjoy higher incomes and access to a wider variety of higher-quality goods. Ordinary people often suffer shortages and poorly made goods.

5. *Additional goals* Central planning has successfully met some goals. It can guarantee jobs and income. It can also be used to jump-start selected industries. For example, Stalin's five-year plans did increase output in heavy industries.

The disadvantages of central planning have caused leaders in many countries to move away from command economies and toward mixed economies. In the next lesson, you will read about today's mixed economies.

>> Millions of Soviet citizens lived in featureless housing that did not allow for individual choice.

▶ **Interactive Gallery**

? CHECK UNDERSTANDING Why do centrally planned economies tend not to be efficient?

ASSESSMENT

1. **Summarize** What economic characteristics does a centrally planned economy oppose that a market economy encourages?

2. **Contrast** How do socialism and communism differ?

3. **Distinguish** What distinguishes an authoritarian government from a democratic one?

4. **Infer** Which economic goal do you think was most important to Karl Marx: efficiency, growth, or equity? Explain.

5. **Draw Conclusions** Who benefits and who suffers most from a centrally planned economy? How?

>> The Lyndon B. Johnson Space Center, near Houston, led in the design and development of the first space shuttle. Space exploration is an example of an activity that was first undertaken by the government.

▶ **Interactive Flipped Video**

As an American, you expect a high degree of economic freedom. But that does not mean you can walk into a convenience store after school and buy a pack of cigarettes. It doesn't mean that you, as a high school student, can get a part-time job operating a forklift in a factory. And it sure doesn't mean that you get to decide whether or not to pay taxes! Why not?

>> **Objectives**

Explain the rise of mixed economic systems.

Explain how government actions affect a circular flow model of a mixed economy.

Compare the mixed economies of various nations along a continuum between centrally planned and free market systems.

Describe the role of free enterprise in the United States economy.

>> **Key Terms**

laissez faire
private property
intellectual property
mixed economy
economic transition
privatization

Mixed Economies

The Reasons for Mixed Economies

Most economies today—including ours—blend a market system with elements of government involvement. You will be learning about why governments step in to provide for your defense or fulfill other needs.

Why Government Gets Involved in the Economy Every economic system has inherent problems in addressing the three basic economic questions. Traditional economies have little potential for growth or change.

Centrally planned economies stifle innovation, do not adequately meet consumer needs, and limit freedom. Even free market economies, with all their advantages, have drawbacks.

Early free market thinkers such as Adam Smith believed that, left alone, the free market would provide the greatest benefit for consumers and raise the standard of living. They favored **laissez faire**, the doctrine that government generally should not intervene in the marketplace. Yet even Smith acknowledged the need for a limited degree of government involvement.

Since Smith's time, government intervention has increased for several reasons. First, some needs of modern society would be difficult to meet in the marketplace. How well, for example, could a free market provide for national defense or highway systems? In addition, governments supply some needs in order to achieve the goal of equity and ensure that all members of society can benefit. For instance, a society could rely solely on private schools to educate its children, but then some families could not afford to send their children to school.

To make sure that all members of society receive a basic education, government in the United States provides public schools. Another example that some governments place in this category is mass transit.

Governments today also play a role in the economy by protecting property rights. For instance, the Fifth and Fourteenth amendments to the Constitution declare that no person may be deprived of "life, liberty, or property, without due process of law." These amendments protect **private property**, or property owned by individuals or companies and not by the government or the people as a whole. The government also protects private property with laws that give individuals control over **intellectual property** such as books, songs, or movies they have created. Private property is a fundamental element of the American economic system.

Governments try to make sure that exchanges in the marketplace are fair. For instance, laws require businesses to give honest information to consumers and block firms from joining together to prevent competition and fix prices.

Finally, people's preferences for redistribution of income have changed. Some governments tax individuals and businesses to fund pension payments for retired workers, those who cannot work because of disabilities, and others.

For all of these reasons, no nation today has a pure free market or command economy. Most economies are mixed. A **mixed economy** is an economic system that has some market-based elements and some government involvement. The degree of government involvement varies from nation to nation.

Balancing Government Involvement and Economic Freedom As you have seen, every society must assess its values and prioritize its economic goals. Some goals are better met by the open market, others through government action. In addition, societies must evaluate the opportunity cost of pursuing each goal.

What are you willing to give up? Are you willing to pay taxes to fund the army? To give money to the unemployed? To give all people an education? Questions like these can spark heated debate.

❓ **IDENTIFY** What is one reason that governments have become involved in otherwise market-based economies?

>> Governments may limit child labor to protect children's health and safety. The Fair Labor Standards Act of 1938 sets U.S. policy on child labor, but states may have additional rules.

IN THE HANDS OF HIS PHILANTHROPIC FRIENDS. 1897
>> In this cartoon from the late 1800s, Uncle Sam (center) represents the government. **Analyze Political Cartoons** What is the cartoonist's view of the other figures and their actions?

Circular Flow Model of a Mixed Economy

To illustrate accurately how most modern economies work, we must add government to our circular flow diagram (**Figure 2.10**). Government enters this flow and interacts with resource owners—firms and households—in a variety of ways.

Government Actions in the Factor Market As you saw in **Figure 2.4**, firms purchase land, labor, and capital from households in the factor market. The same is true of governments. For example, the U.S. government pays nearly 3 million employees over $150 billion a year for their labor. State and local governments also employ large numbers of people. Every time a police officer gets a paycheck, a local government is buying labor in the factor market. The same is true of federal workers like park rangers, scientists, and janitors who clean the halls of Congress.

Government Actions in the Product Market Like households, governments purchase goods and services from firms in the product market. Government offices need telephones and computers. Printing money requires many tons of paper and gallons of ink.

Governments buy services like consulting and waste removal. The vast majority of these purchases are made from private firms.

Governments also provide certain goods and services by combining the factor resources they have purchased. The federal, state, and local governments, for example, have used concrete, steel, and other products to build nearly 4 million miles of roads. Governments provide police and fire protection, education, and health care services as well.

Government Actions Transferring Money Governments collect taxes from both households and businesses. As **Figure 2.11** shows, governments then transfer some of this money to businesses and individuals for a variety of reasons, such as providing funds to save a failing industry or making payments to disabled workers. In recent years, the United States government has paid out over a trillion dollars in Social Security and Medicare benefits annually.

? DESCRIBE How do government actions affect the product market?

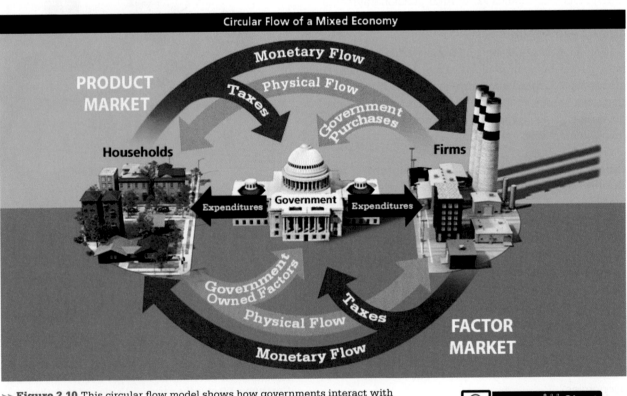

>> **Figure 2.10** This circular flow model shows how governments interact with households and businesses in a mixed economy. **Analyze Charts** How does government affect the monetary flow in a mixed economy?

Interactive Chart

Selected Government Transfer Payments, 2009

PROGRAM	AMOUNT TRANSFERRED
Social Security	$664 billion
Medicare	$500 billion
Unemployment Insurance Payments	$130 billion
Federal Education and Training Assistance Payments	$57 billion
Food Stamps	$55 billion
Veteran's Benefits	$51 billion

SOURCE: United States Census Bureau

>> **Figure 2.11** Government transfers some of the money it collects to people and businesses. **Evaluate Data** Which part of the circular flow model of a mixed economy does this table represent?

Mixed Economies Today

Most modern economies are mixed economies. Governments are involved to some degree, but some are involved more deeply than others. You can see these differences in **Figure 2.12**, which shows a range of mixed economies in today's world.

Mixed Economies with Heavy Government Involvement North Korea represents one extreme of the continuum. Like the former Soviet Union, communist North Korea has an economy almost totally dominated by the government. The government owns all property and all economic output. State-owned industries produce 95 percent of North Korea's goods. Imports are almost totally banned, and production by foreign companies is forbidden.

In China, government long dominated the economy. But in recent decades, China's leaders have loosened their control of the economy, allowing more private ownership of farms and businesses. They have also become more willing to permit foreign firms to invest and operate in China. As a result, China's place on the continuum is closer to the center than North Korea's.

Like many nations that relied on central planning in the past, China is now going through an **economic transition**, a period in which a nation moves from one economic system to another. In China's case, the transition involves privatizing state-owned firms. **Privatization** means selling enterprises operated by the government to individuals, and then allowing them

to compete in the marketplace. Economic transition can be a difficult process.

Mixed Economies Tending Toward Free Markets At the far right of the continuum in **Figure 2.12**, with one of the world's freest markets, is Singapore. The government of this small nation encourages foreign trade and investment while imposing few regulations on commercial activity. This has resulted in strong and steady economic growth in recent years.

Hong Kong is another example of a far-eastern free market powerhouse. Once administered by Great Britain, Hong Kong is now a special administrative region of China. By agreement with the Chinese government, Hong Kong continues to operate largely under the free economic system it had while under British rule. The government protects private property and rarely interferes in the free market.

? RECALL Why is China's economy considered more mixed than North Korea's?

The Economy of the United States

While the American economy is a mixed system, the foundation of the United States economy is the free market. The United States free enterprise system is characterized by individual or corporate ownership of capital goods. Investments in firms are made in a free market by private decision.

The Role of the Government The government of the United States plays a substantial role in the American economy. The American government keeps order, provides vital services, and promotes the general welfare. Federal and state laws protect private property. The marketplace operates with a limited degree of government regulation and some limits government places on business use of private property. For instance, local laws may allow businesses to operate only in certain areas and not in a residential district.

A company planning to shut down a facility may not freely do so if it has 100 or more employees. Federal law requires such a firm to give employees 60 days warning if that shutdown will result in job loss.

Some Americans argue that there is a need for more government services and stricter regulation of business. They want greater regulation of employment practices to protect workers or of business processes to protect consumers or the environment. Many others, however, say that the government already intervenes too much in the economy. They call for relaxation of existing regulations, arguing that government rules drive up the operating and administrative costs of businesses, making them less efficient and less competitive.

Overall Economic Freedom Households and businesses in the United States enjoy a high level of economic freedom—with a few limits. (See **Figure 2.13**.) Individuals can choose what kind of work they want to do (how they wish to enter the factor market for labor) and where they want to live (where they enter that market). Entrepreneurs have the freedom to launch and expand businesses. Both new and existing businesses have the ability to engage in whatever business they want and operate where they want. Though oversight of the banking industry changed somewhat after the 2008 financial crisis, the industry still operates under relatively few restrictions compared to most other nations.

The United States economy is open as well. Foreign investment is encouraged. So, too, is free trade, although the government does protect some domestic industries and does retaliate against trade restrictions imposed by other nations. Foreign-owned banks have few restrictions in addition to those on domestic banks.

? **IDENTIFY MAIN IDEAS** Why is the United States considered to have a mixed economy that tends toward the free market?

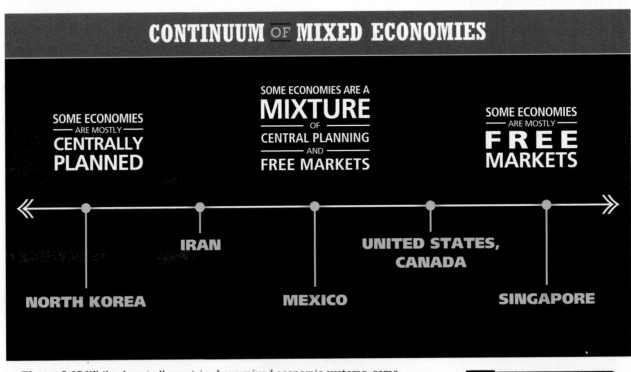

CONTINUUM OF MIXED ECONOMIES

SOME ECONOMIES
— ARE MOSTLY —
CENTRALLY PLANNED

SOME ECONOMIES ARE A
MIXTURE
OF
CENTRAL PLANNING
AND
FREE MARKETS

SOME ECONOMIES
— ARE MOSTLY —
FREE MARKETS

IRAN

UNITED STATES, CANADA

NORTH KOREA   **MEXICO**   **SINGAPORE**

>> **Figure 2.12** While almost all countries have mixed economic systems, some lean farther toward planned economies and others lean more toward free markets. **Analyze Information** How would you describe the location of the United States on this continuum?

▶ **Interactive Gallery**

HOW MUCH FREEDOM?

FEDERAL, STATE, AND LOCAL GOVERNMENTS PLACE SEVERAL LIMITS ON CONSUMERS.

MANY **MEDICINES** CAN BE PURCHASED ONLY WITH A PRESCRIPTION FROM A LICENSED HEALTH-CARE PROVIDER.

IT IS ILLEGAL IN MANY PLACES TO SELL **RAW MILK** MILK THAT HAS NOT BEEN PASTEURIZED.

FINANCIAL PRODUCTS IN GENERAL, CONTRACTS WITH PEOPLE UNDER AGE **18** ARE NOT BINDING SO BANKS DO NOT MAKE LOANS **TO YOUNG PEOPLE.**

>> **Figure 2.13** Even in our free market, government places a number of restrictions on consumers. **Analyze Charts** What is the purpose of government in each of these examples?

ASSESSMENT

1. **Summarize** What are the characteristics of a mixed economy?

2. **Analyze Information** How does the U.S. government protect private property?

3. **Identify Cause and Effect** What are the potential benefits of moving from a command economy to a market-based system?

4. **Paraphrase** What is an example of a government limit on the use of business property?

5. **Infer** Why is privatization not needed in a free market economy?

>> Living in a country with a free enterprise system means that anyone, including you, can become an entrepreneur, start a business, and have a "grand opening."

Picture the dozens of services and products you use every week. Somebody had to think of each one and put it into action. Somebody figured out that people would rather rent movies from a Web site that offers tens of thousands of choices than go to a store that offers far fewer. Somebody invented a way to send photos as well as messages with cellphones.

▶ **Interactive Flipped Video**

>> Objectives

Explain the basic characteristics of the U.S. free enterprise system.

Describe the role of the consumer and the entrepreneur in the American economy.

Identify the protections in the U.S. Constitution that underlie free enterprise.

Describe the role of government in the U.S. free enterprise system.

>> Key Terms

profit motive
open opportunity
legal equality
private property
 rights
free contract
voluntary exchange
interest group
patriotism
eminent domain
public interest
public disclosure
 laws

Benefits of Free Enterprise

Basic Characteristics of Free Enterprise

Now, suppose *you* had one of these brilliant ideas—or just wanted to start your own neighborhood lawn care or baby-sitting service. Could you try to put your plan into action? Since you live in the United States, you can. Every day, American entrepreneurs begin new businesses that earn profits, create jobs, and offer new goods and services. They are a key part of the country's free enterprise system, which is also known as the free market system or capitalism.

The American free enterprise system makes it possible for people who have ideas and persistence to start businesses and make them successful. Now you will examine the vital role that you, as a consumer, play in the free enterprise system.

Opportunity For centuries, people have considered the United States to be a "land of opportunity," where anyone from any background might achieve success. Indeed, this country does offer special opportunities that have allowed businesspeople the freedom to innovate and have contributed to our overall economic prosperity. Today, there are over 27 million businesses in America, including 6 million that are owned by members of minority groups. Many of these were started by a single entrepreneur or a small group of friends or family members.

Why has America been such an economic success? Certainly the United States enjoys many advantages in resources: open land; large reserves of natural resources; and a large, talented labor supply.

But a key factor has also been the American tradition of free enterprise—the social and political commitment to giving people the freedom and flexibility to try out their business ideas and compete in the marketplace. This free enterprise system has several basic characteristics.

Incentives Why do consumers look for lower prices when they shop? That behavior can save them money. Why do workers seek higher wages? That behavior can help them enjoy a better life. Lower prices and higher wages are incentives for consumers and workers to act in certain ways. An incentive is a reward or a cost resulting from specific behavior. For firms, a major incentive is profit. They try to boost their productivity, increase sales, and maintain competitive prices in order to gain the reward of higher profits.

Incentives often involve money, although they can be nonmonetary. For example, the happiness that comes with finding a bargain is an incentive for a consumer to shop. Personal satisfaction is an incentive for an owner to work and build his or her business.

Incentives are often positive, in the form of rewards, but they can also be negative, in the form of costs or penalties. Higher prices for goods and services, for example, are a negative incentive for consumers, as are higher sales taxes. Both can lead consumers to buy less. Higher income taxes can be an incentive for workers to work fewer hours.

Profit Motive The American economy rests on recognition of the profit motive as a key incentive. The **profit motive** drives individuals and businesses to make decisions that improve their material well-being. As you have read, in a centrally planned economic system, the government decides what companies will be formed and how they will be run. In a free enterprise system, business owners and managers make such choices themselves based on what will increase their profits.

Reliance on the profit motive has several benefits. It forces business owners to exercise financial discipline, because they are responsible for their own success or failure. It encourages entrepreneurs to take rational risks and rewards innovation by letting creative companies grow. It also improves productivity by allowing more efficient companies to make more money. As **Figure 2.14** indicates, increasing productivity has been a consistent trend in the U.S. economy.

Competition In order to make a profit, businesses must compete with one another for consumers' money. When faced with several versions of the same product, all of similar quality, consumers will choose the product with the lowest price. If a business expects to compete successfully, it cannot simply raise prices to increase profits. It must set the prices of its products in response to what consumers are willing and able to pay for them.

Competition, then, serves to regulate the free market by keeping prices from rising too high, and in this way it benefits consumers and producers by encouraging them to come together in the marketplace. Competition also encourages businesses to improve the quality of their products in order to attract consumers.

The American economy also benefits from a tradition of **open opportunity**, the principle that anyone can compete in the marketplace. We accept that different people and firms will have different degrees of success. At the same time, we believe that anyone who wants to start a business should have a chance. This allows economic mobility up or down: no matter how much money you start out with, you can end up wealthier or poorer depending on how your business performs.

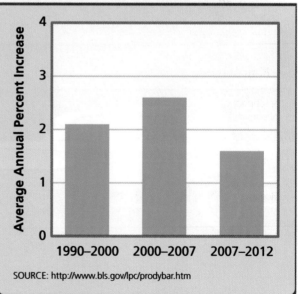

Rates of Productivity Increase in the Business Sector, 1990–2012

SOURCE: http://www.bls.gov/lpc/prodybar.htm

>> **Figure 2.14** While 1990 to 2007 was generally a time of solid economic growth, a deep recession occurred in 2007–2009. **Analyze Graphs** What does this graph tell you about productivity in the period 2007–2012?

▶ **Interactive Chart**

Legal Equality We also have a commitment to **legal equality**—the principle that everyone has the same legal rights. Legal equality benefits the economy by maximizing a country's use of its human capital. Countries that restrict the legal rights of women or minorities lose the productive potential of a large portion of their society.

Private Property Rights In many ways, private property is the cornerstone of the free enterprise system. **Private property rights** give people the right to control their possessions and use them as they wish. The free enterprise system allows people to make their own decisions about the property they have purchased. Personal ownership provides an incentive for property owners to use property wisely and conserve resources.

Economic Freedom The right of **free contract** allows people to decide what agreements they want to enter into. A singer can sign an agreement with any recording company. Consumers are free to choose to enter a credit card agreement with many banks.

The right of **voluntary exchange** allows consumers and producers to decide what, when, and how they buy and sell. Voluntary exchange, in turn, encourages competition, which benefits consumers by

>> The Ford Motor Company had high hopes for the Edsel, a model introduced in 1957. Consumers, however, did not like the car. Ford stopped producing the Edsel in 1960.

providing a larger variety of goods at reasonable prices. Variety of goods and responsive prices, then, are key benefits of the free enterprise system.

? IDENTIFY Which basic characteristic of free enterprise ensures that consumers can choose from a variety of products at acceptable prices?

Key Roles in the Free Enterprise System

You have learned about the powerful dynamics that drive the free enterprise system. Now you will meet two key actors who fill critical roles and exert a strong influence on the economy.

The Role of the Consumer A basic principle of the free enterprise system is that consumers have the freedom to make their own economic choices. Through voluntary exchange, consumers send a signal to businesses, telling them what and how much to produce. Consumers also send a signal when they do not buy a good or service. They are telling the producer that the good or service is not desirable or is priced too high.

Consumers can also make their wishes known by joining an **interest group**, a private organization that tries to persuade public officials to act in ways that benefit its members. One consumer interest group is the Consumers Union, which works to persuade political leaders to pass laws to protect consumers.

Businesses form interest groups as well. For instance, the National Retail Federation represents more than 10,000 firms. Interest groups have also formed around economic issues such as taxation, land use, and aid to farmers.

The Role of the Entrepreneur Entrepreneurs, too, play a vital role in the free enterprise system. They decide how to combine resources—land, labor, and capital—to create new goods and services. By starting new businesses, entrepreneurs fuel economic growth. In the process, they can become some of the most important and celebrated people in our society. Entrepreneurs such as Bill Gates and Oprah Winfrey are widely admired for their success and contributions to our economy and world.

Like any business owner, the entrepreneur seeks to make a profit. Without the profit motive, entrepreneurs would have little incentive to face the challenge of creating and producing new goods and services. Entrepreneurs cannot be sure that consumers will want to buy their product. They know that starting a business is risky and that many new businesses fail. But they also know that successful entrepreneurs, those who correctly gauge consumer wants and needs, can make a large profit from their venture.

? IDENTIFY MAIN IDEAS What key roles do consumers and entrepreneurs play in the free enterprise system?

Economic Freedom and the Constitution

The economic freedoms that American consumers and producers enjoy are an important benefit of the U.S. free enterprise system and a source of **patriotism**, or love of one's country. In the free enterprise system, the right to own property or to become an entrepreneur is as basic to liberty as freedom of speech or the right to vote. According to a leading economist, these rights cannot be separated:

> Economic freedom plays a dual role in the promotion of a free society. On the one hand, freedom in economic arrangements is . . . an end in itself. In the second place, economic freedom is also an indispensable means toward the achievement of political freedom.
>
> — Milton Friedman, *Capitalism and Freedom*

Rights that allow people to engage in business activity are written into the framework of our nation, the Constitution. Perhaps the most important of these is the constitutional recognition of property rights.

Property Rights In many countries, the government has the power to seize property for its own use. To prevent this and ensure economic security, early American leaders protected private property under the Bill of Rights. The Fifth Amendment states that "no person shall be . . . deprived of life, liberty, or property, without due process of law; nor shall private property be taken for public use, without just compensation."

The Fifth Amendment was originally applied only to the federal government. The Fourteenth Amendment, ratified in 1868, extended the same limitations to the state governments.

These due process clauses prevent the government from taking property from its owner except when there is a public reason. For instance, when a state wants to add lanes to a highway, it may take land from people who own property along the route. This right of a

>> In 2013, budding entrepreneur Eesha Kahre (right) won the Intel Foundation Young Scientist Award for inventing a device designed to charge a cell phone in under 30 seconds. She is holding the small device during this television interview.

>> The free enterprise system gives all Americans the right to own property. This couple is pursuing the American dream by looking for a home to purchase.

government to take private property for public use is called **eminent domain**. Even then, the government must pay the person the fair value of the property that has been taken. This protection applies to businesses as well as to individuals.

Taxation The Constitution also spells out how government can tax individuals and businesses. Congress has the power to tax only in the ways the Constitution allows.

Article I gives Congress the power to levy taxes. However, Section 9 once required that direct taxes be apportioned to states according to population. Thus, taxes collected from each state would be based on the number of people living in the state. This rule initially prevented Congress from passing an income tax, which would be a direct tax.

The Sixteenth Amendment, ratified in 1913, first gave Congress the right to set direct taxes based on income. Under current law, both individuals and corporations must pay federal income tax.

Contracts Finally, the Constitution guarantees people and businesses the right to make contracts, which are legally binding agreements between people or businesses. Article I, Section 10 prohibits the states from passing any "Law impairing the Obligation of Contracts." This means that individuals or businesses cannot use the political process to be excused from their contracts. No legislature can pass a law changing the terms of someone's business agreement.

? **IDENTIFY SUPPORTING DETAILS** What constitutional protections make it possible for Americans to conduct business in freedom?

The Limited Role of Government in the Marketplace

The government plays a limited but important part in the American free enterprise system. The government's primary role is to carry out its constitutional responsibilities to protect property rights, contracts, and other business activities. Over time, Americans have come to expect the government to take other actions to promote the **public interest**, or the concerns of society as a whole. The government has passed laws to protect us from economic problems that affect us all, such as pollution or unsafe foods and medicines.

Information and Free Enterprise In a free market system, consumer buying decisions determine what goods get produced. But consumers cannot make informed choices if they do not have basic information about the products they are buying. In other words, educated consumers make the free market system work more efficiently. Because of this, one of the government's important roles in the economy is to make sure that producers provide consumers with information.

Toward this end, Congress has passed **public disclosure laws**, which require companies to give consumers important information about the products or services that they offer. Often this information is attached to the product when it is offered for sale. You may have seen energy efficiency tags on refrigerators, or heard car commercials in which the announcer reads off a long list of terms and conditions. Using this information, consumers can evaluate some important aspects of the products they are thinking about buying.

Other laws require businesses to make the information they supply honest and clear. The Federal Trade Commission Act says that advertisements cannot be deceptive. The Truth-in-Lending Act requires businesses offering loans to disclose certain information to consumers before they sign a loan agreement. Consumers use this information to protect themselves from false claims.

>> The role of government in protecting consumers includes regulations directing car companies to provide detailed information about the vehicles they sell.

Major Federal Regulatory Agencies

AGENCY	DATE	ROLE
Food and Drug Administration (FDA)	1906	Sets standards for food, drugs, cosmetics
Federal Reserve System (FED)	1913	Regulates banking, manages money supply
Federal Deposit Insurance Corporation (FDIC)	1933	Insures deposits, regulates certain bank practices
Federal Aviation Administration (FAA)	1958	Regulates matters related to civil aviation
Environmental Protection Agency (EPA)	1970	Enacts policies to protect health, the environment
Occupational Safety and Health Administration (OSHA)	1970	Enacts policies to protect health and safety of workers
Consumer Product Safety Commission (CPSC)	1972	Enacts policies to reduce risks from consumer products
Nuclear Regulatory Commission (NRC)	1974	Regulates civilian use of nuclear materials
Transportation Security Administration (TSA)	2001	Oversees security in airports, transport systems
Consumer Financial Protection Bureau (CFPB)	2010	Oversees consumer financial products, such as mortgages

>> **Figure 2.15** Over time, government has increased its regulation of the economy. **Determine Relevance** How might the Consumer Financial Protection Bureau help protect the public?

▶ **Interactive Timeline**

Protecting Public Health, Safety, and Well-Being Although the government does not get directly involved in running private businesses, it does place some limits on their actions in the public interest. For example, the federal government and many states are actively involved in passing laws aimed at protecting consumers. The government sets manufacturing standards, requires that drugs be safe and effective, and supervises the conditions in which foods are produced to make sure they are sanitary. Labels on consumer packages must include information about safe operation of equipment or expiration dates for perishables.

A variety of federal and state agencies regulate industries whose goods and services affect the public interest. (See **Figure 2.15**.) For example, in response to growing public concern about the environment, the federal government formed the Environmental Protection Agency (EPA) in 1970.

Businesses must follow certain rules set by the EPA or by state agencies to protect the environment. Gas stations, for example, must dispose of used motor oil properly and ensure that gas tanks cannot leak into surrounding soil.

Both individuals and businesses are subject to local zoning laws. Cities and towns often pass laws designating that certain areas can be used for residential or business purposes only. Zoning laws may forbid homeowners from establishing certain businesses out of their homes. They may block businesses from establishing or operating in certain neighborhoods. These are examples of how government places restrictions on the way businesses and individuals can use their property.

Negative Effects of Regulation During the 1960s and 1970s, popular demand for government protection of consumers and of the environment resulted in the creation of several new governmental agencies and many ordinances and regulations. These placed limits on the establishment and operation of businesses. Government regulation, however, often has negative effects on businesses. Business owners pointed out that the rules were costly to implement, cutting into profits and slowing growth. Highly regulated industries, such as the airlines and telephone companies, said that government rules and regulations stifled competition, resulting in prices that were unnecessarily high. The growth in government oversight of industry also raised government spending, because the government had to hire workers to do the tasks involved in instituting and carrying out the new rules.

In the 1980s and 1990s, public pressure for leaner, less costly government resulted in budget cuts that curtailed some government regulation of industry. Today, the government works to balance concerns raised by businesses with the need to protect the public.

? IDENTIFY MAIN IDEAS Why does the government place some limits on the freedom of businesses?

ASSESSMENT

1. **Infer** What is the key incentive that drives business owners to make sure their firms are operating at their highest level of efficiency?

2. **Draw Conclusions** What is the main benefit to the economy of the principle of open opportunity?

3. **Apply Concepts** How can inequality or discrimination hurt an economy's ability to maximize its human capital? Give an example.

4. **Analyze Context** How do the decisions you make as a consumer affect the economy?

5. **Predict Consequences** How would the right of voluntary exchange be undermined if Congress overturned all public disclosure laws regarding the automobile industry?

2.6 Yesterday you bought a pack of gum . . . or a new guitar . . . or your first car. Your purchase was just one of millions of exchanges that took place across the country that day. Government economists track these patterns of buying and selling in order to assess the state of the American economy.

>> The government has long fostered scientific research, such as the work being carried on in this lab at Texas A&M University. **Express Ideas Clearly** Why do you think the government feels such research is worth supporting?

[▶] **Interactive Flipped Video**

Supporting Economic Growth

Tracking the Economy

Tracking data is one tool government uses to promote growth and stability. As you will see, supporting education is another economic role taken by government. You will also see how your participation in the electoral process can help shape the economy.

Even in our free enterprise system, government intervenes to influence macroeconomic trends. **Macroeconomics** is the study of economic behavior and decision-making in a nation's whole economy. By contrast, **microeconomics** is the study of economic behavior and decision-making in small units, such as households and firms. (The prefix *macro* means "large," while *micro* means "small.")

GDP as a Measure of the Business Cycle One measure of a nation's economic health is **gross domestic product** (GDP), the total value of all final goods and services produced in a country in a given year. In a period of macroeconomic expansion, or growth, a country produces more than it did before, and GDP goes up. In a period of contraction, or decline, the country produces less, and GDP goes down. The alternating pattern of periodic expansion and contraction is called a **business cycle**.

>> **Objectives**

Explain why the government tracks and seeks to influence business cycles.

Analyze how the government promotes economic strength and stability.

Describe the factors that increase productivity.

>> **Key Terms**

macroeconomics
microeconomics
gross domestic
   product
business cycle
referendum
obsolescence
patent
copyright
work ethic

Unlike the day-to-day ups and downs of the stock market, business cycles feature major fluctuations. Each phase can last months or even years, as you can see in **Figure 2.16**.

Forecasting the Business Cycle Changes in business cycles take place because individuals and businesses, acting in their own self-interest, make decisions about factors such as prices, production, and consumption. Business owners who think consumers are going to spend more in the future may increase production and hire more workers. If enough employers take these steps, the economy grows. On the other hand, concern about rising prices might lead consumers to buy fewer goods. If this decrease in consumer spending is widespread and lasts long enough, suppliers might be forced to cut production and to lay off workers.

In Washington, D.C., government economists track where the country is in the business cycle and try to predict what will happen in the future. Public officials use this information to decide what actions to take, if any. Many businesses also make use of the government's economic data.

The U.S. economy has changed dramatically through the country's history, and so has the role of government in the economy. Until the 1900s, the federal government collected relatively little data about the nation's economy. During the Great Depression, the need for more comprehensive economic data became apparent. As a result, the government developed national accounting measures such as GDP. New agencies, such as the Council of Economic Advisers (established in 1946), began helping the president and Congress make better decisions about the economy.

? CHECK UNDERSTANDING Why do government experts track the business cycle?

Encouraging Economic Strength

Because the market is vulnerable to business cycles, the government tries to create public policies that promote economic strength. Again, the nature and extent of these policies have changed over the course of history. For example, in the 1800s, almost every decade brought a new financial crisis, but the federal government could do little to avert these catastrophes. As new agencies were created in the 1900s, the government gained more knowledge about the national economy and more tools to influence it. In general, policymakers today use these tools to promote economic strength by pursuing three main goals: high employment, growth, and stability—stable prices and secure financial institutions.

The Business Cycle, 1930–2012

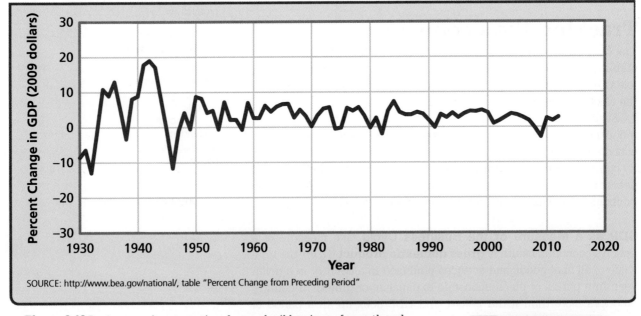

SOURCE: http://www.bea.gov/national/, table "Percent Change from Preceding Period"

>> **Figure 2.16** Business cycles at one time featured wild swings of growth and decline but have in recent decades settled into a moderate pattern. **Analyze Graphs** What has the United States gained—and lost—with the more moderate cycles of recent decades?

▶ **Interactive Chart**

STANDARD MEASURE OF STANDARD OF LIVING

$$\text{STANDARD OF LIVING} = \text{GROSS DOMESTIC PRODUCT} \div \text{TOTAL POPULATION}$$

THESE ITEMS ARE NOT INCLUDED IN THE EQUATION

Education
- Literacy Rates
- Years of Schooling

Poverty Rates
— the number of people who cannot meet basic needs

Income Inequality
— a small number of people owning a large share of the wealth

Health Measures
- Life Expectancy
- Infant Mortality

>> **Figure 2.17** This traditional measure of standard of living does not include many measures that might affect people's quality of life. **Identify Central Issues** How might levels of education, poverty, income inequality, and health impact standard of living?

Maximum Employment One aim of government economic policy is to ensure jobs for everyone who is able to work. In the United States, many economists consider an unemployment rate from 4 percent to 6 percent to be evidence of a healthy economy. If the unemployment rate rises higher than that, government officials may take various steps to encourage job growth.

A Growing Economy Part of the American Dream has always been for each generation to enjoy a higher standard of living than previous generations. For that to happen, the economy must grow to provide additional goods and services. An increasing GDP is a sign of such growth. (See **Figure 2.17** for more about GDP and the concept of standard of living.) To help growth, the government may cut taxes or increase spending. Experts often disagree as to which approach stimulates economic growth more effectively.

Stability The government also seeks to keep the economy stable. Consumers, producers, and investors need to feel confident that economic conditions will not fluctuate unpredictably. If this confidence wavers, economic growth may slow or even stop.

One indicator of economic stability is the general level of prices. A surge in prices puts a strain on consumers, especially people with low or fixed incomes. If prices sink, producers feel the pain. For example, a jump in milk prices hurts consumers, while a plunge in milk prices hurts farmers. Either way, the economy can suffer.

The government thus seeks to prevent sudden, drastic shifts in prices. If it does so wisely, that sector of the economy remains stable, with little effect on consumers or producers. But if it errs, the government can interfere with that sector's economic health, making it difficult for producers to remain in business.

Secure Financial Markets Another sign of economic stability is the security of financial institutions, such as banks or the stock market. Picture yourself going to the bank and finding it boarded up. When we make a deposit or a stock purchase, we want to know that our money will be protected from mismanagement or fraud and shielded from the effects of sudden economic downturns.

To provide such protections, the federal government monitors and regulates banks and other financial institutions. Some regulations protect bank deposits and retirees' pensions. Federal regulators also investigate fraud and manage interest rates and the flow of money through the economy.

Government intervention in the name of economic stability and security comes at a cost. In 2008, when the housing market collapsed, banks found themselves holding billions of dollars' worth of loans borrowers could not repay. The banking system neared collapse, threatening the entire economy. The U.S. government stepped in to shore up the banks, loaning them billions of dollars and making other accommodations. The effort helped keep banks in business, but it was largely funded by U.S. taxpayers. There is a great deal of disagreement over the costs and benefits of this action.

Economic Citizenship Economic policy is made by elected officials and the workers they appoint. But it is the voters who put these officials in office. On a state and local level, voters have an even more direct say. Ballots often include **referendums**, proposed laws submitted directly to the public, on spending or other economic issues.

Voters, then, play a vital role in shaping government economic actions. As you can see in **Figure 2.18**, these actions have contributed to steady, strong growth in the United States over the past century.

Like others in a market economy, voters make choices based on self-interest. To fully determine what policies best serve their interests, Americans must understand the macroeconomic processes that shape our futures.

? LIST What three goals does the government try to meet when promoting economic strength?

Productivity and the Role of Technology

The American economy supports a far higher standard of living than most economies of the world. As you have learned, one way to preserve that high standard is by increasing productivity—producing more outputs from the same or a smaller quantity of inputs.

Technological Progress Improved technology is a key factor in boosting productivity. Technological progress has long enabled the economy of the United States to operate more efficiently, increasing GDP and giving American businesses a competitive advantage in the world.

American history is full of innovations that improved productivity. Thomas Edison's invention of the light bulb made a longer workday possible. Henry Ford's use of the assembly line led to mass production of affordable cars. In recent times, computers have allowed workers to do more work in a shorter amount of time.

Real Gross Domestic Product, 1910–2012

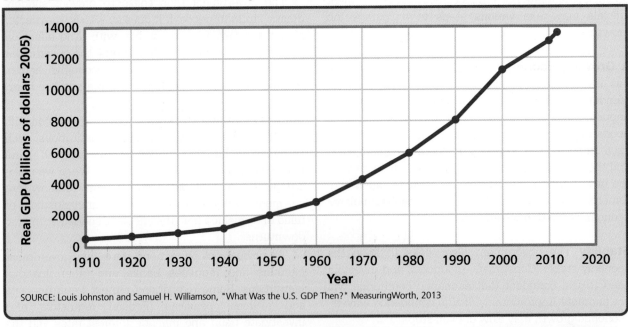

SOURCE: Louis Johnston and Samuel H. Williamson, "What Was the U.S. GDP Then?" MeasuringWorth, 2013

>> **Figure 2.18 Analyze Graphs** How would you characterize GDP growth from 1910 to 2012?

▶ **Interactive Gallery**

Innovation often leads to **obsolescence**, as older products and processes become out-of-date. Workers, too, may be subject to obsolescence. One example is telephone operators who lost their jobs due to computerized dialing systems. Often, these physical and human resources can be used in other ways. Old industrial buildings can be converted into stores or apartments. Workers can be retrained to do other jobs.

Encouraging Innovation To help maintain the country's technological advantage, the government promotes innovation and invention. Federal agencies fund scores of research and development projects at universities. The Morrill Acts of 1862 and 1890 created land-grant colleges that received federal land and money to pursue the study of "agriculture and the mechanical arts." Land-grant schools from the Massachusetts Institute of Technology to Texas A&M University have been powerhouses of innovation.

The government's own research institutions also produce a steady stream of new technologies. Probably the best-known of these federal institutions is the National Aeronautics and Space Administration (NASA). Technologies created by NASA, as part of the effort to send satellites and humans into space, have produced amazing spin-offs, or products with commercial uses. NASA spin-offs range from a muscle stimulator for people with paralysis to a scanner that allows firefighters to see "invisible flames" given off by alcohol or hydrogen fires.

The government also encourages innovation by granting patents and copyrights. A **patent** gives the inventor of a new product the exclusive right to produce and sell it for 20 years. A **copyright** grants an author exclusive rights to publish and sell his or her creative works. Patents and copyrights are an incentive to innovation because they protect people's right to profit from their creativity in the free market.

The American Work Ethic While government incentives may encourage innovation, economic growth cannot occur without individual effort. When asked to account for his success in the movie and recording industries, Will Smith stated:

> I've never really viewed myself as particularly talented. I've viewed myself as slightly above average in talent. And where I excel is ridiculous, sickening worth ethic. You know, while the other guy's sleeping? I'm working. While the other guy's eating? I'm working.

—Will Smith, *60 Minutes* interview

The **work ethic** Smith refers to is a commitment to the value of hard work. It not only means working hard, but also caring about the quality of one's work. The American work ethic has long been seen as a key ingredient in the nation's productivity and economic success.

? EXPRESS IDEAS CLEARLY How does improved technology help the economy?

ASSESSMENT

1. **Apply Concepts** Why would a government decision to increase spending be a matter of macroeconomic policy?

2. **Generate Explanations** How is gross domestic product used to determine the business cycle?

3. **Check Understanding** How do patents act as an incentive to technological innovation?

4. **Make Decisions** Suppose you had a job you did not like. If you read that the economy was in the contracting phase of the business cycle, would you be more or less likely to quit your job and look for a new one? Why or why not?

5. **Apply Concepts** Suppose Congress passed a bill funding research into alternative sources of energy. Which of the three goals of government economic policy would this fulfill?

>> Mail delivery is a service government has provided since the earliest days in the nation's history. **Draw Conclusions** Why do you think the federal government chose to provide this service rather than letting a private company do it?

▶ **Interactive Flipped Video**

You benefit from all kinds of services that federal, state, and local governments provide. You go to school, ride on roads, cross bridges, and use public parks. What would your life be like without these services? Or suppose that you could use a specific road or bridge only if your family had helped pay for it. How much would that complicate your life?

>> **Objectives**

Identify examples of public goods.

Analyze market failures.

Evaluate how the government allocates some resources by managing externalities.

>> **Key Terms**

public good
public sector
private sector
infrastructure
free rider
market failure
externality
poverty threshold
welfare

Public Goods and Externalities

Public Goods

Even in a free market economy, the government must provide certain goods and services that the marketplace cannot. For example, the job of building a bridge would become almost impossible if it had to be done by the joint action of all the people and businesses that would benefit from it. Sometimes, the government has to step in.

Roads and bridges are two of the many examples of public goods the government provides. A **public good** is a shared good or service for which it would be inefficient or impractical (1) to make consumers pay individually and (2) to exclude those who did not pay.

What Makes a Public Good Let us look at the first feature of a public good, the inefficiency or impracticality of making each consumer pay for the good individually. How would you like to receive a bill for your share of launching a space shuttle, cleaning Mount Rushmore, or paying the salary of every soldier in the army? To simplify the funding of government projects in the public interest, the government collects taxes.

What about the second feature of a public good, the inefficiency or impracticality of excluding nonpayers from using the good? Imagine the arguments and traffic delays that would erupt if drivers who refused to pay to use a street were told they had to turn around and drive away. Also, as a society, we believe that certain facilities or services, such as libraries or protection from fire, should be available to all, rich or poor.

In the case of most public goods, it is simply not practical for a private business to provide the good or service, charge those who benefit, and exclude nonpayers from using it. Neither is it efficient. Take, for example, national parks like Yellowstone and Yosemite. These are unique national treasures. If these parks were privately owned, the owner could charge an excessively high admission fee. Also, no other producer could produce a Yellowstone or Yosemite. Thus private ownership would be inefficient, because resources could not be used in a way that would maximize output.

Public goods have another characteristic. Any number of consumers can use them without reducing the benefits to any single consumer. For the most part, increasing the number of consumers does not increase the cost of providing the public good. So, if you are driving on a highway and eight other drivers enter it, they do not significantly reduce the road's benefits to you or increase the government's cost of providing the road.

Public goods are financed by the **public sector**, the part of the economy that involves the transactions of the government. The **private sector**, the part of the economy that involves transactions of individuals and businesses, would have little incentive to produce public goods.

Weighing Costs and Benefits As you have read, governments step in to act in the public interest when they determine that the benefits of a policy outweigh the drawbacks, or the costs. In road construction, the benefits are obvious. Transportation is a vital part of the nation's **infrastructure**, the basic facilities that are necessary for a society and economy to function efficiently and grow. American leaders have long regarded investment in infrastructure not only as a means to provide needed public goods, but also as a way to promote economic growth:

Investing in infrastructure not only makes our roads, bridges, and ports safer and allows our businesses and workers to be as competitive as they need to be in the global economy, it also creates thousands of

good American jobs that cannot be outsourced.

—White House Press Release, February 20, 2013

Transportation improves when governments build needed roads. An economist might say that the government's policy of providing this public good also benefits the economy by increasing efficiency. That is, government investment in road-building uses resources in a way that maximizes the output of roads. The drawback, though, is the economic freedom we give up. None of us individually gets to decide what roads will be built or where. In this case, the advantages clearly outweigh the drawback. In other cases, weighing benefits against costs is more complex.

As **Figure 2.19** shows, understanding the costs and benefits is critical in determining whether something gets produced as a public good. Two cost-benefit criteria must be present.

1. The benefit to each individual is less than the cost that each would have to pay if it were provided privately.
2. The total benefits to society are greater than the total cost.

If just one or a few people got together to fund the project, the cost to each of them would be much higher

>> This bridge is a public good. It benefits society by encouraging commercial and personal links between two populated areas otherwise kept apart by a river.

than the benefits each would gain—whether in the form of profits or some other reward or advantage. In such circumstances, the market would not provide the good.

But if you look at society as a whole, the picture changes. As long as the benefit all people gain exceeds the total cost, it makes sense for government to fund the project.

From the individual's point of view, this situation is better too. The government can fund the project by collecting a small amount of money in taxes from a large number of people. That means the share paid by each person is much less than it would be if they had to fund the project alone or even through a small group.

In economic terms, the need for government to provide public goods is a matter of efficiency, of maximizing the output of goods and services. In the case of public goods, the market cannot be counted on to maximize the output. Private firms have no way of forcing each person who "consumes" the light from a streetlight, for example, to pay for it. For this reason, they cannot produce as many streetlights as consumers need. It would be inefficient to do so. The government, however, can produce streetlights and other public goods efficiently. Through taxes, it can take in enough revenue to produce the needed amount of streetlights.

This does not mean, however, that government will choose to spend its tax revenue on streetlights—or on roads or bridges or public parks. Decisions about how the government uses tax dollars depend on its economic policies. The costs and benefits of any proposed policy must be analyzed to be sure that they fulfill the economic goal of efficiency. The benefits must exceed the costs.

Free-Rider Problem A phenomenon associated with public goods is called the "free-rider problem." A **free rider** is someone who would not be willing to pay for a certain good or service, but would get the benefit of it anyway if it were provided as a public good. Unlike consumers in the free marketplace, free riders consume what they do not directly pay for.

You probably would not voluntarily contribute to build roads in a state you did not live in. Yet when states tax their citizens to build and maintain roads, you share in the benefit. For example, the roads in other states make it easier for trucking companies to bring goods to your state. And if you were traveling through another state on vacation, you would certainly not refuse to drive on its roads. You receive the benefit whether you pay directly or not.

Try another example: Everyone on your street wants fire protection except one penny-pinching neighbor,

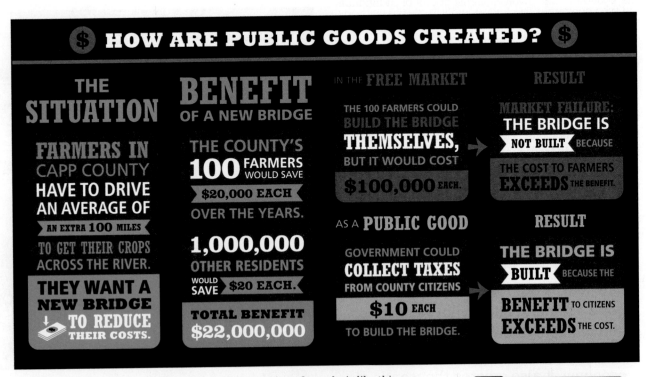

>> **Figure 2.19** Public goods are created after a cost-benefit analysis like this one.
Compare and Contrast Study the fictional event described here. Why was the Capp County bridge built as a public good rather than in the free market?

▶ **Interactive Gallery**

who says it is not worth the money. Don't you want him to have fire protection anyway? If his house catches fire, yours could ignite as well. So local taxes pay for firefighting services for all property in an area, because all residents are better off if the government provides this service. Your free-rider neighbor benefits from this service as well.

The free-rider problem suggests what would happen if the government stopped collecting taxes to fund public services. If it relied on voluntary contributions instead, many people would refuse to give money. Yet they would still use the services. Many public services would then have to be eliminated.

? **IDENTIFY MAIN IDEAS** What two cost-benefit criteria must be met for something to be produced as a public good?

Market Failures

Public goods are examples of what some economists call a market failure. The term does not suggest that the free enterprise system does not work. Rather, **market failure** describes a specific situation in which the free market, operating on its own, does not distribute resources efficiently.

To understand market failure, recall how a successful free market operates: Choices made by individuals determine what goods get made, how they get made, and who consumes the goods. Profit incentives attract producers who, because of competition, provide goods and services that consumers need at prices that are reasonable and responsive to market forces.

In the road-building scenario, are these features present? Generally not. If a company were to build a road, there would be no real competition. So, the company could charge a high price for tolls for those wishing to use the road.

Also, companies would not choose to build roads in sparsely populated areas because there would be little incentive to do so. They would see no chance to earn profits—a low population would mean too few drivers to charge.

As a result, the criteria for a properly functioning market system do not exist. For that reason, the road-building scenario is a market failure.

? **CHECK UNDERSTANDING** In what way are public goods examples of market failure?

>> In the 1930s, utilities had no incentive to string electric lines to isolated areas. Government took on that task with the Rural Electrification Administration. **Infer** Why do you think the government was willing to help bring electricity to rural areas?

Externalities

Out-of-state drivers can travel over roads that they did not pay to have built. Nonpayers as well as payers enjoy the environmental benefits of national parks. Both of these examples involve what economists call externalities. An **externality** is an economic side effect of a good or service that generates benefits or costs to someone other than the person deciding how much to produce or consume. Externalities may be either positive or negative.

Positive Externalities As you have read, public goods generate benefits to many people, not just those who pay for the goods. Such beneficial side effects are positive externalities. Some of the positive externalities associated with building a bridge are shown in **Figure 2.20**.

The private sector—both individuals and businesses—can create positive externalities, too. For instance:

• Walsh Computers hires underprivileged teenagers and trains them to be computer programmers. Walsh set up this training program to serve its own interests. However, the newly trained workers can be hired by other companies, who benefit from the workers' skills without having paid for them.

- Mrs. Ruiz buys an old house that is an eyesore in the neighborhood. She paints the house, cuts the grass, and plants flowers. Her neighbors were not involved in her decision, nor did they share the cost. Yet they receive benefits from it, such as higher property values and a better view.

In fact, many economists believe that the private sector generates positive externalities more efficiently than the public sector can, and at less cost to taxpayers.

Whether private or public, positive externalities allow someone who did not purchase a good to enjoy part of the benefits of that good. In the 1990s, several endangered species, including the bald eagle and the peregrine falcon, were saved from extinction. Protection of species critical to our ecosystem benefits us all.

Negative Externalities Of course, as **Figure 2.20** shows, producing goods and services can also generate unintended costs, called negative externalities. Negative externalities cause part of the cost of producing a good or service to be paid for by someone other than the producer. For example:

- The Enchanted Forest Paper Mill releases chemical wastes into a nearby river, making it

unhealthy. The city of Tidyville, downstream from the mill, is forced to install special equipment at its water-treatment plant to clean up the chemicals. The community, not the polluter, is paying the cost of cleaning up the river.

- Your next-door neighbor, Mr. Fogler, takes up the accordion and holds Friday night polka parties in his backyard. Unfortunately, you hate polka music.

Government's Goals Externalities are a sign of market failure because the costs or benefits of a good or service are not assigned properly. Understanding externalities helps us see another role that the government plays in the American economy.

First, the government may take action to create positive externalities. Education, for example, benefits students directly. Yet society as a whole also benefits from an educated population, because educated workers are generally more productive.

Second, the government aims to limit negative externalities, such as pollution. Pollutants from coal-burning power plants and auto emissions can drift high into the atmosphere and come down in the form of acid rain, which causes ecological damage. Why is acid rain a negative externality? It is part of the cost of producing power and driving cars, but that cost is

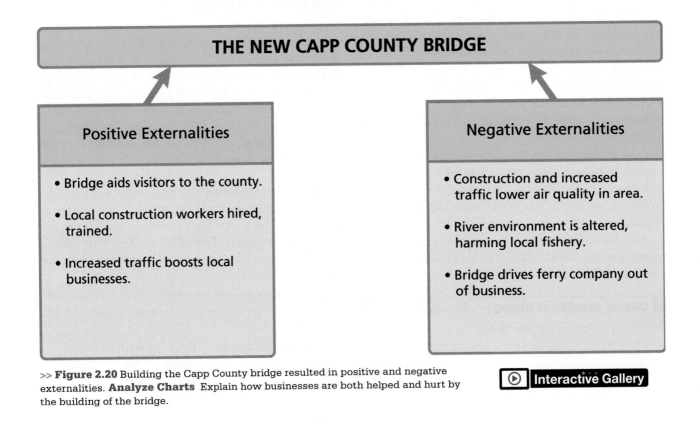

THE NEW CAPP COUNTY BRIDGE

Positive Externalities

- Bridge aids visitors to the county.
- Local construction workers hired, trained.
- Increased traffic boosts local businesses.

Negative Externalities

- Construction and increased traffic lower air quality in area.
- River environment is altered, harming local fishery.
- Bridge drives ferry company out of business.

>> **Figure 2.20** Building the Capp County bridge resulted in positive and negative externalities. **Analyze Charts** Explain how businesses are both helped and hurt by the building of the bridge.

▶ **Interactive Gallery**

imposed upon people other than those who produce the pollution. The cost is damaged trees, lakes, and wildlife.

To address this negative externality, the federal government now requires new cars to have an expensive antipollution device called a catalytic converter. In addition, the Environmental Protection Agency offers incentives to power-plant operators to put "scrubbers" on their smokestacks to cut emissions. These actions transfer the costs of pollution back to its producers. Government management of this negative externality has yielded positive results. For example, emissions of sulfur dioxide, a key trigger of acid rain, decreased by 64 percent between 1990 and 2009.

Government-Driven or Market-Driven Solutions?

As you saw, many economists think that the private sector can better reduce negative externalities than the government can. This belief has spurred debate over how to stop damage to the environment.

Since the 1970s, the government has often tried to halt pollution by creating strict regulations. Many economists say that this approach is inefficient and limits growth, because it increases costs. It also ties the hands of businesses by requiring specific solutions rather than encouraging innovation.

These economists want the government to allow market-driven solutions to environmental problems. In this approach, the government would still play a role by setting standards that industries would have to meet. Individual firms, though, would have more freedom to find ways to meet those goals.

? IDENTIFY SUPPORTING DETAILS What does the government do in response to negative externalities?

The Poverty Problem

You've seen it all around you: on TV shows, in the news, maybe even in your community. There are vast differences between people who have a lot of money, enough money, and very little money. On the average, Americans enjoy a high standard of living. Yet about 15 percent of Americans live in poverty. And for people under the age of 18, the percentage is even higher.

To help the poor, government programs take money from some people and redistribute it to others. Yet critics say such actions violate the economic principle of limited government intervention.

While the free market has proven better than any other economic system at generating wealth, that wealth is spread unevenly throughout society.

>> The government takes steps to limit negative externalities. This costly pollution-control equipment is a response to government rules put forward by the Environmental Protection Agency.

This leaves some people below the **poverty threshold**, an income level below that which is needed to support families. The poverty threshold is determined by the federal government and adjusted periodically. In 2012, the poverty threshold for a single parent under age 65 with one child under age 18 was $15,825 per year. For a four-person family with two children, it was $23,283 per year.

The U.S. Bureau of the Census, part of the Department of Labor, establishes the poverty threshold for families of different sizes and ages. Each year, the poverty threshold is adjusted based on the cost of the goods a family needs to buy. As prices rise, so does the poverty threshold.

The Government's Role As a society, we recognize some responsibilities to the very young, the very old, the sick, the poor, and the disabled. The society tries to provide a safety net for people in these groups, in the form of federal, state, and local government programs. These programs aim to raise people's standard of living, or their level of economic well-being as measured by the ability to purchase goods and services they need and want.

>> Politicians have debated reforming the Social Security system for many years. **Analyze Political Cartoons** Who do you think the person in this cartoon represents, and what is his reaction to the sign on the door?

The Welfare System Since the 1930s, the main government effort to ease poverty has been to collect taxes from individuals and redistribute some of those funds in the form of welfare. **Welfare** is a general term for government aid for the poor. It includes many types of programs that redistribute wealth from some people to others.

The nation's welfare system began under President Franklin Roosevelt during the Great Depression. Welfare spending greatly increased in the 1960s under President Lyndon Johnson's "War on Poverty."

Federal welfare programs came under increasing attack in the 1980s. Critics voiced concern about people becoming dependent on welfare and unable or unwilling to get off it. Some critics also claimed that income redistribution discourages productivity, thus actually aggravating poverty.

In 1996, Congress made sweeping changes to the welfare system. New reforms limited the amount of time people could receive welfare and gave states more freedom to experiment with antipoverty programs.

? RECALL What is the goal of government welfare programs?

ASSESSMENT

1. **Analyze Information** Why is national defense an example of a public good? Give two reasons.

2. **Generate Explanations** Why would the free-rider problem prevent a private business from investing in the building of a city sidewalk?

3. **Compare and Contrast** Why does the construction of a bridge over a river represent a market failure, but the construction of an apartment building does not?

4. **Apply Concepts** How might the government BEST manage the negative externality of litter in the form of bottles and cans?

5. **Infer** What is generally true—in terms of needs and wants—about families whose income is below the poverty threshold?

1. **Explain Basic Economic Problems** Write a paragraph explaining why choice is a basic economic problem faced by every society. In your paragraph, describe an economic situation that our society faces that requires that a choice be made.

2. **Describe Answers to Economic Questions** Write a paragraph that compares the ways in which a free enterprise system and a centrally planned economic system answer the three basic economic questions: What goods and services should be produced? How should these goods and services be produced? Who consumes these goods and services?

3. **Describe and Explain Basic Characteristics of Economic Systems** Write a paragraph that defines and describes economic freedom and explains how economic freedom is a basic characteristic of the U.S. free enterprise system.

4. **Analyze Costs and Benefits of Economic Policies** Write a paragraph evaluating the economic data in the graph. During which period shown on the graph was productivity growth strongest? What further questions concerning the costs and benefits of economic policies related to economic growth does the data on the graph suggest?

Rates of Productivity Increase in the Business Sector, 1990–2012

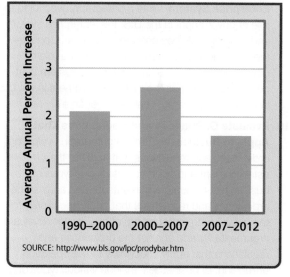

SOURCE: http://www.bls.gov/lpc/prodybar.htm

5. **Examine Socialist Economic Systems** What belief is common to different socialist economic systems? Choose one country that is an example of a current socialist system. What makes this country socialist?

6. **Understand Terms that Describe the U.S. Economic System** Write a paragraph that describes the U.S. economic system in terms of the freedom independent producers and consumers have to make economic decisions. In your paragraph, use each of these terms correctly: free enterprise, free market, and capitalism.

7. **Analyze the Importance and Impact of Economic Philosophers** Using the quotation below, write a paragraph that answers the following: What motivating force is Smith describing in the quotation, and what economic behaviors does it lead to? Identify at least one idea of Smith's that is incorporated by free enterprise systems, such as that of the United States.

"Give me that which I want, and you shall have this which you want . . . it is in this manner that we obtain from one another the far greater part of those good offices [services] which we stand in need of. It is not from the benevolence of the butcher, the brewer, or the baker that we expect our dinner, but from their regard to their own interest."

— Adam Smith, The Wealth of Nations

8. **Explain Basic Characteristics of Economic Systems** Write a paragraph that explains the role competition plays in the way businesses set prices for their goods or services, and in encouraging innovation in the production of goods.

9. **Explain the Benefits of Economic Systems** Write a paragraph that explains the benefits of the U.S. free enterprise system, including variety of goods. Consider why the U.S. free enterprise system offers a wider variety of goods and services than other systems. Explain the concept of consumer sovereignty.

Major Federal Regulatory Agencies

AGENCY	DATE	ROLE
Food and Drug Administration (FDA)	1906	Sets standards for food, drugs, cosmetics
Federal Reserve System (FED)	1913	Regulates banking, manages money supply
Federal Deposit Insurance Corporation (FDIC)	1933	Insures deposits, regulates certain bank practices
Federal Aviation Administration (FAA)	1958	Regulates matters related to civil aviation
Environmental Protection Agency (EPA)	1970	Enacts policies to protect health, the environment
Occupational Safety and Health Administration (OSHA)	1970	Enacts policies to protect health and safety of workers
Consumer Product Safety Commission (CPSC)	1972	Enacts policies to reduce risks from consumer products
Nuclear Regulatory Commission (NRC)	1974	Regulates civilian use of nuclear materials
Transportation Security Administration (TSA)	2001	Oversees security in airports, transport systems
Consumer Financial Protection Bureau (CFPB)	2010	Oversees consumer financial products, such as mortgages

10. **Describe Costs and Benefits of Economic Policies** Describe the costs and benefits of U.S. economic policies related to the economic goals of stability and security. Consider the following in your response: Identify an example of economic stability and describe the economic policies that the government uses to achieve this goal. Describe economic policies that promote security, addressing specifically the security of banking institutions.

11. **Evaluate Government Rules and Regulations in the Free Enterprise System** Using the table above, evaluate government rules and regulations in the U.S. free enterprise system. Consider the following in your response: Evaluate the government's role in regulating the economy over time. Describe the arguments made in opposition to government regulation of the economy.

12. **Identify Government Restrictions on Property** Write a paragraph identifying examples of restrictions that the government places on the way businesses and individuals use property. Consider why such limits are imposed by the government.

13. **Interpret a Circular Flow Model of the Economy** Write a paragraph that interprets the roles of resource owners and firms in a circular flow model of the economy, providing real-world examples to illustrate elements of the model. Consider the following in your response: What role do resource owners play in a circular-flow model of the economy? What role do firms play in a circular-flow model of the economy?

14. **Identify Economic Concepts in the U.S. Constitution** Consider the following questions: What prevents the U.S. government from seizing property for its own use? Under what conditions can a government in the United States take private property for public use?

15. **Describe the Role of Government in the Free Enterprise System** Write a paragraph describing the role of government in the U.S. free enterprise system and how that role has changed over time. Consider the following in your response: How is the role of government in the U.S. free enterprise system best described? How has the role of government in the U.S. free enterprise system changed over time?

16. **Evaluate Ordinances and Regulations That Apply to Businesses** Write a paragraph evaluating ordinances and regulations that apply to the establishment and operation of various types of businesses. Evaluate arguments for and against the ordinances and regulations that apply specifically to the establishing, or founding, of businesses. Evaluate arguments for and against the ordinances and regulations that apply specifically to the operation, or running, of businesses. Include various types of businesses in the examples.

COMPARING AND CONTRASTING SOCIALISM AND COMMUNISM

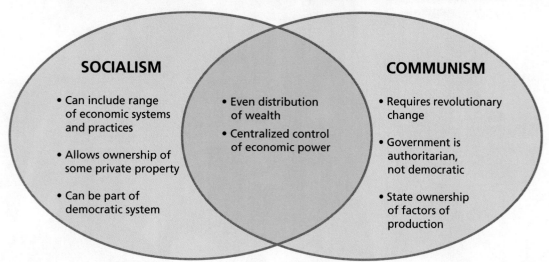

SOCIALISM

- Can include range of economic systems and practices

- Allows ownership of some private property

- Can be part of democratic system

- Even distribution of wealth
- Centralized control of economic power

COMMUNISM

- Requires revolutionary change

- Government is authoritarian, not democratic

- State ownership of factors of production

17. **Compare Economic Systems** Compare the free enterprise system, socialism, and communism using the basic characteristics of economic systems. Using the figure above, write a paragraph addressing the following questions: How do socialism and communism compare in terms of economic freedom and the role of government? How does the free enterprise system compare to socialism and communism in terms of economic freedom and the role of government?

18. **Provide Examples to Illustrate Economic Models** Provide real-world examples to illustrate elements of the circular flow model. Create a circular flow model of the U.S. economy. Include real-world examples and the government's participation in the economy as part of the model.

19. **Identify Economic Concepts in the U.S. Constitution** Write a paragraph expressing and explaining a point of view on the following subject: The government needs more power to take private property for public use. In your paragraph, make reference to the constitutional issues that would be involved.

20. **Describe the Role of Government in the Free Enterprise System and Categorize Economic Information** The new bridge referred to in the chart is a public good. What is the likely role of government in its construction? Analyze externalities by categorizing each of the following entries and saying to which division of

the chart they belong: bridge aids visitors to the county; construction and increased traffic lower air quality in area; local construction workers hired, trained; river environment is altered, harming local fishery; increased traffic boosts local businesses; bridge drives ferry company out of business.

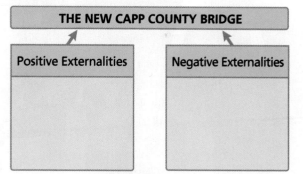

THE NEW CAPP COUNTY BRIDGE

Positive Externalities	Negative Externalities

21. **Write About the Essential Question** **Write an essay on the Essential Question: Who benefits from the free market economy?** Use evidence from your study of this Topic to support your answer.

[ESSENTIAL QUESTION] How do we affect the economy?

3 Demand, Supply, and Prices

Enduring Understandings

- The demand for a good increases or decreases as the price changes. Factors other than price can shift the demand curve to the left or right.

- Businesses can use information about the elasticity of demand of their goods to make intelligent pricing decisions.

- Producers are willing to supply more of a product or service when prices are higher.

- Supply and demand create an equilibrium in the market. When disturbed, prices will change, but in time supply, demand, and prices will move to new equilibrium levels.

- Prices make markets more efficient and help buyers and sellers make informed choices.

>> Shoppers hit the mall to find bargains at a one-day sale.

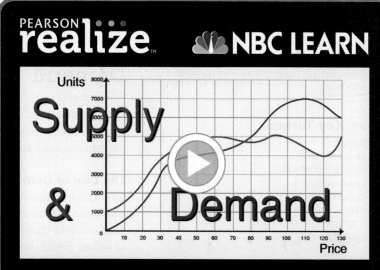

PEARSON realize. ⚡ **NBC LEARN**

Watch the My Story Video on the principles of supply and demand.

PEARSON realize.
www.PearsonRealize.com

Access your digital lessons including:
Topic Inquiry • Interactive Reading Notepad • Interactivities • Assessments

>> These people may have a desire to purchase the goods they see in the store window, but without the ability to pay for them, they do not generate true demand.

Interactive Flipped Video

>> **Objectives**

Understand how the law of demand explains the effects of price on quantity demanded.

Describe how the substitution effect and the income effect influence decisions.

Explore a demand schedule for an individual and a market.

Interpret a demand graph using demand schedules.

>> **Key Terms**

demand
law of demand
substitution effect
income effect
demand schedule
market demand
  schedule
demand curve

Anyone who has ever shopped knows the difference between wanting to have something and being able to pay for it. Sometimes you can buy what you want, and sometimes the price is just too high.

Fundamentals of Demand

Demand

Price changes always affect the quantity demanded because people buy less of a good when its price goes up. By analyzing how the cost of pizza affects how much people are willing to buy, you will see how consumers react to a change in price.

The Law of Demand Demand is the desire to own something and the ability to pay for it. To have demand for a good or service, both of these conditions must be present. We will look at the demand side of markets over the next three lessons. Later, we will look at the actions of sellers, which economists call the supply side. Then, we will look at supply and demand together and study how they interact to establish the prices that we pay for most goods.

Anyone who has ever spent money will easily understand the law of demand. The **law of demand** says that when a good's price is lower, consumers will buy more of it. When the price is higher, consumers will buy less of it. All of us act out this law of demand in our everyday purchasing decisions. Whether your income is $10 or $10 million, the price of a good will strongly influence your decision to buy.

David Henderson, an economics professor who served as a senior economist with the President's Council of Economic Advisers, describes the importance of the law of demand:

> The most famous law in economics, and the one that economists are most sure of, is the law of demand. On this law is built almost the whole edifice of economics.
>
> —David Henderson, "Demand," *The Concise Encyclopedia of Economics*

Now ask yourself a question: Would you buy a slice of pizza for lunch if it cost $2? Many of us would, and some of us might even buy more than one slice. But would you buy the same slice of pizza if it cost $4? Fewer of us would buy it at that price. Even real pizza lovers might reduce their consumption from three or four slices to just one or two. How many of us would buy a slice for $20? Probably very few would pay that amount. As the price of pizza gets higher and higher, fewer of us are willing to buy it. That is the law of demand in action.

The law of demand is the result of not just one pattern of behavior, but two separate patterns that overlap. These two behavior patterns are the substitution effect and the income effect. The substitution effect and the income effect describe two different ways that a consumer can change his or her spending patterns. Together, they explain why an increase in price decreases the amount purchased.

The Substitution Effect When the price of a burrito rises, burritos become more expensive compared with other foods such as salads or tacos. So, as the price of a burrito rises, consumers have an incentive to buy one of those alternatives as a substitute for burritos. This causes a drop in the number of burritos demanded. For example, instead of eating burritos for lunch on Mondays and Fridays, a student could eat a burrito on Mondays and a bagel on Fridays. This change in consumption is known as the substitution effect. The **substitution effect** takes place when a consumer reacts to a rise in the price of one good by consuming less of that good and more of a substitute good.

The substitution effect can also apply to a drop in prices. If the price of a brand of athletic shoes drops, those shoes become cheaper compared to other brands or types of shoes. Consumers will now substitute the athletic shoes for other shoes they may have purchased, causing the demand for those athletic shoes to rise.

The Income Effect Rising prices have another effect that we have all felt. They make us feel poorer. When

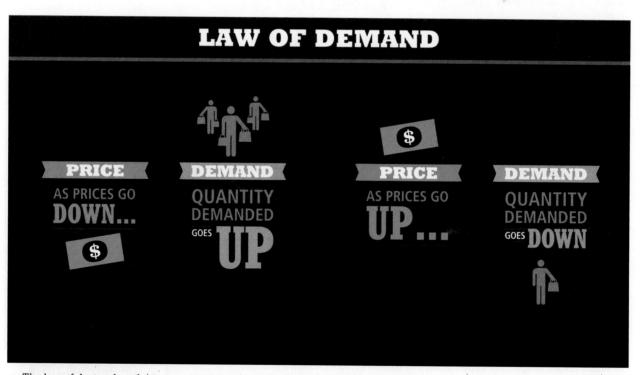

>> The law of demand explains consumer reaction to price increases and decreases.
Paraphrase Restate the law of demand in your own words.

the price of movie tickets, shoes, or pizza increases, your limited budget just won't buy as much as it did in the past. It feels as if you have less money. You can no longer afford to buy the same combination of goods, and you must cut back your purchases of some goods. If you buy fewer slices of pizza without increasing your purchases of other foods, that is the **income effect**.

One important fact to remember is that economists measure consumption in the amount of a good that is bought, not the amount of money spent to buy it. Although you are spending more on pizza, you are consuming fewer slices, so your consumption has gone down. If the price rises from $2 a slice to $4 a slice, you may decide to pay extra and order your usual lunch, but you certainly would not choose to buy more slices than before. When the price goes up, consumers spend more of their money on pizza, but they may demand less of it. Thus, the income effect has led to a decrease in the quantity demanded.

Remember, too, that the income effect also operates when the price is lowered. If the price of pizza falls, you suddenly feel wealthier. If you buy more pizza as a result of the lower price, that's the income effect.

? IDENTIFY If you buy less clothing because the price of clothing at your favorite store has gone up, what has happened?

The Demand Schedule

The law of demand, along with concepts such as the substitution effect and income effect, explains how the price of any item affects the quantity demanded of that item. Before we look at the relationship between price and the quantity demanded for a specific good, we need to look more closely at how economists use the word *demand*.

Understanding Demand To have demand for a good, you must be willing and able to buy it at the specified price. In other words, demand means that you want the good and can afford to buy it. You may desperately want a new car, a laptop computer, or a trip to Alaska, but if you can't truly afford any of these goods, then you do not demand them. You might demand digital music downloads, though, if you want to buy some and have enough money to do so at the current price.

A **demand schedule** is a table that lists the quantity of a good that a person will purchase at various prices in a market. Consider, for example, a consumer named Ashley. She loves and regularly buys pizza. A demand schedule would show the specific quantities of pizza that Ashley is willing and able to purchase at specific prices. You can see such a schedule in **Figure 3.1**. The individual demand schedule on the left tells us that at a price of $4, Ashley's "quantity demanded" of pizza is two slices per day.

The Law of Demand in Action

	PRICE OF APPLES INCREASES		PRICE OF APPLES DECREASES	
	Consumption of Apples	**Consumption of Other Goods**	**Consumption of Apples**	**Consumption of Other Goods**
INCOME EFFECT	↓	↓	↑	↑
SUBSTITUTION EFFECT	↓	↑	↑	↓
COMBINED EFFECT	↓↓	↕	↑↑	↕

>> When price changes, the substitution and income effects influence demand in different ways. **Analyze Charts** In what circumstance do the income and substitution effects lead to the same result?

▶ **Interactive Chart**

Demand Schedules

INDIVIDUAL DEMAND SCHEDULE		MARKET DEMAND SCHEDULE	
Price of a Slice of Pizza	Quantity Demanded	Price of a Slice of Pizza	Quantity Demanded
$1.00	5	$1.00	300
$2.00	4	$2.00	250
$3.00	3	$3.00	200
$4.00	2	$4.00	150
$5.00	1	$5.00	100
$6.00	0	$6.00	50

>> **Figure 3.1** Both individual and market demand schedules record how changing prices affect quantity demanded. **Analyze Data** In these schedules, how much pizza does the market demand at $3 a slice?

Market Demand Schedules If you owned a store, knowing the demand schedule of one customer might not be as helpful as knowing how all of your customers would react to price changes. When you add up the demand schedules of every buyer in the market, you can create a market demand schedule. A **market demand schedule** shows the quantities demanded at various prices by all consumers in the market. A market demand schedule for pizza would allow a restaurant owner to predict the total sales of pizza at several different prices.

The owner of a pizzeria could create a market demand schedule for pizza slices by surveying his or her customers and then adding up the quantities demanded by all individual consumers at each price. The resulting market demand schedule will look like Ashley's demand schedule, but the quantities will be larger, as shown in **Figure 3.1**.

Note that the market demand schedule on the right in **Figure 3.1** contains the same prices as Ashley's individual demand schedule, since those are the possible prices that may be charged by the pizzeria. The schedule also exhibits the law of demand. At higher prices, the quantity demanded is lower. The only difference between the two demand schedules is that the market schedule lists larger quantities demanded because the market demand schedule reflects the purchase decisions of all potential consumers in the market.

? IDENTIFY CENTRAL ISSUES In order for demand for a good to be present, what two conditions must be present?

The Demand Graph

What if you took the numbers in Ashley's demand schedule in **Figure 3.1** and plotted them on a graph? The result would be a demand graph, or curve. A **demand curve** is a graphic representation of a demand schedule.

How do economists create a demand curve? When they transfer numbers from a demand schedule to a graph, they always label the vertical axis with the lowest possible prices at the bottom and the highest price at the top. Likewise, they always label the quantities demanded on the horizontal axis with the lowest possible quantity at the left and the highest possible quantity at the right. All demand graphs show that each pair of price and quantity-demanded numbers on the demand schedule is plotted as a point on the graph. Connecting the points on the graph creates a demand curve.

Reading a Demand Curve Note two facts about Ashley's demand curve shown in **Figure 3.2**. First, the graph shows only the relationship between the price of this good and the quantity that Ashley will purchase.

Graphing Demand

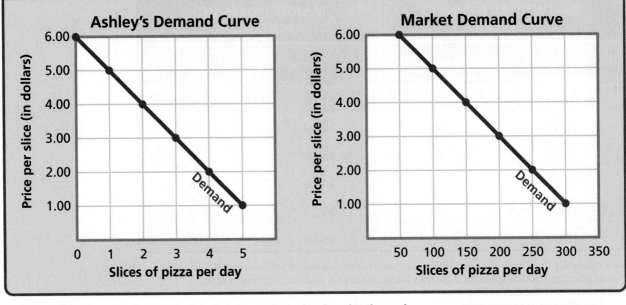

>> **Figure 3.2** These graphs use the data from the individual and market demand schedules to show demand graphically. **Analyze Graphs** How much pizza does Ashley demand at $5 a slice?

Interactive Chart

It assumes that all other factors that would affect Ashley's demand for pizza—like the price of other goods, her income, and the quality of the pizza—are held constant.

Second, the demand curve on the graph slopes downward to the right. If you follow the curve from the top left to the bottom right, you will notice that as price decreases, the quantity demanded increases. All demand schedules and demand curves reflect the law of demand, which states that higher prices will always lead to lower quantities demanded.

Ashley's demand curve in **Figure 3.2** shows her demand for slices of pizza. The market demand curve in **Figure 3.2** shows the quantities demanded by all consumers at the same prices.

Thus, the prices listed on the vertical axis are identical to those in Ashley's demand curve. The quantities listed on the horizontal axis are much larger, corresponding to those in the market demand schedule in **Figure 3.2**.

Limits of a Demand Curve The market demand curve in **Figure 3.2** can predict how people will change their buying habits when the price of a good rises or falls. For example, if the price of pizza is $3 a slice, the pizzeria will sell 200 slices a day.

This market demand curve is only accurate for one very specific set of market conditions. It cannot predict changing market conditions. Next, you will learn how

demand curves can shift because of changes in factors other than price.

? **DEFINE** What is a market demand curve?

ASSESSMENT

1. **Apply Concepts** Demand is more than just the desire to buy something. What else does it require?

2. **Make Generalizations** According to the law of demand, what would you expect to happen in the car market as the price of automobiles goes up?

3. **Express Ideas Clearly** When he saw that the price of the car model he had planned to buy had increased dramatically, Tino decided to purchase another brand instead. Which economic principle does this demonstrate?

4. **Express Ideas Clearly** Because the cost of a taxi ride increased, Martina decided to start packing a lunch instead of ordering out from a nearby restaurant. Which economic principle does this demonstrate?

5. **Describe** What does an individual demand schedule do?

The text message says it all: Raining 2 hrd! Your plans to go out to eat with your friends have suddenly been scuttled. No burger is worth the bother. Not only has your demand for burgers at any price dropped, your demand for home-delivered pizza at any price has risen.

>> The demand curve for this shopper may be changed by the threat of severe weather. As a storm approaches, factors other than price may influence buying decisions.

▶ Interactive Flipped Video

Shifts in Demand

Changes in Demand

Sometimes increases or decreases in demand are not connected to price. On a stormy night, the Burger Barn may be nearly empty while the phone is ringing off the hook at the Pizza Palace with orders for delivery.

Ceteris Paribus When we counted the number of pizza slices that would sell as the price went up or down, we assumed that nothing besides the price of pizza would change. Economists refer to this assumption as **ceteris paribus**, the Latin phrase for "all other things held constant." The demand schedule took into account only changes in price. It did not consider the effects of news reports or any one of thousands of other factors that change from day to day.

A demand curve is accurate only as long as there are no changes other than price that could affect the consumer's decision. In other words, a demand curve is accurate only as long as the *ceteris paribus* assumption is true. When the price changes, we move along the curve to a different quantity demanded.

For example, in **Figure 3.2**, you saw that an increase in price from $2 to $3 per slice will make Ashley's quantity of pizza demanded fall from four slices to three slices per day. This movement along the demand curve is referred to as a *decrease in the quantity demanded*.

>> **Objectives**

Explain the difference between a change in quantity demanded and a shift in the demand curve.

Identify the non-price determinants that create changes in demand and can cause a shift in the demand curve.

Summarize examples of how a change in demand for one good can affect demand for a related good.

>> **Key Terms**

ceteris paribus
normal good
inferior good
demographics
complements
substitutes
non-price
    determinants

By the same reasoning, a decrease in the price of pizza would lead to an *increase in the quantity demanded*.

Demand Shifts When we drop the *ceteris paribus* rule and allow other factors to change, we no longer move along the demand curve. Instead, the entire demand curve shifts. A shift in the demand curve means that at every price, consumers buy a different quantity than before. This shift of the entire curve is what economists refer to as *a change in demand*.

Suppose, for example, that Ashley's town is hit by a heat wave, and Ashley no longer feels as hungry for hot pizza. She will demand fewer slices at every price. The graph on the left in **Figure 3.3** shows her original demand curve and her new demand curve, adjusted for hot weather.

❓ **EXPLAIN** What does a shift in the demand curve indicate about demand for a particular good?

The Non-Price Determinants of Demand

As you have read, a change in the price of a good will change demand. But it does not cause the demand curve to shift. The effects of changes in price are built into the demand curve.

However, several factors can cause demand for a good to change. These are called **non-price determinants**. They are factors that can lead to the shifting of demand up or down. Non-price determinants include income, consumer expectations, population, demographics, and consumer tastes and advertising.

Changes in Income A consumer's income affects his or her demand for most goods. Most items that we purchase are **normal goods**, goods that consumers demand more of when their incomes increase.

In other words, an increase in Ashley's income from $50 per week to $75 per week will cause her to buy more of a normal good at every price level. If we were to draw a new demand schedule for Ashley, it would show a greater demand for slices of pizza at every price. Plotting the new schedule on a graph would produce a curve to the right of Ashley's original curve. For each of the prices on the vertical axis, the quantity demanded would be greater. This shift to the right of the curve is called an *increase in demand*. A fall in income would cause the demand curve to shift to the left. This shift is called a *decrease in demand*.

There are also other goods called inferior goods. They are called inferior goods because an increase in income causes demand for these goods to fall. **Inferior goods** are goods that you would buy in smaller quantities, or not at all, if your income were to rise and you could afford something better. Possible examples of inferior goods include macaroni and cheese, generic cereals, and used cars.

Changes in Demand

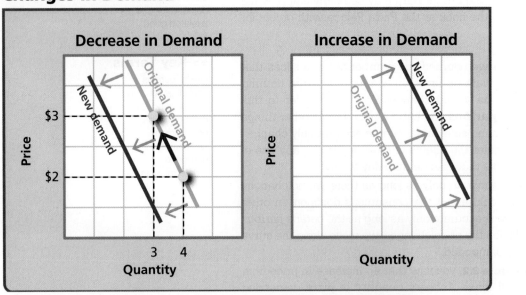

>> **Figure 3.3** The dark blue arrow shows how price affects quantity demanded. The purple lines show actual shifts in demand. **Analyze Graphs** Which type of demand shift would lead to higher prices?

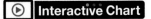

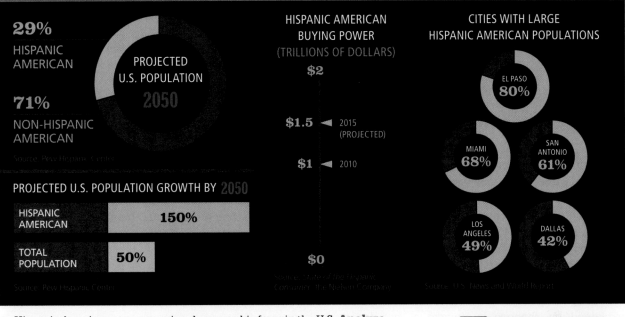

GROWING INFLUENCE OF THE HISPANIC AMERICAN POPULATION

29%
HISPANIC
AMERICAN

71%
NON-HISPANIC
AMERICAN

PROJECTED
U.S. POPULATION
2050

Source: Pew Hispanic Center

PROJECTED U.S. POPULATION GROWTH BY 2050

| HISPANIC AMERICAN | 150% |
| TOTAL POPULATION | 50% |

Source: Pew Hispanic Center

HISPANIC AMERICAN
BUYING POWER
(TRILLIONS OF DOLLARS)

$2

$1.5 ◀ 2015 (PROJECTED)

$1 ◀ 2010

$0

Source: State of the Hispanic
Consumer, the Nielsen Company

CITIES WITH LARGE
HISPANIC AMERICAN POPULATIONS

EL PASO
80%

MIAMI
68%

SAN ANTONIO
61%

LOS ANGELES
49%

DALLAS
42%

Source: U.S. News and World Report

>> Hispanic Americans are a growing demographic force in the U.S. **Analyze Information** How would you expect demand for goods intended to appeal to Hispanic Americans to change in the future?

▶ **Interactive Gallery**

Consumer Expectations Our expectations about the future can affect our demand for certain goods today. Suppose that you have had your eye on a new bicycle for several months. One day you walk into the store to look at the bike, and the salesperson mentions that the store will be raising the price in one week. Now that you expect a higher price in the near future, you are more likely to buy the bike today. In other words, the expectation of a higher price in the future has caused your immediate demand to increase.

If, on the other hand, the salesperson were to tell you that the bike will be on sale next week, your immediate demand for the bicycle would fall to zero. Or perhaps you live in a state that has a so-called tax holiday coming up. You would rather wait to buy the bike when its price to you is lower.

The current demand for a good is positively related to its expected future price. If you expect the price to rise, your current demand will rise, which means you will buy the good sooner. If you expect the price to drop, your current demand will fall, and you will wait for the lower price.

Changes in Demographics Demographics are the statistical characteristics of populations, such as age, race, gender, occupation, and income level. Businesses use this data to identify who potential customers are,

where they live, and how likely they are to purchase a specific product. Demographics also have a strong influence on the packaging, pricing, and advertising for a product.

Growing ethnic groups, like Asian Americans and Hispanic Americans, can create shifts in demand for goods and services. In the United States, Hispanic Americans accounted for about one half of the national population growth between 2000 and 2011. Analysts predict that by 2050, Hispanic Americans will make up 29 percent of the U.S. population.

Such demographic changes have profound implications for the marketplace. As the purchasing power of Hispanic Americans grows, firms will devote more of their resources to producing goods and services demanded by these consumers.

Changes in Population Size Changes in the size of the population will also affect the demand for most products. For example, a growing population needs to be housed and fed. Therefore, a rise in population will increase demand for houses, food, and many other goods and services.

Population trends can have a strong effect on certain goods. For example, when American soldiers returned from World War II in the mid- to late 1940s, record numbers of them married and started families. This trend led to the "baby boom," a jump in the birthrate from 1946 through 1964. Initially, the boom led to higher demand for baby clothes, baby food, and books on baby care. In the 1950s and 1960s, towns built thousands of new schools. Later, universities expanded and opened new campuses to make room for new students.

The baby boomers have now begun to retire. Over the next few decades, the market will face rising demand for the goods and services that are desired by senior citizens, including medical care, recreational vehicles, and homes in the Sunbelt.

Consumer Tastes and Advertising Who can explain why bell-bottom blue jeans were everywhere one year and rarely seen the next? Is it the result of clever advertising campaigns, social trends, the influence of television shows, or some combination of these factors? Although economists cannot always explain why some fads begin, advertising and publicity often play an important role.

Changes in tastes and preferences cannot be explained by changes in income or population or worries about future price increases. Advertising is a factor that shifts demand curves because it plays an important role in many trends. Meanwhile, new media and new technology have led to new trends in advertising.

Although broadcast television is still the biggest advertising medium, viewers can now watch television programs on the Internet, cellphones, or DVD players. Digital media make it easier for consumers to avoid advertisements.

Marketers who want to reach these new media consumers are changing their traditional advertising strategies. Spending for online ads continues to grow. Video is the fastest-growing Internet ad format, topped only by search engine advertising. Ad spending on social network Web sites such as Facebook was estimated at $6.1 billion in 2013.

The popularity of social network Web sites has inspired companies to build their own sites. The goal is to connect with consumers on a personal level while promoting their products and brand names.

Companies spend money on advertising because they hope that it will increase the demand for the goods they sell. Considering the growing sums of money spent on advertising in the United States each year, companies must believe that this investment is paying off.

Prices of Related Goods The demand curve for one good can also shift in response to a change in the demand for another good. There are two types of related goods that interact this way: complements and substitutes.

Growing Power of Social Media

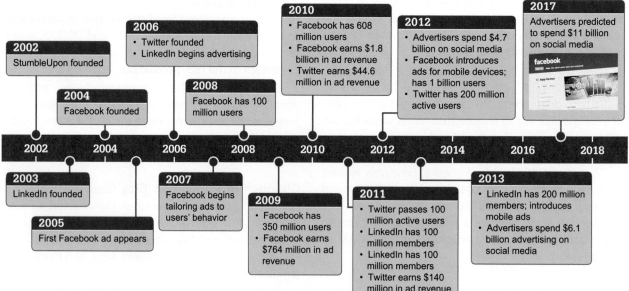

SOURCE: A Brief History of Social Advertising

>> The influence of social media has exploded in the 2000s. **Analyze Data** What evidence can you find that advertisers expect the influence of social media to continue growing?

- **Complements** are two goods that are bought and used together.
- **Substitutes** are goods that are used in place of one another.

When we consider the demand for skis, ski boots are considered a complement. An increase in the price of ski boots will cause people to buy fewer boots. Because skis are useless without boots, the demand for skis will fall at all prices—after all, why buy new skis if you can't afford the ski boots you need?

Now consider the effect on the demand for skis when the price of snowboards rises. Snowboards are a substitute for skis, because consumers will often buy one or the other but not both. A rise in the price of snowboards will cause people to buy fewer snowboards, and, therefore, people will buy more pairs of skis at every price. Likewise, a fall in the price of snowboards will lead consumers to buy fewer skis at all price levels.

❓ **APPLY CONCEPTS** How do non-price determinants affect demand?

>> Snowboards are a product that have both complements—boots and other clothing—and substitutes—skis.

ASSESSMENT

1. **Apply Concepts** How does *ceteris paribus* relate to demand?

2. **Identify Cause and Effect** What effect does a rise in income have on demand?

3. **Distinguish** How does a change in demand relate to a demand curve?

4. **Support Ideas With Examples** Give an example of how businesses use demographic information.

5. **Recall** Think about the way businesses try to influence consumers' behavior. Make a list of all the ways businesses tried to influence you in the past 24 hours. For example, how many ads did you see?

>> This closed Hummer dealership may have fallen victim to falling demand for large, gas-guzzling vehicles that occurred as the cost of gasoline spiked in the 2000s.

▶ **Interactive Flipped Video**

Are there some products that you would continue to buy, even if the price were to rise dramatically? Are there other goods that you would cut back on, or stop buying altogether, if there were just a slight increase in price? How much is too much? No matter how you answer these questions, economists have a way to describe your behavior.

>> Objectives

Explain how to calculate elasticity of demand.

Identify factors that affect elasticity of demand.

Explain how firms use elasticity and revenue to make decisions.

>> Key Terms

elasticity of demand
inelastic
elastic
unitary elastic
total revenue

Elasticity of Demand

Elasticity Defined

In fact, economists have developed a way to calculate just how strongly people react to a change in price. Several factors—including the original price and how much you want or need a particular good—will determine your demand for that product.

The Concept of Elasticity Economists describe the way that consumers respond to price changes as **elasticity of demand**. Elasticity of demand measures how drastically buyers will cut back or increase their demand for a good when the price rises or falls, respectively. If you buy the same amount or just a little less of a good after a large price increase, your demand is **inelastic**, or relatively unresponsive to price changes. If you buy much less of a good after a small price increase, your demand is **elastic**. A consumer with highly elastic demand for a good is very responsive to price changes—both increases and decreases.

How Elasticity Is Calculated In order to calculate elasticity of demand, take the percentage change in the quantity of the good demanded, and divide this number by the percentage change in the price of the good. The result is the elasticity of demand for the good.

The law of demand implies that the result will always be negative. That is because an increase in the price of a good will always decrease the quantity demanded, and a decrease in the price of a good will always increase the quantity demanded. For the sake of simplicity, economists drop the negative sign in the result. You can find the equation for elasticity in **Figure 3.4**.

Price Range The elasticity of demand for a good varies at every price level. Demand for a good can be highly elastic at one price and inelastic at a different price. For example, demand for a glossy magazine will be inelastic when the price rises 50 percent, from $1 to $1.50. The new price is still low, and people will buy almost as many copies as they did before. However, when the price of a magazine increases 50 percent, from $4 to $6, demand will be much more elastic. Many readers will refuse to pay $2 more for the magazine. Yet in percentage terms, the change in the magazine's price is exactly the same as when the price rose from $1 to $1.50.

Elasticity Values We have been using the terms *inelastic* and *elastic* to describe consumers' responses to price changes—including increases and decreases. These terms have precise mathematical definitions. **Figure 3.5** shows how the demand curves for elastic and inelastic demand look—in this case, when prices drop. If the elasticity of demand for a good at a certain price is *less* than 1, we describe demand as inelastic.

If the elasticity is *greater* than 1, demand is elastic. If elasticity is *exactly equal* to 1, we describe demand as **unitary elastic**.

When elasticity of demand is unitary, the percentage change in quantity demanded is exactly equal to the percentage change in the price. Suppose the elasticity of demand for a magazine at $2 is unitary. When the price of the magazine rises by 50 percent to $3, the newsstand will sell exactly half as many copies as before.

Recall **Figure 3.1**, which includes an individual demand schedule—Ashley's demand for pizza. This demand schedule shows that if the price per slice were to rise from $2 to $3, Ashley's quantity demanded would fall from four slices to three slices per day. The change in price from $2 to $3 is a 50 percent increase. The change in quantity demanded from four slices to three is a 25 percent decrease. Dividing the 25 percent decrease in quantity demanded by the 50 percent increase in price gives us an elasticity of demand of 0.5. See **Figure 3.6** for another view of this calculation. This illustration is based on the formula from **Figure 3.4**.

Since Ashley's elasticity of demand at a price change from $2 to $3 is less than 1, we say that Ashley's demand for pizza is inelastic. In other words, price increase has a relatively small effect on the number of slices of pizza she buys.

💲 TO CALCULATE ELASTICITY 💲

STEP 1 **Calculate Percent Change in Price**

$$\frac{\text{ORIGINAL PRICE} - \text{NEW PRICE}}{\text{ORIGINAL PRICE}} \times 100 = \text{PERCENT CHANGE IN PRICE}$$

STEP 2 **Calculate Percent Change in Quantity Demanded**

$$\frac{\text{ORIGINAL QUANTITY DEMANDED} - \text{NEW QUANTITY DEMANDED}}{\text{ORIGINAL QUANTITY DEMANDED}} \times 100 = \text{PERCENT CHANGE IN QUANTITY DEMANDED}$$

STEP 3 **Calculate Percent Change in Elasticity**

$$\frac{\text{PERCENT CHANGE IN QUANTITY DEMANDED}}{\text{PERCENT CHANGE IN PRICE}} = \text{ELASTICITY}$$

>> **Figure 3.4** Economists use the steps shown here to calculate elasticity of demand.
Generate Explanations Why do you think observers may want to be able to measure elasticity precisely?

Suppose we survey another customer and find that when the price of pizza rises by 40 percent, this person's quantity demanded falls by 60 percent. Recall again the formula from **Figure 3.4**: The change in the quantity demanded of 60 percent is divided by the change in price of 40 percent, equaling an elasticity of demand of 1.5 (60 percent/40 percent = 1.5). Since this result is greater than 1, this customer's demand is elastic. In other words, this customer is very sensitive to changes in the price of pizza.

? **DEFINE** How do economists calculate elasticity?

Factors Affecting Elasticity

Why is the demand for some goods so much less elastic than for other goods? Rephrase the question and ask yourself, "What is essential to me? What goods must I have, even if the price rises greatly?" The goods you list might have some traits that set them apart from other goods and make your demand for those goods less elastic. Several different factors, including several non-price determinants, can affect a person's elasticity of demand for a specific good.

Availability of Substitutes If there are few substitutes for a good, then even when its price rises greatly, you might still buy it. You believe you have no good alternatives. For example, if your favorite musical group plans to give a concert that you want to attend, there really is no substitute for that ticket. You could go to a concert to hear some other band, but that would not be as good. You've got to have tickets for this concert, and nothing else will do. Under these circumstances, a moderate change in price is not going to change your mind. Your demand for that concert is inelastic.

Similarly, demand for life-saving medicine is usually inelastic. For many prescription drugs, the only possible substitute is to try an unproven treatment. For this reason, people with an illness will continue to buy as much of the necessary medicine as they can afford, even when the price goes up.

If the lack of substitutes can make demand inelastic, a wide choice of substitute goods can make demand elastic. The demand for a particular brand of apple juice is probably elastic because people can choose from several good substitutes if the price of their preferred brand rises.

Relative Importance A second factor in determining a good's elasticity of demand is how much of your budget you spend on the good. If you already spend a

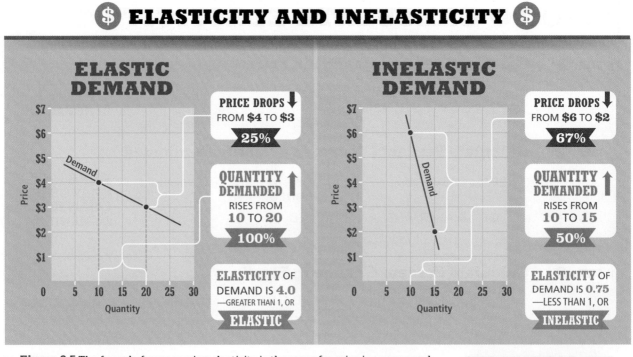

>> **Figure 3.5** The formula for measuring elasticity is the same for price increases and decreases. **Make Generalizations** How do demand curves for elastic demand differ from curves for inelastic demand?

▶ Interactive Chart

ASHLEY'S DEMAND FOR PIZZA
ELASTIC OR INELASTIC?

STEP 1 — **Calculate Percent Change in Price**

$$\frac{\$2 - \$3}{\$2} \times 100 = \textbf{50\% CHANGE IN PRICE}$$

STEP 2 — **Calculate Percent Change in Quantity Demanded**

$$\frac{4 - 3}{4} \times 100 = \textbf{25\% CHANGE IN QUANTITY DEMANDED}$$

STEP 3 — **Calculate Percent Change in Elasticity**

$$\frac{25}{50} = \textbf{.50 ELASTICITY OF DEMAND}$$

CONCLUSION — Ashley's elasticity of demand is less than 1, or inelastic.

>> **Figure 3.6** This chart analyzes the elasticity of Ashley's demand for pizza. **Apply Concepts** How would you describe Ashley's response to a small price increase?

large share of your income on a good, a price increase will force you to make some tough choices. Unless you want to cut back drastically on the other goods in your budget, you must reduce consumption of that particular good by a significant amount to keep your budget under control. The higher the jump in price, the more you will have to adjust your purchases.

If you currently spend half of your budget on clothes, even a modest increase in the cost of clothing will probably cause a large reduction in the quantity you purchase. In other words, your demand will be elastic.

However, if the price of shoelaces doubled, would you cut back on your shoelace purchases? Probably not. You may not even notice the difference. Even if you spend twice as much on shoelaces, they will still account for only a tiny part of your overall budget. Your demand for shoelaces is inelastic.

Necessities Versus Luxuries The third factor in determining a good's elasticity varies a great deal from person to person, but it is nonetheless important. Whether a person considers a good to be a necessity or a luxury has a great impact on a person's elasticity of demand for that good. A necessity is a good people will always buy, even when the price increases. Parents often regard milk as a necessity. They will buy it at any reasonable price. If the price of a gallon of milk rises from $3.49 to $5.49, they will still buy as much milk as

their children need to stay healthy. Their demand for milk is inelastic.

The same parents may regard steak as a luxury. When the price of steak increases slightly, say 20 percent, parents may cut their monthly purchases of steak by more than 20 percent, or skip steak altogether. Steak is a luxury, and consumers can easily reduce the quantity they consume. Because it is easy to reduce the quantity of luxury goods demanded, demand is elastic.

Change Over Time When a price changes, consumers often need time to change their spending habits. Consumers do not always react quickly to a price increase, because it takes time to find substitutes. Because they cannot respond quickly to price changes, their demand is inelastic in the short term. Demand sometimes becomes more elastic over time, however, because people can eventually find substitutes.

Consider the example of gasoline. A person might purchase a large vehicle that requires a greater volume of gasoline per mile to run. This person might work at a job many miles away from home and shop at a supermarket that is not local. These factors determine how much gasoline this person demands, and none can be changed easily.

In the early 1970s, several oil-rich countries cut their oil exports to the United States. Gasoline prices rose quickly. In the short term, people could do little to reduce their consumption of gasoline. They still needed to drive to school and work. At first, drivers were more likely to pay the higher price for gasoline than they were to buy fuel-efficient cars or move closer to their workplaces.

However, because gas prices stayed high for a considerable period of time, some people eventually switched to more fuel-efficient cars, formed car pools, or used public transportation. In the long run, people reduced their consumption of gasoline by finding substitutes. Demand for gasoline, inelastic in the short term, is more elastic in the long term.

The story did not end there. In the early 1980s, the price of a gallon of gas began to fall. Gasoline prices, adjusted for inflation, stayed low for the next two decades. At first, people continued to buy fuel-efficient cars. But over time, many Americans switched to larger vehicles that got fewer miles to the gallon. Because the price of gas remained low, people gradually adjusted their habits and consumed more gasoline. Just as demand for gasoline responded slowly to an increase in price, it also responded slowly to a decrease in price.

In the early 2000s, gasoline prices shot up again and have remained fairly high. At first, consumers were slow to change their car-buying habits and their demand for gasoline. Eventually, however, more fuel-efficient cars, including electrically powered models, gained a foothold in the market. If gas prices remain high over

the long term, economists expect that demand for gasoline will grow increasingly elastic.

? **IDENTIFY** What factors affect elasticity of demand?

How Elasticity Affects Revenue

Elasticity is important to the study of economics because elasticity helps us measure how consumers respond to price changes for different products. Elasticity is also an important tool for business planners, like the pizzeria owner described earlier in this topic. The elasticity of demand determines how a change in prices will affect a firm's total revenue, or income.

Total Revenue A company's **total revenue** is defined as the amount of money the company receives by selling its goods. This is determined by two factors: the price of the goods and the quantity sold. For example, if a pizzeria sells 150 slices of pizza per day at $4 per slice, total revenue would be $600 per day.

Total Revenue and Elastic Demand The law of demand tells us that an increase in price will decrease the quantity demanded. When a good has an elastic demand, raising the price of each unit sold by 20 percent

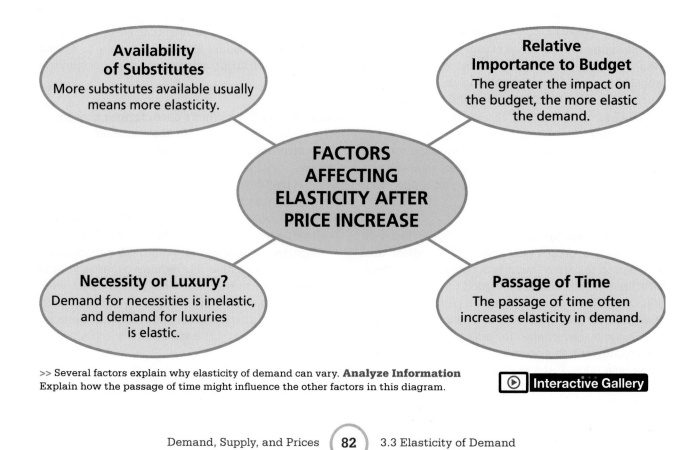

>> Several factors explain why elasticity of demand can vary. **Analyze Information** Explain how the passage of time might influence the other factors in this diagram.

▶ **Interactive Gallery**

Revenue Table

PRICE OF A SLICE OF PIZZA	QUANTITY DEMANDED (PER DAY)	TOTAL REVENUE
$1.00	300	$300
$2.00	250	$500
$3.00	200	$600
$4.00	150	$600
$5.00	100	$500
$6.00	50	$300

>> **Figure 3.7** Achieving higher revenue means finding the best combination of price and quantity demanded. **Analyze Charts** Why does revenue for this restaurant fall when price increases from $4 to $5?

will decrease the quantity sold by a larger percentage, say 50 percent. The quantity sold will drop enough to actually reduce the firm's total revenue.

The revenue table in **Figure 3.7**—drawn from the pizzeria's demand curve—shows how this can happen. An increase in price from $5 to $6, or 20 percent, decreases the quantity sold from 100 to 50, or 50 percent. As a result, total revenue drops from $500 to $300.

The same process can also work in reverse. If the firm were to reduce the price by a certain percentage, the quantity demanded could rise by an even greater percentage. In this case, total revenues could rise.

It may surprise you that a firm could lose revenue by raising the price of its goods. But if the pizzeria started selling pizza at $10 a slice, it would not stay in business very long. Remember that elastic demand comes from one or more of these factors:

- The availability of substitute goods
- A limited budget that does not allow for price changes
- The perception of the good as a luxury item

If these conditions are present, then the demand for the good is elastic, and a firm may find that a price increase reduces its total revenue.

Total Revenue and Inelastic Demand Remember that if demand is inelastic, consumers' demand is not very responsive to price changes. When demand is inelastic, price and total revenue move in the same direction: An increase in price raises total revenue, and a decrease in price reduces total revenue.

Thus, if a firm raises its price by 25 percent, the quantity demanded will fall, but not by enough to lower total revenue. As a result, the firm will have greater total revenues, because the higher price will make up for the lower quantity of sales. The firm brings in more money.

On the other hand, a decrease in price will lead to an increase in the quantity demanded even if demand is inelastic. However, the percentage of increase in the quantity demanded will be less than the percentage of increase in price, and the firm's total revenue will decrease. For example, if you lower the price of socks by 50 percent, you may sell only 20 percent more socks. The increase in the quantity sold does not compensate for the lost revenue.

How Elasticity Affects Pricing Policies Because of these relationships, a firm needs to know whether the demand for its product is elastic or inelastic at a given price. This knowledge helps the firm make pricing decisions that lead to the greatest revenue.

If a firm knows that the demand for its product is elastic at the current price, it knows that an increase in price might reduce total revenues. During the economic crisis of 2008 and 2009, demand for SUVs proved to be elastic. As a result, car manufacturers could not raise prices to compensate for lower sales.

On the other hand, suppose a firm knows that the demand for its product is inelastic at its current price.

The firm may safely conclude that an increase in price will increase total revenue.

❓ IDENTIFY CENTRAL ISSUES Why does a firm need to know whether demand for its product is elastic or inelastic?

ASSESSMENT

1. **Define** What is elasticity of demand?

2. **Draw Conclusions** Suppose demand for a product is elastic at a given price. What will happen to the company's total revenue if it raises the price of that product? Why?

3. **Generate Explanations** (a)How does the percentage of your budget you spend on a good affect its elasticity? (b) Why is this the case?

4. **Make Generalizations** Why does demand generally become more elastic over time?

5. **Interpret** (a) What factors determine a company's total revenue? (b) Do higher prices lead to increased revenues for a company? Explain your answers.

Suppose you were running a business. What would you do if you discovered that customers were still willing to buy your product if you raised the price 20 percent? Would you take an extra day off and only work four days each week? After all, you would still earn the same income with 20 percent less work. Or would you respond like most entrepreneurs would by producing more and increasing your revenue?

>> This warehouse holds goods that help meet consumer demand. **Make Predictions** Consumers' demand is sensitive to price levels. How do you expect price to affect supply? Explain your answer.

▶ **Interactive Flipped Video**

Fundamentals of Supply

The Effect of Price on Supply

Just as the relationship between price and demand is governed by basic economic law, supply and price are directly linked. We will now explore the ways in which changes in price affect supply.

Suppliers Follow the Law of Supply Supply is the amount of a good or service that is available. How do producers decide how much to supply? According to the **law of supply**, producers offer more of a good or service as its price increases and less as its price falls. Economists use the term **quantity supplied** to describe how much of a good or service a producer is willing and able to sell at a specific price. A producer may also be called a supplier, a company, or an owner—whoever supplies a product to the market.

The law of supply develops from the choices of both current and new producers of a good or service. As the price rises, existing firms will produce more in order to earn additional revenue. A price increase is also an incentive for new firms to enter the market to earn their own profits.

If the price of a good or service falls, some firms will produce less, and others might drop out of the market. These two movements—

>> **Objectives**

Understand how the law of supply explains the effect of changes in price on quantity supplied.

Interpret a supply schedule and a supply graph.

Examine the relationship between elasticity of supply and time.

>> **Key Terms**

supply
law of supply
quantity supplied
supply schedule
variable
market supply
   schedule
supply curve
market supply curve
elasticity of supply

individual firms changing their level of production and firms entering or exiting the market—combine to create the law of supply.

The Effect of Price on Production If a firm is already earning a profit by selling a good or service, then an increase in the price—*ceteris paribus*—will increase the firm's profits. The promise of higher revenues generated by each sale encourages the firm to produce more. The pizzeria you read about in prior lessons probably makes a reasonable profit by selling a certain number of slices a day at the market price. If the pizzeria wasn't making a profit, the owner would raise the price or switch from making pizzas to making something more profitable.

If the price of pizza *rises,* but the firm's cost of making pizza stays the same, the pizzeria will earn a higher profit on each slice. Any smart entrepreneur would produce and sell more pizza to take advantage of the higher prices.

Similarly, if the price of pizza goes *down,* the pizzeria will earn less profit per slice or even lose money. The owner will choose to sell less pizza and produce something else, such as calzones, which will yield more profit.

In both cases, the search for profit drives the supplier's decision. When the price goes up, the supplier recognizes the chance to make more money and works harder to produce more pizza. When the price falls, the same supplier is discouraged from producing as much as before.

The Effect of Price on Number of Suppliers Profits appeal both to producers already in the market and to people who may decide to join the market. As you have seen, when the price of pizza rises, a pizzeria provides a good opportunity to make money. If you were thinking about opening your own restaurant, a pizzeria would look like a good move. This is how rising prices draw new firms into a market and add to the quantity supplied of the good or service.

Consider the market for music. In the late 1970s, disco music became popular. The music industry quickly recognized the popularity of disco, and soon, more and more groups released disco recordings. Groups that once recorded soul and rhythm and blues music chose to record disco albums. New entrants crowded the market to take advantage of the potential for profit. Disco, however, was a short-lived fad. By the early 1980s, stores couldn't sell disco albums.

This pattern of sharp increases and decreases in supply occurs again and again in the music industry. In the early 1990s, grunge music emerged from Seattle to become widely popular among high school and college

>> It makes sense for producers to increase quantity supplied when prices rise.
Connect What assumption underlies the decision to increase quantity supplied as price increases?

students across the country. How did the market react? Record labels signed more grunge groups to recording contracts. Music stores devoted more space to grunge music. However, grunge soon lost its appeal, and many groups disbanded or moved on to new styles. Other styles of music, such as hip-hop and independent rock, achieved popularity instead.

In each of these examples, many musicians joined the market to profit from a trend. Their actions reflected the law of supply, which says that the quantity supplied increases as the price of a good increases.

One of the benefits of the economic system of the United States, with its emphasis on free markets, is that markets are open to new suppliers. Entrepreneurs can enter growing markets to respond to these trends as long as they can assemble the needed factors of production and are willing to take the risk.

? GENERATE EXPLANATIONS Why do rising prices for a good or service have the effect of causing firms to increase production?

Understanding Supply Schedules

Similar to a demand schedule, a **supply schedule** shows the relationship between price and quantity supplied for a specific good or service, or how much of a good or service a supplier will offer at various prices. The pizzeria discussed earlier might have a supply schedule that looks like the one in **Figure 3.8**. This table compares two **variables**, or factors that can change: the price of a slice of pizza and the number of slices supplied by a pizzeria. We could collect this information by asking the pizzeria owner how many slices she is willing and able to make at different prices. We could also look at records to see how the quantity supplied has varied as the price has changed. We will almost certainly find that at higher prices, the pizzeria owner is willing to make more pizza. At a lower price, she prefers to make less pizza and devote her limited resources to other, more profitable items.

Like a demand schedule, a supply schedule lists supply for a very specific set of conditions. The schedule shows how the price of pizza, and only pizza, affects the pizzeria's output of pizza. Other factors that could change the restaurant's output of pizza, such as the costs of tomato sauce, labor, and rent, are assumed to remain constant.

Changes in the Quantity Supplied Economists use the word *supply* to refer to the relationship between price and quantity supplied, as shown in the supply

Individual Supply Schedule

PRICE PER SLICE OF PIZZA	SLICES SUPPLIED PER DAY
$1.00	100
$2.00	150
$3.00	200
$4.00	250
$5.00	300
$6.00	350

>> **Figure 3.8** This schedule shows how many slices one pizzeria owner will supply at different prices. **Analyze Charts** What would you expect from this pizzeria if prices rose to $7 a slice?

▶ **Interactive Chart**

>> In the United States, the market is always open to new suppliers of goods and services.

schedule. The pizzeria's supply of pizza includes all possible combinations of price and output. According to this supply schedule, the pizzeria's supply is 100 slices at $1 a slice, 150 slices at $2 a slice, 200 slices at $3 a slice, and so on. The number of slices that the pizzeria offers at a specific price is called the quantity supplied at that price. At $5 per slice, the pizzeria's quantity supplied is 300 slices per day.

A rise or fall in the price of pizza will cause the quantity supplied to change, but not the supply schedule. In other words, a change in a good's price moves the seller from one row to another in the same supply schedule, but it does not change the supply schedule itself. When a factor other than the price of pizza affects output, we have to build a whole new supply schedule to reflect the new market conditions.

All Suppliers and the Market Supply Schedule All of the supply schedules of individual firms in a market can be added up to create a **market supply schedule**. A market supply schedule shows the relationship between prices and the total quantity supplied by *all* firms in a particular market. This information is needed if we want to determine the total supply of pizza at a certain price in a large area, like a city.

The market supply schedule for pizza in **Figure 3.9** shows the supply of pizza for a hypothetical city. It resembles the supply schedule for a single pizzeria, but the quantities are much larger.

This market supply schedule lists the same prices as those in the supply schedule for the single pizzeria,

since all restaurants will charge prices within the same range. The quantities supplied are much larger because there are many pizzerias in the community. Like the individual supply schedule, this market supply schedule reflects the law of supply. Pizzerias supply more pizza at higher prices.

The Supply Graph When we graph the data points in the supply schedule, we create a supply graph—also known as a **supply curve**. A supply curve is a graphic representation of a supply schedule. A supply curve is very similar to a demand curve, except that the horizontal axis now measures the quantity of the good supplied, not the quantity demanded. The graph on the left in **Figure 3.10** shows a supply curve for one pizzeria. The graph on the right shows a **market supply curve,** which applies to all the pizzerias in the city.

The data used to draw the two graphs are from the two supply schedules in **Figure 3.8** and **Figure 3.9**. The prices shown along the vertical axes are the same in both graphs. However, the quantities of pizza supplied at each price are much larger in the market supply curve.

The key feature of the supply curve is that it always rises from left to right. That is, the curve moves toward higher and higher output levels (on the horizontal axis) and higher and higher prices (on the vertical axis) as you move from left to right. This change, of course, illustrates the law of supply, which says that a higher price leads to higher output.

? **SUMMARIZE** What does a supply schedule show?

Market Supply Schedule

PRICE PER SLICE OF PIZZA	SLICES SUPPLIED PER DAY
$1.00	1,000
$2.00	1,500
$3.00	2,000
$4.00	2,500
$5.00	3,000
$6.00	3,500

>> **Figure 3.9** This schedule shows how many slices all pizzerias in a market will supply at different prices. **Analyze Charts** What would you expect to happen in this market if prices dropped to $.50 a slice?

Elasticity of Supply

Earlier you learned that elasticity of demand measures how consumers will react to price changes. Elasticity of supply is based on the same concept.

Elasticity of supply measures how firms will respond to changes in the price of a good or service. The labels *elastic*, *inelastic*, and *unitary elastic* represent the same values of elasticity in relation to supply as they do in relation to demand. When elasticity is greater than 1, supply is very sensitive to changes in price and is considered elastic. If supply is not very responsive to changes in price, and elasticity is less than 1, supply is considered inelastic. When a percentage change in price is perfectly matched by an equal percentage change in quantity supplied, elasticity is exactly 1, and supply is unitary elastic.

What determines whether the supply of a good will be elastic or inelastic? The key factor is time. In the short run, some firms cannot easily change their output

Supply Curves

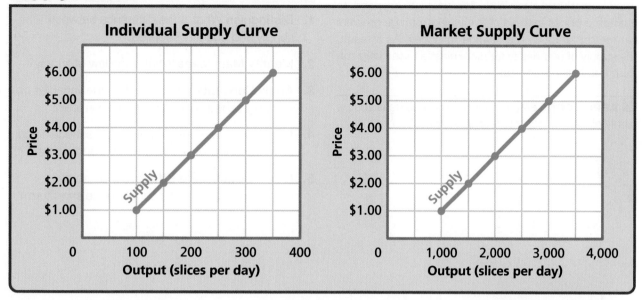

>> **Figure 3.10 Analyze Graphs** a. How much pizza will the individual pizzeria supply per day at $3 a slice? b. How much pizza will the market supply each day at $4 a slice?

▶ **Interactive Chart**

levels, making supply inelastic. In the long run, those firms can be more flexible, and supply becomes more elastic. Of course, different kinds of businesses have more flexibility in the short term, so, for them, supply can be elastic even in the short run.

Elasticity of Supply Over a Short Time An orange grove is one example of a business that has difficulty adjusting to a change in price in the short term. Orange trees take several years to mature and grow fruit. If the price of oranges goes up, an orange grower can buy and plant more trees, but he will have to wait several years for this investment to pay off. However, the grower could still take smaller steps to increase output in the short term. For example, he could use a more effective pesticide. While this step might increase his output somewhat, it would probably not dramatically increase the number of oranges produced.

Economists would say that the orange grower's supply is inelastic in the short run, because he cannot easily change his output. The same factors that prevent the owner of the orange grove from expanding supply would also prevent new growers from entering the market and supplying oranges in the short term.

In the short term, the supply of oranges is also inelastic if the price decreases. If the price of oranges falls, the grove owner has few ways to cut his supply. Years ago, he invested in land and trees, and his grove will provide oranges—not apples or pears or grapefruit—no matter what the price is. Even if the price drops

drastically, the grove owner will probably pick and sell nearly as many oranges as before. His competitors have also invested heavily in land and trees and won't drop out of the market if they can survive.

Other businesses have a more elastic supply even in the short term. For example, a business that provides a service, such as a haircut, is highly elastic. The supply of haircuts is easily expanded or reduced.

If the price rises, barbershops and salons can hire workers fairly quickly or extend their business hours. In addition, new barbershops and salons will open. This means that a small increase in price will cause a large increase in quantity supplied, even in the short term.

If the price of a haircut drops, some shop owners will lay off workers or close earlier in the day. Others will leave the market. Quantity supplied will fall quickly. Because haircut suppliers can quickly change their operations, the supply of haircuts is elastic even in the short run.

Elasticity of Supply Over a Longer Time Like demand, supply becomes more elastic over time. The orange grower could not increase his output much when the price of oranges rose, but he can plant more trees to increase his supply over time. After several years, he will be able to sell more oranges at the higher price.

If the price drops and stays low for several years, orange growers who survived the first two or three years of losses might decide to leave the market and grow something else. With five years to respond to changing prices instead of five weeks, orange growers can better adapt to the change in prices. As a result, the supply of oranges is far more elastic in the long run than it is in the short run.

? **APPLY CONCEPTS** How does a business that is highly elastic respond to a drop in prices?

ASSESSMENT

1. **Distinguish** What is the difference between supply and quantity supplied?

2. **Identify Main Ideas** What is the law of supply?

3. **Apply Concepts** What would be the variables on a supply schedule for a performer on tour?

4. **Contrast** How are a market supply schedule and an individual supply schedule alike and different?

5. **Identify Cause and Effect** Why do some industries have inelastic supply in the short term?

You are making sandwiches for a picnic. The knife is the physical capital. Your labor, the bread, and the sandwich filling are the inputs. In a beanbag factory, the physical capital is one sewing machine and one pair of scissors. Its inputs are workers and materials, including cloth, thread, and beans. Each beanbag requires the same amount of materials. How does the company decide how many beanbags to produce? How many sandwiches should you make?

>> Can adding workers to a factory like this increase marginal returns? **Identify Central Issues** What is helping this woman work productively?

[▶] **Interactive Flipped Video**

Costs of Production

Labor and Output

Producers think about the cost of making one more unit of a good when deciding how to maximize profits. You'll also see what happens when a factory's operating costs are greater than its revenue.

How Many Workers to Hire One basic question that any business owner has to answer is how many workers to hire. Owners have to consider how the number of workers they hire will affect their total production.

For example, at the beanbag factory, one worker can produce four beanbags per hour. Two workers can make a total of ten bags per hour, and three can make a total of 17 beanbags per hour. As each new worker joins the company, total output increases. After the seventh worker is hired, production peaks at 32 beanbags per hour. When the firm hires the eighth worker, however, total output drops to 31 bags per hour.

Marginal Product of Labor The relationship between labor, measured by the number of workers in the factory and the number of beanbags produced, is shown in **Figure 3.11**. This table details the **marginal product of labor**, or the change in output from hiring one more worker. This is called the marginal product because it measures

>> Objectives

Explain how businesses decide how much labor to hire in order to produce a certain level of output.

Analyze the production costs of a business.

Explain how a business chooses to set output.

Identify the factors that a firm must consider before shutting down an unprofitable business.

>> Key Terms

marginal product of
   labor
increasing marginal
   returns
diminishing marginal
   returns
fixed cost
variable costs
total cost
marginal cost
marginal revenue
operating cost
average cost
negative marginal
   return

PEARSON **realize** www.PearsonRealize.com
Access your Digital Lesson.

the change in output at the margin, where the last worker has been hired or fired.

The first worker hired produces four bags an hour, so her marginal product of labor is four bags. The second worker raises total output from four bags per hour to ten, so her marginal product of labor is six. In fact, **Figure 3.11** shows that the marginal product of labor increases for the first three workers, rising from four to seven.

Increasing Marginal Returns The marginal product of labor increases for the first three workers because there are three tasks involved in making a beanbag. Workers cut cloth into the correct shape, stuff it with beans, and sew the bag closed. A single worker performing all these tasks can produce only four bags per hour. Adding a second worker allows each worker to specialize in one or two tasks. If each worker focuses on only one part of the process, she wastes less time switching between tasks and becomes more skillful at her assigned task. Because specialization increases output per worker, the second worker adds more to output than the first. The firm enjoys **increasing marginal returns**.

In our example, there are benefits from specialization. The firm enjoys a rising marginal product of labor for the first three workers.

Diminishing Marginal Returns When workers four through seven are hired, the marginal product of labor is still positive. Each new worker still adds to total output. However, the marginal product of labor shrinks as each worker joins the company. The fourth worker increases output by six bags, while the seventh increases output by only one bag. Why?

After the beanbag firm hires its first three workers, one for each task, the benefits of specialization end. At that point, adding more workers increases total output, but at a decreasing rate. This situation is known as **diminishing marginal returns**. A firm with diminishing marginal returns of labor will produce less and less output from each additional unit of labor. You can observe this effect (and the effect of increasing marginal returns) in graph form in **Figure 3.12**.

The firm suffers from diminishing marginal returns of labor because its workers have a limited amount of capital. Capital—any human-made resource used to produce other goods—is represented by the factory's single sewing machine and its pair of scissors.

With three workers, only one needs to use the sewing machine, so this worker never has to wait to get to work. When there are more than three workers, the factory may assign more than one to work at the sewing machine.

So while one works, the other worker waits. He or she may cut fabric or stuff bags, but every bag must

Marginal Product of Labor

LABOR (NUMBER OF WORKERS)	OUTPUT (BEANBAGS PER HOUR)	MARGINAL PRODUCT OF LABOR
0	0	—
1	4	4
2	10	6
3	17	7
4	23	6
5	28	5
6	31	3
7	32	1
8	31	−1

>> **Figure 3.11** Marginal product of labor is the change in output that results when a unit of labor is added. **Analyze Charts** How does marginal product of labor change when a fourth worker is added?

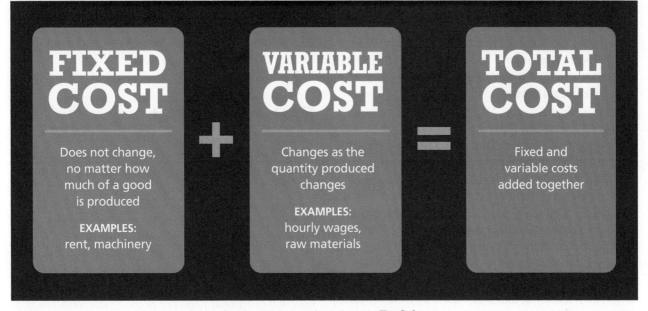

FIXED AND VARIABLE COSTS

FIXED COST

Does not change, no matter how much of a good is produced

EXAMPLES:
rent, machinery

+

VARIABLE COST

Changes as the quantity produced changes

EXAMPLES:
hourly wages, raw materials

=

TOTAL COST

Fixed and variable costs added together

>> All producers need to understand their fixed, variable, and total costs. **Explain** Which categories of cost would increase for a business that decided to extend its hours of operation?

be sewn at some point, so the worker cannot greatly increase the speed of production.

The problem gets worse as more workers are hired and the amount of capital remains constant. Time wasted waiting for the sewing machine or scissors means that additional workers will add less and less to total output.

Negative Marginal Returns As the table in **Figure 3.11** and the graph in **Figure 3.12** show, adding an eighth worker actually decreases output by one bag. This is called **negative marginal return**. At this stage, workers get in each other's way and disrupt production, so overall output decreases. Of course, few companies ever hire so many workers that their marginal product of labor becomes negative.

? **APPLY CONCEPTS** How does the amount of capital in an enterprise affect marginal returns?

Production Costs

Paying workers and purchasing capital are both costs of producing goods. Economists divide a producer's costs into two main categories: fixed costs and variable costs. These ideas are described below.

Fixed Costs A **fixed cost** is a cost that does not change, no matter how much of a good is produced. Most fixed costs involve the property or production facility—the cost of building and equipping a factory, office, store, or restaurant. Examples of fixed costs include rent, machinery repairs, property taxes, and the salaries of workers who run the business even when production temporarily stops.

Variable Costs **Variable costs** are costs that rise or fall depending on the quantity produced. They include the costs of raw materials and some labor. For example, to produce more beanbags, the firm must purchase more beans and hire more workers. If the company wants to produce less and cut costs, it can buy fewer beans or reduce weekly hours for some workers. The cost of labor is a variable cost because it changes with the number of workers, which changes with the quantity produced. Electricity and heating bills are also variable costs, because the company only uses heat and electricity during business hours.

Total Cost Costs for the firm that produces beanbags are shown in **Figure 3.13**. The firm's factory is fully equipped to produce beanbags. How does the cost of producing beanbags change as the output increases?

In our example, the fixed costs are the costs of the factory building and all the machinery and equipment. As shown in the second column in **Figure 3.13**, the fixed costs are $36 per hour.

Variable costs include the cost of beans, fabric, and most of the workers. As shown in the third column, variable costs rise with the number of beanbags produced. Fixed and variable costs added together make up the **total cost**, shown in the fourth column.

Marginal Cost If we know the total cost at several levels of output, we can determine the marginal cost of production at each level. **Marginal cost** is the additional cost of producing one more unit.

In **Figure 3.13**, you see that even if the firm makes no beanbags, it still must pay $36 per hour in fixed costs. If the firm produces one beanbag per hour, its total cost rises by $8, from $36 to $44 per hour. The marginal cost of the first beanbag is $8.

For the first three beanbags, marginal cost falls as output increases. The marginal cost is $4 for the second beanbag and $3 for the third. Each additional beanbag is cheaper to make because of increasing marginal returns resulting from specialization.

At four beanbags per hour, marginal cost starts to rise. The marginal cost of the fifth beanbag per hour is $7, the sixth costs $9, and the seventh, $12. The rising marginal cost reflects diminishing returns of labor. The benefits of specialization are exhausted at three beanbags per hour. Diminishing returns set in as more workers share a fixed production facility.

? **CHECK UNDERSTANDING** Why might a closed factory still have production costs?

Setting Output

Behind all of the hiring decisions is the firm's basic goal: to maximize profits. Profit is defined as total revenue minus total cost. A firm's total revenue is the money the firm gets by selling its product. Total revenue is equal to the price of each good multiplied by the number of goods sold. Total revenue when the price of a beanbag is $24 is shown in **Figure 3.13**. To find the level of output with the highest profit, we look for the biggest gap between total revenue and total cost. The gap is greatest and profit is highest when the firm makes 9 or 10 beanbags per hour. At this rate, the firm can expect to make a profit.

Marginal Revenue and Marginal Cost Another way to find the best level of output is to find the output level where marginal revenue is equal to marginal cost. **Marginal revenue** is the additional income from selling one more unit of a good.

If the firm has no control over the market price, marginal revenue equals the market price. Each beanbag sold at $24 increases the firm's total revenue by $24, so marginal revenue is $24. According to the table, price equals marginal cost with ten beanbags, so that is the quantity that maximizes profit at $98 per hour.

To understand how an output of ten beanbags maximizes the firm's profits, suppose that the firm made only four beanbags per hour. Is it making as much money as it can?

From **Figure 3.13**, we know that the marginal cost of the fifth beanbag is $7. The market price for a beanbag is $24, so the marginal revenue from that beanbag is $24. The $17 difference between the marginal revenue and marginal cost represents pure profit for the company from the fifth beanbag. The company should increase production to five beanbags an hour to capture that profit on the fifth beanbag.

The same calculations show that the company can capture a profit of $15 by producing a sixth beanbag per hour. The price of the seventh beanbag is $12 higher than its marginal cost, so that beanbag earns an additional $12 in profit for the company. The profit is available any time the company receives more for the

Marginal Returns

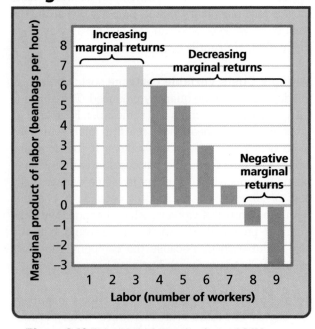

>> **Figure 3.12** This graph shows the rise and fall in marginal product of labor for the beanbag factory. **Analyze Graphs** What is the marginal product of labor when a fifth worker is added?

[▶] **Interactive Chart**

Production Costs

BEANBAGS PER HOUR	FIXED COST	VARIABLE COST	TOTAL COST	MARGINAL COST	MARGINAL REVENUE	TOTAL REVENUE	PROFIT PER HOUR
0	$36	$0	$36	—	$24	$0	$-36
1	36	8	44	$8	24	24	-20
2	36	12	48	4	24	48	0
3	36	15	51	3	24	72	21
4	36	20	56	5	24	96	40
5	36	27	63	7	24	120	57
6	36	36	72	9	24	144	72
7	36	48	84	12	24	168	84
8	36	63	99	15	24	192	93
9	36	82	118	19	24	216	98
10	36	106	142	24	24	240	98
11	36	136	172	30	24	264	92
12	36	173	209	37	24	288	79

>> **Figure 3.13** Producers must identify costs and revenues to calculate profit—total revenues minus total costs. **Apply Concepts** Why might this factory *not* seek the highest possible revenue?

Interactive Illustration

last beanbag than the cost to produce it. Any rational entrepreneur would take this opportunity to increase profit.

Now suppose that the firm is producing so many beanbags per hour that marginal cost is higher than price. If the firm produces eleven beanbags per hour, it receives $24 for that eleventh beanbag, but the $30 cost of producing that beanbag wipes out the profit. The firm actually loses $6 on the sale of the eleventh beanbag. Because marginal cost is increasing and price is constant in this example, the losses get worse at higher levels of output. The company would be better off producing less and keeping costs down.

The ideal level of output is where marginal revenue (price) is equal to marginal cost. Any other quantity of output would generate less profit. Profit can be determined by subtracting total cost from total revenue. We can also determine profit by comparing price and average cost. **Average cost** is total cost divided by the quantity produced. At an output of 10 beanbags per hour, the average cost is $14.20 ($142—total cost—divided by 10). Profit is the difference between market price and average cost ($24 — 14.20 = $9.80) multiplied by the quantity ($9.80 X 10 = $98). Again, these numbers appear in **Figure 3.13**.

Responding to Price Changes What happens if the price of a beanbag rises from $24 to $37? Thinking

at the margin, the firm would probably increase production to 12 beanbags per hour. At that quantity, marginal cost is equal to the new, higher price. At the original price of $24, the firm would not produce more than ten beanbags, according to **Figure 3.14**. When the price rises to $37, marginal revenue soars above marginal cost at that output level. By raising production to 12 beanbags per hour, the firm earns profits on the eleventh and twelfth beanbags.

This example shows the law of supply in action. An increase in price from $24 to $37 causes the firm to increase the quantity supplied from 10 to 12 beanbags per hour.

The Shutdown Decision Consider the problems faced by a factory that is losing money. The factory is producing at the most profitable level of output, where marginal revenue is equal to marginal cost. However, the market price is so low that the factory's total revenue is still less than its total cost, and the firm is losing money. Should this factory continue to produce goods and lose money, or should its owners shut the factory down?

In fact, there are times when keeping a money-losing factory open is the best choice. The firm should keep the factory open if the total revenue from the goods the factory produces is greater than the cost of keeping it open.

For example, if the price of beanbags drops to $7 and the factory produces at the profit-maximizing level of five beanbags per hour, the total revenue drops from $120 per hour to $35 per hour. Weigh this against the factory's **operating cost**, the cost of operating the facility. Operating cost includes the variable costs the owners must pay to keep the factory running, but not fixed costs, which the owners must pay whether the factory is open or closed.

According to **Figure 3.13**, if the factory produces five beanbags per hour, the variable cost is $27 per hour. Therefore, the benefit of operating the facility (total revenue of $35) is greater than the variable cost ($27), so it makes sense to keep the facility running.

Consider the effects of the other choice. If the firm shuts down the factory, it would still have to pay all of its fixed costs. The factory's total revenue would be zero, because it produces nothing for sale. Therefore, the firm would lose an amount of money equal to its fixed costs.

For this beanbag factory, the fixed costs equal $36 per hour, so the factory would lose $36 for each hour it is closed. If the factory produced five beanbags per hour, its total cost would be $63 ($36 in fixed costs

plus $27 in variable costs) per hour, but it would lose only $28 ($63 in total cost minus $35 in revenue) for each hour it is open. The factory would lose less money while producing because the total revenue ($35) would exceed the variable costs ($27), leaving $8 to cover some of the fixed costs. Although the factory would lose money either way, it would lose less money by continuing to produce and sell beanbags.

When will a business replace a factory that is operating at a loss? The firm will build a new factory and stay in the market only if the market price of beanbags is high enough to cover all the costs of production, including the cost of building a new factory.

Note also that a business that owns an unprofitable property can sell it. There are costs to disposing of business property—for example, the loss of the opportunity to take advantage of future market conditions. But disposing of business property can also yield benefits, such as income from sale of the property and relief from the fixed costs. These costs and benefits must be considered in any shutdown decision.

? EXPRESS IDEAS CLEARLY Under what circumstances should a firm keep a money-losing factory open?

Output and a Change in Price

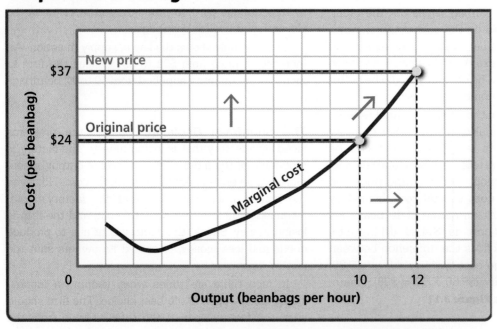

>> **Figure 3.14** Changes in price lead to a change in the ideal level of output. **Analyze Graphs** Based on this graph, what should output be if the price fell to $20?

ASSESSMENT

1. **Describe** What would be some examples of fixed costs and variable costs for a farm?

2. **Solve Problems** Suppose you were advising a company that is experiencing a decline in marginal returns. What two steps might you recommend?

3. **Express Problems Clearly** Why is it sometimes not a good idea for a company to simply produce more of a good or service?

4. **Identify Central Ideas** What should be the basic goal of a firm when it sets a level of output?

5. **Apply Concepts** Explain the effect an increase in prices in the market would have on a factory's level of production.

You own a collection of original action figures from a popular movie. You notice that the price of these figures is increasing rapidly on Web auction sites. Should you sell the figures now, or wait? How would your decision affect the supply of these action figures?

>> Many companies try to grow by capturing customers in foreign markets. **Infer** Why would a soft-drink company want to locate operations in China?

▶ **Interactive Flipped Video**

>> Objectives

Explain how factors such as input costs create change in supply.

Identify three ways that the government can influence the supply of goods.

Identify other non-price determinants that create changes in supply.

Explain how firms choose a location to produce goods.

>> Key Terms
subsidy
excise tax
regulation

Changes in Supply

Input Costs and Changes in Supply

Several factors, including the number of suppliers in a market, can lead to a shift in the supply curve. Government actions and global events also have an impact on supply. A very important influence on supply, though, is suppliers' input costs.

Any change in the cost of an input used to produce a good—such as raw materials, machinery, or labor—will affect supply. A rise in the cost of an input will cause a fall in supply at all price levels because the good has become more expensive to produce. On the other hand, a fall in the cost of an input will cause an increase in supply at all price levels.

The Effect of Input Costs on Supply Think of the effects of input costs on the relationship between marginal revenue (price) and marginal cost. A supplier sets output at the most profitable level, where price is equal to marginal cost. Since marginal cost includes the cost of the inputs that go into production, a rise in the cost of labor or raw materials will result in a higher marginal cost. If the cost of inputs increases enough, the marginal cost may become higher than the price, and the firm may not be as profitable.

If a firm has no control over the price, the only solution is to cut production and lower marginal cost until marginal cost equals the lower price. Supply falls at each price, and the supply curve shifts to the left, as illustrated in **Figure 3.15**.

The Effect of Technology on Input Costs Input costs can drop as well. Advances in technology can lower production costs in many industries. Automation, including the use of robotic tools, has spread throughout the manufacturing sector, saving on labor costs. Computers have simplified tasks and cut costs in many fields. Web-based conferencing makes it possible for individuals in different locations to meet while eliminating travel costs. Future advances promise to decrease production costs even further.

Technology lowers costs and increases supply at all price levels. This effect is seen in a rightward shift in the supply curve in **Figure 3.15**.

? ANALYZE CHARTS The rightward shift in the supply curve associated with lower input costs signifies what kind of change in supply?

Government Policies and Changes in Supply

The government has the power to affect the supplies of many types of goods. By raising or lowering the cost of producing goods, the government can encourage or discourage an entrepreneur or an industry within the country or abroad.

Subsidies and Supply One method governments use to affect supply is to give subsidies to producers of a good. A **subsidy** is a government payment that supports a business or market. Government often pays a producer a set subsidy for each unit produced. Subsidies generally lower costs, allowing a firm to produce more goods. They are particularly common with food production.

Governments have several reasons for subsidizing producers, and these reasons can change over time. During and after World War II, European countries faced food shortages.

Today, European governments protect farms so that some will be available to grow food in case cheaper imports are ever restricted. The French government subsidizes small farms to protect the lifestyle and character of the French countryside.

Governments in developing countries often subsidize manufacturers to protect young, growing industries from strong foreign competition. Countries such as Indonesia and Malaysia have subsidized a

Shifts in the Supply Curve

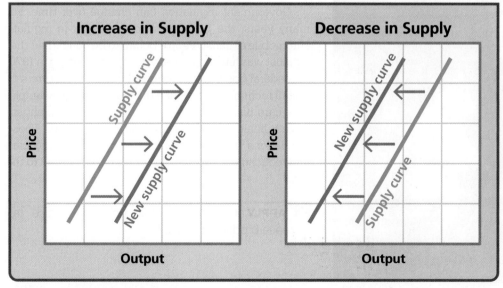

>> **Figure 3.15** Non-price determinants that alter supply shift the entire curve to the right or left. **Check Understanding** How do supply shifts differ from changes in quantity supplied based on price?

national car company as a source of pride, even though imported cars were less expensive. In Western Europe, banks and national airlines were allowed to suffer huge losses with the assurance that the government would cover their debts. In recent years, many governments have stopped providing industrial subsidies in the interest of free trade and fair competition.

In the United States, the federal government subsidizes producers in many industries. Farm subsidies are particularly controversial, especially when farmers are paid to take land out of cultivation to keep prices high.

In these cases, more efficient farmers are penalized, and farmers use more herbicides and pesticides on lands they do cultivate to compensate for production lost on the acres the government pays them not to plant.

Excise Taxes and Supply A government can reduce the supply of some goods by placing an excise tax on them. An **excise tax** is a tax on the production or sale of a good. An excise tax increases production costs by adding an extra cost for each unit sold.

Excise taxes are sometimes used to discourage the sale of goods that the government thinks are harmful to the public good, like cigarettes, alcohol, and high-pollutant gasoline. Excise taxes are indirect—they are built into the price of the good—so consumers may not realize that they are paying them. Like any increase in cost, an excise tax causes the supply of a good to decrease at all price levels, shifting the supply curve to the left.

The Role of Government Rules and Regulations

In the case of subsidies and excise taxes, government directly affects supply by changing revenue or production costs. Government can also raise or lower supply through indirect means. Government regulation often has the effect of raising costs. **Regulation** is government intervention in a market that affects the price, quantity, or quality of a good.

Some government regulation aims to ensure the safety of products. The federal government's Food Safety Inspection Service, for instance, inspects livestock, poultry, and eggs to ensure that the food supply is healthy. The Consumer Product Safety Commission works to minimize the risk of injury to people who use a wide variety of consumer products.

Government regulation has its drawbacks, however. Even members of government recognize the burden that regulation can place on business. In a 2006 speech to the Economic Club of New York, Treasury Secretary Henry M. Paulson Jr. described how over-regulation of business can affect economic progress:

> Excessive regulation slows innovation, imposes needless costs on investors, and stifles competitiveness and job creation.
>
> —Henry M. Paulson Jr., Secretary of the Treasury, washingtonpost.com, Nov. 11, 2006

Government regulation can change over time. For many years, the government did nothing to regulate automobile exhaust. People began to be concerned that exhaust was harming the environment. Starting in 1970, the federal government required car manufacturers to install technology to reduce this pollution. For example, new cars had to use lead-free fuel because scientists linked health problems to lead in gasoline. These regulations increased the cost of manufacturing cars and reduced the supply. The supply curve shifted to the left.

? **APPLY CONCEPTS** How does an excise tax increase production costs?

>> Regulations about the removal and disposal of hazardous wastes from factories add cost to business that can affect supply.

[▶] **Interactive Gallery**

SUPPLY AND THE EXPECTATION OF FUTURE PRICES

IF FUTURE **PRICES** ARE EXPECTED TO **RISE...** SUPPLY WILL **FALL** IN THE **SHORT TERM.**

IF FUTURE **PRICES** ARE EXPECTED TO **FALL...** SUPPLY WILL **RISE** IN THE **SHORT TERM.**

>> **Summarize** How does expectation of future prices affect supply?

Other Non-Price Determinants That Create Changes in Supply

While input costs and government can have an important influence on the supply of goods, there are other important factors that influence supply. They include changes in the global economy and the number of competitors in a market.

Changes in the Global Economy and Supply A large and rising share of goods and services consumed by Americans is imported. Naturally, the supply of imported goods is affected by conditions in other countries. Here are just two examples of possible changes in the supply of products imported by the United States.

- The U.S. imports carpets from India. An increase in the wages of Indian workers would decrease the supply of carpets to the U.S. market, shifting the supply curve to the left.

- The United States imports oil from Russia. A new oil discovery in Russia could increase the supply of oil to the U.S. market and shift the supply curve to the right.

Import restrictions also affect supply. The total supply of a product equals the sum of imports and domestically produced products. An import ban on

sugar would eliminate foreign sugar suppliers from the market, shifting the market supply curve to the left. If government restricted imports by establishing an import quota rather than a ban, the supply curve would shift to the left, but to a smaller degree.

Expectations About Prices and Supply If you were a soybean farmer, and you expected the price of soybeans to double next month, what would you do with the crop that you just harvested? Most farmers would store their soybeans until the price rose, cutting back supply in the short term.

If a seller expects the price of a good to rise in the future, the seller will store the goods now in order to sell more in the future at a higher price. But if the price of the good is expected to drop in the near future, the suppliers will earn more money by selling their goods immediately, before the price falls. Expectations of higher prices reduce supply now and increase supply later. Expectations of lower prices have the opposite effect.

Inflation is a condition of generally rising prices. During periods of inflation, the value of the cash in a person's pocket decreases from day to day as prices rise. Over many years, inflation has reduced the value of the dollar.

However, some goods continue to hold their value if they can be stored for a long period of time. When faced with inflation, suppliers prefer to hold on to these goods that maintain their value rather than sell them for cash that is losing its value rapidly. In this way, inflation affects supply by encouraging suppliers to hold on to goods as long as possible. In the short term, supply can fall dramatically.

During the Civil War, the South faced terrible inflation. There were shortages of food, and shopkeepers knew that prices on basic items like flour, butter, and salt would rise each month. A few decided to hoard these goods and wait for higher prices. They succeeded too well; the supply of food fell so much that prices rose out of the reach of many families. Riots broke out in Virginia and elsewhere when hungry people decided they weren't going to wait for the food to be released from the warehouses, and the shopkeepers lost their goods and their profits.

Changes in the Number of Competitors and Supply Another factor to consider when looking at changes in supply is the number of suppliers in the market. If more suppliers enter a market to produce a certain good, the market supply of the good will rise, and the supply curve will shift to the right. However, if suppliers stop producing the good and leave the market, the supply will decline. There is a positive relationship between the number of suppliers in a market and the market supply of the good.

❓ **IDENTIFY CAUSE AND EFFECT** Explain what happens to supply if the price of a good is expected to rise in the near future.

Deciding Where to Locate

So far, we have ignored the issue of where firms locate their production facilities. For many firms, the key factor is the cost of transportation—both the cost of transporting inputs to a production facility and the cost of transporting the finished product to consumers. Firms locate close to input suppliers when inputs, such as raw materials, are expensive to transport. They locate close to consumers when output is more costly to transport.

Consider the example of a firm that processes tomatoes into tomato sauce. Suppose that the firm uses seven tons of tomatoes to produce one ton of sauce. The firm locates its plant close to the tomato fields—and far from its consumers— because it is much cheaper to ship one ton of sauce to consumers than to ship seven tons of tomatoes to a faraway plant. Tomato sauce producers cluster in places like California's Central Valley, where weather and soil conditions are favorable for the growing of tomatoes.

Now consider the example of a firm that bottles soft drinks. The firm combines concentrated syrup with local water, so the firm's output (bottled drinks) weighs more than its transportable input (syrup). As a result, the firm locates close to its consumers—and far from its syrup supplier—because it saves more on transporting soft drinks than it pays to transport its syrup. In general, if a firm's output is bulky or perishable, the firm will locate close to its consumers.

Other firms establish themselves close to inputs that cannot be transported at all. Some firms locate near concentrations of specialized workers such as artists, engineers, and computer programmers. Other firms are pulled toward locations with low energy costs. Many firms locate in urban areas because of the rich variety of workers and business services available there.

❓ **CATEGORIZE** What kind of firm is most likely to locate near sources of supply?

>> It is common for multiple businesses to supply the same product in the same area.

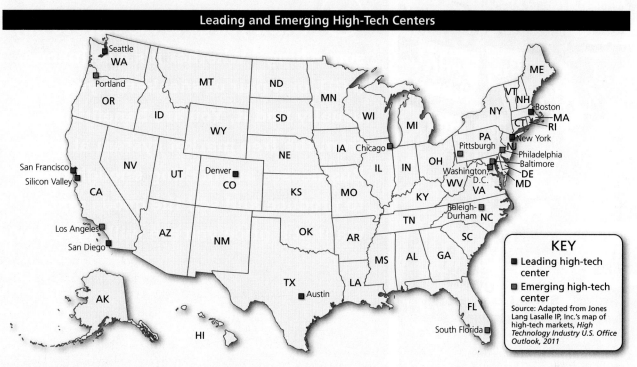

>> Businesses of a particular industry often cluster near critical inputs. **Express Ideas Clearly** What inputs do you think the cities and regions shown offer high-tech companies?

ASSESSMENT

1. **Describe** Why do rising input costs shift the supply curve to the left?

2. **Make Generalizations** Why does adoption of new technology tend to increase supply?

3. **Identify Central Ideas** How do subsidies generally affect the supply curve? Why?

4. **Predict Consequences** What would be the impact on the supply curve of oil if a major oil-producing country banned all exports to the United States?

5. **Summarize** What factors influence firms in their decision about where to locate operations?

When you go to the store to buy something—whether it's a cellphone, a CD, or a pair of sneakers—you can usually find it. You are benefiting from the free market system at work. Businesses are making enough profit to produce and sell the goods you want at a price you are willing to pay.

>> Building owners with few rental units—"small owners"—protest against rent control in New York City.

▶ **Interactive Flipped Video**

>> Objectives

Explain how supply and demand create equilibrium in the marketplace.

Describe what happens to prices, quantities demanded, and quantities supplied when equilibrium is disturbed.

Identify two ways that the government intervenes in markets to control prices and restricts the use of individual property.

Analyze the impacts of price ceilings and price floors on the free market.

>> Key Terms

equilibrium
disequilibrium
shortage
surplus
price ceiling
rent control
price floor
minimum wage

Equilibrium and Price Controls

Achieving Equilibrium

Prices are affected by the laws of supply and demand and by government action. Using the market for pizza as an example, you will see how free markets provide goods and services at the right price and in sufficient quantities. You will also see examples of how government intervention affects the wages of some workers and the rent that some people pay.

Just as buyers and sellers come together in a market, supply and demand also have a close relationship. Your knowledge of supply and demand will help you understand how markets operate and how markets can turn competing interests into a positive outcome for both sides. You'll also see why free markets usually produce some of their best outcomes when they are left to operate on their own, free from government intervention.

We begin by looking at a supply and demand schedule. As you know, a demand schedule shows how much of a good consumers are willing to buy at various prices. A supply schedule shows how much firms are willing to sell at various prices. Comparing these schedules will help us to find common ground for the two sides of the market.

Balancing Supply and Demand The point at which demand and supply come together is called the equilibrium. **Equilibrium** is the point of balance at which the quantity demanded equals the quantity supplied. At equilibrium, the market for a good is stable.

To find the equilibrium price and quantity, simply look for the price at which the quantity supplied equals the quantity demanded. In the combined supply and demand schedule for a pizza market in **Figure 3.16**, this occurs at a price of $3 per slice.

As you know, supply and demand schedules can be graphed. Look at the three graphs in **Figure 3.17**. The first two graphs are the demand curve and the supply curve for pizza slices from earlier lessons. The third graph, Finding Equilibrium, combines the first two graphs. This graph shows both the number of slices that consumers in a market will buy at various prices and the number of slices that pizzerias will supply.

To find the equilibrium price and quantity on the graph, locate the point at which the supply curve and the demand curve intersect. At that point, quantity supplied equals quantity demanded. As you can see, the supply and demand curves intersect at $3 per slice. At that price and only at that price, the quantity demanded and the quantity supplied are equal, at 200 slices per day. At that price, the market is in a state of equilibrium.

Benefits to Buyers and Sellers In any market, supply and demand will be equal at only one price and one quantity. At this equilibrium price, buyers will purchase exactly as much of a good as firms are willing to sell.

Buyers who are willing to purchase goods at the equilibrium price will find ample supplies on store shelves. Firms that sell at the equilibrium price will find enough buyers for their goods. When a market is at equilibrium, both buyers and sellers benefit.

? IDENTIFY CENTRAL ISSUES At what point on a combined supply and demand graph is the market at equilibrium?

Effects of Disequilibrium

If the market price or quantity supplied is anywhere but at the equilibrium, the market is in a state of disequilibrium. **Disequilibrium** occurs when quantity supplied is not equal to quantity demanded in a market. In **Figure 3.17**, disequilibrium occurs at any price other than $3 per slice and at any quantity other than 200 slices. Disequilibrium can produce one of two outcomes: shortage or surplus.

Shortage The problem of **shortage**—also known as excess demand—exists when the quantity demanded in a market is more than the quantity supplied. When the actual price in a market is below the equilibrium price, you have a shortage, because the low price encourages buyers and discourages sellers. For example, in **Figure 3.17**, a price of $2 per slice of pizza will lead to a quantity demanded of 250 slices per day

Combined Supply and Demand Schedule

PRICE OF A SLICE OF PIZZA	QUANTITY DEMANDED	QUANTITY SUPPLIED	RESULT
$1.00	300	100	Shortage from excess demand
$2.00	250	150	
$3.00	200	200	Equilibrium
$4.00	150	250	Surplus from excess supply
$5.00	100	300	
$6.00	50	350	

>> **Figure 3.16** Market equilibrium is found at the price where quantity demanded equals quantity supplied. **Analyze Data** How many slices are sold at equilibrium?

but a quantity supplied of only 150 slices per day. At this price, there is a shortage of 100 slices per day.

When customers want to buy 100 more slices of pizza than restaurants are willing and able to sell, these customers will have to wait in long lines for their pizza, and some will have to do without. In the graph on the far left of **Figure 3.18**, we have illustrated the shortage at $2 per slice by drawing a dashed line across the graph at that price.

If you were running the pizzeria, and you noticed long lines of customers waiting to buy your pizza at $2 per slice, what would you do? Assuming that you like to earn profits, you would probably raise the price. As the price increased, you would be willing to work harder and bake more pizzas, because you would know you could earn more money for each slice you sell.

Moving From Shortage to Equilibrium Of course, as the price rises, customers will buy less pizza, since it is becoming relatively more expensive. When the price reaches $3 per slice, you will find that you are earning more profit and can keep up with demand, but the lines are much shorter. Some days you may throw out a few leftover slices, and other days you may have to throw an extra pizza or two in the oven to keep up with customers, but on the whole, you are meeting the needs of your customers. In other words, the market is now at equilibrium.

As long as there is a shortage and the quantity demanded exceeds the quantity supplied, suppliers will keep raising the price. When the price has risen enough to close the gap, suppliers will have found the highest price that the market will bear. They will continue to sell at that price until some factor changes either the demand or the supply curve, creating new pressures to raise or lower prices and, eventually, a new equilibrium.

Non-price determinants that can shift the demand curve include changes in income, consumer expectations, and population. Factors that can shift the supply curve include changes in input costs, government regulations, and the number of suppliers.

Surplus If the price is too high, the market will face the problem of surplus, also known as excess supply. A **surplus** exists when quantity supplied exceeds quantity demanded and the actual price of a good is higher than the equilibrium price. (See **Figure 3.19**.) For example, at a price of $4 per slice of pizza, the quantity supplied of 250 slices per day is much greater than the quantity demanded of 150 slices per day. This means that pizzeria owners will be making 100 more slices of pizza each day than they can sell at that price.

The relatively high price encourages pizzeria owners to make more pizza, but it discourages customers from buying pizza, since it is relatively more expensive than other menu items. Some customers will buy one slice instead of two, while others will eat elsewhere. At the

Finding Equilibrium

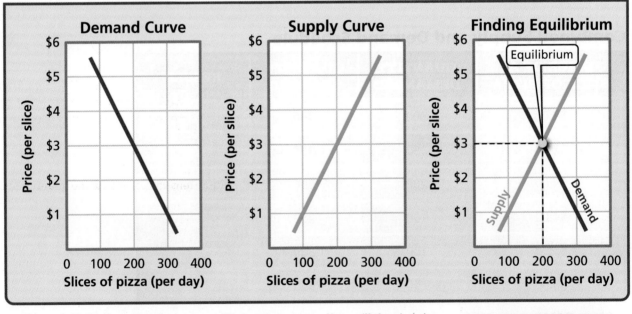

>> **Figure 3.17 Analyze Graphs** a. At equilibrium, how many slices will the pizzeria supply? b. At what price will the pizzeria supply it?

▶ **Interactive Chart**

Shortage

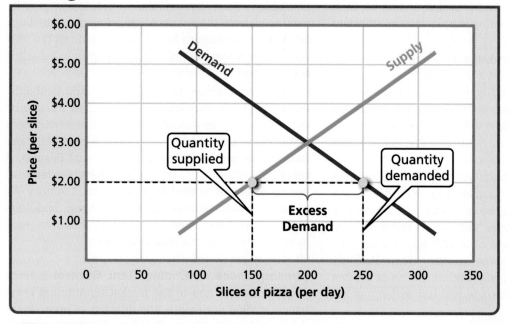

>> **Figure 3.18** Shortage results when quantity demanded in a market exceeds quantity supplied. **Analyze Graphs** What is the shortage when pizza is sold at $2 per slice?

▶ **Interactive Chart**

end of the day, it is likely that 100 slices will have to be thrown out.

Moving From Surplus to Equilibrium Before long, pizzeria owners will get tired of throwing out unsold pizza and will cut their prices. As the price falls, the quantity demanded will rise, and more customers will buy more pizza. At the same time, pizzeria owners will supply fewer pizzas. This process will continue until the price reaches the equilibrium price of $3 per slice. At that price, the amount of pizza that pizzeria owners are willing and able to sell is exactly equal to the amount that their customers are willing and able to buy.

Whenever the market is in disequilibrium and prices are flexible, market forces will push the market toward the equilibrium. Sellers do not like to waste their resources on a surplus, particularly on goods that cannot be stored for long, like pizza. And when there is a shortage, profit-seeking sellers realize that they can raise prices to earn more profits. For these reasons, market prices move toward the equilibrium level.

❓ IDENTIFY MAIN IDEAS What market condition might cause a pizzeria owner to throw out many slices of pizza at the end of the day?

Price Ceilings

Markets tend toward equilibrium, but in some cases the government intervenes to control prices. The government can impose a **price ceiling**, or a maximum price that can be legally charged for a good or service. The price ceiling is set below the equilibrium price.

Effects of Government Rent Control A price ceiling is a maximum price, set by law, that sellers can charge for a good or service. The government places price ceilings on some goods that are considered "essential" and might become too expensive for some consumers.

For example, in the early 1940s, New York City introduced **rent control**, or price ceilings placed on apartment rents, to prevent inflation during a housing crisis. Later, other cities imposed rent control to help the poor cut their housing costs and enable them to live in neighborhoods that they could not otherwise afford. Let's examine how rent control affects the quantity and quality of housing available to consumers.

The housing market data for a hypothetical city are shown in **Figure 3.20**. Look at the graph on the left side of this illustration. The supply and demand curves for two-bedroom apartments meet at the point where the rental price is $900 a month. At this equilibrium rent, consumers will demand 30,000 apartments and suppliers will offer 30,000 apartments for rent.

Suppose that the city government passes a law that limits the rent on two-bedroom apartments to $600 per month. This price ceiling is below the equilibrium price.

The effect on the market is shown in the graph on the right in **Figure 3.20**. At a price of $600, the quantity of apartments demanded is 45,000, and the quantity supplied is 15,000. At such a low price, apartments seem inexpensive. Many people will try to rent apartments instead of living with their families or investing in their own houses.

However, some landlords will have difficulty earning profits or breaking even at these low rents. Fewer new apartment buildings will be built, and older ones might be converted into offices, stores, or condominiums. The result is a shortage of 30,000 apartments. The price ceiling increases the quantity demanded but decreases the quantity supplied. Since rents are not allowed to rise, this shortage will last as long as the price ceiling holds.

Cost of Rent Control When the price cannot rise to the equilibrium level, the market must determine which 15,000 of the 45,000 households will get an apartment, and which 30,000 will do without.

Although governments usually pass rent control laws to help renters with the greatest need, few of these renters benefit from rent control. Methods besides

prices—including long waiting lists, discrimination by landlords, a lottery system, and even bribery—may be used to allocate the scarce supply of apartments. Luck becomes an important factor, and sometimes the only way to get a rent-controlled apartment is to inherit it from a parent or grandparent.

In addition, since the rent controls limit landlords' profits, landlords may try to increase their income by cutting costs. Why should a landlord give a building a fresh coat of paint and a new garden if he or she can't earn the money back through higher rent? Besides, if there's a waiting list to get an apartment, the landlord has no incentive to work hard and attract renters. As a result, many rent-controlled apartment buildings become run-down, and renters may have to wait months to have routine problems fixed.

Consequences of Ending Rent Control If rents were allowed to rise to the market equilibrium level, which is $900 per month, the quantity of apartments in the market would actually rise to 30,000 apartments. The market would be in equilibrium, and people who could afford $900 a month would have an easier time finding vacant apartments. Instead of spending time and money searching for apartments and then having to accept an apartment in a poorly maintained building, many renters would be able to find a wider selection of apartments. Landlords would also have a

Surplus

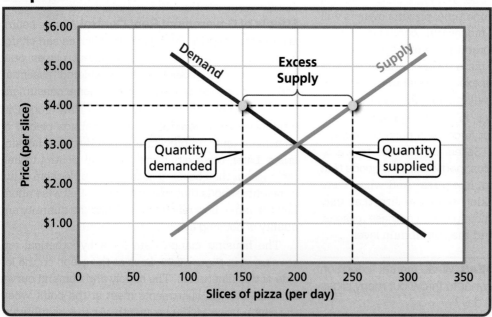

>> **Figure 3.19** At a certain price, quantity supplied exceeds quantity demanded, creating a surplus. **Analyze Graphs** How might the pizzeria solve the problem of excess supply?

THE EFFECTS OF RENT CONTROL

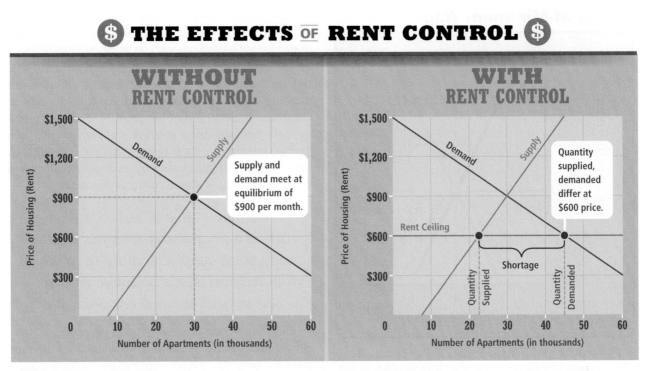

>> **Figure 3.20** In these graphs, a price ceiling of $600 for rent-controlled apartments is below the equilibrium price. **Analyze Graphs** Why does rent control lead to a shortage of desirable apartments?

greater incentive to properly maintain their buildings and invest in new construction.

On the other hand, once rent control is ended, people living in formerly rent-controlled apartments may no longer be able to afford the higher rents. As soon as the neighborhood improves, these renters may be priced out of their apartments and replaced by people willing to pay the equilibrium price.

Certainly, the end of rent control benefits some people and hurts others. Nearly all economists agree that the benefits of ending rent control exceed the costs, and suggest that there are better ways to help poor households find affordable housing.

? **SUMMARIZE** What is one positive and one negative effect of government intervention in the rental market in the form of price ceilings?

Price Floors

A **price floor** is a minimum price, set by government, that must be paid for a good or service. Governments set price floors to ensure that certain sellers receive at least a minimum reward for their efforts. Sellers can include workers, who sell their labor.

The Minimum Wage One well-known price floor is the **minimum wage**, which sets a minimum price employers can pay for one hour of labor. (The federal government sets a minimum wage, but states can make theirs higher.) A full-time worker paid the federal minimum wage will earn less than government says is necessary to support a couple with one child. Still, the minimum wage does ensure a lower limit for workers' earnings.

But do the benefits of a minimum wage outweigh the loss of some jobs? The supply and demand curves for labor are combined in **Figure 3.21**. This theoretical supply curve shows the workers available at various wage rates. The demand curve shows the workers employers will hire at various wages. (In this example, the worker is the supplier of labor purchased by an employer.) If the minimum wage is set above the market equilibrium wage rate, the demand for workers will go down.

If the equilibrium wage for low-skilled labor is $6.60 per hour, and the minimum wage is set at $7.25, the result is a surplus of labor. Firms will employ 2 million fewer low-skilled workers than they would at the equilibrium wage rate, because the price floor keeps the wage rate artificially high. If the minimum wage is below the equilibrium rate, it will have no effect,

Effects of Minimum Wage

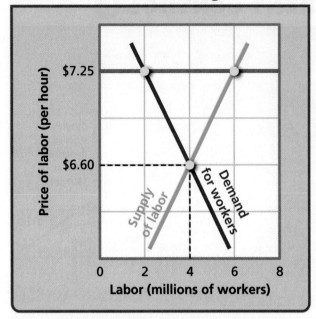

>> **Figure 3.21** A minimum wage law can set the price of labor above the equilibrium price. **Analyze Graphs** In this graph, what happens to the supply of labor with a minimum wage of $7.25 per hour?

because employers would have to pay the equilibrium rate anyway to find workers in a free market.

Remember, **Figure 3.21** is a theoretical model of the effects of a minimum wage. The real world is more complex, and some economists believe the actual effect of the minimum wage on employment rates is not as severe as in this example.

Agricultural Price Supports Agricultural price supports are another example of price floors used for farm products. Like the minimum wage, price supports have supporters and opponents.

During the Great Depression of the 1930s, the federal government began setting minimum prices for many commodities. Unlike the minimum wage, these price floors were not legal minimums set for buyers. Instead, whenever prices fell below a certain level, the government created demand by buying excess crops.

Supporters of price floors believed they were necessary because American farms would not easily

survive in a freely competitive market. If many American farms were to go out of business, the United States would have to depend on other nations for food.

Opponents of price supports argued that the regulations were a burden to farmers. Government dictated what and how much farmers should produce. Congress voted to phase out most of these programs in 1996 because they seemed to conflict with free market principles. Some people worried that without government stepping in to buy excess crops, farmers would overproduce. One farmer commented:

> When you have bumper crops, if it truly is a supply-and-demand market, and you're supplying more than what the demand is, it's financial suicide.
>
> —Brian Romsdahl, Minnesota Public Radio, 1998

Despite efforts to end price supports, many commodities remain relatively untouched by the new laws. For example, government has periodically bought surplus milk to help keep the price from dropping below the set minimum. In addition, government often responds to low prices by providing emergency financial aid to farmers.

❓ DEFINE Why is the minimum wage considered to be a price floor?

ASSESSMENT

1. **Define** Under what conditions is a market at equilibrium?

2. **Identify Central Ideas** What two conditions can lead to disequilibrium in a free market?

3. **Check Understanding** In a free market, what impact does a shortage have on producers?

4. **Identify Main Ideas** In what two ways can the government intervene to control prices?

5. **Recall** What is the main argument for agricultural price supports?

>> A cold snap in a region where citrus fruit is grown can cause a sharp decline in the supply of oranges.

(3.8) Have you ever stood in a long line to buy concert tickets or the latest video game? Do you anxiously scan the signs at the pump to see if the price of gas is up or down? Have you ever seen ads trumpeting the words "Great Bargains . . . Everything Must Go!"? These are all elements of the market system at work. And often, the one who gets the benefit—or pays the price—is you.

▶ **Interactive Flipped Video**

Changes in Market Equilibrium

Tending Toward Equilibrium

Changes in supply and demand upset market equilibrium and cause prices to change. Sometimes prices go up, and sometimes prices go down. But either way, the principle of market equilibrium is at work. As you will see, changes in supply and demand affect a variety of products, from digital cameras to toys.

Economists say that a market will tend toward equilibrium, which means that the price and quantity will gradually move toward their equilibrium levels. Why does this happen? Remember that a shortage will cause firms to raise prices. Higher prices cause the quantity supplied to rise and the quantity demanded to fall until the two values are equal. On the other hand, a surplus will force firms to cut prices. Falling prices cause quantity demanded to rise and quantity supplied to fall until, once again, they are equal. Through these relationships, the market price of a good and the quantity supplied will move toward their equilibrium values.

As you learned earlier, such changes in demand and supply are changes along a demand or supply curve. Assuming that a market starts at equilibrium, there are two factors that can push it into

>> **Objectives**

Explain why a free market naturally tends to move toward equilibrium.

Analyze how a market reacts to an increase or decrease in supply.

Analyze how a market reacts to an increase or decrease in demand.

>> **Key Terms**

inventory
search cost

PEARSON **realize** www.PearsonRealize.com
Access your Digital Lesson.

disequilibrium: a shift in the entire demand curve or a shift in the entire supply curve.

❓ IDENTIFY MAIN IDEAS What changes can push a market out of equilibrium?

Increasing Supply

You have learned about the different non-price determinants that can shift a supply curve to the left or to the right—that is, decrease or increase supply of a good or service in the marketplace. These factors include advances in technology, new government taxes and subsidies, and changes in the prices of the raw materials and labor used to produce the good or service.

You know that market equilibrium occurs at the intersection of a demand curve and a supply curve. This means that a shift of the entire supply curve will change the quantity supplied and demanded and the equilibrium price. In other words, a shift in the supply curve to the left or the right creates a new equilibrium point. Markets tend toward equilibrium, so a change in supply will set into motion market forces that lead the market to a new equilibrium price and quantity sold.

>> Early digital cameras combined high prices with low-quality. **Predict Consequences** What do you think will happen to the supply curve for digital cameras as technology improves?

To illustrate these market forces, we will present an example of what happens when supply shifts to the right. We will look at a familiar product that has undergone a radical market change in a relatively short period of time: the digital camera.

Market Changes Digital cameras were first introduced into the consumer market in 1994. These early digital cameras were far less sophisticated than the ones that people use today. They produced grainy pictures of lower quality than cameras that used film. The first digital cameras were also expensive, at a cost of well over $700 each.

Gradually, improved technology for producing digital cameras caused prices to fall. By 2000, a consumer could purchase a midrange digital camera for $500; just two years later, a similar camera cost about $350. Today, a camera like the one that cost over $700 in 1994 would sell for well under $100. Consumers have their pick of many models at a low cost.

At the same time, the quality of digital cameras has improved. For a fraction of that original $700 cost, you can now get a digital camera that has many more features and produces far better photographs than the first digital cameras. In fact, many smartphones today contain cameras that exceed the quality of the early, expensive devices.

Why has this happened? Advances in technology have lowered the cost of manufacturing digital cameras by reducing some of the input costs, such as computer chips. Advances in production have allowed manufacturers to produce digital cameras at lower costs. These lower costs have been passed on to consumers in the form of lower prices.

We can use the graphing tools developed in an earlier lesson to show the effect of these changes on the digital camera market's supply curve. As shown in **Figure 3.22**, the supply curve shifted to the right as manufacturers continued to offer a greater supply of digital cameras at lower prices.

In 2000, no digital cameras were offered for $100. They were simply too expensive to develop and manufacture. Today, manufacturers can offer millions of cameras at this price and still make a profit.

Finding a New Equilibrium Digital cameras evolved from an expensive luxury good to a midrange good when a new generation of computer chips reduced the cost of production. These lower costs shifted the supply curve to the right, where, at each price, producers are willing to supply a larger quantity.

A graph can show you how the shifts in supply threw the market into disequilibrium. **Figure 3.23** represents what happens in this situation. (The numbers used

Falling Prices and the Supply Curve

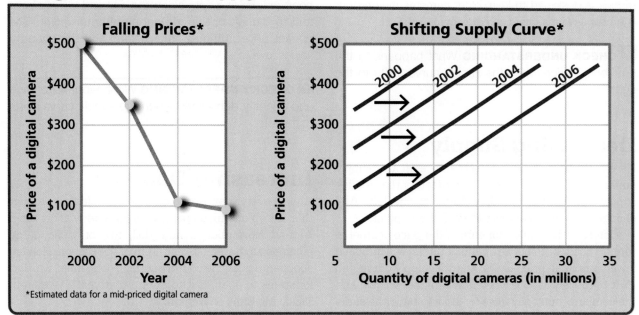

Falling Prices*

Price of a digital camera: $500, $400, $300, $200, $100

Year: 2000, 2002, 2004, 2006

*Estimated data for a mid-priced digital camera

Shifting Supply Curve*

Price of a digital camera: $500, $400, $300, $200, $100

2000, 2002, 2004, 2006

Quantity of digital cameras (in millions): 5, 10, 15, 20, 25, 30, 35

>> **Figure 3.22** As digital cameras became cheaper and easier to produce, the supply increased. **Draw Conclusions** Why do you think the pace of the falling prices began to slow in 2004?

here are fictional to help provide a clear representation of the market forces.) After the shift, suppliers were willing to offer 4,000,000 cameras per year at the original equilibrium price of 2,000,000.

In **Figure 3.23**, the increase in quantity supplied at the original equilibrium price is shown as the change from point *a* to point *b*. However, the quantity demanded at this price has not changed, and consumers will buy only 2,000,000 digital cameras. If this original equilibrium price is not changed, unsold digital cameras—or **inventory**, the quantity of goods that a firm has on hand—will begin to pile up in the warehouse. When quantity supplied is greater than quantity demanded at a given price, there is a surplus. Something will have to change to bring the market to equilibrium.

As you know, suppliers will respond to a surplus by reducing prices. As the price falls from $900 to $450, more consumers buy digital cameras, and the quantity demanded rises. The combined movement of falling prices and increasing quantity demanded can be seen in **Figure 3.23** as a change from point *a* to point *c*. Notice that this change is a movement along the demand curve, not a shift of the entire demand curve.

At point *c*, the price has fallen to a level where quantity supplied and quantity demanded are equal. Surplus is no longer a problem. This new equilibrium point marks a lower equilibrium price and a higher

equilibrium quantity supplied than before the supply curve shifted. This is how equilibrium changes when supply increases, and the entire supply curve shifts to the right.

Changing Equilibrium As improved technology caused the price of digital cameras to fall, sales increased. Market equilibrium then started moving gradually downward and to the right, where the quantities demanded and supplied are higher and prices are lower.

The supply curve for digital cameras has been moving to the right ever since the first cameras were sold. The curve continues to shift today as new technology drives down the production cost and market price of the most basic cameras.

In real-life markets, equilibrium is usually not an unchanging, single point on a graph. The equilibrium in the digital camera market has always been in motion. The market equilibrium follows the intersection of the demand curve and the supply curve as that point moves downward along the demand curve.

Equilibrium is a "moving target" that changes as market conditions change. Manufacturers and retail sellers of digital cameras are constantly searching for a new equilibrium as technology and methods of production change. Consumers can easily recognize the impact of this search by the frequent price changes, sales, and rebates for digital cameras. Each of these tactics is designed to keep older cameras moving out of stores as fast as new cameras come in.

❓ CHECK UNDERSTANDING What happens to the equilibrium price when the supply curve shifts to the right?

Decreasing Supply

New technology or lower costs can shift the supply curve to the right. However, other factors that reduce supply can shift the supply curve to the left. Any change in supply changes the equilibrium point.

Consider the market for cars. If the price of steel or rubber rises, automobile manufacturers will produce fewer cars at all price levels, and the supply curve will shift to the left. If auto workers win higher wages, and the company must pay more for labor to build the same number of cars, supply will decrease. If the government imposes a new tax on car manufacturers, supply will decrease. In all of these cases, the supply curve will move to the left, because the quantity supplied is lower at all price levels.

When the supply curve shifts to the left, the equilibrium price and quantity sold will change as well. This process is the exact opposite of the change that results from an increase in supply. As the supply curve shifts to the left, suppliers raise their prices, and

A Change in Supply

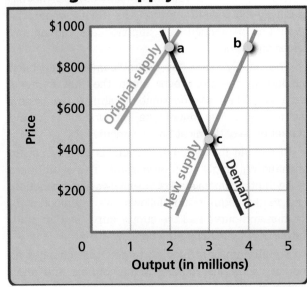

>> **Figure 3.23** This graph shows how a change in supply affects the original equilibrium point (a). **Analyze Graphs** a. What does point b on this graph represent? b. What does point c represent?

▶ Interactive Gallery

the quantity demanded falls. The new equilibrium point will be at a spot along the demand curve above and to the left of the original equilibrium point. The market price is higher than before, and the quantity sold is lower.

❓ CHECK UNDERSTANDING What happens to price and quantity demanded when the supply curve shifts to the left?

Increasing Demand

Almost every year, we experience a new fad—a product that enjoys enormous popularity for a fairly short time. Around November, a new doll, toy, or video game emerges as the "must-buy" item of the season. Holiday shoppers across the country stand in long lines, waiting for stores to open, just to obtain that year's version of Tickle Me Elmo or Webkinz®.

You know that fads reflect the impact of consumer tastes and advertising on consumer behavior. Fads like these, in which demand rises quickly, are real-life examples of a rapid, rightward shift in a market demand curve. **Figure 3.24** shows how a swift, unexpected increase in market demand can affect the equilibrium in a market for a hypothetical, trendy new toy.

Shortages **Figure 3.24** shows how the fad causes a sudden increase in market demand and a shift of the demand curve to the right. This shift reflects a shortage at the original price of $24 (point b). Before the fad began, quantity demanded and quantity supplied were equal at 300,000 toys (point a). On the graph, the shortage appears as a gap at the $24 price level between the quantity supplied of 300,000 toys and the new quantity demanded of 500,000 toys, shown at point b. The fad has caused the quantity demanded to increase by 200,000.

In the stores that carry the toy, the shortage appears as empty shelves or long lines. Shortage also appears in the form of **search costs**—the financial and opportunity costs that consumers pay in searching for a product or service. Driving to or calling different stores to find an available toy are examples of search costs. Today, the Internet has dramatically reduced search costs for many items, but finding the exact product you want can still be a costly and time-consuming process.

In the meantime, the available toys must be distributed in some other manner. In this case, long lines, limits on the quantities each customer may buy, and "first come, first serve" policies are used to distribute a limited number of toys among customers.

A Change in Demand

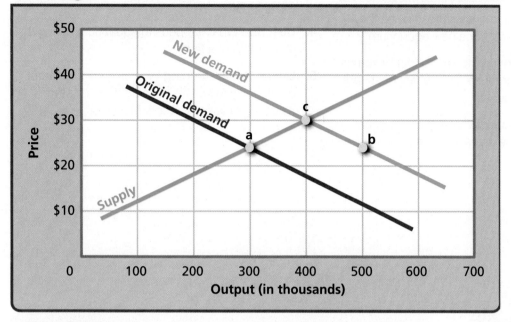

>> **Figure 3.24** Observe how a change in demand affects the original equilibrium point (*a*). **Analyze Graphs** a. What do points *b* and *c* on this graph represent? b. How has the increased demand affected price?

Interactive Chart

Return to Equilibrium In time, firms will react to the signs of shortage by increasing their prices and the quantity supplied. Customers may actually push prices up on their own if there is "bidding" in the market, as there is for real estate, antiques, fine art, and rare items. For example, if parents cannot find the toy they want at the store, they might offer the storekeeper an extra $10 to guarantee getting a toy from the next shipment. Through methods like this, the market price will rise until the quantity supplied equals the quantity demanded at 400,000 toys. All of these toys are sold at the new equilibrium price of $30, shown at point *c* in **Figure 3.24**.

When demand increases, both the equilibrium price and the equilibrium quantity also increase. The demand curve has shifted, and the equilibrium point has moved, setting in motion market forces that push the price and quantity toward their new equilibrium values.

? IDENTIFY CENTRAL IDEAS How is equilibrium restored after a shortage?

Decreasing Demand

When a fad passes its peak, demand can fall as quickly as it rose. The shortage turns into a surplus for the once-popular toy, as parents look for new, trendier gifts

for their children. Overflowing store shelves and silent cash registers, the symptoms of a surplus, replace long lines and policies that limit purchases.

As demand falls, the demand curve shifts to the left. Suppliers will respond to decreased demand for the once-fashionable toy by cutting prices on their inventory. Price and quantity supplied slide down to the equilibrium point shown at point *a* in **Figure 3.24**. The end of the fad has restored the original price and quantity supplied.

New technology can also lead to a decrease in consumer demand. Digital camera sales captured just 18 percent of the market in 2000. But in 2012, digital camera sales accounted for 99 percent of the market. Digital technology has led to a steep decline in film camera sales. Some firms have switched to digital camera production while others have left the market.

Digital technology has also changed the music industry. While sales of music CDs dropped by 20 percent in early 2007, digital sales of individual songs increased by 54 percent during the same period. New technology has caused the supply curve for CDs to shift to the left. However, in the future, new technology may lead to a change in demand for both digital cameras and digital music.

? DESCRIBE How does a demand curve change to reflect decreased demand?

ASSESSMENT

1. **Interpret** What do economists mean when they say firms are "searching for a new equilibrium"?

2. **Make Generalizations** When a product becomes more expensive to produce, what effect does that have on the supply curve?

3. **Compare and Contrast** What is the difference between a shift of the demand curve and movement of the equilibrium point along the demand curve?

4. **Describe** What happens to equilibrium during the rise and fall of a fad?

5. **Check Understanding** What is likely true about demand if you see a sign in a store that says "Great Bargains—All Boots Must Go!"

The price system is a delicate balance of supply and demand in which consumers, producers, and sellers all play a role. How does the price system affect you as a consumer?

>> This store wants its consumers to be confident that the prices they find are low by offering a low-price guarantee.

>> **▶ Interactive Flipped Video**

Prices at Work

The Price System

Prices and Consumers Consider this example: You want to buy a pair of athletic shoes, so you go to a local mall to compare prices. A discount shoe store offers low-end sneakers for $20. At other stores, you find that you can spend as little as $50 for brand-name sneakers, or more than $200 for a pair of designer basketball shoes. Basing your decision on the available supply, the price, and your demand, you buy the $50 sneakers.

Later, through online research, you find a pair of sneakers similar to the pair you bought, on sale for $5 less, including shipping. You buy the online sneakers with your credit card and return the sneakers you bought at the mall.

Prices in a Free Market In a free market economy, prices offer a number of advantages to both consumers and producers. Simple purchases would be much more complicated and inefficient without the price system to help us make informed decisions. In this lesson, you will see how prices affect consumer behavior and how producers respond. You will also see how profits act as an incentive.

Earlier in this topic, you read about how supply and demand interact to determine the equilibrium price and quantity sold in a market. You also read about how prices change over time, based on

>> **Objectives**

Identify the many roles that prices play in a free enterprise system.

List the advantages of a price-based system.

Examine how a price-based system leads to a wider choice of goods and more efficient allocation of resources than systems such as barter or rationing.

Describe the relationship between prices and the profit incentive.

>> **Key Terms**

supply shock
rationing
black market
barter

shifts in the demand curve or supply curve. As **Figure 3.25** shows, prices are a key element of equilibrium. Price changes can move markets toward equilibrium and solve problems of shortage and surplus.

In a free market, prices are a tool for distributing goods and resources throughout the economy. Prices are nearly always the most efficient way to allocate, or distribute, resources. Prices help move land, labor, and capital into the hands of producers and finished goods into the hands of buyers. The alternative method for distributing goods and resources, namely a centrally planned economy, is not nearly as efficient as a market system based on prices.

As you will see, prices play other vital roles in a free market economy. Prices serve as a language, as an incentive, and as a signal of economic conditions. The price system is flexible and free, and it allows for a wide diversity of goods and services.

? **LIST** three roles that prices play in a free market system.

The Benefits of the Price System

Prices provide a common language for buyers and sellers. Could you conceive of a marketplace without prices? Without prices as a standard measure of value,

a seller would have to **barter**—that is, exchange one type of good or service for another. Under a barter system, one customer might offer two pairs of shoes in exchange for one sweater, but another customer might be willing to trade three pairs of shoes for the same sweater. The supplier would have no consistent and accurate way to measure demand for a product. Such a system would be inconvenient, impractical, and inefficient.

Prices Provide Incentives Buyers and sellers alike look at prices to find information on a good's demand and supply. The laws of supply and demand describe how people and firms respond to a change in prices. In these cases, prices are signals that tell producers or consumers how to adjust. Prices communicate to buyers and to sellers whether goods are in short supply or readily available.

In the example of the "fad" toy discussed in the preceding lesson, the sudden increase in demand for the toy told suppliers that people wanted more of those toys, and soon! However, the signal that producers respond to is not simply the demand but also the high price consumers are willing to pay for the toy, well above the usual retail price. This higher price tells firms not only that people want more of the toys, but also that the firms can earn more profit by producing more toys, because they are in demand. Therefore, rising prices in a market will provide an incentive for existing firms to produce more of the goods that are in demand and will encourage new firms to enter a market.

Prices Serve as Signals Think of prices as a traffic light. A green light means "go," and a red light means "stop." A relatively high price is a green light that tells producers that a specific product is in demand and that they should use their resources to produce more. New suppliers will also join the market. But a low price is a red light to producers, signaling that a good is being overproduced. In this case, low prices tell a supplier that he or she might earn higher profits by using existing resources to produce a different product.

For consumers, a low price is a green light to buy more of a product. A low price indicates that the product carries a low opportunity cost for the consumer and offers a chance to get a good deal. By the same token, a high price is a red light that tells consumers to stop and think carefully before buying.

Prices Are Responsive and Flexible Another important aspect of prices is that they are responsive to market conditions. When a supply shift or a demand shift changes the equilibrium in a market, price and quantity supplied need to change to solve problems of

Using Price to Restore Equilibrium

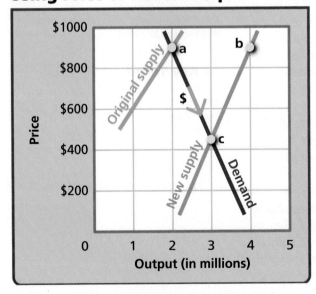

>> **Figure 3.25** Price changes can move markets back to equilibrium, solving shortages and surpluses. **Analyze Graphs** Which problem is price solving in this graph? Explain, using the points on the graph.

$ THE PRICE SYSTEM DOES ALL OF THIS $

ALLOCATES RESOURCES EFFICIENTLY

PROVIDES INCENTIVES TO BUY, SELL

IS RESPONSIVE AND FLEXIBLE

SERVES AS A "COMMON LANGUAGE"

HELPS CONSUMERS CHOOSE

AND THE PRICE SYSTEM IS "FREE"

>> The price system provides consumers and producers with many benefits. **Explain** How can the price system do all of this and still be "free"?

▶ Interactive Chart

too much or too little demand. In many markets, prices are much more flexible than output levels. Prices can easily be increased to solve a problem of shortage, and they can just as easily be decreased to eliminate a problem of surplus.

For example, a **supply shock** is a sudden shortage of a good such as gasoline or wheat. A supply shock creates a shortage because suppliers can no longer meet consumer demand. The immediate problem is how to divide up the available supply among consumers.

What are the options? Increasing supply can be a time-consuming and difficult process. For example, wheat takes time to plant, grow, and harvest. **Rationing**, a system of allocating goods and services using criteria other than price, is expensive and can take a long time to organize. Rationing is the basis of central planning, an economic system in which a central authority, rather than a free market, makes basic economic decisions for a society. Rationing has also been used at times in U.S. history.

Raising prices is the quickest way to resolve a shortage. A quick increase in prices can reduce quantity demanded to the same level as quantity supplied and avoid the problem of distribution. The people who have enough money and value the product most highly will pay the most for it. These consumers will be the only consumers still in the market at the higher price, and the market will settle at a new equilibrium.

The Price System Is "Free" A free market distribution system, based on prices, costs nothing to administer. Central planning, however, requires many administrators to collect information on production and decide how resources are to be distributed. In the former Soviet Union, the government employed thousands of bureaucrats in an enormous agency called GOSPLAN to organize the economy. During World War II, the United States government set up a similar agency, called the Office of Price Administration, to prevent inflation and coordinate the rationing of important goods.

The price system has many benefits. Unlike central planning, free market pricing distributes goods through millions of decisions made daily by consumers and suppliers. At the beginning of the lesson, looking at the prices of sneakers helped you decide which product to buy and which supplier to buy them from. A farmer looks at prices listed in crop reports and decides whether to grow corn instead of soybeans next year. Everyone is familiar with how prices work and knows how to use them. In short, prices help goods flow through the economy without a central plan.

? IDENTIFY CENTRAL IDEAS How does the price system provide incentives for producers and for consumers?

Choice and Efficiency

One benefit of a market-based economy is the diversity of goods and services that consumers can buy. Prices help consumers choose among similar products. You could have bought footwear along a wide range of prices, from the cheap $20 pair to the $200 designer basketball shoes. Based on your income, you decided on a pair of sneakers at the lower end of the price range. The prices provided an easy way for you to narrow your choices to a certain price range. Prices also allow producers to target the audience they want with the products that will sell best to that audience.

Another benefit of the U.S. free enterprise system is responsive prices. That is, prices go up or down in response to consumer demand. In a command economy, however, one organization decides what goods are produced and how much stores will charge for those goods. To limit their costs, central planners restrict production to a few varieties of each product.

As a result, consumers in the former Communist states of Eastern Europe and the Soviet Union had far fewer choices of goods than consumers in Western Europe and the United States. The government of the Soviet Union even built whole neighborhoods of identical apartment blocks and supermarkets with names such as "Supermarket No. 3."

Rationing and Shortages Although goods in the Soviet Union were inexpensive, consumers could not always find them. When they did, they often had to wait hours for eggs or soap, and years for apartments or telephones. The United States experienced similar, although far less severe, problems when the federal government instituted temporary price controls during World War II.

The needs of the U.S. armed forces for food, metal, and rubber during World War II created tremendous shortages at home. In order to ensure that enough resources were available for military use, the government controlled the distribution of food and consumer goods.

Rationing in the United States was only a short-term hardship. Still, like rationing in the Soviet Union, it was expensive and inconvenient and left many consumers unhappy. Choices were limited, and consumers felt, rightly or wrongly, that some people fared better than others. However, rationing was chosen because a price-based system might have put food and housing out of the reach of some Americans, and the government wanted to guarantee every civilian a minimum standard of living during wartime.

The Black Market Despite the World War II ration system, the federal government was unable to control the supply of all goods passing through the economy. A butcher could sell a steak without asking for ration points, or a landlord might be willing to rent an apartment at the rate fixed by the government only if the renter threw in a cash "bonus" or an extra two months' rent as a "deposit."

When people conduct business without regard for government controls on price or quantity, they are said to do business on the **black market**. Black markets allow consumers to pay more so they can buy a product when rationing makes it otherwise unavailable. Although black markets are a nearly inevitable consequence of rationing, such trade is illegal and strongly discouraged by governments.

Efficient Resource Allocation All of the advantages of a free market allow prices to allocate, or distribute, resources efficiently. Efficient resource allocation means that economic resources—land, labor, and capital—will be used for their most valuable purposes. A market system, with its responsive prices, ensures that resources go to the uses that consumers value most highly. A price-based system also ensures

>> In a market-based economy, consumers have a diversity of goods and services available to them. Consumers use prices to help them make choices among similar goods and services.

▶ Interactive Gallery

that resource use will adjust relatively quickly to the changing demands of consumers.

These changes take place without any central control, because the people who own resources—landowners, workers who sell their labor, and people who provide capital to firms—seek the largest possible returns. How do people earn the largest returns? They sell their resources to the highest bidder. The highest bidder will be that firm that produces goods that are in the highest demand. Therefore, the resources will flow to the uses that are most highly valued by consumers. This flow is the most efficient way to use our society's scarce resources in a way that benefits both producers and consumers.

❓ IDENTIFY SUPPORTING DETAILS How does the practice of rationing address a shortage of goods?

"BUT WE SPEND ALL OUR MONEY CREATING TOXIC WASTE. WE WERE HOPING SOMEONE ELSE WOULD FIGURE OUT HOW TO DETOXIFY IT."

>> Waste is a negative externality of some manufacturing. **Analyze Political Cartoons** Who is the "someone else" who has taken on the cost of cleaning up toxic waste?

Prices and the Profit Incentive

In a free market, efficient resource allocation goes hand in hand with the profit incentive. Suppose that scientists predicted extremely hot weather for the coming summer. In most parts of the country, consumers would buy up air conditioners and fans to prepare for the heat. Power companies would buy reserves of oil and natural gas to supply these appliances with enough power. Since demand would exceed supply, consumers would bid up the price of fans, and power plants would bid up the price of fuel.

Suppliers would recognize the possibility for profit in the higher prices charged for these goods, and they would produce more fans and air conditioners. Oil and natural gas fields would hire workers to produce more fuel for power plants. Eventually, more fans, air conditioners, and fuel would move into the market. The potential heat wave would have created a need among consumers for certain goods, and the rise in prices would have given producers an incentive to meet this need.

As we previously noted, efficient resource allocation occurs naturally in a market system as long as the system works reasonably well. Landowners tend to use their scarce property in the most profitable manner. Workers usually move toward higher-paying jobs, and capital will be invested in the firms that pay the highest returns.

The Wealth of Nations Adam Smith wrote about the profit incentive in *The Wealth of Nations*, published in 1776. Smith explained that it is not because of charity that the baker and the butcher provide people with food. Rather, they provide bread and meat because prices are such that they profit from doing so. In other words, businesses prosper by finding out what people want and then providing it. Smith's observations have been highly influential, and the system he championed has proved to be more efficient than any other that has been tried in the modern era.

Market Problems There are some exceptions to the idea that markets lead to an efficient allocation of resources. One problem is imperfect competition: If only a few firms are selling a product, there might not be enough competition to lower market prices to the true equilibrium point. If there is only one producer in a market, he or she will usually charge a higher price than we would see in a market with competing businesses.

A second problem involves negative externalities. These are side effects of production that impose unintended costs. Examples of negative externalities include air and water pollution. Negative externalities affect people who have no control over how much of a product is produced or consumed. Since producers do not have to pay these unintended costs, their total costs seem artificially low, and they will produce more than the equilibrium quantity of the good. The extra costs will be paid by consumers or, in some cases, by society at large.

Imperfect information is a third problem that can prevent markets from operating smoothly. If buyers and sellers do not have enough information, they may not make the choice that is best for them.

❓ IDENTIFY SUPPORTING DETAILS Under what circumstances may the free market system fail to allocate resources efficiently?

ASSESSMENT

1. **Analyze Information** What does a higher price for a good tell a producer?

2. **Paraphrase** Why do economists say that the price system is "free"?

3. **Interpret** Read and interpret the following statement: Prices also allow producers to target the audience they want with the products that will sell best to that audience.

4. **Integrate Information** Do you think rationing worked better than a price system would have during World War II? Why or why not?

5. **Draw Conclusions** How can a negative externality such as water pollution lead to disequilibrium?

A Change in Supply

A Change in Supply

A graph titled with Price on the vertical axis ($0 to $1000, marked at $200, $400, $600, $800, $1000) and Output (in millions) on the horizontal axis (0 to 5). Lines labeled Original supply, New supply, and Demand. Points a (at approximately 2, $900), b (at approximately 4, $900), and c (at approximately 3, $450).

1. **Interpret a Graph, Create Economic Models, and Transfer Information** Using the graph above as an example, create a supply and demand graph that presents economic information and data of your own invention. When you have finished, transfer the information from the graph into a supply and demand schedule, using appropriate computer software if available.

2. **Understand the Effect of Changes in Price** Write a paragraph that explains the effect changes in price have on the quantity of a good or service demanded, Include the economic term for this phenomenon. Explain the *substitution effect* and the *income effect* in the context of the effect of changes in price on quantity demanded.

3. **Understand the Effect of Changes in Price** Explain the effect of changes in price on the quantity supplied. What do economists mean by the term *quantity supplied*? What is the effect on quantity supplied of higher and lower prices?

4. **Identify Non-Price Determinants** List the non-price determinants that create changes in supply and demand. Then, create a brief written presentation that describes how government rules and regulations can act as non-price determinants, providing at least one example.

5. **Understand the Effect of Changes in Price and Create an Oral Presentation** Write a paragraph in which you describe the effect of retail sales and price discounts and explain how they relate to the effect of changes in price on the quantity demanded. Use your written paragraph to create an oral presentation of your findings.

Supply and Demand Graph

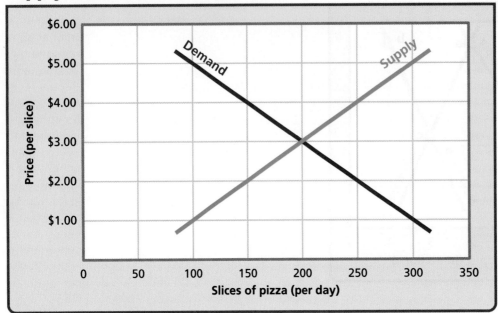

6. **Interpret a Graph** Using the graph above, answer the following: What is the shortage when pizza is sold at $1.00 per slice? What is the surplus when pizza is sold at $4.00 per slice? By how much is the surplus increased when pizza is sold at $5.00 per slice over when it is sold at $4.00 per slice?

7. **Explain the Benefits of the U.S. Free Enterprise System** Write a paragraph that answers the following: How do retail sales and price discounts illustrate the responsiveness of prices? How do responsive prices benefit both consumers and producers in a free enterprise system? In circumstances such as a supply shock, how do responsive prices provide a better alternative than rationing?

8. **Describe Characteristics of Economic Systems** How do prices act as an incentive for both producers and consumers? What is the profit motive and how does it function as an incentive in the economy?

9. **Evaluate Government Rules and Regulations** Responding to the quotation, write a brief evaluation of the potential costs and benefits of government regulation. Use real-life examples to support your point of view.

"Excessive regulation slows innovation, imposes needless costs on investors, and stifles competitiveness and job creation."

— *Henry M. Paulson, Jr., Secretary of the Treasury, washingtonpost.com, Nov. 11, 2006*

Items Rationed in U.S. During World War II

- Tires and rubber footwear
- Bicycles and cars
- Gasoline, kerosene, and other fuels
- Sugar, coffee
- Various processed and canned foods
- Meats, fats, fish, and cheese
- Stoves and typewriters

10. **Evaluate Government Rules and Regulations and Economic Data** Using the figure above, answer the following: Why might the government impose regulations to ration goods during wartime? Why might the government regulate a product through rationing? How would you evaluate the information in the table as an indicator of which materials were in high demand during World War II?

11. **Analyze the Importance of Economic Philosophers** In what work did Adam Smith write about the profit incentive? Explain Adam Smith's reasoning concerning the profit incentive. How does the text explain the profit incentive as the basis of an economic system?

12. **Identify Non-Price Determinants** Write a paragraph that answers the following: How do farm subsidies act as a non-price determinant? What is the general effect of subsidies on costs and supply?

13. **Identify Restrictions and Describe the Role of Government and Changes in That Role** Identify an action government has taken that places a restriction on the use of individual property because of environmental concerns. How has government action in this area changed over time?

14. **Write About the Essential Question** **Write an essay on the Essential Question: How do we affect the economy?** Use evidence from your study of this Topic to support your answer.

[**ESSENTIAL QUESTION**] How does competition affect markets?

4 **Competition and Market Structures**

>> Monitors and other goods are displayed in an electonics store.

Enduring Understandings

- Perfect competition exists when a market has many buyers and sellers of the same good so that no one buyer or seller can affect the price.

- Monopolies exist when one seller controls a market. Monopolies are so powerful that the government strictly regulates them.

- Monopolistic competition is similar to perfect competition, except the goods are not identical and firms have a small amount of control over prices.

- An oligopoly is a market made up of only a few large producers who have some control over the pricing of the goods they sell.

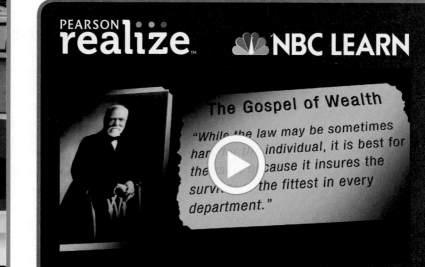

PEARSON
realize™   NBC LEARN

The Gospel of Wealth

"While the law may be sometimes har... individual, it is best for the ... cause it insures the surv... the fittest in every department."

Watch the My Story Video and learn about Andrew Carnegie and how he came to dominate the American steel industry.

PEARSON
realize™
www.PearsonRealize.com

Access your digital lessons including:
Topic Inquiry • Interactive Reading
Notepad • Interactivities • Assessments

>> Farmer's markets usually have easy market entry and exit. New vendors can easily set up tables to sell their goods and then leave them whenever they choose.

▶ Interactive Flipped Video

You have decided to cook dinner. As you shop for produce at the local farmer's market, you see many fruits and vegetables being offered by several different suppliers. Yet each supplier charges the same price for these fruits and vegetables. On the way home, you wonder why buying a leather jacket, a car, or a high-definition television isn't as simple as buying produce at the local farmer's market.

>> **Objectives**

Describe the characteristics and give examples of perfectly competitive markets.

List two common barriers that prevent firms from entering a market.

Describe prices and output in a perfectly competitive market.

>> **Key Terms**

pure competition
commodity
barrier to entry
imperfect
   competition
start-up costs

Perfect Competition

Conditions for Pure Competition

A market has a few basic elements. Producers supply goods and services. Consumers demand goods and services to satisfy their wants and needs. The interaction of supply and demand sets price. That interaction often features another key component of a market system: competition. Competition is, quite simply, the effort of each supplier to be the one who meets the demand of as many consumers as possible.

The farmer's market, with its identical goods and many buyers and sellers, is a rare, real-world example of a market in pure competition. **Pure competition,** also called perfect competition, is the simplest market structure. A market with pure competition is one in which a large number of firms all produce essentially the same product. In pure competition, the market is in equilibrium, and all firms sell the same product for the same price. However, each firm produces so little of that product compared with the total supply that no single firm can hope to influence price. The only decision such producers can make is how much to produce, given their production costs and the market price.

While few industries meet all the conditions for pure competition, some come close. Examples include markets for many farm products and the stocks traded on the New York Stock Exchange.

These examples fulfill the four strict conditions for a market with pure competition:

- Many buyers and sellers participate in the market.
- Sellers offer identical products.
- Buyers and sellers are well informed about products.
- Sellers are able to enter and exit the market easily.

Many Buyers and Sellers Markets with pure competition require many participants on both the buying and the selling sides. This condition leads to an important feature of purely competitive markets—the inability of any buyer or seller to control price. No individual can be powerful enough to buy or sell enough goods to influence the total market quantity or the market price. Everyone in the market must accept the market price as given.

As you have read, supply and demand interact to determine both price and output. If a market has many independent buyers and sellers, it is not very likely that large enough groups of either buyers or sellers will work together to bargain for better prices.

Instead, the market determines price as a result of the total supply and demand of all individual suppliers and consumers. Any given individual supplier or consumer has no more influence on price than any other supplier or consumer.

Identical Products In a purely competitive market, there are no differences between the products sold by different suppliers. This is the second condition for pure competition. If a rancher needs to buy corn to feed his cattle, he will not care which farmer grew the corn, as long as every farm is willing to deliver the corn he needs for the same price. If an investor buys a share of a company's stock, she will not care which particular share she is buying.

A product that is considered the same regardless of who makes or sells it is called a **commodity.** Examples of commodities include low-grade gasoline, notebook paper, sugar, and silicon chips. Identical products are a key to pure competition for one reason: the buyer will not pay extra for one particular company's goods. The buyer will always choose the supplier with the lowest price.

Informed Buyers and Sellers The third condition for a purely competitive market is that buyers and sellers know enough about the market to find the best deal. Under conditions of pure competition, the market provides the buyer with full information about the features of the product and its price. For the market

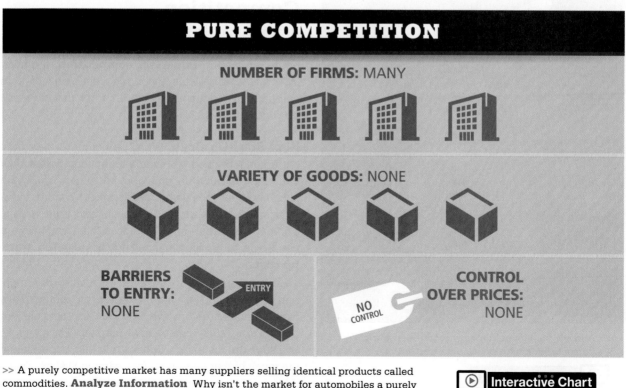

PURE COMPETITION

NUMBER OF FIRMS: MANY

VARIETY OF GOODS: NONE

BARRIERS TO ENTRY: NONE

ENTRY

NO CONTROL

CONTROL OVER PRICES: NONE

>> A purely competitive market has many suppliers selling identical products called commodities. **Analyze Information** Why isn't the market for automobiles a purely competitive market?

▶ Interactive Chart

>> Beyond having a bike and a phone, entry costs for a bicycle delivery service are minimal. Some cities do require any person providing this service to obtain a license, however.

>> A movie production company requires so much equipment that it usually has high start-up costs.

▶ **Interactive Chart**

to work effectively, both buyers and sellers have clear incentives to gather as much information as possible.

In most markets, a buyer's willingness to find information about prices and availability represents a trade-off. The time spent gathering information must be worth the amount of money that will be saved. For example, most buyers would not search the Internet or visit a dozen convenience stores to save five cents on a pack of chewing gum.

Easy Market Entry and Exit The final condition of a purely competitive market is that firms must be able to enter it when they can make money and leave it when they can't earn enough to stay in business. For example, if a new farmer's market opened in a town, a farmer or other vendor would probably not have much trouble setting up a spot to sell her goods. If that vendor was unable to make much money at the market, however, she could just as easily decide to leave it.

Studies show that markets with more firms, and thus more competition, have lower prices. When one firm can keep others out of the market, it can sell its product at a higher price.

? IDENTIFY CENTRAL IDEAS What controls price in a market with pure competition?

Barriers to Entry and Competition

Factors that make it difficult for new firms to enter a market are called **barriers to entry.** Barriers to entry can lead to **imperfect competition,** a market structure that fails to meet the conditions of pure competition. Common barriers to entry include start-up costs and technology.

High Start-Up Costs When launching a new firm, entrepreneurs need to invest money long before they can start earning income. Before a new sandwich shop can open, the owner needs to rent a store; buy a refrigerator, a freezer, and an oven; and print menus. The expenses that a new business must pay before it can begin to produce and sell goods are called **start-up costs.**

When the start-up costs in a market are high, entrepreneurs are less likely to enter that market. As a result, markets that involve high start-up costs are less likely to be purely competitive markets. For example, the start-up costs for a lumber mill or a supermarket are much higher than those for a sandwich shop. That's why more entrepreneurs open sandwich shops than they do lumber mills or supermarkets.

Use of the Internet reduced start-up costs in many markets, including books and music. However, many entrepreneurs discovered that a Web page did not attract and hold customers as easily as a shop window. The high costs of advertising, shipping, and discounting goods pushed many out of business. With a few exceptions, the Internet-based companies that have succeeded paid substantial start-up costs.

Complex Technology When a school group needs to raise money, its members can sell cookies or candy. Some technically skilled students might offer to fix cars or bicycles. But very few student groups would be able to raise money by creating and selling a new computer word-processing program.

Some markets require a high degree of technological know-how—the knowledge and skills needed to create or repair something. A carpenter, pharmacist, or electrician can spend years in training before he or she has learned all the necessary skills. Computer software engineers need extensive training to develop, create, and customize computer software and manage computer network systems.

As a result, new entrepreneurs cannot easily enter these markets without a lot of preparation and study. Technological barriers to entry can keep a market from becoming purely competitive.

? IDENTIFY MAIN IDEAS Give an example of a business with high start-up costs and one with low start-up costs.

Price, Output, and Purely Competitive Markets

One of the primary characteristics of purely competitive markets is that they are efficient. Competition within these markets keeps both prices and production costs low. Firms must use all inputs—land, labor, organizational skills, machinery and equipment—to their best advantage. As a result, the prices that consumers pay and the revenue that suppliers receive accurately reflect how much the market values the inputs used to produce the product. In a purely competitive market, prices correctly represent the opportunity costs of each product.

Prices in a purely competitive market are the lowest sustainable prices possible. Because many sellers compete to offer their commodities to buyers, intense

Market Equilibrium in Pure Competition

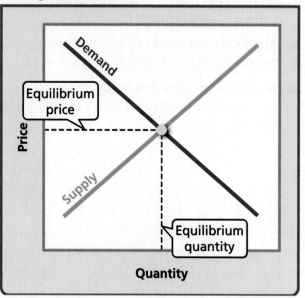

>> **Figure 4.1** Under pure competition, supply and demand set the equilibrium price and equilibrium quantity. **Analyze Information** Would the entry of a new firm change the equilibrium price? Why or why not?

competition forces prices down to the point where the prices just cover the most efficient sellers' costs of doing business.

As you have learned, this equilibrium is usually the most efficient state a market can achieve. Equilibrium in a perfectly competitive market is shown in **Figure 4.1.**

Producers generally earn their highest profits when they produce enough that their cost to produce one more unit exactly equals the market price of the unit. Since no supplier can influence prices in purely competitive markets, producers will make their output decisions based on their most efficient use of available land, labor, capital, and management skills.

In the long run, output in a purely competitive market will reach the point where each supplying firm just covers all of its costs and earns only the minimally acceptable profit. This outcome is not very desirable from the point of view of the owners, however.

? COMPARE POINTS OF VIEW Who likes a purely competitive market more, consumers or producers? Why?

1. **Summarize** What are the four conditions of a purely competitive market?

2. **Apply Concepts** Give two examples of a commodity other than petroleum and milk.

3. **Analyze Information** Why would a unique product not be possible in a purely competitive market?

4. **Analyze Information** Do you think that the dairy industry is an example of a purely competitive market? Why or why not? If not, what industry is?

5. **Identify Cause and Effect** Why are suppliers in purely competitive markets efficient? What is the result of that efficiency?

Unfortunately, you have been diagnosed with a rare and serious infection. The doctor prescribes a ten-day supply of a new medication. At the pharmacy, you discover that the medicine costs $97.35—nearly ten dollars per pill! There are no substitutes, so you buy the medicine. Later, you learn that only one company has the right to produce that drug. The company says that revenue from the medicine pays for the research and development costs of producing it.

>> The Texas Rangers are one of two Major League Baseball teams in Texas. Major League Baseball is allowed to limit the number of teams in each state, even though that is a type of monopoly.

▶ **Interactive Flipped Video**

Monopolies

Characteristics of a Monopoly

While there are different types of monopolies, all are characterized by a single seller that controls an entire market. This arrangement allows monopolies to control output and charge higher prices.

A **monopoly** forms when barriers prevent firms from entering a market that has a single supplier. While a purely competitive market has many buyers and sellers, monopoly markets have only one seller but any number of buyers. In fact, barriers to entry are the principal condition that allows monopolies to exist.

Economists use a strict set of requirements to characterize a monopoly. Besides having a single seller and barriers to entry, a monopoly is also characterized by supplying a unique product. But suppliers may only appear to have a unique product, because if we take a broader view, we may uncover alternatives.

For example, you might think that a convenience store on a highway in the middle of the desert has a monopoly. However, travelers can carry their own supplies in their car instead of paying high prices for items at the store. Or, if they have enough money, they can take an airplane across the desert and bypass the store altogether. In other words, there are options. In a monopoly, the good or service provided has no close substitute.

The problem with monopolies is that they can take advantage of their market power and charge high prices. Given the law of demand,

>> Objectives

Describe the characteristics and give examples of a monopoly.

Describe how monopolies, including government monopolies, are formed.

Explain how a firm with a monopoly makes output decisions.

Explain why monopolists sometimes practice price discrimination.

>> Key Terms

monopoly
economies of scale
natural monopoly
government
   monopoly
patent
franchise
license
price discrimination
market power

this means that the quantity of goods sold is lower than in a market with more than one seller. For this reason, the United States has outlawed some monopolistic practices.

Economies of Scale All monopolies have one trait in common: a single seller in a market. However, different market conditions can create different types of monopolies.

If a firm's start-up costs are high, and its average costs fall for each additional unit it produces, then it enjoys what economists call economies of scale. **Economies of scale** are characteristics that cause a producer's average cost to drop as production rises.

Figure 4.2 shows an average total cost curve for a firm without economies of scale. Follow the curve from left to right. As output increases from zero, the average cost of each good drops, and the curve initially slopes downward. This is because large, initial, fixed costs, like the cost of the factory and machinery, can be spread out among more and more goods as production rises. If the factory cost $1,000 to build and each unit of output costs $10 to make, producing one unit will cost $1,010, but producing two units will cost $1,020, or only $510 each. However, if the industry has limited economies of scale, output will eventually rise to a level at which the limited-scale economies are exhausted, and the cost of making each unit will rise. The average cost of producing each good increases as output increases, and the curve slopes upward to match the rising cost per unit.

A factory in an industry with economies of scale never reaches this second stage of rising costs per unit. As production increases, the firm becomes more efficient, even at a level of output high enough to supply the entire market. **Figure 4.2** shows how cost and output are related in economies of scale. Follow the curve from left to right. As output increases, the cost per unit falls, and continues to fall.

A good example is a hydroelectric plant, which generates electricity from a dam on a river. A large dam is expensive to build. However, once the dam is built, the plant can produce energy at a very low additional cost simply by letting water flow through the dam. The average cost of the first unit of electricity produced is very high because the cost of the dam is so high. As output increases, the fixed costs of the dam can be spread over more units of electricity, so the average cost drops.

In a market with economies of scale, bigger is better. An industry that enjoys economies of scale can easily become a natural monopoly.

However, new strategies are emerging. Some business leaders now favor sidestepping economies of scale:

Effect of Economies of Scale

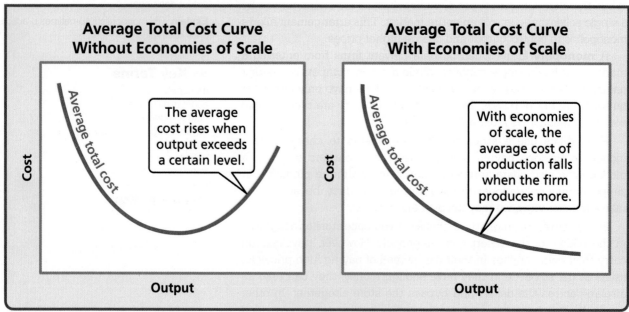

>> **Figure 4.2** With economies of scale, production costs continue to fall as output increases. **Analyze Graphs** Describe the cost curve for a firm without economies of scale.

> Many business leaders are re-examining their assumptions about the benefits of scale. Scaling down, not up, and building "disposable factories" and even "disposable strategies" are becoming new keys to lowering costs and boosting performance.

—George Stalk, *5 Future Strategies You Need Right Now,* Harvard Business School Press, 2008

Natural Monopolies A **natural monopoly** is a market that runs most efficiently when one large firm provides all of the output. If a second firm enters the market, competition will drive down the market price charged to customers and decrease the quantity each firm can sell. One or both of the firms will not be able to cover their costs and will go out of business.

Public water provides a good example of a natural monopoly. In a competitive market, different water companies would invest huge amounts of money to dig reservoirs and set up overlapping networks of pipes and pumping stations to deliver water to the same town. Companies would use more land and water than necessary. Each company would have to pay for all of the unneeded pipes and would serve customers no better than a single network.

In cases like this, the government often steps in to allow just one firm in each geographic area to provide these necessary services. The government action ensures that resources are not wasted by building additional plants when only one is needed. In return for monopoly status, a firm with a natural monopoly agrees to let government control the prices it can charge and what services it must provide.

Technology and Change Sometimes the development of a new technology can destroy a natural monopoly. A new innovation can cut fixed costs and make small companies as efficient as one large firm.

When telephone calls were carried by thick copper wires, local telephone service was considered a natural monopoly. No one wanted to build more than one network of wires to connect thousands of homes and businesses. In the 1990s, more and more consumers began using cellular phones, which are portable and can carry phone calls via radio waves rather than through wires. Cellular technology reduced the barriers to entry in the local telephone market.

Now that cellular phone companies can link to thousands or millions of customers with a few well-placed towers, they don't need to invest in an expensive infrastructure of cables and telephone poles.

>> Mass transit systems such as subways, commuter rails, and buses are examples of natural monopolies, which are often regulated by the government.

▶ **Interactive Gallery**

Cellular phone companies have become as efficient as traditional wire-based phone services. In addition, Internet phone service, which sends phone calls over the Internet, is another technological innovation that has changed the telephone industry.

? DETERMINE CENTRAL IDEAS What is one characteristic all types of monopolies have in common?

The Role of Government

In the case of a natural monopoly, the government allows the monopoly to form and then regulates it. In other cases, however, government actions themselves can create barriers to entry in markets and thereby create monopolies. A **government monopoly** is a monopoly created by the government.

Technological Monopolies One way that the government can give a company monopoly power is by issuing a patent. A **patent** gives a company exclusive rights to sell a new good or service for a specific period of time. Suppose that Leland Pharmaceuticals developed a new, effective asthma medication called BreatheDeep that helped people with asthma to breathe more easily. If Leland's researchers could prove to the government that they had invented BreatheDeep, the government would grant Leland a patent. This patent would give Leland the exclusive right to sell BreatheDeep for 20 years.

Why would the government want to give a company monopoly power? Patents guarantee that companies can profit from their own research without competition. For this reason, patents encourage firms to research and develop new products that benefit society as a whole, even though the research and development costs may be very high. The patent allows firms to set prices that maximize their opportunity to make a profit. By protecting patent rights, the government encourages innovations in industries such as pharmaceuticals, where a number of new drugs have been developed to treat different types of cancer and other diseases.

Franchises and Licenses A **franchise** is a contract issued by a local authority that gives a single firm the right to sell its goods within an exclusive market. National companies often grant franchises to entrepreneurs, who then sell that company's product in a local market.

A government entity can also grant a franchise. For example, the National Park Service picks a single firm to sell food and other goods at national parks such as Yellowstone, Yosemite, and the Everglades. Your school may have contracted with one bottled-water company to install and stock vending machines. The franchise may include a condition that no other brand of water

will be sold in the building. Governments, parks, and schools use franchises to keep small markets under control.

On a larger scale, governments can issue a **license** granting firms the right to operate a business, especially where scarce resources are involved. Examples of scarce resources that require licensing include land, as well as radio and television broadcast frequencies. The Federal Communications Commission issues licenses for individual radio and television stations. Local governments might give a single firm a license to manage all of their public parking lots.

Industrial Organizations In rare cases, the government allows the companies in an industry to restrict the number of firms in a market. For example, the United States government lets Major League Baseball and other sports leagues restrict the number and location of their teams. The government allows team owners of the major professional sports leagues to choose new cities for their teams and does not charge them with violating the laws that prevent competitors from working together.

Major League Baseball has an exemption from these laws, which are known as antitrust laws, because they were originally passed to break up an illegal form of monopoly known as a trust. Other sports leagues do not have an official exemption, but the government treats them as it treats baseball. The restrictions that the leagues impose help keep team play orderly and

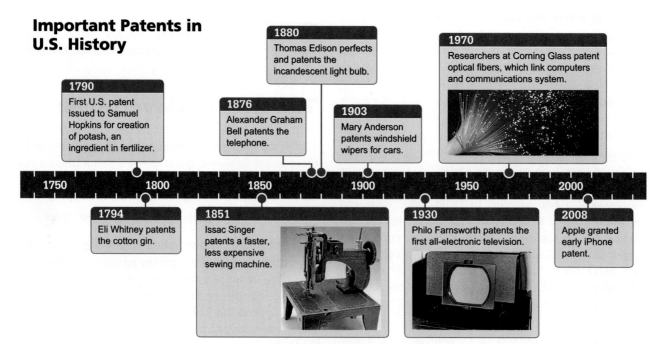

Important Patents in U.S. History

1790 First U.S. patent issued to Samuel Hopkins for creation of potash, an ingredient in fertilizer.

1794 Eli Whitney patents the cotton gin.

1851 Issac Singer patents a faster, less expensive sewing machine.

1876 Alexander Graham Bell patents the telephone.

1880 Thomas Edison perfects and patents the incandescent light bulb.

1903 Mary Anderson patents windshield wipers for cars.

1930 Philo Farnsworth patents the first all-electronic television.

1970 Researchers at Corning Glass patent optical fibers, which link computers and communications system.

2008 Apple granted early iPhone patent.

>> The patents shown here have given their inventors monopolies for a limited period of time. **Analyze Information** How do patents such as these encourage new ideas?

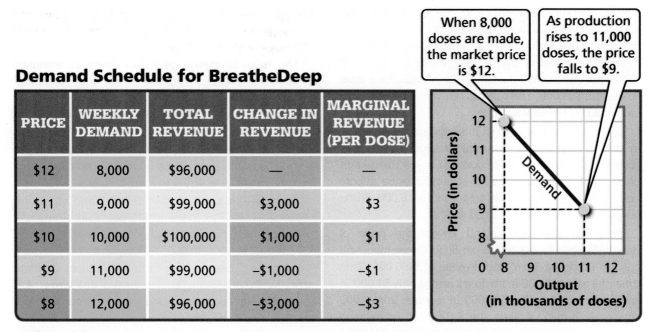

Demand Schedule for BreatheDeep

PRICE	WEEKLY DEMAND	TOTAL REVENUE	CHANGE IN REVENUE	MARGINAL REVENUE (PER DOSE)
$12	8,000	$96,000	—	—
$11	9,000	$99,000	$3,000	$3
$10	10,000	$100,000	$1,000	$1
$9	11,000	$99,000	-$1,000	-$1
$8	12,000	$96,000	-$3,000	-$3

When 8,000 doses are made, the market price is $12.

As production rises to 11,000 doses, the price falls to $9.

>> **Figure 4.3** By increasing output, a monopolist lowers the price of the good. Above a certain output, revenue begins to decrease. **Analyze Data** How does producing fewer goods benefit a monopolist?

stable by preventing other cities from starting their own major-league teams and crowding the schedule.

The problem with this type of monopoly is that team owners may charge high prices for tickets. In addition, if you're a sports fan in a city without a major league team, you're out of luck.

? **SUMMARIZE** How does having a patent give a company a monopoly?

Output Decisions

If you had severe asthma, which can be fatal, what would BreatheDeep be worth to you? You would probably want the medicine no matter how much it cost. So Leland, the company that invented and patented the drug, could charge a very high price for its new medication. The resulting profits would give the company a reason, or incentive, for inventing the new medication in the first place. But could Leland sell as much medication as it wanted to at whatever price it chose?

Even a monopolist faces a limited choice—it can choose either output or price, but not both. The monopolist looks at the big picture and tries to maximize profits. This usually means that, compared to a purely competitive market for the same good, the monopolist produces fewer goods at a higher price.

The Monopolist's Dilemma The law of demand states that buyers will demand more of a good at lower prices and less at higher prices. A possible demand curve for BreatheDeep is shown in **Figure 4.3,** with prices in dollars on the vertical axis and doses on the horizontal axis. Many people with life-threatening asthma will pay whatever the medicine costs. But some people with milder asthma will choose a cheaper, weaker medicine if the price of a stronger one rises too high.

Trace the demand curve from left to right. At $12 per dose, consumers might demand 8,000 doses of BreatheDeep each week. But at $9 per dose, as many as 11,000 doses will sell. The law of demand means that when the monopolist increases the price, it will sell less, and when it lowers the price, it will sell more. Another way to interpret this graph is that if a monopolist produces more, the price of the good will fall, and if it produces less, the price will rise.

Falling Marginal Revenue To maximize profits, a seller should set its marginal revenue, or the amount it earns from the last unit sold, equal to its marginal cost, or the extra cost from producing that unit. This same rule applies to a firm with a monopoly. The key difference is that in a purely competitive market, marginal revenue is always the same as price, and each firm receives the same price no matter how much it produces. Neither assumption is true in a monopoly.

To understand how this happens, consider **Figure 4.3.** When BreatheDeep is sold at $12 per dose, consumers buy 8,000 doses per week, providing $96,000 in revenue. If Leland lowers the price of BreatheDeep to $11 per dose, 9,000 doses will be bought, for a total revenue of $99,000. The sale of 1,000 more doses brings Leland $3,000 in new revenue.

Marginal revenue in most markets is equal to price. In this monopoly, the marginal revenue at a market price of $11 is roughly $3 per dose, far below the market price. This is because the lower market price affects both the 1,000 new doses sold and the 8,000 doses people buy for $11 each instead of $12.

Now suppose that Leland lowers the price of BreatheDeep from $11 to $10 per dose. Consumers will buy 10,000 doses, for a total revenue of $100,000. This time, the sale of 1,000 more doses brings only $1,000 in additional revenue. The $10,000 in revenue from 1,000 new sales barely exceeds the $9,000 fall in revenue from selling the 9,000 doses for $10 each, not $11. The market price is $10 per dose, but the marginal revenue has fallen to a mere $1 for each dose of BreatheDeep sold.

As you've seen, when a firm has some control over price—and can cut the price to sell more—marginal revenue is less than price. In contrast, in a purely competitive market, the price would not drop at all as output increased, so marginal revenue would remain the same as price. The firm's total revenue would increase at a steady rate with production.

The table in **Figure 4.3** lists marginal revenues for several different prices. Note that marginal revenue actually becomes negative when the quantity demanded is greater than 10,000 doses per week.

Setting a Price Leland will choose a level of output that yields the highest profits. This is the point at which marginal revenue is equal to marginal cost.

In **Figure 4.3,** we plotted the demand at market prices of $8, $9, $10, $11, and $12 per dose. According to **Figure 4.3,** output per week at these prices will be 12,000, 11,000, 10,000, 9,000, and 8,000 doses, respectively. These points form the market demand curve for BreatheDeep, shown in red in **Figure 4.3.** Then, based on these data, we plotted Leland's marginal revenue at these levels of output.

These points form the marginal revenue curve shown in blue in **Figure 4.4.** The marginal revenue curve is at the bottom of the graph, because a monopolist's marginal revenue is lower than the market price.

Marginal cost equals marginal revenue at point *a* in **Figure 4.4.** This is the most profitable level of output. The monopolist produces 9,000 units, the quantity at which marginal revenue and marginal cost are both $3. According to the market demand curve, the market price is $11 when 9,000 units are sold (point *b*). Therefore, the monopolist will set the price of each dose at $11 or set production at 9,000 units.

If dozens of firms sold BreatheDeep and the market were purely competitive, price and output would be different, as shown in **Figure 4.4.** In a purely competitive market, marginal revenue is always equal to market price, so the marginal revenue curve would be the same as the demand curve. Firms will set output where marginal revenue is equal to marginal cost, shown at point *c.* As you can see, a purely competitive market for BreatheDeep would have more units sold *and* a lower market price than a monopoly.

Profits How much profit does the monopolist earn? Well, profit can be determined by comparing price and average cost. For Leland, the company that makes BreatheDeep, the profit per dose is the difference between the market price and the average cost at that level of production. Suppose the average cost of producing 9,000 doses is $5, or slightly higher than the marginal cost. Each dose is sold for $11. The monopolist

Price Setting in a Monopoly

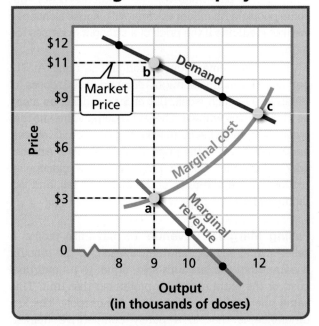

>> **Figure 4.4** A monopolist sets output at point *a*, where marginal revenue equals marginal cost. **Analyze Graphs** How does point *c* show the benefits to consumers in a purely competitive market?

▶ **Interactive Chart**

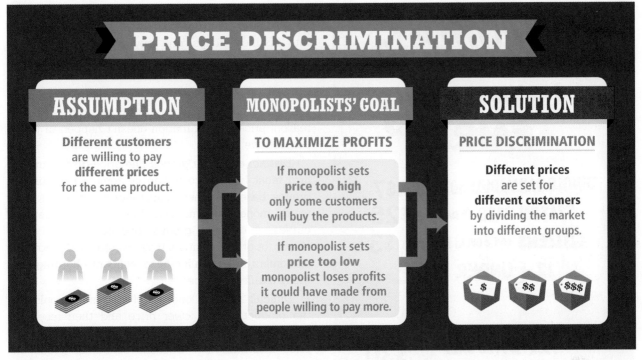

PRICE DISCRIMINATION

ASSUMPTION

Different customers are willing to pay **different prices** for the same product.

MONOPOLISTS' GOAL

TO MAXIMIZE PROFITS

If monopolist sets **price too high** only some customers will buy the products.

If monopolist sets **price too low** monopolist loses profits it could have made from people willing to pay more.

SOLUTION

PRICE DISCRIMINATION

Different prices are set for **different customers** by dividing the market into different groups.

$ $$ $$$

>> **Analyze Charts** Would a monopolist benefit from setting the same price for every person? Why or why not?

will earn a profit of $6 per dose ($11 - $5), so the total profit is $54,000, or $6 per dose for 9,000 doses.

❓ DRAW CONCLUSIONS What happens if a monopolist increases the price of a good?

Price Discrimination

The previous example assumed that the monopolist must charge the same price to all consumers. But in some cases, the monopolist may be able to divide consumers into two or more groups and charge a different price to each group. This practice is known as **price discrimination.**

Price discrimination is based on the idea that each customer has a maximum price that he or she will pay for a good. If a monopolist sets the good's price at the highest maximum price of all the buyers in the market, the monopolist will sell only to the one type of customer willing to pay that much. If the monopolist sets a low price, the monopolist will gain a lot of customers but will lose the profits it could have made from the customers who bought at the low price but were willing to pay more.

Although price discrimination is a feature of monopoly, it can be practiced by any company with market power. **Market power** is the ability to control

prices and total market output. As you will read in the next section, many companies have some market power without having a true monopoly. Market power and price discrimination may be found in any market structure except for pure competition.

Targeted Discounts In the monopolist's ideal world, the firm could charge each customer the maximum that he or she is willing to pay, and no less. However, this is impractical, so companies divide consumers into large groups and design pricing policies for each group. The different prices that firms charge each group for the same good or service are not related to production costs.

One common form of price discrimination identifies some customers who are not willing to pay the regular price and offers those customers a discount. Price discrimination can also mean that a company finds the customers who need the good the most, and charges them more for that good. Here are some examples of price discrimination.

Discounted airline fares Airlines offer discounts to travelers who buy tickets several weeks in advance or are willing to spend a Saturday night at their destinations. Business travelers would prefer not to stay over on a Saturday night, but these tickets are appealing to vacationers who wouldn't otherwise pay to fly and don't mind the restrictions.

Welcome to Lake County FAIR

SINGLE DAILY ADULT ADMISSION $7

SEASON PASS (5 DAYS) $25

CITIZENS (65 & OVER) DAILY $3

12 & UNDER FREE

PURCHASE MEMBERSHIP TICKETS IN FAIR OFFICE ONLY $30

>> This sign for a county fair shows targeted discounts for senior citizens, children, and people who want to visit the fair on multiple days.

Manufacturers' rebate offers At times, manufacturers of refrigerators, cars, televisions, and other items will refund a small part of the purchase price to buyers who fill out a rebate form and mail it back. People who take the time to fulfill the rebate requirements are likely more price-conscious than those who don't and may be unwilling to pay full price.

Senior citizen or student discounts Many retirees and students have lower incomes than people who work full time. Zoos, theaters, museums, and restaurants often offer discounts to people in these groups, because they are unlikely to be able to pay full price for what some consider luxuries.

Children fly or stay free promotions Families with young children spend more of their income on food, clothing, and school expenses. As a result, they have less money to spend on vacations. Once again, firms would rather have their business and earn lower profits than earn no profits at all, so they offer discounts for families with children.

Limits of Price Discrimination For price discrimination to work, a market must meet three conditions. Firms that use price discrimination must have some market power, customers must be divided into distinct groups, and buyers must not be in a position in which they can easily resell the good or service.

Some market power For price discrimination to work, firms must have some control over prices. For this reason, price discrimination doesn't happen in purely competitive markets.

Distinct customer groups The price-discriminating firm must be able to divide customers into distinct groups based on their sensitivity to price. In other words, monopolists must be able to guess the demand curves of different groups, one of which is more elastic, or price-sensitive, than the others. By grouping customers, firms can increase profits by charging each group a different price.

Difficult resale If one set of customers could buy the product at the lower price and then resell the product for a profit, the firm could not enforce its price discrimination. Because consumer goods like shoes, groceries, and clothes are easily resold, price discrimination works best in marketing services that are consumed on the spot. Examples include theme-park admissions and restaurant meals. Airlines can offer senior discounts because the company can ask for identification and proof of age before letting the customer board the plane.

Although most forms of price discrimination are perfectly legal, sometimes firms use price discrimination to drive other firms out of business. This illegal form of the practice is called predatory pricing.

❓ **PARAPHRASE** Price discrimination can only work if

ASSESSMENT

1. **Identify Cause and Effect** How can technology affect a monopoly?

2. **Categorize** What government actions can lead to the creation of monopolies?

3. **Determine Central Ideas** What is the most profitable level of output for a monopolist?

4. **Draw Conclusions** Why do monopolists practice price discrimination?

5. **Determine Central Ideas** How does price discrimination benefit producers and consumers?

At the supermarket, you roam through aisles filled with various brands of soap, toothpaste, and paper towels. Although they are produced by different companies, these everyday products are very similar. To compete, producers find ways to make their products unique to attract customers like you.

>> The market for jeans is monopolistically competitive because jeans can vary by size, color, style, and designer.

▶ **Interactive Flipped Video**

Monopolistic Competition and Oligopoly

Characteristics of Monopolistic Competition

While monopolistic competition is similar to pure competition, oligopoly describes a market with only a few large producers. These are the market structures most familiar to consumers.

In **monopolistic competition,** many companies compete in an open market to sell products that are similar but not identical. Each firm is monopolistic—it holds a monopoly over its own particular product design. You can think of monopolistic competition as a modified version of pure competition with minor differences in products.

The differences between pure competition and monopolistic competition arise because monopolistically competitive firms sell goods that are similar enough to be substituted for one another but are not identical. Monopolistic competition does not involve identical commodities. An example of a monopolistically competitive market is the market for jeans. All jeans can be described as denim pants,

>> **Objectives**

Describe characteristics and give examples of monopolistic competition.

Explain how firms compete without lowering prices.

Understand how firms in a monopolistically competitive market set output.

Describe characteristics and give examples of oligopoly.

>> **Key Terms**

monopolistic competition
differentiation
non-price competition
oligopoly
price war
collusion
price fixing
cartel

but in stores, buyers can choose from a variety of brand names, styles, colors, and sizes.

Unlike pure competition, monopolistic competition is a fact of everyday life. You and your friends probably buy from monopolistically competitive firms several times a week. Common examples include bagel shops, ice-cream stands, gas stations, and retail stores.

Four Conditions of Monopolistic Competition

Monopolistic competition develops from four conditions. As you read about the types of markets that favor monopolistic competition, note how similar they are to the rules that define pure competition.

Many firms As a rule, monopolistically competitive markets are not marked by economies of scale. They do not have high start-up costs. Because firms can begin selling goods and earning money after a small initial investment, new firms spring up quickly to join the market.

Few artificial barriers to entry Firms in a monopolistically competitive market do not face high barriers to entry. Patents do not protect anyone from competition, either because they have expired or because each firm sells a product that is distinct enough to fall outside the zone of patent protection. Just like a purely competitive market, a monopolistically competitive market includes so many competing firms

that producers cannot work together to keep out new competitors.

Little control over price In a monopolistically competitive market structure, each firm's goods are a little different from everyone else's, and some people are willing to pay more for the difference. For this reason, firms have a bit of freedom to raise or lower their prices. However, unlike a monopoly, a monopolistically competitive firm has only limited control over price. If the price rises too high, consumers will buy a rival's product, because close substitutes are readily available. For example, many customers will choose a carton of brand-name orange juice over the store brand even if it costs $0.50 more per carton. If the difference in price rose to $2, however, most people would think seriously about buying the store brand of orange juice or some other drink altogether.

Differentiated products Firms have some control over their selling price because they can differentiate, or distinguish their goods from the other products in the market. The ability to differentiate goods is the main way that monopolistic competition differs from pure competition. **Differentiation** enables a monopolistically competitive seller to profit from the differences between his or her products and competitors' products.

? RECALL A monopolistically competitive firm has some control over price because

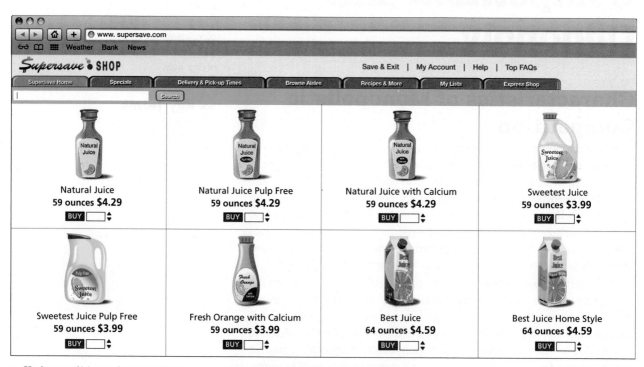

>> Under conditions of monopolistic competition, prices of similar products are not identical but are usually close to one another.

Non-price Competition

The ability to differentiate products means that firms do not have to compete on price alone. The alternative is **non-price competition,** or competition through ways other than lower prices. Non-price competition takes several different forms.

Physical characteristics The simplest way for a firm to distinguish its products is to offer a new size, color, shape, texture, or taste. Running shoes, pens, cars, and toothpaste are good examples of products that can be easily differentiated by their physical characteristics. A pen is always a writing tool that uses ink, but many people will pay extra for a pen that looks or writes differently. Similarly, you can probably describe a "car" in only a few words, but factories around the world manufacture thousands of car models to fit a range of personalities, jobs, families, and incomes.

Location Real-estate agents say that the three most important factors when buying property are "location, location, location." Some goods can be differentiated by where they are sold. Gas stations, movie theaters, and grocery stores succeed or fail based on their locations. A convenience store in the middle of a desert differentiates its product simply by selling it hundreds of miles away from the nearest competitor. Such a location allows the seller to charge a lot more for a quart of water.

Service level Some sellers can charge higher prices because they offer their customers a high level of service. Conventional restaurants and fast-food restaurants both offer meals to customers. However, conventional restaurants provide servers who bring the food to your table, whereas fast-food restaurants offer a more bare-bones, do-it-yourself atmosphere. Conventional restaurants and fast-food chains sell many of the same food items, but fast-food chains sell their meals for less. Customers at conventional restaurants pay more for the service and the relaxing atmosphere.

Advertising, image, or status Firms often use advertising to point out differences between their own offerings and other products in the marketplace. These product differences are often more a matter of perception than reality. For example, a designer can apply his or her name to a plain white T-shirt and charge a higher price, even if the quality of fabric and stitching is no different than what generic T-shirts offer. Customers will pay extra for a designer or a brand-name T-shirt because the image and status that go with the name are worth the extra money to them.

? **CATEGORIZE** A hotel that offers a complimentary fruit basket and an employee who will help you plan your activities is an example of what kind of non-price competition?

>> **Analyze Political Cartoons** How is this cartoon an illustration of monopolistic competition?

>> Location is one characteristic of non-price competition. Stores located on Rodeo Drive, the exclusive shopping area in Beverly Hills, California, shown here, sell many expensive goods.

▶ **Interactive Gallery**

Prices, Output, and Profits

Economists study prices, output, and profits when comparing market structures. They find that under monopolistic competition, the market looks very much as it would under pure competition.

Prices Prices under monopolistic competition will be higher than they would be in pure competition, because firms have some power to raise prices. However, the number of firms and ease of entry prevent companies from raising prices as high as they would if they were a true monopoly. As you have read, if a monopolistically competitive firm raised prices too high, most customers would buy the cheaper product. Because customers can choose from among many substitutes, monopolistically competitive firms face more elastic demand curves than true monopolists do.

Output The law of demand says that output and price are negatively related. As one rises, the other falls. Monopolistically competitive firms sell their products at higher prices than do purely competitive firms, but at lower prices than a monopoly. As a result, total output under monopolistic competition falls somewhere between that of monopoly and that of pure competition.

Profits Like purely competitive firms, monopolistically competitive firms earn just enough to cover all of their costs, including salaries for the workers. If a monopolistically competitive firm started to earn profits well above its costs, two market trends would work to take those profits away.

First, fierce competition would encourage rivals to find new ways to differentiate their products and lure customers back. If one company hires a basketball star to promote its soft drink, a rival might hire a popular singer. The rivalries among firms prevent any one firm from earning excessive profits for long.

Second, new firms will enter the market with slightly different products that cost less than the market leader's. If the original good costs too much, consumers will switch to these substitutes. You've seen this happen when a brand-name line of clothing or a video game becomes popular. Competitors quickly flood the market with cheap imitations to appeal to people who can't afford the original or don't care about the difference in quality.

Although monopolistically competitive firms can earn profits in the short run, they have to work hard to keep their product distinct to stay ahead of their rivals. Often, they do not succeed.

Production Costs and Variety Firms in monopolistic competition may not be able to produce their goods at the lowest possible average cost. Monopolistically competitive markets have many firms, each producing too little output to minimize costs and use resources efficiently. But consumers in these markets benefit from having a wide variety of goods from which to choose.

❓ **IDENTIFY CAUSE AND EFFECT** Why can't a monopolistically competitive firm raise prices as high as a true monopoly can?

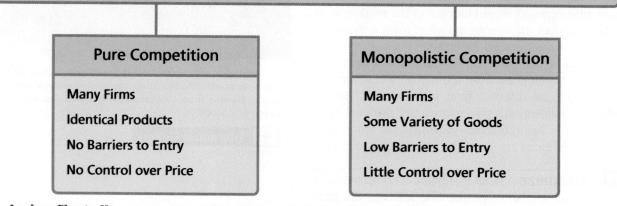

COMPARING MONOPOLISTIC COMPETITION AND PURE COMPETITION

Pure Competition	Monopolistic Competition
Many Firms	Many Firms
Identical Products	Some Variety of Goods
No Barriers to Entry	Low Barriers to Entry
No Control over Price	Little Control over Price

>> **Analyze Charts** How are pure competition and monopolistic competition similar? How are they different?

Top Music Companies, 2012

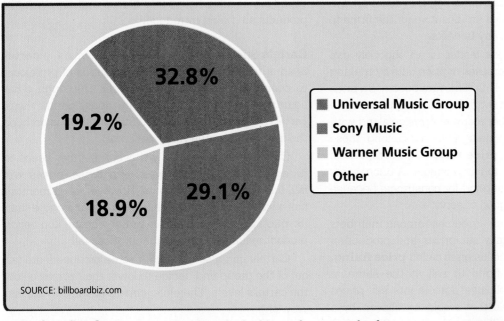

- Universal Music Group
- Sony Music
- Warner Music Group
- Other

32.8%
19.2%
18.9%
29.1%

SOURCE: billboardbiz.com

>> **Analyze Graphs** Are the music companies in this graph an example of an oligopoly? Why or why not?

Interactive Illustration

Characteristics of Oligopoly

Oligopoly describes a market dominated by a few large, profitable firms. Oligopoly looks like an imperfect form of monopoly. Some economists call an industry an oligopoly if the four largest firms produce at least 70 to 80 percent of the output.

Acting on their own or as a team, the biggest firms in an oligopoly may well set prices higher and output lower than in a purely competitive market. Examples of oligopolies in the United States include the markets for air travel, automobiles, breakfast cereals, and household appliances.

Barriers to Entry An oligopoly can form when significant barriers to entry keep new companies from entering the market to compete with existing firms. These barriers can be technological, or they can be created by a system of government licenses or patents.

In other cases, the economic realities of the market lead to an oligopoly. Take the video game console industry, for example. The three big game console manufacturers have invested so much money to develop their brand names and products associated with those games that few companies can successfully challenge such a grip on the market.

High start-up costs such as expensive machinery and large production facilities present additional barriers to entry. Many small airlines have had trouble competing with larger, better-financed rivals because airplanes are very expensive to buy and maintain. The biggest airlines compound the problem because they often own the most desirable gates at the airport, and already enjoy name recognition and the trust of the consumer.

Some oligopolies occur because of economies of scale. As you have read, when a firm experiences economies of scale, the average cost of production decreases as output increases.

Greater economies of scale mean that there will be fewer firms in an industry. In a monopoly market, only one company can produce enough goods to earn a profit. In an oligopoly, perhaps three or four companies can reach a profitable level of output before the market becomes too crowded and revenue falls below costs.

Cooperation and Collusion Oligopoly presents a big challenge to government, because oligopolistic firms often *seem* to work together as a monopoly, even when they are not actually doing so. Many government regulations try to make oligopolistic firms act more like competitive firms. When determined oligopolists work together illegally to set prices and bar competing firms from the market, they can become as damaging to the consumer as a monopoly.

The three practices that concern government the most are price leadership, collusion, and cartels. While these three practices represent ways that firms in an oligopoly can try to control a market, they don't always work. Each tactic includes an incentive for the firms to cheat and thereby undo any benefits.

Sometimes the market leader in an oligopoly can start a round of price increases or price cuts by making its plans clear to other sellers. This firm becomes a price leader. Price leaders can set prices and output for entire industries as long as other member firms go along with the leader's policy. But disagreements among those companies can spark a **price war,** when competitors cut their prices very low to win business. A price war is harmful to producers but good for consumers because they will pay less for a good or service.

Collusion refers to an agreement among members of an oligopoly to illegally set prices and production levels. One outcome of collusion is called **price fixing,** an agreement among firms to sell at the same or very similar prices. Collusive agreements set prices and output at the levels that would be chosen by a monopolist. Collusion is illegal in the United States, but the lure of monopolistic profits can tempt businesses to make such agreements despite the illegality and risks.

Collusion is not, however, the only reason for nearly identical pricing in oligopolistic industries. Such pricing may actually result from intense competition, especially if advertising is vigorous and new lines of products are being introduced.

Cartels Stronger than a collusive agreement, a **cartel** is an agreement by a formal organization of producers to coordinate prices and production. Although other countries and international organizations permit them, cartels are illegal in the United States. OPEC is perhaps the most familiar international cartel.

Cartels can survive only if every member keeps to its agreed-upon output levels. Otherwise, prices will fall, and firms will lose profits. However, each member has a strong incentive to cheat and produce more than its quota. If every cartel member cheats, too much product reaches the market, and prices fall.

Cartels can also collapse if some producers are left out of the group and decide to lower their prices below the cartel's levels. Therefore, cartels usually do not last very long.

❓ INTERPRET Why is a price war harmful to producers?

OPEC Oil Production, 2012

OPEC NATIONS	OIL PRODUCTION (IN THOUSANDS OF BARRELS PER DAY)
Algeria	1,875
Angola	1,872
Ecuador	505
Iran	3,589
Iraq	2,987
Kuwait	2,797
Libya	1,483
Nigeria	2,524
Qatar	1,579
Saudi Arabia	11,726
United Arab Emirates	3,213
Venezuela	2,489

World Oil Production, 2012

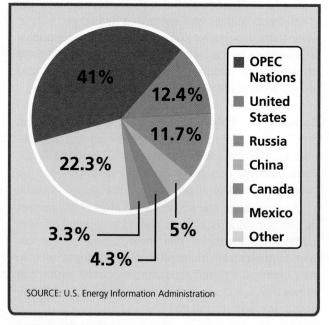

SOURCE: U.S. Energy Information Administration

>> **Analyze Data** Based on the amount of oil that each nation produces, which two OPEC nations are most important to the cartel?

ASSESSMENT

1. **Express Ideas Clearly** Why is it relatively easy for firms to enter and leave a monopolistically competitive market?

2. **Identify Supporting Details** What role does advertising play for monopolistically competitive firms?

3. **Identify Steps in a Process** What keeps monopolistically competitive firms from making high profits?

4. **Identify Cause and Effect** Name three barriers to entry in a market that can lead to the formation of an oligopoly.

5. **Distinguish** What power does a market leader in an oligopoly have?

THE SOAP-AND-WATER CURE.

>> As president, Theodore Roosevelt began vigorous enforcement of the Sherman Antitrust Act. **Analyze Political Cartoons** Why did the cartoonist show him scrubbing an eagle?

▶ **Interactive Flipped Video**

>> Objectives

Explain why firms might try to increase their market power.

List three market practices that the government regulates or bans to protect competition.

Define *deregulation,* and list its effects on several industries.

>> Key Terms

predatory pricing
antitrust laws
trust
merger
deregulation

4.4   As a consumer, you have choices. You can choose from a variety of cellphone plans or Internet service providers. But you still have no choice when it comes to cable television service. Congress passed a law in 2007 that stated that no company could control more than 30 percent of the cable television market. Two years later, a major cable company successfully argued in court that it had competition from other sources, such as satellite television. So the court removed the 30-percent limit, opening the door for cable companies to gain a larger share of the market.

Government Regulation and Competition

Government and Competition

Sometimes the government takes steps to promote competition, but the limits of its actions can be tested in court. In this section, you will read about the tools the government uses to combat anticompetitive practices.

Market Power Monopolies and oligopolies have market power. Recall that market power is the ability of a firm to control prices and total market output. This can be bad for the consumer and for the economy as a whole. Markets dominated by one firm or a few large ones tend to have higher prices and lower output than markets with many sellers. Competition is reduced. Before we look at antitrust policies, let's look at ways in which a firm might try to increase its market power.

To control prices and output like a monopoly, the leading firms in a market can merge with one another, form a cartel, or set the market price below their costs for the short term to drive competitors out of business. The last practice is known as **predatory pricing.** Economists are skeptical about most claims of predatory pricing, because the predator loses money each time it drives an endless series of rivals out of business.

Antitrust Laws The federal government has a number of policies that keep firms from controlling the price and supply of important goods. If a firm controls a large share of a market, the Federal Trade Commission and the Department of Justice's Antitrust Division will watch the firm closely to ensure that it does not unfairly force out its competitors. These government policies are known as **antitrust laws.** A **trust** is a business combination similar to a cartel.

In 1890, Congress passed the Sherman Antitrust Act, which outlawed mergers and monopolies that limit trade between states. This and other laws gave the government the power to regulate industry, to stop firms from forming cartels or monopolies, and to break up existing monopolies. Over the years, Congress passed new laws to outlaw other anticompetitive practices. Even though these actions have restricted businesses' actions, they have generally benefited consumers.

Despite the antitrust laws, companies have used many strategies to gain control over their markets. Some firms require a customer who buys one product to buy other products from the same company, whether or not the customer wants them. For example, the manufacturer of a popular tennis shoe can demand

that a chain also buy and resell its brand-name shirts, windbreakers, and watches if it wants to sell its shoes. Buying out competitors is another strategy used by many large firms.

Regulating Business Practices The government has the power to regulate all of these practices if they give too much power to a company that already has few competitors. Microsoft is such a company. It sells operating systems, software that tells a computer how to run. In 1997, the Department of Justice accused Microsoft of using its near-monopoly over the operating-system market to try to take control of the browser market. A browser is a program that allows people to access Web sites.

Microsoft insisted that computer manufacturers selling its operating system must also include its browser. The government accused Microsoft of predatory pricing, because the company gave away its browser for free, a policy that could ruin the other browser company, Netscape. Microsoft's power in one market gave it a big—and possibly unfair—advantage in a related market.

Microsoft argued that the browser was part of its operating system and could not be sold separately. Microsoft's defenders said that companies do compete with Microsoft, and people buy Microsoft software because they like it. In November 1999, a federal

Comparing Browser Usage

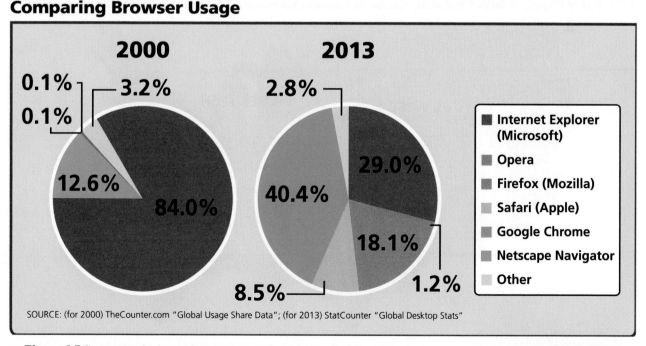

SOURCE: (for 2000) TheCounter.com "Global Usage Share Data"; (for 2013) StatCounter "Global Desktop Stats"

>> **Figure 4.5** Consumers had more browsers to choose from in 2013 than they had in 2000. **Analyze Graphs** What do these graphs suggest about the effect of the government lawsuit against Microsoft?

▶ **Interactive Cartoon**

judge ruled against Microsoft. The company appealed, and in 2001, the Justice Department and Microsoft reached an agreement to settle the case. According to the settlement, Microsoft could link its browser to its operating system but could not force computer manufacturers to provide only Microsoft software on new computers. The Microsoft browser had a large share of the market at the time. Partly as a result of the settlement, competing browsers have entered the market and attracted a fair share of users, as **Figure 4.5** shows.

Splitting Up Monopolies In 1911, the government used the Sherman Antitrust Act to break up two monopolies, John D. Rockefeller's Standard Oil Company and the American Tobacco Company. The Supreme Court ordered these powerful monopolies to split apart into competing firms. Antitrust laws have been put to use many times since then. These laws have generally helped companies that tried to compete with the monopolies, and as a result, have lowered prices and given more options to consumers.

In 1982, the government reached an agreement with American Telephone and Telegraph (AT&T) to break up the company into seven regional phone companies. Two years later, in 1984, the new companies, including BellSouth, US West, and Pacific Telesis, began operating. Because the government had treated local telephone service as a natural monopoly, AT&T had legally controlled all the cables and networks that linked telephones in homes and businesses. The government stepped in only when AT&T used its legal monopoly on local phone service to take control of other markets for long-distance phone calls and communications equipment.

Today, the larger telephone companies offer plans that include nationwide long-distance along with local phone service. However, numerous smaller firms still compete in the market for long-distance service. Although the breakup of AT&T cost thousands of workers their jobs, consumers have benefited from lower prices and improved technology.

Assessing Mergers In addition to breaking up existing monopolies, the government has the power to prevent the rise of monopolies. The government does this by blocking mergers that might reduce competition and lead to higher prices. A **merger** occurs when a company joins with another company or companies to form a single firm. Government regulators also follow the effects of past mergers to check that they do not lead to unfair market control. You read earlier that prices often fall when the number of firms in a market

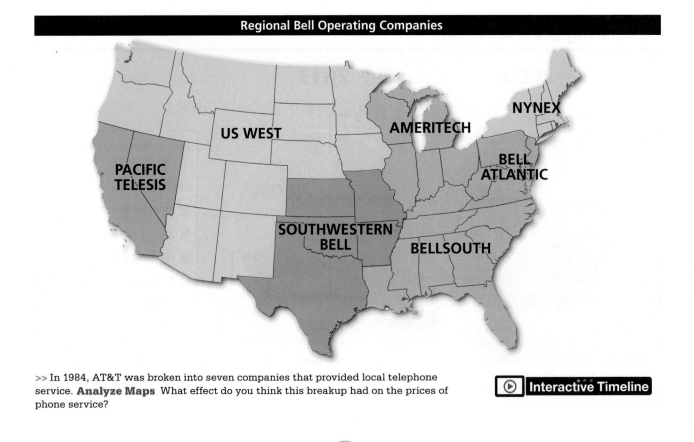

Regional Bell Operating Companies

>> In 1984, AT&T was broken into seven companies that provided local telephone service. **Analyze Maps** What effect do you think this breakup had on the prices of phone service?

▶ Interactive Timeline

GOVERNMENT ACTIONS

REGULATION

Enforce antitrust laws

Break up monopolies

Challenge business practices that limit competition

Block mergers that create unfair market power

DEREGULATION

Cut regulations that reduce competition

Eliminate price controls, allowing prices to fall

Remove barriers to entry, allowing new firms to enter the market

MORE COMPETITION

>> Supporters of regulation and of deregulation both argue that the result is more competition. **Analyze Information** Choose one entry from each column and explain how it boosts competition.

increases. The reverse is also true. Prices often rise when the number of firms in a market decreases.

When the government considers whether or not to approve a merger, it tries to predict the effects of the merger on prices and service. Sometimes it determines that the effects will be minimal. In 2000, the Federal Trade Commission (FTC) and the Federal Communications Commission both approved the merger of media giants America Online (AOL) and Time Warner. Approval came with several conditions designed to ensure consumer choice. Two years later, the government drew a different conclusion when the FTC blocked the merger of the glassware makers Libbey and Anchor Hocking. The FTC argued that the merger would create a monopoly. A federal court agreed, and the deal fell apart.

Merger Guidelines Although some mergers hurt consumers by reducing competition, others can actually benefit consumers. In these cases, corporate mergers will lower overall average costs and lead to lower prices, more reliable products or service, and a more efficient industry. The government must act carefully to make the right decision.

In 1992, the Justice Department and the FTC released guidelines for proposed mergers. The basic theme of the guidelines was that "mergers should not be permitted to create or enhance market power." As revised in 1997, the guidelines gave companies the chance to prove that the merger would generate efficiencies, leading to lower costs and prices.

IDENTIFY What kinds of rules and regulations does the government use to break up monopolies?

Deregulation

In the late 1970s and 1980s, Congress decided that some government regulation was reducing competition. It passed laws to deregulate several industries. **Deregulation** means that the government no longer decides what role each company can play in a market and how much it can charge its customers.

Over several years, the government deregulated the airline, trucking, banking, railroad, natural gas, and television broadcasting industries. Depending on the degree of deregulation, the government's action allowed—or forced—firms in these industries to compete by eliminating many price controls and barriers to entry.

Deregulation weakens government control, and antitrust laws strengthen it. Yet the government uses both deregulation and antitrust laws for the same purpose: to promote competition.

Many critics say that government efforts to regulate industries have created inefficiencies. In some cases, the economic facts that created the need for regulation in the first place have changed. In an earlier Lesson, you read about how cellular phones challenged the natural monopoly of local phone service and opened the market to new companies. The trucking industry was also regulated as a natural monopoly from the early 1900s until 1978. By then, many people had decided that the government was regulating industries that were not natural monopolies at all.

Judging Deregulation Deregulation has met with mixed success. In most cases, many new firms entered the deregulated industries right away. Competition certainly increased in the airline, trucking, and banking industries. Typically, years of wild growth were followed by the disappearance of some firms. This weeding out of weaker players is considered healthy for the economy, but it can be hard on workers in the short term.

In the 1990s, several states deregulated their electricity markets to allow private, competing companies to produce and sell energy to homeowners. In some markets, energy prices fell, but elsewhere, customers paid more. California experienced a massive energy crisis in 2000 that forced the state to pay extraordinarily high rates for electricity. Many attributed this crisis to private energy companies,

such as Enron, that may have used deregulation rules to create an electricity shortage. Enron later declared bankruptcy, and several of its executives faced criminal charges. California reacted to the crisis by reinstating some limits on competition.

Airline Deregulation: Mixed Results Many new airlines started operating after President Carter deregulated the industry in 1978, but some eventually failed or were acquired by other companies. Freed from regulatory restriction, many of the large airlines competed aggressively for the busiest routes. For most travelers, increased competition created lower prices. However, many busy airports now have one or two dominant airlines. In some cases, fares are actually higher than before deregulation.

In the early 2000s, changing conditions transformed the airlines. Over-expansion and sharply rising labor costs squeezed profits. The terrorist hijackings of four commercial passenger jets on September 11, 2001, caused many people to stop flying. Revenues plunged while costs for security, insurance, and fuel rose. Several major airlines filed for bankruptcy.

For several airlines, the solution to their financial difficulties was to merge with another airline. The early 2000s saw several mergers of major airlines. These included American Airlines and TWA in 2001 and Delta and Northwest Airlines in 2008. Another merger proposed in 2013 between American Airlines

Average Round-Trip Airfare, 1979–2011

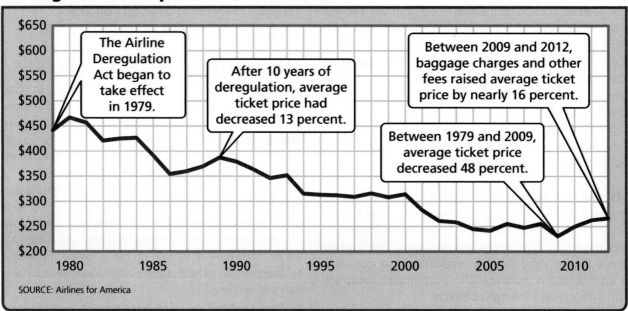

SOURCE: Airlines for America

>> The average cost of flying generally decreased after the Airline Deregulation Act took effect. **Analyze Graphs** Why did airline deregulation lead to lower prices for consumers?

and US Airways triggered an antitrust lawsuit filed by the Justice Department. The settlement of that suit involved the airlines' reducing their dominant positions at certain large airports. That meant giving up control of gates and slots. Gates are where passengers depart from and arrive at airports; slots are runways. These changes promised to open up space for new airlines and thus increase competition.

? CHECK UNDERSTANDING How does deregulation encourage competition in a market?

ASSESSMENT

1. **Infer** What do firms stand to gain by increasing their market power?

2. **Cite Evidence** In 1997, the government accused Microsoft of predatory pricing. Does the rule against predatory pricing make sense in this case? Why or why not?

3. **List** three market practices that the government regulates or bans to protect competition.

4. **Make Predictions** What do you think policymakers expected would happen when they deregulated the trucking industry?

5. **Evaluate Arguments** Critics argue that deregulation gives some companies too much power and hurts competition. Evaluate that argument, using airline deregulation as an example.

1. **Describe Basic Characteristics** Using the image provided, write a paragraph that applies economics-related terminology, standard grammar, spelling, sentence structure, and punctuation to describe the characteristics of economic systems, including competition, that must be present in order for the action in the photo to take place. Consider such things as: What types of products are for sale? Are all of the products the same? Why are consumers evaluating the products? What might producers do to increase sales of their product in this market?

2. **Describe Characteristics** Why do monopolies result in consumers having less satisfactory choices than in competitive markets? In a market dominated by a monopoly, what choices does the consumer typically have? What factors prevent more than one firm from supplying a product to the market? What factors influence a firm's decision to enter a market?

3. **Identify and Evaluate Examples** What is the Sherman Antitrust Act, and why was it enacted? What business practices does the Sherman Antitrust Act limit? In what ways might the Sherman Antitrust Act restrict the use of business property?

4. **Describe Basic Characteristics** Write a paragraph that describes the characteristics of economic systems that result in the outcome described in the quotation. Consider such things as: Given the number of suppliers at the farmer's market, does any one supplier have the market power to control prices? Do the suppliers offer very different items for sale, or do they sell similar goods? Why are the suppliers (competitors) charging the same price for their produce?

   "As you shop for produce at the local farmer's market, you see many fruits and vegetables being offered by several different suppliers. Yet each supplier charges the same price for these fruits and vegetables."

5. **Give Examples** Give an example of pure competition in agriculture and describe why it is a purely competitive market.

6. **Describe Characteristics** Describe the factors that prevent more than one firm from supplying a product to the market. What factors influence a firm's decision to enter a market?

7. **Analyze and Evaluate Primary Sources** What economic information does the cartoon convey? Is the cartoon's point of view neutral or one-sided? How would you evaluate the validity of economic information in this cartoon?

8. **Give Examples** Write a paragraph that gives an example of a natural monopoly and describes it. Consider such things as: What conditions lead to the emergence of natural monopolies? What is one example of a natural monopoly?

9. **Describe Characteristics** How do monopolistically competitive firms that facilitate competition by preventing monopolies from arising? Consider such things as: How is competition affected by start-up costs? Why do relatively low start-up costs characterize markets with monopolistic competition? What is the effect of relatively low start-up costs for markets characterized by monopolistic competition?

10. **Give Examples** Write a paragraph that gives an example of monopolistic competition in clothing students might wear. Consider such things as: What is one item of clothing students typically wear to school? Are all examples of that item the same? What makes something a substitute for that item?

11. **Describe Characteristics** Referring to the quotation, write a paragraph that describes the role of information in a system of pure competition. Consider such things as: In what way would full information about the market among producers lead to pure competition? In what way would full information about the market among consumers lead to pure competition? In what way would a lack of information about the market among producers and/or consumers inhibit competition?

"The third condition for a purely competitive market is that buyers and sellers know enough about the market to find the best deal."

12. **Describe Characteristics** Describe the characteristics of oligopoly. What makes an industry an oligopoly? Consider such things as: In what way do barriers to entry affect the number of firms in an oligopoly? What is the effect of having this number of firms on prices?

Average Round-Trip Airfare, 1979–2011

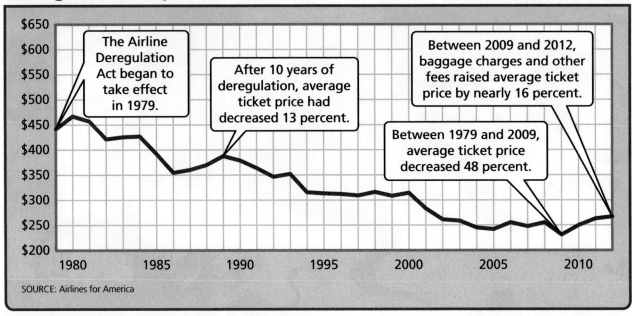

SOURCE: Airlines for America

Callouts in graph:
- The Airline Deregulation Act began to take effect in 1979.
- After 10 years of deregulation, average ticket price had decreased 13 percent.
- Between 2009 and 2012, baggage charges and other fees raised average ticket price by nearly 16 percent.
- Between 1979 and 2009, average ticket price decreased 48 percent.

13. **Analyze and Evaluate Secondary Sources and Evaluate Rules and Regulations** Using the line graph, write a paragraph that evaluates government rules and regulations in the U.S. free enterprise system. What industry does the graph focus on? What does the line in the graph represent? Does the information in the graph show any signs of propaganda, bias, or point of view? What effect did the regulation of the airline industry have on prices before deregulation?

14. **Give Examples** Give an example of an oligopoly in the transportation industry. What form of transportation do many individuals own and use to travel from one location to another? What factor would make the market for that product oligopolistic?

15. **Identify and Evaluate Ordinances, Rules, and Regulations** Write a paragraph that identifies and evaluates the regulations that apply to the establishment and operation of firms that are created through corporate mergers. Consider such things as: What is a corporate merger? What threats do mergers pose to any market? Why are mergers regulated? What is the goal of such regulation?

16. **Write About the Essential Question Write an essay on the Essential Question: How does competition affect markets?** Use evidence from your study of this Topic to support your answer.

Go online to PearsonRealize.com and use the texts, quizzes, interactivities, Interactive Reading Notepads, Flipped Videos, and other resources from this Topic to prepare for the Topic Test.

	Texts
	Quizzes
	Interactivities
	Interactive Reading Notepads
	Flipped Videos

While online you can also check the progress you've made learning the topic and course content by viewing your grades, test scores, and assignment status.

5 Business and Labor

>> A self-emplyeed fashion designer calculates bills in her studio.

Enduring Understandings

- In a sole proprietorship, one owner makes all the decisions and profits while accepting all the responsibilities and debts. In partnerships, two or more owners share the benefits and responsibilities.

- A corporation is owned by its stockholders and run by professional managers.

- Nonprofit organizations function like businesses, but do not operate for the purpose of generating profit.

- The labor market changes over time as the types of jobs available to workers change and as the composition of the labor force changes.

- Unions arose during the days of the Industrial Revolution and fought to improve working conditions, wages, and benefits.

PEARSON realize.™ NBC LEARN

Watch the My Story Video to learn how one entrepreneur founds and builds a business.

PEARSON realize™
www.PearsonRealize.com

Access your digital lessons including:
Topic Inquiry • Interactive Reading
Notepad • Interactivities • Assessments

>> A music instructor who is a sole proprietor must not only be a good teacher, but may also need other skills. He may need to advertise, schedule lessons, and take care of accounting.

You may be one of the lucky people who is able to turn something you really like to do into a business. Imagine launching a Web site that reviews video games, or opening a baseball camp or a car detailing business. One of the many challenges you will face is finding the best way to organize your business.

>> **Objectives**

Explain the characteristics of a sole proprietorship.

Analyze the advantages of a sole proprietorship.

Analyze the disadvantages of a sole proprietorship.

Analyze the economic rights and responsibilities involved in starting a small business.

>> **Key Terms**

sole proprietorship
business
   organization
business license
zoning laws
liability
fringe benefits

Sole Proprietorships

The Role of Sole Proprietorships

The easiest business to set up is the one in which you are the only owner. In this section, you will learn that being your own boss has its advantages as well as its disadvantages.

A **sole proprietorship** is a business owned and managed by a single individual. In this type of **business organization,** which is the ownership structure of a company or firm, the lone entrepreneur earns all of the firm's profits and is responsible for all of its debts. This type of company is by far the most popular in the United States. According to the Internal Revenue Service, more than 70 percent of all businesses are organized as sole proprietorships.

Most sole proprietorships are small, however. All together, they generate only about 4 percent of all sales in the United States.

Many types of businesses can flourish as sole proprietorships. Look around your neighborhood or town. It is more likely than not that your local bakery, your barber shop or hair salon, your bike-repair shop, and the corner grocery store are all sole proprietorships.

Entrepreneurial Spirit In some ways, the word *spirit* in the term *entrepreneurial spirit* says it all. There is a difference between people who expect to spend their lives working for someone else and those who want to work for themselves. Some people are driven by an idea or ambition to create their own jobs. But ambition is only a starting point. To be successful, sole proprietors have to be risk takers. They have to be willing to risk failure for greater satisfaction, and perhaps greater financial gain.

The profile of an entrepreneur includes other essential qualities. The person hoping to start a business has to be able to answer "yes" to a series of questions. Are you organized? Are you responsible? Are you energetic? Are you goal-oriented? Do you know how to run a business? You may be the best cook in the world, but if you know nothing about the business end of running a restaurant, you are likely to fail.

Steve Case, co-founder of America Online, is a model of the successful entrepreneur who believed in himself and had the vision that a company could thrive on the Internet.

> If you're doing something new, you've got to have a vision. You've got to have a perspective. You've got to have some North Star you're aiming for, and you just believe somehow you'll get there . . . . You've got to stick with it, because these things are not overnight successes . . . .

—from an interview with Academy of Achievement, July 12, 2004

Even though sole proprietorships can be started with an idea and a lot of determination, small business owners are taking on a number of economic responsibilities. If you have employees besides yourself, you'll need to pay them. You are responsible for making this payroll. By the same token, you are economically responsible for paying your bills. You will likely have rent and utilities to cover.

Small businesses benefit from government services just like individuals. Therefore, a small business has an economic responsibility to pay taxes to the government, just as individuals do. Small businesses with employees must also pay employment taxes, which include Social Security and Medicare taxes and federal unemployment taxes.

? **IDENTIFY** What is the most common form of business organization in the United States?

Advantages of Sole Proprietorships

While you need to do more than just hang out a sign to start your own business, a sole proprietorship is simple to establish. It also offers the owner several advantages.

Easy to Start and End Easy start-up is the main advantage of the sole proprietorship. With just a

Sizes of Sole Proprietorships (by Tax Return)

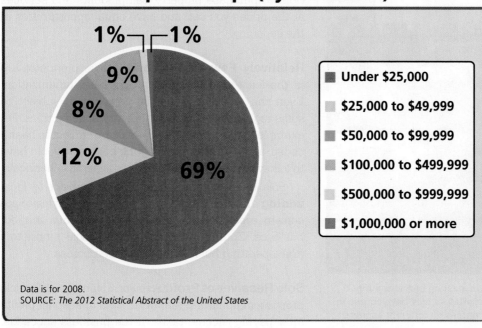

1% 1%
9%
8%
12%
69%

■ Under $25,000
□ $25,000 to $49,999
■ $50,000 to $99,999
▨ $100,000 to $499,999
□ $500,000 to $999,999
■ $1,000,000 or more

Data is for 2008.
SOURCE: *The 2012 Statistical Abstract of the United States*

>> **Analyze Graphs** Based on the graph, how would you describe the size of most sole proprietorships?

 **Interactive Gallery**

>> Some sole proprietorships need to be licensed. The owner of a food truck must be licensed to sell food and must submit to inspections to ensure that safety guidelines are followed.

>> The Small Business Administration provides support for small businesses. Sole proprietors may have access to loans, grants, and training courses on different aspects of running a business.

small amount of paperwork and legal expense, just about anyone can start such a business. The exact requirements vary from city to city and state to state. Typically, though, sole proprietors must meet the following minimum requirements:

Authorization Many sole proprietors must obtain a **business license,** which is an authorization from the local government to operate a business. Certain professionals, such as doctors and day-care providers, may also need a special license from the state.

Site permit If not operating the business out of his or her home, a sole proprietor must obtain a certificate of occupancy to use another building for business. Some zoning laws prohibit doing business in a residential area.

Name If not using his or her own name as the name of the business, a sole proprietor must register a business name.

This paperwork often takes only a day or two to complete. Because they require little legal paperwork, sole proprietorships are usually the least expensive form of ownership to establish.

The federal government offers aid to entrepreneurs to help their businesses grow. Once a business has been started, the federal government's Small Business Administration provides a variety of loan programs and other support.

When you start a small business like a sole proprietorship, you have economic rights. The economic rights of small businesses are protected by laws and regulations that allow businesses to open and operate freely. These economic rights include the right to purchase property, sell products and services at the prices you set, and have equal opportunities in the economy.

Relatively Few Regulations A sole proprietorship is the least-regulated form of business organization. Even the smallest business, however, is subject to some regulation, especially industry-specific rules. For example, a soft pretzel stand would be subject to health codes, and a furniture refinishing business would have to follow laws about disposing of dangerous chemicals.

Sole proprietorships may also be subject to local **zoning laws.** Cities and towns often designate certain areas, or zones, for residential use and for business. Zoning laws may prohibit sole proprietors from operating businesses out of their homes.

Sole Receiver of Profit A major advantage of the sole proprietorship is that the owner gets to keep all profits after paying income taxes. If the business succeeds, the owner does not have to share the success with anyone else. The desire for profits motivates many people to start their own businesses.

Full Control Another advantage of sole proprietorship is that sole proprietors can run their businesses as they wish. This high degree of freedom appeals to entrepreneurs. Fast, flexible decision making allows sole proprietors to take full advantage of sudden opportunities. These entrepreneurs can respond quickly to changes in the marketplace. Finally, if sole proprietors decide to stop operations and do something else for a living, they can do so easily. They must, of course, pay all debts and other obligations, such as taxes, but they do not have to meet any other legal obligations to stop doing business.

Many small businesses rent office or storefront space, but there are advantages to purchasing it as well. For example, it can be difficult and expensive to adapt a rental space to the particular needs of your business. However, if you purchase the property, you have the ability to make the changes you want more easily. If you rent, you will not receive anything in return when you move out. If you purchase, the property belongs to you, and you will be able to sell it. Although the upfront cost may be higher, purchasing can be a good option.

✎ DRAW CONCLUSIONS Why are sole proprietorships easy to start and end?

Disadvantages of Sole Proprietorships

As with everything else, there are trade-offs with sole proprietorships. The independence of this form of business organization comes with a high degree of responsibility.

Unlimited Personal Liability The biggest disadvantage of sole proprietorship is unlimited personal liability. **Liability** is the legal obligation to pay debts. Sole proprietors are fully and personally responsible for all their business debts. If the business fails, the owner may have to sell personal property— such as a car or home—to cover any outstanding obligations. Business debts can ruin a sole proprietor's personal finances.

Limited Access to Resources Suppose you start a landscaping business that grows quickly. You might need to expand your business by buying more equipment. But as a sole proprietor, you may have to pay for that equipment out of your own pocket. Banks are sometimes unwilling to offer loans to a business

>> This sole proprietor enjoys full control, including a flexible work schedule. **Analyze Political Cartoons** How does the cartoon show a major disadvantage of a sole proprietorship?

>> Business costs can be high for a sole proprietor. This floor installer must pay for new equipment out of his own pocket or by taking out a loan for which he is personally liable.

Survival of Sole Proprietorships

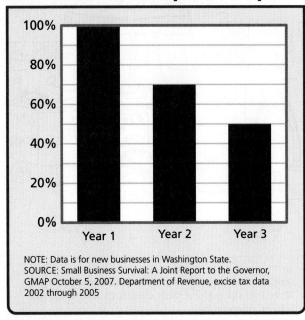

NOTE: Data is for new businesses in Washington State.
SOURCE: Small Business Survival: A Joint Report to the Governor, GMAP October 5, 2007. Department of Revenue, excise tax data 2002 through 2005

>> **Analyze Graphs** Suppose that 80 new sole proprietorships were started in a city in 2014. Based on this graph, how many of these would you expect to still be in business after three years?

▶ **Interactive Chart**

that has not been operating for very long. This makes it difficult or impossible for many sole proprietorships to expand quickly.

Physical capital may not be the only resource in short supply. Human capital may be lacking, too. A sole proprietor, no matter how ambitious, may lack some of the skills necessary to run a business successfully. For example, you may be great at sales but not at accounting. You may love working outdoors as a landscaper but hate to call on people to drum up business. Some aspects of the business suffer if the owner's skills do not match the needs of the business.

Finally, as a sole proprietor, you may have to turn down work because you simply do not have enough hours in the day or enough workers to keep up with demand. A small business often presents its owner with too many demands, and that can be exhausting, both personally and financially.

Lack of Permanence A sole proprietorship has a limited life. If a sole proprietor dies or retires, the business simply ceases to exist if there is no one willing to buy it or run it. The same can happen if the owner suffers an extended illness or loses interest in the business.

Sole proprietorships often have trouble finding and keeping good employees. Small businesses generally cannot offer the security and advancement opportunities that many employees look for in a job. In addition, a sole proprietorship usually has limited access to capital, which means that most small business owners lack the resources to offer workers fringe benefits. **Fringe benefits** are payments to employees other than wages or salaries, such as paid vacation, retirement pay, and health insurance. Lack of experienced employees can hurt a business. Once again, the other side of total control is total responsibility: a sole proprietor cannot count on anyone else to maintain the business.

❓ **SUMMARIZE** What are the disadvantages of sole proprietorships?

ASSESSMENT

1. **Describe** What is a sole proprietorship?

2. **Explain** How might the inability to provide fringe benefits affect a sole proprietor's ability to run a business?

3. **Express Ideas Clearly** A sole proprietor wants to take out a loan so she can buy a small restaurant and open her own cafe. What are some benefits and costs of buying the restaurant property?

4. **Identify** What is an example of a government regulation that might prevent a sole proprietor from opening a used furniture store in his or her home?

5. **Support Ideas with Examples** How is having the economic right to start a sole proprietorship connected to the economic responsibility of starting a sole proprietorship?

5.2 Have you ever thought about setting up your own business? Suppose the idea is very appealing, but you aren't sure that you want to take on all the responsibilities needed to be successful. You may be great at doing the work, like repairing computers, but you may dread all the paperwork that goes along with being in business. Do you have to give up your dream? Some business owners overcome obstacles that block them from starting a business, whether it is a shortage of money or of specific skills, by taking on a partner who supplies what is lacking.

>> Partners sometimes divide work responsibilities to suit their experience and abilities. One may focus on production and the other on sales and marketing, for example.

▶ **Interactive Flipped Video**

Partnerships and Franchises

The Characteristics of Partnerships

A **partnership** is a business organization owned by two or more persons who agree on a specific division of responsibilities and profits. In the United States, partnerships account for nearly 10 percent of all businesses. They generate almost 15 percent of all receipts and just over a quarter of all the income earned by all businesses.

Partnerships are a good choice if owners are willing to share both the responsibility of running the business and the economic right to enjoy the profits it earns. They can also be a good choice if the partners get along well and have skills that complement each other.

Partnerships fall into three categories: general partnerships, limited partnerships, and limited liability partnerships. Each divides responsibility and liability differently.

General Partnership The most common type of partnership is the **general partnership.** In this type, all partners share equally in both responsibility and liability. Partners share some of the economic responsibility of the business based on how much they contribute to launching the partnership. Similarly, they share proportionately

>> **Objectives**

Explain the characteristics of different types of partnerships.

Analyze the advantages of partnerships.

Analyze the disadvantages of partnerships.

Describe how a business franchise operates.

>> **Key Terms**

partnership
general partnership
limited partnership
limited liability
   partnership
articles of
   partnership
assets
business franchise
royalties

in the rewards from the business. Many of the same kinds of businesses that operate as sole proprietorships can operate as general partnerships. Doctors, lawyers, accountants, and other professionals often form partnerships. Small retail stores, farms, construction firms, and family businesses often form partnerships as well.

Limited Partnership In a **limited partnership,** only one partner is required to be a general partner. That is, only one partner has unlimited personal liability for the firm's actions. The remaining partner or partners contribute only money. If the business fails, they can lose only the amount of their initial investment. If the business succeeds, though, limited partners share in the profits.

A limited partnership must have at least one general partner but may have any number of limited partners. Limited partners play no role in managing the business. The general partner runs the company. That control is the main advantage of being a general partner. The main drawback, of course, is the unlimited liability that the general partner has.

Limited Liability Partnerships The **limited liability partnership** (LLP) is a newer type of partnership recognized by many states. In this type of partnership, all partners are limited partners. An LLP functions like a general partnership, except that all partners have limited personal liability in certain situations, such as another partner's mistakes. Not all types of businesses are allowed to register as limited liability partnerships. Most states allow professionals such as attorneys, physicians, dentists, and accountants to register as LLPs.

❓ CONTRAST What is the chief financial difference between a general partner and a limited partner?

Advantages of Partnerships

Partnerships are easy to establish and are subject to few government regulations. They provide entrepreneurs with a number of advantages.

Ease of Start-Up Like proprietorships, partnerships are easy and inexpensive to establish. The law does not require a written partnership agreement. Most experts, however, advise partners to work with an attorney to develop **articles of partnership,** or a partnership agreement. This legal document spells out each partner's economic rights and responsibilities. It outlines how partners will share profits or losses. It may also address other details, such as the ways new partners can join the firm, the duration of the partnership, and tax responsibilities.

If partners do not develop their own articles of partnership, they will fall under the rules of the Uniform Partnership Act (UPA). The UPA is a law adopted by most states to establish rules for partnerships. The UPA requires common ownership interests, profit and loss sharing, and shared management responsibilities.

Like sole proprietorships, partnerships are subject to little government regulation. The partnership may face

Liability in Different Types of Partnerships

TYPE OF PARTNERSHIP	BUSINESS LOSS	PARTNERS' PERSONAL LIABILITY		
General Partnership	$150,000	General Partner A $50,000	General Partner B $50,000	General Partner C $50,000
Limited Partnership	$150,000	General Partner A $75,000	General Partner B $75,000	Limited Partner W $0
Limited Partnership	$150,000	General Partner A $150,000	Limited Partner W $0	Limited Partner X $0

>> The table shows how the same business loss might be shared by partners in three different partnerships. **Synthesize** Why does the personal liability of the partners differ in these scenarios?

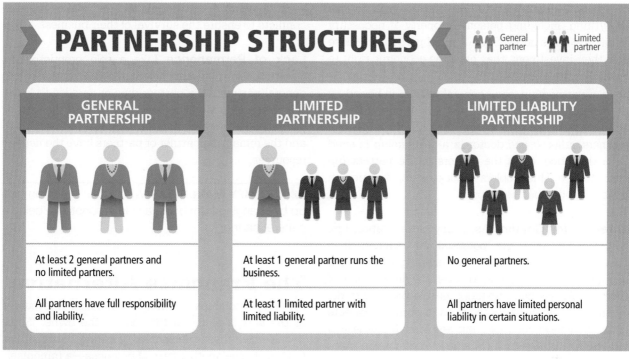

PARTNERSHIP STRUCTURES

General partner | Limited partner

GENERAL PARTNERSHIP

At least 2 general partners and no limited partners.

All partners have full responsibility and liability.

LIMITED PARTNERSHIP

At least 1 general partner runs the business.

At least 1 limited partner with limited liability.

LIMITED LIABILITY PARTNERSHIP

No general partners.

All partners have limited personal liability in certain situations.

>> **Compare and Contrast** How do limited liability partnerships differ from the other two types of partnerships?

certain government regulations because of the nature of its work. Medical partnerships, for instance, must follow government regulations regarding safe handling of biomedical waste. Some kinds of businesses face limits on their operations due to zoning laws. The government does not dictate how partnerships conduct business, however. Partners have the right to distribute profits in whatever way they wish, as long as they abide by the partnership agreement or by the UPA.

Financial Impact A major advantage of partnerships is the ability to raise capital. In a partnership, more than one person contributes **assets,** or money and other valuables. As a result, these businesses can raise more capital than a sole proprietorship. In addition, partnerships have improved ability to borrow funds for operations or expansion.

Partnerships offer advantages to employees as well. They can attract and keep talented employees more easily than sole proprietorships can. Graduates from top accounting schools, for example, often seek jobs with large and prestigious accounting LLPs, hoping to become partners themselves someday. Partnerships, like sole proprietorships, are not subject to any special taxes. Partners do have the legal and economic responsibility to pay taxes on their share of the income that the partnership generates, of course. The business itself does not have to pay taxes, however.

Shared Decision Making In a sole proprietorship, the owner has the burden of making all business decisions. In a partnership, the responsibility for the business may be shared. A sole proprietorship requires the owner to wear many hats, some of which might not fit very well. For example, the sole proprietor may have good managerial abilities but lack marketing skills and experience. In a successful partnership, each partner brings different strengths and skills to the business.

? CONTRAST Why are partnerships better able to raise capital than sole proprietorships?

Disadvantages of Partnerships

Partnerships also present some disadvantages. Many of the disadvantages of sole proprietorships are present in partnerships. Limited liability partnerships have fewer disadvantages than partnerships with general partners. All partnerships, however, have the potential for conflict.

Unlimited Liability Unless the partnership is an LLP, at least one partner has unlimited liability. As in a sole proprietorship, any general partner has full responsibility for any financial obligations the firm takes on. General partners have the potential to lose everything, including personal property, if necessary to pay the firm's debts. Since limited partners can lose only their investment, they have the economic right to avoid this threat.

In a partnership, each general partner is bound by the acts of all other general partners. If one partner's actions cause the firm losses, then all of the general partners suffer. If one doctor in a partnership is sued for malpractice, all of the doctors in the partnership stand to lose. This problem is not present, of course, in limited liability partnerships.

Potential for Conflict As in any close relationship, partnerships have the potential for conflict. If a business has more than one general partner, each one has only partial control over the firm. None of them enjoys as much freedom as sole proprietors do. Partnership agreements address technical aspects of the business, such as profit and loss. Many issues vital to the success of the business exist outside these guidelines, however. Partners need to ensure that they agree on matters such as work habits, management style, ethics, and general business philosophies.

Still, friction between partners often arises and can be difficult to resolve. Many partnerships dissolve because of these interpersonal conflicts. Partners must learn to communicate openly and find ways to resolve conflicts to ensure the survival of their business.

Lack of Permanence Like a sole proprietorship, a partnership may not outlast the life of one of the general partners. If a partner dies or decides to leave, the partnership might cease to exist unless the articles of partnership state that the business can continue and the remaining partner or partners have the needed resources.

? IDENTIFY MAIN IDEAS What does a person give up by changing from being a sole proprietor to being a general partner?

The Franchise Alternative

Sole proprietorships can suffer from a lack of resources or the lack of skills on the part of the owner. Some people solve these problems by forming partnerships. Others choose another form of business—a franchise.

What Is a Franchise? As you learned earlier, a franchise is a contract issued by a local authority that gives a single firm the right to sell its goods within an exclusive market. One type of franchise is issued by government authorities. These franchises give one firm the sole right to sell its goods within a limited

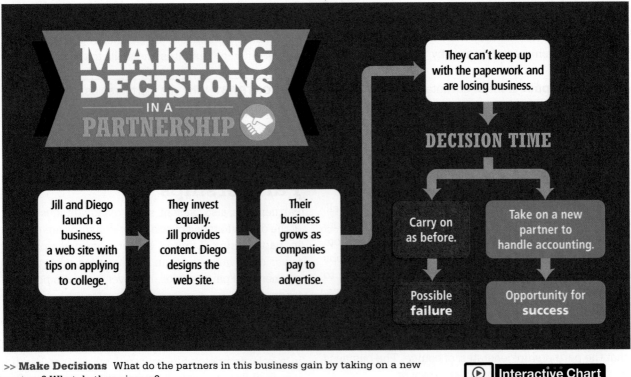

>> **Make Decisions** What do the partners in this business gain by taking on a new partner? What do they give up?

▶ **Interactive Chart**

HOW A FRANCHISE WORKS

PARENT COMPANY

Training and support, advertising, standardized quality, financial assistance, savings on materials

FRANCHISE OWNER

Royalties and fees

>> **Analyze Information** Which aspect of franchising might be helpful for a relatively inexperienced entrepreneur?

▶ **Interactive Illustration**

market, such as within a national park. In business, too, a franchise signals exclusive rights. A **business franchise** is a semi-independent business that pays fees to a parent company. In return, the business is granted the exclusive right to sell a certain product or service in a given area. Franchises offer a wide array of goods and services, from fast-food restaurants to stores that sell diamonds.

In this arrangement, the parent company is called a franchiser. The franchiser develops the products and systems to produce them to improve efficiency and reliability. Franchisers then work with local franchise owners to help them produce and sell their products. Each owner is called a franchisee.

Franchising has become popular in recent years. This is because franchises allow each owner a degree of control. At the same time, the owners benefit from the support of the parent company. Of course, franchises offer both advantages and disadvantages.

Advantages of Franchises A franchise provides certain advantages that a completely independent business cannot have. First, a franchise comes with a built-in reputation. Consumers may already be familiar with the product and brand. Other advantages help the franchisee assume the responsibilities of the business by supporting him or her in running the business:

- *Management training and support* Franchisers help owners gain the experience they need to succeed by running training and support programs.

- *Standardized quality* Most parent companies require franchise owners to follow certain rules and processes to guarantee product quality. High-quality products attract customers.

- *National advertising programs* Parent companies pay for advertising campaigns to establish their brand names. These ads can increase sales for each franchisee.

- *Financial assistance* Some franchisers provide financing to help franchise owners start their businesses. This aid can help people with fewer resources enjoy the economic right of becoming business owners.

- *Centralized buying power* Franchisers buy materials in bulk for all of their franchise locations. They pass on the savings to their franchisees.

Disadvantages of Franchises The biggest disadvantage of a franchise is that the owner must sacrifice some freedom in return for the parent company's guidance. Other disadvantages include:

- *High franchising fees and royalties* Buying into a franchise carries significant economic

Comparing Profits in Different Types of Businesses

	SOLE PROPRIETORSHIP	PARTNERSHIP (2 EQUAL PARTNERS)	FRANCHISE
Revenue	$500,000	$500,000	$500,000
Costs	−$400,000	−$400,000	−$400,000
Profit	$100,000	$100,000	$100,000
Franchise fee (5% of revenue)	n/a	n/a	−$25,000
Marketing fee (2% of revenue)	n/a	n/a	−$10,000
Profit to owner	$100,000	$50,000 per partner	$65,000

>> The chart compares profits when the same revenue is earned by three types of businesses. **Analyze Charts** Why does the franchise owner have less profit than the sole proprietor?

responsibilities. Franchisers often charge high fees for the right to use the company name. They also charge franchise owners a share of their earnings, or **royalties.**

- *Strict operating standards* Franchise owners have the responsibility to follow all the rules laid out in the franchising agreement for such matters as hours of operation, employee dress codes, and operating procedures. If they do not, they may lose the franchise.

- *Purchasing restrictions* Franchise owners must often buy their supplies from the parent company or from approved suppliers.

- *Limited product line* Franchise agreements allow franchisees to offer only approved products. Franchisees usually cannot launch new product lines that might appeal more to local customers.

? COMPARE What disadvantage do franchisees share with partnerships but not with sole proprietorships?

ASSESSMENT

1. **Identify Main Ideas** What financial right does someone give up when changing a business from a sole proprietorship to a partnership?

2. **Infer** What ethical responsibilities do general partners have to one another? Why?

3. **Summarize** What do limited partners in a business give up? What do they gain?

4. **Identify** What are three advantages of forming a partnership?

5. **Synthesize** What are three disadvantages of partnerships?

5.3 Every day you use goods and services provided by a variety of businesses, both large and small. Did the bread you ate today come from a local bakery or a huge multinational food producer? Some goods can be provided by either. But what about the car or bus you took to school? Some products can be produced only by big businesses.

>> A large corporation has the capital to build factories and hire many workers. As a result, it can produce and sell goods on a large scale.

▶ **Interactive Flipped Video**

Corporations

The Characteristics of Corporations

Goods and services that require huge amounts of capital to produce require a special kind of business organization, or ownership structure. Sole proprietorships and partnerships lack the resources to carry out expensive processes, such as making cars, or having operations that reach across the country or around the world. What form of business organization do these companies have? Most of these businesses are corporations.

The most complex form of business organization is the corporation. A **corporation** is a legal entity, or being, owned by individual stockholders, each of whom has limited liability for the firm's debts. Stockholders own **stock,** a certificate of ownership in a corporation. Each person who owns stock is a part-owner of the corporation issuing it. If a corporation issues 1,000 shares of stock, and you purchase 1 share, you own 1/1000th of the corporation.

Sole proprietorships have no identity beyond that of the owners. A corporation, on the other hand, does have a legal identity separate from the identities of its owners. Legally, it is regarded much like an individual. A corporation may engage in business, make contracts, sue other parties or be sued by others, and pay taxes.

In the United States, corporations account for about 20 percent of all businesses but more than 80 percent of all sales. They generate nearly 60 percent of the net income earned in the nation. Because of the advantages of corporations, most large business firms do incorporate, or become corporations.

Types of Corporations Some corporations issue stock to only a few people, often family members. These stockholders rarely trade their stock, but instead pass it on, typically within the family. Such corporations are called **closely held corporations.** They are also known as privately held corporations.

A **publicly held corporation,** however, has many shareholders who can buy or sell stock on the open market. Stocks are bought and sold in financial markets called stock exchanges, such as the New York Stock Exchange or the Tokyo Stock Exchange.

Corporate Structure While the exact organization varies from firm to firm, all corporations have the same basic structure. The owners—the stockholders—elect a board of directors. The board of directors makes all the major decisions of the corporation. It appoints corporate officers such as the chief executive officer or president.

These officers run the corporation and oversee its operations. Corporate officers, in turn, hire managers and employees, who work in various departments such as finance, sales, research, marketing, and production.

? **SUMMARIZE** A publicly held corporation has

Advantages of Incorporation

Incorporation, or forming a corporation, offers advantages to both stockholders and the corporation itself. These advantages include limited liability for owners, transferable ownership, ability to attract capital, and long life.

Advantages for Stockholders The primary reason that entrepreneurs choose to form a corporation is to gain the benefit of limited liability. Individual stockholders do not carry personal responsibility for the corporation's actions. They can lose only the amount of money they have invested in the business. If a corporation is sued and loses the case, it must pay the money award, but the assets of individual stockholders cannot be touched.

Corporations usually also provide owners with more flexibility than other forms of ownership. Shares of stock are easily transferable. That is, stockholders can easily sell their stock to others and get money in return.

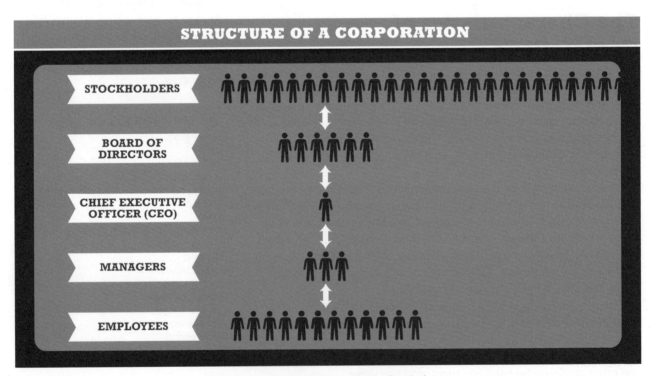

STRUCTURE OF A CORPORATION

STOCKHOLDERS

BOARD OF DIRECTORS

CHIEF EXECUTIVE OFFICER (CEO)

MANAGERS

EMPLOYEES

>> **Categorize** In a corporation, who chooses the board of directors, and who chooses the chief executive officer?

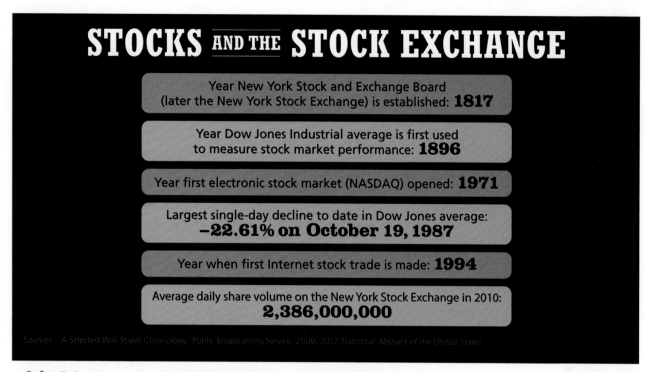

STOCKS AND THE STOCK EXCHANGE

Year New York Stock and Exchange Board
(later the New York Stock Exchange) is established: **1817**

Year Dow Jones Industrial average is first used
to measure stock market performance: **1896**

Year first electronic stock market (NASDAQ) opened: **1971**

Largest single-day decline to date in Dow Jones average:
−22.61% on October 19, 1987

Year when first Internet stock trade is made: **1994**

Average daily share volume on the New York Stock Exchange in 2010:
2,386,000,000

Sources: "A Selected Wall Street Chronology," Public Broadcasting Service, 2009, 2012 Statistical Abstract of the United States

>> **Infer** Before the introduction of modern technology, stocks were traded in person. What effect do you think Internet trading has had on the stock market?

That is not the case with other forms of business organization.

Advantages for Corporations The corporate structure also presents advantages for the firm itself. Corporations have more potential for growth than other business forms. By selling shares on the stock market, corporations can raise large amounts of capital.

Corporations can also raise money by borrowing it. They do this by selling bonds. A **bond** is a formal contract issued by a corporation or other entity that includes the promise to repay borrowed money with interest at fixed intervals.

Because ownership is separate from the running of the firm, corporate owners—that is, stockholders— do not need any special managerial skills. Instead, the corporation can hire various experts—the best financial analysts, the best engineers, and so forth.

Corporations also have the advantage of long life. Because stock is transferable, corporations are able to exist longer than simple proprietorships or even partnerships. Unless it has stated in advance a specific termination date, the corporation can do business indefinitely.

? **RECALL** How do corporations raise capital?

Disadvantages of Incorporation

Corporations do have some disadvantages, including expense and difficulty of start-up, double taxation, potential loss of control by the founders, and more legal requirements and regulations.

Difficulty and Expense of Start-Up Businesses that wish to incorporate must first file for a state license known as a **certificate of incorporation,** or corporate charter. The application includes crucial information such as corporate name, statement of purpose, length of time that the business will run (usually "for perpetuity," or without limit), founders' names and addresses, where business is based, method of fundraising, and rules for management.

Once state officials review and approve the application, they grant the corporation its charter. Then the corporation organizes itself to produce and sell a good or service. Corporate charters can be difficult, expensive, and time-consuming to create. Though most states allow people to form corporations without legal help, few experts would recommend this shortcut.

Double Taxation The law considers corporations legal entities separate from their owners. Corporations, therefore, must pay taxes on their income.

"The IRS is here to bite the hand that feeds it."

>> The Internal Revenue Service (IRS) collects taxes from corporations and investors. **Analyze Political Cartoons** In what sense is this company the "hand that feeds" the IRS?

▶ **Interactive Chart**

>> President George W. Bush signs the Sarbanes-Oxley Act of 2002, which instituted regulations encouraging corporate responsibility, especially with regard to accounting practices.

Corporate earnings are taxed a second time as well. When corporations determine their profits, they often choose to pay a share of those profits to stockholders in payments called **dividends.** These dividends count as income for the stockholder, and the stockholder must pay personal income tax on them. This double taxation keeps many firms from incorporating.

When stockholders sell shares, they must compare the selling price to how much they paid for them. If the selling price is higher, they have earned what is called a capital gain. That gain is also taxed.

Some owners form **limited liability corporations** (LLCs). These businesses have the advantage of limited liability for owners, which all corporations enjoy. They also have tax advantages because the firm does not pay corporate income tax.

Loss of Control The original owners of a corporation often lose control of the company. Corporate officers and boards of directors, not owners, manage corporations. These managers do not always act in the owners' best interests. They might be more interested in protecting their own jobs or salaries today than in making difficult decisions that would benefit the firm tomorrow.

More Regulation Corporations face more regulations than other types of businesses. They must hold annual meetings for stockholders and keep records of all business transactions. Publicly held corporations are required to file quarterly and annual reports with the Securities and Exchange Commission (SEC). The SEC is a federal agency that regulates the stock market.

Corporations must also abide by government regulations that affect the use of business property. For example, a corporation that opens a new factory in a city must abide by the zoning laws of that city. It must also make sure that the factory meets regulations designed to ensure that employees work in a safe environment. It must make sure that the factory abides by laws that regulate the safe handling of industrial waste.

? IDENTIFY SUPPORTING DETAILS In order to do business, what is one regulation that corporations have to follow?

Corporate Mergers

Corporations can grow very large. One way to grow is to raise money by selling stocks or bonds. Corporations may also grow by merging, or combining, with another corporation. The three kinds of mergers are horizontal mergers, vertical mergers, and conglomerates.

A TYPICAL CORPORATE MERGER

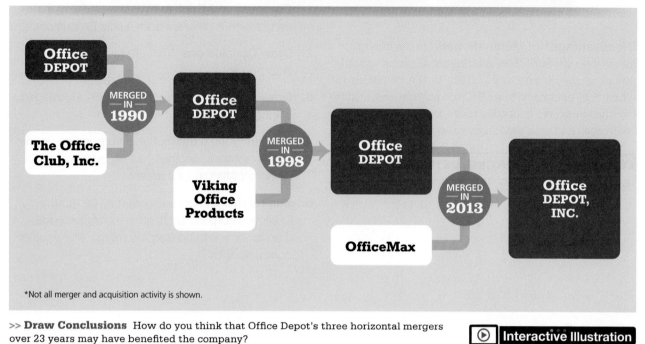

*Not all merger and acquisition activity is shown.

>> **Draw Conclusions** How do you think that Office Depot's three horizontal mergers over 23 years may have benefited the company?

Interactive Illustration

Horizontal Mergers In a **horizontal merger,** two or more firms competing in the same market with the same good or service join together. In 2013, Office Depot, an office-supply store, merged with OfficeMax, another office-supply store. This was a horizontal merger. Two firms might choose to merge if the newly established firm would result in economies of scale or would otherwise improve efficiency.

The federal government watches horizontal mergers carefully. The resulting single firm might gain monopoly power in its market. If that is the case, the government might try to block the merger in court. Judges then listen to arguments and read evidence to decide whether to allow the merger.

Vertical Mergers In a **vertical merger,** two or more firms involved in different stages of producing the same good or service join together. A vertical merger can allow a firm to operate more efficiently. A vertically combined firm can control all phases of production, rather than relying on the goods or services of outside suppliers. Sometimes firms take this step out of fear that they may otherwise lose crucial supplies. Antitrust regulators become concerned when firms in the same industry merge vertically, especially if supplying firms suffer. Most vertical mergers do not substantially lessen competition, however.

Some companies grow larger through a combination of horizontal and vertical mergers.

Conglomerates Sometimes firms buy other companies that produce totally unrelated goods or services. When three or more unrelated businesses are involved, this combination is called a **conglomerate.** In a conglomerate, no one business earns the majority of the firm's profits. The government usually allows this kind of merger because it does not result in decreased competition.

? IDENTIFY CAUSE AND EFFECT What is one advantage of a vertical merger?

Multinational Corporations

The world's largest corporations produce and sell their goods and services in more than one country. They are called **multinational corporations** (MNCs). MNCs usually have headquarters in one country and branches in other countries. Multinationals must obey laws and pay taxes in each country in which they operate.

In 2007, U.S. multinational firms employed 32 million workers. The largest multinational companies in the world include General Electric, Royal Dutch Shell, BP, Exxon Mobil, and Toyota.

Advantages of Multinationals Multinationals benefit consumers and workers by providing jobs and products around the world. Often the jobs they provide help people in poorer nations enjoy better living standards. Multinational corporations (MNCs) also spread new technologies and production methods across the globe.

Disadvantages of Multinationals On the downside, many people feel that multinational firms unduly influence the culture and politics in the countries in which they operate. While MNCs do provide jobs, critics say that in poorer countries those jobs are marked by low wages and poor working conditions.

? IDENTIFY SUPPORTING DETAILS Describe a potential disadvantage of multinational corporations.

1. **Compare and Contrast** What is one way that a corporation is different from a sole proprietorship?

2. **Draw Conclusions** What are four advantages of incorporating?

3. **Draw Conclusions** What are the disadvantages of incorporation?

4. **Explain** When a multinational corporation opens a new factory in another country, what economic responsibilities must it meet?

5. **Summarize** The government may be more likely to allow a corporation to form a conglomerate than to allow it to horizontally merge with another company. Why?

Any time you go to a museum, the zoo, or a hospital, you are benefiting from a business organization whose main goal is to provide a service to you rather than to make a profit for itself. If you meet certain criteria, you may join a credit union, whose main purpose is to benefit its members. Although these various institutions may seem no different from other businesses, they are not quite the same.

>> The International Committee of the Red Cross is a nonprofit NGO that provides humanitarian aid. These Philippine Red Cross workers are helping victims of a typhoon in their home country.

▶ **Interactive Flipped Video**

Cooperatives and Nonprofits

Cooperatives

Success in business is not measured only in dollars and cents. Some businesses are not organized to maximize profits. Instead their goals are to work for the good of all their members or to work for the good of society in general. In this Lesson, you will learn about these other kinds of business organizations, classified as cooperatives and nonprofits.

Ben Franklin, one of our nation's founders, was a remarkable innovator. In 1752, he organized a company that collected money from its members in order to make payments to any one of them who suffered losses from a fire.

This group was America's first cooperative. Franklin explained the nature of this group in a letter to a Boston newspaper.

I would leave this to the Consideration of all who are concern'd for their own or their Neighbour's Temporal Happiness; and I am humbly of Opinion, that the Country is ripe for many such *Friendly Societies,* whereby every

>> **Objectives**

Identify the different types of cooperative organizations.

Understand the purpose of nonprofit organizations, including professional and business organizations.

>> **Key Terms**

cooperative
consumer
   cooperative
service cooperative
producer
   cooperative
nonprofit
   organization
professional
   organization
business association
trade association

Man might help another, without any
Disservice to himself.

—*The New-England Courant*, August 13, 1722

A **cooperative** is a business organization owned and operated by a group of individuals for their shared benefit. In other words, working together, the individuals help one another. Cooperatives are based on several principles, which include:

- voluntary and open membership;
- democratic control of the organization by its members;
- sharing of contributions and benefits by members.

Cooperatives enjoy some tax benefits. Like all businesses, cooperatives have earnings. But since they are not corporations, cooperatives do not pay income tax on their earnings as long as they handle those earnings in certain ways. At least 20 percent must be paid out to members. Members, of course, must then pay personal income taxes on that money. The cooperative invests as much as 80 percent of its earnings to maintain or expand its operations.

Cooperatives, or co-ops, are found in many industries, from farming and energy to healthcare and child care. They fall into three main categories: consumer cooperatives, service cooperatives, and producer cooperatives. Any group of consumers or producers with common social or economic goals can band together to form a cooperative.

Consumer Cooperatives Retail outlets owned and operated by consumers are called consumer cooperatives. They are also known as purchasing cooperatives. **Consumer cooperatives** sell merchandise to their members at reduced prices.

By purchasing goods in large quantities, these cooperatives can obtain goods at a lower cost. They then pass the savings on to members by setting prices low. Examples of consumer cooperatives include discount price clubs, compact disc or book clubs, some health food stores, and housing cooperatives.

Some co-ops charge an annual fee for membership. Others require members to work a small number of hours to maintain membership. For example, your health food store may require you to work 20 hours per month to remain in the cooperative. Consumer co-ops range in size from small buying clubs to Fortune 500 businesses.

Service Cooperatives Cooperatives that provide a service rather than goods are called **service cooperatives.** Some service co-ops offer discounted insurance, banking services, healthcare, legal help, or baby-sitting services.

Credit unions, or financial cooperatives, are a special kind of service cooperative. People deposit money in these institutions. The credit unions then use those funds to lend money to members at reduced rates.

Producer Cooperatives **Producer cooperatives** are agricultural marketing cooperatives that help members sell their products. These co-ops allow members

Comparing Corporations and Cooperatives

CORPORATION	COOPERATIVE
Owned by individual stockholders	Owned by its members, a group of individuals
Decisions are made by a board of directors	Decisions are made by members
Main purpose is to maximize profits	Main purpose is to help its members
Distributes a portion of profits to stockholders	Distributes a portion of profits to members
Pays income taxes on earnings	Does not pay income taxes on earnings

>> **Analyze Charts** How is being a member of a cooperative the same as being a stockholder in a corporation? How is it different?

▶ **Interactive Chart**

to focus their attention on growing crops, raising livestock, and catching fish. The co-ops, meanwhile, market these goods for the highest prices possible. In a recent year, producer cooperatives sold more than $235 billion worth of crops, livestock, and seafood. These groups are involved in marketing dairy products, grain, beef and chicken, fish, and many other products. Some co-ops have more than a million members.

? RECALL How do members benefit from each type of cooperative?

Nonprofits

Some institutions function much like business organizations but do not operate for the purpose of generating profit. For that reason, they are called **nonprofit organizations.** Nonprofit organizations have no owner. They are often run by a board of directors. Nonprofits are usually in the business of providing some benefit to the public. Examples include museums, public schools, the American Red Cross, hospitals, adoption agencies, churches, synagogues, YMCAs, and many other groups and charities. Almost all of them provide services rather than goods.

The government exempts nonprofit organizations from income taxes. The government gives this tax break in order to encourage organizations to meet needs that for-profit businesses might not otherwise provide, such as food or shelter for those who cannot afford them. Nonprofits must meet certain requirements to qualify for this tax-exempt status.

Nonprofits cannot issue stock, so any profits that they make cannot be distributed to stockholders. Profits have to be invested in the organization. The group must devote its activities exclusively to those that the Internal Revenue Service says will qualify. For instance, a charity must act only to help people, such as the poor or those disabled by illness or injury. An educational nonprofit, such as a private college, must devote itself to the advancement of learning.

Some nonprofits are nongovernmental organizations (NGOs). The International Committee of the Red Cross and Greenpeace are examples. NGOs are independent groups that raise money and use it to fund and carry out programs. They are typically international organizations and operate in countries other than those in which they have headquarters. You will learn more about NGOs elsewhere in the course. Other nonprofit organizations provide support to particular occupations or geographical areas. These include professional organizations, business associations, trade associations, and labor unions.

>> A food cooperative may depend on members who volunteer their time to work at the cooperative. Here, volunteers sort vegetables at a food co-op in California.

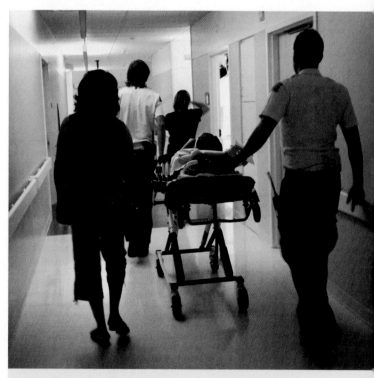

>> Nonprofit hospitals like this one seek to make money. They invest some of that profit in new technology and expansion, but much of it goes to charity care and community health programs.

 **Interactive Gallery**

>> Professional organizations such as the American Library Association often sponsor conferences at which members can network, attend workshops, and learn about trends in their field.

>> Chambers of commerce support businesses through events such as this Business Expo in Miami, Florida. They also work with government to promote pro-business policies.

Nonprofits have some limits on their political activity. Charities and religious groups, for instance, can meet with members of Congress to try to influence laws being considered. They cannot devote too much of their resources to this lobbying activity, however.

Professional Organizations Some nonprofits are **professional organizations** that work to improve the image, working conditions, and skill levels of people in particular occupations. Examples of this kind of nonprofit include the National Education Association for public school, college, and university workers; the American Veterinary Medical Association for veterinary professionals; the American Bar Association for lawyers; and the American Management Association for business professionals.

Professional organizations keep their members up-to-date on industry trends. Many of these organizations provide members with employment-related services such as job boards, training workshops, and networking opportunities. They also set codes of conduct that members are expected to follow.

For example, the American Medical Association sets guidelines for certain kinds of advertising. It wants doctors to present a professional, authoritative, and caring image as they seek new patients. The American Bar Association does not favor law firms that advertise their services for personal injury complaints.

Business Associations Organizations called **business associations** promote the collective business interests of a city, state, or other geographical area, or of a group of similar businesses. A city or state chamber of commerce, for instance, works with government officials to try to promote policies that will help businesses grow and thrive. Business associations may also address codes of conduct, just as professional associations do. Your local Better Business Bureau (BBB), sponsored by local businesses, is a nonprofit group. It aims to protect consumers by promoting an ethical and fair marketplace. Consumers who have complaints about the actions of a local business can take them to the BBB. Workers there will contact the business and try to work out a solution that satisfies both parties.

Trade Associations Nonprofit organizations that promote the interests of particular industries are called **trade associations.** The American Marketing Association, for example, aims to improve the image of companies that sell goods and services. All kinds of industries, from publishing to food processing, enjoy the support of trade associations. Many of these nonprofits hire lobbyists to work with state legislatures and the U.S. Congress. Lobbyists provide legislators with information about an industry and try to influence laws that affect that industry. Trade associations also hold meetings that members can attend to improve their skills or learn about industry trends.

Labor Unions A labor union is an organized group of workers whose aim is to improve working conditions, hours, wages, and fringe benefits for members. You will read about their history and role in another Lesson.

? COMPARE How do professional organizations differ from trade associations?

ASSESSMENT

1. **Draw Conclusions** One principle basic to cooperatives is democratic control of the organization by its members. How do you think important decisions are made in a cooperative?

2. **Solve Problems** A farmer must decide whether to sell his milk to a multinational food conglomerate or to join with other farmers to form a dairy cooperative. What incentive might the farmer have for selling through a cooperative rather than selling to a large corporation?

3. **Contrast** Show how cooperatives and nonprofits are different by identifying who benefits from each type of organization.

4. **Infer** How might professional organizations benefit consumers?

5. **Make Decisions** Why might a mayor or town council decide to fund the formation of a business association?

>> Colleges and universities often hold job fairs to help students make career choices and find employment. Having a college degree can mean greater earning opportunities.

▶ **Interactive Flipped Video**

>> Objectives

Describe how trends in the labor force are tracked.

Analyze past and present occupational trends.

Summarize how the U.S. labor force is changing.

Explain trends in the wages and benefits paid to U.S. workers.

>> Key Terms

labor force
outsourcing
offshoring
learning effect
screening effect
contingent
  employment
guest workers

Have you considered how you want to earn a living when you get out of school? You may be one of those people who has been focused on a career goal for as long as you can remember, or you may not have a clue. Is your goal to help others, make a lot of money, or travel? Whatever career you decide on, you will have to be prepared for change.

The Labor Force

Tracking the Labor Force

Economic trends affect workers in many ways. Over the past two decades, the U.S. economy has shifted from a manufacturing economy toward a service-producing economy. As jobs in industries such as technology and financial services have soared, the number of manufacturing jobs has dwindled.

How do we know the direction of changes in the job market? Each month, the Bureau of Labor Statistics (BLS) of the United States Department of Labor surveys households to assemble information on the labor force. Economists define the **labor force** as all nonmilitary people who are employed or unemployed.

Employment and Unemployment Economists consider people to be employed if they are 16 years or older and meet at least one of the following requirements:

- they worked at least one hour for pay in the past week;
- they worked 15 or more hours without pay in a family business, such as a farm or a family-owned store; and
- they held jobs but did not work due to illnesses, vacations, labor disputes, or bad weather.

People who have more than one job are counted only once. In 2013, about 6.7 million people held more than one job.

People who do not meet these criteria are counted as unemployed if they are either temporarily without work or are not working but have looked for jobs within the last four weeks. To be counted as unemployed, then, a person either must have work lined up for the future, or must be actively searching for a new job.

Some groups of people are considered to be outside the labor force. The BLS uses the term "discouraged workers" to describe people who once sought work but have given up looking for a job. They are not counted in employment statistics. In addition, full-time students, parents who stay at home to raise children, and retirees are not considered unemployed, and thus are not counted in employment statistics. **Figure 5.1** summarizes the groups that make up the U.S. labor force.

The Labor Market Today The Bureau of Labor Statistics provides answers to two important economic questions. First, it says how many people are in the labor force. Second, it tells us how many are employed and unemployed at any given time. You can find BLS data at the Web site for the Bureau of Labor Statistics.

The BLS provides information about historical trends. For example, the percentage of the U.S. population in the labor force has increased from 59.2 percent in 1950 to 63.2 percent in 2013. The number of employed civilians in the United States in 2013 was close to 144 million. About 76 million of these workers were men. About 68 million were women.

The BLS also reports the unemployment rate each month. Economists studying the health of the economy monitor these monthly unemployment figures. In July 2007, the unemployment rate was 4.6 percent. The highest unemployment rate from 1997 to 2007 was 6.3 percent in June of 2003.

Beginning in 2008, however, the rate of unemployment in the United States began to rise. In just one year, the rate jumped from 5.8 percent in 2008 to a staggering 9.3 percent in 2009. Then, in 2010, it reached its highest number in nearly 30 years, peaking at 9.6 percent. Since that time, however, it has been slowly but steadily decreasing. In November of 2013, it stood at 6.6 percent.

? **RECALL** Give two examples of employment data that the Bureau of Labor Statistics provides information about.

Occupational Trends

The job market does not stay the same all the time. It grows as the nation's economy and population grow. The jobs that make up the job market also change. New

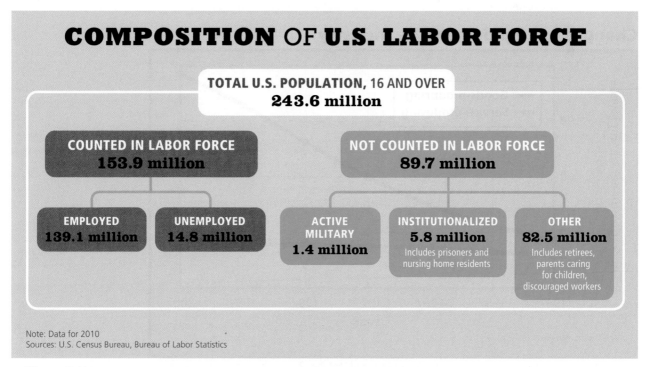

COMPOSITION OF U.S. LABOR FORCE

TOTAL U.S. POPULATION, 16 AND OVER
243.6 million

COUNTED IN LABOR FORCE
153.9 million

NOT COUNTED IN LABOR FORCE
89.7 million

EMPLOYED
139.1 million

UNEMPLOYED
14.8 million

ACTIVE MILITARY
1.4 million

INSTITUTIONALIZED
5.8 million
Includes prisoners and nursing home residents

OTHER
82.5 million
Includes retirees, parents caring for children, discouraged workers

Note: Data for 2010
Sources: U.S. Census Bureau, Bureau of Labor Statistics

>> **Figure 5.1** The chart shows that more than a third of the population 16 and over is not in the labor force. **Analyze Charts** How is being unemployed different from not being in the labor force?

technologies or new industries bring new jobs to life—and cause others to fade. Shifts in the job market reflect major shifts in what our economy produces. You can better understand these changes by looking at them in a historical context.

A Changing Economy At its founding, the United States was a nation of farmers. Most people had few job opportunities beyond the corn, wheat, cotton, and tobacco fields. In the 1800s in the North, however, this focus on agriculture gradually yielded to the Industrial Revolution. The coming of the machine age energized the economy and created new jobs in textile mills, shoe factories, and other new manufacturing enterprises.

By the early decades of the 1900s, heavy manufacturing had become the powerhouse of the U.S. economy. New corporate empires were born: John D. Rockefeller's Standard Oil in 1863; Andrew Carnegie's steelworks in the 1870s; Henry Ford's automobile company in 1903. These huge firms employed thousands of workers.

The mid-twentieth-century boom in electronics—led by radio and television—produced a new surge of factory jobs. Employment growth centered in the Northeast and Midwest, in companies such as General Electric, Westinghouse, Carrier, and Goodyear.

In the 1970s, the revolution in personal computers opened another new horizon for employment. As computer use continues to rise, the demand for computer-related occupations continues to grow. In this "Information Age," even some traditional jobs, from trucking to farming to car sales, now require some computer skills. By the early 2000s, over half of American workers reported using computers on the job. More than a quarter of all workers in the agriculture, forestry, fishing, and construction industries used computers.

Fewer Goods, More Services The spread of computers is not the only change that has transformed the American economy. In the past one hundred or so years, the United States has shifted from a manufacturing economy to a service economy. Our production of services is increasing faster than our production of goods. (See **Figure 5.2**.) In 2005, five workers produced services for every one who produced goods. The service sector includes financial services, banking, education, and online services.

Effects of International Competition While the number of service jobs has increased, the United States has lost manufacturing jobs. In 1990, almost 17.7 million Americans worked in manufacturing industries. Fifteen years later, the number had fallen to 14.2 million. Many workers have been laid off due to plant closings

Changes in Employment, by Industry

SOURCE: Bureau of Labor Statistics

>> **Figure 5.2** The graph compares the growth of service-producing and goods-producing industries over time. **Analyze Graphs** About how many service-producing jobs were added in the period shown?

▶ **Interactive Gallery**

Industry in the United States

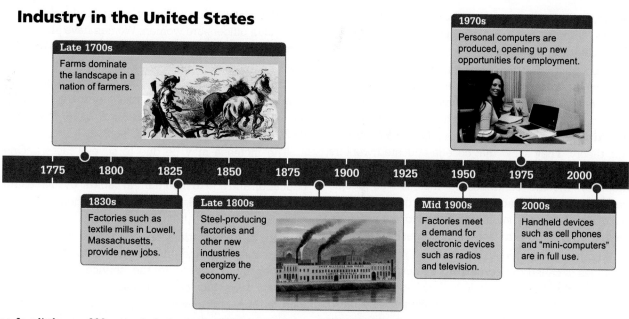

Late 1700s
Farms dominate the landscape in a nation of farmers.

1830s
Factories such as textile mills in Lowell, Massachusetts, provide new jobs.

Late 1800s
Steel-producing factories and other new industries energize the economy.

1970s
Personal computers are produced, opening up new opportunities for employment.

Mid 1900s
Factories meet a demand for electronic devices such as radios and television.

2000s
Handheld devices such as cell phones and "mini-computers" are in full use.

1775 1800 1825 1850 1875 1900 1925 1950 1975 2000

>> In a little over 200 years, industry in the United States has changed dramatically. **Analyze Information** What 50-year period do you think has seen the most change and innovation, and why?

or moves, too little work, or the replacement of jobs by new technology.

These conditions can be the result of **outsourcing,** in which companies contract with another company to do a specific job that would otherwise be done by a company's own workers. Most companies will outsource work in some way.

In the past, limits on the mobility of capital and labor meant that most goods sold in the United States were made by American workers in American factories. Today, capital and labor can be easily moved from place to place—and even from country to country. The movement of some of a company's operations, or resources of production, to another country is known as **offshoring.** American firms can build factories and hire workers in countries where wages and other costs are lower. American stores can buy a wide range of goods made in foreign countries to sell in the United States.

As less-skilled manufacturing jobs moved overseas, the Americans who had filled these jobs had to find new work. Many went back to school or entered job training programs to gain new skills.

These shifts in demand for workers are another example of supply and demand in operation. Demand for skilled service workers is rising, so wages for skilled workers go up. These higher wages persuade more people to train for these jobs to meet the demand. Meanwhile, as demand for manufacturing workers drops off, there is a surplus of these workers who find

that they must become more skilled in order to compete in the job market.

In recent years, businesses have looked abroad not only for factory workers, but also for the labor of highly skilled workers. By the early 2000s, companies increasingly looked offshore for computer engineers, software programmers, and other high-skilled jobs. This trend has affected other fields, such as auto design and some medical services, as well.

❓ RECALL Why do companies engage in offshoring?

The Changing Labor Force

Not only have jobs changed; workers have also changed. In the 1950s, a typical American worker was a white man who had graduated from high school and had found a secure 40-hour-a-week job where he probably hoped to stay until retiring at age 65. Not anymore. Today, more women and members of minority groups are in the workforce. In addition, someone entering the workforce can expect to have four or five different jobs during his or her working life.

College Graduates To get jobs, people must have human capital—the education, training, and experience that make them useful in the workplace. More and more, a high school diploma alone is not enough to prepare a person for financial success. To get—and succeed in—a job, people need more education. Getting a good education, however, requires money, time, and effort. Higher earnings compensate these workers for their advanced-training costs.

Economists offer two explanations for the connection between educational advancement and higher wages. The theory that education increases efficiency of production and thus results in higher wages is called the **learning effect.** The statistics in **Figure 5.3** support this theory. They show that college-educated workers have a higher median weekly income than high-school dropouts. Income continues to increase as people gain even more education. People with doctorates and professional degrees, such as doctors and lawyers, earn more than people with bachelor's degrees.

Another theory about the relationship of education to wages is called the **screening effect.** This theory suggests that the completion of college signals to employers that a job applicant is intelligent and hard-working. The skills and determination necessary to complete college may also be useful qualities for employees to have. According to this theory, a college degree does not increase productivity, but simply identifies people who may be good employees because of their perseverance and innate skills.

Women at Work The changing face of the labor force can be seen at your local bank. A few decades ago, men greeted customers at the tellers' windows and served as loan officers. Today, most bank tellers and many loan officers are women. Women have also taken a greater role in national defense and in police and fire departments across the country.

These changes over the past several decades are clearly shown in labor statistics numbers. In 1960, almost 38 percent of women belonged to the labor force. By 2012, that rate was nearly 58 percent.

The increase may be due to several factors. One is that women were encouraged to pursue a higher education and add to their human capital. By increasing their human capital, they increased their potential earnings.

With the expectation of earning more, more women entered the workforce. In addition, as more and more jobs become available in the service sector of the economy, fewer jobs call for physical strength. Instead, jobs require brainpower and personal skills, placing men and women on equal footing.

In recent times, economists believe that women are being affected by the same economic problems as men, including layoffs and offshoring. Nevertheless, for women in their prime working years, there appears to be little change in employment. In 2011, the Bureau of Labor Statistics reported that 69 percent of women ages 25 to 54 were employed. This was down from 74.9 percent in 2000.

Education and Income, 2012

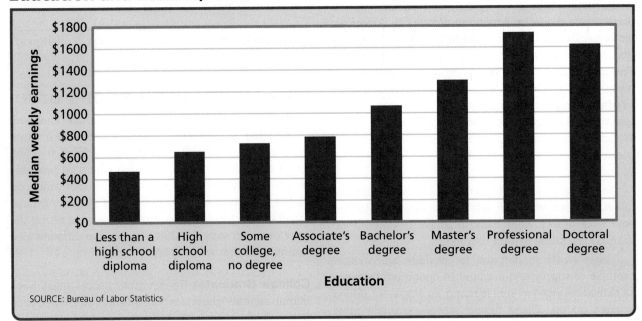

SOURCE: Bureau of Labor Statistics

>> **Figure 5.3** More education corresponds to greater income. **Analyze Graphs** How do the earnings of someone with a professional degree compare to those of someone with a high school diploma?

Part-time Employees in the United States, 2002–2012

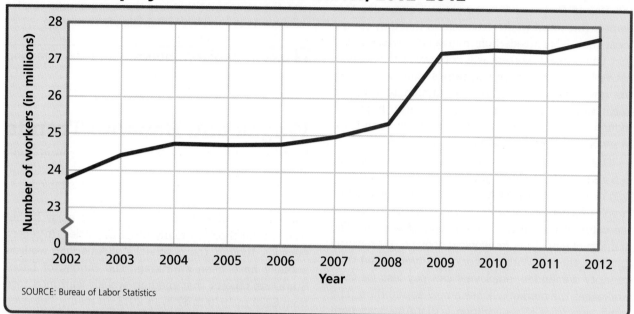

SOURCE: Bureau of Labor Statistics

>> Part-time employment has increased since 2002. **Analyze Graphs** By about how much did the number of part-time workers change between 2008 and 2009?

Temporary Workers In another important trend, more and more businesses are replacing permanent, full-time workers with part-time and temporary workers. These temporary and part-time jobs are known as **contingent employment.**

Some temporary workers come from "temp" agencies. These are companies that have a pool of experienced workers who can be hired out to organizations on a short-term basis. The organization that needs the workers pays the temp agency. The agency, in turn, pays the worker a share of that fee, keeping the rest to cover expenses and profit.

Other temporary workers are hired directly by firms as contract workers, people hired for a specified time period or to complete a certain task.

Contingent employment is becoming more common even in occupations that had been very secure jobs. For example, some software engineers and attorneys are now hired as contract workers. When the workers complete their part of the project they were hired for, they are released. These highly skilled workers are generally well paid, with some earning as much as permanent workers.

Experts have identified several reasons for the increased use of temporary employees.

- Flexible work arrangements allow firms to easily adjust their workforce to changing demand for their output. At times of reduced demand, they can easily lay off temporary workers or reduce workers' hours instead of paying employees who are idle. When business picks up, companies can rehire whatever workers they need.

- Temporary workers in many industries are paid less and given fewer benefits (if any) than permanent, full-time workers. Thus, hiring more temporary workers cuts costs.

- Discharging temporary workers is easier and less costly than discharging regular, permanent employees. Many employers give full-time employees severance pay of several weeks' worth of wages or salary when they lay off workers. They do not have to make these payments to temporary workers.

- Some workers actually prefer these flexible arrangements to traditional, permanent jobs. The market, then, reflects their preferences. On the other hand, BLS studies show that a majority of temporary workers would prefer permanent jobs.

The Impact of Foreign-Born Workers One topic that has received much attention in recent years is the impact of foreign-born workers on the labor force. In 2005, foreign-born workers numbered about 22 million people, nearly 15 percent of all workers in the United States.

Many immigrant workers are able to become permanent residents. Some foreign-born workers are

guest workers. They are allowed to live and work in the United States only temporarily. Companies that want to hire guest workers must show that they cannot meet their labor needs from native-born workers and that using guest workers will not lower the wages of native-born workers. If companies can prove this, the government gives them permission to bring in guest workers. Guest workers hold jobs in high-tech industries that demand highly skilled workers, and also in lower-skilled work such as agricultural labor.

The impact of immigrants on the labor force is hotly debated. Some analysts say that immigrant workers hold down the wages of Americans. This effect shows supply and demand at work. As more immigrants enter the country, they increase the supply of workers. The demand of employers for workers does not necessarily increase, though. With greater quantity supplied than quantity demanded, employers can pay less for their workers as the market reaches a new equilibrium. The result, say critics of immigration, is that American-born workers see their wages drop. They also face stiffer competition for jobs.

Other analysts say that immigrant workers fill an important role in the economy. First, they say, lower-skilled immigrant workers do jobs that Americans are unwilling to do because the wages are low. As a result, important work gets done that would not be done otherwise. Second, because immigrants take those jobs, the companies that hire them can charge less for their goods or services, which benefits everyone.

? CHECK UNDERSTANDING How is the screening effect beneficial to employers?

Wages and Benefits Trends

Labor economists study not only who is in and out of the workforce, but how they are doing in terms of earnings and benefits. Today, the picture is mixed.

Real Wages Down American workers enjoy higher wages than those in many other countries. In recent decades, though, the paychecks of American workers actually have been shrinking. The Bureau of Labor Statistics reports that median weekly earnings rose from $232 in 1979 to $770 in 2013. In reality, however, there has been no actual increase. To make a better comparison, economists make calculations to hold the value of the dollar constant. This takes away the effect of inflation—the rise of prices over time. In constant 1982–1984 dollars, median wages actually declined, from a value of $335 per week in 1979 to $332 in 2013. In other words, real weekly wages have fallen about $3 in 34 years.

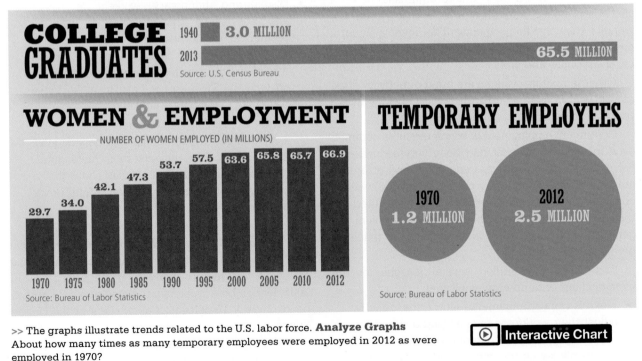

LABOR FORCE TRENDS IN THE UNITED STATES

COLLEGE GRADUATES
1940 — 3.0 MILLION
2013 — 65.5 MILLION
Source: U.S. Census Bureau

WOMEN & EMPLOYMENT
NUMBER OF WOMEN EMPLOYED (IN MILLIONS)

1970	1975	1980	1985	1990	1995	2000	2005	2010	2012
29.7	34.0	42.1	47.3	53.7	57.5	63.6	65.8	65.7	66.9

Source: Bureau of Labor Statistics

TEMPORARY EMPLOYEES
1970 — 1.2 MILLION
2012 — 2.5 MILLION
Source: Bureau of Labor Statistics

>> The graphs illustrate trends related to the U.S. labor force. **Analyze Graphs** About how many times as many temporary employees were employed in 2012 as were employed in 1970?

▶ **Interactive Chart**

Why have average real wages decreased in the last couple of decades? One reason, as you have read, is that greater competition from foreign companies has decreased the demand for workers. Deregulation of many domestic industries, such as trucking, air travel, and telecommunications, may have forced firms to cut employees' wages as competition has intensified. The increased use of temporary work has also held down wages.

Cost of Benefits For many workers, benefits such as pensions and health insurance are a significant share of total compensation. This share rose fairly steadily during the 1900s and early 2000s. By 2005, employer-provided benefits added $7.87 an hour to the cost of workers. Benefits now make up nearly 30 percent of workers' compensation. This adds up to a large cost for employers—especially since benefits like health insurance are becoming more expensive.

Social Security and Medicare taxes are included in these benefits, since they are used to pay benefits to retired and disabled workers. Most workers know that Social Security taxes are deducted from their paychecks each month.

Did you know that employers pay a matching amount? Thus, workers and employers share this cost. In addition, Social Security and Medicare tax rates have risen substantially in recent decades, causing further increases in employers' benefits costs.

Employers are finding that these rising benefits costs increase the cost of doing business and thus cut into their profits. As a result, some types of contingent employees, such as independent contractors, become an attractive labor resource for companies because these workers do not have to be paid benefits. Offshoring and outsourcing also help firms to cut their expenses. If benefits costs continue to rise, companies will be pressured to pursue these steps to a greater extent. Those responses may prove unpopular with workers.

? IDENTIFY SUPPORTING DETAILS Who pays Social Security taxes?

ASSESSMENT

1. Who makes up the labor force?

>> Because real wages have actually gone down in recent years, the average worker is able to purchase less with a paycheck than he or she would have been able to purchase in 1979.

2. Harry is a 34-year-old sergeant in the United States Air Force. He has been employed full time with the Air Force since graduating from college. Is Harry considered to be part of the U.S. labor force? Why or why not?

3. Ignacio owns a small business that employs 12 full-time workers. He has recently been told by his financial advisor that he would benefit financially from adopting a contingent employment strategy. What would Ignacio have to do in order to take his financial advisor's advice?

4. What does the learning effect demonstrate about continuing education?

5. Why are contracted workers often a more attractive alternative for employers?

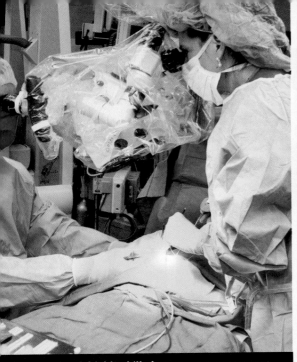

>> A highly skilled neurosurgeon can earn over $500,000 per year. Neurosurgeons must complete four years of medical school and several more years of residency training.

▶ Interactive Flipped Video

How important is it to you to make a lot of money? If it is very important, then you had better think carefully about what you want to do for a living. Some jobs and professions are very well paid. In 2012, the mean annual salary for surgeons was about $230,000; but surgeons may earn much more. A lawyer might make $600 for a one-hour consultation, while the clerk at the local convenience store might make $8.00 an hour. What will determine the size of your paycheck?

>> Objectives

Analyze how supply and demand in the labor market affect wage levels.

Describe how skill levels and education affect wages.

Explain how laws against wage discrimination affect wage levels.

Identify other factors affecting wage levels, such as minimum wage and workplace safety laws.

>> Key Terms

derived demand
productivity of labor
equilibrium wage
unskilled labor
semi-skilled labor
skilled labor
professional labor
glass ceiling
labor union
featherbedding

Labor and Wages

Supply, Demand, and the Labor Market

The law of supply and demand applies to the world of labor and wages. What people earn for what they do is largely a matter of how many people are willing and able to do the job and how much that job is in demand. Like eggs or airplanes or pet iguanas, labor is a commodity that is bought and sold.

In a free market economy, the market finds its own equilibrium price for labor. In a mixed economy, the government also plays a role.

Employment or unemployment in a labor market depends on how closely the demand for workers—the number of available jobs—meets the supply of workers seeking jobs. Let's examine how supply and demand operate in labor markets.

Labor Demand The demand for labor comes from private firms and government agencies that hire workers to produce goods and services. In most labor markets, dozens, or even hundreds, of firms compete with one another for workers.

Demand for labor is called a **derived demand,** because it is derived, or set, by the demand for another good or service. In this case, that other demand is the demand for what a worker produces. For example, the demand for cooks in a market depends on the demand for restaurant meals.

In a competitive labor market, workers are usually paid according to the value of what they produce. For example, competition among restaurants results in a wage for cooks that reflects the cook's productivity. **Productivity of labor** is the quantity of output produced by a unit of labor.

The productivity of a cook's labor, for example, can be measured as the cost of a meal. Suppose that most of the restaurants in a city pay $12 an hour for cooks and that each cook generates $20 an hour in revenue for the restaurants. The possibility of profit will attract other entrepreneurs to open restaurants. Competition will push up the wage for cooks. As a result, cooks will be paid close to the value of their productivity of labor.

Now look at the demand curve for labor, shown in **Figure 5.4**. Notice that it is negatively sloped, reflecting the law of demand. The higher the price of labor, the smaller the quantity of labor demanded by employers. Restaurants are more likely to hire more cooks at $12 an hour than at $16 an hour, because the lower cost means they can earn more profits on each cook's labor.

Labor Supply The supply of labor comes from people willing to work for wages. As the graph in **Figure 5.5** shows, the supply curve is positively sloped, reflecting the law of supply. In other words, the higher the wage, the larger the quantity of labor supplied.

This is logical. It simply means that the higher the wage for a job, the greater the number of people who will be attracted to that job. A higher wage for cooks encourages people who would choose other occupations to acquire the training required to become a cook.

Equilibrium Wage We know that at market equilibrium, the quantity of a good supplied will equal the quantity demanded. Economic factors—the supply of labor and the demand for it—combine to determine an equilibrium price. Because the equilibrium price makes the quantity that suppliers want to sell equal to the quantity that demanders want to buy, there is a tendency for the price or quantity not to change. That stability applies to the equilibrium price in one market, though. These factors may be different in different parts of the country, or at different times.

The **equilibrium wage** is the wage rate, or price of labor services, that is set when the supply of workers meets the demand for workers in the labor market. On a graph, the equilibrium wage is shown by the intersection of the supply and demand curves. (See **Figure 5.6**.) At equilibrium, there is no pressure to raise or lower wages.

Labor Demand

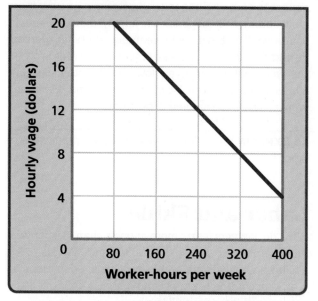

>> **Figure 5.4** The graph shows a demand curve for restaurant cooks. **Analyze Graphs** If each cook works a 40-hour workweek, how many cooks will be hired at $12 an hour and at $16 an hour?

Labor Supply

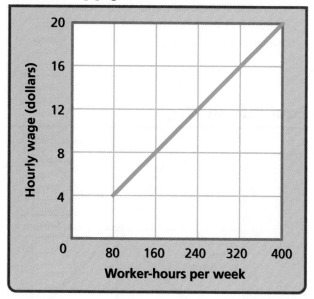

>> **Figure 5.5** The graph shows a supply curve for restaurant cooks. **Analyze Graphs** Why is the supply curve positively sloped?

How do these theories affect how much you should expect to earn working in a pet store or a grocery store next summer? It depends on supply and demand in your area. If stores do not hire many additional workers during the summer and a lot of teenagers want to work, the wage will be relatively low. On the other hand, if stores want to hire a lot of teenagers and few teens want to work, the wage will be higher.

? EXPLAIN What determines the equilibrium wage of labor?

Labor and Skills

Why do lawyers earn more money than carpenters, and carpenters more than cashiers? Wages vary according to workers' skill levels and education, as well as according to supply and demand. Jobs are often categorized into four skill levels:

- **Unskilled labor** requires no specialized skills, education, or training. Workers in these jobs usually earn an hourly wage. They include dishwashers, messengers, janitors, and many farmworkers.
- **Semi-skilled labor** requires minimal specialized skills and education, such as the operation of certain types of equipment. Semi-skilled workers usually earn an hourly wage.

They include lifeguards, word processors, short-order cooks, and many construction and factory workers.

- **Skilled labor** requires specialized abilities and training to do tasks such as operating complicated equipment. Skilled workers need little supervision, yet usually earn an hourly wage. They include auto mechanics, bank tellers, plumbers, firefighters, chefs, and carpenters.
- **Professional labor** demands advanced skills and education. Professionals are usually white-collar workers who receive a salary. Professionals include managers, teachers, bankers, doctors, actors, professional athletes, and computer programmers.

Labor supply and demand can create a significant difference in pay scales for workers with various skills. For example, the labor market for medical doctors is relatively high compared to the market for construction workers. Because the supply of doctors is relatively low and the demand is relatively high, there is a high equilibrium wage.

By comparison, the supply of construction workers is high relative to the demand for them. Hence, the equilibrium wage for construction workers would be much lower than that for doctors.

Doctors and other highly educated workers—and those with extensive training and experience—enjoy demand for their services that is high relative to the supply, leading to higher earnings. The demand for workers with less education and training tends to be lower relative to the supply, so their earnings are lower. Experienced workers are desirable because they tend to be more productive than those newer to that job.

Another reason that earnings vary is differences in working conditions. The level of danger in doing a job, the physical or emotional stress involved, and the location of the work can all change the equilibrium wage.

Economic studies have shown that jobs with high accident and fatality rates pay relatively high wages. Workers who do dangerous jobs require compensation for the risk they take. Thus, there is a higher equilibrium wage rate for dangerous jobs, as shown in **Figure 5.7**.

? EXPRESS IDEAS CLEARLY How do education, training, and experience affect wages?

Equilibrium Wage

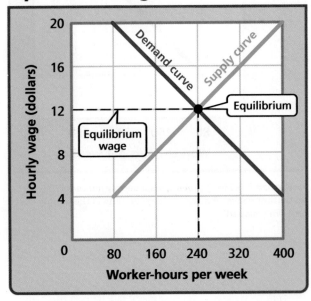

>> **Figure 5.6** The graph shows the equilibrium wage for cooks in a labor market. **Analyze Graphs** What is the equilibrium wage, and how many cooks working a 40-hour week would make that wage?

 **Interactive Chart**

Comparison: Wages for High-Risk, Low-Risk Jobs

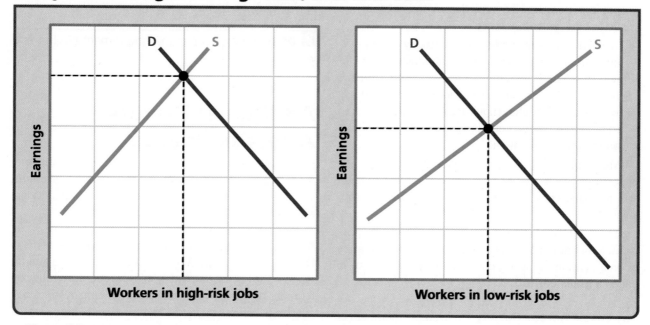

>> **Figure 5.7** The graphs show how wages compare for similar jobs with different degrees of risk. **Analyze Graphs** How do the demand curves in the two graphs compare? What can you conclude?

Discrimination in the Labor Market

As we have seen, wages for a particular job should end up at the equilibrium price of labor for that job. However, some people are paid less because of the social group they belong to. For instance, in the past, women and members of minority groups often received lower wages than white male workers for the same work. This practice is wage discrimination.

Some employers defended wage discrimination against women by claiming that men needed the money to support families, while women were simply working to earn extra cash. Discrimination against minority workers reflected racial and ethnic prejudice in society. In recent decades, national or state legislators have tried to end these practices by passing laws prohibiting wage discrimination.

Laws Against Wage Discrimination In the 1960s, the United States Congress passed several anti-discrimination laws that prevent companies from paying lower wages to some employees based on factors that are not related to skill or productivity, like gender or race. The Equal Pay Act of 1963 required that male and female employees in the same workplace performing the same job receive the same pay. Title VII of the Civil Rights Act of 1964 prohibited job discrimination

on the basis of race, sex, color, religion, or nationality. (Religious institutions and small businesses are exempt from the law.) The Civil Rights Act also established the Equal Employment Opportunity Commission (EEOC) to enforce the provisions of the law. Workers who feel they have been discriminated against can complain to the EEOC, which will investigate the matter. If necessary, the commission can take companies to court to force them to comply with the law.

Pay Levels for Women Despite protections, women still earn less than men. This earnings gap has persisted over time. Historically, it has been the result of three factors:

- *"Women's work."* Women have historically been discouraged from entering certain high-paying professions, such as medicine, law, and corporate management. Instead, they have been encouraged to pursue careers such as teaching, nursing, and clerical work. With so many women seeking work in these occupations, the labor supply has been generally high. As you know, a large supply of labor tends to produce a relatively low equilibrium wage.

- *Human capital.* Overall, women have had less education, training, and experience than men. This lack of human capital makes women's labor, in economic terms, less productive. As a result, fewer women are eligible for the higher-paying, traditionally male-dominated jobs in fields such as engineering.

- *Women's career paths.* Even today, some employers assume that female employees are not interested in career advancement. This perception can be a roadblock for women in the workplace. The challenges many women face in trying to balance child-rearing and a career adds to this perception.

Much progress has been made in creating job opportunities for women. Yet some qualified women still find that they cannot receive promotions to top-level jobs.

This unofficial barrier that sometimes prevents women and minorities from advancing to the top ranks of organizations that are dominated by white men is called a **glass ceiling.**

Pay Levels Across Society On average, members of minority groups tend to receive lower pay than whites do. Part of the wage gap has been caused by a history of racial discrimination. On average, whites have had access to more education and work experience, enabling them to develop skills that are in demand. Nondiscrimination laws, in part, are designed to give minority workers improved access to education and job opportunities so they can develop more human capital and lessen the wage gap. (See **Figure 5.8**.) The entire

economy benefits when all workers have a higher level of skill and can be more productive.

❓ DESCRIBE How has the government tried to end wage discrimination?

Additional Factors Affecting Wages

In addition to laws forbidding discrimination, several other factors can affect wages. These include minimum wage laws, workplace safety laws, employer actions, and labor unions.

Minimum Wage Laws In 1938, Congress passed the Fair Labor Standards Act. This law created a minimum wage—the lowest amount employers could lawfully pay for most types of work—and required employers to pay overtime for work beyond 40 hours a week. Many states also have their own minimum wage laws. Because of these laws, employers may be forced to pay more than the equilibrium wage for unskilled labor.

Supporters of the minimum wage argue that it helps the poorest American workers earn enough to support themselves. Opponents say that artificially increasing the price of labor actually causes a decrease in quantity demanded. In other words, individual employees will earn more, but companies will hire fewer of them.

Median Income by Gender and Ethnicity, 2009

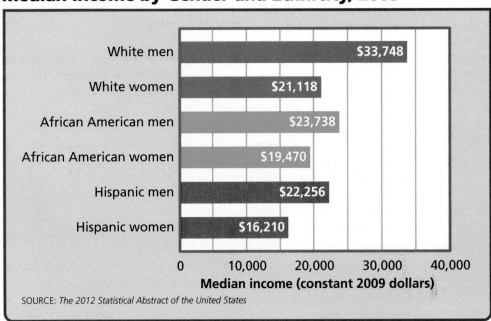

Group	Median income (constant 2009 dollars)
White men	$33,748
White women	$21,118
African American men	$23,738
African American women	$19,470
Hispanic men	$22,256
Hispanic women	$16,210

SOURCE: *The 2012 Statistical Abstract of the United States*

>> **Figure 5.8 Analyze Graphs** According to the bar graph, which group has the lowest median income?

Safety Laws The federal government created the Occupational Safety and Health Administration (OSHA) in 1970 to establish standards for safer working conditions. OSHA policies were issued in an effort to save lives, prevent injuries, and protect the health of workers in the private sector. All laws requiring certain minimum levels of safety also could have an impact on wages.

If a law or policy increases safety at work, it may also decrease wages because workers are willing to work for lower wages when jobs are safer. By holding down wages, the law lowers an employer's costs. Of course, the employer will usually have to spend money to comply with safety regulations, which may more than offset the employer's savings from any wage reduction.

Employers Respond to Wage Levels Employers may also take actions to try to affect wage levels. For example, a company might try to cut labor costs by substituting machines for people. In other words, employers can replace human capital with physical capital.

Take furniture making, for example. In countries where labor is relatively cheap, furniture may be handmade by workers. In the United States, where labor is relatively expensive, manufacturers have substituted sophisticated machinery for more expensive human labor. Another increasingly common substitution involves customer service call centers, where automated answering services have replaced live telephone operators to direct incoming calls.

Other examples of substituting physical capital for human capital include automated teller machines (ATMs), which take the place of bank tellers, and mechanized assembly lines, which can eliminate the need for some manufacturing workers. These technological advances have greatly reduced the number of employees that banks and manufacturing companies hire.

Even if firms cannot use technology to replace labor, they may be able to reduce their labor costs in other ways. For instance, companies may outsource jobs to other parts of the world where labor is more plentiful and therefore cheaper. They may also choose to hire temporary workers.

Unions Workers who are unhappy with their wages also have several choices. In a competitive labor market, they might get higher-paying jobs from another employer. Some people change careers, either by choice or out of necessity. Although labor unions are becoming less of a force in the American economy, workers might decide to join a union and press for higher pay.

>> **Analyze Political Cartoons** What does the cartoon illustrate about the different opportunities for men and women in some corporations?

>> In 1938, unionized garment workers in San Francisco went on a strike that resulted in their obtaining higher wages, better hours, and improved working conditions.

>> Many teachers belong to unions that negotiate teacher contracts with school districts. Contracts focus on specific items such as salary, sick leave, and vacation.

▶ **Interactive Gallery**

A **labor union** is an organization of workers that tries to improve working conditions, wages, and benefits for its members. One of the key goals of unions is to get wage increases for their members. As you will learn, unions allow workers to negotiate wage levels as a group rather than having to deal individually with employers. Their combined bargaining power is sometimes more effective at persuading employers to raise wages.

Nationally, union members do tend to earn higher wages than nonunion workers in similar jobs. In 2012, the median weekly earnings for workers represented by unions were about $200 higher than the median weekly earnings for nonunion workers. That amounts to a difference of $5 an hour for a 40-hour workweek.

Some economists argue that unions depress the wages of nonunion workers. They offer this reasoning:

1. Unions press employers to raise their members' wages.

2. When wages go up, the quantity of labor demanded goes down. Thus, the number of union jobs decreases.

3. As union jobs are cut, more workers are forced to seek nonunion jobs.

4. An increase in the supply of nonunion workers causes the wage rate for nonunion jobs to fall.

In addition, some unions have engaged in **featherbedding,** negotiating labor contracts that keep unnecessary workers on the company payroll. A notable example of this practice occurred in the railroad industry. In the early days of railroads, a "cabooseman" had to ride at the back of the train to operate a rear brake that stopped the train. Yet even after design changes allowed the engineer at the front of the train to operate rear brakes, unions managed to keep caboosemen on the payroll. These workers received full wages and benefits for doing nothing.

People who support unions counter that without the ability to organize, workers have little power compared to that of employers. Unless workers join together, they say, employers can dictate wage levels and working conditions. Since they can usually find replacement workers, their employees might have little real choice. In a later Lesson, you will learn more about the history of unions in the United States. You will also learn about the advantages and disadvantages of unions.

? **SUMMARIZE** What three actions can employers take to reduce the cost of wages?

ASSESSMENT

1. **Cite Evidence** Why is the demand for labor called a derived demand?

2. **Analyze Information** If an advertising business buys new computers for its employees, how might its productivity of labor be affected?

3. **Analyze Information** What generally happens to the equilibrium wage when demand for workers decreases and supply rises?

4. **Identify** What term describes an unofficial barrier that sometimes prevents qualified women from receiving promotions to top-level jobs?

5. **Explain** How might union employers benefit from workplace safety laws?

What comes to mind when you think of Labor Day? Do you think of the holiday as summer's last hurrah—a final weekend spent frolicking at the beach or enjoying a summer picnic at the park before school gets underway? The origins of the holiday can be traced to 1882, when labor leader Peter J. McGuire suggested a day celebrating the American worker. On September 5, 1882, some 10,000 workers marched in New York City in a parade sponsored by a labor group called the Knights of Labor. Twelve years later, Congress made Labor Day a federal holiday to be spent any way workers wished, including going to the beach or a picnic at the park.

>> Textile workers in North Carolina march in a parade on Labor Day in 1934.

▶ **Interactive Flipped Video**

Labor Unions

Organized Labor

Labor unions support the interests of workers with respect to wages, benefits, and working conditions. They provide workers with the power of collective bargaining, which has proven to be an effective tool to extract concessions from employers.

Shifts in the U.S. economy, however, have had a major impact on unions. The loss of manufacturing-sector jobs and the increased number of women in the workplace have been major factors contributing to the steep decline in union membership over the past 50 years.

As you read earlier, wages are determined by the forces of supply and demand. Competition among firms keeps a worker's wages close to his or her level of productivity. In general, workers who command the highest wages are those with specialized skills and those who are in short supply.

What about employees who feel that they are paid too little, work too many hours, or labor in unsafe conditions? What can these employees do? One option is to seek better wages and working conditions with a different employer. Many economists, in fact, argue that a competitive labor market helps prevent low pay and dangerous working conditions, because workers will leave companies with these characteristics to work elsewhere.

>> Objectives

Explain why American workers have formed labor unions.

Summarize the history of the labor movement in the United States.

Analyze the reasons for the decline of the labor movement.

Explain how labor and management negotiate contracts.

>> Key Terms

strike
right-to-work law
blue-collar worker
white-collar worker
collective bargaining
mediation
arbitration

Many American workers have tried to gain some control over their wages and working conditions by forming labor unions. They reason that an individual worker does not have the power to change how an employer acts but that by banding together, workers can win gains from employers. In 2012, only about 11 percent of workers in the United States belonged to a labor union. In the past, though, unions had a strong influence on the nation's economy. In order to understand the role of labor unions today, we will look at how labor unions rose to power.

IDENTIFY MAIN IDEAS Why do workers join labor unions?

>> Dolores Huerta cofounded an important farmworkers' union. She continued to support the rights of unionized farmworkers and has been awarded the Presidential Medal of Freedom.

The History of the Labor Movement

The union movement took shape over the course of more than a century. It faced many obstacles along the way, including violence and legal challenges from companies.

Working Conditions in the 1800s Labor unions arose largely in response to changes in working conditions brought on by the Industrial Revolution in the early and mid-1800s. The spread of manufacturing in this period introduced factory work to the United States.

By today's standards, this work was not enviable. In garment factories, iron plants, and gunpowder mills, laborers worked 12- to 16-hour days, 7 days a week, for meager wages. Working conditions were poor. Men, women, and children as young as five years old operated machines so dangerous that many people lost fingers and limbs. Injured workers often lost their jobs.

Today, many firms try to retain their most skilled workers by treating them well. In 1855, however, that was hardly the case. One factory boss bluntly summarized his attitude toward workers:

> I regard people just as I regard my machinery. So long as they can do my work for what I choose to pay them, I keep them, getting out of them all that I can.
>
> —manager of a textile mill in Fall River, Massachusetts, 1855

>> In the nineteenth century, children were forced to work in factories.

Unions Take Hold As early as the 1790s, whispers of worker discontent grew into organized protests. Skilled workers began to form unions to protect their interests.

Key Events in the U.S. Labor Movement

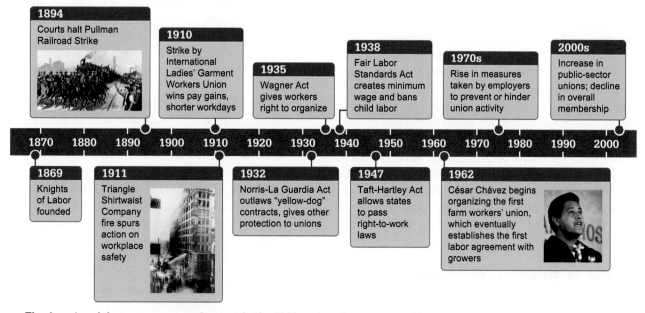

1894 Courts halt Pullman Railroad Strike

1910 Strike by International Ladies' Garment Workers Union wins pay gains, shorter workdays

1935 Wagner Act gives workers right to organize

1938 Fair Labor Standards Act creates minimum wage and bans child labor

1970s Rise in measures taken by employers to prevent or hinder union activity

2000s Increase in public-sector unions; decline in overall membership

1870 1880 1890 1900 1910 1920 1930 1940 1950 1960 1970 1980 1990 2000

1869 Knights of Labor founded

1911 Triangle Shirtwaist Company fire spurs action on workplace safety

1932 Norris-La Guardia Act outlaws "yellow-dog" contracts, gives other protection to unions

1947 Taft-Hartley Act allows states to pass right-to-work laws

1962 César Chávez begins organizing the first farm workers' union, which eventually establishes the first labor agreement with growers

>> The American labor movement got its start in the 1800s, when dangerous working conditions prevailed. **Infer** Why do you think the early years of the labor movement were marked by violence?

The chief tool of these early unions was the **strike,** an organized work stoppage intended to force an employer to address union demands. Employers responded by firing and replacing workers who tried to organize. Workers could not find help in the courts because the courts treated unions as illegal.

An important leader in the early years of the United States labor movement was Samuel Gompers. The young cigarmaker rose within union ranks in New York City, focusing on three goals: higher wages, shorter hours, and safer work environments. In 1886, he founded the American Federation of Labor (AFL).

Employer Resistance Attempts to unionize brought swift responses from employers. Viewing strikers as threats to free enterprise and social order, companies identified and fired union organizers. They forced workers to sign so-called yellow-dog contracts, in which workers promised not to join a union. (Yellow was slang for "cowardly.") Companies also used court orders called injunctions to force striking employees back to work. Some companies hired their own militias to harass union organizers or fight striking workers.

A Thriving Movement As the nation struggled through the Great Depression in the 1930s, Congress passed a number of measures that favored unions. The expansion of workers' rights in the 1930s contributed to a new rise in union strength. Membership grew, reaching about 35 percent of the nation's non-farm workforce in the 1940s.

Unions became a dominant force in many industries. They controlled the day-to-day operations of activities from shipbuilding to garbage collection to steel production. Unions amassed billions of dollars in union dues to cover the costs of union activities including organizing, making political donations, and providing aid to striking workers.

? RECALL Why did union membership rise in the 1930s?

The Decline in Labor Union Membership

As they grew, some unions began to abuse their power. Some sought to preserve outdated and inefficient production methods in order to protect jobs. As you read earlier, some unions managed to preserve job positions that were unnecessary—called "featherbedding"—in order to keep more members employed. As a result, companies that badly needed to improve efficiency to stay competitive found that unions could be an obstacle.

The reputation of unions suffered further because of their links to organized crime. Corrupt crime bosses gained a foothold in many local unions and used union funds to finance illegal operations.

"Right-to-Work" Laws In an effort to curb union power, Congress passed the Taft-Hartley Act in 1947. This act allowed states to pass **right-to-work laws,** measures that ban mandatory union membership. Today, most right-to-work states are in the South, which has a lower level of union membership than other regions.

Right-to-work laws may be one of several reasons for a decline in union membership in recent decades. By 2005, union membership had dropped to about 8 percent of the labor force. Today, unionism in the United States is far more limited than in many other countries.

Decline of Traditional Strongholds One theory suggests that structural changes in the U.S. economy have caused union membership to decline. For example:

- Unions have traditionally been strongest among **blue-collar workers.** These workers perform manual labor, often in a manufacturing job, and earn an hourly wage. The decline of manufacturing activity, shown in **Figure 5.9,** has caused union jobs to disappear.

- Unions are weakest among white-collar employees. A **white-collar worker** is someone in a professional or clerical job who usually earns a weekly salary. While white-collar workers generally do not belong to unions, workers in the public sector are an exception. Unionization among government workers has increased in recent decades. This growth of union membership has partially made up for losses in the private sector. Some people object when public-sector workers like teachers go on strike. Members of these unions argue that, just as in the private sector, these unions are needed to promote the interests of their workers.

- Certain manufacturing industries, such as automobiles, steel, and textiles, have traditionally employed large numbers of union workers. These industries have been hurt by foreign competition in recent years, and automation, including the use of robots, has increased. As a result, many industries have laid off union workers, which has cut into union strength. As you saw earlier, the percentage of workers belonging to unions has fallen in recent years.

- The rising proportion of women in the labor force (see **Figure 5.10**) also has affected union membership, since women have been less likely to join unions.

- Seeking to reduce their production costs, some industries have relocated from the

U.S. Manufacturing as a Percentage of GDP, 1959 and 2012

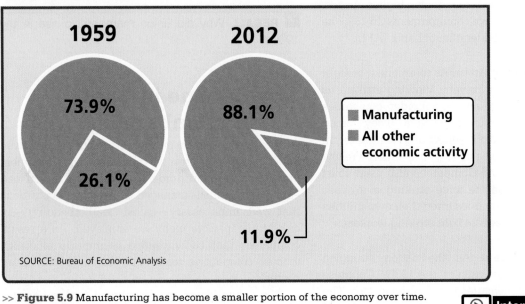

SOURCE: Bureau of Economic Analysis

>> **Figure 5.9** Manufacturing has become a smaller portion of the economy over time. **Analyze Data** How is the decline in union membership related to the decline of manufacturing?

▶ **Interactive Chart**

Gender Makeup of the U.S. Labor Force, 1970 and 2011

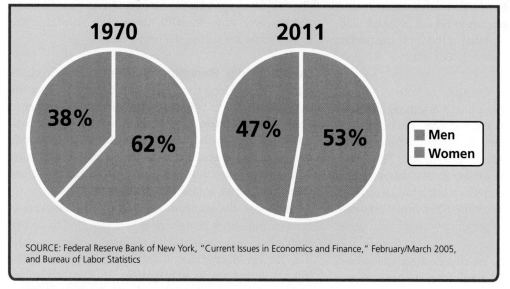

SOURCE: Federal Reserve Bank of New York, "Current Issues in Economics and Finance," February/March 2005, and Bureau of Labor Statistics

>> **Figure 5.10** More women are in the workforce now than in the past. **Analyze Information** How has this change affected union membership?

Northeast and Midwest to the South, which has historically been less friendly to unions.

Reduced Need for Unions Another theory for union decline is that other institutions now provide many of the services that had been won in the past through union activity. For example, the government has passed laws setting workplace safety standards and a shorter workweek. It provides unemployment insurance and Social Security. More nonunionized employers offer benefits such as medical insurance.

? CHECK UNDERSTANDING What are three explanations for the decline in union membership?

Labor and Management

A union gains the right to represent workers at a company when a majority of workers in a particular work unit, such as a factory, vote to accept the union. After that, the company is required by law to bargain with the union in good faith to negotiate an employment contract.

The Bargaining Process Picture a room and, on each side of a table, a team of lawyers and trained negotiators determined to get what they want—or at least part of it. This is **collective bargaining,** the process in which union and company management meet to negotiate a new labor contract.

Union contracts generally last two to five years and can cover hundreds of issues. The resulting contract spells out each side's rights and responsibilities for the length of the agreement. Generally the union comes to the bargaining table with certain goals that set the agenda for collective bargaining talks. Let's examine those goals.

Wages and benefits. The union negotiates on behalf of all members for wage rates, overtime rates, planned raises, and benefits. In seeking higher wages, the union is aware that if wages go too high, there may be consequences. If the workers succeed in getting higher wages and benefits, the company will have higher costs, which can reduce its competitiveness in the free market. If the company can't compete with other companies, it runs the risk of bankruptcy. As a result, the company may lay off workers to reduce costs.

Working conditions. Safety, comfort, worker responsibilities, and many other workplace issues are negotiated and written into the final contract.

Job security. One of the union's primary goals is to secure its members' jobs, so the contract spells out the conditions under which a worker may be fired. If a union member is discharged for reasons that the union believes to be in violation of the contract, the union might file a grievance, or formal complaint.

The union contract specifies how such grievances are handled. The procedure usually involves hearings by a committee of union and company representatives.

Strikes When a contract is about to expire, or when the union is negotiating its first agreement with a company, the negotiators can wind up in tough late-night bargaining sessions. Most of the time, the parties manage to reach an agreement. But when a deadlock occurs, tensions escalate.

The union may ask its members to vote to approve a strike. A strike is the union's ultimate weapon. A strike, particularly a lengthy one, can cripple a company. Some firms can continue to function by using managers to perform key tasks. They may hire workers who do not belong to the union, called "strikebreakers." If a company can withstand a strike, it is in a good bargaining position. Most firms, however, cannot produce goods and services without their union workers.

A long strike can also be devastating to workers, since they do not get paid while they are not working. Many unions do make some payments to their members during a strike, funded by the dues the union has collected. These payments can help workers, but they are generally much smaller than what the members would have earned while working.

It may seem as though workers strike frequently since strikes are often front-page news when they do occur. In fact, the collective bargaining process usually goes smoothly, with few work stoppages due to strikes.

As shown in the graph in **Figure 5.11**, the number of work stoppages in the United States has declined sharply over time. In 2010, there were only 11 major work stoppages across the entire nation.

Outside Help Reaching Settlements If a strike continues for a long time, the two sides sometimes call in a third party to help settle the dispute. They might agree to **mediation,** a settlement technique in which a neutral person, the mediator, meets with each side to try to find a solution that both sides will accept. A mediator often can help each side understand the other's concerns, leading to an agreement.

However, the decision reached by the mediator is nonbinding—that is, neither side is required to accept it. If either side rejects the mediator's decision, the dispute could continue indefinitely. Sometimes, the talks will end up in **arbitration.** In this settlement technique, a neutral third party listens to both sides and then imposes a decision. Since the company's management and the union had agreed to enter the arbitration stage, the decision is legally binding for both sides. It can be a risky step, because the decision might be seen as more favorable to one side than the other.

? IDENTIFY MAIN IDEAS What issues are addressed in collective bargaining?

U.S. Work Stoppages, 1950–2010

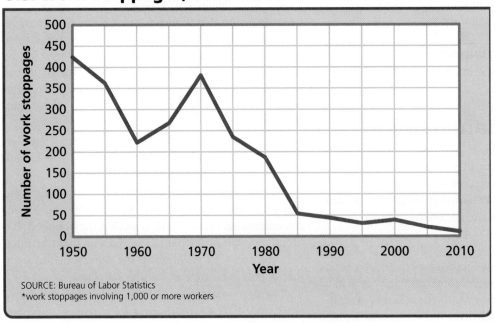

SOURCE: Bureau of Labor Statistics
*work stoppages involving 1,000 or more workers

>> **Figure 5.11** Work stoppages were once common, but they have become rare. **Analyze Graphs** Which 25-year period showed the greatest decline in the number of work stoppages?

▶ **Interactive Illustration**

ASSESSMENT

1. **Check Understanding** How do right-to-work laws diminish union power?

2. **Recall** How do blue-collar workers and white-collar workers differ in the types of work they perform? Give examples of each.

3. **Distinguish** In working toward a strike settlement, the two sides seek mediation and sometimes arbitration. How do the two techniques differ?

4. **Compare** What is the difference between the need for labor unions now and in the 1800s?

5. **Identify Central Issues** Some manufacturing companies have been moving their factories to countries where nonunion labor is cheap. They say they do this to reduce costs and compete with foreign companies. United States unions have opposed the cuts in U.S. jobs, insisting that companies must care for their workers. Which side would you support if you were an investor in a company moving a factory to a different country? Explain your reasoning for each response.

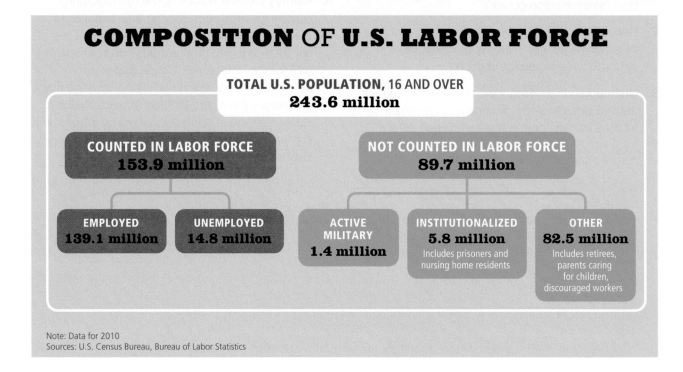

COMPOSITION OF U.S. LABOR FORCE

TOTAL U.S. POPULATION, 16 AND OVER
243.6 million

COUNTED IN LABOR FORCE
153.9 million

NOT COUNTED IN LABOR FORCE
89.7 million

EMPLOYED
139.1 million

UNEMPLOYED
14.8 million

ACTIVE MILITARY
1.4 million

INSTITUTIONALIZED
5.8 million
Includes prisoners and nursing home residents

OTHER
82.5 million
Includes retirees, parents caring for children, discouraged workers

Note: Data for 2010
Sources: U.S. Census Bureau, Bureau of Labor Statistics

1. **Interpret Data and Create Visual Presentations**
   Using the infographic, create a new visual representation of the unemployment rate within the United States labor force. Consider these questions: What information does this chart show? How does it show this information? How could the data concerning the employment within the labor force be presented in a circle graph? Why might the 2010 unemployment rate have concerned economists?

2. **Evaluate Rules and Regulations** Evaluate government rules and regulations concerning Social Security and Medicare benefits and the costs to businesses in providing the benefits. Consider these questions: What responsibility do businesses have in relation to funding Social Security and Medicare? How does the government regulate retirement benefits? Why might one support or oppose government policies in providing benefits to citizens through Social Security and Medicare?

3. **Explain and Analyze Sole Proprietorships** Write a paragraph that explains the characteristics of sole proprietorships and that analyzes their advantage in relation to other types of business organizations. Consider these questions: How do sole proprietorships differ from other forms of business organizations? Who makes most or all decisions in a sole proprietorship? What happens to profits made in sole proprietorships? How does this method of distributing profits compare to methods for profit-sharing in other types of business structures?

4. **Explain and Analyze Sole Proprietorships** Write a paragraph that explains and analyzes the disadvantages of sole proprietorships compared to other types of business organizations. Consider these questions: Who makes decisions, and bears responsibility for those decisions, in sole proprietorships? Do sole proprietorships protect business owners in the event the business goes into default or gets sued?

5. **Evaluate Examples of Restrictions** Write a paragraph that evaluates examples of government restrictions on the use of business property. Consider these questions: What type of restrictions might government place on businesses in order to ensure worker safety? What costs might come with laws concerning worksite safety for workers? How might businesses evaluate the costs and benefits of such restrictions?

Unemployment Rate, 1970–2013

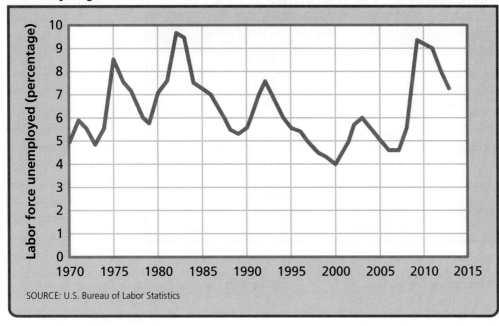

SOURCE: U.S. Bureau of Labor Statistics

6. **Explain Corporations and Create Oral Presentations** Write a paragraph that explains how corporations raise money through selling stocks and bonds. Then use the paragraph as an outline for an oral presentation about corporations. Consider these questions: How do corporations raise the capital needed to operate and expand through selling stocks? How do corporations raise the capital needed to operate and expand through selling bonds? What are the uses of money raised through selling stocks and bonds?

7. **Interpret Data** Interpret economic data, including the unemployment rate. Referring to the graph, write a paragraph that interprets the evolution of the unemployment rate between 1970 and 2013. Consider these questions: What is the unemployment rate? What are the two highest points of unemployment shown on the graph? What does that data suggest about the strength of the overall economy and well-being of workers?

8. **Analyze Partnerships** Write a paragraph that analyzes the disadvantages of partnerships. Consider these questions: What are the primary disadvantages of partnerships? What personal dynamics can threaten partnerships in all walks of life? What happens to liabilities when a partnership business ends? How does this method of operating a business run risks that sole proprietorships do not?

9. **Identify Examples of Restrictions** Write a paragraph in which you identify examples of restrictions that the government places on the use of business property in cities. Consider these questions: What is one example of how government can regulate businesses' operations in a city? Based on the quotation, what is one way the government can place restrictions on the use of business property within cities?

"Some kinds of businesses face limits on their operations due to zoning laws."

10. **Explain and Analyze Corporations** Explain the characteristics of corporations and analyze the advantages of the corporate form of business. Consider these questions: What are the primary characteristics of corporations? How do these characteristics represent the advantages of running a corporation? How do corporations raise money for investing in the future?

Liability in Different Types of Partnerships

TYPE OF PARTNERSHIP	BUSINESS LOSS	PARTNERS' PERSONAL LIABILITY		
General Partnership	$150,000	General Partner A $50,000	General Partner B $50,000	General Partner C $50,000
Limited Partnership	$150,000	General Partner A $75,000	General Partner B $75,000	Limited Partner W $0
Limited Partnership	$150,000	General Partner A $150,000	Limited Partner W $0	Limited Partner X $0

11. Explain and Analyze Partnerships Using the table, explain the characteristics of partnerships and analyze the advantages of this type of business organization in comparison with others. Consider these questions: What is a partnership? In what way do partnerships benefit from the differing abilities of the partners? If business owners often invest in their business to get it started, why might partnerships often have stronger financial foundations than sole proprietorships?

12. Analyze Advantages Using the infographic below, write a paragraph that analyzes at least one advantage of sole proprietorships. Consider these questions: Based on the infographic, who receives profits in a sole proprietorship? In what way does the distribution of profits reflect the degree of control a sole proprietor has over his or her business?

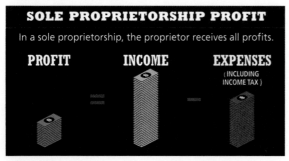

SOLE PROPRIETORSHIP PROFIT

In a sole proprietorship, the proprietor receives all profits.

PROFIT   INCOME   EXPENSES (INCLUDING INCOME TAX)

13. Evaluate Charitable Giving and Create Written Presentations Using the quotation, evaluate the costs and benefits of charitable giving by preparing a written presentation. Consider these questions: What type of business structure allows an organization to receive in charitable gifts? What are the costs and benefits of giving money to charitable organizations?

"Nonprofits are usually in the business of providing some benefit to the public....Almost all of them provide services rather than goods."

14. Analyze Corporations Analyze the disadvantages of corporations. Consider these questions: What is the level of difficulty in starting a corporation? How are corporations taxed? How do owners influence the activities of corporations? How are corporations affected by government rules and regulations?

15. Analyze Economic Rights and Responsibilities Analyze the economic rights and responsibilities of businesses, focusing on those involved in starting a small business. Consider these questions: What rights do small businesses have? What responsibilities do small businesses have? How are rights balanced by the responsibilities businesses have?

16. Write About the Essential Question Write an essay on the Essential Question: How can businesses and labor best achieve their goals? Use evidence from your study of this Topic to support your answer.

Go online to PearsonRealize.com and use the texts, quizzes, interactivities, Interactive Reading Notepads, Flipped Videos, and other resources from this Topic to prepare for the Topic Test.

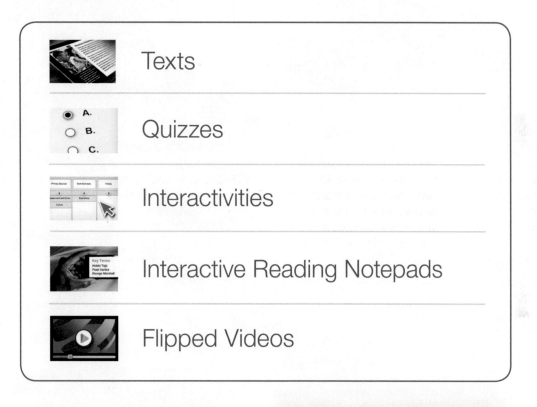

Texts

Quizzes

Interactivities

Interactive Reading Notepads

Flipped Videos

While online you can also check the progress you've made learning the topic and course content by viewing your grades, test scores, and assignment status.

6 **Money, Banking, and Financial Markets**

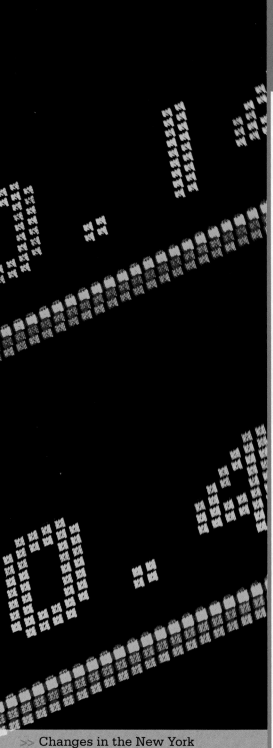

Enduring Understandings

- Money provides a medium through which individuals and societies enter into basic economic activities.

- The policies and actions of major banking institutions, including the Federal Reserve, have important effects on the U.S. and world economies.

- Modern banks offer consumers a wide range of opportunities for saving and for borrowing.

- Financial institutions provide consumers with opportunities to invest savings in ways that can create economic growth.

- The stock market and bond trading markets provide means for corporations to raise money that can then be invested for further growth.

>> Changes in the New York Stock Exchange appear in this electronic display.

PEARSON realize. **NBC LEARN**

Watch the My Story Video to learn more about Warren Buffet, one of the most successful investors of all time.

PEARSON realize.
www.PearsonRealize.com

Access your digital lessons including:
Topic Inquiry • Interactive Reading
Notepad • Interactivities • Assessments

>> Because money serves as a store of value, it will keep its value when you deposit it into a checking or savings account at your local bank.

▶ **Interactive Flipped Video**

6.1 It's been a hot day, and you have just arrived at your neighborhood store after playing basketball. You grab a soda and search the pockets of your jeans for some money. You find a pen, keys, and a chewing gum wrapper, but, unfortunately, no money. Then you reach into your jacket pocket. Finally!—a crumpled dollar bill. You hand the money to the clerk and take a long, cold drink.

>> Objectives

Describe the uses and functions of money.

List the characteristics of money, including its commodity and representative forms.

Analyze the positive and negative aspects of currency, as well as other media of exchange.

>> Key Terms

money
medium of
  exchange
barter
unit of account
store of value
currency
commodity money
representative
  money
specie
fiat money

The Role of Money

The Three Uses of Money

Money, like the dollar you used to buy the soda, serves the needs of individuals and society in many ways. It provides a means for comparing values of goods and services, and it serves as a store of value. Without it, we can't get the things we need and want. That's not the whole story of money, as you will see. In fact, money has functions and characteristics that you might never have thought about.

If you were asked to define *money*, you would probably think of the coins and bills in your wallet. Economists define *money* in terms of its three uses. To an economist, **money** is anything that serves as a medium of exchange, a unit of account, and a store of value.

Money as a Medium of Exchange A **medium of exchange** is anything that is used to determine value during the exchange of goods and services. Without money, people acquire goods and services through **barter,** or the direct exchange of one set of goods or services for another. A barter agreement can be very useful when neither party in a transaction has money to pay for the other's services or goods. It can also lead to cost savings. For example, a baker's cost to bake a cake might be only $5. If he trades that cake for a $25 haircut, it is a savings to him of $20. Similarly, the barber received a $25 cake for the time it took him to cut a head of hair. Barter is still used in many parts of the world, especially in traditional economies in Asia, Africa, and

Latin America. It is also sometimes used informally in the United States.

For example, a person might agree to mow a neighbor's lawn in exchange for vegetables from the neighbor's garden. In general, however, as an economy becomes more specialized, it becomes too difficult to establish the relative value of items to be bartered.

To appreciate how much easier money makes exchanges, suppose that money did not exist, and that you wanted to trade your portable DVD player for a brand-new mountain bike. You probably would have a great deal of trouble making the exchange. First, you would need to find a person who wanted to both sell the model of mountain bike you want and buy your particular DVD player. Second, this person would need to agree that your DVD player is worth the same as his or her bike. As you might guess, people in barter economies spend a great deal of time and effort exchanging the goods they have for the goods they need and want. That's why barter generally works well only in small, traditional economies. In those small economies, people can devote much of their time to exchanging goods.

Now consider how much easier your transaction would be if you used money as a medium of exchange. All you would have to do is find someone who is willing to pay you $100 for your DVD player. Then you could use that money to buy a mountain bike from someone else. The person selling you the bike could use the $100 however he or she wished. By the same token, the person who pays $100 for your DVD player could raise that money however he or she wished. Because money makes exchanges so much easier, people have been using it for thousands of years.

Money as a Unit of Account In addition to serving as a medium of exchange, money serves as a **unit of account.** That is, money provides a means for comparing the values of goods and services. For example, suppose you see a jacket on sale for $30. You know this is a good price because you have checked the price of the same or similar jackets in other stores.

You can compare the cost of the jacket in this store with the cost in other stores because the price is expressed in the same way in every store in the United States—in terms of dollars and cents. Similarly, you would expect seeing a movie in a theater to cost about $8, a new DVD rental about $3.50, and so forth.

Other countries have their own forms of money that serve as units of account. The Japanese quote prices in terms of yen, the Russians in terms of rubles, Mexicans in terms of pesos, and so forth.

Money as a Store of Value Money also serves as a **store of value.** This means that money keeps its value if you decide to hold on to—or store—it instead of spending it. For example, when you sell your DVD player to purchase a mountain bike, you may not have a chance to purchase a bike right away. In the meantime, you can keep the money in your wallet or in a bank. The money will still be valuable and will be recognized as a medium of exchange weeks or months from now when you go to buy the bike.

Money serves as a good store of value with one important exception. Sometimes economies experience a period of rapid inflation, or a general increase in prices. For example, suppose the United States experienced 10-percent inflation during a particular year. If you sold your DVD player at the beginning of that year for $100, the money you received would have 10 percent less value, or buying power, at the end of the year. Inflation would have caused the price of the mountain bike to increase by 10 percent during the year, to $110. The $100 you received at the beginning of the year would no longer be enough to buy the bike.

In short, when an economy experiences inflation, money does not function as well as a store of value. You

>> Money makes the purchase of goods and services very easy.

will read more about the causes and effects of inflation later.

? DEFINE What does it mean to say that money serves as a store of value?

The Six Characteristics of Money

The coins and paper bills used as money are called **currency.** In the past, societies have also used an astoundingly wide range of other objects as currency. Cattle, salt, dried fish, furs, precious stones, gold, and silver have all served as currency at various times in various places. So have porpoise teeth, rice, wheat, seashells, tulip bulbs, and olive oil.

These items all worked well in the societies in which they were used. None of them, however, would function very well in our economy today. Each lacks at least one of the six characteristics that economists use to judge how well an item serves as currency. These six characteristics are durability, portability, divisibility, uniformity, limited supply, and acceptability.

Money Is Durable. Objects used as money must withstand the physical wear and tear that comes with

being used over and over again. If money wears out or is easily destroyed, it cannot be trusted to serve as a store of value.

Unlike wheat or olive oil, coins last for many years. In fact, some collectors have ancient Roman coins that are more than 2,000 years old. Although our paper money may not seem very durable, its rag (cloth) content helps $1 bills typically last at least a year in circulation. When paper bills wear out, the United States government can easily replace them.

Of course, nothing is indestructible. Anyone who's ever had paper currency accidentally go through washing machine and dryer cycles knows that it doesn't always come out in "spendable" condition. One negative aspect of currency is that it can wear out in this way.

Money Is Portable. People need to be able to take money with them as they go about their daily business. They also must be able to transfer money easily from one person to another when they use money for purchases. Paper money and coins are very portable, or easy to carry, because they are small and light.

Money Is Divisible. To be useful, money must be easily divided into smaller denominations, or units of value. When money is divisible, people can use only

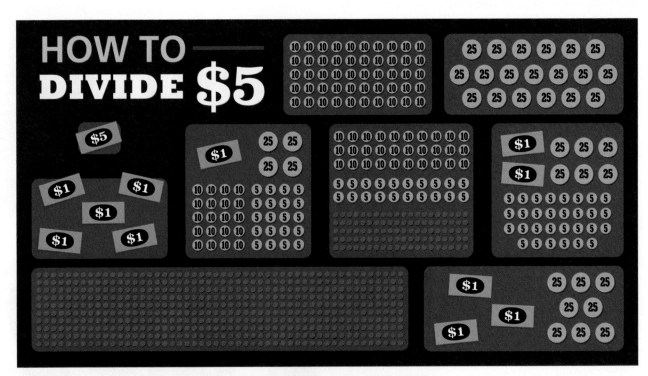

>> One characteristic of money is that it is divisible into smaller amounts. Divisibility of money into small amounts such as coins means that you can pay the exact amount for something that you buy.

as much of it as necessary for any exchange. In the sixteenth and seventeenth centuries, people actually used parts of coins to pay exact amounts for their purchases. Spanish dollars, widely circulated in the American colonies, were often cut into as many as eight "bits," or pieces. For this reason, these coins came to be called "pieces of eight."

Today, of course, if you use a $20 bill to pay for a $5 lunch, the cashier will not rip your bill into four pieces in order to make change. That's because American currency, like currencies around the world, consists of various denominations—$5 bills, $10 bills, and so on.

There are circumstances in which money may not be conveniently divisible. All of the five- and ten-dollar bills in the world, for instance, would not do one much good at a parking meter that only accepts quarters.

Money Is Uniform. Any two units of money must be uniform—that is, the same—in terms of what they will buy. In other words, people must be able to count and measure money accurately.

Suppose everything were priced in terms of dried fish. One small dried fish might buy an apple. One large dried fish might buy a sandwich. This method of pricing is not a very accurate way of establishing the standard value of products, because the size of a dried fish can vary. Picture the arguments people would have when trying to agree whether a fish was small or large. A dollar bill, however, always buys $1 worth of goods.

There Is a Limited Supply of Money. Suppose a society uses certain pebbles as money. These rare pebbles have been found only on one beach.

One day, however, someone finds an enormous supply of similar pebbles on a different beach. Now anyone can scoop up these pebbles by the handful. Since these pebbles are no longer in limited supply, they are no longer useful as currency.

In the United States, the Federal Reserve System controls the supply of money in circulation. By its actions, the Federal Reserve is able to keep just the right amount of money available. You'll read more about the Federal Reserve System later in this Topic.

Money Is Acceptable as a Form of Payment. Finally, everyone in an economy must be able to take the objects that serve as money and exchange them for goods and services. When you go to the store, why does the person behind the counter accept your money in exchange for a carton of milk or a box of pencils? After all, money is just pieces of metal or paper. Your money is accepted because the owner of the store can spend it elsewhere to buy something he or she needs or wants.

>> The characteristic of uniformity means that bills of the same denomination not only look exactly the same, but also buy the same amount of goods or services.

▶ **Interactive Gallery**

There are, of course, instances when your currency may not be accepted. We've all seen signs in smaller stores that read "No bills over $20," or "No payment with pennies."

In general, though, in the United States, we expect that other people in the country will continue to accept paper money and coins in exchange for our purchases. This acceptability is one positive aspect of currency.

❓ **IDENTIFY** Who controls the supply of money in circulation in the United States?

Sources of Money's Value

Think about the bills and coins in your pocket. They are durable and portable. They are also easily divisible, uniform, in limited supply, and accepted throughout the country. As convenient and practical as they may be, however, bills and coins have very little value in and of themselves. What, then, makes money valuable? The answer is that there are actually several possible sources of money's value, depending on whether it is commodity money, representative money, or fiat money.

Commodity Money A commodity is an object. **Commodity money** consists of objects that have value in and of themselves and that are also used as money. For example, various societies have used salt, cattle, and precious stones as commodity money. The usefulness of objects is what gives them value. If not used as money, salt can preserve food and make it tastier. Cattle can be slaughtered for their meat, hides, and horns. Gems can be made into beautiful jewelry. Tobacco, corn, and cotton all served as commodity money in the American colonies.

As you can guess, commodity money tends to lack several of the characteristics that make objects good to use as money. Take cattle, for example. Cows and bulls are not all that portable, or even durable. A cow is not divisible, at least not if you want to keep it alive. That's why commodity money only works in simple economies. As the American colonies developed more complex economic systems, tobacco and other objects were no longer universally accepted as money. The colonies needed a more convenient payment system. They turned to representative money to meet their needs.

Representative Money Representative money

makes use of objects that have value solely because the holder can exchange them for something else of value. For example, if your brother gives you an IOU for $20, the piece of paper itself is worth nothing. The promise that he will do all of your chores for a month may be worth quite a lot, however. The piece of paper simply represents his promise to you.

Early representative money took the form of paper receipts for gold and silver. Gold or silver money was heavy and thus inconvenient for customers and merchants to carry around. Each time someone made a transaction, the coins would have to be weighed and tested for purity. People therefore started to leave their gold in goldsmiths' safes. Customers would carry paper ownership receipts from the goldsmith to show how much gold they owned. After a while, merchants began to accept goldsmiths' receipts instead of the gold itself. In this way, the paper receipts became an early form of paper money.

Colonists in the Massachusetts Bay Colony first used representative money in the late 1600s, when the colony's treasurer issued bills of credit to lenders to help finance King William's War. The bills of credit showed the exact amount that colonists had loaned to the Massachusetts government. Holders of these bills could redeem the paper for **specie,** or coins made of gold or silver.

Representative money was not without its problems. During the American Revolution, the Second Continental Congress issued representative money called Continentals to finance the war against England. Unfortunately, few people were able to redeem these early paper currencies for specie because the federal government had no power to collect taxes. Until the Constitution replaced the Articles of Confederation in 1789, the federal government depended on the states' voluntary contributions to fill the treasury. As a result, the federal treasury held very little gold or silver to back the Continentals. People even began to use the phrase "not worth a Continental" to refer to something of no value.

During the summer of 1780, this wretched "Continental" currency fell into contempt. As Washington said, it took a wagon-load of money to buy a wagon-load of provisions. At the end of the year 1778, the paper dollar was worth 16 cents in the northern states and twelve cents in the south. Early in 1789 its value had fallen to two cents and before the end of the year it took ten paper dollars to make a cent. A

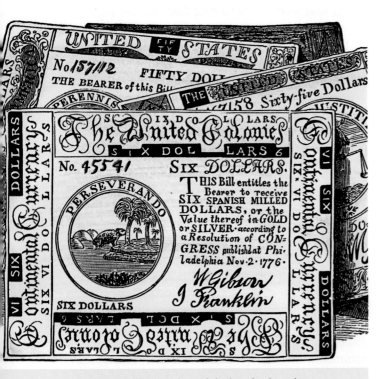

>> These bills were issued during the American Revolution and could be redeemed for gold, silver, or Spanish currency.

barber in Philadelphia papered his shop with bills.

—John Fiske, *The American Revolution*, 1896

Later, the United States government issued representative money in the form of silver and gold certificates. These certificates were "backed" by gold or silver. In other words, holders of such certificates could redeem them for gold or silver at a local bank. The United States government thus had to keep vast supplies of gold and silver on hand to be able to convert all paper dollars to gold if the demand arose. Some silver certificates circulated until 1968, but for the most part, the government stopped converting paper money into silver or gold in the 1930s.

Fiat Money If you examine a dollar bill, you will see George Washington's picture on one side. To the left of the portrait are the words "This note is legal tender for all debts, public and private." In essence, these words mean that this Federal Reserve Note is valuable because our government says it is.

United States money today is fiat money. A fiat is an order or decree. **Fiat money,** also called "legal tender," has value because a government has decreed that it is an acceptable means to pay debts. Furthermore, citizens have confidence that the money will be accepted. It remains in limited supply, and therefore valuable, because the Federal Reserve controls its supply. This control of the money supply is essential for a fiat system to work. If the money supply grows too large, the currency may become worthless due to inflation.

? EXPLAIN Although in some societies cattle are used as a type of "money," why are cattle not a good source of money?

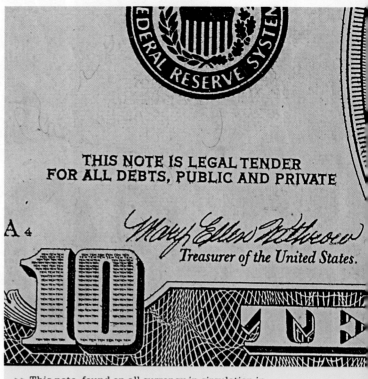

>> This note, found on all currency in circulation in the United States, means that our government stands behind the value of the bill.

ASSESSMENT

1. **Compare and Contrast** What is one disadvantage of bartering over using currency to purchase goods?

2. **Explain** Why do objects used as money need to be in limited supply?

3. **Define** What does it mean to say that money is an acceptable form of payment?

4. **List** What are the six characteristics of money?

5. **Apply Concepts** If you write your friend an IOU for a loan of twenty dollars, what type of money have you given her?

>> Alexander Hamilton, a Federalist, was a staunch supporter of a strong federal government and, therefore, of a strong central bank.

[▶] **Interactive Flipped Video**

If you need a large sum of cash to make a purchase, do you get it from under your mattress, under a floorboard, or inside a cookie jar? These options are unlikely in today's world. In the past, many Americans kept their savings hidden in such places. However, times have changed. Today, almost all Americans prefer to entrust their savings to a bank—an institution for receiving, keeping, and lending money.

>> Objectives

Describe the shifts between centralized and decentralized banking in the United States before the Civil War.

Explain how government reforms stabilized the banking system in the later 1800s.

Describe changes in banking in the early 1900s, including the abandonment of the gold standard.

Explain the causes of two recent banking crises.

>> Key Terms

bank
national bank
bank runs
greenbacks
gold standard
central bank
Federal Reserve
   Banks
member banks
Federal Reserve
   Board
short-term loans
Federal Reserve
   Notes
foreclosures

Changes in American Banking

American Banking Before the Civil War

Over time, the American banking system has changed in order to meet new challenges. In earlier days, people distrusted banks because they sometimes distributed worthless money and caused financial panics. In this section, you will see how government regulations helped increase confidence in American banks. You will also see how American banking has developed over the years to meet the needs of a growing and changing population.

During the first part of our nation's history, local banks were informal businesses that merchants managed in addition to their regular trade. For example, a merchant who sold cloth, grain, or other goods might allow customers to deposit money. The merchant would then charge a small fee to keep the money safe. These informal banks were not completely safe, however. If a merchant went out of business or invested deposits in risky schemes, customers could lose all of their savings.

Opposing Views of Banking After the American Revolution, the leaders of the new nation agreed on the need to establish a safe, stable banking system. Such a system was important for ensuring the economic growth of the new United States. The nation's leaders did not, however, agree on how that goal should be accomplished. The debate on banking between followers of Alexander Hamilton and followers of Thomas Jefferson was part of a larger political debate about the role of government in the young country.

As you may remember from your study of American history, the Federalists believed that the country needed a strong central government to establish order. The Antifederalists favored leaving most powers in the hands of the states. These two groups viewed the country's banking needs quite differently.

The Federalists, led by Alexander Hamilton, believed that a centralized banking system was a key to promoting industry and trade. After President Washington appointed Hamilton secretary of the treasury in 1789, Hamilton proposed a **national bank**—a bank chartered, or licensed, by the federal government. The bank would have the power to issue a national currency, manage the federal government's funds, and monitor other banks throughout the country.

The Antifederalists, led by Thomas Jefferson, opposed this plan. They feared that the wealthy would gain control of the bank and use its resources to increase their power. They supported a decentralized banking system. In this system, the states would establish and regulate all banks within their borders.

The First Bank of the United States At first, the Federalists were successful in creating a strong central bank. In 1791, Congress set up the Bank of the United States, granting it a 20-year charter to operate. The United States Treasury used the Bank to hold the money that the government collected in taxes and to issue representative money in the form of bank notes, which were backed by gold and silver. The Bank also supervised state-chartered banks, making sure they held sufficient gold and silver to exchange for bank notes should the demand arise.

The Bank succeeded in bringing stability to American banking. However, opponents of the Bank charged that ordinary people who needed to borrow money to maintain or expand their farms and small businesses were being refused loans.

In addition, the Antifederalists pointed out that the Constitution does not explicitly give Congress the power to create a national bank. Therefore, they argued, the Bank was unconstitutional. When Alexander Hamilton died in a famous duel with Vice President Aaron Burr in 1804, the Bank lost its main backer. The Bank functioned only until 1811, when its charter ran out.

Financial Chaos in America Once the Bank's charter expired, state banks (banks chartered by state governments) began issuing bank notes that they could not back with specie—gold or silver coins. The

Developments in American Banking

DATE	DEVELOPMENT
1791	First Bank of the United States established with 20-year charter.
1811–1816	Period of instability follows expiration of First Bank's charter.
1816	Second Bank of the United States reestablishes stability; 20-year charter.
1836–1860s	President Jackson vetoes recharter of Second Bank; Free Banking Era begins.
1863–1864	National Banking Acts establish national banking system and national currency.
1913	President Wilson signs the Federal Reserve Act.
1929	The Great Depression begins.
1933	President Franklin D. Roosevelt establishes the FDIC.
1940s–1960s	Period of government regulation and long-term stability.
1980s	Period of deregulation; savings and loans face bankruptcies.
2000s	Subprime loans lead to foreclosures and the worst economic crisis since WWII.

>> **Analyze Charts** What does the chart suggest about the role of government in banking during the twentieth century?

▶ **Interactive Timeline**

states also chartered many banks without considering whether these banks would be stable and creditworthy.

Without any kind of regulation, financial confusion resulted. Prices rose rapidly. Neither merchants nor customers had confidence in the value of the paper money in circulation. Different banks issued different currencies, and bankers always faced the temptation to print more money than they had gold and silver to back.

The Second Bank of the United States To eliminate this financial chaos, Congress chartered the Second Bank of the United States in 1816. Like the first Bank, the Second Bank was limited to a 20-year charter. The Second Bank slowly managed to rebuild the public's confidence in a national banking system. Nicholas Biddle, who became president of the Second Bank in 1823, was responsible for restoring stability. If Biddle thought that a particular state bank was issuing bank notes without enough gold and silver reserves, he would surprise the bank with a great number of its notes all at once, asking for gold or silver in return. Some state banks, caught without the necessary reserves, went out of business. Others quickly learned to limit how many notes they issued.

Still, many Americans continued to be wary of the federal government's banking powers. They believed that the bank was a tool for the wealthy to further increase their wealth. Although the Supreme Court had ruled a national bank constitutional in 1819, President Andrew Jackson agreed with the bank's opponents. In 1832, Jackson vetoed its renewal.

The Free Banking Era The fall of the Second Bank once again allowed state-chartered banks to flourish. For this reason, the period between 1837 and 1863 is known as the Free Banking, or "Wildcat," Era. Between 1830 and 1837 alone, the number of state-chartered banks nearly tripled. As you might expect, the sheer number of banks gave rise to a variety of problems.

Bank runs and panics State-chartered banks often did not keep enough gold and silver to back the paper money that they issued. This sometimes led to **bank runs**—widespread panics in which great numbers of people try to redeem their paper money at the same time. Many banks failed as a result, and public confidence plummeted.

Wildcat banks Some banks were located on the frontier. They were called wildcat banks because people joked that only wildcats lived in such remote places. Wildcat banks were inadequately financed and had a high rate of failure.

Fraud A few banks engaged in out-and-out fraud. They issued bank notes, collected gold and silver money from people who bought the notes, and then disappeared. Customers who were left holding the notes lost their money.

Many different currencies State-chartered banks—as well as cities, private banks, railroads, stores, churches, and individuals—were allowed to issue currency. Notes of the same denomination often had different values, so that a dollar issued by the "City of Atlanta" was not necessarily worth the same as a dollar issued by the "City of New York." The profusion of currencies made it easier to create counterfeits, or worthless imitations of real notes.

? IDENTIFY Which group succeeded in creating a strong central bank in 1791?

Stability in the Later 1800s

By 1860, an estimated 8,000 different banks were circulating currency. To add to the confusion, the federal government played no role in providing paper currency or regulating reserves of gold or silver. The Civil War, which erupted in 1861, made existing problems worse.

Currencies of the Civil War During the Civil War, both the Union and Confederacy needed to raise money

>> During the years when there was no central bank, individual states and banks issued currency that was not backed by gold or silver, which led to financial confusion and chaos.

to finance their military efforts. In 1861, the United States Treasury issued its first paper currency since the Continental. The official name of the currency was "demand notes," but people called them **greenbacks** because they were printed with green ink.

In the South, the Confederacy issued currency backed by cotton, hoping that a Confederate victory would ensure the currency's value. As the war weakened the Confederate economy, however, Confederate notes became worthless.

National Banking Acts With war raging, the federal government enacted reforms aimed at restoring confidence in paper currency. These reforms resulted in the National Banking Acts of 1863 and 1864. Together, these Acts gave the federal government the power to charter banks, the power to require that banks hold adequate gold and silver reserves to cover their bank notes, and the power to issue a single national currency. The new national currency led to the elimination of the many different state currencies in use and helped stabilize the country's money supply.

The Gold Standard Despite the reforms made during the Civil War, money and banking problems still plagued the country. In the 1870s, the nation adopted a **gold standard**—a monetary system in which paper money and coins had the value of certain amounts of gold. The gold standard set a definite value for the dollar, so that one ounce of gold equaled about $20. Since the value was set, people knew that they could redeem the full value of their paper money at any time.

Now, the government could issue currency only if it had enough gold in the treasury to back the notes. Because of the limited supply of gold, the government was prevented from printing an unlimited number of notes. The gold standard thus fulfilled an essential requirement of a banking system: a stable currency that inspires the confidence of the public.

The gold standard, however, could not survive tougher times to come.

❓ **IDENTIFY SUPPORTING DETAILS** With the gold standard in place, the government could issue currency only if _____.

Banking in the Early 1900s

Reforms such as creating a single national currency and adopting the gold standard helped stabilize American banking. They did not, however, provide for a central decision-making authority. Such an authority could

>> For many years, gold bars like these were used to establish the value of paper money and coins.

help banks provide funds for growth and manage the money supply based on what the economy needed.

Continuing problems in the nation's banking system resulted in the Panic of 1907. Lacking adequate reserves, many banks had to stop exchanging gold for paper money. Several long-established New York banks failed, and many people lost their jobs because businesses could not borrow money to invest in future projects.

The Federal Reserve System The Federal Reserve Act of 1913 established the Federal Reserve System. The Federal Reserve System, or Fed, served as the nation's first true **central bank,** or bank that can lend to other banks in times of need. It reorganized the federal banking system as follows:

Federal Reserve Banks The system created as many as 12 regional Federal Reserve Banks throughout the country. All banks chartered by the national government were required to become members of the Fed. The Federal Reserve Banks are the central banks for their districts. **Member banks**—banks that belong to the Fed—store some of their cash reserves at the Federal Reserve Bank in their district.

Federal Reserve Board All of the Federal Reserve Banks were supervised by a Federal Reserve Board appointed by the President of the United States.

Short-Term Loans Each of the regional Federal Reserve Banks allowed member banks to borrow money to meet short-term demands. This helped prevent bank failures that occurred when large numbers of depositors withdrew funds during a panic.

Federal Reserve Notes The system also created the national currency we use today in the United States—Federal Reserve notes. This allowed the Federal Reserve to increase or decrease the amount of money in circulation according to business needs.

You will read more about the role of the Federal Reserve and how the system works today in the next Lesson.

Banking and the Great Depression The Fed helped restore confidence in the nation's banking system. It was unable, however, to prevent the terrifying Great Depression—the severe economic decline that began with a stock market crash in 1929 and lasted more than a decade.

During the 1920s, banks loaned large sums of money to many high-risk businesses. Many of these businesses were unable to pay back their loans. Because of hard times on the nation's farms, many farmers also failed to repay bank loans.

Then, the 1929 stock market crash led to widespread bank runs as depositors in all parts of the country rushed to withdraw their money. The combination of unpaid loans and bank runs resulted in the failure of thousands of banks across the country.

FDR Reforms After becoming President in 1933, Franklin D. Roosevelt acted to restore public confidence in the nation's banking system. Only days after his inauguration, Roosevelt closed the nation's banks. This "bank holiday" was a desperate last resort to restore trust in the nation's financial system. Within a matter of days, sound banks began to reopen.

Later in 1933, Congress passed the act that established the Federal Deposit Insurance Corporation (FDIC). The FDIC insures customer deposits if a bank fails. By 2008, each depositor's basic accounts in one bank were insured up to $250,000.

In an attempt to increase the money supply, Roosevelt also issued an executive order that effectively ended the nation's use of the gold standard.

In 1933, the United States nationalized all gold owned by private citizens and restricted individuals' ability to redeem dollars for gold. The results of these actions were an increase in gold's value and a decrease in the value of the dollar. Going off the gold standard also allowed the Federal Reserve to maintain a money supply at adequate levels to support a growing economy. These actions, which meant that the nation moved away from representative money and moved toward a system of fiat money, helped the nation recover somewhat but did not end the Great Depression.

? DESCRIBE What was the purpose of the FDIC?

Two Crises for Banking

As a result of the many bank failures of the Great Depression, banks were closely regulated from 1933 through the 1960s. The government restricted the interest rates banks could pay depositors and the rates that banks could charge consumers for loans. By the 1970s, bankers were eager for relief from federal regulation.

The Savings and Loan Crisis In the late 1970s and 1980s, Congress passed laws to deregulate, or remove some restrictions on, several industries. Unfortunately, this deregulation contributed to a crisis in a class of banks known as Savings and Loans (S&Ls). Government regulation had protected S&Ls from some of the stresses of the marketplace. Thus, they were unprepared for the intense competition they faced after deregulation.

>> As the Great Crash of 1929 sent stock prices tumbling, people flooded into the Wall Street area of New York City.

Subprime Mortgages, 1998 to 2008

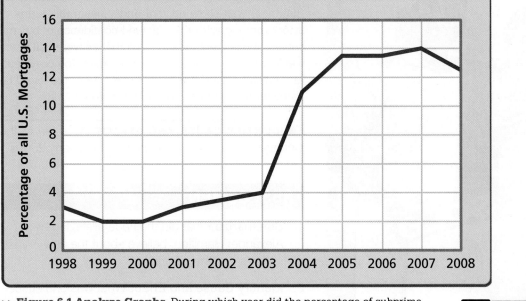

>> **Figure 6.1 Analyze Graphs** During which year did the percentage of subprime mortgages increase the most?

Interactive Gallery

There were other reasons for the crisis. During the 1970s, S&Ls had made long-term loans at low rates of interest. By the 1980s, interest rates had skyrocketed. This meant that S&Ls had to pay large amounts of interest to their depositors.

The S&L industry made many risky loans in the early 1980s. Losses on bad loans forced many banks out of business. A few S&L managers also used S&L funds for their own personal gain.

In 1989, Congress passed legislation that essentially abolished the independence of the savings and loan industry. This legislation expanded the insurance responsibilities of the FDIC.

Financial "Meltdown," Bailout, and "Recovery" In late 2006, problems in the U.S. banking industry began to threaten the housing market. The episode quickly spiraled into a full-fledged crisis, the most serious threat to the U.S. economy since the Great Depression.

Beginning in the 1990s, U.S. banks decided to issue "subprime" loans to people seeking to purchase homes. The term "subprime" refers to loans that are made to borrowers with an unfavorable credit history. The higher interest rate banks charge because of the greater risk makes these loans more profitable.

Banks began to market these loans aggressively to people who did not qualify for standard loans. **Figure 6.1** shows the significant increase in subprime mortgages beginning around 2003. Bankers also devised ways of packaging these mortgages so that

they could be sold off to investors. The value of these bundled mortgages, of course, depended on the ability of individual homeowners to repay their loans.

The situation reached a crisis point when many homeowners had trouble repaying their loans. This led to a sharp rise in **foreclosures,** the seizure of property from borrowers who are unable to repay their loans. In addition, housing prices dropped significantly, and some people owed more money on their mortgages than their homes were worth. This condition became known as having an "underwater mortgage."

The increase in foreclosures hurt investors who had bought the mortgage bundles. A number of the nation's largest financial institutions that had invested heavily in subprime mortgages were forced into bankruptcy. The ripple effect was great, as hundreds of thousands of U.S. workers lost their jobs. Businesses and individuals found it difficult to get credit.

By late 2008, the U.S. economy was on the edge of a financial catastrophe. It was officially in a recession. Treasury Secretary Henry M. Paulson, President George W. Bush, and U.S. lawmakers organized a $700 billion bailout of banks, automakers, and Wall Street financial firms. The money was used to help them avoid bankruptcy and to restart the flow of credit to businesses and individuals. In 2009, President Obama signed into law a $787 billion stimulus package, the largest in U.S. history. Approximately one third of the package was devoted to tax cuts; the rest went to spending increases. These included infrastructure

>> Although the recovery from the meltdown was uneven, by 2013, the real estate market had bounced back in many parts of the country and people were again able to purchase homes.

Five years after the meltdown, things in the U.S. economy had improved. The real estate market, for instance, was showing real and measurable signs of strengthening with the renewed confidence of buyers, sellers, and lenders. However, big banks were still much too large, excessive debt was still much too prevalent, and household savings rates were still far too low. The recovery was coming slowly and incrementally.

? IDENTIFY CAUSE AND EFFECT What led to the increase in mortgage foreclosures in the early 2000s?

ASSESSMENT

1. **Summarize** What did the Federalists, led by Alexander Hamilton, believe about the new nation's system of banking?

2. **Identify Cause and Effect** What was one effect of President Jackson's veto of the Second Bank of the United States?

3. **Describe** What was the gold standard?

4. **Summarize** What were the effects of the government policies that limited people's ability to redeem paper money for gold during the Depression?

5. **Hypothesize** What might have happened if banks had not issued large numbers of subprime loans in the 1990s and early 2000s?

projects and support for state healthcare obligations. Despite this, recovery has been slow.

It's Saturday night, and you've gone out to a movie with friends. Now everyone wants to eat, but you realize that you have only a dollar and some change left. What can you do? If you have access to an ATM, you could get cash out of your bank account. Here's a crazy thought—what if your bank runs out of money? What can *it* do?

>> Janet Yellen succeeded Ben Bernanke as Chairman of the Fed in 2014.

The Federal Reserve System

A Review of U.S. Banking History

As you will learn, when American banks need emergency cash, they turn to the Federal Reserve System for a loan. The Federal Reserve System is organized to provide this and a host of essential services to banks, to the federal government, and, most importantly, to the national economy.

The Federal Reserve in American History The Federal Reserve System is the central bank of the United States. It has many important tasks, but the most prominent one is to act as the main spokesperson for the country's monetary policy. **Monetary policy** refers to the actions that the Fed takes to influence the level of real GDP and the rate of inflation in the economy.

The role of a central bank in the U.S. economy has been hotly debated since 1790, when Federalists lined up in favor of establishing a central bank. The first Bank of the United States issued a single currency. It also reviewed banking practices and helped the federal government carry out its duties and powers. Partly because of the impassioned debate over state versus federal powers, however, the

>> Objectives

Describe banking history in the United States.

Explain the structure of the Federal Reserve System.

Explain how the Federal Reserve System's policies affect the money supply and the broader economy.

Analyze the basic tools used by the Federal Reserve System to carry out United States monetary policy.

>> Key Terms

monetary policy
reserves
reserve
   requirements
check clearing
bank holding
   company
federal funds rate
discount rate

first Bank lasted only until 1811. At that time, Congress refused to extend its charter.

Congress established the Second Bank of the United States in 1816 to restore order to the monetary system. However, many people still feared that a central bank placed too much power in the hands of the federal government. Political opposition toppled the Second Bank in 1836 when its charter expired.

A period of confusion followed. States chartered some banks, while the federal government chartered and regulated others. Banks had to keep a certain amount of reserves on hand. **Reserves** are deposits that a bank keeps readily available as opposed to lending them out. **Reserve requirements**—the amount of reserves that banks are required to keep on hand—were difficult to enforce, however, and the nation experienced several serious bank runs. The Panic of 1907 finally convinced Congress that it had to act.

The nation's banking system needed to address two issues. First, consumers and businesses needed greater access to funds to encourage business expansion. Second, banks needed a source of emergency cash to prevent depositor panics that resulted in bank runs.

❓ **IDENTIFY MAIN IDEAS** Why did some Americans oppose the idea of creating a central bank?

The History of the Federal Reserve System

Attempting to prevent problems such as the Panic of 1907, Congress passed the Federal Reserve Act in 1913. The resulting Federal Reserve System, now often referred to simply as "the Fed," consisted of a group of 12 independent regional banks. These banks could lend to other banks in times of need.

Structural Weaknesses Revealed The Great Depression was exactly the situation Congress had hoped to avoid by creating the Federal Reserve System. The system did not work well in that economic crisis, however, because the regional banks each acted independently. Their separate actions often canceled one another out.

For example, in 1929 and 1930, the Governors of the Federal Reserve Banks of New York and Chicago wanted the Fed to lower interest rates. Many of the assets used to make business loans had lost value as a result of the stock market crash. Lowering interest rates would address that problem by making more money available to banks.

However, the Federal Reserve Board of Governors was against lowering interest rates. Concerned about the growth of the stock market, the board favored a contractionary monetary policy—that is, a policy that did not promote rapid economic growth. They also

Central Banks of the United States

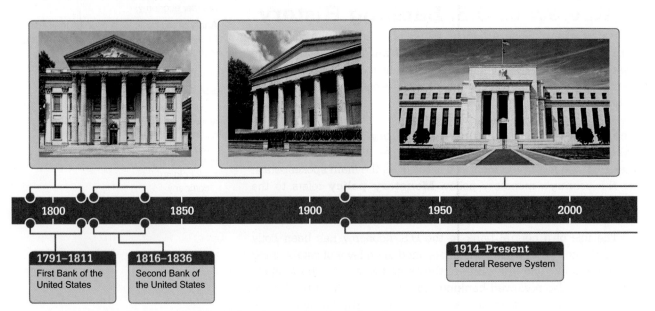

1791–1811	1816–1836	1914–Present
First Bank of the United States	Second Bank of the United States	Federal Reserve System

>> After the end of the second national bank, it took many decades before Congress created a new central bank. **Analyze Data** About how long has the Federal Reserve System been in place?

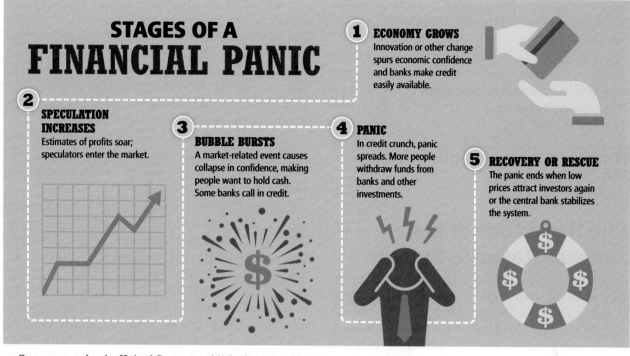

STAGES OF A
FINANCIAL PANIC

1 ECONOMY GROWS
Innovation or other change spurs economic confidence and banks make credit easily available.

2 SPECULATION INCREASES
Estimates of profits soar; speculators enter the market.

3 BUBBLE BURSTS
A market-related event causes collapse in confidence, making people want to hold cash. Some banks call in credit.

4 PANIC
In credit crunch, panic spreads. More people withdraw funds from banks and other investments.

5 RECOVERY OR RESCUE
The panic ends when low prices attract investors again or the central bank stabilizes the system.

>> One reason why the United States established a central banking system was to avoid financial speculation and panics. **Analyze Information** How can a central bank help achieve that goal?

restrained the New York board from taking strong action. Many economists believe that the failure of the Fed to act contributed to the deepening of the financial crisis.

Strengthening the Fed In response to the ongoing depression, Congress adjusted the Federal Reserve's structure in 1935 so that the system could respond more effectively to future crises. These reforms created the Federal Reserve System as we know it today. The new Fed enjoyed more centralized power so that the regional banks were able to act consistently with one another while still representing their own districts' banking concerns. One example shows how the new Fed helped fight a Depression-era crisis in a small Minnesota town. Picture this scene:

Outside a bank in the town, a large crowd was growing frantic. A large number of withdrawals had badly depleted the bank's supply of cash. Inside the bank, a worried banker phoned the Federal Reserve Bank in Minneapolis—200 miles away—and begged officials there to send him money. Fed officers snapped into action. They hired an airplane and loaded it with half a million dollars packed in satchels.

Upon approaching the town the pilot guided the plane low over the main

street to dramatize its arrival and then landed in a nearby field. From there the Fed officials were ceremoniously escorted into town by the police and the money was stacked along the bank's teller windows. The sight of all that money piled up inside the bank quelled the customers' fears and saved the bank from failing.

— "Born of a Panic: Forming the Federal Reserve System," Federal Reserve Board, Minneapolis

More Recent Fed Changes The Fed has continued to change since the Depression. In the early 1950s, the Fed had a sharp disagreement with President Harry Truman and his Treasury Department over whether the Fed or the Treasury would control interest rates on Treasury bonds. The Fed won, allowing it to act more independently in setting monetary policy. In 1980, a new law gave the Fed the authority to set reserve requirements for all banks, even those that are not members.

In 1987 and the early 2000s, the Fed acted aggressively to try to reassure investors that it would support financial institutions in times of crisis. That determination was demonstrated in 2008, when the Fed played a leading role in responding to the financial crisis that arose.

It made emergency loans to banks that needed funds, purchased large amounts of Treasury bonds, and even bought mortgage-related financial instruments. These actions helped reduce the impact of the financial crisis at that time.

? **DESCRIBE** Why did the Fed fail to respond to the Great Depression?

The Structure of the Federal Reserve System

The Federal Reserve System is privately owned by the member banks themselves, but it is publicly controlled by the federal government. Like so many American institutions, the structure of the Federal Reserve System represents compromises between centralized power and regional powers. **Figure 6.2** illustrates that structure.

The Board of Governors The Federal Reserve System is overseen by the Board of Governors of the Federal Reserve. The Board of Governors is headquartered in Washington, D.C. Its seven governors, or members,

are appointed for staggered 14-year terms by the President with the advice and consent of the Senate. The terms are staggered to prevent any one President from appointing a full Board of Governors and to protect board members from day-to-day political pressures. Members cannot be reappointed after serving a full term. Geographical restrictions on these appointments ensure that no one district is overrepresented.

The President also appoints, and the Senate confirms, the chair of the Board of Governors from among these seven members. Chairs serve four-year terms, which can be renewed.

Recent chairs of the Fed have been economists from the business world, the academic world, or government. They have a keen sensitivity toward public opinion and an ability to use the media to affect it. Alan Greenspan, a former head of an economics consulting firm and chair of the President's Council of Economic Advisers (CEA), has been the most notable chair of the Fed in modern times. He took office in 1987 and served both Republican and Democratic administrations. After Greenspan resigned in 2006, President George W. Bush replaced him with Ben Bernanke, the head of the Council of Economic Advisers and a former professor of economics. Bernanke learned about monetary policy and the ideas of Milton Friedman as a graduate student.

In 2013, President Barack Obama nominated Janet Yellen as the first female chair of the Federal Reserve

>> **Figure 6.2** The Federal Reserve System is made up of three levels. **Analyze Charts** At which level would a nationally chartered bank in your community fit?

▶ **Interactive Illustration**

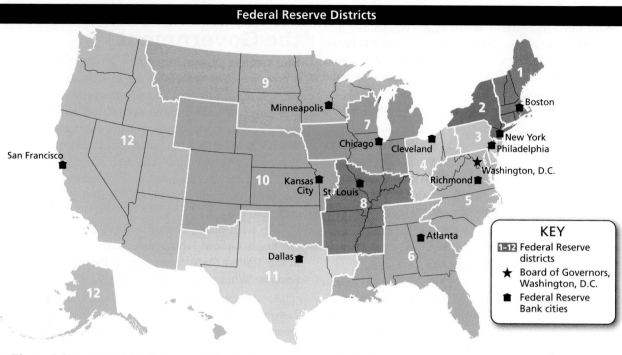

>> **Figure 6.3** The 12 District Banks are different sizes as measured by their assets. The New York Reserve Bank has a small geographic area but the largest number of assets.

System. Prior to her nomination, Yellen was the Vice Chair of the Federal Reserve Board of Governors and the President of the Federal Reserve District Bank in San Francisco.

Twelve Federal Reserve Banks The Federal Reserve Act divided the United States into 12 Federal Reserve Districts, as shown in **Figure 6.3.** One Federal Reserve Bank is located in each district, though it may have branches in other cities in the district as well. Each of these banks monitors and reports on economic and banking conditions in its district.

Each Federal Reserve District is made up of more than one state. The Federal Reserve Act aimed to establish a system in which no one region could exploit the central bank's power at another region's expense.

Congress regulates the makeup of each Reserve Bank's board of nine directors to make sure that the board represents many interests. The nine directors consist of three sets of three persons each.

The first set of three represents commercial banks, and they are elected by the district's member banks. The member banks also elect the second set—three people who represent the interests of groups such as industry, commerce, labor, services, and consumers. The third set of directors is appointed by the Board of Governors of the Federal Reserve. These three represent the same broad public interests as the second group.

The Board of Governors selects one of the nine directors to serve as chair of the Reserve Bank's board. Each board of directors appoints a president of the Reserve Bank, subject to approval by the Board of Governors.

Member Banks All nationally chartered banks are required to join the Federal Reserve System. The remaining members are state-chartered banks that join voluntarily. Since 1980, all banks have equal access to Fed services, whether or not they are Fed members. These services include reserve loans to banks in need of short-term cash.

Each of the approximately 2,400 Fed member banks contributes a small amount of money to join the system. In return, it receives stock in the system. This stock earns the bank dividends from the Fed at a rate of up to 6 percent. The fact that the banks themselves, rather than a government agency, own the Federal Reserve gives the system a high degree of political independence. This independence helps the Fed to make decisions that best suit the interests of the country as a whole.

The Federal Open Market Committee The Federal Open Market Committee (FOMC) makes key monetary policy decisions about interest rates and the growth of the money supply in the United States. The committee meets about eight times a year in private to discuss the cost and availability of credit, for businesses and consumers, across the country. Announcements of the FOMC's decisions can affect financial markets and rates for home mortgages, as well as many economic institutions around the world.

Members of the Federal Open Market Committee are drawn from the Board of Governors and the 12 district banks. All seven members of the Board of Governors sit on the FOMC, as do five of the 12 district bank presidents. The president of the New York Federal Reserve Bank is a permanent member.

The four other district presidents serve one-year terms on a rotating basis. The Board of Governors holds a majority of the seats on the FOMC, giving it effective control over the committee's actions.

After meeting with the FOMC, the chair of the Board of Governors announces the committee's decisions to the public. The Federal Reserve Banks and financial markets spring into action as they react to Fed decisions.

? IDENTIFY What is the role of each of the 12 Federal Reserve Banks?

>> The Federal Reserve is the banker for the United States government. The Fed processes all checks that the government writes, such as payments to members of the military.

The Fed's Roles: Serving the Government

Your summer job is going great—you like the work, and it pays well. The trouble is, the paychecks are handed out just once a month, and you desperately need that first paycheck. Finally, the end of the month arrives, and you rush to your bank to cash your paycheck. But the bank teller has an unpleasant surprise for you. The bank will not credit the amount to your account until the paycheck clears. It will take at least two days, the teller says, for the check-clearing process to be completed.

The teller doesn't explain—probably because he or she doesn't know—that most check-clearing functions in the United States are handled through the Federal Reserve. What else does the Fed do?

As the central bank of the United States, the 12 district banks that make up the core of the Federal Reserve System carry out several important functions. Among the most important of these functions is to provide banking and fiscal services to the federal government.

Acting as the Government's Banker and Agent The United States government pays out about $1.2 trillion each year to support such social insurance programs as Medicare, Social Security, and veterans' benefits. To handle its banking needs when dealing with such enormous sums, the federal government turns to the Federal Reserve. The Fed maintains a checking account for the Treasury Department that it uses to process Social Security checks, income tax refunds, and other government payments. For example, if you receive a check from the federal government and cash it at your local bank, it is the Federal Reserve that deducts the amount from the Treasury's account.

The Federal Reserve also serves as a financial agent for the Treasury Department and other government agencies. The Fed sells, transfers, and redeems securities such as government bonds, bills, and notes. It also makes interest payments to the people holding these securities.

The Treasury Department auctions off government bills, bonds, and notes to finance the many programs of the U.S. government. Funds raised from these auctions are automatically deposited into the Federal Reserve Bank of New York.

Issuing Currency for the Government Only the federal government can issue currency. The Treasury Department issues coins minted at the United States Mint. The district Federal Reserve Banks issue paper currency. You may have one now—the bill says "Federal

Noncash Transactions (in Billions)

	2000	2006	2009
Checks	42.5	30.5	24.5
Debit cards	8.2	25.0	37.9
Credit cards	15.2	21.7	21.6
Electronic payments	5.6	14.6	19.1
Prepaid cards	.1	3.3	6.0
Total	**71.6**	**95.2**	**109.0**

SOURCE: Federal Reserve System, The 2010 Federal Reserve Payments Study: Noncash Payment Trends in the United States: 2006–2009, Federal Reserve System, 2011, p 11

>> Between 2000 and 2009, consumers' use of checks decreased while most other types of noncash transactions increased. **Analyze Charts** What technological developments occurred during these years that made the changes in non-cash transactions possible?

▶ **Interactive Illustration**

Reserve Note." As bills become worn out or torn, the Fed takes them out of circulation and replaces them with fresh ones.

? RECALL How does the Federal Reserve serve as the government's banker?

The Fed's Roles: Serving and Regulating Banks

The Federal Reserve also provides services to banks throughout the nation. It clears checks, safeguards bank resources, and lends funds to help banks that need to borrow in order to maintain their legally required reserves. It also coordinates the activities of a number of state and federal regulatory authorities.

Clearing Checks Check clearing is the process by which banks record whose account gives up money and whose account receives money as a result of a customer writing a check. The Fed can clear millions of checks at any one time using high-speed equipment. Most checks clear within two days—a remarkable achievement when you consider that the Fed processes about 18 billion checks per year.

Supervising Banking Practices To ensure stability of the banking system, the Federal Reserve monitors banks' reserves. Each of the 12 Federal Reserve Banks

sends out bank examiners to check up on lending and other financial activities of member banks.

As part of the Fed's role in supervising banks, the Board of Governors studies proposed bank mergers and bank holding company charters to ensure competition in the banking and financial industries. A **bank holding company** is a company that owns more than one bank. The Board of Governors approves or disapproves mergers and charters based on the findings and recommendations of the Reserve Banks.

Acting as Lender of Last Resort Under normal circumstances, banks lend each other money on a day-to-day basis, using money from their reserve balances. These funds are called federal funds. The interest rate that banks charge each other for these loans is the **federal funds rate.**

Banks also borrow from the Federal Reserve, especially in financial emergencies such as recessions. The Fed acts as a lender of last resort, making emergency loans to commercial banks so that they can maintain required reserves. The rate the Federal Reserve charges for these loans is called the **discount rate.**

The Fed's Expanded Role A serious financial crisis erupted in 2008. It began because many banks had made home loans that borrowers were unable to repay. As the crisis deepened, corporations and other borrowers could not obtain loans from banks, and the financial system ceased to function effectively.

The Federal Reserve responded to this crisis by changing the size and scope of its involvement in the economy. When banks stopped lending each other money, the Fed fulfilled its role as lender of last resort.

It also began purchasing assets, as total assets increased during 2008 from less than $1 trillion to over $2 trillion. Prior to the financial crisis, most of the Fed's assets consisted of government securities. To help the mortgage market through the financial crisis, the Fed bought mortgage-backed securities. In 2010, the Fed held over $1 trillion of these financial instruments.

The Fed took two other significant steps during the financial crisis. The Federal Reserve worked with some central banks in other countries to create "swap lines." In these arrangements, the Fed loaned dollars to the foreign banks for a short period of time. The foreign banks could lend those funds in their own countries but had to repay the Fed—with interest—in a specified time period.

The second unusual measure was that the FOMC reduced the discount rate nearly to 0 percent in late 2008. This move aimed at lowering interest rates in the hopes of jump-starting the economy. The FOMC kept the rate at this extremely low level late into 2013.

Monitoring Reserves United States banks operate under a fractional reserve system. Banks hold in reserve only a fraction of their funds—just enough to meet customers' expected daily needs. Banks then lend their remaining funds, charging interest to earn returns.

Each financial institution that holds deposits for customers must report daily to the Fed about its reserves and activities. The Fed uses these reserves to control how much money is in circulation.

Conducting Bank Examinations The Federal Reserve and other regulatory agencies also examine banks periodically to ensure that each institution is obeying laws and regulations. Examiners may make unexpected bank visits to ensure that banks are following sound lending practices.

Bank examiners can force banks to sell risky investments or to declare loans that will not be repaid as losses. If examiners find that a bank has taken excessive risks, they may classify that institution as a problem bank and force it to undergo more frequent examinations.

The Federal Reserve also protects consumers by enforcing truth-in-lending laws, which require lenders to provide full and accurate information about loan terms. Under a provision called Regulation Z, consumers receive useful information about retail credit terms, automobile loans, and home mortgages.

? **IDENTIFY CENTRAL IDEAS** Why does the Federal Reserve conduct bank examinations?

The Effect of Different Reserve Requirements

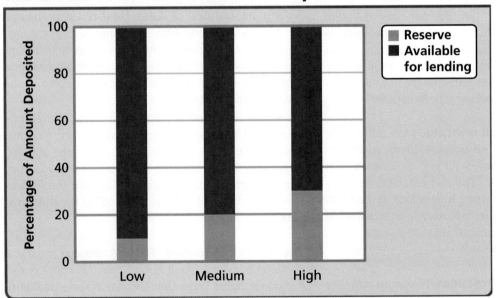

>> **Analyze Graphs** What effect does the reserve requirement have on banks' ability to lend?

Prime Interest Rate, 1995–2013

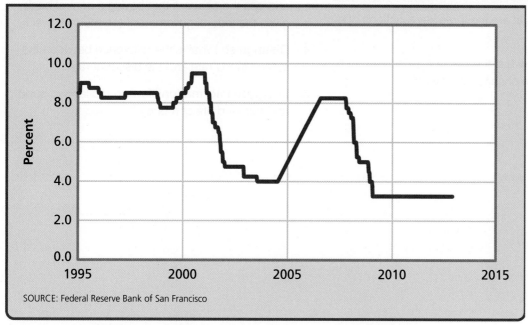

SOURCE: Federal Reserve Bank of San Francisco

>> The prime interest rate is not set by the Fed but by banks: it is the rate charged by the top 25 commercial banks. **Analyze Charts** When was it cheaper to borrow money, in 2000 or 2010? Why?

The Fed's Roles: Regulating the Money Supply

The Federal Reserve is best known for its role in regulating the nation's money supply. To do so, it uses several tools: setting the discount rate, setting reserve requirements, setting the federal funds rate target, and using open market operations to meet that target. Economists and the Fed watch several indicators of the money supply. M1 is a measure of the funds that are easily accessible or in circulation. M2 includes the funds counted in M1 as well as money market accounts and savings instruments. You will read more about these measurements in the next Lesson. The Fed compares various measures of the money supply with the likely demand for money to determine when and how to use these tools.

The Demand for Money People and firms need to have a certain amount of cash on hand to make purchases—to buy groceries, supplies, clothing, and so forth. The more of your wealth you hold as money, the easier it will be to make these transactions.

Of course, we can't earn interest on money that we hold as cash. As interest rates rise, it becomes more expensive to hold money as cash rather than placing it in assets that pay returns. That is, not investing when interest rates are high means you don't realize earnings you otherwise would realize. So, as interest rates rise, people and firms will generally keep their wealth in assets such as bonds, stocks, or savings accounts rather than in cash. The higher that interest rates are, the lower the demand for money.

The final factor that influences money demand is the general level of income. As GDP or real income rises, families and firms keep more of their wealth or income in cash.

Stabilizing the Economy The laws of supply and demand affect money, just as they affect everything else in the economy. Too much money in the economy leads to inflation. In inflationary times, it takes more money to purchase the same goods and services. It is the Fed's job to keep the money supply stable.

Ideally, if real GDP grew smoothly and the economy stayed at full employment, the Fed would increase the money supply just enough to match the growth in the demand for money, thus keeping inflation low. It is difficult to predict economic effects. however. The Fed has to be careful in using monetary policy to regulate the money supply.

? IDENTIFY What is the effect of too much money in circulation?

ASSESSMENT

1. **Summarize** What are the three key functions of a central bank?

2. **Synthesize** How has the role of the Federal Reserve System changed over time?

3. **Cite Evidence** How does the structure of the Fed address the concern that having a central bank gives the federal government too much power?

4. **Distinguish** What is the difference between the federal funds rate and the discount rate?

5. **Integrate Information** How do the laws of supply and demand affect money?

It's Friday. You just got your paycheck for the week. You take it to the bank, where you fill out a deposit slip and then stand in line and wait . . . and wait . . . and wait for the next available teller. Hold on a minute. That scenario is out-of-date! You don't have time for standing in line. You deposit your check quickly at an ATM. Or better yet, you have arranged to have your week's pay electronically deposited directly into your bank account.

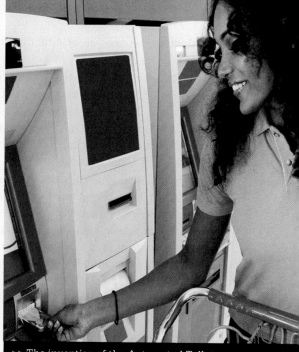

>> The invention of the Automated Teller Machine (ATM) has made withdrawing money and conducting other banking activities more convenient than in the past.

▶ **Interactive Flipped Video**

The Functions of Modern Banks

The Money Supply

Financial institutions provide these electronic services—and many others suited to the computer age. They issue credit cards, make loans to businesses, and provide mortgages to prospective home buyers. They also manage automated teller machines that enable a person to deposit or withdraw money in almost any place on the globe. In this text, you'll learn more about electronic transactions, the fractional reserve system, and other aspects of banking today.

You are familiar with paying for the items you need with currency—the bills and coins in your pocket. Currency is money. So are traveler's checks, checking account deposits, and a variety of other components. All of these components make up the United States **money supply**—all the money available in the United States economy. To more easily keep track of these different kinds of money, economists divide the money supply into several categories. The main categories are called M1 and M2.

M1 As you can see from **Figure 6.4,** M1 represents money that people can gain access to easily and immediately to pay for goods and services. In other words, M1 consists of assets that have **liquidity,**

>> **Objectives**

Identify different types of financial institutions, and the services they provide.

Explain the benefits provided by financial institutions in the context of our free enterprise system.

Describe the development of electronic banking.

>> **Key Terms**

money supply
liquidity
demand deposits
money market
  mutual funds
fractional reserve
  banking
default
mortgage
credit card
interest
principal
debit card
creditor

or the ability to be used as, or directly converted into, cash.

About 45 percent of M1 is made up of currency held by the public, that is, all currency held outside of bank vaults. Another large component of M1 is deposits in checking accounts. Funds in checking accounts are also called **demand deposits,** because checks can be paid "on demand," that is, at any time.

Until the 1980s, checking accounts did not pay interest. When they began paying interest, the Fed introduced a new component to measure M1, called *other checkable deposits,* to describe those accounts. Today this category is not as meaningful as it once was, since many checking accounts only pay interest if the balance is sufficiently high.

Traveler's checks make up a very small part of M1. Unlike personal checks, traveler's checks can be easily turned into cash.

M2 As you can see in **Figure 6.5,** M2 consists of all the assets in M1 plus several additional assets. These additional M2 funds cannot be used as cash directly but can be converted to cash fairly easily. M2 assets are also called *near money.*

For example, deposits in savings accounts are included in M2. They are not included in M1 because they cannot be used directly in financial exchanges. You cannot hand a sales clerk your savings account passbook to pay for a new backpack. You can, however, withdraw money from your savings account and then use that money to buy a backpack.

Deposits in **money market mutual funds** are also included as part of M2. These are funds that pool money from a large number of small savers to purchase short-term government and corporate securities. They earn interest and can be used to cover checks written over a certain minimum amount, such as $250.

❓ IDENTIFY Which category of the money supply includes deposits in money market mutual funds?

Functions of Financial Institutions

Banks and other financial institutions are essential to managing the money supply. They perform many functions and offer a wide range of services to consumers.These services benefit both businesses and households, which is a term economists use to describe ordinary consumers

Storing Money Banks provide a safe, convenient place for people to store money. Banks keep cash in fireproof vaults and are insured against the loss of money in the event of a robbery. As you have already read, FDIC

M1 Components

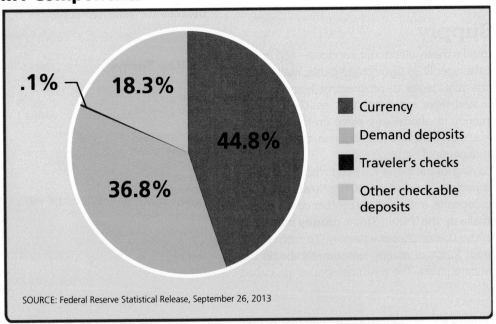

.1% 18.3% 44.8% 36.8%

- Currency
- Demand deposits
- Traveler's checks
- Other checkable deposits

SOURCE: Federal Reserve Statistical Release, September 26, 2013

>> **Figure 6.4** M1 consists of cash and assets that can be directly converted into cash. The term demand deposits refers to money in checking accounts. **Analyze Graphs** Which type of asset makes up most of M1?

M2 Components

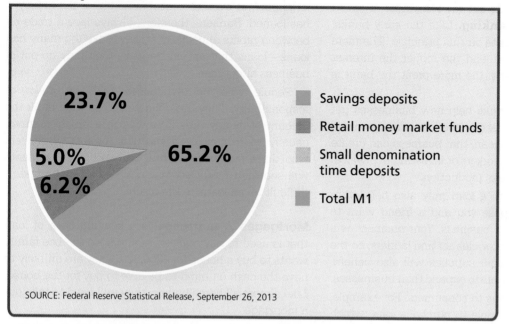

Savings deposits

Retail money market funds

Small denomination time deposits

Total M1

23.7%

5.0%

6.2%

65.2%

SOURCE: Federal Reserve Statistical Release, September 26, 2013

>> **Figure 6.5** M2 consists of M1 assets plus funds that cannot be easily converted into cash. **Analyze Graphs** Which type of asset makes up most of M2?

insurance protects people from losing their money if the bank is unable to repay funds.

Saving Money Banks offer a variety of ways for people to save money. Four of the most common ways are savings accounts, checking accounts, money market accounts, and certificates of deposit (CDs).

Savings accounts and checking accounts are the most common types of bank accounts. They are especially useful for people who need to make frequent withdrawals. Savings accounts and most checking accounts pay interest at an annual rate. These accounts offer practically no risk, but the financial cost of them is that the interest rates are very low.

Money market accounts and certificates of deposit (CDs) are special kinds of savings accounts that pay a higher rate of interest than savings and checking accounts. Money market accounts allow you to save and to write a limited number of checks. Interest rates are not fixed; they can move up or down. CDs, on the other hand, offer a guaranteed rate of interest. Funds placed in a CD, however, cannot be removed until the end of a certain time period, such as one or two years. CDs, like savings anc checking accounts, have little risk, but customers who remove their money before that time pay a penalty for early withdrawal.

Interest allows consumers to earn money from their savings when they maintain bank accounts or purchase CDs. For example, a person with $25,000 in a savings

account with an annual interest rate of 3 percent will earn $750 in a year.

Over time, these earnings will add up and increase savings. Consumers can use these savings to put a down payment on a house, pay for college, or fund their retirement. Savings are also helpful when something unforeseen, like a job layoff, happens.

Making Loans Banks also perform the important service of providing loans. As you have read, the first banks started doing business when goldsmiths issued paper receipts. These receipts represented gold coins that the goldsmiths held in safe storage for their customers. They would charge a small fee for this service.

In early banks, those receipts were fully backed by gold—every customer who held a receipt could be sure that the goldsmith kept the equivalent amount of gold in his safe. Gradually, however, goldsmiths realized that their customers seldom, if ever, asked for all of their gold on one day. Goldsmiths could thus lend out half or even three quarters of their gold at any one time and still have enough gold to handle customer demand. Why did goldsmiths want to lend gold? The answer is that they charged interest on their loans. By keeping just enough gold reserves to cover demand, goldsmiths could run a profitable business lending deposits to borrowers and earning interest.

A banking system that keeps only a fraction of its funds on hand and lends out the remainder is called **fractional reserve banking.** Like the early banks, today's banks also operate on this principle. The more money a bank lends out, and the higher the interest rate it charges borrowers, the more profit the bank is able to make.

By making loans, banks help new businesses get started, and they help established businesses grow. When a business gets a loan, that business can create new jobs by hiring new workers or investing in physical capital in order to increase production.

A business that gets a loan may also help other businesses grow. Suppose you and a friend want to start a window-washing business. Your business will need supplies, like window cleaner and ladders, so the companies that make your supplies will also benefit. They may even hire workers to expand their businesses.

Banks also make loans to consumers. For example, banks lend money to people to purchase cars, which are expensive and difficult to pay for all at once. Consumers also borrow money from banks to purchase homes, make improvements to their homes, and pay for college. Banks earn money on the interest they charge to consumers.

Bankers must, however, consider the security of the loans they make. Suppose borrowers **default,** or

fail to pay back their loans. Then the bank may lose a large part, or even the entire amount, of the money it has loaned. Bankers, therefore, always face a trade-off between profits and safety. If they make too many bad loans—loans that are not repaid—they may go out of business altogether.

People who borrow money take on a lot of responsibility. They are obligated to pay the bank the amount of money they borrowed in a timely manner, usually on a monthly basis, plus interest. Borrowers who don't repay their loans or make late payments will see their credit scores suffer, which will make it difficult to get loans in the future.

Mortgages A **mortgage** is a specific type of loan that is used to buy real estate. Suppose the Lee family wants to buy a house for $250,000. They are unlikely to have the cash on hand to be able to pay for the house. Like almost all home buyers, they will need to take out a mortgage.

The Lees can afford to make a down payment of 20 percent of the price of the house, or $50,000. After investigating the Lees' creditworthiness, their bank agrees to lend them the remaining $200,000 so that they can purchase their new house. Mortgages usually last for 15, 25, or 30 years. According to the terms of their loan, the Lees are responsible for paying back

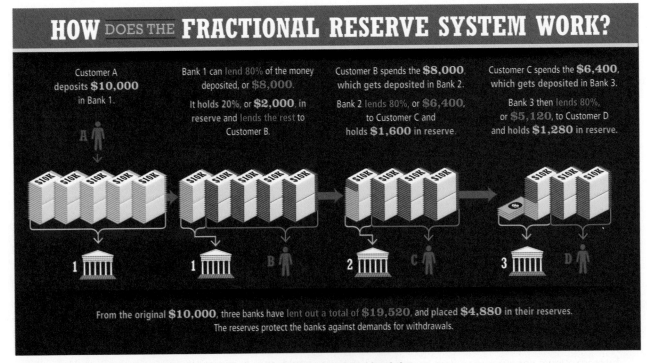

HOW DOES THE FRACTIONAL RESERVE SYSTEM WORK?

Customer A deposits **$10,000** in Bank 1.

Bank 1 can lend 80% of the money deposited, or **$8,000.**
It holds 20%, or **$2,000,** in reserve and lends the rest to Customer B.

Customer B spends the **$8,000,** which gets deposited in Bank 2.
Bank 2 lends 80%, or **$6,400,** to Customer C and holds **$1,600** in reserve.

Customer C spends the **$6,400,** which gets deposited in Bank 3.
Bank 3 then lends 80%, or **$5,120,** to Customer D and holds **$1,280** in reserve.

From the original **$10,000,** three banks have lent out a total of **$19,520,** and placed **$4,880** in their reserves. The reserves protect the banks against demands for withdrawals.

>> The Fed requires banks to keep a fraction of their funds on hand and lend the remainder to customers. **Analyze Information** What could happen if banks kept only 5 percent in reserve?

Mortgage Rates

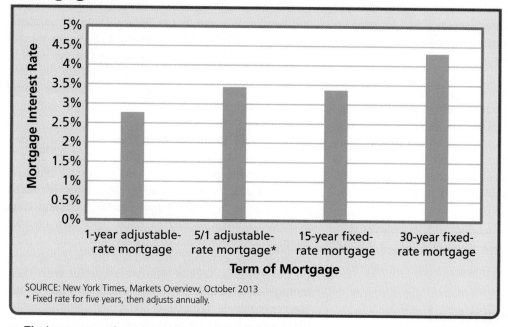

Mortgage Interest Rate vs. Term of Mortgage

- 1-year adjustable-rate mortgage
- 5/1 adjustable-rate mortgage*
- 15-year fixed-rate mortgage
- 30-year fixed-rate mortgage

SOURCE: New York Times, Markets Overview, October 2013
* Fixed rate for five years, then adjusts annually.

>> The interest rate that a bank charges depends on the term of the loan. **Analyze Graphs** Why is the interest rate on a 30-year fixed-rate mortgage higher than the rate on a 15-year fixed-rate mortgage?

the loan, plus whatever interest the bank charges, in regular monthly payments over a period of 25 years.

Buying a home can provide many benefits, but it also can come with costs. One benefit is stability. Unlike renters, homeowners with a fixed-rate mortgage can expect to pay the same amount every year for the duration of the loan. Because homes typically increase in value over time, people often make money when they sell their home. However, many home buyers have to use a large portion of their savings for a down payment. They also have less mobility than renters. For example, a renter who finds a new job in a different city will be able to relocate more easily than a homeowner.

Credit Cards Another service that banks provide is issuing **credit cards**—cards entitling their owners to buy goods and services based on the owners' promises to pay. How do credit cards work? Suppose you buy a sleeping bag and tent for $150 on May 3. Your credit card bill may not arrive until June. You do not actually pay for the gear until you pay that bill. In the meantime, however, the credit card issuer (often a bank) will have paid the sporting-goods store. Your payment repays the bank for the "loan" of $150. If you do not pay your credit card bill in full when you receive it, you will end up paying a high rate of interest on that loan.

A positive aspect of credit cards is that they give people the ability to purchase goods they might not have

been able to afford otherwise. For example, you might want to purchase $500 worth of gear for a camping trip next weekend. Because you won't have that amount of money in your checking account until you get paid in two weeks, you can use a credit card. Using a credit card will help build credit, which is needed for getting a loan to buy a car or house.

A negative aspect of credit cards is that items purchased with credit cards sometimes wind up costing more than their price tag. If you purchased the camping gear with a card that had a 15 percent interest rate and you sent your credit card company $50 a month for 11 months, the total you would pay for the gear would be about $538. People who frequently make purchases with credit cards run the risk of incurring high debts that are difficult to pay back.

Interest As you have read, **interest** is the price paid for the use of borrowed money. The amount borrowed is called the **principal.** Simple interest is interest paid only on principal. For example, if you deposit $100 in a savings account at 5 percent simple interest, you will make $5 in a year (assuming that interest is paid annually).

Suppose that you leave the $5 in interest in the bank, so that at the end of the year you have $105 in your account—$100 in principal and $5 in interest. Compound interest is interest paid on both principal and accumulated interest. That means that in the second year, as long as you leave both the principal and the interest in your account, interest will be paid on $105. In **Figure 6.6,** you can see how an account paying compound interest grows over time.

Making a Profit The largest source of income for banks is the interest they receive from customers who have taken loans. Banks, of course, also pay out interest on customers' savings and most checking accounts. The amount of interest they pay out, however, is less than the amount of interest they charge on loans. The difference in the amounts is how banks cover their costs and make a profit.

? IDENTIFY What type of loan helps a person purchase a home?

Types of Financial Institutions

Several kinds of financial institutions operate in the United States. These include commercial banks, savings and loan associations, mutual savings banks, and credit unions.

Commercial Banks Commercial banks, which traditionally served businesses, offer a wide range of services today. Commercial banks offer checking accounts, accept deposits, and make loans to businesses and to individuals. Some commercial banks are chartered by states and are regulated by state authorities and by the Federal Deposit Insurance Corporation (FDIC). About one third of all commercial banks are national banks and are part of the Federal Reserve System. Commercial banks provide the most services and play the largest role in the economy of any type of bank.

Savings and Loan Associations Savings and loan associations (S&Ls), which you read about in Text 2, were originally chartered to lend money for building homes during the mid-1800s. Members of S&Ls deposited funds into a large general fund and then borrowed enough money to build their own houses. Savings and loan associations are also called thrifts because they originally enabled "thrifty" working-class people—that is, people who were careful with their money—to save up and borrow enough to build or buy their own homes. Over time, S&Ls have taken on many of the same functions as commercial banks.

Savings Banks Mutual savings banks (MSBs) originated in the early 1800s to serve people who made smaller deposits and transactions than commercial banks wished to handle. Mutual savings banks were owned by the depositors themselves, who shared in any profits. Later, many MSBs began to sell stock to raise additional capital. These institutions became simply savings banks because depositors no longer owned them.

Compound Interest

YEAR	PRINCIPAL AMOUNT	INTEREST EARNED AT 5%	PRINCIPAL AT END OF YEAR
1	$100.00	$5.00	$105.00
2	$105.00	$5.25	$110.25
3	$110.25	$5.51	$115.76
5	$121.55	$6.08	$127.63
10	$155.13	$7.77	$162.90
15	$197.99	$9.90	$207.89

>> **Figure 6.6** A $100 deposit, when compounded yearly at 5 percent, will more than double in value over 15 years. **Analyze Charts** Would a higher interest rate encourage people to save more or less? Why?

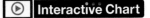 **Interactive Chart**

Banks in the United States, 2012

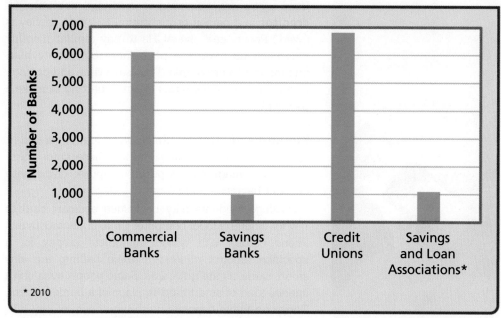

* 2010

>> Savings banks and S&Ls have become less common because they don't differ significantly from other banks. **Analyze Graphs** About how many more commercials banks are there in the United States than savings banks?

Although savings banks were traditionally concentrated in the Northeast, they had an important influence on the national economy. In 1972, the Consumer's Savings Bank of Worcester, Massachusetts, introduced a Negotiable Order of Withdrawal (NOW) account, a type of checking account that pays interest. NOW accounts became available nationwide in 1980.

Credit Unions Credit unions are cooperative lending associations usually established by and for particular groups, usually employees of a specific firm or government agency. Some are open to an entire community. Credit unions are commonly fairly small and specialize in consumer loans, usually at interest rates favorable to members. Some credit unions also provide checking account services.

Finance Companies Finance companies make installment loans to consumers. These loans spread the cost of major purchases such as computers, cars, and large appliances over a number of months. Because people who borrow from finance companies more frequently fail to repay the loans, finance companies generally charge higher interest rates than banks do.

? **IDENTIFY** Which type of financial institution plays the largest role in the economy?

Electronic Banking

Banks began to use computers in the early 1970s to keep track of transactions. As computers have become more common in the United States, their role in banking has also increased dramatically. In fact, computerized banking may revolutionize banking in much the same way that paper currency changed banking long ago.

Automated Teller Machines If you use an Automated Teller Machine (ATM), you are already familiar with one of the most common types of electronic banking. ATMs are computers that customers can use to deposit money, withdraw cash, and obtain account information at their convenience. Instead of having to conduct banking business face-to-face with a teller during the bank's hours of operation, you can take care of your finances at an ATM.

ATMs are convenient both for banks and for customers, since they are available 24 hours a day and reduce banks' labor costs. Their popularity has made them a standard feature of modern banking.

Debit Cards At an ATM, bank customers can use a **debit card** to withdraw money from an account. They can also use a debit card in stores equipped with special machines. When you "swipe" your debit card through one of those machines, the card sends a message to your bank to debit, or subtract money

writing checks. An ACH transfers funds automatically from customers' accounts to creditors' accounts. (A **creditor** is a person or institution to whom money is owed.) People can use ACHs to pay regular monthly bills such as mortgage payments, rent, utility bills, and insurance premiums. They save time and postage costs, and end any worries about forgetting to make a payment.

Stored-Value Cards Stored-value cards, or smart cards, are similar to debit cards. These cards carry embedded magnetic strips or computer chips with account balance information.

College students may be issued a smart card to pay for cafeteria food, computer time, or photocopying. Phone cards, with which customers prepay for a specified amount of long-distance calling, are also smart cards, as are gift cards. Some people even use a special kind of smart card in place of a bank account. They can make deposits, withdraw cash, or pay bills with the card.

Will stored-value smart cards someday replace cash altogether? No one can know for sure, but private companies and public facilities continue to explore new uses for smart card technology.

? **DESCRIBE** How does a debit card work?

>> Smartphone credit card readers have made it easier for small businesses to accept credit card payments.

▶ **Interactive Chart**

from, your checking account. The money goes directly into the store's bank account. For security, debit cards require customers to use personal identification numbers, or PINs, to authorize financial transactions.

Home Banking More and more people are using the Internet to conduct their financial business. Many banks, credit unions, and other financial institutions allow people to check account balances, transfer money to different accounts, automatically deposit their paychecks, and pay their bills via computer. Many Americans have also opened accounts with private online bill-paying services and money-transfer services that allow them to send money instantly over the Internet.

Automated Clearing Houses Automated Clearing Houses (ACHs), located at Federal Reserve Banks and their branches, allow consumers to pay bills without

ASSESSMENT

1. **Summarize** Describe a situation in which a person would need a mortgage from a bank.

2. **Determine Central Ideas** When would you pay interest?

3. **Identify Supporting Details** List at least three services that are available through home banking over the Internet.

4. **Summarize** (a) What kinds of money are included in M1 and M2? (b) Why do economists use these different categories?

5. **Compare and Contrast** (a) In what ways are debit cards and stored-value cards similar? (b) How are they different?

Right now, you are making a huge investment. You are investing your time and energy in your education. This investment is likely to pay off later, in the form of a satisfying career. In the same way, businesses and governments look to the future. If a firm builds a new plant, it invests money today for the sake of earning more money later. If the government builds a new dam, it invests money today to ensure that people will have hydroelectric power in the future.

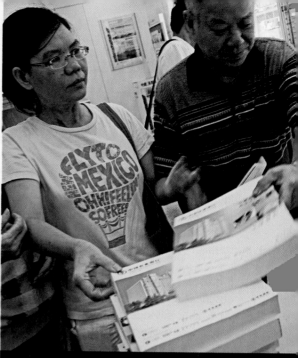

>> These people are picking up prospectuses of a company that is issuing stock for the first time. Wise investors study prospectuses carefully to choose how to invest their money.

▶ **Interactive Flipped Video**

Investing

Investment and Free Enterprise

There are both benefits and risks to savings and investment. The savings you put in the bank will grow with almost no risk to the principle.

However, as this section points out, a properly timed investment can bring a much greater reward than the same money put away in savings. On the other hand, if your investment is wrongly placed or ill-timed, you may wish you had never taken the money out of the bank.

In its most general sense, **investment** is the act of redirecting resources from being consumed today so that they may create benefits in the future. In more narrow, economic terms, investment is the use of assets to earn income or profit.

One of the benefits of the free enterprise system is that it provides investment opportunities. Investment promotes economic growth and helps to create wealth. When people deposit money in a savings account in a bank, for example, the bank may then lend the funds to businesses. The businesses, in turn, may invest that money in new plants and equipment to give them the resources to increase production. As these businesses use their investments to purchase new capital equipment for expansion and growth, they create new

>> **Objectives**

Describe how investing contributes to the free enterprise system.

Explain how investing brings together savers and borrowers in the free enterprise system.

Explain how different types of financial institutions serve as intermediaries between savers and borrowers.

Analyze liquidity, return, and risk within the free enterprise system.

>> **Key Terms**

investment
financial system
financial asset
financial
   intermediary
mutual fund
hedge fund
diversification
portfolio
prospectus
return

and better products and provide new jobs, all of which helps create wealth throughout society.

? DESCRIBE What role does investment play in the free enterprise system?

The Financial System

In order for investment to take place, an economy must have a financial system. A **financial system** is the network of structures and mechanisms that allows the transfer of money between savers and borrowers.

Financial Assets When people save, they are, in essence, lending funds to others. Whether they put cash in a savings account, purchase a certificate of deposit, or buy a government or corporate bond, savers obtain a document that confirms their purchase or deposit. These documents may be passbooks, monthly statements, bond certificates, or other records.

Such documents represent claims on the property or income of the borrower. These claims are called **financial assets,** or securities. If the borrower fails to pay back the loan, these documents can serve as proof in court that money was borrowed and that commitments were made that were not fulfilled.

Savers and Borrowers Figure 6.7 shows how the financial system brings together savers and borrowers, fueling investment and economic growth. On one side are savers—households, individuals, and businesses that lend out their savings in return for financial assets, such as the promise of regular interest payments.

On the other side are investors—governments and businesses—who invest the money they borrow to build roads, factories, and homes. Investors may also use these funds to develop new products, create new markets, or provide new services.

Interest allocates savings to its most productive use. The interest that savers earn is the reason why they save money in a bank or invest it, rather than spending it or holding cash. Financial institutions then invest those savings in businesses that use it productively to create more wealth. Long-term interest rates are higher than short term rates, which can also help use money productively. Without the higher rates, people might not be willing to invest money for long periods of time. When businesses can have that money for longer periods, they can use in productive ways that require more time, such as building new facilities or investing in equipment that may take a while to pay off.

? CHECK UNDERSTANDING How can a saver such as an individual, a household, or a business put savings to their most productive use?

FINANCIAL INTERMEDIARIES

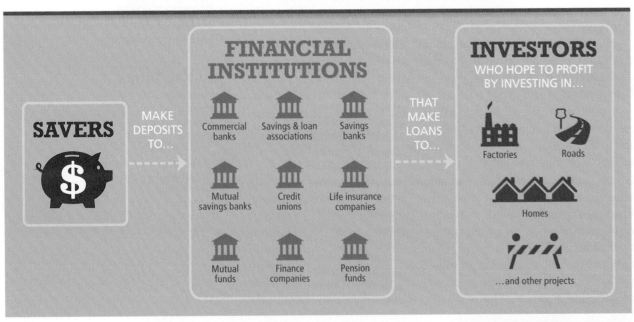

>> **Figure 6.7 Analyze Information** Why do investors typically borrow money from financial institutions rather than directly from savers?

▶ Interactive Illustration

Americans' Saving Rate

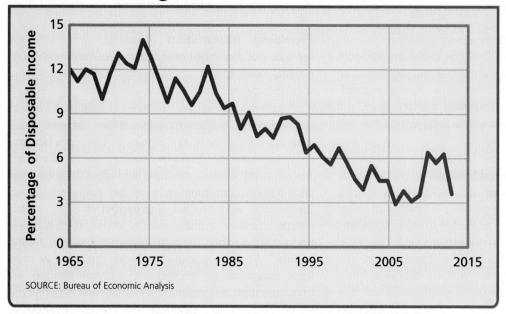

SOURCE: Bureau of Economic Analysis

>> Individuals' savings is one important part of our financial system. **Analyze Graphs**
How would you describe the trend in the percentage that Americans saved between
1975 and 2005?

Financial Intermediaries

Savers and borrowers may be linked directly. As you examine **Figure 6.7,** you will notice that borrowers and savers may also be linked through a variety of institutions pictured as "in between" the two. These **financial intermediaries** are institutions that help channel funds from savers to borrowers. They include the following:

Banks, savings and loan associations (S&Ls), credit unions, and finance companies Banks, S&Ls, and credit unions take in deposits from savers and then lend out some of these funds to businesses and individuals. Finance companies make loans to consumers and small businesses.

Mutual funds A **mutual fund** pools the savings of many individuals and invests this money in a variety of stocks, bonds, and other financial assets. Mutual funds allow people to invest in a broad range of companies in the stock market. Investing in this way is less risky than purchasing the stock of only one or two companies that might do poorly.

Hedge funds A **hedge fund** is a private investment organization that employs risky strategies that often make huge profits for investors. These investors are generally wealthy and often are knowledgeable about investing. Because hedge funds are private, they have not been regulated by the SEC and have not had to reveal information about themselves to the public.

Life insurance companies The main function of life insurance is to provide financial protection for the family or other people named as beneficiaries of the insured. Working members of a family, for example, may buy life insurance policies so that, if they die, money will be paid to survivors to make up for lost income. Insurance companies collect payments called premiums from the people who buy insurance. They lend out to investors part of the premiums that they collect.

Pension funds A pension is income that some retirees receive after working a certain number of years or reaching a certain age. In certain cases, injuries may qualify a working person for pension benefits. Employers may set up pension funds in a number of ways. They may contribute to the pension fund on behalf of their employees, they may withhold a percentage of workers' salaries to deposit in a pension fund, or they may do both. Employers set up pension funds to collect deposits and distribute payments. Pension fund managers invest those deposits in stocks, bonds, and other financial assets.

Now that you know something about the types of financial intermediaries, you may wonder why savers don't deal directly with investors. The answer is that, in general, dealing with financial intermediaries offers three advantages. Intermediaries share risks, provide information, and provide liquidity.

Sharing Risk As a saver, you may not want to invest your entire life savings in a single company or enterprise. For example, if you had $500 to invest and your neighbor was opening a new restaurant, would you give her the entire $500? Since it is estimated that more than half of all new businesses fail, you would be wise not to risk all of your money in one investment. Instead, you would want to spread the money around to various businesses. This would reduce your chances of losing your entire investment.

This strategy of spreading out investments to reduce risk is called **diversification.** If you deposited $500 in the bank or bought shares of a mutual fund, those institutions could pool your money with other people's savings and put your money to work by making a variety of investments. In other words, financial intermediaries can diversify your investments and thus reduce the risk that you will lose all of your funds if a single investment fails.

Financial intermediaries such as banks weigh risks when determining if it will be worthwhile to invest money in a given business venture. They will take a risk if the opportunity merits it. Because financial institutions diversify their investments, they can take risks that individuals would probably be unwilling to take. They can invest a portion of money into a risky venture, because they know that it could be a very profitable and productive use of the money. Financial intermediaries generally know more than individuals about potential risks and rewards of investments, so these institutions are more likely to invest in ventures that will have a productive outcome.

Providing Information Financial intermediaries are also good sources of information. Your local bank collects information about borrowers by monitoring their income and spending.

Finance companies collect information when borrowers fill out credit applications. Mutual fund managers know how the stocks in their **portfolios,** or collections of financial assets, are performing. As required by law, all intermediaries provide this and other information to potential investors in an investment report called a **prospectus.** The typical prospectus also warns potential investors that "past performance does not necessarily predict future results." An investment that looks great today may fizzle tomorrow. As economic conditions change, an investment once considered safe may look very risky.

By providing vital data about investment opportunities, financial intermediaries reduce the costs in time and money that lenders and borrowers would pay if they had to search out such information on their own. The information, however, is sometimes provided in lengthy documents with small type. So the careful investor must be knowledgeable and must study whatever information has been provided.

Providing Liquidity Financial intermediaries also provide investors with liquidity. Liquidity is the ability to convert an asset into cash. Suppose, for example,

Types of Risk

NAME	DESCRIPTION	EXAMPLE
Credit risk	Borrowers may not pay back the money they have borrowed, or they may be late in making payments.	You lend $20 to your cousin, who promises to pay you back in two weeks. When your cousin fails to pay you on time, you don't have money for the basketball tickets you had planned to buy.
Liquidity risk	You may not be able to convert the investment back into cash quickly enough for your needs.	Your cell phone is worth $100. You need cash to buy concert tickets, so you decide to sell the phone. To convert your cell phone into cash on short notice, you have to discount the price to $75.
Inflation rate risk	Inflation rates erode the value of your assets.	Ricardo lends Jeff $1,000 for one year at 10 percent interest. If the inflation rate is 12 percent, Ricardo loses money.
Time risk	You may have to pass up better opportunities for investment.	Lili invests $100 in May's cleaning business, to be repaid at 5 percent interest one year later. Six months later, Lili is unable to invest in Sonia's pet-sitting business, which pays 10 percent interest, because she has already invested her savings.

>> Investing money almost always comes with some type of risk. **Analyze Charts** How are a liquidity risk and a time risk similar? How are they different?

▶ **Interactive Chart**

that you decide to invest in a mutual fund. Two years later, you need cash to pay your college tuition. You can get cash quickly by selling your shares in the mutual fund. Other investments are not so liquid. If you had purchased an investment-quality painting instead, you would need to find another investor who would buy the art from you. As you can see, financial intermediaries and the liquidity they provide are crucial to meeting borrowers' and lenders' needs in our increasingly complex financial system.

? IDENTIFY CENTRAL IDEAS Why do savers and investors generally work through financial intermediaries?

Liquidity, Return, and Risk

As you have read, most decisions involve trade-offs. For example, the trade-off for not going to a movie may be two additional hours of sleep. Saving and investing involve trade-offs as well.

Liquidity and Return Suppose you save money in a savings account. Savings accounts are good ways to save when you need to be able to get to your cash for immediate use. On the other hand, savings accounts pay relatively low interest rates, about 2 to 3 percentage points below a certificate of deposit (CD). In other words, savings accounts are liquid, but they have a low return. **Return** is the money an investor receives above and beyond the sum of money that has been invested.

What if, however, you unexpectedly inherit $5,000? You do not need ready access to those funds, since your part-time job pays your day-to-day expenses.

If you are willing to give up some degree of ready access to your money, you can earn a higher interest rate than you would earn if you put the money into a savings account. For example, you can invest your money in a CD that pays 4 percent interest. You would not be allowed to withdraw your money for, say, two years without paying a penalty. Therefore, before buying the CD, you would want to weigh the greater return on your investment against the loss of liquidity.

Risk and Return Certificates of deposit (up to $250,000) are considered very safe investments because they are insured by the federal government. When you buy a CD valued at less than $250,000, you are giving up liquidity for a certain period of time, but you are not risking the loss of your money. What if, however, you decided to invest the money in a new company that your friends are starting? You must consider the risk you are now incurring. If the company succeeds, you could double your investment. However, it may take years before it is

>> **Analyze Political Cartoons** How does this investment advisor misinterpret the term *liquidity*?

>> Certificates of Deposit provide a greater rate of return than savings accounts. The trade-off is that CDs are not liquid, so investors cannot access their money until the CD matures.

clear that the company is successful. If it fails, however, you could lose all or part of the money you invested.

The government does not insure you against the risk of an investment gone bad. You may benefit from the rewards of a good investment, but you face the risks of a bad one.

To take another example, suppose your savings account is earning 2 percent interest. Would you be willing to lend money to your friend Emily for that same 2 percent interest rate, knowing that she rarely pays back loans on time? Probably not. For you to lend Emily the money, she would have to offer you a higher return than the bank could offer. This higher return would help offset the greater risk that Emily will not repay the loan on time—or that she does not repay the loan at all. Likewise, a large investor, such as a big company, might be willing to pay a higher rate of return on a riskier investment. In this way, the higher return encourages savers to put their money in parts of the economy that might be very productive but are also riskier.

Whenever individuals evaluate an investment, they must balance the risks involved with the rewards they expect to gain from the investment. In general, the higher the potential return on an investment, the riskier the investment.

Balancing this risk may be exceedingly tricky. Yet it's important to remember that investors will put their savings into an array of higher- and lower-risk investments while always trying to make the investments solid. By investing in this range, their savings are allocated to their most productive use. As *Forbes* magazine has commented:

> The risk/return tradeoff could easily be called the 'ability-to-sleep-at-night test.' While some people can handle the equivalent of financial skydiving without batting an eye, others are terrified to climb the financial ladder without a secure harness. Deciding what amount of risk you can take while remaining comfortable with your investments is very important ....
>
> —Forbes, "The Risk-Return Tradeoff"

? CHECK UNDERSTANDING Which investment has greater liquidity, a savings account or a certificate of deposit?

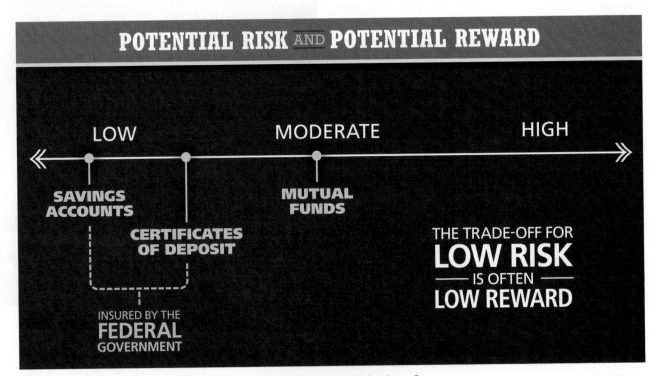

>> Investors need to think carefully about the level of risk that is right for them. Lower risk investments typically have low rewards. As risk increases however, so does potential reward.

ASSESSMENT

1. **Identify Central Ideas** What role do financial intermediaries play in the free enterprise system?

2. **Make Generalizations** What relationship does risk have to return?

3. **Compare and Contrast** (a) How are mutual funds and hedge funds similar? (b) How are they different?

4. **Identify Central Ideas** What role do households play in the financial system?

5. **Formulate Questions** If you had $500 to invest, what questions would you have as you decided how to invest your money?

>> Traders around the world use computer programs to sell financial assets on primary and secondary markets.

▶ Interactive Flipped Video

It is 1942, and the world is at war. The United States has thrown all of its resources into the Allied effort to defeat the Axis powers. To keep the armed forces equipped, the government needs money. To raise that money, the Treasury Department begins selling savings bonds.

>> Objectives

Describe the characteristics of bonds as financial assets.

Explain how corporations raise money through bonds.

Describe the characteristics of other types of financial assets.

List four different types of financial asset markets.

>> Key Terms

coupon rate
maturity
par value
yield
savings bond
inflation-indexed
  bond
municipal bond
corporate bond
junk bond
capital market
money market
primary market
secondary market

Bonds and Other Financial Assets

Bonds as Financial Assets

Americans from every walk of life support the war effort by buying these "war bonds." Even though money is tight, you manage to do your part by bringing a few nickels and dimes to school to buy war stamps. Added to the money that other students bring, the class collects enough stamps to buy a bond.

Why are bonds bought and sold? Like the war bonds that helped finance our effort in World War II, bonds are sold by governments or corporations to finance projects.

Using the example of a community that needs to construct a major road, you will see how municipal bonds offer the best method of financing expensive community projects. You will also learn another advantage of bonds. They are a type of investment that usually provides a higher return, but a greater risk, than a savings account.

Bonds are basically loans, or IOUs, that represent debt that the seller, or issuer, must repay to an investor. Bonds typically pay the investor a fixed amount of interest at regular intervals for a specific amount of time. Bonds are generally lower-risk investments. As you might expect from your reading about the relationship between risk and return, the rate of return on bonds is usually also lower than for many other investments.

The Three Components of Bonds Bonds have three basic components:

Coupon rate The **coupon rate** is the interest rate that a bond issuer will pay to a bondholder.

Maturity The time at which payment to a bondholder is due is called the bond's **maturity.** The length of time to maturity varies with different bonds. Bonds usually mature in 10, 20, or 30 years.

Par value A bond's **par value,** assigned by the issuer, is the amount to be paid to the bondholder at maturity. Par value is also called face value or principal.

Suppose that you buy a $1,000 bond from the corporation Jeans, Etc. The investor who buys the bond is called the holder. The seller of a bond is the issuer. You are, therefore, the holder of the bond, and Jeans, Etc. is the issuer. The components of this bond are as follows:

Coupon rate: 5 percent, paid to the bondholder annually

Maturity: 10 years

Par value: $1,000

How much money will you earn from this bond, and over what period of time? The coupon rate is 5 percent of $1,000 per year.

This means that you will receive a payment of $50 (0.05 x $1,000) each year for 10 years, or a total of $500 in interest. In 10 years, the bond will have reached maturity, and the company's debt to you will have ended. Jeans, Etc. will now pay you the par value of the bond, or $1,000. Thus, for your $1,000 investment, you will have received $1,500 over a period of 10 years.

Not all bonds are held to maturity. Over their lifetime they might be bought or sold, and their price may change. Because of these shifts in price, buyers and sellers are interested in a bond's yield, or yield to maturity. **Yield** is the annual rate of return on a bond if the bond is held to maturity (5 percent in the earlier example involving Jeans, Etc.).

Buying Bonds at a Discount In the free enterprise system, investors earn money from interest on the bonds they buy. They can also earn money by buying bonds at a discount, called a discount from par. In other words, if Nate were buying a bond with a par value of $1,000, he may have to pay only $960 for it. When the bond matures, Nate will redeem the bond at par, or $1,000. He will thus have earned $40 on his investment, in addition to interest payments from the bond issuer.

Why would someone sell a bond for less than its par value? The answer lies in the fact that interest rates

continually change. For example, suppose that Sharon buys a $1,000 bond at 5 percent interest, the current market rate. A year later, she needs to sell the bond to help pay for a new car. By that time, however, interest rates have risen to 6 percent. No one will pay $1,000 for Sharon's bond at 5 percent interest when they could go elsewhere and buy a $1,000 bond at 6 percent interest. For Sharon to sell her bond at 5 percent, she will have to sell it at a discount. (See **Figure 6.8.**)

Bond Ratings How does an investor decide which bonds to buy? Investors can check bond quality through independent firms that publish bond issuers' credit ratings. These firms include Standard & Poor's and Moody's.

They rate bonds on a number of factors, focusing on the issuer's financial strength—its ability to make future interest payments and its ability to repay the principal when the bond matures.

Their rating systems rank bonds from the highest investment grade (AAA in Standard & Poor's system and AAA in Moody's) through the lower grades. An investment-grade bond is considered safe enough for banks to invest in. The lowest grade generally means that the bond is in default—that is, the issuer has not

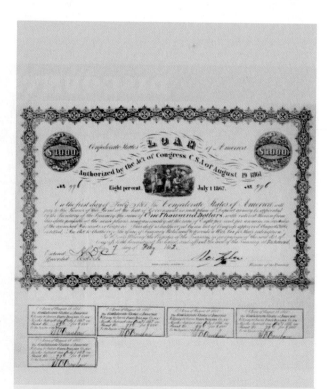

>> Historically, bond owners cut out coupons that were printed on bonds (shown here) and redeemed the coupons for interest payments. Today, the interest rate is still called the coupon rate.

kept up with interest payments or has defaulted on paying principal.

The higher the bond rating, the lower the interest rate the company usually has to pay to get people to buy its bonds. For example, an AAA (or "triple A") bond may be issued at a 5 percent interest rate. A BBB bond, however, may be issued at a 7.5 percent interest rate. The buyer of the AAA bond trades off a lower interest rate for lower risk. The buyer of the BBB bond trades greater risk for a higher interest rate.

Similarly, the higher the bond rating, the higher the price at which the bond will sell. For example, a $1,000 bond with an AAA rating may sell at $1,100. A $1,000 bond with a BBB rating may sell for only $950 because of the increased risk that the seller could default.

Holders of bonds with high ratings who keep their bonds until maturity face relatively little risk of losing their investment. Holders of bonds with lower ratings, however, take on more risk in return for potentially higher interest payments.

Costs and Benefits of Issuing Bonds From the point of view of the investor, bonds are good investments because they are relatively safe. Bonds are desirable from the issuer's point of view as well, for two main reasons:

1. Once the bond is sold, the coupon rate for that bond will not go up or down. For example, when Jeans, Etc. sells bonds, it knows in advance that it will be making fixed payments for a specific length of time.

2. Unlike stockholders, bondholders do not own a part of the company. Therefore, the company does not have to share profits with its bondholders if the company does particularly well.

On the other hand, bonds also pose two main disadvantages to the issuer:

1. The company must make fixed interest payments, even in bad years when it does not make money. In addition, it cannot change its interest payments even when interest rates have gone down.

2. If the firm does not maintain financial health, its bonds may be downgraded to a lower bond rating and, thus, may be harder to sell unless they are offered at a discount.

? CHECK UNDERSTANDING Why do some people invest in bonds with a low interest rate?

Types of Bonds

Despite risks to the issuer, when corporations or governments need to borrow funds for long periods, they often issue bonds. There are several different types of bonds.

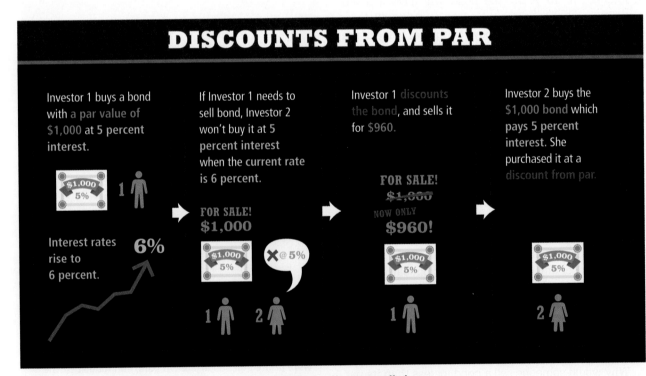

>> **Figure 6.8** Investors can earn money by buying bonds at a discount, called discount from par. **Analyze Information** How do interest rates affect bond prices?

Types of Government Debt

	TREASURY BOND	TREASURY NOTE	TREASURY BILL
Term	Long-term	Intermediate-term	Short-term
Maturity	30 years	2, 5, or 10 years	4, 13, 26, or 52 weeks
Liquidity and safety	Safe	Safe	Liquid and safe
Minimum purchase	$100	$100	$100
Denomination	$100	$100	$100

>> **Figure 6.9** Treasury bonds, notes, and bills represent debt that the government must repay the investor. **Analyze Charts** Which of these three types of government securities is the most liquid?

▶ **Interactive Chart**

Savings Bonds You may already be familiar with savings bonds, which are sometimes given to young people as gifts. **Savings bonds** are low-denomination ($50 to $10,000) bonds issued by the United States government. The government uses funds from the sale of savings bonds to help pay for public works projects such as buildings, roads, and dams. Like other government bonds, savings bonds have virtually no risk of default, or failure to repay the loan.

The federal government pays interest on savings bonds. In the past, the rate of interest on savings bonds changed every six months. Since 2005, bonds earn a fixed rate of interest for 30 years, which means that investors can know far in advance what their investment will earn.

Treasury Bonds, Bills, and Notes The United States Treasury Department issues Treasury bonds, as well as Treasury bills and notes (T-bills and T-notes). These investments offer different lengths of maturity, as shown in **Figure 6.9.** Backed by the "full faith and credit" of the United States government, these securities are among the safest investments in terms of default risk.

One possible problem with bonds (and investments in general) is inflation. The purchase price and return on Treasury securities are governed by changing interest rates and market conditions. As a result, the value of Treasury securities as an investment must be carefully understood. If a Treasury bond pays you 5 percent interest per year, but the inflation rate is 3 percent, you are really getting just 2 percent interest on the bond.

One type of bond issued mainly by the government seeks to protect against inflation—a general rise in prices. The **inflation-indexed bond** links the principal and interest to an inflation index—a measure of how fast prices are rising. If the index rises by 3 percent, this bond's par value will also rise by 3 percent. As a result, you will receive the return on the bond that you expected when you bought it.

Municipal Bonds State and local governments and municipalities (government units with corporate status) issue bonds to finance such projects as highways, state buildings, libraries, parks, and schools. These bonds are called **municipal bonds,** or "munis."

Because state and local governments have the power to tax, investors can assume that these governments will be able to keep up with interest payments and repay the principal at maturity. Standard & Poor's and Moody's therefore consider most municipal bonds to be safe investments. In addition, the interest paid on municipal bonds is not subject to income taxes at the federal level or in the issuing state.

Because they are relatively safe and are tax-exempt, "munis" are very attractive to investors as a long-term investment. A high-quality municipal bond can pay a good return for quite a long time.

Corporate Bonds As you have already read, corporations issue bonds to help raise money to expand their businesses. These **corporate bonds** are generally issued in denominations of $1,000 or $5,000.

The interest on corporate bonds is taxed as ordinary income.

Unlike governments, corporations have no tax base to help guarantee their ability to repay their loans. Thus, these bonds have moderate levels of risk. Investors in corporate bonds must depend on the success of the corporation's sales of goods and services to generate enough income to pay interest and principal.

In the free enterprise system, a corporation often needs to improve and expand its capital resources in order to grow. Using profits is one way to accomplish this, but sometimes a corporation needs more money than their profits can provide.

If, for example, it wants to hire more workers, build new offices, or update its equipment, raising money through a bond issue is an option. By making improvements such as these, the corporation can grow its business substantially and earn more money than it borrows from the bondholders.

Corporations that issue bonds are watched closely not only by the independent ratings firms, but also by the Securities and Exchange Commission (SEC). The SEC is an independent government agency that regulates financial markets and investment companies. It enforces laws prohibiting fraud and other dishonest investment practices.

Each bond is issued with an indenture agreement. It sets forth all the features associated with the bond. The interest rate is specified on the indenture agreement.

Junk Bonds Bonds with a fairly high risk of default but a potentially high yield are known as **junk bonds.** These non-investment-grade securities became especially popular investments during the 1980s and 1990s, when large numbers of aggressive investors made—but also sometimes lost—large sums of money buying and selling them.

Junk bonds have been known to pay more than 12 percent interest at a time when government bonds were yielding only about 8 percent. On the other hand, the speculative nature of most junk bonds makes them very risky. Investors in junk bonds face a strong possibility that some of the issuing firms will default on their debt. Nevertheless, issuing junk bonds has enabled many companies to undertake activities that would otherwise have been impossible to complete. Junk bond funds, which pool large numbers of individual high-risk bonds, may reduce the risk somewhat for the average investor. Still, investment in junk bond funds can be hazardous.

? CHECK UNDERSTANDING Which type of bond might have been used to fund the construction of your school?

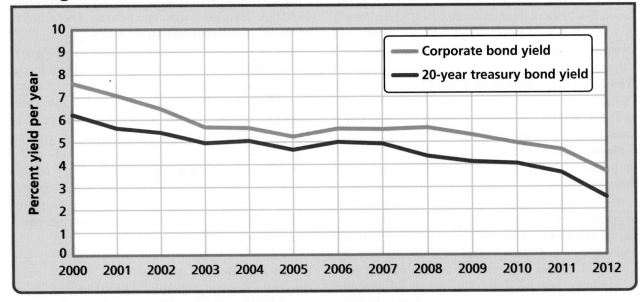

Average Bond Yields, 2000–2012

>> Since 2000, yields for corporate and treasury bonds have dropped significantly.
Analyze Graphs Which of these two types of bonds would you expect to carry less risk? Why?

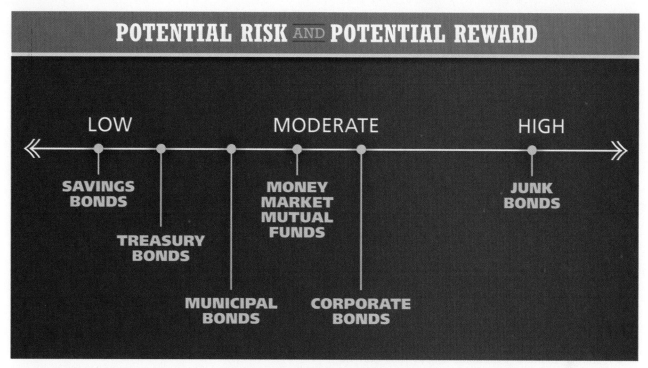

POTENTIAL RISK AND POTENTIAL REWARD

| LOW | MODERATE | HIGH |

SAVINGS BONDS

TREASURY BONDS

MUNICIPAL BONDS

MONEY MARKET MUTUAL FUNDS

CORPORATE BONDS

JUNK BONDS

>> Investments with lower risk usually have lower reward as well. Bonds issued by the government are generally less risky than bonds issues by corporations.

Other Types of Financial Assets

In addition to bonds, investors may choose other financial assets. These include certificates of deposit and money market mutual funds, as well as stock. You will read more about stock later in this Topic.

Certificates of Deposit Certificates of deposit (CDs) are one of the most common forms of investment. As you have read, CDs are available through banks, which lend out the funds deposited in CDs for a fixed amount of time, such as six months or two years.

CDs are attractive to small investors because they can deposit as little as $100. Investors can also choose among several terms of maturity. This means that if an investor foresees a future expenditure, he or she can buy a CD that matures just before the expenditure is due.

Money Market Mutual Funds Money market mutual funds are special types of mutual funds. Financial intermediaries collect money from individual investors and then buy stocks, bonds, or other financial assets to form a mutual fund.

In the case of money market mutual funds, intermediaries buy short-term financial assets. Investors receive higher interest on a money market mutual fund than they would receive from a savings account. On the other hand, money market mutual funds are not covered by FDIC insurance. (As you read earlier in this Topic, FDIC insurance protects bank deposits up to $250,000 per account.) This lack of insurance makes them slightly riskier than savings accounts.

? **CONTRAST** What is one advantage and one disadvantage of a money market mutual fund as compared with a savings account?

Financial Asset Markets

Financial assets, including bonds, certificates of deposit, and money market mutual funds, are traded on financial asset markets. The various types of financial asset markets are classified in different ways.

Capital Markets and Money Markets One way to classify financial asset markets is according to the length of time for which funds are lent. This type of classification includes both capital markets and money markets.

Capital markets Markets in which money is lent for periods longer than a year are called **capital markets.** Financial assets that are traded in capital markets include long-term CDs and corporate and government bonds that require more than a year to mature.

Money markets Markets in which money is lent for periods of one year or less are called **money markets.** Financial assets that are traded in money markets include short-term CDs, Treasury bills, and money market mutual funds.

Primary and Secondary Markets Markets may also be classified according to whether assets can be resold to other buyers. This type of classification includes primary and secondary markets.

Primary markets Financial assets that can be redeemed only by the original holder are sold on **primary markets.** Examples include savings bonds, which cannot be sold by the original buyer to another buyer. Small certificates of deposit are also in the primary market because investors would most likely cash them in early rather than trying to sell them to someone else.

Secondary markets Financial assets that can be resold are sold on **secondary markets.** This option for resale provides liquidity to investors. If there is a strong secondary market for an asset, the investor knows that the asset can be resold fairly quickly without a penalty,

thus providing the investor with ready cash. The secondary market also makes possible the lively trade in stock that is the subject of the next Lesson.

? CLASSIFY What are two ways of classifying financial asset markets?

ASSESSMENT

1. **Identify Central Issues** Name two advantages of bonds for their issuers.

2. **Summarize** Why does the United States government issue savings bonds?

3. **Interpret** When would it be a good investment to sell bonds at a discount from par?

4. **Describe** (a) How are bonds rated? (b) How do you think these ratings are helpful to investors?

5. **Contrast** (a) What kinds of financial assets are traded in capital markets? (b) How are these different from the financial assets traded in money markets?

You hear it on the news every day: "Stock prices fell today in heavy trading" or "The bulls controlled Wall Street today as the Dow surged." Lots of long faces follow a drop in the stock market. A substantial rise prompts smiles and general enthusiasm. Lots of people—maybe even you—are interested in the stock market. But is the stock market a place where you should invest your precious resources?

>> Americans can find up-to-the-minute information about stocks in many places—from newspapers to television to mobile devices.

▶ **Interactive Flipped Video**

Stocks

Investing in Stock

If you want to know how the stock market works, you will not lack sources of information and advice. Newspapers often include a business section that lists the price of various stocks. Television news broadcasts highlight the latest price changes. You may even see stock prices crawling across the bottom of your TV screen. But just what is stock, exactly how is it traded, and when is it a good investment?

You have read about how corporations, when they need money to expand their business, will often borrow it by selling bonds. A bond carries with it a promise to investors to repay the borrowed money, with interest. Corporations can also raise funds by issuing stock, which is a certificate of ownership in a corporation. Unlike someone who buys a bond, an investor who buys stock in a corporation becomes a part-owner of that corporation. Stock is issued in portions known as **shares.** By selling shares of stock, corporations raise money to start, run, and expand their businesses.

Benefits of Investing in Stock There are two ways for stockholders to make a profit:

Dividends As you read in an earlier Lesson, many corporations pay out part of their profits as dividends to their stockholders. Dividends are usually paid four times per year (quarterly). The size of

>> Objectives

Describe how stocks are traded.

Describe the benefits and risks of investing in stock.

Explain how corporations raise money through stocks and bonds.

Explain how stock performance is measured.

Assess the ways to be a wise investor in the stock market.

>> Key Terms

share
capital gain
capital loss
stock split
stockbroker
brokerage firm
stock exchange
futures
options
call option
put option
bull market
bear market
speculation

the dividend depends on the corporation's profit. The higher the profit, the larger the dividend per share of stock.

Capital gains A second way an investor can earn a profit is to sell the stock for more than he or she paid for it. The difference between the higher selling price and the lower purchase price is called a **capital gain.** An investor who sells a stock at a price lower than the purchase price, however, suffers a **capital loss.**

Types of Stock Stock may be classified in several ways, such as whether or not it pays dividends.

Income stock By paying dividends, this stock provides investors with regular income.

Growth stock This stock pays few or no dividends. Instead, the issuing company reinvests its earnings in its business. The business (and its stock) thus grows in value over time.

Stock may also be classified as to whether or not the stockholders have a vote in company policy.

Common stock Investors who buy common stock are usually voting owners of the company. They usually receive one vote for each share of stock owned. They may use this vote, for example, to help elect the company's board of directors. In some cases, a relatively small group of people may own enough shares to give them control over the company.

Preferred stock Investors who buy preferred stock are usually nonvoting owners of the company. Owners of preferred stock, however, receive dividends before the owners of common stock. If the company goes out of business, preferred stockholders get their investments back before common stockholders.

Stock Splits Owners of common stock may sometimes vote on whether to initiate a stock split. A **stock split** means that each single share of stock splits into more than one share. A company may seek to split a stock when the price of stock becomes so high that it discourages potential investors from buying it.

For example, suppose you own 200 shares in a sporting goods company called Ultimate Sports. Each share is worth $100. After a 2-for-1 split, you own 400 shares of Ultimate Sports, or two shares of stock for every single share you owned before. Because the price is divided along with the stock, however, each share is now worth only $50. Thus a stock split does not immediately result in any financial gain. Shareholders like splits, however, because splits usually demonstrate that the company is doing well, and the lower stock price tends to attract more investors.

Risks of Investing in Stock Purchasing stock is risky, because the firm selling the stock may earn lower profits than expected, or it may lose money. If so, the

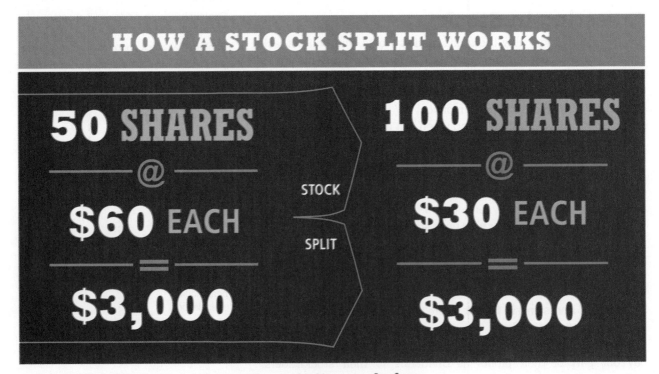

HOW A STOCK SPLIT WORKS

50 SHARES @ **$60** EACH = **$3,000**

STOCK
SPLIT

100 SHARES @ **$30** EACH = **$3,000**

>> A stock split doubles the amount of shares that a stockholder owns. **Analyze Information** Why does the value of the stock not also double?

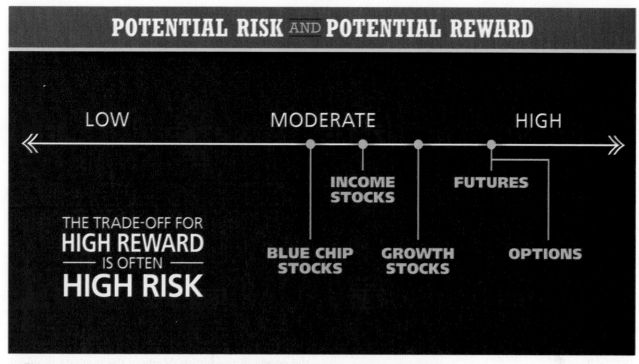

POTENTIAL RISK AND POTENTIAL REWARD

LOW   MODERATE   HIGH

THE TRADE-OFF FOR
HIGH REWARD
— IS OFTEN —
HIGH RISK

INCOME STOCKS

FUTURES

BLUE CHIP STOCKS

GROWTH STOCKS

OPTIONS

>> This continuum shows that the potential reward of buying stocks and stock-related products is fairly high, but so is the risk. **Analyze Charts** Which type of stock shown here is the safest?

dividends will be smaller than expected or nothing at all, and the market price of the stock will probably decrease. If the price of the stock decreases, investors who choose to sell their stock will get less than they paid for it, experiencing a capital loss.

How do the risk and rate of return on stocks compare with the risk and rate of return on bonds? As you have read, investors expect higher rates of return when they take on greater risk.

Because of the laws governing bankruptcy, stocks are more risky than bonds. When a firm goes bankrupt, it sells its assets (such as land and equipment) and then pays its creditors, including bondholders, first. Stockholders receive a share of the assets only if there is money left over after bondholders are paid. As you might expect, because stocks are riskier than bonds, the return on stocks is generally higher.

? RECALL What are two ways to make a profit from investing in a stock?

Stock Trading

Suppose you decide that you want to buy stock. How do you get started? Do you call up the company and place an order? Probably not, because very few companies sell stock directly. Instead, you would contact a

stockbroker, a person who links buyers and sellers of stock. Stockbrokers usually work with individual investors, advising them to buy or sell particular stocks.

Stockbrokers work for **brokerage firms,** or businesses that specialize in trading stocks. Stockbrokers and brokerage firms cover their costs and earn a profit by charging a commission, or fee, on each stock transaction. Sometimes, they also act as dealers of stock, meaning that they buy shares at a lower price and sell them to investors at a slightly higher price, profiting from the difference, or "spread."

Stock Exchanges A market for buying and selling stock is known as a **stock exchange.** Stock exchanges act as secondary markets for stocks and bonds. That is, stocks and bonds are not sold directly by corporations through the stock exchange but are resold by investors. Most newspapers and many Web sites publish data on transactions in major stock exchanges. (See **Figure 6.10** to learn how to read an online stock market report.) Major United States stock exchanges include the New York Stock Exchange (NYSE) and Nasdaq. In addition, a large number of people trade stocks on the Internet, using online brokerage firms or special trading software. The ease of this approach also makes it very risky, because snap judgments can often be wrong—and very costly.

New York Stock Exchange The New York Stock Exchange (NYSE) is probably the country's best known exchange. The NYSE began in 1792 as an informal, outdoor exchange in New York's financial district.

Over time, as the financial market developed and the demand to buy and sell financial assets grew, the exchange moved indoors and became restricted to a limited number of members who bought "seats" allowing them to trade on the exchange. In 2013, the NYSE was purchased by the Intercontinental Exchange (ICE) an Atlanta-based company that runs commodities and other types of exchanges around the world.

The NYSE handles stock and bond transactions for the top companies in the United States and in the world. The largest, most financially sound, and best-known firms listed on the NYSE are referred to as blue chip companies. Blue chip stocks are often in high demand, because investors expect the companies to continue to do business profitably for a long time.

Nasdaq Despite the importance of organized markets like the New York Stock Exchange, many stocks, as well as bonds, are not traded on the floor of stock exchanges. Instead, they are traded directly, on the over-the-counter (OTC) market. Using a telephone or the Internet, investors may buy directly from a dealer or broker who will search other dealers or brokers on the OTC market for the best price.

The Nasdaq (National Association of Securities Dealers Automated Quotation) system was created in 1971 to help organize the OTC market through the use of automation. It grew rapidly in the 1990s, in part by focusing on new-technology stocks. Today, the Nasdaq Stock Market (as it became known) is the second-largest securities market in the country and the largest electronic market for stocks. It handles more trades on average than any other American market. True to its OTC roots, Nasdaq has no physical trading floor. Instead it has a telecommunications network through which it broadcasts trading information to computer terminals throughout the world.

Futures and Options **Futures** are contracts to buy or sell commodities at a particular date in the future at a price specified today. For example, a buyer and seller might agree today on a price of $4.50 per bushel for soybeans that would not reach the market until six or nine months from now. The buyer would pay some portion of the money today, and the seller would deliver the goods in the future. Many of the markets in which futures are bought and sold are associated with grain and livestock exchanges. These markets include the New York Mercantile Exchange and the Chicago Board of Trade.

Similarly, **options** are contracts that give investors the choice to buy or sell stock and other financial assets. Investors may buy or sell a particular stock at a

Best Performing Stocks

View: Most Active | Tracked on the: DJIA

Company	Last	Chg % | $	Volume	52 Week Range	Div	Yld
MFST Microsoft Corp.	$33.87	2.40%/$0.80	32.4M	26.26 – 36.42	$1.13	3.3%
CSCO Cisco Systems Inc.	$23.07	2.53%/$0.57	31.3M	16.68 – 26.48	$0.68	2.9%
INTC Intel Corp.	$23.11	2.30%/$0.52	30.1M	19.23 – 25.98	$0.90	3.9%
GE General Electric Co.	$24.20	2.65%/$0.63	27.2M	19.87 – 24.95	$0.76	3.1%
T AT&T Inc.	$34.04	0.86%/$0.29	19.6M	32.71 – 39.00	$1.80	5.4%

Best Performing Mutual Funds | Best Performing Exchange Traded Funds

>> **Figure 6.10 Analyze Charts** Wise investors benefit from being able to read stock tables such as this one. Which of these stocks paid the highest dividend at this time?

Interactive Illustration

OPTIONS

CALL OPTION	PUT OPTION

TODAY

Investor pays fee for option to **buy** stock six months from now at today's price.

Investor pays fee for option to **sell** stock six months from now at today's price.

SIX MONTHS LATER

If stock price **rises**, investor can buy at the lower price and earn a profit.

If stock price drops, investor does not have to use option.

If stock price **drops**, investor can sell at the higher price and earn a profit

If stock price rises, investor does not have to use option.

>> Both types of options have a "safety valve," a way of ensuring that the investor does not lose money—other than the fee paid for the option. **Analyze Charts** How does this "safety valve" work?

particular price up until a certain time in the future— usually three to six months.

The option to buy shares of stock until a specified time in the future is known as a **call option.** For example, you may pay $10 per share today for a call option.

The call option gives you the right, but not the obligation, to purchase a certain stock at a price of, say, $100 per share. If at the end of six months, the price has gone up to $115 per share, your option still allows you to purchase the stock for the agreed-upon $100 per share. You thus earn $5 per share ($15 minus the $10 you paid for the call option). If, on the other hand, the price has dropped to $80, you can throw away the option and buy the stock at the going rate.

The option to sell shares of stock at a specified time in the future is called a **put option.** Suppose that you, as the seller, pay $5 per share for the right to sell a particular stock that you do not yet own at $50 per share. If the price per share falls to $40, you can buy the share at that price and require the contracted buyer to pay the agreed-upon $50. You would then make $5 per share on the sale ($10 minus the $5 you paid for the put option). If the price rises to $60, however, you can throw away the option and sell the stock for $60.

Day Trading Most people who buy stock hold their investment for a significant period of time—sometimes many years—with the expectation that it will grow in value. Day traders use a different strategy. They might make dozens of trades per day, sometimes holding a stock for just minutes or even seconds. The typical day trader, sitting in front of a computer, hopes to ride a rising stock's momentum for a short time and then sell the stock for a quick profit. Day trading is a bit like gambling—it is a very risky business in which traders can lose a great deal of money. As the United States Securities and Exchange Commission has warned:

While day trading is neither illegal nor is it unethical, it can be highly risky. Most individual investors do not have the wealth, the time, or the temperament to make money and to sustain the devastating losses that day trading can bring.

—"Day Trading, Your Dollars at Risk," U.S. Securities and Exchange Commission

? IDENTIFY What two kinds of contracts allow investors to buy and sell commodities or financial assets at some later date?

Tracking Stock Performance

You may have heard newscasters speak of a "bull" or "bear" market or of the market rising or falling. What do these terms mean, and how can an investor track increases and decreases in the sale of stocks?

Bull and Bear Markets When stock prices in general steadily rise for a period of time, a **bull market** exists. On the other hand, when stock prices steadily fall or stagnate for a period of time, analysts call it a **bear market.** In a bull market, investors expect an increase in profits and, therefore, buy stock. During a

>> Large gains on the stock market are often followed by large losses. **Analyze Political Cartoons** What object in this cartoon symbolizes the stock market? Why did the cartoonist choose it?

bear market, investors sell stock in expectation of lower profits.

The 1980s and 1990s brought the longest sustained bull market in the nation's history. Between 2000 and 2006, the market went through brief cycles of bear and bull markets.

Then general concerns about the economy, and the subprime mortgage crisis, led to a bear market lasting from October 2007 to March 2009. During that time, the stock market lost some 54 percent of its value. After that, a strong bull market developed.

Dow Jones Industrial Average When newscasters say "the stock market rose today," they are often referring to the Dow Jones Industrial Average, a measure of stock performance known simply as "the Dow." The Dow is the average value of a particular set of stocks, and it is reported as a certain number of points. For example, on a good day, the Dow might rise 60 points.

The group of stocks listed on the Dow is intended to represent the market as a whole. To make sure it does, some of the stocks are periodically dropped and others added. Today, those stocks represent 30 large, very strong, and influential companies in various industries, such as food, energy, and technology.

S&P 500 The S&P 500 (Standard & Poor's 500) gives a broader picture of stock performance than the Dow. It tracks the price changes of 500 different stocks as a measure of overall stock market performance. The S&P 500 reports mainly on stocks listed on the NYSE, but some of its stocks are traded on the Nasdaq market.

? DEFINE What do investors tend to do during a bull market?

The Great Crash and Beyond

Like the 1980s and 1990s, the 1920s saw a long-term bull market. Unfortunately, this period ended in a horrifying collapse of the stock market known as the Great Crash of 1929. The causes of this collapse contain important lessons for investors in the twenty-first century.

Investing During the 1920s When President Herbert Hoover took office in 1929, the United States economy seemed to be in excellent shape. The booming economy had dramatically changed the lives of Americans. Factories produced a steady stream of consumer products, including washing machines, toasters, and automobiles. The stock market was soaring. In 1925, the market value of all stocks had been $27 billion. By early October 1929, combined stock values had hit $87 billion.

Despite widespread optimism about continuing prosperity, there were signs of trouble. A relatively small number of companies and families held much of the nation's wealth, while many farmers and workers were suffering financially. In addition, many ordinary people went into debt buying consumer goods such as refrigerators and radios—new and exciting inventions at the time—on credit. Finally, industries were producing more goods than consumers could buy. As a result, some industries, including the important automobile industry, developed large surpluses of goods, and prices began to slump.

Another economic danger sign was the debt that investors were piling up by playing the stock market. The dizzying climb of stock prices encouraged widespread **speculation,** the practice of making high-risk investments with borrowed money in hopes of getting a big return.

Before World War I, only the wealthy had bought and sold shares in the stock market. Now, however, the press was reporting stories of ordinary people making fortunes in the stock market. Small investors thus began speculating in stocks, often with their life savings.

One man described how he began speculating in the following way:

One day, one of my customers showed me how much money he was making in the market.... I bit with what you folks call 'hook, line and sinker.' All the money I took in, I put into stocks. The first day of October in 1929 made me feel like I was rich. The stocks I bought had gone up and up.?

—*American Life Histories: Manuscripts from the Federal Writers' Project, 1936–1940*

To attract less-wealthy investors, stockbrokers encouraged a practice called buying on margin. Buying on margin allowed investors to purchase a stock for only a fraction of its price and borrow the rest from the brokerage firm. The Hoover administration did little to discourage such risky loans.

The Crash By September 3, 1929, the Dow had reached an all-time high of 381 points. The rising stock prices dominated the news. Prices for many stocks soared

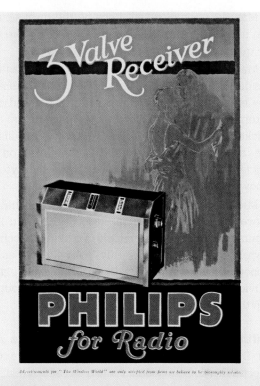

>> In the 1920s, consumers went into debt to buy the latest innovations, including radios like the one advertised here.

far above their real values in terms of the company's earnings and assets.

After their peak in September, stock prices began to fall. Some brokers demanded repayment of loans. When the stock market closed on Wednesday, October 23, 1929, the Dow had dropped 21 points in an hour. The next day, worried investors began to sell, and stock prices fell further. Although business and political leaders told the public not to worry about their losses, widespread panic began.

By Monday, October 28, 1929, shares of stock were dropping in value to a fraction of what people had paid for them. Investors all over the country were racing to get what was left of their money out of the stock market. On October 29, 1929, forever known as Black Tuesday, a record 16.4 million shares were sold, compared with the average 4 to 8 million shares per day earlier in the year. The Great Crash had begun.

In the Wake of the Crash During the bull market that led up to the Crash, about 4 million people had invested in the stock market. Although they were the first to feel the effects of the Crash, eventually the whole country was affected. The Crash was one cause of the Great Depression, in which millions of Americans lost their jobs, homes, and farms.

Massive unemployment became the most obvious sign of the deepening depression. By 1933, more than one quarter of the labor force was out of work.

Many Americans lost their homes as well as their jobs during the Great Depression. Desperate for shelter, they erected shacks of scrap wood, old tin, and other materials that they could scavenge. As more and more shacks sprang up, they formed shabby little villages. The residents, who blamed their troubles on the policies of President Hoover, called these shantytowns "Hoovervilles."

Mistakes in monetary policy slowed the nation's recovery. In 1929, the Federal Reserve ("the Fed") had begun limiting the money supply in order to discourage speculation. It continued this policy, even as the economy worsened. With too little money in circulation, individuals and businesses could not spend enough to help the economy improve.

Shifting Attitudes Toward Owning Stocks After the Depression, many people saw stocks as risky investments to be avoided. As late as 1980, a relatively small percentage of American households held stock. Gradually, however, attitudes began to change. For one thing, the development of mutual funds made it easy to own a wide range of stocks. Americans became more comfortable with stock ownership.

After a period of very strong growth, stocks crashed again on "Black Monday," October 18, 1987. The Dow lost 22.6 percent of its value that day—nearly twice the one-day loss that began the Great Crash of 1929.

However, this time the market rebounded on each of the next two days, and the impact on the economy was much less severe. The Fed moved quickly to add liquidity and reduce interest rates to stimulate economic growth. The shock of the 1987 crash wore off quickly. Within two years, the Dow had returned to pre-crash levels.

Starting in 1990, stock prices began to soar on the strength of a growing economy and a technology boom. Many people bought stock for the first time, investing heavily in internet-based companies and other new, high-tech enterprises. A so-called dot.com boom raised stock prices of Internet-based securities to wildly unrealistic levels. At the end of the 1990s, almost half of American households owned mutual funds.

Scandals Rock the Stock Market By that time, however, investors had begun worrying that many companies—especially the new ones—could not make enough money to justify their high stock prices. Those prices began dropping, and a lot of investors lost most or all of their prior gains. In 2001, an economic downturn and the September 11 terrorist attacks further battered the stock market.

History of the Dow

>> The Great Depression left many people afraid of buying stocks. That fear faded in the 1980s. **Analyze Graphs** What is the highest point value reached by the Dow during the period shown?

▶ **Interactive Timeline**

That same year, the stock market took yet another hit. An enormous energy-trading company named Enron filed for bankruptcy in December after revealing that it had falsely reported profits for several years in order to cover up huge losses. The price of its once high-flying stock fell from $90 per share to less than $1. Soon, several other large firms faced similar financial scandals.

In 2002, Congress responded to the scandals with the Sarbanes-Oxley Act. This legislation was aimed at reforming lax accounting practices. As a result of Sarbanes-Oxley, top corporate leaders now have to verify that financial reports are accurate or face criminal charges.

A Market in Turmoil In time, the stock market recovered and reached new heights, boosted by a red-hot real estate market. In October 2006, the Dow passed the 11,700-point mark. It reached 14,000 in 2007. Then, as investors realized the full extent of the subprime mortgage crisis, the stock market again nosedived.

By the end of 2008, it had plunged back to the 8,000 range. Trillions of dollars worth of investments were lost, and people saw their retirement savings lose much of their value. Safe investments, such as corporate and municipal bonds, also were badly hit. The financial crisis even caused the collapse of the renowned investment firm Lehman Brothers. Although the stock market slowly recovered, the market turmoil left investors uneasy.

? SUMMARIZE What was the Great Crash of 1929?

ASSESSMENT

1. **Identify Steps in a Process** What has to happen for you to have a capital gain?

2. **Compare and Contrast** How are futures similar to options? How are they different?

>> The terrorist attacks on the World Trade Center and the Pentagon on September 11, 2001, left Americans in shock and battered the stock market.

3. **Formulate Questions** Your uncle announces at a family gathering that he is thinking of becoming a day trader. What might you ask him to help him assess the wisdom of that choice?

4. **Apply Concepts** Would you buy stock during a bear market? Why or why not?

5. **Support Ideas With Evidence** How did the Federal Reserve apply lessons learned from the Great Crash to the crash of 1987?

TOPIC 6 ASSESSMENT

1. **Analyze Changes** Using the graph provided, analyze the change in savings rates since the onset of the 2008 financial crisis. Consider such questions as the following: What effect did the 2008 financial crisis have on savings rates? What impact did the 2008 financial crisis have on employment? Why might people increase their savings rate after the crisis?

Americans' Saving Rate

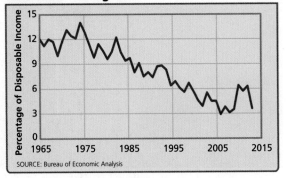

SOURCE: Bureau of Economic Analysis

2. **Explain the Benefits** Referring to the quotation, write a paragraph about investment opportunities available to companies in the U.S. free enterprise system that increase the capacity to generate future wealth. Consider such questions as the following: How does the free enterprise system make funds available for investment? In what ways can future wealth be created out of current investment? In what forms is this future wealth generated?

"When people deposit money in a savings account in a bank, for example, the bank may then lend the funds to businesses."

3. ***Examine Credit and Explain Responsibilities** Write a paragraph that examines the positive and negative aspects of using credit cards and the owner's responsibilities of borrowing money. Consider such questions as the following: Why do people use credit instead of cash or other forms of payment? What is the cost of using credit? What responsibilities are incurred in the use of credit cards? What are the benefits and dangers of using credit cards?

4. ***Explain Obligations, Develop Strategies, and Examine** Explain the obligations of borrowing money and describe a strategy for becoming a low-risk borrower, by avoiding credit card debt in general and eliminating it when it has accumulated. Consider such questions as the following: In what sense does a credit card user borrow money? Why is a borrower obligated to repay his or her debt? What occurs if an individual using credit cannot afford to pay off the balance in full in a short amount of time? What is the best way to avoid credit card debt? How might a person eliminate credit card debt if he or she allows it to accumulate?

5. **Describe Functions** Referring to the quotation, describe how money functions in a modern economy to allow consumers to compare different goods, and how producers set prices for the products and services they provide. Consider such questions as the following: How do consumers determine what is a good buy? How do consumers compare the value of different goods? How do producers determine the selling price of the goods or services they provide?

"You can compare the cost of the jacket in this store with the cost in other stores . . . "

6. **Explain the Structure** Explain how the structure of the Federal Reserve System affects the ability of the Federal Open Market Committee to represent a balanced view of the nation's banking system in its policy decisions. Consider such questions as the following: How is the Federal Reserve System structured? What role does the Federal Open Market Committee have within the Federal Reserve system? How are members of the Federal Open Market Committee selected?

7. ***Examine Investment Options** Examine the different investment options available to people for their personal retirement. Include three facts about each retirement plan—401(k), IRA, and Social Security. Write three or four sentences examining the positive and negative aspects of investment options available in a personal retirement plan.

8. ***Assess the Transition from Renting to Home Ownership** Conduct your own research to write a paragraph of three to four sentences that assesses the financial challenges an individual faces when transitioning from renting a home to owning a home.

*For help in answering these questions, refer to the **Personal Finance Handbook** at the end of your textbook.

9. **Describe the Characteristics of Money, Including Fiat Money** Using the image shown, describe the characteristics of fiat money that makes it an acceptable means to buy and sell goods. Consider such things as the following: In what way does this image show that the currency is accepted as a medium of exchange? In what way is the value of this type of money guaranteed?

10. **Analyze Basic Tools** Analyze how the discount rate and federal funds rate are used to carry out U.S. monetary policy. Consider the following questions: What are the goals of monetary policy? What are the discount and federal funds rates and how are banks affected by them? How does the Federal Reserve use the discount and federal funds rates to implement monetary policy?

11. **Explain the Actions** Explain how the actions of the Federal Reserve affect the nation's money supply. Write a paragraph that explains how and why the Federal Reserve uses its policies to affect the money supply.

12. **Analyze the Dollar** Analyze the decline in value of the U.S. dollar by examining the abandonment of the gold standard. Consider such questions as the following: How does a gold standard serve to stabilize the value of a currency? What is the relationship between a gold standard and the money supply? What has occurred to the value of the U.S. dollar since going off the gold standard in the 1930s?

13. **Explain How Corporations Raise Money** Explain how corporations raise money through issuing preferred stocks. Consider such questions as the following: What incentives do investors have to buy preferred stocks? In what ways are preferred stocks similar to and different from other stocks?

14. **Explain Functions** Explain the function of financial intermediaries. Consider such questions as the following: What is one common type of financial institution common in the U.S. economy? How do financial intermediaries meet the needs of savers? What happens to the money savers put into financial intermediaries?

15. **Analyze the Role** Analyze the role of interest in allocating savings to its most productive uses. Consider questions such as the following: What determines the interest rates, or returns, that savers earn? How does a variety of interest rates ensure savings go to the most productive uses?

16. **Describe Characteristics and Examine Aspects** Referring to the quotation, write a paragraph that describes the characteristics of fiat money by examining its positive and negative aspects with respect to inflation. Consider such questions as the following: What allows a currency to function as a store of value over time? What determines the value of this Federal Reserve note? Explain how, without careful oversight of the money supply, currency can lose its value through inflation. In what way is the government's ability to maintain a currency's value through policy changes a positive aspect of fiat money?

"If the money supply grows too large, the currency may become worthless due to inflation."

17. ***Identify Loans, Evaluate Costs and Benefits, and Assess Financial Aspects** Identify and evaluate the costs and benefits of taking a mortgage versus continuing to rent, and assess the financial aspects of making the transition from rent to home ownership. Consider such questions as the following: What are the costs and benefits of buying a home? What is involved in the transition from renting to buying?

18. ***Examine Financial Accounts** Create a chart that organizes and examines the types, risks, costs, and benefits associated with savings, checking, and investment accounts available to consumers from financial institutions.

---

*For help in answering these questions, refer to the **Personal Finance Handbook** at the end of your textbook.

Use words to write the payment amount.

Write the name of the payee.

Write the current date.

Use numerals to enter the payment amount.

1027

Tomás Q. Public
123 Main Street
Anywhere, USA 45678

October 14, 2014 DATE

$ 25.99

PAY TO THE ORDER OF GameOh!

Twenty-five and 99/100 —————————————— DOLLARS

Security Features Details on Back.

Main Street Bank
321 Main Street
Anywhere, USA 45678

Tomás Q. Public

FOR game rental

⑆222222222⑆ 000 111 555⑈ 1027

Sign your check.

Write additional information about the payment or payee, such as a reason or an account number.

19. **Examine Financial Accounts** Write a paragraph examining the following: types of available financial accounts, risks of maintaining financial accounts, monetary costs of maintaining financial accounts, benefits of maintaining financial accounts.

20. ***Maintain a Checking Account** Using the image of the check, describe how to maintain a checking account and reconcile a bank statement.

21. ***Examine, Explain, and Assess Personal Investment Options** Write a paragraph that examines, explains, and assesses how to be a wise. Consider such questions as the following: What type of savings and investment options are available? What levels of risk and return are associated with these saving and investment options? What does it mean to be a wise investor? What saving and investment options make sense for a personal retirement plan?

22. ***Evaluate Insurance Options** Evaluate the costs and benefits of buying insurance, such as life insurance. Consider such questions as the following: What is the purpose of life insurance? Who benefits from life insurance in the event it pays a benefit? How do life insurance companies benefit from offering these policies?

23. ***Evaluate Buying a Home** Write a paragraph that evaluates the costs and benefits of home ownership. In your paragraph, make sure to list three benefits of buying a home. List three costs of buying a home.

24. ***Explain How to Begin a Savings Program** Referring to the quotation, explain in three to four sentences how to begin a savings program. Be specific and complete in your explanation.

Mia has just landed her first job at a local fast food restaurant. She is looking to establish a savings account at the local bank to save money for a car and college. She asks you for advice on how to begin a savings account. What can you tell her?

25. **Write About the Essential Question Write an essay on the Essential Question: How can you make the most of your money?** Use evidence from your study of this Topic to support your answer.

*For help in answering these questions, refer to the **Personal Finance Handbook** at the end of your textbook.

Go online to PearsonRealize.com and use the texts, quizzes, interactivities, Interactive Reading Notepads, Flipped Videos, and other resources from this Topic to prepare for the Topic Test.

Texts

Quizzes

Interactivities

Interactive Reading Notepads

Flipped Videos

While online you can also check the progress you've made learning the topic and course content by viewing your grades, test scores, and assignment status.

7 Economic Performance and Challenges

>> This sculpture, located near Wall Street, represents the power of a surging stock market.

Enduring Understandings

- The gross domestic product and other economic indexes provide a way to measure the health of the economy.

- Throughout its history, the country has undergone recurring periods of economic expansion and contraction.

- Economic growth provides a whole society with improved quality of life.

- There are different types of unemployment, but the unemployment rate is one of the key indicators of economic health.

- Inflation, a rise in prices, cuts into a person's ability to purchase the things they want or need.

- The poverty threshold divides those who can support a family or household from those who cannot.

PEARSON realize. **NBC LEARN**

Watch the My Story Video to learn more about unemployment, a key measure of the health of any economy.

PEARSON realize
www.PearsonRealize.com

Access your digital lessons including:
Topic Inquiry • Interactive Reading
Notepad • Interactivities • Assessments

>> Aggregate supply is the total amount of goods and services available at all price levels in the economy.

▶ Interactive Flipped Video

How much attention do you pay to the economic news? If you're like most people your age—or most Americans in general—your answer is probably, "Not much." After all, you'd have to be some kind of genius to keep track of the GDP, the GNP, the NNP, the NI, the DPI, and the rest of the economic alphabet soup. Who has the time? And who cares anyway?

>> Objectives

Explain how gross domestic product (GDP) is calculated.

Interpret GDP data.

Identify factors that influence GDP.

Describe other output and income measures.

>> Key Terms

national income accounting
gross domestic product
intermediate goods
durable goods
nondurable goods
nominal GDP
real GDP
gross national product
depreciation
price level
aggregate supply
aggregate demand

Gross Domestic Product

Economic Measures

But, whether you care or not, the GDP, the NI, and the rest do affect you. What's more, you affect them. Every time you buy a shirt or rent a movie or get a paycheck, you toss your bit into the alphabet soup.

Economists have developed many tools to monitor the nation's economic performance. They even have a way to measure how much money families like yours have to spend. You will learn what these measures tell us—and don't tell us—about the economy.

Economists use a system called **national income accounting** to monitor the U.S. economy. They collect and organize macroeconomic statistics on production, income, investment, and savings. The Department of Commerce then presents these data in the form of National Income and Product Accounts (NIPA). The government uses NIPA data to determine economic policies.

What is GDP? The most important measure in NIPA is **gross domestic product** (GDP), which is the dollar value of all final goods and services produced within a country's borders in a given year. To help you understand GDP, let us examine each part of this definition:

Dollar value refers to the total cash value of the sales of all goods and services produced in a country's households, firms, and government in a calendar year. Since different quantities of goods such as oranges, computers, and movie tickets are sold at different prices, economists figure out the average prices of these items and the total number sold during the year. These cash figures are then used to calculate GDP.

Final goods and services are products in the form sold to consumers. They differ from **intermediate goods,** which are products used in the production of final goods. The memory chips that a computer maker buys to put into its machines are intermediate goods; the computer is a final good.

Produced within a country's borders is especially important to remember. Because we are trying to find the country's gross *domestic* product, we can look only at the goods and services produced within that country. For example, the GDP of the U.S. economy includes cars made in Ohio by a Japanese car company but not cars made in Brazil by an American automaker.

In a given year takes into account when a good was produced. Suppose your neighbor sells you his used car. When the car was originally made, it was counted in the GDP of that year. Thus, it would be inaccurate to count it toward GDP again this year when it was resold.

The Expenditure Approach Government economists calculate GDP two ways. In one method, they use the expenditure approach, sometimes called the output-expenditure approach. First, economists estimate the annual expenditures, or amounts spent, on four categories of final goods and services:

1. consumer goods and services
2. business goods and services
3. government goods and services
4. net exports

Two of these categories need explanation. First, bear in mind that consumer goods include two kinds of goods. They are **durable goods**—those that last for a relatively long time, such as refrigerators and DVD players—and **nondurable goods**—those that last a short period of time, such as food, light bulbs, and sneakers.

Net exports are found by adding up exports—goods produced in the country but purchased in other countries—and then subtracting imports. Imports, of course, were produced in another country.

After finding the value of those four categories, economists add them together to arrive at the total expenditures on goods and services produced during the year. This total equals GDP. **Figure 7.1** provides a simplified example of calculating GDP with the expenditure approach.

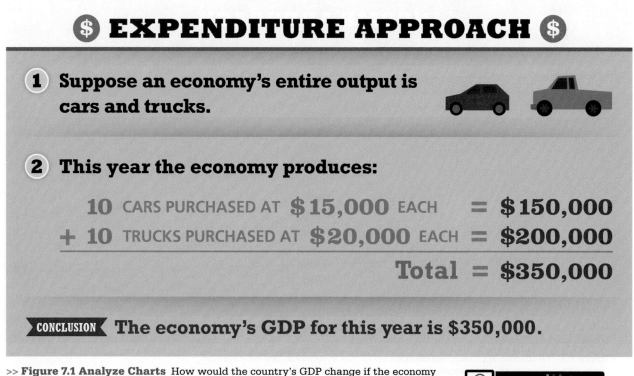

💲 EXPENDITURE APPROACH 💲

1 **Suppose an economy's entire output is cars and trucks.**

2 **This year the economy produces:**

    10 CARS PURCHASED AT **$15,000** EACH = **$150,000**
+ 10 TRUCKS PURCHASED AT **$20,000** EACH = **$200,000**
                                              Total = $350,000

CONCLUSION **The economy's GDP for this year is $350,000.**

>> **Figure 7.1 Analyze Charts** How would the country's GDP change if the economy produced trucks that were purchased for $25,000 each instead of $20,000 each?

▶ **Interactive Chart**

The Income Approach The second method to calculate GDP, known as the income approach, is shown in **Figure 7.2**. This method calculates GDP by adding up all the incomes in the economy. The rationale for this approach is that when a firm sells a product or service, the selling price minus the dollar value of goods and services purchased from other firms represents income for the firm's owners and employees.

Suppose your neighbor bought a newly built house for $200,000. That $200,000 (minus what the builder spent on lumber, plaster, etc.) is income shared by all of the people who helped build and sell the house—including the contractor, the bricklayer, the roofers, and the real estate broker. Each of these people may get only a small share of the house's selling price. However, if we added up all those shares, we would arrive at $200,000 (minus what the builder spent on lumber, plaster, etc.) worth of income generated by the sale.

This same logic holds for all goods and services. Thus, we may calculate GDP by adding up all income earned in the economy.

In theory, calculating GDP with the income approach and the expenditure approach should give us the same total. In fact, there are usually differences because of errors in the underlying data. Economists who work in the federal government take those differences into account. They first determine GDP using both approaches. Then they compare the two totals and make adjustments to offset the differences. This gives them a more accurate result.

? EXPLAIN Why are imports not included in gross domestic product?

Two Measures of GDP

Government officials use gross domestic product to find out how well the economy is performing. To help them understand what is really going on in the economy, economists distinguish between two measures of GDP, nominal and real.

Calculating Nominal GDP In **Figure 7.1** and **Figure 7.2**, we calculated **nominal GDP**—that is, GDP measured in current prices. Because it is based on current prices, this type of GDP is also called "current GDP." To calculate nominal GDP, we simply use the current year's prices to calculate the value of the current year's output. **Figure 7.3** shows how the definition of nominal GDP applies to the small economy that produces only cars and trucks.

Calculating Real GDP The data in **Figure 7.3** reveal a problem with nominal GDP. The GDP of Year 2 is higher

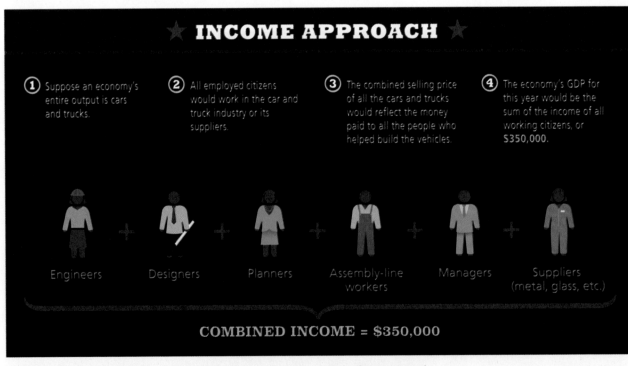

★ **INCOME APPROACH** ★

① Suppose an economy's entire output is cars and trucks.

② All employed citizens would work in the car and truck industry or its suppliers.

③ The combined selling price of all the cars and trucks would reflect the money paid to all the people who helped build the vehicles.

④ The economy's GDP for this year would be the sum of the income of all working citizens, or $350,000.

Engineers + Designers + Planners + Assembly-line workers + Managers + Suppliers (metal, glass, etc.)

COMBINED INCOME = $350,000

>> **Figure 7.2** The income approach, which adds up all the incomes in the economy, is generally more accurate than the expenditure approach. **Analyze Charts** How would cutting workers affect GDP?

NOMINAL AND REAL GDP

YEAR 1: NOMINAL GDP

1 Suppose an economy's entire output is cars and trucks.

2 This year the economy produces:

10 CARS AT
$15,000 EACH = $150,000

+ 10 TRUCKS AT
$20,000 EACH = $200,000

TOTAL = **$350,000**

3 Nominal GDP for Year 1 is $350,000.

YEAR 2: NOMINAL GDP

1 The next year, the economy's output increases, and so do the prices of cars and trucks.

12 CARS AT **$16,000** EACH = $192,000
+ 12 TRUCKS AT **$21,000** EACH = $252,000

TOTAL = **$444,000**

2 Nominal GDP for Year 2 is $444,000, but this sum includes price increases. Economists prefer a measure of GDP that is not affected by price changes.

YEAR 2: REAL GDP

1 Economists establish constant prices by choosing one year as a base year. To correct for an increase in prices, we calculate real GDP for Year 2 using Year 1 prices:

12 CARS AT **$15,000** EACH = $180,000
+ 12 TRUCKS AT **$20,000** EACH = $240,000

TOTAL = **$420,000**

2 Real GDP for Year 2, therefore, is $420,000, showing an increase of $70,000 in real dollars over the previous year.

>> **Figure 7.3** Although nominal GDP offers useful information, real GDP corrects for increases in prices. **Analyze Charts** What is the difference between nominal and real GDP for Year 2?

than that of Year 1 even though the output of cars and trucks in the two years is the same. The difference is due to an increase in prices. As a result of these price increases, the higher GDP figure in the second year is misleading. To correct for this distortion, economists determine **real GDP,** which is GDP expressed in constant, or unchanging, prices.

Look at the third section of **Figure 7.3**. Notice that GDP in Year 2 is based on the prices from Year 1. By using real GDP, economists can discover whether an economy is actually producing more goods and services, regardless of changes in the prices of those items. In **Figure 7.3**, we can quickly see that output did not increase in Year 2.

❓ **IDENTIFY** What problem is solved by using real GDP?

What GDP Doesn't Measure

Even though GDP is a valuable tool, it is not a perfect yardstick. For instance, GDP does not take into account certain economic activities or aspects of life. These include nonmarket activities, the underground economy, negative externalities, and quality of life.

Nonmarket Activities GDP does not measure goods and services that people make or do themselves, such as caring for children, mowing the lawn, cooking dinner, or washing the car. GDP does rise, however, when people pay someone else to do these things for them. When these nonmarket activities are shifted to the market, GDP goes up, even though production has not really increased.

The Underground Economy A large amount of production and income is never recorded or reported to the government. For instance, transactions on the black market—the market for illegal goods—are not counted. Income from illegal gambling goes unreported. So do "under the table" wages that some companies pay workers to avoid paying business and income taxes.

Many legal, informal transactions are also not reported, for example, selling your bike to a friend or trading that bike for a stereo. If you earned money baby-sitting, mowing lawns, or shoveling snow, those payments are not included in the GDP either, even though goods and services were produced and income was earned.

Negative Externalities Unintended economic side effects, or externalities, have a monetary value that often is not reflected in GDP. For example, a power plant that emits smoke and dust is polluting the air. That negative result is not subtracted from GDP.

Quality of Life Although some economists and politicians interpret rising GDP as a sign of rising well-being, we should remember that additional goods and services do not necessarily make people any happier. In fact, some things that are not counted in GDP contribute greatly to most people's quality of life, such as pleasant surroundings, ample leisure time, and personal safety.

All of these limitations suggest that GDP is a somewhat flawed measure of output and income and doesn't fully measure the personal well-being of all. Nevertheless, while the measure may be imperfect, when calculated consistently over a period of time, GDP helps reveal economic growth rates. For this reason, economists and policymakers closely watch the nation's GDP.

? **SYNTHESIZE** Cleaning your house is an example of what type of activity?

Other Economic Measures

As you have read, our system of National Income and Product Accounts provides numerous measurements of the performance of the nation's economy. While gross

domestic product is the primary measure of income and output, economists also look at other measures to focus on specific parts of the economy. Many of these other yardsticks are derived from GDP. **Figure 7.4** shows how GDP is used to determine five other economic measures.

The first is **gross national product** (GNP), the annual income earned by a nation's firms and citizens. GNP is a measure of the market value of all goods and services produced by Americans in one year. Study the chart to see how GNP is related to GDP.

GNP does not account for **depreciation,** or the loss of the value of capital equipment that results from normal wear and tear. The cost of replacing this physical capital slightly reduces the value of what we produce. GNP minus the cost of depreciation of capital equipment is called net national product (NNP). NNP measures the net output for one year, or the output made after the adjustment for depreciation.

Once they have calculated NNP, government economists adjust their figures to account for minor discrepancies between different sources of data. After making these minor adjustments to NNP, they get another measure, called national income (NI).

From NI, we can find out how much pretax income businesses actually pay to U.S. households. This is found by subtracting the profits that firms reinvest in the business and the income taxes and Social Security

MEASURES OF THE MACROECONOMY

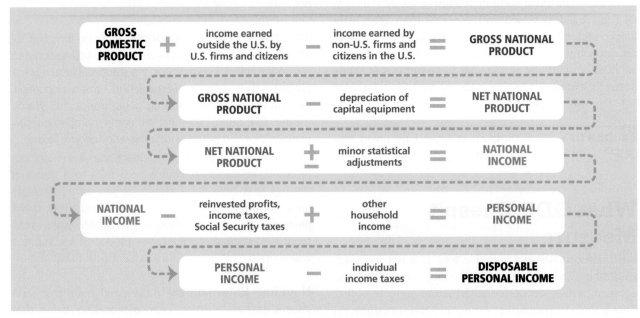

>> **Figure 7.4** These equations summarize formulas for calculating some of these key indicators. **Analyze Charts** Which measure includes depreciation in its calculation?

taxes they pay out. What remains is called personal income (PI).

Finally, we want to know how much money people actually have to spend after they pay *their* taxes, a figure called disposable personal income (DPI). To find DPI, we take personal income and subtract individual income and Social Security taxes.

See how far we have come? Beginning with GDP, the value of all goods and services produced in a year, we wind up knowing how much cash Americans have to spend or put in the bank.

? **DESCRIBE** What is disposable personal income?

Factors That Affect GDP

So far, we have defined GDP, calculated it, and learned about its limitations. One important issue remains, however: What influences GDP? That is, in a real economy, what factors can make GDP go up or down? These questions go to the heart of macroeconomics.

Aggregate Supply As you read earlier, market supply is the amount of a particular good or service available for purchase at all possible prices in an individual market. But how do we look at supply and prices on a macroeconomic level? Think of aggregate supply as a supply curve for the whole economy.

First, economists add up the total supply of goods and services produced for sale in the economy—in other words, GDP. Then they calculate the **price level,** the average of all prices in the economy. Now they can determine **aggregate supply,** the total amount of goods and services in the economy available at all possible price levels.

In a nation's economy, as the prices of most goods and services change, the price level changes. Firms respond by changing their output. For example, if the price level rises, which means that the prices of most goods and services are rising, firms have an incentive to increase their output. Similarly, as prices throughout the economy fall, companies' profits shrink. In response, they reduce output. You can see this effect in the aggregate supply (AS) curve in **Figure 7.5**. As the price level rises, real GDP, or aggregate supply, rises. As the price level falls, real GDP falls.

Aggregate Demand **Aggregate demand** is the amount of goods and services in the economy that will be purchased at all possible price levels. As price levels in the economy move up and down, individuals and businesses change how much they buy—in the opposite direction that aggregate supply changes.

Aggregate Supply

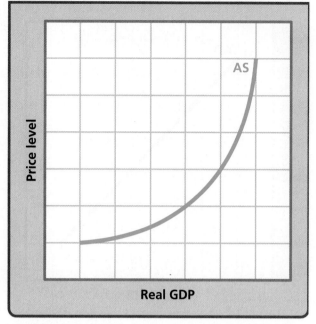

>> **Figure 7.5 Analyze Graphs** What does the positive slope of the graph mean?

For example, a lower price level translates into greater purchasing power for households, because the real value of money rises as price levels drop. The dollars that we hold are worth more at lower price levels than they are at higher price levels. Therefore, falling prices increase wealth and demand. This scenario is called the wealth effect.

On the other hand, as the price level rises, purchasing power declines, causing a reduction in the quantity of goods and services demanded. The aggregate demand (AD) curve shows this relationship between price and real GDP demanded. As you can see from **Figure 7.6**, this curve is negatively sloped; that is, it moves downward to the right. Consumers account for most of aggregate demand, but business spending on capital investment, government spending, and foreigners' demand for export goods all play roles, too.

Aggregate Supply/Aggregate Demand Equilibrium When we put together the aggregate supply (AS) and aggregate demand (AD) curves, we can find the AS/AD equilibrium in the economy as a whole. Look at **Figure 7.7**. The intersection of the AS and AD curves indicates an equilibrium price level of P1 and an equilibrium real GDP of Q1.

Now consider how GDP might change. Any shift in either the AS or AD curve will cause real GDP to change. For example, the graph shows aggregate demand falling from line AD1 to line AD2. As a

Aggregate Demand

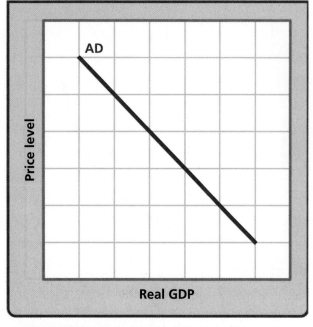

>> **Figure 7.6 Analyze Graphs** What does the negative slope of the graph mean?

Aggregate Supply/Aggregate Demand Equilibrium

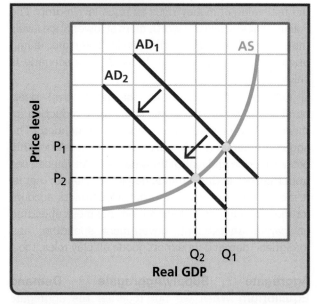

>> **Figure 7.7 Analyze Graphs** If the country whose economy is shown on this graph went to war and government demand for many kinds of goods increased, how might real GDP and price levels be affected?

▶ **Interactive Chart**

result, the equilibrium GDP (Q2) falls, and so does the equilibrium price level (P2). Any shift in aggregate supply or aggregate demand will have an impact on real GDP and on the price level. In the next Lesson, we will discuss some factors that may cause such shifts.

❓ **CATEGORIZE** What four types of demand are included in aggregate demand?

ASSESSMENT

1. **Infer** Why are intermediate goods not included in GDP?

2. **Compare and Contrast** How does nominal GDP differ from real GDP?

3. **Evaluate Data** If aggregate demand rises, what happens to real GDP?

4. **Compare and Contrast** How does gross domestic product differ from gross national product?

5. **Draw Conclusions** Why do economists calculate GDP by both the expenditure approach and the income approach?

Sometimes, you don't have to read the newspaper to tell how the economy is doing. You can see the signs all around you. They may be *Help Wanted* signs in front of local stores and factories—when the economy is doing well, businesses hire, and it's easier for you to find a part-time job. Or they may be *Closed* or *Going Out of Business* signs in the windows of those same businesses. You might even get an idea by counting the number of *For Sale* or *Foreclosure* signs where you live. The ups and downs of the economy affect us all.

>> An oil drilling boom in North Dakota is an external shock that has drawn thousands to the state's booming economy.

▶ **Interactive Flipped Video**

Business Cycles

Business Cycle Phases

The national economy undergoes periodic cycles of good times, then bad times, and then good times again. Recognizing this pattern, economists try to predict what the economy will do in the future—what can be done to make the good times last longer and keep the bad times brief. You will learn what factors affect these ups and downs and how they have shaped the country's economy. You will also see how the actions of ordinary consumers and borrowers can affect the phases of the economy and how long these phases last.

A **business cycle** is a period of macroeconomic expansion followed by a period of macroeconomic contraction. Economists also call these periods of change "economic fluctuations."

Business cycles are not minor, day-to-day ups and downs. They are major changes in real gross domestic product above or below normal levels. As you can see in **Figure 7.8**, the typical business cycle consists of four phases: expansion, peak, contraction, and trough.

Expansion An **expansion** is a period of economic growth as measured by a rise in real GDP. To economists, **economic growth** is a steady, long-term increase in real GDP. In the expansion phase, jobs are plentiful, the unemployment rate falls, and businesses prosper.

Peak When real GDP stops rising, the economy has reached its **peak,** the height of an economic expansion.

>> **Objectives**

Analyze business cycles using economic data.

Describe four factors that keep business cycles going.

Explain how economists predict changes in business cycles.

Analyze the impact of business cycles in U.S. history.

>> **Key Terms**

business cycle
expansion
economic growth
peak
contraction
trough
recession
depression
stagflation
business investment
leading indicators

Contraction After reaching its peak, the economy enters a period of **contraction,** an economic decline marked by falling real GDP. Falling output generally causes unemployment to rise.

Trough When the economy has "bottomed out," it has reached the **trough** (trawf), the lowest point in an economic contraction. At that point, real GDP stops falling and a new period of expansion begins.

During a contraction, GDP is always falling. But other economic conditions, such as price levels and the unemployment rate, may vary. Economists have created terms to describe contractions with different characteristics and levels of severity. They include:

Recession If real GDP falls for two consecutive quarters (at least six straight months), the economy is said to be in a recession. A **recession** is a prolonged economic contraction. Generally lasting from 6 to 18 months, recessions are typically marked by unemployment reaching the range of 6 percent to 10 percent.

Depression If a recession is especially long and severe, it may be called a **depression.** The term has no precise definition but usually refers to a deep recession with features such as high unemployment and low economic output.

Stagflation This term combines parts of *stagnant*—a word meaning "unmoving" or "decayed"—and *inflation*. **Stagflation** is a decline in real GDP (output) combined with a rise in the price level (inflation).

Although economists know much about business cycles, they cannot predict how long the phases in a particular cycle will last. The only certainty is that a growing economy will eventually experience a downturn, and that a contracting economy will eventually bounce back.

❓ INTERPRET If real GDP has fallen for three consecutive quarters, and the unemployment rate is nearing 10 percent, what period of economic fluctuation is the economy in?

What Drives Business Cycles?

The shifts that occur during a business cycle have many causes, some more predictable than others. Often, two or more factors will combine to push the economy into the next phase of a business cycle. Typically, a sharp rise or drop in some important economic variable will set off a series of events that bring about the next phase. Business cycles are affected by four main economic variables:

1. business investment
2. interest rates and credit
3. consumer expectations
4. external shocks

Tracking a Business Cycle

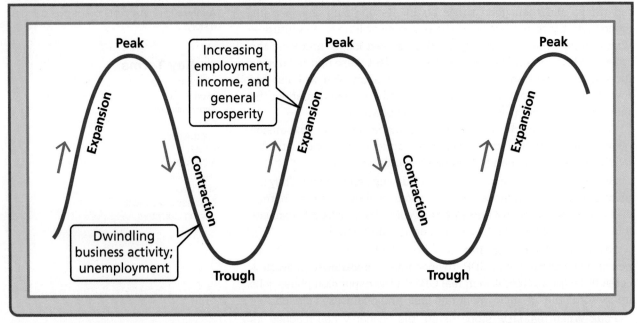

>> **Figure 7.8 Analyze Information** What is the point of slowest business activity in a business cycle called?

▶ **Interactive Chart**

Why Businesses Make Investments When the economy is expanding, businesses might expect to increase the goods or services they produce. Therefore, they may invest heavily in building new plants and buying new equipment. Or they may invest in the expansion of old plants in order to increase the plants' productive capacity. All of this **business investment** spending creates additional output and jobs, helping to increase GDP and maintain the expansion.

At some point, however, firms may decide that they have expanded enough or that demand for their products is dropping. They cut back on investment spending; as a result, aggregate demand falls. The result is a decline in GDP and also in the price level. The drop in business spending reduces output and income in other sectors of the economy.

When that occurs, industries that produce capital goods slow their own production and begin to lay off workers. Other industries might follow, causing overall unemployment to rise. Jobless workers cannot buy new cars, eat at restaurants, or perhaps even pay their rent. If the downward spiral picks up speed, a recession results.

The Cost of Credit In the United States economy, consumers often use credit to purchase "big ticket" items—from new cars and houses to home electronics and vacations. The cost of credit is the interest rate that financial institutions charge their customers. If the interest rate rises, consumers are less likely to buy those new cars and appliances. Consumers who do purchase items using credit cards can find themselves paying much more for the items they buy because high interest rates and fees increase the cost.

Businesses, too, look to interest rates in deciding whether or not to purchase new equipment, expand their facilities, or make many other large investments. When interest rates are low, companies are more willing to borrow money. When interest rates climb, business borrowing falls. One result of rising interest rates, then, is less output. Such a result may lead to a contraction phase.

Consider one example of the impact of interest rates on the business cycle. In the early 1980s, high consumer interest rates helped bring on the worst economic slump in the United States since the Great Depression.

Some credit card interest rates reached 21 percent. As a result, the cost of expensive items usually purchased using credit was too high for many Americans. With reduced consumer spending, the economy entered a recession that pushed unemployment rates over 9 percent—the highest since the Depression.

>> In a downturn, consumers may have a harder time with credit card debt. **Analyze Political Cartoons** Why does the cartoonist portray the man as looking so nervous?

Expectations Affect Spending Consumer spending is determined partly by consumers' expectations. If people expect the economy to begin contracting, they may reduce their spending because they expect layoffs and lower incomes.

This reduced spending can actually help bring on a contraction, as firms respond to reduced demand for their products. Thus consumer expectations often become self-fulfilling prophecies, creating the very outcome that consumers fear. In the summer of 2007, consumer confidence fell. By September, consumer confidence was the lowest it had been in two years. This low level of consumer confidence affected the holiday shopping season at the end of the year.

High consumer confidence has the opposite effect on the economy. If people expect a rapidly growing economy, they will also expect abundant job opportunities and rising incomes. Thus, they will buy more goods and services, pushing up gross domestic product.

Effects of External Shocks Of all the factors that affect the business cycle, perhaps most difficult to predict are external shocks. External shocks can dramatically affect an economy's aggregate supply. Examples of negative external shocks include disruptions of the oil supply, wars that interrupt trade, and droughts that severely reduce crop harvests.

Let's consider what might happen if a shock occurred. Suppose that the nation's supply of imported oil was suddenly cut off. Immediately, the price of any remaining oil would skyrocket. This rapid increase would have a powerful ripple effect on the economy.

Oil is used to produce many goods, and petroleum products fuel the trucks, trains, and airplanes that transport goods from factories to stores. The oil shortage and high prices would force firms to reduce production and raise prices. In other words, GDP declines and the price level rises. This economic condition is particularly harmful to businesses and households, and is difficult for policymakers to fix.

Of course, an economy may also enjoy positive external shocks. The discovery of a large deposit of oil or minerals will contribute to a nation's wealth. A growing season with a perfect mix of sun and rain may create bountiful harvests that drive food prices down. Positive shocks tend to shift the Aggregate Supply curve to the right, lowering the price level and increasing real GDP.

External shocks usually come without much warning. The other key factors capable of pushing an economy from one phase of the business cycle to another are more predictable. So economists track business investment, interest rates, and consumer expectations in order to more accurately forecast new stages of the business cycle.

? INFER A major thunderstorm destroyed Midland Farm's summer crop of corn, greatly affecting the business's overall profits. What type of economic variable would this storm be considered?

Forecasting Business Cycles

Predicting changes in a business cycle is difficult. For example, in the summer of 1929, John J. Raskob, Senior Financial Officer of General Motors, declared his firm belief that the United States was on the verge of the greatest industrial expansion in its history.

> In my opinion the wealth of the country is bound to increase at a very rapid rate . . . . Anyone who believes that opportunities are now closed and that from now on the country will get worse instead of better is welcome to the opinion—and whatever increment it will bring. I think that we have scarcely started . . . . I am firm in my belief that anyone not only can be rich but ought to be rich.
>
> —John Jakob Raskob, interview in the *Ladies Home Journal,* August 1929

Less than two months later, the stock market crashed, setting off the worst depression in American history.

Economists today know a lot more about the workings of our economy than Raskob did in 1929. However, economic predictions are still tricky. To predict the next phase of a business cycle, forecasters must anticipate movements in real GDP before they occur. This is no easy task, given the large number of factors that influence the level of output in a modern economy.

Government and business decision makers need economic predictions to be accurate, however, so they can respond properly to changes in a business cycle. If businesses expect a contraction, they may postpone building new factories. If government policymakers expect a contraction, they may take steps to try to prevent a recession.

>> When the business cycle that brought expansion in the 1920s began to contract, the Great Depression followed.

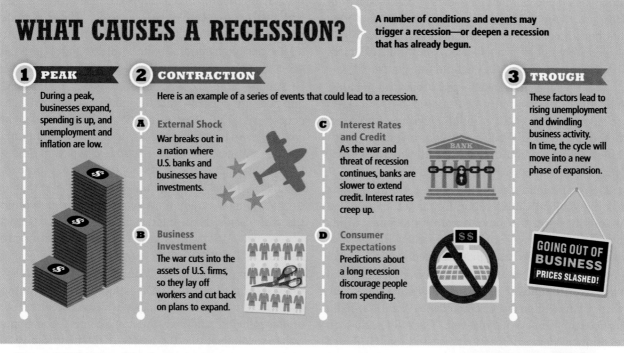

WHAT CAUSES A RECESSION? 〉 A number of conditions and events may trigger a recession—or deepen a recession that has already begun.

1 PEAK

During a peak, businesses expand, spending is up, and unemployment and inflation are low.

2 CONTRACTION

Here is an example of a series of events that could lead to a recession.

A External Shock
War breaks out in a nation where U.S. banks and businesses have investments.

B Business Investment
The war cuts into the assets of U.S. firms, so they lay off workers and cut back on plans to expand.

C Interest Rates and Credit
As the war and threat of recession continues, banks are slower to extend credit. Interest rates creep up.

D Consumer Expectations
Predictions about a long recession discourage people from spending.

3 TROUGH

These factors lead to rising unemployment and dwindling business activity. In time, the cycle will move into a new phase of expansion.

BANK

GOING OUT OF BUSINESS PRICES SLASHED!

>> **Figure 7.9 Analyze Charts** How do expectations by business leaders and consumers contribute to a recession?

▶ Interactive Chart

Economists have many tools available for making these predictions. The **leading indicators** are a set of key economic variables that provide economists with economic data to predict future trends in a business cycle, but as you can see in **Figure 7.9** many factors can contribute to a recession.

The stock market is one leading indicator. Typically, the stock market turns sharply downward before a recession begins. For example, the crash of the Nasdaq exchange in 2000 preceded the recession of 2001. Interest rates are another indicator. As you have seen, interest rates have a strong effect on consumer and business spending.

The Conference Board, a private business research organization, maintains an index of economic data from the ten leading economic indicators, including stock prices, interest rates, and manufacturers' new orders of capital goods. Economists and policymakers closely watch this index, which is updated monthly. However, like the other important tools used to forecast changes in the business cycle, it is not altogether reliable.

? IDENTIFY What do the stock market and interest rates have in common?

Business Cycles in the United States

Economic activity in the United States has indeed followed a cyclical pattern. Periods of GDP growth alternate with periods of GDP decline.

The Great Depression As you read earlier, before the 1930s many economists believed that when an economy declined, it would quickly recover on its own. This explains why, when the U.S. stock market crashed in 1929, and the economy took a nosedive, President Herbert Hoover felt little need to change his economic policies.

However, the Great Depression did not rapidly cure itself. Rather, it was the most severe economic downturn in the history of industrial capitalism. As **Figure 7.10** indicates, the effects went beyond the United States. Between 1929 and 1933, GDP fell by about a quarter, and unemployment rose sharply. In fact, one out of every four American workers was jobless, and those who could find work often earned very low wages.

As the effects of the Great Depression spread throughout the world, it affected economists' beliefs about the macroeconomy. The Depression, along with the publication of John Maynard Keynes's *The General Theory of Employment, Interest, and Money*, pushed economists to consider the idea that modern market economies could fall into long-lasting contractions. In addition, many economists accepted Keynes's idea that government intervention might be needed to pull an economy out of a depression. You will read more about Keynes and his ideas later in this course.

The Depression also affected American politics. Rejecting Hoover, voters in 1932 elected the Democratic governor of New York, Franklin Delano Roosevelt, to the presidency. Roosevelt soon began a series of government programs, known as the New Deal, designed to get people back to work.

Programs such as the Works Progress Administration and the Civilian Conservation Corps got able-bodied workers back on the job and earning income, which they then spent supporting their families. In this way, spending increased throughout the economy.

Still, although the New Deal relieved some of the effects of hard times, it did not end the Great Depression. Not until the United States entered into World War II did the economy achieve full recovery. The sudden surge in government defense spending boosted real GDP well above pre-Depression levels.

More Recent Recessions Thankfully, no economic downturns since the 1930s have been nearly as severe as the Great Depression. We have had recessions, though.

In the 1970s, an international cartel, the Organization of Petroleum Exporting Countries (OPEC),

placed an embargo on oil shipped to the United States and quadrupled the price of its oil. These actions caused external shocks in the American oil market. As oil prices skyrocketed, raw material costs rose, and the economy quickly contracted into a period of stagflation.

Reeling from higher-than-ever prices for gasoline and heating fuel, Americans began looking for ways to conserve energy. They turned down their heat; bought smaller, more fuel-efficient cars; and began researching energy alternatives to petroleum. When the United States and other nations developed more of their own energy resources, OPEC finally lowered its oil prices.

As you read earlier, there was another recession in the early 1980s. High interest rates and other factors caused real GDP to fall and the unemployment rate to rise to over 9 percent in the early 1980s.

Following a brief recession in 1991, the U.S. economy grew steadily, with real GDP rising each year during the 1990s. The country enjoyed record growth, low unemployment, and low inflation. Some economists began to suggest that the nature of the business cycle had changed. Perhaps we had learned how to control recessions and promote long-term growth.

Much of this growth was fueled by the rise of Internet companies, called "dot.coms," after part of their Internet address. As the dot.com boom of the 1990s ended, however, U.S. economic growth slowed. Businesses and individuals invested billions of dollars in new technology that proved to be unprofitable and,

Effects of the Great Depression

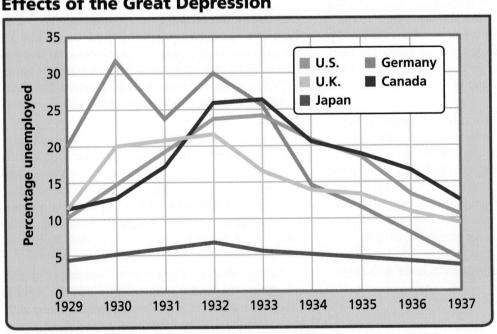

>> **Figure 7.10 Analyze Graphs** Which nations had the highest and lowest levels of unemployment in 1930? Which had the highest and lowest in 1937?

Visitor Spending in NYC, 1998–2010

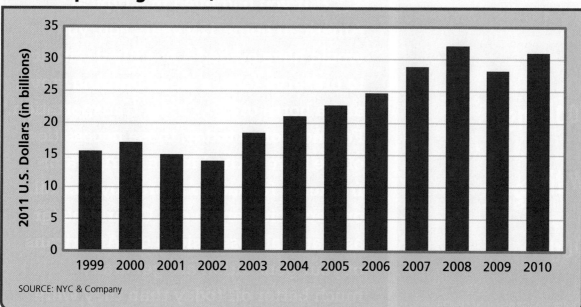

SOURCE: NYC & Company

>> **Analyze Graphs** If this chart included data through 2012, what would you expect it to show? Explain your answer.

in some cases, worthless. The negative effects of the technology crash spread throughout the economy to other industries. In March 2001, the country slipped into a recession.

Economists hoped this decline would prove short-lived, but then the terrorist attacks of September 11, 2001, resulted in a sharp drop in consumer spending. The hotel, airline, and tourism industries were especially affected. Many companies blamed their performance problems on September 11.

The Present-Day Business Cycle The recession ended in November 2001 when the economy began to grow slowly. Historically low interest rates prevented the economy from slipping back into a recession. However, unemployment continued to rise steadily over the following years as companies laid off more workers and kept spending low. Growth was not strong enough to dispel the feeling of bad times even though the recession had ended.

The economy did recover, though. By late 2003, it was surging, with GDP growing at an annual rate of 7.5 percent over three months. After that, growth slowed, though it did continue. High gasoline prices in 2006 caused the economy's growth to slow even further. Difficulties in the home mortgage market spiraled into a financial crisis and economic recession in 2008. In the following years the economy improved slowly, though the unemployment rate remained high.

❓ IDENTIFY CAUSE AND EFFECT What effect did the embargo placed on oil shipped to the United States by OPEC in the 1970s have on the economy?

ASSESSMENT

1. **Trace** In the early 1980s, what brought on the worst economic slump in the United States since the Great Depression?

2. **Identify Cause and Effect** What is the effect on consumer spending when interest rates rise?

3. **Identify** The discovery of a large oil deposit off a nation's shores would be what type of economic variable?

4. **Identify** What event brought an end to the Great Depression, returning the economy to a full recovery?

5. **Check Understanding** What do economists hope to predict by keeping track of stock prices, interest rates, orders of capital goods, and other leading economic indicators?

WE'RE HIRING

Solve problems.

Learn new things.

Do good.

>> Job fairs are events at which companies find workers with the skills, experience, and education they need.

▶ Interactive Flipped Video

7.3 If you had lived in a typical American home 125 years ago, you would have owned a box filled with ice to preserve food, a wood-burning stove, and a horse or bicycle for transportation. For most of us today, those necessities of life have turned into a refrigerator-freezer; a furnace powered by gas, oil, or electricity; and a car. Clearly, as far as material possessions go, Americans of your generation are generally much better off today than they were 100 years ago. The biggest reason is economic growth.

>> Objectives

Analyze how economic growth is measured.

Analyze how productivity, technology, and trade relate to economic growth.

Summarize the impact of population growth and government policies on economic growth.

Analyze how saving and investment are related to economic growth.

Explain how the functions of financial institutions affect households and businesses.

>> Key Terms

real GDP per capita
capital deepening
saving
savings rate
technological
  progress
capital formation

Economic Growth

Measuring Economic Growth

Economic growth allows successive generations to have more and better goods and services than their parents had. Economic growth enables an entire society to make major improvements in its quality of life.

The basic measure of a nation's economic growth rate is the percentage of change in real GDP over a period of time. For example, real GDP in 1996 was $8.3 trillion, and in 2006, it was $11.3 trillion. The economic growth rate for this decade was about 36 percent ($11.3 trillion − $8.3 trillion) ÷ $8.3 trillion x 100).

GDP and Population Growth To satisfy the needs of a growing population, real GDP must grow at least as fast as the population does. This is one reason that economists prefer a measure that takes population growth into account. For this, they rely on **real GDP per capita,** which is real GDP divided by the total population of a country (*per capita* means "for each person"). **Figure 7.11** shows growth in real GDP per capita.

Real GDP per capita is considered the most accurate measure of a nation's standard of living. As long as real GDP is rising faster than the population, real GDP per capita will rise, and so will the standard of living. Economists can see how the standard of living has changed over time by comparing real GDP per capita from two different time periods. They can also examine the growth rates of real GDP per capita to compare the economic strength of two different nations.

GDP and Quality of Life GDP measures standard of living, which relates to material goods. We cannot use it, however, to measure people's quality of life. GDP excludes many factors that affect the quality of life, such as the state of the environment or the level of stress people feel in their daily lives.

In addition, while real GDP per capita represents the average output per person in an economy, it tells us nothing about how that output is distributed across the population. There are a number of ways that economists measure how income is distributed in the United States, such as "personal income distribution" and "functional income distribution." These measures, while complicated, are important. If most of the income in a nation goes to relatively few people while the majority earn next to nothing, the typical person will not enjoy a very high standard of living even if the real GDP per capita figure is high.

Despite these facts, real GDP per capita is a good starting point for measuring a nation's quality of life. People who live in nations with greater availability of goods and services usually enjoy better nutrition, safer and more comfortable housing, lower infant mortality, longer life spans, better education, greater job opportunities, and other indicators of a favorable quality of life.

Since economic growth has an enormous impact on quality of life, economists devote significant resources to figuring out what causes a nation's real GDP to rise. They focus on the roles of capital goods, technology, and a few related factors.

? ANALYZE INFORMATION How is high GDP per capita linked to quality of life?

Capital Deepening

Physical capital, the equipment used to produce goods and services, makes an important contribution to the output of an economy. With more physical capital, each worker can be more productive, producing more output per hour of work. Economists use the term *labor productivity* to describe the amount of output produced per worker.

Even if the size of the labor force does not change, more physical capital will lead to more output—in other words, to economic growth. This process of increasing the amount of capital per worker, called **capital deepening,** is one of the most important sources of growth in modern economies. (See **Figure 7.12**.) This process is also known as capital formation. Human capital, the productive knowledge and skills acquired

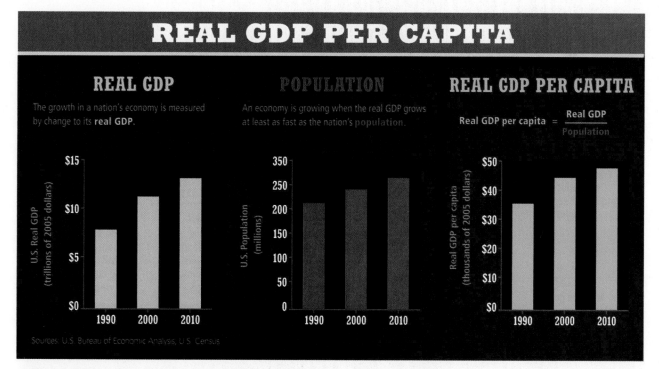

>> **Figure 7.11 Analyze Graphs** Is it possible for real GDP per capita to grow if the population remains the same? Explain your answer.

by a worker through education and experience, also contributes to output. Firms, and employees themselves, can deepen human capital through training programs and on-the-job experience. Better-trained and more-experienced workers can produce more output per hour of work.

Along with increasing output per worker, capital deepening tends to increase job opportunities and workers' earnings. To understand why this happens, consider the effect of greater worker productivity on the demand for workers. If workers can produce more output per hour, they become more valuable to their employers. As a result, employers will demand more workers. This increase in demand will increase the equilibrium wage rate in the labor market.

Therefore, with a labor force of a given size, capital deepening will increase output and workers' wages. How, then, does an economy increase its stock of capital per worker? It does so through saving and investment.

? DRAW CONCLUSIONS Why does capital deepening work with human capital?

Saving and Investment

To see how saving and investment are related, consider an economy with no government sector and no foreign trade. In this simplified economy, consumers and business firms purchase all output. In other words, output can be used for consumption (by consumers) or investment (by firms). Income that is not used for consumption is called **saving.**

Since output can only be consumed or invested, whatever is not consumed must be invested. Therefore, in this simplified economy, saving is equal to investment. The proportion of disposable income that is saved is called the **savings rate.**

To see this another way, look at an individual's decision, as shown in **Figure 7.13**. Shawna had an after-tax income of $30,000 last year, but she spent only $25,000. That left her with $5,000 available for saving. She used some of her leftover income to purchase shares in a mutual fund, giving her ownership of some stocks and bonds. She put the rest of the money into a savings account at her bank.

Through her mutual-fund firm, her bank, and other intermediaries, Shawna's $5,000 was made available to businesses. The firms used the money to invest in new plants and equipment. So, when Shawna chose not to spend her entire income, the amount that she saved became available for business investment.

If we consider the economy as a whole, the process works the same way. If total saving rises, more investment funds become available to businesses. This accumulation of savings made available for investment is called **capital formation.** Those firms will use most

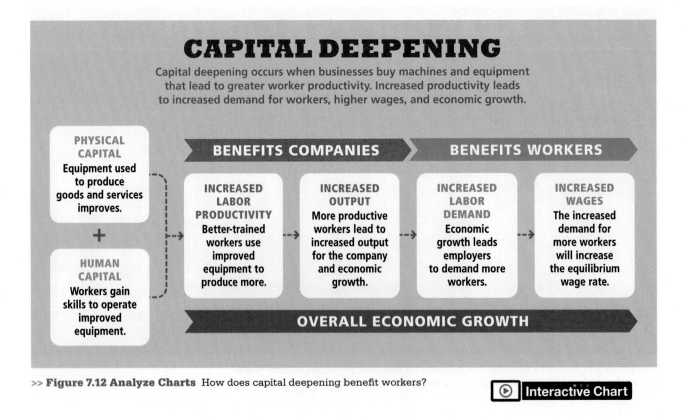

>> **Figure 7.12 Analyze Charts** How does capital deepening benefit workers?

▶ **Interactive Chart**

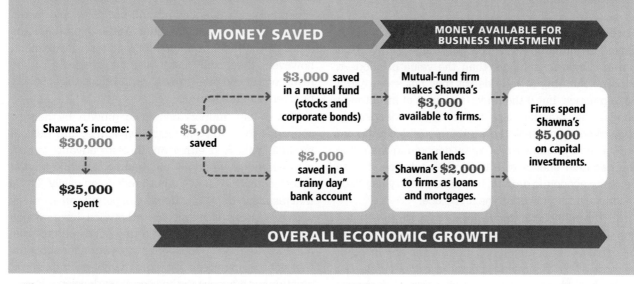

HOW SAVING LEADS TO CAPITAL DEEPENING When individuals save or invest money, that money becomes available to businesses. Firms can use this money to buy new plants or equipment. This capital deepening leads to greater productivity and growth for the whole economy.

MONEY SAVED

MONEY AVAILABLE FOR BUSINESS INVESTMENT

Shawna's income: $30,000 → $5,000 saved

$3,000 saved in a mutual fund (stocks and corporate bonds) → Mutual-fund firm makes Shawna's $3,000 available to firms.

Firms spend Shawna's $5,000 on capital investments.

$25,000 spent

$2,000 saved in a "rainy day" bank account → Bank lends Shawna's $2,000 to firms as loans and mortgages.

OVERALL ECONOMIC GROWTH

>> **Figure 7.13 Analyze Charts** What actually happens to the money Shawna saves?

of these funds for capital investment. That is, they will expand the stock of capital in the business sector.

Higher saving, then, leads to higher investment, and thus to higher amounts of capital per worker. In other words, higher saving leads to capital deepening, or capital formation. Now we can understand why most nations promote saving. In the long run, more saving will lead to higher output and income for the population, raising GDP and the standard of living.

The United States has a low savings rate. To obtain the investment funds they need, businesses and the government borrow from other countries with higher savings rates.

? **IDENTIFY CAUSE AND EFFECT** How is saving linked to capital deepening?

The Effects of Population, Government, and Trade

Now we will consider a slightly more realistic economy that has population growth, a government sector, and foreign trade. First, think about the effect of population growth on capital accumulation.

Population Growth Population growth does not necessarily preclude economic growth. However, if the population grows while the supply of capital remains

constant, the amount of capital per worker will shrink. This process, the opposite of capital deepening, leads to lower living standards. In fact, some relatively poor countries, such as Bangladesh, have large labor forces but small capital stocks.

The result is that output per worker— and earnings per worker—are relatively low. Conversely, a nation with low population growth and expanding capital stock will enjoy significant capital deepening.

Government Government can affect capital formation in several ways. If government raises tax rates to pay for additional services or to finance a war, households will have less money. People will reduce saving, thus reducing the money available to businesses for investment. In these cases, the government is taxing households in order to pay for its own consumption spending. The net effect is reduced investment.

On the other hand, a different result occurs if government invests the extra tax revenues in public goods such as roads and telecommunications. These public goods are called infrastructure, the underlying necessities of modern life. Spending on infrastructure increases investment. To see why, consider what share of income the average household saves.

Suppose that, on average, households save 10 percent of their income. In this case, for every extra dollar in tax revenue the government collects, household saving (and investment) drops by 10 cents. However, government investment in infrastructure rises by $1. The net result is an increase in total investment of 90 cents. This kind of spending, then, is capital deepening, since the government is taxing its citizens to provide investment goods.

Foreign Trade Foreign trade can result in a trade deficit, a situation in which the value of goods a country imports is higher than the value of goods it exports. Running a trade deficit may not seem like a wise practice, but if the imports consist of investment goods, the practice can foster capital deepening. Investment goods are the structures and equipment purchased by businesses. Capital deepening can offset the negative effects of a trade deficit by helping to generate economic growth, helping a country pay back the money it borrowed in the first place.

In the mid-1800s, for example, the United States financed the building of the transcontinental railroad in part by borrowing funds from investors in other countries. The borrowing created a trade deficit, but it also helped create a much higher rate of economic growth than would have occurred otherwise. The railroad promoted new industries and opened up vast areas to farming, leading to a huge increase in the nation's farm output.

Of course, not all trade deficits promote capital deepening. In this regard, trade deficits are similar to government taxation. Whether they encourage capital deepening and economic growth depends on how the funds are used. If they are used for short-term consumption, the economy will not grow any faster, and it will not have any additional GDP to pay back the debts. If the funds are used for long-term investment, however, they will foster capital deepening. The resulting economic growth will bring the country prosperity in the future.

Trade can support economic growth by helping countries focus on producing what they are best at producing (having either an absolute advantage or a comparative advantage) and trading it, while buying other goods that they cannot produce as easily. Trade that results in importing goods can provide an economy with resources it might not otherwise have, which helps the economy grow. Exporting goods can enlarge a market for those goods, creating a stronger economy that is built on access to bigger markets. For example, a nation with access to the sea might develop a strong fishing industry and export some of the catch to a landlocked country. The landlocked country might have abundant forests from which to export wood products. Such trade can grow the economies of both countries. Trade is essential for economies to specialize in what they are most efficient at producing.

? EXPRESS IDEAS CLEARLY Do higher taxes increase or reduce investment?

Technological Progress

Another key source of economic growth is technological progress. This term usually brings to mind new inventions or new ways of performing a task, but in economics, it has a more precise definition. **Technological progress** is an increase in efficiency gained by producing more output without using more inputs.

Technological progress occurs in many ways. It can result from new scientific knowledge—for example, nanotechnology, making computer chips smaller and smaller—that has practical uses. It can be a new invention that allows workers to produce goods more efficiently. It could even be a new method for organizing production. All of these advances raise a nation's productivity. Increased productivity means producing more output with the same amounts of land, labor, and capital. With technological progress, a society enjoys higher real GDP per capita, which leads to a higher standard of living.

>> Port dredging is an example of investment in infrastructure. Dredging deepens the port, which allows larger ships and increased trade.

Technological Progress Boosts GDP

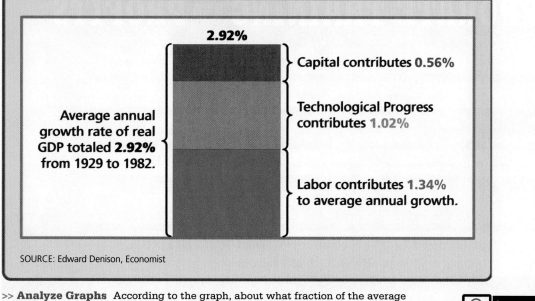

2.92%

Average annual growth rate of real GDP totaled **2.92%** from 1929 to 1982.

Capital contributes 0.56%

Technological Progress contributes 1.02%

Labor contributes 1.34% to average annual growth.

SOURCE: Edward Denison, Economist

>> **Analyze Graphs** According to the graph, about what fraction of the average annual growth rate of real GDP from 1929 to 1982 was due to technological progress?

▶ **Interactive Gallery**

Measuring Technological Progress In most modern economies, the amount of physical and human capital changes all the time. So do the quantity and quality of labor and the technology used to produce goods and services. These interconnected variables work together to produce economic growth. How, then, can we isolate and measure the effects of technological progress?

Robert Solow, a Nobel Prize–winning economist from the Massachusetts Institute of Technology, developed a method for doing so. Solow's method was to determine how much growth in output comes from increases in capital and how much comes from increases in labor. He concluded that any remaining growth in output must then come from technological progress.

Between 1929 and 1982, the average annual growth rate of real GDP was 2.92 percent. Using Solow's method, economist Edward Denison has estimated that technological progress boosted the real GDP 1.02 percent per year, on average.

Denison determined that increases in capital and labor were responsible for 0.56 percent and 1.34 percent of the average annual growth, respectively (2.92 — 0.56 —1.34 = 1.02). Technological progress, then, was the second most important factor in promoting economic growth in that period.

Causes of Technological Progress Since technological progress is such an important source of economic growth, economists have looked for its causes. They have found a variety of factors that influence technological progress.

Scientific research Scientific research can generate new or improved production techniques, improve physical capital, and result in better goods and services.

Innovation When new products and ideas are successfully brought to the market, output goes up, boosting GDP and business profits. Yet innovation often requires costly research. Companies willing to carry out that research need assurance that they will profit from the products they develop.

The government issues patents to provide that assurance. A patent is a set of exclusive rights to produce and sell a product for a particular period of time. It is given to people who can show that they have discovered or invented a new product or process. Currently, patents last 20 years. A patent helps a company recover the cost of research by earning profits before its competitors can copy its new products.

Government aids innovation in several other ways as well. Through organizations such as the National Science Foundation and the National Institutes of Health, the United States government sponsors *basic research*. This term describes theoretical research that is often expensive and might not bring a new product to market in a timely way.

Scale of the market Larger markets provide more incentives for innovation, since the potential profits are greater. For this reason, larger economies will come up with more technological advances.

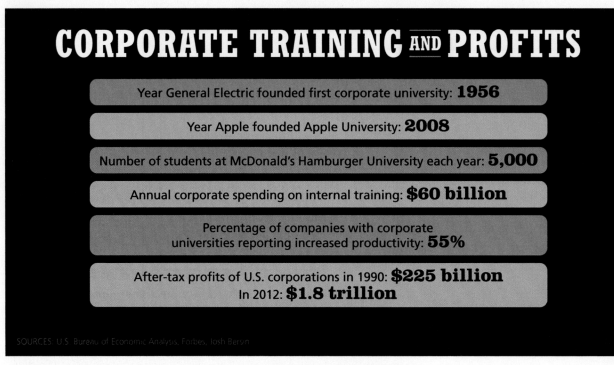

CORPORATE TRAINING AND PROFITS

Year General Electric founded first corporate university: **1956**

Year Apple founded Apple University: **2008**

Number of students at McDonald's Hamburger University each year: **5,000**

Annual corporate spending on internal training: **$60 billion**

Percentage of companies with corporate universities reporting increased productivity: **55%**

After-tax profits of U.S. corporations in 1990: **$225 billion**
In 2012: **$1.8 trillion**

SOURCES: U.S. Bureau of Economic Analysis, Forbes, Josh Bersin

>> **Analyze Charts** Why are companies willing to spend such large amounts of resources on training?

*Education and experience*As you read earlier, firms increase their human capital by providing education and on-the-job experience for their employees. Human capital makes workers more productive, which accelerates economic growth. It can also stimulate growth in another way. A more educated and experienced workforce can more easily handle technological advances and may well create some new advances, too.

Natural resource use Increased use of natural resources can create a need for new technology. For example, new technology can turn previously useless raw materials into usable resources. It can also allow us to obtain and use resources more efficiently, develop substitute resources, and discover new resource reserves. Because price is based on the cost of obtaining a resource (and not necessarily on its scarcity), new technology can also lead to lower prices.

? IDENTIFY MAIN IDEAS What are the main factors in technological progress?

ASSESSMENT

1. **Analyze Data** Based on your completed table, how does the economy grow?

2. **Apply Concepts** Suppose an uncle left you $500, and you had three choices for how to use the money. You could (1) save the $500 in a bank, (2) buy computer equipment, or (3) keep it in your closet. How would each of these actions affect the growth of the economy?

3. **Analyze Data** What is real GDP per capita, and why do economists measure it?

4. **Summarize** What is capital formation, and how much does it contribute to economic growth?

5. **Describe** What role does savings play in the process of economic growth?

Many people face unemployment at some point in their lives. For the jobless worker, it is a very personal issue. For the government, it is a national economic issue. Economists measure the health of the economy by tracking the number of people who are out of work. The government pays close attention to these statistics so that it can take actions that will spur economic recovery.

>> Workers displaced by Hurricane Katrina line up to attend a job fair in Arlington, Texas, in 2005.

[►] **Interactive Flipped Video**

Unemployment

Types of Unemployment

It is important to understand the causes of unemployment in order to foster a better job market. General economic conditions, lengthy job searches, and seasonal production schedules are some of the factors that cause unemployment.

Economists look at four categories of unemployment: frictional, seasonal, structural, and cyclical. Sometimes, factors outside the economy can cause unemployment. The various kinds of unemployment have different effects on the economy as well as on the people who are unemployed.

Frictional Unemployment Unemployment always exists, even in a booming economy. **Frictional unemployment** occurs when people take time to find a job. For example, people might change jobs, be laid off from their current jobs, or need some time to find the right position after they finish their schooling. They might be returning to the workforce after a long period of time. In the following examples, all three people are considered frictionally unemployed.

Hannah was not satisfied working as a nurse in a large hospital. Last month she left her job to look for a position at a small health clinic.

Since Jorge graduated from law school three months ago, he has interviewed with various law firms to find the one that best suits his needs and interests.

>> **Objectives**

Interpret economic data relating to the unemployment rate.

Differentiate between frictional, seasonal, structural, and cyclical unemployment.

Explain why full employment does not mean that every worker is employed.

Explain the costs and benefits of U.S. economic policies related to the goal of full employment.

>> **Key Terms**

frictional
   unemployment
structural
   unemployment
globalization
seasonal
   unemployment
cyclical
   unemployment
unemployment rate
full employment
underemployed
discouraged worker

Liz left her sales job two years ago to care for an aging parent. Now she is trying to return to the workforce.

None of these three people found work immediately. While they look for work, they are frictionally unemployed. In the large, diverse U.S. economy, economists expect to find many people in this category. Unemployment insurance, which provides income to laid-off workers seeking new jobs, may contribute slightly to frictional unemployment. A worker receiving unemployment insurance faces somewhat less financial pressure to find a new job immediately.

Structural Unemployment The structure of the American economy has changed over time. Two centuries ago, people needed basic farming skills to survive. As the country developed an industrial economy, farm workers moved to urban areas to work in factories. Today, service industries are rapidly replacing manufacturing industries, and information services are expanding at breakneck speed.

All these shifts lead to upheavals in the labor market. When the structure of the economy changes, the skills that workers need to succeed also change. Workers who lack the necessary skills lose their jobs. **Structural unemployment** occurs when workers'

>> Maria Contreras-Sweet was nominated to head the U.S. Small Business Administration in January 2014. According to the SBA, small businesses create two out of three new jobs.

skills do not match those needed for the jobs that are now available.

There are five major causes of structural unemployment.

The development of new technology New inventions and ideas often push out older ways of doing things. For example, downloading music has hurt the sales of compact discs. Firms making CDs have let workers go, and those workers must find jobs in another field.

The discovery of new resources New resources replace old resources. The discovery of petroleum in Pennsylvania in 1859 severely hurt the whale-oil industry. Whaling-ship crews lost their jobs and did not have the skills needed for the petroleum industry.

Changes in consumer demand Consumers often stop buying one product in favor of another. Many people now favor athletic shoes over more traditional kinds of shoes. As a result, traditional shoemaking jobs have declined.

Globalization The mobility of capital and labor has fueled a shift from local to international markets. Countries have become more open to foreign trade and investment in a trend called **globalization.** As a result, companies often relocate jobs or entire facilities to other countries where costs are lower. Celia, for example, spent many years working on an automobile assembly line in Michigan. When her company moved much of its auto assembly work to Mexico, where labor is less expensive, Celia lost her job. Unfortunately, there were no local jobs that matched Celia's skills.

Lack of education People who drop out of school or fail to acquire the minimum skills needed for today's job market may find themselves unemployed, employed part time, or stuck in low-wage jobs. For example, Martin barely managed to graduate from high school.

When he was hired as a clerk by a local clothing store, he had trouble using the computerized checkout register. The store manager fired Martin after just two months because he lacked the skills needed for the job.

Policymakers in the 1990s and 2000s recognized that computer technology, globalization, and other structural changes threatened the futures of many workers. As a result, they developed job-training programs to help workers gain new skills, especially computer skills.

Retraining takes time, however, and the new skills do not ensure that the trainees will obtain high-wage jobs. Some companies offer their own training programs. In this way, they can teach trainees the specialized skills they need to become valued employees.

Seasonal Unemployment Gregory is a brick mason for a small construction company in the northeastern United States. Every winter Gregory's employer lays off all seven of his employees when cold weather forces an end to outdoor work. In the spring, he hires them back again for the new construction season. Gregory and his co-workers are examples of people who experience seasonal unemployment.

In general, **seasonal unemployment** occurs when industries slow or shut down for a season or make seasonal shifts in their production schedules. Seasonal unemployment can also occur as a result of harvest schedules or vacations. When this school year ends, you or your friends may need some time to find the perfect summer job. Until you do so, economists will count you as seasonally unemployed.

As with frictional unemployment, economists expect to see seasonal unemployment throughout the year. Government policymakers do not take steps to prevent this kind of unemployment, because it is a normal part of a healthy economy.

Still, the lives of seasonally unemployed workers can be extremely difficult. Migrant agricultural workers, for example, travel throughout the country to pick fruits and vegetables as various crops come into season.

They know that their work will likely end when winter arrives. Migrant workers can also have periods of unemployment even during harvest season, depending on the weather. Heat, cold, rain, and drought can ruin harvest schedules by causing fruits and vegetables to ripen sooner or later than expected. Instead of moving smoothly from crop to crop, migrant workers might lose work time waiting for a crop to be ready for picking.

Cyclical Unemployment Unemployment that rises during economic downturns and falls when the economy improves is called **cyclical unemployment.** During recessions, or downturns in the business cycle, the demand for goods and services drops. The resulting slowdown in production causes the demand for labor to drop as well, and companies begin to lay off employees. Many of these laid-off employees will be rehired when the recession ends and the business cycle resumes an upward trend. Although economists expect cyclical unemployment, it can severely strain the economy and greatly distress the unemployed.

The most damaging example of cyclical unemployment in the twentieth century was the Great Depression. During the Great Depression, one out of every four workers was unemployed. Many remained jobless for years. In 1935, President Franklin D. Roosevelt proposed, and Congress passed, the Social Security Act. In addition to providing monthly payments for retirees and people who could not support themselves, the Social Security Act established a program of unemployment insurance.

>> A counselor at a summer day camp is an example of a seasonal worker.

▶ **Interactive Chart**

Today, unemployment insurance still provides weekly payments to workers who have lost their jobs. The payments usually provide about half of a worker's lost wages each week for a limited amount of time.

Circumstances Outside the Economy Sometimes events outside the economy can cause unemployment. The September 11, 2001, terrorist attacks on the World Trade Center and the Pentagon cost the country an estimated 1.5 to 2 million jobs. Many of the lost jobs were in the travel and tourism industries.

About 20 percent of the lost jobs were in the airline industry. In Manhattan, the area around the World Trade Center site was hit especially hard, and New York City lost some 150,000 jobs.

Natural disasters also affect employment. In October 2005, Hurricane Katrina slammed into the Gulf Coast region. The powerful storm caused widespread destruction, and thousands of people lost their jobs. Many families were relocated to other areas while their communities were being rebuilt. Months later, unemployment among people affected by Hurricane Katrina was still higher than the national average.

? **COMPARE AND CONTRAST** How is cyclical unemployment different from seasonal unemployment?

The Unemployment Rate

The amount of unemployment in the nation is an important clue to the health of the economy. For this reason, the government keeps careful track of how many people are unemployed, and why.

To measure employment, the United States Bureau of the Census conducts a monthly household survey for the Bureau of Labor Statistics (BLS). For this survey, called the Current Population Survey, interviewers poll 60,000 families about employment during that month. This sample is designed to represent the entire population of the United States. The BLS, a branch of the U.S. Department of Labor, analyzes the data from the survey to identify how many people are employed and how many are unemployed. Using these numbers, the BLS computes the **unemployment rate,** or the percentage of the nation's labor force that is unemployed.

Interpreting the Unemployment Rate The labor force is composed of civilians age 16 and older who have a job or are actively looking for a job. To determine the unemployment rate, BLS officials add up the number of employed and unemployed people. That figure equals the total labor force. Then they divide the number of unemployed people by the total labor force and multiply by 100. The result is the percentage of people who are unemployed.

For example, in September 2007, the Current Population Survey showed that 146.3 million people were employed, and 7.2 million were unemployed. The total labor force, therefore, was 153.5 million. Dividing 7.2 million by 153.5 million and then multiplying the result by 100 yields an unemployment rate of 4.7 percent for that month.

Adjusting the Unemployment Rate When you see the unemployment rate for a particular month, it has usually been "seasonally adjusted." This means that the rate has been increased or decreased to take into account the level of seasonal unemployment.

Taking this step allows economists to more accurately compare unemployment rates from month to month. This comparison helps them better detect changing economic conditions.

The unemployment rate is only an average for the nation. It does not reflect regional differences. Some areas, such as the coal-mining region of Appalachia in the southeastern United States, have long had a higher-than-average unemployment rate. The BLS and individual state agencies therefore establish unemployment rates for states and other geographic

CALCULATING THE UNEMPLOYMENT RATE

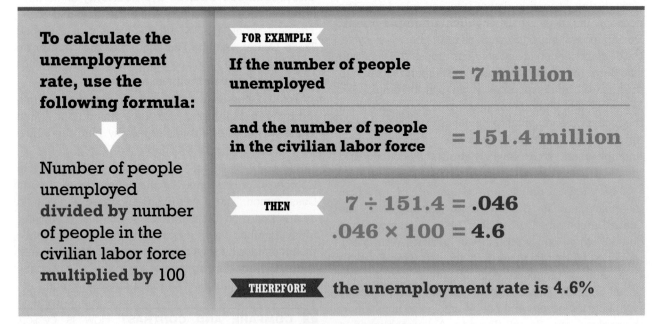

To calculate the unemployment rate, use the following formula:

Number of people unemployed **divided by** number of people in the civilian labor force **multiplied by 100**

FOR EXAMPLE

If the number of people unemployed = **7 million**

and the number of people in the civilian labor force = **151.4 million**

THEN $7 \div 151.4 = .046$
$.046 \times 100 = 4.6$

THEREFORE the unemployment rate is **4.6%**

>> **Analyze Charts** How would the unemployment rate change if the number of unemployed people stayed the same but the number of people in the civilian labor force increased?

Unemployment and Underemployment, 1996–2012

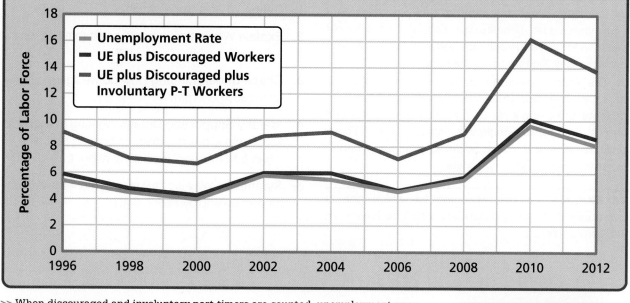

>> When discouraged and involuntary part-timers are counted, unemployment goes up. **Analyze Charts** What was the unemployment rate with discouraged and involuntary part-timers in 2010?

Interactive Chart

areas. These rates help pinpoint trouble areas on which policymakers can focus attention.

? EXPLAIN Why do states keep track of their own unemployment rates?

The Goal of Full Employment

Zero unemployment is not an achievable goal in a market economy, even under the best of circumstances. Economists generally agree that in an economy that is working properly, an unemployment rate of around 4 to 6 percent is normal. Such an economy would still experience frictional, seasonal, and structural unemployment. In other words, **full employment** is the level of employment reached when no cyclical unemployment exists.

Underemployment Full employment means that nearly everyone who wants a job has a job. But are all those people satisfied with their jobs? Not necessarily. Some people working at low-skill, low-wage jobs may be highly skilled or educated in a field with few opportunities. They are **underemployed,** that is, working at a job for which they are overqualified, or working part time when they desire full-time work.

For example, Jim, a philosophy major, earned a graduate degree in philosophy. When he left school, Jim found that although the economy was booming, he could not find jobs in which he could apply his knowledge of philosophy. Jim found a part-time job that did not pay well and did not challenge his mind. He was underemployed.

Underemployment also describes the situation of people who want a permanent, full-time job but have not been able to find one. Many part-time workers and seasonal workers fit into this category.

Discouraged Workers Some people, especially during a long recession, give up hope of finding work. These **discouraged workers** have stopped searching for employment and may rely on other family members or savings to support them. Although they are without jobs, discouraged workers do not appear in the unemployment rate determined by the Bureau of Labor Statistics because they are not actively looking for work.

If underemployed and discouraged workers were included, the unemployment rate would be much higher than reported. Some estimates are that the 2009 unemployment rate would have been above 17 percent.

United States economic policy encourages full employment in various ways. Monetary and fiscal policies, for example, aim to promote strong but sustainable growth, which in turn will keep employment rates high. Full employment benefits individuals and society as a whole because more people can provide for themselves and their families and pay taxes. Full employment also benefits the economy as a whole because employed people are better able to save and invest money, leading to capital formation.

The federal government also spends money to improve infrastructure such as highways. Such projects promote fuller employment and increasing economic output due to the improved infrastructure. These projects come at the cost, however, of higher eventual taxes to cover the projects' costs.

? **EXPLAIN** Working at a job for which one is overqualified, or working part time when full-time work is desired, refers to

ASSESSMENT

1. **Define** What is globalization?

2. **Explain** Why is the unemployment rate seasonally adjusted?

3. **Check Understanding** How do we figure out the unemployment rate?

4. **Identify Supporting Details** Working at a job for which one is overqualified, or working part time when full-time work is desired, refers to

5. **Synthesize** Why isn't full employment the same as zero unemployment?

At first, the changes are hardly noticeable. You pay more for lunch at your favorite eatery. Your personal grooming products are more expensive. Clothing prices are higher. A movie ticket costs two dollars more. You realize that as a result of these steady price increases, your money doesn't buy as much as it did just a few months ago.

>> During hyperinflation, money becomes almost worthless. In September 2008, the International Monetary Fund set the annual rate of inflation in Zimbabwe at 489 billion percent.

▶ **Interactive Flipped Video**

Inflation and Deflation

How Rising Prices Affect You

As you will see, you cannot escape rising prices. Economists believe that the money supply, changes in demand, and increased production costs all contribute to a rise in prices throughout the economy. Higher prices can affect your life.

Inflation Josephine and Jack Barrow have owned the same house for 50 years. Recently, they had a real estate agent estimate their home's present market value. The Barrows were astounded. The house that they had bought for $12,000 was now worth nearly $150,000—a rise in value of more than 1,100 percent.

How could the value of a house, or anything else, increase so much? The main reason is inflation. **Inflation** is a general increase in prices across an economy. Over the years, prices generally go up. Since World War II, real estate prices have risen greatly.

The Barrows were pleased their house was worth so much. Then they realized that inflation had raised the prices of all houses, just as it had also raised wages and the prices of most other goods and services. As a result, they could not buy a similar house in their area for $12,000 or even $120,000.

>> **Objectives**

Interpret data that reflect the rate of inflation.

Explain the effects of rising prices.

Identify the causes of inflation.

Describe recent trends in the rate of inflation.

>> **Key Terms**

inflation
purchasing power
price index
Consumer Price
  Index
market basket
inflation rate
core inflation rate
hyperinflation
quantity theory
wage-price spiral
fixed income
deflation

PEARSON realize www.PearsonRealize.com Access your Digital Lesson.

Purchasing Power Another way to look at the Barrows' situation is that inflation had shrunk the value, or purchasing power, of the Barrows' money. **Purchasing power** is the ability to purchase goods and services. As prices rise, the purchasing power of money declines. That is why $12,000 buys much less now than it did 50 years ago.

? GENERATE EXPLANATIONS Why does inflation cause purchasing power to decrease over time?

Price Indexes

Housing costs are just one element that economists consider when they interpret economic data that reflect inflation and other price changes. The economy has thousands of goods and services, with millions of individual prices. How do economists compare the changes in all these prices in order to measure inflation? The answer is that they do not compare individual prices; instead, they compare price levels. Price level is the cost of goods and services in the entire economy at a given point in time.

To help them calculate price level, economists use a price index. A **price index** is a measurement that shows how the average price of a standard group of goods changes over time. A price index produces an average that economists compare to earlier averages to see how much prices have changed over time.

How Price Indexes Are Used Price indexes help consumers and business owners make economic decisions. For example, after Marina read in the newspaper that prices for consumer goods had been rising, she increased the amount of money she was saving for a new car. She wanted to be sure that when

the time came to buy the car, she had saved enough money to pay for it.

The government also uses indexes in making policy decisions. A member of Congress, for example, might push for an increase in the minimum wage if she thinks inflation has reduced purchasing power.

The Consumer Price Index Although there are several price indexes, the best-known index focuses on consumers. The **Consumer Price Index** (CPI) is computed each month by the Bureau of Labor Statistics (BLS). The CPI is determined by measuring the price of a standard group of goods meant to represent the "market basket" of a typical urban consumer. This **market basket** is a representative collection of goods and services. By looking at the CPI, consumers, businesses, and the government can compare the cost of a group of goods this month with what the same or a similar group cost months or even years ago.

As you can see from **Figure 7.14**, the CPI market basket is divided into eight categories of goods and services. These categories, and a few examples of the many items in each, are shown.

About every ten years, the items in the market basket are updated to account for shifting consumer buying habits. The BLS determines how the market basket should change by conducting a Consumer Expenditure Survey. The BLS conducted one such survey from 2000 to 2001, collecting spending information from 10,000 families. Another 7,500 families kept diaries, noting everything they purchased during a two-week period for both years. This process created the list of market basket items used today.

Calculating the Inflation Rate Economists also find it useful to calculate the **inflation rate**—the

Food Prices in Dollars, 1990–2010*

	MARCH 1990	MARCH 2000	MARCH 2010
Bread, white (1 lb.)	0.68	0.92	1.37
Butter, stick (1 lb.)	2.05	2.41	1.82
Bacon, sliced (1 lb.)	1.99	2.78	3.67

* U.S. City average
SOURCE: Bureau of Labor Statistics

>> **Analyze Graphs** What happened to the price of a 1 lb loaf of white bread between 1990 and 2010?

CATEGORY	EXAMPLES
Food and Beverages	cereals, coffee, chicken, milk, restaurant meals
Housing	rent, homeowner's costs, bedroom furniture
Apparel	men's shirts, women's dresses, jewelry
Transportation	airfares, new vehicles, gasoline, auto insurance
Medical Care	prescription medicines, eyecare, physicians' services
Recreation	televisions, toys, sports equipment
Education and Communication	tuition, postage, telephone services, computer
Other Goods and Services	haircuts, funeral expenses

>> **Figure 7.14 Analyze Information** In what category do you think the CPI market basket would place money spent for a home Internet connection? Why?

percentage rate of change in price level over time. The inflation rate can be calculated between any two points in time, typically between two years. An inflation rate calculated from one year to the next gives a snapshot of current economic conditions. An inflation rate calculated from many years ago to today shows how inflation has changed over a longer period of time. To calculate the inflation rate, use the following formula: CPI for Year A – CPI for Year B/ CPI for Year B x 100.

Since the CPI is the most familiar price index, we will focus on it. How does the BLS determine the CPI and use it to calculate the inflation rate?

Calculating CPI To determine the CPI, the BLS establishes a base period to which it can compare current prices. Currently, the base period is 1982–1984.

The cost of the market basket for that period is assigned the index number 100. Every month, BLS representatives update the cost of the same market basket of goods and services by rechecking all the prices. Each updated cost is compared with the base-period cost to determine the index for that month. As costs rise, the index rises.

The BLS determines the CPI for a given year using the following formula:

CPI = updated cost ÷ base-period cost x 100

For example, suppose the market basket cost $200 during the base period and costs $360 today. The CPI for today would be:

$360 ÷ $200 x 100 = 180

In this example, the CPI rose from 100 in the base period to 180 today.

Types of Inflation Inflation rates in the United States have changed greatly over time as you can see in **Figure 7.15** . When the inflation rate stays low—between 1 and 3 percent—it does not typically cause problems for the economy.

In this environment, businesses and governments can make plans. When the inflation rate exceeds 5 percent, however, the inflation rate itself becomes unstable and unpredictable. This makes planning very difficult.

Sometimes the inflation rate spikes sharply, as in 1974 and 1980. These sharp increases in the inflation rate were due in part to increases in prices in world food and oil markets. In order to study long-term trends in the inflation rate, analysts need to set aside temporary spikes in food and fuel prices. To do this, economists have developed the concept of a core inflation rate. The **core inflation rate** is the rate of inflation excluding the effects of food and energy prices.

By far the worst kind of inflation is **hyperinflation,** or inflation that is out of control. During periods of hyperinflation, inflation rates can go as high as 100 or even 500 percent per month, and money loses much of its value. This level of inflation is rare, but when it occurs it often leads to a total economic collapse.

? **CONSTRUCT** How is the Consumer Price Index calculated?

Identifying Causes of Inflation

Where does inflation come from? Price levels can rise steeply when demand for goods and services exceeds the supply available at current prices, such as during wartime. They can also rise steeply when productivity is restricted—for example, when a long drought leads to poor harvests.

Nobody can explain every instance of rising price levels. However, economists have several theories about the causes of inflation. These include the growth of the money supply, changes in aggregate demand, and changes in aggregate supply. Economists look at all of these elements when they try to understand the inflation process.

Growth of the Money Supply The **quantity theory** of inflation states that too much money in the economy causes inflation. Therefore, the money supply should be carefully monitored to keep it in line with the nation's productivity as measured by real GDP.

Economists at the University of Chicago developed a popular version of this theory in the 1950s and 1960s. They maintained that the money supply could be used to control price levels in the long term. The key to stable prices, they said, was to increase the supply of money at the same rate as the economy was growing.

Changes in Aggregate Demand Aggregate demand is the amount of goods and services in the economy that will be purchased at all possible price levels. Inflation can occur when demand for goods and services exceeds existing supplies.

During wartime, for example, the government's need for military supplies puts pressure on producers. The heavy demand for new equipment, supplies, and services increases the value of those items, pushing prices up. Wages also rise as the demand for labor increases along with the demand for goods.

Changes in Aggregate Supply Finally, inflation occurs when producers raise prices in order to meet increased costs. Higher prices for raw materials can cause costs to increase. Wage increases, however, are most often the biggest reason, because wages are the largest single production cost for most companies.

One cause of wage increases is low unemployment. Employers must then offer higher wages to attract and retain workers. Wage increases can also occur as a result of collective bargaining.

For example, Jen is a union laborer at Am-Gro Fertilizer. The union she belongs to recently won a large wage increase from the company. The increased cost for labor led Am-Gro to raise its prices in order to maintain its profits.

Such a situation can lead to a spiral of ever-higher prices, because one increase in costs leads to an

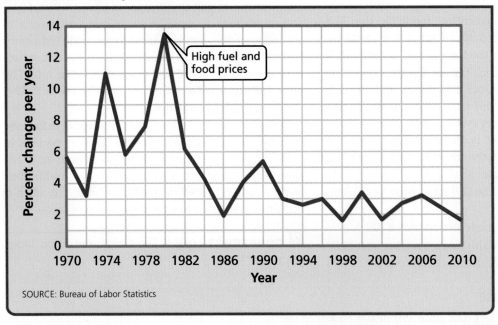

Inflation Rate, 1970–2010

SOURCE: Bureau of Labor Statistics

>> **Figure 7.15 Analyze Graphs** According to the graph, when was the last time inflation topped 4 percent?

Interactive Gallery

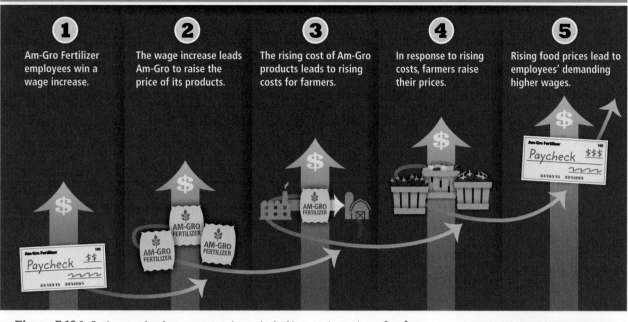

WAGE-PRICE SPIRAL

1 Am-Gro Fertilizer employees win a wage increase.

2 The wage increase leads Am-Gro to raise the price of its products.

3 The rising cost of Am-Gro products leads to rising costs for farmers.

4 In response to rising costs, farmers raise their prices.

5 Rising food prices lead to employees' demanding higher wages.

>> **Figure 7.16** Inflation can lead to a wage-price spiral of increasing prices. **Analyze Charts** How might the global labor market and outsourcing affect the wage-price spiral?

Interactive Chart

increase in prices, which leads to another increase in costs, and on and on. The process by which rising wages cause higher prices, and higher prices cause higher wages, is known as the **wage-price spiral.** The effect of a wage-price spiral on Am-Gro Fertilizer is shown in **Figure 7.16**.

? IDENTIFY Which three factors affect inflation?

Interpreting Effects of Inflation

High inflation is a major economic problem, especially when inflation rates change greatly from year to year. Buyers and sellers find planning for the future difficult, if not impossible. The effects of inflation can be seen mainly in purchasing power, income, and interest rates.

Effects on Purchasing Power You have seen, in the example of Jack and Josephine Barrow's house, how inflation can erode purchasing power. In an inflationary economy, a dollar will not buy the same number of goods that it did in years past. When there is no inflation, $1 buys the same amount of goods it did in the previous year. If the inflation rate is 10 percent this year, however, $1 will buy the equivalent of only

$.90 worth of goods today. In this case, the purchasing power of a dollar has fallen.

Effects on Income Inflation sometimes, but not always, erodes income. If wage increases match the inflation rate, a worker's real income stays the same. People who do not receive their income as wages, such as doctors, lawyers, and businesspeople, can often increase their incomes by raising the prices they charge in order to keep up with inflation.

Not all people are so fortunate. If workers' wages do not increase as much as inflation does, they are in a worse economic position than before. Since prices are higher, their income has less purchasing power.

People living on a fixed income are hit especially hard by inflation. A **fixed income** is income that does not increase even when prices go up. The Barrows, for example, who are retired, are hurt by high inflation. The portion of their income from Social Security payments rises with the price level, because the government raises Social Security benefits to keep up with inflation. Much of their income, however, comes from a pension fund that pays them a fixed amount of money each month. Inflation steadily eats away at the real value of that pension check.

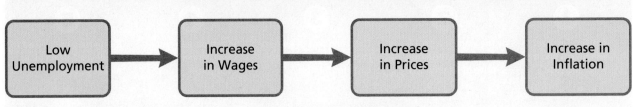

UNEMPLOYMENT AND INFLATION

| Low Unemployment | → | Increase in Wages | → | Increase in Prices | → | Increase in Inflation |

>> **Analyze Charts** How would you expect high unemployment to affect inflation?

Effects on Interest Rates People receive a given amount of interest on money in their savings accounts, but their true return depends on the rate of inflation. For example, Sonia had her savings in an account that paid 7 percent interest. At the same time, the annual inflation rate was 5 percent. As a result, the purchasing power of Sonia's savings increased that year by only 2 percent, because 5 percent of her interest was needed to keep up with inflation.

When a bank's interest rate matches the inflation rate, savers break even. The amount they gain from interest is taken away by inflation. However, if the inflation rate is higher than the bank's interest rate, savers lose money.

☑ ANALYZE DATA What is the true return on a savings account for the year if the interest rate is 6 percent and the inflation rate is 2 percent?

Recent Trends in the Rate of Inflation

Americans under age 30 have experienced fairly low inflation rates for most of their lifetimes. In the late 1990s, unemployment levels were low. Typically, low unemployment leads to higher inflation because companies compete for scarce workers by offering higher wages. Rising wages can push the inflation rate up, as you know from the discussion of the wage-price spiral. However, inflation crept along at less than 3 percent. Some economists suggested that the economy was going through a lucky streak. Others argued that the economy was returning to the normal levels of unemployment that had existed in the 1950s and 1960s.

Deflation As the economy entered a period of recession and slow growth in the 2000s, inflation fell to less than 2 percent. Rising unemployment and falling capital investment removed two factors that might have led to inflation due to increases in aggregate supply. Prices at times seemed to be falling. Some experts even predicted a period of **deflation,** or a sustained drop in the price level. However, the economy recovered.

Although inflation remained relatively low through 2007, by mid-2008, soaring energy costs had pushed the inflation rate past 4 percent. The CPI recorded its biggest monthly gain since 1982. Consumers, pressured by sharp price increases for food and gasoline, had less demand for big-ticket items such as household appliances and automobiles.

The 2008 Recession By the end of 2008, the economy was in crisis. A severe recession led to a slowdown in economic activity. Global demand for oil dropped, and the price of gasoline plunged by 30 percent in one month. The CPI was 3 percent lower than it had been just three months earlier. The record decline in retail prices and sales put added pressure on the federal government to solve the economic crisis and avoid a deflationary spiral in prices.

☑ EXPLAIN How does low unemployment lead to higher inflation?

ASSESSMENT

1. **Contrast** What is the purpose of calculating the core inflation rate and the inflation rate separately?

2. **Interpret** How does inflation influence purchasing power?

3. **Describe** What are three possible effects of inflation?

4. **Identify Cause and Effect** What causes a wage-price spiral, and how does it affect the economy?

5. **Analyze Data** Suppose the market basket cost $800 during the base period and $1,800 today. What is the CPI for today?

The United States has millions of people living in poverty. It also has one of the highest per capita GDPs in the world. How can that be? Looking at poverty rates among different groups of Americans reveals some important reasons.

>> Private groups also work to alleviate poverty, independent of government help. High school students from a church group cook and serve a meal at a homeless shelter.

Interactive Flipped Video

Poverty and Income Distribution

Living in Poverty

Statistically, you are at greater risk for living in poverty if you come from a single-parent home, live in the inner city, or do not have at least a high school education. Other factors, including the way that income is distributed, also affect the poverty rate.

As you have read, the United States Bureau of the Census conducts extensive surveys to gather data about the American people. Its economists then analyze the data and organize them to reveal important characteristics.

One key feature they look at is how many families and households live in poverty. The Census Bureau defines a *family* as a group of two or more people related by birth, marriage, or adoption who live in the same housing unit. A *household* is all people who live in the same housing unit, regardless of how they are related.

What is Poverty? According to the government, a poor family is one whose total income is less than the amount required to satisfy the family's minimum needs. The Office of Management and Budget determines the income level, known as the poverty threshold, required to meet those minimum needs. The **poverty threshold** is the income

>> **Objectives**

Define who is poor, according to government standards.

Describe the causes of poverty.

Analyze the distribution of income in the United States.

Analyze the costs and benefits of U.S. economic policy related to the goal of equity.

>> **Key Terms**

poverty threshold
poverty rate
income distribution
food stamp program
Lorenz Curve
enterprise zone
block grants
workfare
welfare
cash transfers
in-kind benefits
medical benefits
grant

level below which income is insufficient to support a family or household.

The poverty threshold, or poverty line, varies with the size of the family. For example, in 2013, the poverty threshold for a single parent under age 65 with one child was $15,510. For a family of four with two children, it was $23,550. If a family's total income is below the poverty threshold, everyone in the family is counted as poor. The Census Bureau determines how many people and families are living below the poverty line.

Measuring Poverty Trends in the national poverty rate are shown in **Figure 7.17**. The **poverty rate** is the percentage of people who live in households with income below the official poverty threshold.

Poverty rates for various groups are shown in **Figure 7.18**. We can use poverty rates to discover whom the government considers to be poor and what factors seem to contribute to poverty. Poverty rates differ sharply by groups, according to several different indicators:

Race and ethnic origin The poverty rate among African Americans, Hispanics, and Native Americans is more than twice the rate for white Americans.

Type of family Families with a single mother have a poverty rate more than four times greater than that of two-parent families.

Age The percentage of children living in poverty is significantly larger than that for any other age group.

U.S. Poverty Rate, 1992–2012

SOURCE: www.census.gov

>> **Figure 7.17** In 2012, the poverty rate was about 15 percent. **Analyze Graphs** What happened to the poverty rate from 1994 to 2000?

[▷] **Interactive Chart**

Adults between the ages of 18 and 64 are the next largest group.

Residence Inner-city residents have double the poverty rate of those who live outside the inner city. People who live in rural areas also have a higher poverty rate, especially in regions where job prospects are limited.

? **DEFINE** What is the poverty rate?

What Causes Poverty?

Put simply, a family is poor when the adults in the family fail to earn enough income to provide for its members' basic needs. This failure to earn adequate income is often the result of unemployment.

Millions of Americans are unemployed for a variety of reasons. While they are out of a job, their families might well fall below the poverty threshold. Many other poor adults are not even considered a part of the labor force. Some suffer from chronic health problems or disabilities that prevent them from working. Others are discouraged workers who are no longer looking for work.

Many poor adults do have jobs, however. In fact, more than half of poor households have someone who works at least part time, and one in five have a full-time, year-round worker.

For these "working poor," the problem is usually low wages or a limited work schedule, rather than the lack of a job. For example, Ray makes $9 an hour as a full-time clerk in a clothing store. While he is at work, his wife stays at home with their two young children. Although Ray works 40 hours per week, and his salary is well above the minimum wage, his annual earnings amount to just $18,720, which is below the poverty threshold for a family of four.

Economists agree that poverty and lack of income go hand in hand, but they have different ideas about the causes of poverty. Here are some of the most important explanations for why some people are poor.

Changes in Family Structure Single-parent families are more likely to live in poverty than two-parent families. That is especially the case when the lone parent is a single mother. The divorce rate has risen significantly since the 1960s, as has the number of children born to unmarried parents. These demographic shifts tend to result in more single-parent families and more children living in poverty.

Where People Live In most American cities, racial minorities are concentrated in the inner cities, far from

Poverty Rate by Group, 2012

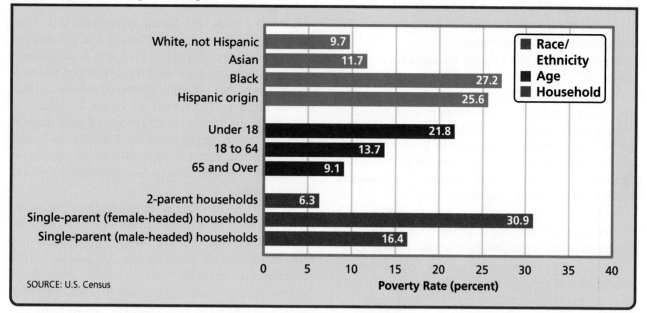

Race/Ethnicity
- White, not Hispanic: 9.7
- Asian: 11.7
- Black: 27.2
- Hispanic origin: 25.6

Age
- Under 18: 21.8
- 18 to 64: 13.7
- 65 and Over: 9.1

Household
- 2-parent households: 6.3
- Single-parent (female-headed) households: 30.9
- Single-parent (male-headed) households: 16.4

Poverty Rate (percent)

SOURCE: U.S. Census

>> **Figure 7.18 Analyze Graphs** Which group in each category has the highest poverty rate? Which groups have the lowest?

the higher-wage jobs in suburban areas. Many of these inner-city residents do not own cars, and mass-transit systems are often not an efficient means of commuting from the inner city to the suburbs. As a result, people who live in the inner city earn less than people living outside the inner city. Similar obstacles exist for many people living in rural areas, where there is little business or industry.

Unequal Treatment White workers generally earn higher salaries than minority workers, and men generally earn more than women. Much of this income inequality can be explained by differences in hours worked, education, and work experience. Part of the inequality, however, results from racial and gender discrimination. Even when all the workers in a group are equally productive, whites are often paid more than African Americans, and men are often paid more than women. Economists agree, however, that discrimination based on race or gender has been diminishing.

Low-Wage Service Jobs In the past, less-educated people could earn good wages working in manufacturing jobs. Globalization, the decline in manufacturing, and the rise of the service economy have led to a decline in the number of higher-paying manufacturing jobs. More workers with less education now work in low-skill service jobs, where wages are often not as high as they are for factory jobs.

Lack of Education The median income in 2011 for full-time workers between the ages of 25 and 34 who did not complete high school was $22,860, which was below the poverty threshold for a family of four in that year. Those with high school diplomas or the equivalent earned median incomes of nearly $30,000 a year for full-time work, while college graduates earned a median of nearly $45,000 a year, or more than twice as much as those who did not complete high school.

? IDENTIFY CAUSE AND EFFECT Why are racial and gender discrimination a cause of poverty?

Household Income

The estimated median household income in the United States between 2008 and 2012 was $53,046, which means that half the households earned more than this amount and half earned less. This figure tells only part of the income story. To fully understand poverty in this country, you also need to understand **income distribution,** or how the nation's total income is distributed among its population.

Income Distribution Income distribution figures do not reflect the effects of taxes or non-cash government aid such as housing subsidies, healthcare, or food stamps. The **food stamp program** helps low-income people buy food. Benefits are provided on an electronic card that is accepted at most food stores.

Look at **Figure 7.19**. To compute the numbers in the table, economists take four steps.

First, they rank the nation's households according to income.

Then, they divide the list into fifths, or quintiles, with equal numbers of households in each fifth. The lowest fifth, which appears at the top of the list, includes the poorest 20 percent of households. The highest fifth, shown at the bottom of the list, includes the richest 20 percent of households. The first column in **Figure 7.19** shows this division into quintiles.

Next, they compute each group's average income by adding up the incomes of all the households in the group and then dividing by the number of households.

Finally, they compute each group's share, or percentage, of total income by dividing the group's total income by the total income of all the groups. The second column shows each group's share. The third column shows the cumulative total. (For example, the lowest two fifths of households earned 12 percent of the total income.) Compare the share of the poorest fifth with that of the richest fifth. If you divide richest by poorest, you will see that the richest fifth receives nearly 15 times the income of the poorest fifth.

Now look at **Figure 7.20**. It shows that the numbers for shares of total income, when they are plotted on a graph, form a curve. This graph, called the **Lorenz Curve,** illustrates the distribution of income in the economy.

Let's see what this Lorenz Curve tells you. First, read the label on each axis. Then look at the straight line running diagonally across the graph. This reference line represents complete equality. Under conditions of complete equality, each quintile would receive one fifth of total income. That means the lowest 20 percent of households would receive 20 percent of total income, as shown by the point (lowest, 20). Similarly, the lowest 40 percent (the first two quintiles) would receive 40 percent of total income, as shown by the point (second, 40), and so on.

In 2010, the distribution of income was not equal, as the Lorenz Curve indicates. For example, the point (lowest, 3.3) shows that the lowest 20 percent, or one fifth, of households received just 3.3 percent of the nation's total income.

The point (second, 11.8) shows that the lowest 40 percent, or two fifths, of households received only 11.8 percent of the income. The area on the graph between the line of equality and the Lorenz Curve represents the amount of inequality in income distribution. The larger the area between the curves, the greater the income inequality.

Differences in Income As you can see from **Figure 7.19** and **Figure 7.20**, the wealthiest fifth of American households earned more income (50.2 percent) than the bottom four fifths combined. Why are there such

Percent of Total Income by Quintile, 2010

QUINTILE	PERCENT OF INCOME FOR QUINTILE	CUMULATIVE PERCENT OF INCOME FOR THIS AND LOWER QUINTILES
Lowest fifth	3.3%	3.3%
Second fifth	8.5%	11.8%
Third fifth	14.6%	26.4%
Fourth fifth	23.4%	49.8%
Highest fifth	50.2%	100%

NOTE: Because of rounding, totals may be greater than or less than 100 percent.
SOURCE: U.S. Census Bureau

>> **Figure 7.19** This table shows what percentage of the nation's total income is earned by people with different levels of income. **Analyze Data** What percentage of total income earned in the United States did the lowest three fifths of households make in 2010?

Lorenz Curve

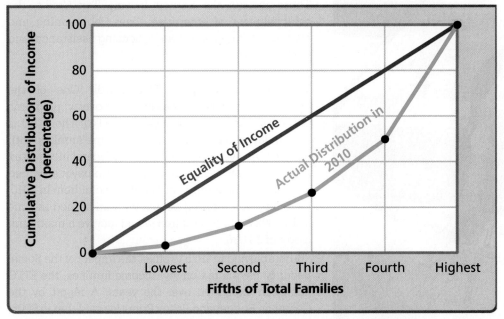

>> **Figure 7.20 Analyze Graphs** What would a Lorenz Curve that curved more deeply to the right tell you about distribution of income?

differences in income among Americans? Here are some factors.

Differences in skills and education Some people are more highly skilled than others, so they earn higher wages. Labor skills are determined by education, training, and a worker's natural ability.

Inheritances Some people inherit large sums of money and earn income by investing it. Others inherit businesses that produce income from profits.

Field of work Wages are determined by the demand for labor. Labor demand is a "derived demand" because it is set by demand for what people produce. People who produce goods with a low market value usually earn lower wages.

James Webb, a former United States senator from Virginia, commented on the growing income gap:

America's top tier has grown infinitely richer and more removed over the past 25 years . . . . The top 1 percent now takes in an astounding 16 percent of national income, up from 8 percent in 1980.

—James Webb, the *Wall Street Journal,* Nov. 15, 2006

In fact, in the last two decades, the distribution of income has become less equal. Since 1977, the share of

income earned by the lowest three fifths has decreased by 12 percent, while the share earned by the top 1 percent has more than doubled.

? IDENTIFY Name one program the government uses to help alleviate income inequality.

The Economic Goal of Equity

The government spends billions of dollars on programs designed to reduce poverty. This money is spent mainly on cash assistance, education, medical benefits, and non-cash benefits such as food stamps and subsidized housing. The stated goal of these programs is not to provide equal distribution of wealth. Rather, it is to ensure a basic standard of living for all and to provide the poor an opportunity to improve their condition.

Critics of antipoverty programs argue that the programs themselves harm some of the people they are intended to help by encouraging people to remain dependent on government programs. Some analysts say the programs raised unrealistic hopes of eradicating poverty. The costs of the programs have increased as the programs have expanded. Some critics do not object to the antipoverty programs as much as they object to the increase in the size of the government required to administer the programs.

>> Americans receive the Earned Income Tax Credit in the form of a tax refund. Here, a clerk scans tax returns for processing.

▶ **Interactive Timeline**

>> Executives from smartphone makers Motorola and Google with Governor Rick Perry of Texas. Low taxes and business-friendly policies encourage businesses to locate in Texas.

The criticisms have led to new policies. These include the Earned Income Tax Credit, the establishment of enterprise zones, job training and other employment assistance, housing assistance, and welfare reform.

The Earned Income Tax Credit One of the government's most successful antipoverty programs is the Earned Income Tax Credit (EITC). The EITC is a refundable tax credit that low-income families with children receive when they file their federal income tax return. Eligibility is based on the taxpayer's earned income and the number of qualifying children. In 2010, for example, a married couple with an earned income of $40,363 and two children would receive a maximum credit of $5,036.

Established in 1975 to offset the impact of the Social Security payroll tax on low-income families, the EITC has been expanded over the years. A report by the Center on Budget and Policy Priorities said that in 2005, the EITC lifted more than four million people above the official poverty line and was "the nation's most effective antipoverty program for working families."

Enterprise Zones Areas where companies can locate and be free of certain state, local, and federal taxes and restrictions on business operations called **enterprise zones,** became popular in the 1980s. Zones benefit businesses by lowering their costs. They help local people by making it easier for them to find work. By providing jobs, these zones can help revitalize areas such as inner cities.

Job Training In recent decades, federal and state governments have designed job-training programs to help workers who lack the skills to earn an adequate income. In addition, the federal government has made a minimum wage mandatory since 1938. The minimum wage ensures that workers' hourly pay will not fall below a certain point.

Affordable Housing The government also has programs to help poor people obtain affordable housing. In one approach, the government makes payments to landlords who then lower the rent they would otherwise charge. In another program, poor people receive vouchers that cover part of the rent they pay. The third approach is government-owned housing, which charges low rental fees.

Welfare to Workfare Poor people often cannot afford basic needs such as food and medical care. The United States has long had a welfare system that provides for those basic needs, especially for children and the elderly.

Federal Minimum Wage: Nominal and Real (2013) Dollars

YEAR	NOMINAL DOLLARS	REAL DOLLARS	YEAR	NOMINAL DOLLARS	REAL DOLLARS
Mar. 1956	1.00	8.52	Jan. 1980	3.10	9.10
Sept. 1961	1.15	8.76	Jan. 1981	3.35	8.81
Sept. 1963	1.25	9.31	Apr. 1990	3.80	6.88
Feb. 1967	1.40	9.73	Apr. 1991	4.25	7.35
Feb. 1968	1.60	10.77	Oct. 1996	4.75	7.03
May 1974	2.00	9.42	Sept. 1997	5.15	7.47
Jan. 1975	2.10	9.22	July 2007	5.85	6.61
Jan. 1976	2.30	9.45	July 2008	6.55	6.94
Jan. 1978	2.65	9.70	July 2009	7.25	7.90
Jan. 1979	2.90	9.72	July 2013	7.25	7.25

SOURCE: U.S. Dept. of Labor

>> **Analyze Charts** How did the minimum wage in real dollars change between 1980 and 2013?

That system underwent major reform when President Bill Clinton signed the Personal Responsibility and Work Opportunity Reconciliation Act of 1996.

This welfare-reform plan responded to criticisms that welfare encouraged poor people to remain unemployed in order to keep receiving aid. It replaced the traditional antipoverty program for poor families (Aid to Families with Dependent Children, or AFDC) with a new program called Temporary Assistance for Needy Families (TANF). TANF eliminated cash assistance for poor families. Instead, the federal government provides **block grants,** or lump sums of money, to the states. The states are now responsible for designing and implementing programs to move most poor adults from welfare dependence to employment. TANF also set a five-year limit on receipt of benefits.

The plan calls for a shift from welfare to **workfare**—a program requiring work in exchange for temporary assistance from the government. It was hoped that this reform would reduce poverty by providing poor Americans with labor skills and access to a steady, adequate income.

Addressing Poverty The federal government has several major types of redistribution programs to help the poor, elderly, and disadvantaged. State and federal governments provide **cash transfers,** or direct payments of money to poor, disabled, or retired people. The following examples are cash transfer programs:

Temporary Assistance for Needy Families (TANF) Launched in 1996, TANF does not provide direct federal welfare payments to the poor. Instead, federal money goes to the states, which design and run their own welfare programs. States must adhere to federal rules that create work incentives and establish a lifetime limit for benefits. TANF aims to move people from depending on welfare to joining the workforce.

Social Security The Social Security program was created in 1935, during the Great Depression. At the time, many elderly people lost their life savings and had no income. The program collects payroll taxes from current workers and then redistributes that money to current recipients. Those who receive Social Security include retired people, people unable to work because of a disability, and, in some cases, the widowed spouses or orphaned children of such individuals.

Unemployment insurance Unemployment insurance is funded by taxes paid by employers. Compensation checks provide money to workers who have lost their jobs. Recipients must offer proof that they have made efforts to get work. As with TANF, states set the rules for this program. The program is supposed to supply only temporary help. As a result, most states pay benefits to workers for only 26 weeks. In periods of high unemployment, however, the government may decide to pay the benefits longer.

Workers' compensation This program is an insurance program for workers injured or disabled on the job. It is

>> Some work, such as the job being done by this roofer, have increased risks for injury. Workers' compensation programs provide them with insurance.

>> EBT (electronic benefit transfer) cards allow people who qualify for food stamps to use their benefits to purchase food at this farmer's market.

mandated, or required, by state law. Most employers pay workers' compensation insurance to cover future claims by employees.

In-Kind Benefits The government also provides poor people with **in-kind benefits,** goods and services provided for free or at greatly reduced prices. One example is the food stamp program. People who qualify receive a debit card or smart card that they can use to help meet food expenses.

Another type of in-kind benefit is subsidized housing. Poor people are allowed to rent housing for less than the regular rent. The government pays the difference to the landlord.

Legal aid is legal advice given at no charge. This in-kind benefit covers contracts and other business matters. Poor people charged with a crime may be represented in court by public defenders, who are paid with tax dollars. The right of an accused person to have legal counsel is guaranteed by the Sixth Amendment.

Another social service that the U.S. government provides is **medical benefits,** meaning health insurance for children and people who are elderly, disabled, or poor. Medicare covers Americans over age 65 and disabled people. Medicaid covers some poor people who are unemployed or not covered by their employer's insurance plans. Administered under the Social Security program, Medicare and Medicaid are enormously expensive programs.

A program called the Children's Health Insurance Program (CHIP) provides health insurance for children who are uninsured. CHIP is funded by both state and federal governments. States write the rules for the program within federal guidelines. The program covers more than 6.5 million children.

Education Programs Federal, state, and local governments all provide educational opportunities to those who need aid. The federal government funds programs from preschool to college. State and local programs aid students with learning disabilities.

Education programs add to the nation's human capital and labor productivity. As explained earlier, improved education and technology can make an entire economy more productive.

? **RECALL** Who pays for the Children's Health Insurance Program?

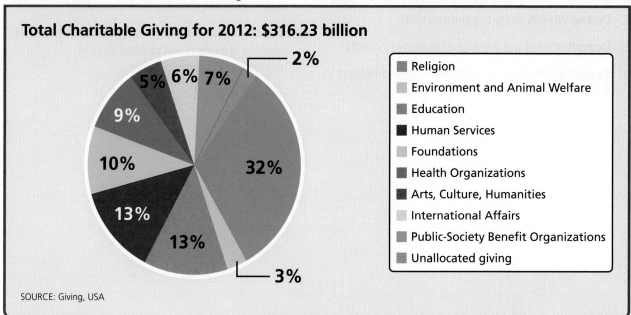

Charitable Contributions by Sector, 2012

Total Charitable Giving for 2012: $316.23 billion

- Religion — 32%
- Environment and Animal Welfare — 3%
- Education — 13%
- Human Services — 13%
- Foundations — 10%
- Health Organizations — 9%
- Arts, Culture, Humanities — 5%
- International Affairs — 6%
- Public-Society Benefit Organizations — 7%
- Unallocated giving — 2%

SOURCE: Giving, USA

>> **Analyze Charts** What portion of charitable contributions in 2012 went toward human services?

Charitable Donations

In addition to providing direct assistance to the needy, federal and state governments also encourage private action to help people in need. Federal tax law allows both individuals and corporations to take tax deductions for charitable donations. This policy provides an economic incentive to give money and property to relief organizations, as well as to other nonprofit groups such as churches, hospitals, colleges, libraries, or museums. In 2012, American individuals and organizations gave more than $316 billion in tax-deductible charitable contributions.

There are opportunity costs associated with donating to charity. Money given away cannot be spent or invested in other productive ways. In addition, governments lose vital tax revenues by allowing deductions for charitable giving. Still, governments encourage it. As one tax expert noted:

> It's always better to give than receive. The glory of charitable donations is that you give and receive at the same time.

—Jeff Schnepper, "Give and Grow Rich With Charitable Deductions"

The government may also provide grants and other assistance to organizations that provide social services. A **grant** is a financial award given by a government agency to a private individual or group in order to carry out a specific task. Many people believe that private groups do a more effective job of helping people than the government can.

In 2001, President George W. Bush announced a new initiative that allowed religious organizations to receive federal funding support for programs to alleviate poverty. The President believed that these groups provided a special compassion that made their programs particularly successful. Bush established an Office of Faith-Based and Neighborhood Partnerships to help religious groups work more effectively with the federal government. He also encouraged the states to create similar offices. Still, not everyone supported faith-based initiatives. Critics said that giving government money to religious organizations violated the First Amendment.

? EXPRESS IDEAS CLEARLY Why did President Bush allow religious organizations to compete for federal funds?

1. **Define** What is the poverty threshold?

2. **Describe** What are the major causes of poverty?

3. **Evaluate Data** Why is it important to understand income distribution?

4. **Analyze Information** How do enterprise zones help both businesses and workers?

5. **Classify** Legal aid, food stamps, and subsidized housing are examples of what kind of redistribution program?

Fighting Poverty in the United States, 1916–2008

YEAR	PROGRAM
1916	Worker's compensation for federal employees
1933	Federal Emergency Relief Administration
1935	Social Security, Aid to Dependent Children, and unemployment compensation
1950	Social Security extended to 3.5 million recipients
1964	Head Start preschool education
1965	Medicare and Medicaid
1974	Food Stamp program extended nationwide
1975	Earned Income Tax Credit (EITC)
1996	Temporary Assistance to Needy Families (TANF)
2001	White House Office of Faith-Based and Community Initiatives
2008	Emergency Unemployment Compensation program

1. **Describe the Role and Describe Changes** Using the table, write a paragraph that describes the role of government in the U.S. economy and the changes in that role over time. Address the following: Describe three major ways in which government devotes resources to address the problem of poverty. What is one recent way the national government has promoted private efforts to combat poverty?

2. **Describe Economic Systems** Describe the role the government plays in our economic system, specifically in the area of fighting poverty. Provide at least three specific examples of government antipoverty programs. What criticisms have been made concerning government antipoverty programs?

3. **Analyze the Importance and Impact of Economic Philosophers** Write a paragraph that analyzes the importance of John Maynard Keynes, and analyzes Keynes's impact on the U.S. economy. Address the following: Before the Great Depression, what was the prevailing view about how economic systems recovered from declines? How did the Great Depression change that view? Analyze John Maynard Keynes's role in the U.S. government's response to the Great Depression.

4. **Analyze Costs and Benefits** Analyze the costs and benefits of U.S. economic policies related to the economic goals of full employment. Answer the following questions: How does the United States promote full employment through its economic policies? What is a potential cost to policies promoting full employment?

5. **Interpret Economic Data and Analyze Information** Using the line graph provided, write a paragraph that answers the following questions: During which years, approximately, did the U.S. GDP show a significant decline? What generalization can you make about GDP in the United States in recent decades, and what prediction can you make about the future, according to the graph?

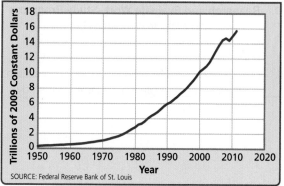

Gross Domestic Product (GDP)

SOURCE: Federal Reserve Bank of St. Louis

Tracking a Business Cycle

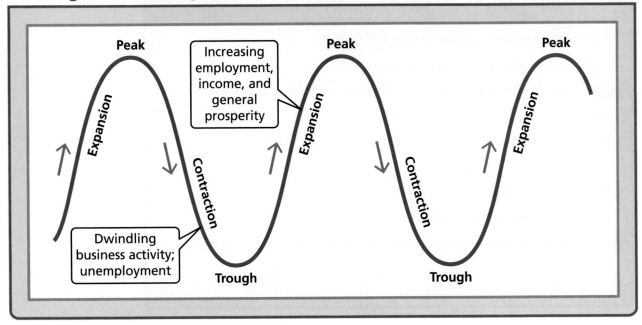

6. **Analyze Business Cycles** Using the graph provided, address the following questions: What are some key economic indicators of where in a business cycle a given economy is? At what points on the graph has the GDP stopped rising?

7. **Interpret Economic Data** Answer the following questions: What is GDP per capita, and why do economists prefer this as a measure of economic growth and national wealth? How is GDP per capita interpreted to measure a nation's standard of living?

8. **Analyze and Compare Student Loans** Write two sentences comparing private student loans with federal student loans. Write two sentences analyzing why an individual might choose a private student loan in addition to a federal student loan.

9. **Research and Evaluate Work-Study Programs** Research and evaluate work-study program opportunities. Be sure to answer the following questions: How would you research work-study opportunities for college? After doing your research, how would you evaluate the available work-study opportunities?

10. **Interpret Economic Data and Analyze Economic Information** Use the line graph to respond to the following questions in an oral presentation: During which years shown on the graph would the inflation rate have been considered unstable and unpredictable? What was noteworthy about the inflation rate in 1974 and 1980? What might be the explanation, and how would economists have taken the information into account in their interpretations? Referring to the graph, what prediction can you make about the rate of inflation in future years?

Inflation Rate, 1970–2010

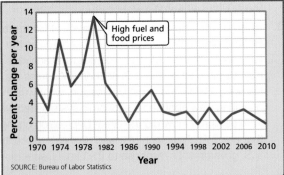

SOURCE: Bureau of Labor Statistics

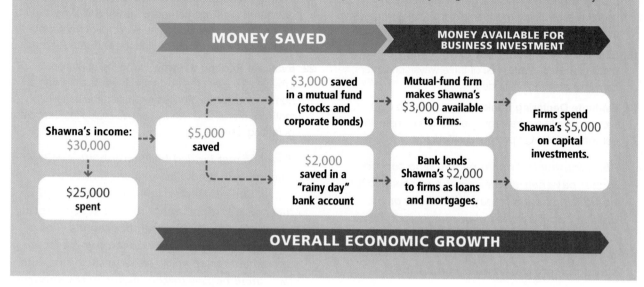

HOW SAVING LEADS TO CAPITAL DEEPENING

When individuals save or invest money, that money becomes available to businesses. Firms can use this money to buy new plants or equipment. This capital deepening leads to greater productivity and growth for the whole economy.

MONEY SAVED

MONEY AVAILABLE FOR BUSINESS INVESTMENT

Shawna's income: $30,000

$25,000 spent

$5,000 saved

$3,000 saved in a mutual fund (stocks and corporate bonds)

$2,000 saved in a "rainy day" bank account

Mutual-fund firm makes Shawna's $3,000 available to firms.

Bank lends Shawna's $2,000 to firms as loans and mortgages.

Firms spend Shawna's $5,000 on capital investments.

OVERALL ECONOMIC GROWTH

11. **Explain the Functions of Financial Institutions** Use the infographic to answer the following questions: What role do financial institutions play in allowing households to contribute to capital deepening? What role do financial institutions play in allowing capital deepening to benefit businesses?

12. **Interpret Economic Data and Create Written Presentations** Create a brief written presentation in which you describe the uses and limits of GDP and GDP per capita as interpretative tools. Include in your presentation an interpretation of how GDP per capita may be useful as a measure of national wealth.

13. **Interpret Economic Data** Write a paragraph in which you interpret economic data, including rate of inflation. Answer the following questions: What is the inflation rate? How do economists interpret the inflation rate using different periods of time? How is an inflation rate between 1 and 3 percent interpreted? How is an inflation rate that exceeds 5 percent interpreted?

14. **Analyze Productivity and Growth** Analyze the process by which capital deepening leads to economic growth. Focus your analysis on the role of productivity, and make references to both physical and human capital.

15. **Analyze Technology and Growth** Create a visual presentation based on the following prompts: Identify at least three general sources of technological progress in economic activity. Analyze the way changes in technology affect economic growth. Create a cause-and-effect graphic organizer to accurately present your analysis.

16. **Identify Loans and Explain Borrowing Responsibilities** Write a paragraph in which you identify the types of loans available to consumers, and explain the responsibilities and obligations of borrowing money. Be sure to three types of loans available to potential borrowers.

17. Examine Aspects of Credit Cards Write a paragraph that examines the positive and negative aspects of using credit cards and ways to avoid credit card debt. Consider the following questions: What are some positive aspects of credit cards? What are some negative aspects of credit cards? How can an individual avoid credit card debt? Examine at least two strategies.

18. Examine Credit Card Debt Examine ways to eliminate credit card debt. Write a list of three ways consumers can eliminate credit card debt.

19. Evaluate Declaring Bankruptcy Using the quote provided, write a paragraph evaluating the costs and benefits of declaring personal bankruptcy.

"Bankruptcy laws help people who can no longer pay their creditors get a fresh start-by liquidating assets to pay their debts or by creating a repayment plan. Bankruptcy laws also protect troubled businesses and provide for orderly distributions to business creditors through reorganization or liquidation."

—*United States Federal Courts Web site*

20. Develop Strategies to Become a Low-Risk Borrower Using the chart, answer the following questions about how consumers can reduce their risk when borrowing: What is a personal credit score, and how can it affect you? What are two strategies you can develop to improve your credit score?

How Do You Score?

- 35% Payment history
- 30% Amounts owed
- 15% Length of credit history
- 10% New credit
- 10% Types of credit used

SOURCE: www.myfico.com

21. Understand How to Complete the FAFSA Write a paragraph that explains how to complete the Free Application for Federal Student Aid (FAFSA) provided by the United States Department of Education. Answer the following questions: Why should all students who plan on attending college complete the FAFSA? What basic information do you need to have in order to complete the FAFSA? Where can you find the FAFSA?

22. Evaluate Renting a Home Using the quotation provided, evaluate the costs and benefits of renting a home. Write two sentences evaluating the benefits of renting a home, and two sentences evaluating the costs of renting a home.

Ziva has just landed her first job after college. The job is in a new city, so she'll have to move. She's talked with a local realtor and has made arrangements to look at four rental properties in different neighborhoods. The rental properties vary between two-bedroom apartments in the city, close to the office, and two small houses further away, in the suburbs.

23. Analyze Trade and Growth Write a paragraph in which you analyze how trade relates to growth. Answer the following question: How can trade support economic growth? Analyze the importance of specialization in your response.

24. Analyze Costs and Benefits and Use a Problem-Solving Process Analyze U.S. economic policies related to the economic goals of full employment. Create an outline for a written presentation in which you identify the problem, gather information, list and consider options, consider advantages and disadvantages, and speculate on different solutions and their effectiveness.

25. Explain Savings and Capital Formation Explain how the amount of savings in an economy is the basis of capital formation. What happens when an individual puts savings in a bank. How is this process reflected when considering the economy as a whole? Make reference to *capital formation* in your response.

26. Analyze and Compare Student Grants Using the scenario, write a paragraph analyzing and comparing student grant options. Write three to four sentences analyzing what Jon should know about student grants. Compare student grant options in your analysis.

Jon is hoping to attend the local trade school after graduating from high school. He does not want to take out a loan to pay for college and is hoping a grant will pay for the tuition instead. He plans to live at home and commute to college. Though he will spend money on commuting, he hopes to save the money he would otherwise have spent to live at the college dorm.

27. Research and Evaluate Scholarships Research and evaluate various scholarship opportunities. Using the scenario and your own research, write an email to Ella, giving her advice on how to find information about scholarships. In your email, make sure to: Offer general suggestions about researching scholarship opportunities. Provide a list of at least five different groups that offer scholarships that Ella can research for more information. Explain to Ella how she can evaluate which scholarship opportunities are best for her needs.

Ella is applying to several colleges in hopes of finding the best one to fit her interests and budget. She has some money saved, but it is not enough to cover the cost of tuition, books, room and board, food, and other incidental expenses

A friend of Ella's suggested that she apply for scholarships. Ella discussed this with her parents and they agree that scholarships would help to offset some of her expenses for college. Ella, however, does not know where to start looking for scholarship opportunities. She is also concerned about how to evaluate each scholarship.

28. Investigate Nontraditional Payments Investigate nontraditional methods of paying for college or postsecondary education and training. Referring to the scenario, write a paragraph addressing the following: Identify two types of nontraditional methods of paying for college that Marcus might use. What are the advantages of these methods? Explain why Kristen suggests investigating nontraditional methods of paying for college.

Marcus is very interested in attending the local college following high school graduation. He applied for a grant and received an award that will pay for the first semester. He does not want to apply for a loan to cover the cost of the second semester. Marcus asks his friend Kristen for some suggestions on where he can find the needed funds to pay for the second semester. Kristen suggests that he investigate nontraditional methods to pay for his college studies.

29. Write About the Essential Question **Write an essay on the Essential Question: Why should we care how the economy is doing?** Use evidence from your study of this Topic to support your answer.

APRIL

15

Morning
8:00

105/260 WEEK 16

Taxes Du

[**ESSENTIAL QUESTION**] Can and should the government be fair to everyone?

8 **Taxes and Spending**

>> On April 15 every year is the deadline for Americans to file their individual tax returns.

Enduring Understandings

- Governments collect taxes to pay for programs, but taxes can have powerful effects on the general economy.

- The federal government taxes income, the manufacture or sale of some goods, imports, and other sources of wealth.

- The national government spends tax money on mandatory outlays, including entitlements such as Social Security, and on discretionary spending.

- State taxes provide money for education, public safety, transportation, and other public goods.

- Local governments tax residents in order to pay for police, fire protection, education, and other public goods.

Watch the My Story Video to learn more about how taxes relate to income and affect people across the country.

PEARSON realize™
www.PearsonRealize.com

Access your digital lessons including:
Topic Inquiry • Interactive Reading
Notepad • Interactivities • Assessments

319

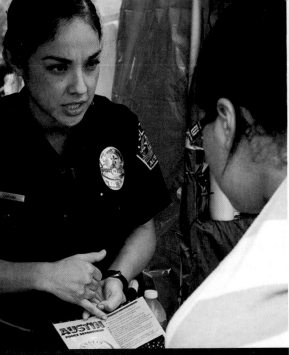

>> Taxes help fund essential services such as law enforcement.

Interactive Flipped Video

8.1 You're looking forward to getting your first paycheck. You figure that at $7 per hour, you should be getting $140 for the 20 hours you worked. When you open the envelope, you find that the check is for much less than $140. Where did the money go? The answer is: taxes! A tax is a required payment to a local, state, or national government. The federal government and most state governments levy taxes on personal income. Is this fair?

>> Objectives

Identify the sources of the government's authority to tax in the U.S. Constitution.

Describe types of tax bases and tax structures.

Identify who bears the burden of a tax.

Describe the key characteristics of a tax.

>> Key Terms

tax
revenue
progressive tax
proportional tax
regressive tax
tax base
individual income
  tax
corporate income
  tax
property tax
sales tax
incidence of a tax

Understanding Taxes

The Importance of National Taxes

Fairness, or equity, is one of the main goals of a tax system. But what is fair to one person may not be fair to another. For example, some would argue that fairness requires that all people be taxed at the same rate. Others say that the person who earns more money should pay a higher percentage of income in taxes. In fact, this concept, known as progressive taxation, has been at the base of our income tax system since its beginnings. (You will read more about progressive taxation and the concept of equity shortly.)

The Impact of Taxation Looking at all of the taxes taken from your paycheck can be discouraging. You worked hard for that money, and now it is being taken away. Similar feelings of frustration over taxes helped persuade American colonists to declare their independence from Britain.

Unlike those colonists, however, an overwhelming majority of citizens today consent to having a portion of their earnings taken by the government. We authorize the federal government, through the Constitution and our elected representatives in Congress, to raise money in the form of taxes.

In fact, taxation is the primary way that the government collects money. Taxes give the government the money it needs to operate. The income received by a government from taxes and other nontax sources is called **revenue.**

Without revenue from taxes, the government would not be able to provide the goods and services that we not only benefit from, but also expect the government to provide. For example, we authorize the government to spend well over $3.5 trillion a year. This money helps provide national defense, highways, education, and law enforcement. We also ask the government to provide help to people in need. All of these goods and services cost money—in workers' salaries, in materials, in land and labor. All members of our society share these costs through the payment of taxes.

The national taxes we pay and the spending they help make possible have a large macroeconomic impact. Total government spending in the United States was over 32 percent of gross domestic product in fiscal year 2013. Federal outlays alone topped 20 percent of GDP. The way these huge sums are collected and then spent can have a number of effects on economic growth—helping to spur it in some cases and dampening it in others.

The Power to Tax Taxation is a powerful tool. The founders of the United States thought long and hard before giving this tool to their new national government. The Constitution they created assigned each branch of the government certain powers and responsibilities. The powers of the legislative branch—Congress—appear in Article I, Section 8. The very first clause in this section grants Congress the power to tax. This clause is the basis for all federal tax laws.

Limits on the Power to Tax The Constitution also spells out specific limits on the government's power to tax. Two of those limits are in the taxation clause. First, the purpose of a tax must be "to pay the debts and provide for the common defense and general welfare of the United States." A tax cannot bring in money that goes to individual interests. Second, federal taxes must be the same in every state. The federal gas tax, for example, cannot be 4 cents per gallon in Maryland and 10 cents per gallon in South Dakota.

Other provisions of the Constitution also limit the kinds of taxes Congress can levy, or impose. For example, Congress cannot tax religious services, because that would violate the freedom of religion promised by the First Amendment. The Twenty-Fourth Amendment prohibits "poll taxes," or tax payments required in order to vote.

Another clause of the Constitution prohibits taxing exports—goods sent out of the United States to foreign customers. The government can collect taxes only on imports—goods brought into the United States. (Congress can restrict or prohibit the export of certain goods, however, such as technology or weapons.)

Yet another clause of the Constitution (Article 1, Section 9, Clause 4) prohibits Congress from levying a capitation, or "head," tax, which is a tax to be paid by every single person. This same clause also prohibited direct taxes unless they were divided among the states according to population.

A direct tax is one paid directly by a taxpayer to the government rather than indirectly—say, to a shopkeeper who later sends the money to the government. But, the Sixteenth Amendment legalized a direct tax on citizens' personal income. This income-tax amendment was ratified in 1913.

? **IDENTIFY MAIN IDEAS** According to the Constitution, for what purpose can government collect taxes?

Tax Structures and Tax Bases

Despite the constitutional limits on its power, the government actually collects a wide variety of taxes. Economists describe these taxes in different ways. First, they describe how the tax is structured. Economists describe three different tax structures: progressive, proportional, and regressive. Second, they describe a tax according to the object taxed—the tax base.

Americans throwing the Cargoes of the Tea Ships into the River, at Boston

>> On December 16, 1773, American colonists protested British tax policy by dumping chests of tea into the Boston Harbor—an event known as the Boston Tea Party.

▶ **Interactive Chart**

Progressive Taxes A **progressive tax** is a tax for which the percentage of income paid in taxes increases as income increases. People with higher incomes pay a higher percentage of their income in taxes. People with very small incomes might pay no tax at all. In the United States, the federal income tax is structured this way.

Figure 8.1 illustrates a progressive tax system. Notice that the tax rate in this example rises from 15 to 25 and then to 30 percent for that portion of income above certain levels. This is a progressive tax rate structure because as income rises, the percentage of income paid in taxes also rises.

Proportional Taxes A **proportional tax** is a tax for which the percentage of income paid in taxes remains the same at all income levels. Selena Diaz, a corporate executive, earns $350,000 per year. Tony Owens, a nurse, earns $50,000 per year. If government levied a 6 percent proportional tax on both their incomes, Selena would pay 6 percent of $350,000, or $21,000, in taxes. Tony would pay 6 percent of $50,000, or $3,000, in taxes. With a proportional income tax, whether income goes up or down, the percentage of income paid in taxes stays the same.

Regressive Taxes A **regressive tax** is a tax for which the percentage of income paid in taxes decreases as income increases. The **sales tax** levied on the sale of goods and services in many states is generally regressive—even though the sales tax rate remains constant. This is because higher-income households typically spend a lower proportion of their incomes on the goods and services that are taxable under a sales tax. As a result, although wealthier people may pay more actual dollars in sales taxes, the proportion of their incomes spent on sales taxes is lower than that of lower-income households.

Selena Diaz, for example, may pay $8,000 in sales taxes while Tony Owens pays $3,500. But Tony is paying 7 percent of his income in sales taxes while Selena is paying only about 2 percent.

Tax Bases A **tax base** is the income, property, good, or service that is subject to a tax. Different taxes have different bases. The **individual income tax** is based on a person's earnings. The **corporate income tax** uses a company's profits as its base. The **property tax** is based on real estate and other property. The tax base for the sales tax is goods or services that are sold. When government policymakers create a new tax, they

PROGRESSIVE TAXATION

INCOME $25,000

$25,000 — TAX RATE **15%** $3,750

TOTAL TAXES $3,750

INCOME $75,000

$50,000 — TAX RATE **25%** $12,500

$25,000 — TAX RATE **15%** $3,750

TOTAL TAXES $16,250

INCOME $100,000

$25,000 — TAX RATE **30%** $7,500

$50,000 — TAX RATE **25%** $12,500

$25,000 — TAX RATE **15%** $3,750

TOTAL TAXES $23,750

>> **Figure 8.1** The progressive structure shown here is similar—but not identical—to the federal income tax. **Analyze Graphs** What percentage of total income does each earner shown on this graph pay?

▶ **Interactive Chart**

Who Bears the Tax Burden: Inelastic Demand

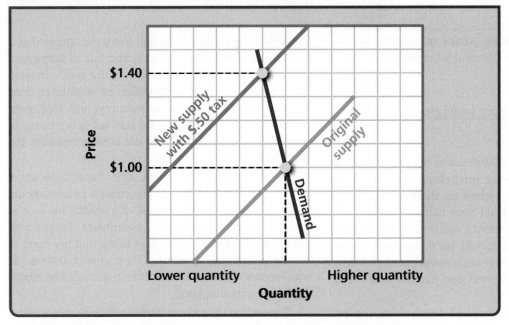

>> **Figure 8.2** This graph shows the effect of a tax when the demand for the good being taxed is inelastic. **Analyze Graphs** Do you think consumers or businesses will pay the larger share of the tax? Explain.

first decide what the base will be for the tax: income, profits, property, sales, or some other category.

❓ RECALL Is the federal individual income tax proportional, progressive, or regressive?

The Tax Burden

Government tax policies have a real impact on millions of individuals and businesses. These impacts can affect the entire economy. Thus, it is important to think about who actually bears the burden of a tax. This is not necessarily the person who sends in the money to pay the tax bill. How can we know who is actually bearing the burden of a tax? The answer lies in supply-and-demand analysis.

For the purpose of this analysis, consider this example: Suppose the government imposes a gasoline tax of $.50 per gallon and collects the tax from service stations. You may think the burden of the tax falls only on the service stations, because they send the tax money to the government. But you will see that this is not always the case.

Figure 8.2 shows the original supply curve (in green) and a supply curve after the $.50 tax is imposed (in blue). You see that before the tax, the market was

at equilibrium, and gas cost $1.00 per gallon. The new supply curve reflects the fact that when a tax is imposed on a good, the cost of supplying the good increases. Quantity supplied will decrease at every price level.

Notice the steep demand curve in **Figure 8.2**. This is what you would see if demand for gas were inelastic—that is, if consumers bought about the same amount no matter what the price. So, when demand is inelastic, the tax will increase the price of each gallon by a relatively large amount, and consumers will bear a large share of the tax. The $.50 tax will increase the equilibrium price by $.40 (from $1.00 to $1.40). In other words, consumers will pay about four fifths of the tax.

In contrast, if demand is relatively elastic, the demand curve will be relatively flat, as in **Figure 8.3**. Consumers will pay a relatively small part of the tax. In this case, a $.50 tax increases the equilibrium price by only $.10 (from $1.00 to $1.10). Consumers pay only one fifth of the tax. Businesses pay the other four fifths.

This example shows the **incidence of a tax**— that is, the final burden of a tax. When policymakers consider a new tax, they examine who will actually bear the burden. As in the example above, producers can "pass on" a portion of the burden to consumers. Generally, the more inelastic the demand, the more easily the seller can shift the tax to consumers. The more elastic the demand, the more the seller bears the burden.

❓ RECALL Who bears the greater burden of a tax on a good or service when demand is inelastic?

Key Characteristics of a Tax

Although it is sometimes difficult to decide whether a specific tax is proportional, progressive, or regressive, economists do generally agree on the qualities a tax ought to have. A tax should have four characteristics: simplicity; efficiency; certainty; and equity, or fairness.

Simplicity. Tax laws should be simple and easily understood. Taxpayers and businesses should be able to keep the necessary records and pay the taxes on a predictable schedule.

Efficiency. Government administrators should be able to assess and collect taxes without spending too much time or money. Similarly, taxpayers should be able to pay taxes without giving up too much time or paying too much money in fees.

Certainty. Certainty is also a characteristic of a good tax. It should be clear to the taxpayer when a tax is due, how much money is due, and how the tax should be paid.

Equity. The tax system should be fair, so that no one bears too much or too little of the tax burden.

Determining Equity Although everyone agrees that a tax system should be equitable and fair to taxpayers, people often disagree on what *equity* really means. Does it require equal distribution of wealth, or does it simply demand equal opportunity and treatment for all? Over time, this debate has led economists to propose two different ideas about how to measure the fairness of a tax.

The first idea is called the benefits-received principle. According to this principle, a person should pay taxes based on the level of benefits he or she expects to receive from the government. People who drive, for example, pay gasoline taxes that are used to build and maintain highways. In this way, the people who receive the most benefit from the roads contribute the most to their upkeep.

The second idea about fairness is called the ability-to-pay principle. According to this principle, people should pay taxes according to their ability to pay. This is the principle behind a progressive income tax: People who earn more income pay more taxes.

Achieving equity in a tax system for a nation the size of the U.S. is a huge challenge. Many complain about the number and complexity of taxes we are

Who Bears the Tax Burden: Elastic Demand

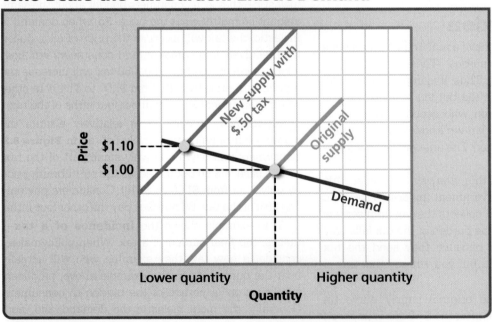

>> **Figure 8.3** Here we see the impact of a tax when demand for the taxed good is elastic. **Analyze Graphs** Do you think consumers or businesses will pay the larger share of the tax? Explain.

subject to. Some of this complexity is the result of efforts to achieve equity.

Balancing Tax Revenues and Tax Rates How much revenue does a good tax generate? The answer is "enough, but not too much." That is, enough so that citizens' needs are met, but not so much that the tax discourages production.

For example, if a company has to pay $100,000 in taxes, it will not be able to use that $100,000 to expand production. If tax rates are lower, however, the company can use more of its income to stimulate production rather than to pay taxes. Ultimately, many people argue, the economy benefits from lower tax rates.

The debate over the appropriate level of taxation is a vigorous one. In this country—and around the world—people have widely different views on this subject.

? **CHECK UNDERSTANDING** What four characteristics do economists believe a tax should possess?

>> The government's Internal Revenue Service (IRS) has a "long form" and a simpler "short form" for filing taxes. **Analyze Political Cartoons** What does this cartoon suggest about the tax system?

ASSESSMENT

1. **Summarize** What does the United States Constitution say about government's power to tax?

2. **Draw Conclusions** Suppose Michelle earns $40,000 per year and Rosa earns $100,000 per year. Under a proportional tax, who would pay a greater percentage of her income in taxes?

3. **Cite Evidence** Cite evidence from your reading that illustrates the economic importance of national taxes in the United States.

4. **Contrast** How do progressive taxes differ from regressive taxes?

5. **Predict Consequences** Suppose the government imposed a new tax on an item for which demand is typically inelastic. Who would probably end up bearing the incidence of the tax? Why?

>> Our tax system promotes equity, but its complexity makes it necessary for many people to get help preparing their taxes. This couple is meeting with a professional tax preparer.

Interactive Flipped Video

8.2 The United States has a government "of the people, by the people, for the people." For that government to function, it needs the economic backing of the American people. If you work and pay income taxes, you are helping to support the work the government does. Taxes are of great economic importance to the nation.

Federal Taxes

Individual and Corporate Income Taxes

The income tax is one category of revenue and one of several taxes collected by the federal government. As you will read, individual taxpayers like you are not the only source of federal tax revenues. The federal government also receives revenue from corporate income taxes, social insurance taxes, excise taxes, estate and gift taxes, and taxes on imports.

Individual Income Taxes The government's main source of revenues is the federal tax on individuals' taxable income. As **Figure 8.4** shows, 46 percent of the federal government's receipts for 2014 were expected to come from the payment of individual income taxes. The graph shows the other sources of government receipts, as well.

It is important to note that today, the receipts shown in **Figure 8.4** rarely cover the full cost of government. In recent decades, the federal government has borrowed huge sums of money virtually every year to cover budget deficits.

The amount of federal income tax a person owes is determined on an annual basis. In theory, the federal government could wait until the end of the tax year to collect individual income taxes. In reality, that would be a problem for both taxpayers and the government. Like other employers, the government has to pay regularly for rent, supplies, services, and employees' salaries. A single annual payment from all the nation's taxpayers at once would make meeting these expenses difficult.

Similarly, many people might have trouble paying their taxes in one large sum. For these reasons, federal income tax is collected in a "pay-as-you-earn" system. This means that individuals usually pay most of their income tax throughout the calendar year as they earn income. They have until mid-April of the following year to pay any additional income taxes they owe.

Individual Tax Brackets The federal income tax is a progressive tax, which is aimed at the economic goal of equity. In other words, the tax rate rises with the amount of taxable income. You can see this progressive structure in **Figure 8.5.** This table gives the rates for an unmarried filer who is not the head of a household. Married couples who file their taxes jointly have a different set of tax rates.

The schedule you see here shows seven rates. Each applies to a different range of income, or tax bracket. For example, a person subject to this tax table and with a taxable income of $8,925 or less would pay 10 percent income tax. If that person earned more than $400,000 in taxable income, he or she would pay the highest rate—39.6 percent—on earnings in excess of that amount. (The person would pay lower rates on the income below $400,000.) Each year, the IRS publishes new tax rate schedules that reflect any changes in the federal tax code.

Supporters of our progressive system argue that it helps promote the economic goal of equity. Others, however, say progressive rates reduce the incentive to work hard and earn more. Our progressive tax system may add cost in the form of complexity. One recent study claimed Americans spend $140 and 7.6 billion hours annually on their federal taxes alone. Not all of this time and money is a result of the progressive tax code, but some of it is.

Tax Withholding Employers are responsible in part for carrying out the system of collecting federal income taxes. They do so by **withholding,** or taking payments out of your pay before you receive it. The amount they withhold is based on an estimate of how much you will owe in federal income taxes for the entire year. After withholding the money, the employer forwards it to the federal government as an "installment payment" on your upcoming annual income tax bill.

Filing a Tax Return After the calendar year ends, employers give their employees a report stating how much income tax has already been withheld and sent to the government. The employee uses that information to complete a tax return. A **tax return** is a form used to

Federal Receipts, 2014 (Estimated)

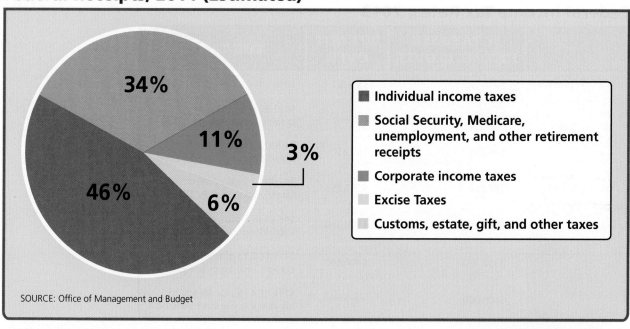

34%

11%

3%

46%

6%

- Individual income taxes
- Social Security, Medicare, unemployment, and other retirement receipts
- Corporate income taxes
- Excise Taxes
- Customs, estate, gift, and other taxes

SOURCE: Office of Management and Budget

>> **Figure 8.4 Analyze Graphs** Based on this graph, what effect would an economic downturn, with lower corporate and individual earnings, have on government receipts? Explain.

▶ Interactive Chart

file income taxes. On it, you declare your income to the government and figure out how much of that income is taxable.

Taxable income is a person's gross (or total) income minus exemptions and deductions. Gross income includes earned income—salaries, wages, tips, and commissions. It also includes income from investments such as interest on savings accounts and dividends from stock. **Personal exemptions** are set amounts that you subtract from your gross income for yourself, your spouse, and any dependents.

Tax deductions are amounts that you can subtract, or deduct, from your gross income. Commonly taken deductions include mortgage interest, large medical expenses, and state and local tax payments.

Taxpayers may also deduct charitable donations. By creating a tax benefit for charitable giving, the government creates a positive incentive and lowers the cost of giving money away. The government created this incentive because, while charitable giving costs donors money they could use for other purposes, it also provides great benefits to the organizations that receive the money, the people those organizations serve, and society at large.

Once you determine how much tax you owe, you can apply available tax credits. A **tax credit** is an amount that you can subtract from the total amount of your income tax. You can claim a credit for such things as a portion of the cost of child care and higher education.

Completing a tax return allows you to determine whether the amount of income taxes you have already paid is higher or lower than the actual amount owed. If you have paid more than you owe, the government sends you a refund. If you have paid less than you owe, you must pay the balance. All federal income tax returns must be sent to the Internal Revenue Service, or IRS, by midnight on April 15 (or the next business day if April 15 falls on a weekend or holiday).

Corporate Income Taxes Like individuals, corporations must pay federal income tax on their taxable income. Recall, **Figure 8.4** showed that corporate taxes were expected to account for 11 percent of federal receipts in 2014.

Determining corporate taxable income can be a challenge, because businesses can take many deductions. That is, they can subtract many expenses from their income before they reach the amount of income that is subject to taxation. For example, companies deduct the cost of employees' health insurance. Many other costs of doing business can also be deducted.

Like individual income tax rates, corporate income tax rates are progressive. For 2013, rates begin at 15 percent on the first $50,000 of taxable income. On the

Federal Income Tax Rates, 2013

	IF TAXABLE INCOME IS OVER	BUT NOT OVER	THE TAX IS
For Unmarried People Who Are Not Heads of Households	$0	$8,925	10%
	$8,925	$36,250	$892.50 plus 15% of taxable income over $8,925
	$36,250	$87,850	$4,991.25 plus 25% of taxable income over $36,250
	$87,850	$183,250	$17,891.25 plus 28% of taxable income over $87,850
	$183,250	$398,350	$44,603.25 plus 33% of taxable income over $183,250
	$398,350	$400,000	$115,586.25 plus 35% of taxable income over $398,350
	$400,000	no limit	$116,163.75 plus 39.6% of taxable income over $400,000

SOURCE: Internal Revenue Service

>> **Figure 8.5 Analyze Charts** Assuming this schedule applied to you, in what range would your taxable income fall if you were in the 28 percent tax bracket?

Two Views on Corporate Taxes

"Today, large **U.S. corporations** report more than **$1 trillion** in cash or liquid assets. They have the funds to invest in new jobs, should they choose to do so. We found **no evidence** that cutting the tax rate on corporate profits induces firms to **create new jobs** in the United States."

—Center for Effective Government, "The Corporate Tax Rate Debate," December 2013

"**American manufacturers** are at a distinct **disadvantage** to competitors headquartered in other countries. Specifically, foreign manufacturers uniformly face a **lower corporate tax rate** than U.S. manufacturers, and virtually all operate under territorial systems which **encourage investment** both abroad and at home."

—Susan Ford, Corning, Inc. executive, testimony before Congress, July 2012

>> Views on corporate income taxes vary widely. **Compare Points of View** How might Susan Ford reply to the views expressed in the quote from the Center for Effective Government?

highest corporate income, above $18,333,333, the tax rate is 35 percent.

? DEFINE What is a person's or corporation's taxable income?

Social Security, Medicare, and Unemployment Taxes

In addition to withholding money for income taxes, employers withhold money for taxes authorized under the Federal Insurance Contributions Act, or FICA. FICA taxes fund two large government social-insurance programs, Social Security and Medicare. Employees and employers share FICA payments.

Social Security Taxes Most of the FICA taxes you pay go to the Social Security Administration to fund Old-Age, Survivors, and Disability Insurance (OASDI), or Social Security. Social Security was established in 1935 to ease the hardships of the Great Depression.

From the start, Social Security provided old-age pensions and unemployment insurance to workers. Today, it also provides benefits to surviving family members of wage earners and to people whose disabilities keep them from working.

Each year the government establishes an income cap for Social Security taxes. In 2013, the cap was $113,700. No Social Security taxes could be withheld from a taxpayer's wages and salaries above that amount.

Medicare Taxes FICA taxes also fund Medicare. The Medicare program is a national health insurance program that helps pay for healthcare for people over age 65. It also covers people with certain disabilities. Both employees and self-employed people pay the Medicare tax on all their earnings. There is no ceiling as there is for Social Security payments. In spite of this fact, Medicare is experiencing a growing gap between receipts in tax payments and expenditures. You will learn more about this shortly.

Unemployment Taxes The federal government also collects an unemployment tax, which is paid by employers. In effect, the tax pays for an insurance policy for workers.

If workers are laid off from their jobs through no fault of their own, they can file an "unemployment compensation" claim and collect benefits for a fixed number of weeks. In order to collect unemployment benefits, an unemployed person usually must show that he or she is actively looking for another job. The unemployment program is financed by both state and federal unemployment taxes.

? **CATEGORIZE** Who benefits from Medicare taxes?

Other National Taxes

What are the taxes on gasoline and cable television service called? If you inherit money from your great aunt, will you have to pay a tax? Why are some imported products so expensive? To answer these questions, you need to look at excise, estate, gift, and import taxes.

Excise Taxes An excise tax is a general revenue tax on the sale or manufacture of a good. Federal excise taxes apply to gasoline, cigarettes, alcoholic beverages, telephone services, cable television, and other items.

Estate Taxes An **estate tax** is a tax on the estate, or total value of the money and property, of a person who has died. It is paid out of the person's estate before the heirs receive their share. A person's estate includes not only money, but also real estate, cars, furniture, investments, jewelry, paintings, and insurance.

As of 2013, if the total value of an estate is $5,250,000 or less, there is no federal estate tax. Because an estate tax is a progressive tax, the rate rises with increasing value. That is, a larger estate will be taxed by the federal government at a higher rate than a smaller one.

Gift Taxes The **gift tax** is a tax on the money or property that one living person gives to another. The goal of the gift tax, established in 1924, was to keep people from avoiding estate taxes by giving away their money before they died. The tax law sets limits on gifts but still allows the tax-free transfer of fairly large amounts each year. Under current law, a person can give up to $14,000 a year tax-free to each of several different people.

Tariffs—Taxes on Imported Goods Taxes on imported goods (foreign goods brought into the country) are called **tariffs.** Tariffs were once the most important source of federal revenue, but that is no longer the case. Today they represent a tiny share of federal revenues.

Today, most tariffs are intended to protect American farmers and industries from foreign competitors rather than to generate revenue. Tariffs raise the prices of foreign items, which helps keep the prices of American products competitive.

Taxes That Affect Behavior The basic goal of taxation is to create revenue. However, governments sometimes use tax policy to discourage the public from buying harmful products. They also use taxes to encourage constructive behavior. The use of taxation to discourage or encourage behavior is called a **tax incentive.** One example you learned about earlier is the available tax deduction for charitable giving.

Federal taxes on tobacco products and alcoholic beverages are examples of so-called sin taxes. Their main purpose is to discourage people from buying and using these products.

Incentives also come in the form of tax credits. Congress tries to encourage energy conservation by offering a variety of credits to consumers and industry. To persuade people to purchase more fuel-efficient cars, buyers of some electric and plug-in hybrid vehicles may receive an income tax credit. Owners of homes and commercial buildings can also claim credits for improvements that decrease the use of oil and other fossil fuels, including insulation and replacement windows. Under the Affordable Care Act, the sweeping healthcare law passed in 2010, the purchase of health insurance may lead to a tax credit for some. Those who fail to purchase coverage may face a penalty.

? **COMPARE AND CONTRAST** How has the role of tariffs changed over history?

"One day all this will be someone else's."

>> **Analyze Political Cartoons** How would you summarize this cartoon's view of the estate tax?

▶ **Interactive Gallery**

ASSESSMENT

1. **Compare and Contrast** How would a single person with a taxable income of $15,000 per year and a single person with a taxable income of $300,000 per year be treated differently—and similarly—in terms of national taxes?

2. **Express Ideas Clearly** Why do people in the United States pay unemployment taxes?

3. **Draw Conclusions** What is the purpose of tax incentives?

4. **Identify** What are the main sources of federal government receipts?

5. **Express Ideas Clearly** What is an example of how the U.S. tax system attempts to promote the goal of economic equity?

Suppose that each year you were given a million dollars to spend on serious expenses. So much money! So many choices! Where would you begin? The federal government, with a budget that approaches $4 trillion, faces a similar "dilemma" every year.

>> Many military veterans are entitled to pensions based on their service to the country.

[▷] **Interactive Flipped Video**

>> **Objectives**

Analyze categories of expenditures in the U.S. federal budget.

Describe major entitlement programs.

Identify major types of discretionary spending in the federal budget.

>> **Key Terms**

mandatory spending
discretionary
  spending
entitlement

Federal Spending

Mandatory and Discretionary Spending

Through the democratic process, the American public chooses between candidates who often have different ideas on how the federal government should spend its income. As you will read, government spending meets numerous needs. Our elected leaders have decided that much of the money should provide for our health and welfare.

In reality, when the government considers the huge sum of money it collects to fund the budget, most of it is already accounted for. After the government fulfills all its legal obligations, only about a third of the money remains to be spent.

Figure 8.6 shows the major categories of federal spending in the 2012 budget year. Some of these categories, such as Social Security and Medicare, are mandatory. **Mandatory spending** refers to money that Congress is mandated, or required, by existing law to spend on certain programs or to use for interest payments on the national debt. Other categories, such as defense and education, are discretionary. **Discretionary spending** is spending about which lawmakers are free to make choices.

In general, the percentage of federal spending that is mandatory has grown in recent years. The percentage of discretionary spending has decreased.

? **EXPRESS IDEAS CLEARLY** Explain why government does not truly get to decide how to spend all the money in its budget.

Government Entitlements

Except for interest on the national debt, most of the mandatory spending items in the federal budget are for entitlement programs. **Entitlements** are social welfare programs that people are "entitled to" and benefit from if they meet certain eligibility requirements, such as being at a particular income level or age. The federal government guarantees assistance for all those who qualify. As the number of people who qualify rises, mandatory spending rises as well. As a result, managing the cost of entitlement programs has become a major concern.

Some, but not all, entitlements are "means-tested." In other words, people with higher incomes may receive lower benefits or no benefits at all. Medicaid, for instance, is means-tested. Social Security is not. A retired person who has worked and paid Social Security taxes is entitled to certain benefits. Similarly, military veterans and retired federal employees are entitled to receive pensions from the government.

Entitlements are a largely unchanging part of government spending. Once Congress has set the requirements, it cannot control how many people become eligible for each kind of benefit. Congress can change the eligibility requirements or reduce the amount of the benefit in order to try to keep costs down. Such actions, however, require a change in the law.

Social Security Social Security makes up a huge portion of all federal spending. About 58 million Americans receive monthly benefits from the Social Security Administration. Of those beneficiaries, some are disabled workers, but the great majority are retired workers. Many of those retirees rely solely on their Social Security checks to support themselves.

The Social Security system faces an uncertain future today. To understand the uncertainty, you must understand how the Social Security system is set up. American workers pay into the system through taxes. Those taxes go toward benefits for people who are no longer working. That is, the money that you pay into Social Security today does not go into a fund for your own future retirement. It goes toward supporting people who have already retired.

For the system to function properly, there must be enough workers paying in to support all the retired workers receiving benefits. Although the system has worked well, changes in the U.S. population threaten to undermine it. A key reason for this is the so-called baby

Federal Spending, 2012

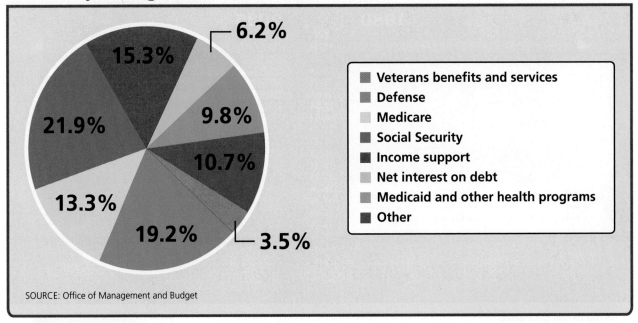

- Veterans benefits and services
- Defense
- Medicare
- Social Security
- Income support
- Net interest on debt
- Medicaid and other health programs
- Other

6.2%
15.3%
9.8%
21.9%
10.7%
13.3%
19.2%
3.5%

SOURCE: Office of Management and Budget

>> **Figure 8.6 Analyze Graphs** What is the largest spending category in the budget represented here?

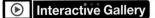 ▶ **Interactive Gallery**

boom—the generation born following World War II. This large demographic group has been the backbone of the workforce. But they did not have children at anywhere near the rate of their parents, and the oldest baby boomers are entering retirement. Millions more will soon follow. As this happens, the ratio of existing workers to retirees will fall.

The system may not reach crisis levels for some time. But unless something is done, today's high school students might receive only limited benefits from Social Security when they retire. At the same time, making changes to the program is politically difficult. Proposals for doing so typically meet significant opposition.

Medicare Medicare serves about 47 million people, most of them over 65 years old. The program pays for hospital care and for the costs of physicians and medical services. It also pays healthcare bills for people who suffer from certain disabilities and diseases.

Like Social Security, Medicare is funded by taxes withheld from people's paychecks. Monthly payments paid by people who make certain levels of taxable income and receive Medicare benefits also help pay for the program.

Medicare costs have been growing rapidly, partly as a result of expensive technology, but also because people are living longer. The basic problem facing Medicare is the same as the one facing Social Security: a falling ratio of workers to beneficiaries.

Medicaid Medicaid benefits low-income families, some people with disabilities, and elderly people in nursing homes. It is the largest source of funds for medical and health-related services for America's poorest people. The federal government shares the costs of Medicaid with state governments.

Other Mandatory Spending Programs Other means-tested entitlements benefit people and families whose incomes fall below a certain level. Requirements vary from program to program. Federal programs include the Supplemental Nutrition Assistance Program and the National School Lunch Program. The federal government also pays retirement benefits and insurance for federal workers, as well as veterans' pensions and unemployment insurance.

Some members of Congress have pushed for additional government programs related to healthcare. One reason is that healthcare costs have increased at more than twice the rate of inflation over the last few decades. The average expenditure for healthcare rose from $891 per person in 1960 to $8,680 in 2011. To keep pace, health insurance costs have skyrocketed.

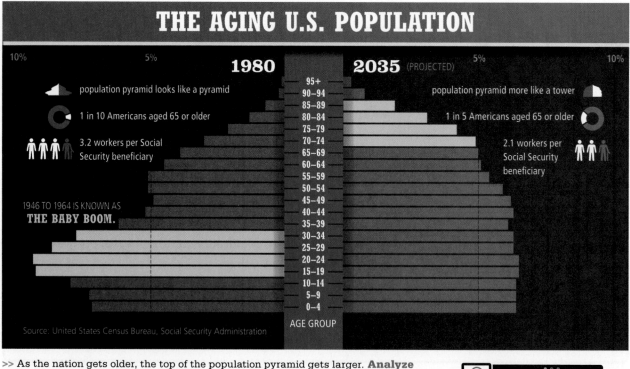

THE AGING U.S. POPULATION

1980		2035 (PROJECTED)

population pyramid looks like a pyramid

1 in 10 Americans aged 65 or older

3.2 workers per Social Security beneficiary

1946 TO 1964 IS KNOWN AS **THE BABY BOOM.**

population pyramid more like a tower

1 in 5 Americans aged 65 or older

2.1 workers per Social Security beneficiary

AGE GROUP

Source: United States Census Bureau, Social Security Administration

>> As the nation gets older, the top of the population pyramid gets larger. **Analyze Data** Compared to 1980, how will the ratio of workers to Social Security recipients have changed by 2035?

▶ **Interactive Chart**

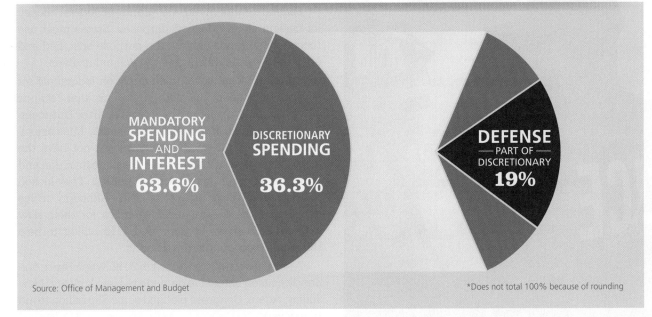

DEFENSE SPENDING AS A PART OF DISCRETIONARY SPENDING 2012*

MANDATORY SPENDING AND INTEREST
63.6%

DISCRETIONARY SPENDING
36.3%

DEFENSE PART OF DISCRETIONARY
19%

Source: Office of Management and Budget

*Does not total 100% because of rounding

>> **Figure 8.7 Analyze Graphs** About what percentage of discretionary spending went to defense in the budget year shown?

As a result, some 48 million Americans had no health insurance in 2011.

Over the years, leaders have proposed a range of solutions to these issues—from single-payer systems organized by the government, to expansion of healthcare tax credits to help make insurance more affordable. Others have insisted we rely on market forces to correct problems. In 2010, President Obama signed a new law called the Affordable Care Act. This law requires Americans who lack certain health insurance coverage to purchase it through competitive private exchanges in their state or through a federal insurance marketplace. The program also seeks to expand the Medicaid program and offers subsidies to help lower-income people afford health insurance. It remains to be seen how this program will affect healthcare costs or access for previously uninsured Americans.

? DESCRIBE What key demographic challenge faces the largest entitlement programs in the United States?

Spending on Discretionary Programs

As you have read, the majority of the federal budget is devoted to mandatory spending. The remaining funds available for discretionary spending are divided among a wide variety of programs.

Defense Spending Of the categories of discretionary spending, defense spending is the largest. (See **Figure 8.7.**) Defense spending has dropped somewhat since the end of the Cold War in the late 1900s as a percentage of the total federal budget. As you can see from the graph, defense spending consumes about 19 percent of the federal budget. However, you can also see that defense accounts for more than half of discretionary spending.

The Department of Defense spends most of the defense budget. It pays the salaries of all the men and women in the army, navy, air force, and marines, as well as the department's civilian employees. Defense spending, of course, also buys weapons, missiles, battleships, tanks, airplanes, and other equipment.

Other Discretionary Spending Look again at **Figure 8.7.** After mandatory and defense spending, you may be surprised at how small a portion of federal spending goes into the category that could be labeled "everything else." Some of the many programs that this category of federal spending includes are education and training, scientific research, student loans, law enforcement, environmental cleanup, and disaster aid.

This part of the federal budget also pays the salaries of the millions of people who work for the civilian branches of the federal government. They include park rangers, FBI agents, file clerks, senators and members of Congress, geologists, CIA agents, Cabinet secretaries, meat inspectors, and many others.

>> Inspectors prepare to examine shipping containers for terrorist threats. **Express Problems Clearly** Why is the share of the budget that funds such discretionary activities shrinking?

healthcare, employment training, and dozens of other programs.

Federal grants-in-aid are grants of federal money for certain closely defined purposes. States must use these federal funds only for the purpose specified and obey the federal guidelines for which aid is given.

State and local governments rely on federal aid for a variety of needs. But nothing reveals that reliance as vividly as a disaster. For example, after Hurricane Katrina slammed into coastal Louisiana, Mississippi, and Alabama in 2005, those states did not have the resources to deal with the widespread destruction and human misery that the storm left behind. They looked to the federal government for help. Although critics denounced the federal relief agencies for their slow response, Congress appropriated $116 billion to help the states recover from the disaster.

A similar scenario occurred in 2012, when Hurricane Sandy caused extensive damage in New York and New Jersey. Again, Congress pledged some $50 billion to aid in recovery.

? **DESCRIBE** Describe the key features of the discretionary portion of the federal budget.

Federal Aid to State and Local Governments

Some federal tax money finds its way to state and local governments—much of it from the discretionary portion of the federal budget. In 2011, about $625 billion in federal grants went to the states. This is an average of about $2,000 per person and represents nearly 40 percent of state and local expenditures.

As you have read, state and federal governments share the cost of some entitlement programs, including Medicaid and unemployment compensation. They also share funding in other social programs. Additional federal money goes to the states for education, lower-income housing, highway construction, mass transit,

ASSESSMENT

1. **List** Name at least three examples of federal discretionary spending.

2. **Describe** How are the Social Security benefits of today's retirees funded?

3. **Contrast** How are mandatory funding and discretionary funding different?

4. **Identify Supporting Details** What are at least three programs in which state governments and the federal government share funding?

5. **Express Problems Clearly** Explain why entitlement programs challenge the federal budgeting process.

You and your family are thinking about colleges. Which one offers the courses you want? How much does it cost? During your research, you find that colleges within your state's university system are far less expensive than private schools. The reason is that your state government pays part of the cost of running the state colleges. In fact, funds for higher education represent a sizeable part of state expenditures.

>> State tax revenues support state parks, which provide recreational and educational opportunities for people all across the country.

▶ **Interactive Flipped Video**

State and Local Taxes and Spending

Budgeting at the State Level

Because they are democracies, state and local governments manage their money in accordance with priorities set by elected government officials. In this Lesson, you will examine these priorities. For example, you will see that funding education is a priority for state and local legislators. Although school-related tax increases can be painful to the taxpayer, the programs they fund help ensure that students receive a quality education.

Operating Budgets Like families and individuals, governments must plan their spending ahead of time. That planning involves drawing up a budget. A **budget** is an estimate of future revenues and expenses. The federal government has just one budget for planned revenue and expenses. States, however, have two budgets: operating budgets and capital budgets.

A state puts together an **operating budget** to plan for its day-to-day spending needs. Those expenses include salaries of state employees and supplies needed to run the government, such as computers and paper. They also include the maintenance of state facilities such as recreation areas and parks.

>> **Objectives**

Explain how states use a budget to plan spending.

Examine the major categories of state spending.

Identify the types and economic importance of state taxes.

Describe local government, and the types and economic importance of local taxes.

>> **Key Terms**

budget
operating budget
capital budget
balanced budget
tax exempt
real property
personal property
tax assessor

Capital Budgets A state also draws up a **capital budget** to pay for major capital, or investment, spending. If the state builds a new bridge, the money likely comes from this budget. Most of these expenses are met by long-term borrowing or the sale of bonds. The planning process for projects covered by the capital budget may begin years before the project itself begins.

Balancing State Budgets In most states, the governor prepares the budget with the help of a budget agency. The legislature then discusses and eventually approves the budget. Unlike the federal government, 48 states require **balanced budgets**—budgets in which revenues are equal to spending. These laws, however, apply only to the operating budget, not the capital budget. That makes it easier to balance the overall state budget than to balance the federal budget.

> ? **CHECK UNDERSTANDING** Would the construction of a new courthouse come out of a state's operating budget or capital budget? Explain.

State Spending Categories

Spending policies differ among the 50 states. You are probably most familiar with state spending on education, highways, police protection, and state recreation areas. There are many other categories of state spending, as you will read.

Education Every state spends taxpayer money to support at least one public state university. Some, such as Texas and California, have large systems with many campuses throughout the state. In many states, tax dollars also support agricultural and technical colleges, teachers colleges, and two-year community colleges. Spending on higher education is especially important to maintaining economic growth. Public colleges and universities offer an education at much lower tuition than most private institutions. Lower tuition enables large numbers of people to get the training and skills they need to contribute to the economy.

State governments also provide financial help to their local governments, which run public elementary, middle, and high schools. The total amount of money spent per student varies among the states. The national average was $10,560 per student per year in 2011.

Spending on education is the most significant expenditure in state budgets. **Figure 8.8** shows that it represents about 30 percent of state spending nationwide.

Public Safety State police are a familiar sight along the nation's highways. The state police enforce traffic laws and help motorists in emergencies. State police

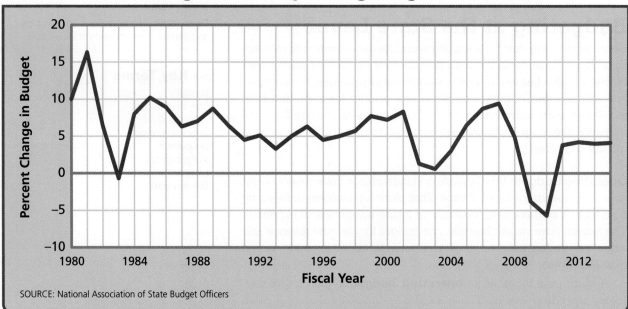

Annual Percent Change in State Operating Budgets, 1980–2014

SOURCE: National Association of State Budget Officers

>> Changes in state budgets tend to reflect changes in the national economy. **Analyze Graphs** What can you infer about the national economy in the years 1981–1983 and 2007–2010?

State Spending, 2011

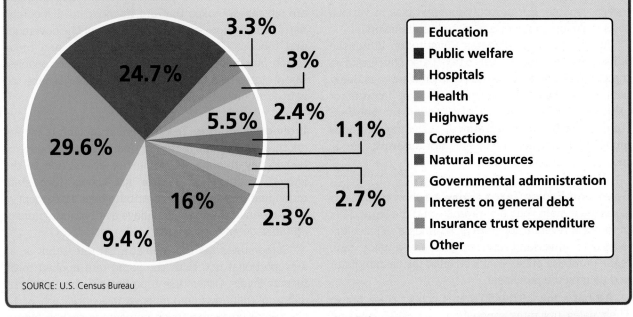

SOURCE: U.S. Census Bureau

Legend:
- Education
- Public welfare
- Hospitals
- Health
- Highways
- Corrections
- Natural resources
- Governmental administration
- Interest on general debt
- Insurance trust expenditure
- Other

Values shown: 3.3%, 3%, 2.4%, 1.1%, 24.7%, 5.5%, 29.6%, 16%, 9.4%, 2.3%, 2.7%

>> **Figure 8.8** This graph shows combined spending by category for all the states. **Analyze Graphs** Based on this graph, what would you say is the states' highest priority?

▶ **Interactive Gallery**

also maintain crime labs that can assist local law-enforcement agencies. State governments build and run corrections systems. These institutions house people convicted of state crimes.

Transportation Building and maintaining highway systems is another major state expense. State crews resurface roads and repair bridges. Some money for roads comes from the federal government. In turn, states contribute money to federal and interstate highway systems.

States pay at least some of the costs of other kinds of transportation facilities, such as waterways and airports. Money for such projects may also comes from federal and local government budgets.

Health and Welfare States look after the health and welfare of the public in various ways. State funds support some public hospitals and clinics. State regulators inspect water supplies and test for pollution.

As you have read, states also help pay for many of the federal programs that assist individuals, such as unemployment compensation benefits. Because states determine their own benefits, they can meet local needs better than the federal government can. For example, during a local recession, they may decide to extend the number of weeks that people can claim benefits.

Arts and Recreation If you've hiked in a state forest or picnicked in a state park, you've enjoyed another benefit of state tax dollars. Nature reserves and parks preserve scenic and historic places for people to visit and enjoy. States also run museums and help fund music and art programs.

Administration Besides providing services, state governments need to spend money just to keep running. Like the federal government, state governments have an executive branch (the governor's office), a legislative branch, and a court system. State tax revenues pay the salaries of all these and other state workers, including judges, maintenance crews in state parks, the governor, and professors in state universities.

? **IDENTIFY CENTRAL IDEAS** Explain how state universities contribute to economic growth.

Revenue for State Budgets

For every dollar a state spends, it must take in a dollar in revenue. Otherwise, it cannot maintain a balanced budget. The 50 states took in almost $2.3 trillion from various sources in 2011. Where does this money come from? The circle graph in **Figure 8.9** shows the major sources of state revenue. The largest portion is intergovernmental revenue, mostly money from the federal government. Income from insurance trusts—used to pay pension and other benefits—is another key revenue source. But as you can see, taxes of various sorts make up an important share of state revenues.

Just as the United States Constitution limits the federal government's power to tax, it also puts limits on the states. Because trade and commerce are considered national enterprises, states cannot tax imports or exports. They also cannot tax goods sent between states. Nonprofit organizations, including religious groups and charities, are usually **tax exempt;** that is, they are not subject to taxes.

Sales and Excise Taxes **Figure 8.9** shows that sales taxes are a main source of revenue, and the largest tax in terms of revenue, for state governments. A sales tax is a tax on goods and services. The tax—a percentage of the purchase price—is added on at the cash register and paid by the purchaser.

All but a few of the 50 states collect sales taxes. Their sales tax rates range from 2.9 to 7.5 percent. Some local governments have their own, additional sales tax. In every state, some categories of products are exempt from sales tax. For example, many states do not charge sales tax on basic needs such as food and clothing. Exemption of everyday items that most people buy in similar quantities helps make sales taxes less regressive.

Even states without a sales tax impose excise taxes that apply to specific products and activities. Some are sin taxes—taxes that are intended to discourage harmful behavior—on products like alcoholic beverages and tobacco. Other taxes apply to hotel and motel rooms, automobiles, rental cars, and insurance policies. Many states also tax gasoline. This state gasoline tax is in addition to the federal tax.

Individual Income Tax Individual income taxes are another large contributor to many states' budgets. People pay this state income tax in addition to the federal income tax. **Figure 8.9** shows that state individual income taxes contribute over 11 percent of state revenue. As such, they have a substantial impact on the economy of the state.

Some states tax incomes at a flat rate—that is, as a proportional tax, with the same rate applied to all income levels. Others use a progressive tax, either by creating their own progressive rate structure or by charging taxpayers a given percentage of their federal income tax. A handful of states have no state income tax. A couple tax only interest and dividends from investments, not wages and salaries.

Corporate Income Tax Most states collect income taxes from corporations that do business in the state. Some states levy taxes on business profits at a fixed,

State Revenue, 2011

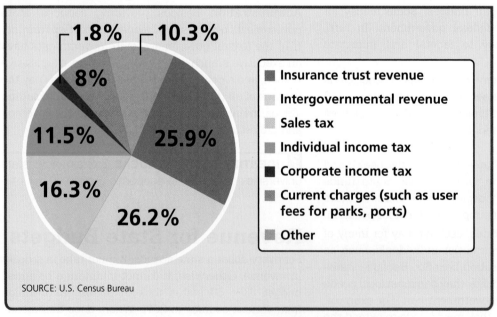

SOURCE: U.S. Census Bureau

>> **Figure 8.9** This graph shows the ways that the states, collectively, get their revenues. **Analyze Graphs** What is the most significant source of tax revenue at the state level?

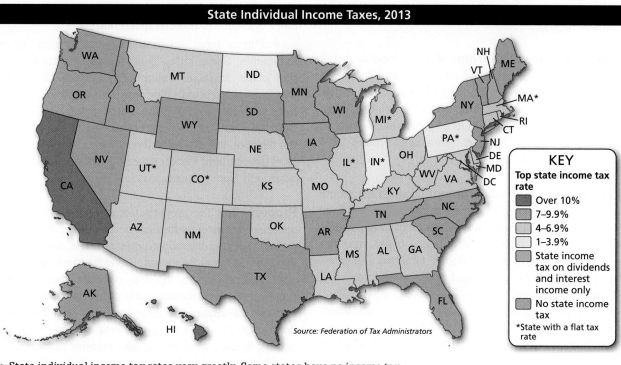

KEY

Top state income tax rate

- Over 10%
- 7–9.9%
- 4–6.9%
- 1–3.9%
- State income tax on dividends and interest income only
- No state income tax

*State with a flat tax rate

Source: Federation of Tax Administrators

>> State individual income tax rates vary greatly. Some states have no income tax. **Analyze Maps** In which range does the largest number of states set their top individual income tax rate?

flat rate. A few charge progressive rates—higher tax rates for businesses with higher profits.

As you have seen in **Figure 8.9,** corporate income taxes make up only a small portion of state revenues—about 2 percent. Nevertheless, the level of corporate income taxes can exert a strong influence on a state's economy.

Low corporate taxes, along with a well-educated workforce and efficient public services, can make it easier to attract entrepreneurs and new businesses to a state. Politicians keep this fact in mind when they determine their state's taxing policies.

Other State Taxes Besides the corporate income tax, businesses pay a variety of other state taxes and fees. Do you want to be a hairdresser, a carpenter, or a building contractor? If so, you will have to pay a licensing fee. A licensing fee is a kind of tax that people pay to carry on different kinds of business within a state.

Some states charge a transfer tax when documents such as stock certificates are transferred and recorded. Other states tax the value of the stock shares that corporations issue.

As you read earlier, the federal government taxes the estate of a person who has died. Some states, in turn, charge an inheritance tax on the value of the property that goes to each heir.

Some states also tax property. That includes real estate, or **real property**—land and any permanent structures on the land to which a person has legal title. It also includes **personal property**—movable possessions or assets—such as jewelry, furniture, and boats. Some states even tax property that is intangible (meaning "not able to be touched"), such as bank accounts, stocks, and bonds. Today, however, most property taxes, especially on real estate, are levied by local governments.

? RECALL What kind of tax raises the price of cigarettes and no other goods or services?

Local Government Spending and Revenue

Your local government plays a part in many aspects of everyday life, including your town's public schools. Like state governments, local governments draw up a budget to organize their spending. The revenue they collect through taxes allows them to hire police and firefighters. Tax revenue also enables local governments to build roads; operate libraries, hospitals, and jails; and pay teachers. Even though this is the level of government closest to you, it may be the one you know the least about.

Forms of Local Government You probably think of "local government" as a town or city. There are other types as well, including townships, counties, and special districts such as school districts. Today, there are more than 90,000 local government units in the United States. Together they collect around $600 billion in tax revenues.

The Jobs of Local Government Local governments carry major responsibilities in many areas, such as public school systems, law enforcement (local police, county sheriff's departments, park police), and fire protection. They manage public facilities (libraries, airports, public hospitals) and parks and recreational facilities (beaches, swimming pools, zoos). They monitor public health (restaurant inspection, water treatment, sewer systems), public transportation, elections (voter registration, ballot preparation, election supervision, vote counting), record keeping (birth/death certificates, wills, marriage licenses), and social services (food stamps, child care, welfare).

From this listing of tasks, you can see that local governments touch our lives every day. Many of the tasks are reflected in **Figure 8.10.** In some towns and

cities, separate commissions or private corporations carry out some of these responsibilities.

Fulfilling local government's responsibilities is expensive. Some cities have found that their debts and other financial obligations are out of control. Stockton, California, filed for bankruptcy in 2012. Detroit, Michigan, did the same thing in 2013. In Detroit's case, a key cause of financial difficulties was the flight of its citizens to the suburbs. As a result, the local government lost an enormous amount of revenue, especially from property taxes.

Property Tax The property tax is the most significant source of tax revenue for local governments. **Figure 8.11** shows that this tax contributes about a quarter of all local government revenues. Property taxes are levied on property owners in local communities to offset the expense of services such as street construction and maintenance. An official called a **tax assessor** determines the value of the property. Property taxes are usually figured as a fixed dollar amount per $1,000 of the assessed value. They are a main source of funding for public schools.

Other Local Taxes Local taxes are similar to the types of taxes imposed by the states. Besides property taxes, local governments levy sales, excise, and income taxes. Some of these taxes affect not only residents of a

Local Spending, 2011

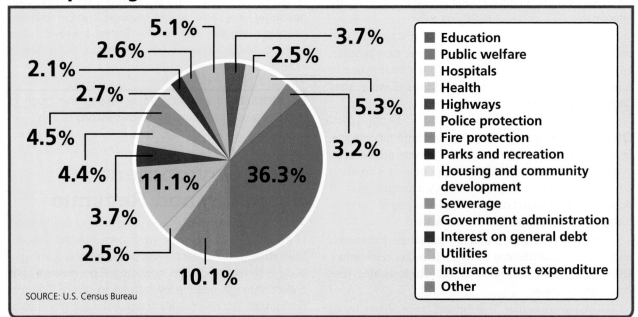

SOURCE: U.S. Census Bureau

>> **Figure 8.10** Local governments supply a variety of services to many different people. **Analyze Graphs** Based on this graph, what do you think is the largest priority of local governments?

Local Revenue, 2011

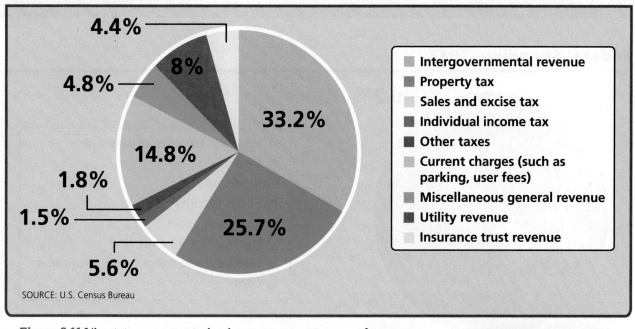

- 4.4%
- 8%
- 4.8%
- 33.2%
- 14.8%
- 1.8%
- 1.5%
- 25.7%
- 5.6%

Legend:
- Intergovernmental revenue
- Property tax
- Sales and excise tax
- Individual income tax
- Other taxes
- Current charges (such as parking, user fees)
- Miscellaneous general revenue
- Utility revenue
- Insurance trust revenue

SOURCE: U.S. Census Bureau

>> **Figure 8.11** Like state governments, local governments get revenue from many sources. **Analyze Graphs** What is a key similarity between local government revenue and state government revenue shown in Fig. 8.9?

▶ **Interactive Chart**

community but also visitors. In fact, many are designed specifically to raise revenue from nonresidents. In this way, tourists and others from outside the local area help boost local economies.

Suppose you've gone on a school trip to New York City. The room rate for your hotel is $200 a night. When you see the bill in the morning, however, it's $233! Three different taxes have been added—a 4.0 percent state sales tax, a 4.5 percent city sales tax, and a 5.875 percent hotel room occupancy tax. In addition, the city charges a Metropolitan Commuter Transportation District surcharge of 0.375 percent, for a total tax of 14.75 percent. The state and city also collect room fees totaling $3.50. Many other cities have taxes aimed at tourists and business travelers. Besides hotel taxes, they include sales taxes on rental cars, airport taxes, and taxes on movie or theater tickets.

A few thousand cities and other types of local governments assess a tax on individual income. It takes the form of a payroll tax. Usually the rate is low, but this tax can still produce a significant amount of revenue.

Some cities have debated the idea of instituting a congestion tax on vehicles. The local government would charge drivers a fee for entering a congested, or overcrowded, area of the city between certain hours. Supporters of a congestion tax say many commuters would opt to use mass transit instead of automobiles.

This would not only help clear clogged streets, but would also decrease the emission of gases that contribute to local air pollution into the atmosphere.

Critics counter that the city's businesses would be hurt, as many people would decide to stay out of the downtown area—and spend their money elsewhere.

? **RECALL** What type of local tax is a main source of funding for public schools?

ASSESSMENT

1. **Make Predictions** Which budget—capital or operating—do you think a state would draw from to fund the cleanup after a natural disaster? Why?

2. **Evaluate Arguments** Is it fair that nonprofit organizations are exempt from taxes? Why or why not?

3. **Make Generalizations** Do states generally help local governments carry out their responsibilities?

4. **Generate Explanations** Why might local governments design taxes to raise revenue from nonresidents?

5. **Contrast** In what ways do local government taxes differ from state taxes?

Federal Spending, 2012

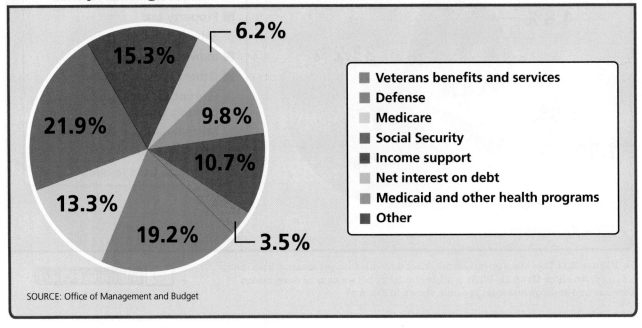

SOURCE: Office of Management and Budget

Legend:
- ■ Veterans benefits and services
- ■ Defense
- ■ Medicare
- ■ Social Security
- ■ Income support
- ■ Net interest on debt
- ■ Medicaid and other health programs
- ■ Other

Pie values: 6.2%, 15.3%, 9.8%, 21.9%, 10.7%, 13.3%, 19.2%, 3.5%

1. **Analyze Expenditures and Attribute Ideas and Information** Analyze the categories of expenditures in the U.S. federal budget. Consider these questions: What information does the chart show? What source provided this information? Use the information in the chart to analyze why the federal government might have difficulty funding new social programs in the future.

2. **Analyze Costs and Benefits** Write a paragraph in which you analyze the costs and benefits of the purchase, use, and disposal of business property. Consider these questions: How is the purchase, use, and disposal of business property affected by taxes? What rights does the business property bring? In what way can the use of business property affect its value? What are possible benefits of disposing of business property?

3. **Analyze Costs and Benefits** Analyze the costs and benefits of the purchase, use, and disposal of personal property. Consider these questions: How is the purchase, use, and disposal of personal property affected by taxes? What rights does the purchase of personal property bring? In what way can using personal property affect its value? In what way might a person benefit from disposing of personal property?

4. **Identify Economic Concepts** Identify how the U.S. Constitution incorporates the economic concept of taxation. Consider these questions: To what branch of government does the United States Constitution give the power to tax? Is the constitutional power to tax limited or unlimited? Why is the power of taxation given to the government?

5. **Analyze Costs and Benefits** Using the quotation provided, analyze the costs and benefits of U.S. economic policies related to the economic goals of equity. Consider these questions: In what way is the United States' income tax progressive? In what way does a progressive income tax promote relatively equal outcomes in family wealth? In what sense does a progressive tax oppose the equality of opportunity? Why would the progressive income tax be seen as fair by some and unfair by others?

"But what is fair to one person may not be fair to another."

6. **Identify Economic Importance** Write a paragraph in which you identify the economic importance of national taxes. Consider these questions: What types of taxes does the federal government collect from businesses and individuals? In what way does the amount of taxes raised by the national government have important implications for the economy as a whole? In what ways might national taxes introduce inefficiencies into a free market?

Federal Receipts, 2014 (Estimated)

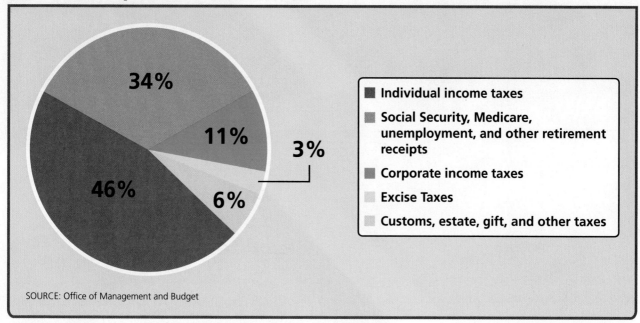

34%

11%

3%

46%

6%

- ■ **Individual income taxes**
- ■ **Social Security, Medicare, unemployment, and other retirement receipts**
- ■ **Corporate income taxes**
- ■ **Excise Taxes**
- ■ **Customs, estate, gift, and other taxes**

SOURCE: Office of Management and Budget

7. **Analyze Revenues** Using the graph provided, analyze the categories of revenues in the U.S. federal budget. Consider these questions: What sources of revenue does the federal government have? What percentage of federal receipts did corporate income taxes provide in 2014? An increase in both personal wages and corporate profits would have what effect on the federal government's revenue?

8. **Analyze Expenditures and Create Presentations** Using the quotation below, write an outline for presentation that you might give, in which you analyze the categories of expenditures in the U.S. federal budget. Consider these questions: What are some examples of major types of expenditures the federal government makes? What is the difference between mandatory and discretionary spending? What is one major limitation on discretionary spending by the federal government?

"In reality, when the government considers the huge sum of money it collects to fund the budget, most of it is already accounted for. After the government fulfills all its legal obligations, only about a third of the money remains to be spent."

9. **Analyze Costs and Benefits and Transfer Information and Create Presentations** Referring to the quotation provided, analyze the costs and benefits

of U.S. tax policies as they relate to the economic goal of equity. Consider these things: What information is communicated in the quotation? In what sense does this type of tax system aim to achieve the goal of economic equity? What are the costs and benefits of national income tax policy for people with different income levels?

"People with higher incomes pay a higher percentage of their income in taxes. People with very small incomes might pay no tax at all."

10. **Identify Economic Importance** Using the quotation provided, write a paragraph in which you identify the economic importance of types of local taxes. Consider these questions: What idea or information is communicated in the quotation? In referring to taxes, is there any reason not to include local taxes as a concern in the quotation? What author can the ideas or information in the quotation be attributed to?

"The power to tax involves the power to destroy."

11. **Write About the Essential Question** Write an essay on the Essential Question: **Can and should government be fair to everyone?** Use evidence from your study of this Topic to support your answer.

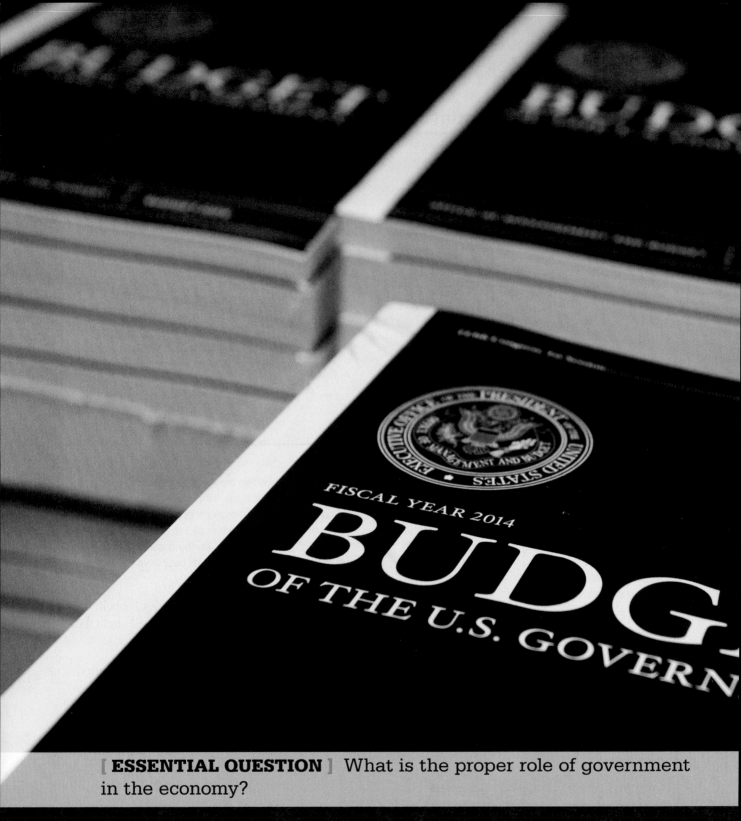

[**ESSENTIAL QUESTION**] What is the proper role of government in the economy?

⑨ Fiscal and Monetary Policy

Enduring Understandings

- The government uses fiscal policy to promote full employment and maintain stable prices.

- Demand-side economists believe that government spending will improve the economy during times of economic weakness. Supply-side economists believe instead in using tax cuts to boost the economy.

- Deficits and the national debt can cause problems for a nation.

- The Federal Reserve uses monetary policy tools to regulate the nation's money supply.

- Monetary policy can lessen the frequency and amplitude of the fluctuations in the economy if it is implemented at the right time.

>> The proposed federal budget is published every year and printed in book-like format.

PEARSON realize™ **NBC LEARN**

U.K. Polar

Watch the My Story Video to learn more about John Maynard Keynes, an economist whose work has shaped economic policies since the Great Depression.

PEARSON realize™
www.PearsonRealize.com

Access your digital lessons including:
Topic Inquiry • Interactive Reading
Notepad • Interactivities • Assessments

>> Congressional staff members receive massive copies of the proposed 2012 budget.

▶ **Interactive Flipped Video**

Does your family have a household budget? Have you ever tried to budget your own money? Either way, you know that you have to take a close look at how much money you have coming in and how much you have to spend. Your goal is to get those two figures in line. But it's not easy. Sometimes it requires giving something up. Sometimes—although you try to avoid it—it may even require borrowing money. No matter what, making a budget takes time. Somebody has to sit down with a calculator, a stack of bills, a checkbook, and a calendar to figure it all out.

>> **Objectives**

Describe how the federal budget is created.

Analyze the impact of expansionary and contractionary fiscal policy on the economy.

Identify the limits of fiscal policy.

>> **Key Terms**

fiscal policy
federal budget
fiscal year
appropriations bill
expansionary policy
contractionary policy

The Federal Budget and Fiscal Policy

The Federal Budget and Fiscal Policy

Now, imagine how much more effort it would take if your expenses were $3.5 *trillion* per year. Suppose everyone in the house had to agree on every single item in the budget, and you had to send it to somebody else for final approval. Now you have an idea what the U.S. federal government must do before it can spend your tax money.

Unlike a family, the federal government is not just interested in making income meet expenses. As you will see, the government may also use its taxing and spending policies to speed up economic growth—or even to slow it down.

Fiscal Policy The federal government takes in and spends huge amounts of money. In fact, it spends an average of about $10 billion every day. This tremendous flow of cash into and out of the economy has a large impact on aggregate supply and aggregate demand.

The government's taxing and spending decisions are shaped both by budgetary needs and by fiscal policy. **Fiscal policy** is the use of government spending and revenue collection to influence the economy. Fiscal policy is a tool used to expand or to slow economic growth, to achieve full employment, and to maintain price stability. The federal government makes key fiscal policy decisions—how much to spend and how much to tax—each year when it creates the federal budget.

Federal Budget Basics The **federal budget** is a written document estimating the federal government's revenue and authorizing its spending for the coming year. Like any organization's budget, it lists expected income and shows exactly how the money will be spent. In effect, the budget reflects the nation's priorities—the tasks and goals it finds most pressing and worthy of financial support. **Figure 9.1** helps illustrate this point by showing how the federal budget in one year was distributed among broad spending categories. It also shows how spending has changed over time.

The federal government prepares a new budget for each fiscal year. A **fiscal year** is a 12-month period used for budgeting purposes. It is not necessarily the same as the January-to-December calendar year. The federal government uses a fiscal year that runs from October 1 through September 30.

Step 1: Agencies Submit Spending Proposals
The federal budget takes about 18 months to prepare. During this time, citizens, Congress, and the President debate the government's spending priorities. In fact,

the budget reflects the nation's commitment to different priorities.

There are several basic steps in the federal budget process. These steps are outlined in **Figure 9.2**.

The federal budget must fund many offices and agencies in the federal government, and Congress cannot know all of their needs. So, before the budget is put together, each federal agency writes a detailed estimate of how much it expects to spend in the coming fiscal year.

These spending proposals are sent to a special unit of the executive branch, the Office of Management and Budget (OMB). Created in 1970, the OMB is part of the Executive Office of the President.

As its name suggests, the OMB is responsible for managing the federal government's budget. Its most important job is to prepare that budget.

Step 2: Executive Branch Draws Up a Budget The OMB reviews the federal agencies' spending proposals. Representatives from the agencies may explain their spending proposals to the OMB and try to persuade the OMB to give them as much money as they have requested. Usually, the OMB suggests giving each agency less than it requests.

The OMB then works with the President's staff to combine all of the individual agency budgets into a

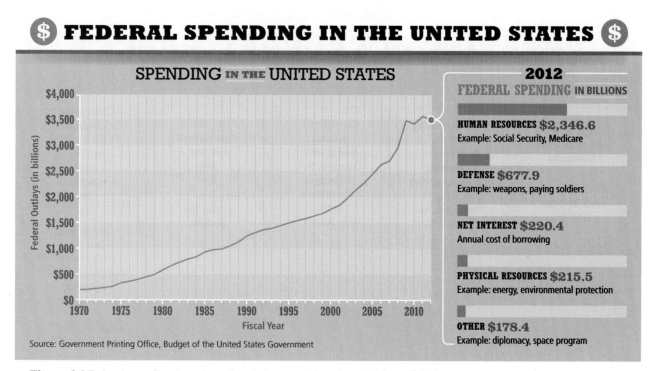

FEDERAL SPENDING IN THE UNITED STATES

SPENDING IN THE UNITED STATES

Federal Outlays (in billions): $4,000 / $3,500 / $3,000 / $2,500 / $2,000 / $1,500 / $1,000 / $500 / $0

Fiscal Year: 1970 1975 1980 1985 1990 1995 2000 2005 2010

Source: Government Printing Office, Budget of the United States Government

2012
FEDERAL SPENDING IN BILLIONS

HUMAN RESOURCES $2,346.6
Example: Social Security, Medicare

DEFENSE $677.9
Example: weapons, paying soldiers

NET INTEREST $220.4
Annual cost of borrowing

PHYSICAL RESOURCES $215.5
Example: energy, environmental protection

OTHER $178.4
Example: diplomacy, space program

>> **Figure 9.1** Federal spending has risen sharply in recent decades. **Analyze Graphs** Based on this data, which category is most likely responsible for the steep growth in spending? Explain your answer.

single budget document. This document reveals the President's overall spending plan for the coming fiscal year. The President presents the budget to Congress in January or February.

Step 3: Congress Debates The President's budget is only a starting point. The number of changes Congress makes to the President's budget depends on the relationship between the President and Congress. Congress carefully considers, debates, and modifies the President's proposed budget. For help, members of Congress rely on the assistance of the Congressional Budget Office (CBO). Created in 1974, the CBO gives Congress independent economic data to help with its decisions.

Much of the work done by Congress is done in small committees. Working at the same time, committees in the House of Representatives and the Senate analyze the budget and hold hearings at which agency officials and others can speak out about the budget. The House Budget Committee and Senate Budget Committee combine their work to propose one initial budget resolution, which must be adopted by May 15, before the beginning of the fiscal year. This resolution is not intended to be final. It gives initial estimates for revenue and spending to guide the legislators as they continue working on the budget.

Then, in early September, the budget committees propose a second budget resolution that sets binding spending limits. Congress must pass this resolution by September 15, after which Congress cannot pass any new bills that would spend more money than the budget resolution allows.

Finally, the Appropriations Committee of each house submits bills to authorize specific spending, based on the decisions Congress has made. By this time, the new fiscal year is about to start, and Congress faces pressure to get these **appropriations bills** adopted and submitted to the President before the previous year's funding ends on September 30. If Congress cannot finish in time, it must pass short-term emergency spending legislation known as "stopgap funding" to keep the government running. If Congress and the President cannot even agree on temporary funding, the government "shuts down," and all but the most essential federal offices close.

Step 4: Back to the White House Once Congress approves the appropriations bills, they are sent to the President, who can sign the bills into law. If the President vetoes any of the bills, Congress has two options. It can vote to override the President's veto—a difficult task, because an override requires the votes of two thirds of each chamber. More often, Congress

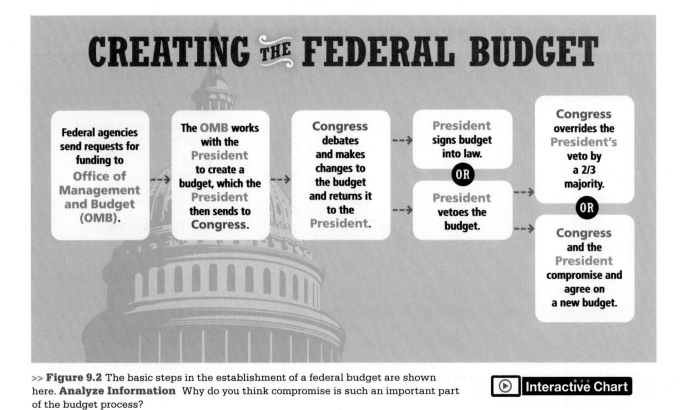

>> **Figure 9.2** The basic steps in the establishment of a federal budget are shown here. **Analyze Information** Why do you think compromise is such an important part of the budget process?

▶ **Interactive Chart**

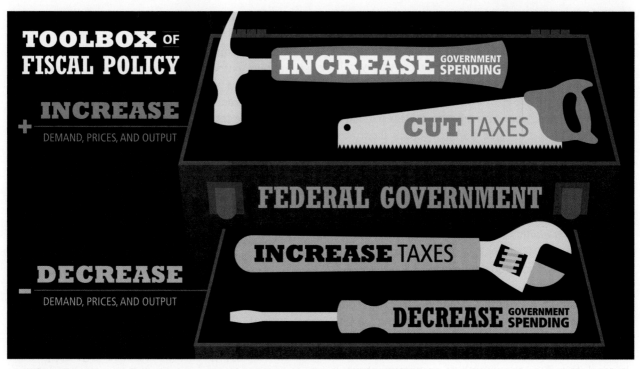

>> **Figure 9.3** When implementing fiscal policy, government has several tools at its disposal. **Analyze Information** If government leaders wanted to spur economic activity, which tools would they select? Explain.

works with the President to write an appropriations bill on which both sides can agree. Once that is completed, the President signs the new budget into law.

? LIST What two offices provide information that helps the President and Congress make budget decisions?

How Fiscal Policy Decisions Impact the Economy

Government officials who take part in the budget process debate how much should be spent on specific programs such as defense or education. They also consider how much should be spent in all. These decisions do not affect only the specific programs in the budget—they affect the entire economy. Government spending increases or decreases can affect the nation's total economic output. Similarly, the raising or lowering of taxes may help reduce or boost output. (See **Figure 9.3**.)

Fiscal policy that tries to increase output is known as **expansionary policy**. Fiscal policy intended to decrease output is called **contractionary policy**. By carefully choosing to follow expansionary or contractionary fiscal policy—and considering the

costs of each—the federal government tries to make the economy grow as smoothly and sustainably as possible.

Expansionary Fiscal Policy Governments use an expansionary fiscal policy to raise the level of output in the economy. That is, they use expansionary policy to encourage growth, either to try to prevent a recession or to move the economy out of a recession. Recall that a recession is the part of the business cycle that occurs when output declines for at least two quarters, or three-month periods, in a row. Expansionary fiscal policy involves increasing government spending, cutting taxes, or both.

If the federal government increases its spending, or buys more goods and services, it triggers a chain of events that raises output and creates jobs. Government spending increases aggregate demand, which causes prices to rise, as shown in **Figure 9.4**. According to the law of supply, higher prices encourage suppliers of goods and services to produce more. To do this, firms will hire more workers. In short, an increase in demand should lead to lower unemployment and to an increase in output. The economy will expand.

Tax cuts can work in a similar way to encourage economic expansion. If the federal government cuts taxes, individuals keep more of their income, and businesses keep more of their profits. Consumers have more money to spend on goods and services, and firms have more money to spend on land, labor, and capital. If consumers and businesses spend the money they gain through tax cuts, this spending will increase demand, prices, and output.

The U.S. government's response to the recession that began after the 2008 financial crisis illustrates expansionary fiscal policy. The American Recovery and Reinvestment Act both increased government spending and cut taxes. The act provided funding for road construction and repair, for scientific research, and for many other projects. It also cut payroll taxes, provided a tax credit for new home buyers, and offered other tax breaks. The goal was to increase demand, lower unemployment, and spur economic output.

Contractionary Fiscal Policy Under some circumstances, the government may employ a contractionary fiscal policy. Contractionary fiscal policy tries to decrease aggregate demand and, by decreasing demand, to reduce the growth of economic output. If contractionary fiscal policy is strong enough, it may slow the growth of output to zero or even lead to a fall in gross domestic product (GDP). (See **Figure 9.5**.)

Why would the government try to decrease economic output? The government sometimes tries

to slow down the economy to fight inflation, a rapid increase in prices.

When demand exceeds supply, producers respond by raising output and raising prices. If producers cannot expand production enough, they will raise their prices, which can lead to high inflation. Left unchecked, inflation cuts into consumers' purchasing power and discourages economic growth and stability.

Contractionary fiscal policy aimed at slowing the growth of total output generally involves two alternatives. The Federal government can decrease spending or raise taxes—or both.

If the federal government spends less, or buys fewer goods and services, it triggers a chain of events that may lead to slower GDP growth. As **Figure 9.6** indicates, government spending represents a significant share of GDP. A decrease in government spending leads to a decrease in aggregate demand, because the government is buying less than before. Decreased demand tends to lower prices. According to the law of supply, lower prices encourage suppliers to cut their production and possibly lay off workers. Lower production lowers the growth rate of the economy and may even reduce GDP.

This chain of events is the exact opposite of what happens when the government increases spending. The government uses the same tools to try to influence

Effects of Expansionary Fiscal Policy

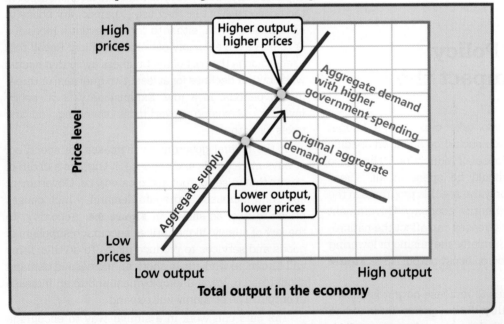

>> **Figure 9.4** The goal of expansionary fiscal policy is to achieve higher aggregate demand—and higher output and prices. **Analyze Graphs** In this graph, what causes the effect of increased demand, output, and prices?

▶ **Interactive Chart**

To contract the economy, government buys fewer goods and services.

Companies that sell goods and services to the government have lower profits and less money available to pay workers.

Workers and investors have less money to spend on goods and services.

Decreased demand tends to lead to lower prices, forcing suppliers to cut production and lay off workers.

The growth rate of the economy slows.

>> **Figure 9.5 Infer** What can you infer about the amount of goods and services purchased by government from outside companies?

the economy in both cases, but in different ways and with very different goals.

When the federal government raises taxes, individuals have less money to spend on goods and services or to save for the future. Firms keep less of their profits and have less money to invest in land, labor, and capital. As a result of these decreases in demand, prices tend to fall. Producers of goods and suppliers of services tend to cut production. This slows the growth of GDP.

? IDENTIFY CENTRAL IDEAS What are the two main tools that government uses to implement fiscal policy?

The Limits and Costs of Fiscal Policy

Fiscal policy can be a powerful tool that can keep the economy in balance, but it can also be clumsy and difficult to put into practice. In addition, fiscal policy decisions come at a cost.

The Reality of Entitlements Increasing or decreasing federal spending is not an easy task. Many spending categories in the federal budget are entitlements that are fixed by law. Over half the federal budget is set aside for programs such as Medicaid, Social Security, and veterans' benefits before Congress even begins

the budget process. Government cannot change spending for entitlements under current law. Also, it must continue to pay interest on the large debt the nation has incurred. As a result, significant change in federal spending generally must come from the smaller discretionary spending part of the federal budget. This gives government little fiscal leeway.

Knowing the Future Governments use fiscal policy to prevent big changes in the level of GDP. Despite the statistics, however, it is difficult to know the current state of the economy. No one can know for sure how quickly the business cycle will move from one stage to the next, nor can anyone identify exactly where in the cycle the economy is at any particular time.

Predicting future economic performance is even more difficult.

If economists forecast well, then the lag would not matter. They could tell Congress in advance what the appropriate fiscal policy is. But economists do not forecast well. Most economists, for example, badly under predicted both the rise in unemployment in 1981 and the strength of the recovery that began in late 1982. Absent accurate forecasts, attempts to use discretionary fiscal policy to counteract business cycle fluctuations are as likely to do harm as good.

—David N. Weil, Professor of Economics at Brown University

Delayed Results Although changes in fiscal policy affect the economy, changes take time. Once officials decide to change fiscal policy, they have to put the changes into effect within the federal budget, which takes more than a year to develop. Finally, they have to wait for the changes to affect the economy.

As **Figure 9.7** shows, by the time a new policy takes effect, the economy might be moving in the opposite direction. Government could propose massive public spending on highways and other infrastructure in the middle of a recession, only to have the economy recover before construction begins. In cases like this, fiscal policy would only strengthen the new trend, instead of correcting the original problem. If government continued to spend freely on highways in the middle of a recovery, it could lead to high inflation and a labor shortage.

Political Pressures The President and the members of Congress, who develop the federal budget and the federal government's fiscal policy, are elected officials. If they wish to be reelected, they must make decisions that please the people who elect them—not necessarily decisions that are good for the overall economy.

For example, government officials have an incentive to boost spending or lower taxes. Expansionary fiscal policies are often popular with voters. Government spending benefits firms that receive government contracts and individuals who receive direct government payments. Lower taxes leave more disposable income in people's pockets.

On the other hand, contractionary fiscal policy, which decreases government spending or raises taxes, is often unpopular. Firms and individuals who expect income from the government are not happy when the income is reduced. No one likes to pay higher taxes, even when the revenue is spent on a highly valued good or service.

Coordinating Fiscal Policy For fiscal policy to be effective, various branches and levels of government must work together. For example, if the federal government is pursuing contractionary policy, state and local governments should, ideally, pursue a similar fiscal policy. However, this does not always happen. For example, after the federal government cut income taxes in 2001 and 2003, many state and local

2010 GDP (in billions of dollars)

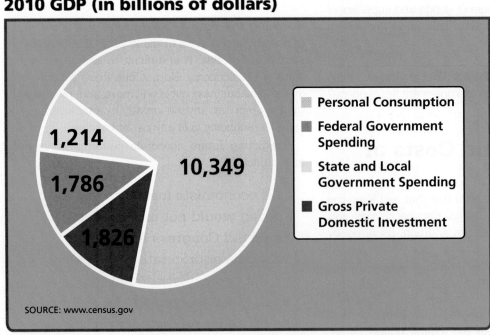

Personal Consumption

Federal Government Spending

State and Local Government Spending

Gross Private Domestic Investment

1,214

1,786

1,826

10,349

SOURCE: www.census.gov

>> **Figure 9.6 Analyze Graphs** What percentage of GDP did spending by federal and state and local governments amount to in the year shown?

Delayed Results and Fiscal Policy

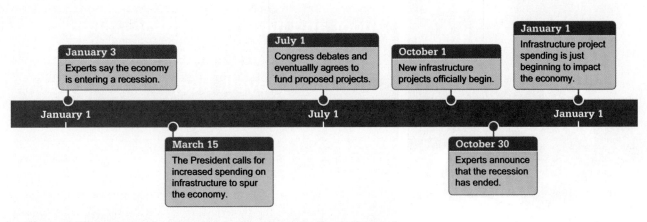

January 3
Experts say the economy is entering a recession.

March 15
The President calls for increased spending on infrastructure to spur the economy.

July 1
Congress debates and eventuallly agrees to fund proposed projects.

October 1
New infrastructure projects officially begin.

January 1
Infrastructure project spending is just beginning to impact the economy.

October 30
Experts announce that the recession has ended.

January 1 — July 1 — January 1

>> **Figure 9.7** Using fictional events, this timeline illustrates the challenge of mounting a fiscal response to an economic downturn. **Summarize** Summarize the difficulty with fiscal policy that is represented by the events on this timeline.

governments raised income and property taxes in order to fund their budgets and avoid deep spending cuts. The federal government was willing to cut taxes and run a deficit in poor economic times, but most state and local governments were legally forbidden to do so.

Businesspeople, politicians, and economists often disagree about how well the economy is performing and what the goals of fiscal policy should be. Also, different regions of the country can experience different economic conditions. Some states may have high unemployment while others face a labor shortage.

In addition, in order for the federal government's fiscal policy to be effective, it must also be coordinated with the monetary policy of the Federal Reserve. You will learn more about monetary policy elsewhere.

Governments must recognize that short-term effects of fiscal policy will differ from long-term effects. These differing effects must be considered in evaluating the overall cost of any fiscal policy. For example, a tax cut or increased spending may give a quick boost to production and to employment. However, as the economy returns to full employment, continued high levels of government spending or increased market spending may lead to high inflation and interest rates.

Similarly, an increase in taxes or fees or a decrease in government spending may "cool" the economy and avoid inflation. In the short run, reduced government spending and higher taxes may even contribute to a recession. But at the same time, such fiscal policies may create opportunities for private investment spending that could lead to higher economic growth in the long run. In this way, slow growth or even recession in the short term can lead to prosperity and more jobs in the future.

? **EXPRESS PROBLEMS CLEARLY** What challenge do policy-makers face when contemplating large changes in spending levels for the federal budget?

ASSESSMENT

1. **Define** What is fiscal policy?

2. **Express Ideas Clearly** How does the government use the federal budget to implement its fiscal policy?

3. **Apply Concepts** Describe a hypothetical government budget that employs an expansionary policy.

4. **Summarize** Explain how fiscal policy decisions impact the economy.

5. **Identify** Identify at least one cost and one benefit of using fiscal policy as a tool to pursue the goal of economic growth.

>> During the Great Depression, government spending helped people like the family shown here. **Generate Explanations** Why do you think some people turn to the government for aid when times are difficult?

▶ **Interactive Flipped Video**

>> Objectives

Compare and contrast classical economics and demand-side economics.

Analyze the importance of John Maynard Keynes and his economic theories.

Explain the basic principles of supply-side economics and the importance of Milton Friedman.

Analyze the impact of fiscal policy decisions on the economy of the United States.

>> Key Terms

classical economics
productive capacity
demand-side
  economics
Keynesian
  economics
multiplier effect
automatic stabilizer
supply-side
  economics
deficit spending
John Maynard
  Keynes
Arthur Laffer
Milton Friedman
John Kenneth
  Galbraith

Fiscal Policy Options

Classical Economics

During the Great Depression, it was clear that millions of people needed help. Less clear was the answer to this question: Who should provide it? A factory owner? The local supermarket? A religious institution or maybe the neighbors? What about the government? Would *you* expect the government to spend large amounts of money to give your father or mother—as well as thousands of other people—a job?

Nowadays, many of us are used to the idea that the government might use its spending power to stimulate the economy. But at the time of the Depression, this was a radical new idea. And today, there are plenty of people who think that there are better ways the government can stimulate the economy than by spending. In this text, you will look at two very different fiscal policy options the government can pursue.

In a free market, people act in their own self-interest, causing prices to rise or fall so that supply and demand will always return to equilibrium. This idea that free markets regulate themselves is central to the school of thought known as **classical economics**. Adam Smith, David Ricardo, and Thomas Malthus all contributed basic ideas to this school. For well over a century, classical economics dominated economic theory and government policies. Some aspects of classical economic thought are still widely followed today.

The Great Depression, which began in 1929, challenged the classical theory. Prices fell over several years, so demand should have increased enough to stimulate production as consumers took advantage of low prices.

Instead, demand also fell as people lost their jobs and bank failures wiped out their savings. **Figure 9.9** highlights the widespread economic devastation. According to classical economics, the market should have reached equilibrium, with full employment. But it didn't, and millions suffered from unemployment and other hardships. Farmers lost their farms because corn was selling for seven cents a bushel and beef for two and a half cents a pound. Yet even with these low prices, many people were too poor to buy food.

The Great Depression highlighted a problem with classical economics: It did not address how long it would take for the market to return to equilibrium. Classical economists recognized that it could take some time and looked for equilibrium to reestablish itself "in the long run"—over time. One economist, who was not satisfied with the idea of simply waiting for the economy to recover on its own, commented, "In the long run we are all dead." That economist was **John Maynard Keynes** (pronounced CANES).

? IDENTIFY What event challenged the dominance of the classical economics school of thought?

Keynesian Economics

British economist John Maynard Keynes developed a new theory of economics to explain the Great Depression. Keynes presented his ideas in 1936 in a book called *The General Theory of Employment, Interest, and Money*. He wanted to develop a comprehensive explanation of macroeconomic forces. Such an explanation, he argued, should tell economists and politicians how to get out of economic crises like the Great Depression. In sharp contrast to classical economics, Keynes wanted to give government a tool it could use immediately to boost the economy in the short run. His theories have had a huge impact on the changing role of government in the U.S. free enterprise system.

Keynes Versus Classical Economics Classical economists had always looked at how the equilibrium of supply and demand applied to *individual products*. In contrast, Keynes focused on the workings of the economy *as a whole*.

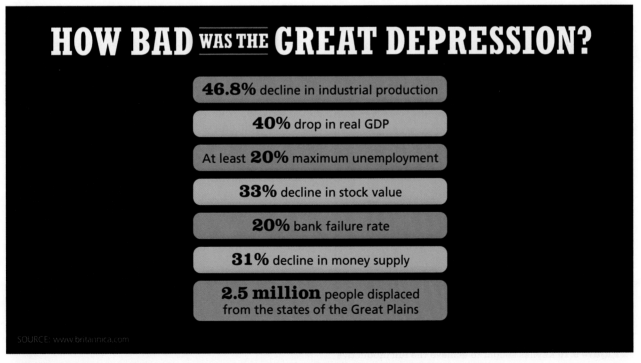

HOW BAD WAS THE GREAT DEPRESSION?

46.8% decline in industrial production

40% drop in real GDP

At least **20%** maximum unemployment

33% decline in stock value

20% bank failure rate

31% decline in money supply

2.5 million people displaced from the states of the Great Plains

SOURCE: www.britannica.com

>> **Figure 9.9** Classical economics taught that a struggling economy would recover on its own. But the Great Depression lasted for many years. **Analyze Data** Why do you think the economy took so long to recover during the Great Depression?

Keynes looked at the productive capacity of the entire economy. **Productive capacity**, often called full-employment output, is the maximum output that an economy can sustain over a period of time without increasing inflation. Keynes attempted to answer the difficult question posed by the Great Depression: Why does actual production in an economy sometimes fall far short of its productive capacity?

Keynes argued that the Depression continued because neither consumers nor businesses had an incentive to spend enough to cause an increase in production. After all, why would a company spend money to increase production when demand for its products was falling? How could consumers significantly increase demand when they had barely enough money to survive?

The only way to end the Depression, Keynes thought, was to find a way to boost aggregate demand. Economists who agreed with the idea that demand drives the economy developed a school of thought known as **demand-side economics**. They asked themselves this question: Who could spend enough to spur demand and revitalize production?

Changing Government's Role in the Economy

Keynes thought that the answer to that question was: the federal government. (See **Figure 9.10**.) He reasoned that in the early 1930s, only the federal government still had the resources to spend enough to affect the whole economy.

The government could, in effect, make up for the drop in private spending by buying goods and services on its own. This, Keynes argued, would encourage production and increase employment. Then, as people went back to work, they would spend their wages on more goods and services, leading to even higher levels of production. This ever-expanding cycle would carry the economy out of the Great Depression. Once the crisis was over, Keynes believed, the government could step back and reduce its spending.

These ideas form the core of Keynes's approach to resolving problems with the economy. **Keynesian economics** uses demand-side theory as the basis for encouraging government action to help the economy. In other words, Keynesian economics proposes that government can and should use fiscal policy to help the economy. Keynes argued that fiscal policy can combat the two fundamental macroeconomic problems: periods of recession and periods of inflation.

Avoiding Recession The federal government, Keynes argued, should keep track of the total level of spending by consumers, businesses, and government. If total spending begins to fall far below the level required to keep the economy running at full capacity, the government should watch out for the possibility of recession.

The government can respond by increasing its own spending until spending by the private sector returns to a higher level. Or it can cut taxes so that spending and investment by consumers and businesses increase. Raising government spending and cutting taxes are expansionary fiscal policies.

After he was elected President in 1932, Franklin D. Roosevelt carried out expansionary fiscal policies. His New Deal put people to work—whether planting forests, building dams and schools, or painting murals. The federal government paid for all these programs.

Classical economists criticized these programs. Even today, many people argue that instead of creating new jobs, such public works projects only shift employment from the private to the public sector. The dispute over Keynes's ideas is generally reflected today in the philosophies of the two political parties. Republicans generally have been associated with using tax cuts to stimulate the economy. Democrats generally have favored more expansive government programs to stimulate the economy.

Keynes and Inflation Keynes also argued that the government could use a contractionary fiscal policy to

Keynesian Economics

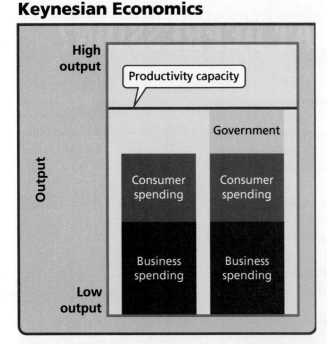

>> **Figure 9.10** Keynes sought to achieve the full productive capacity of the economy. **Analyze Graphs** According to Keynes, what could fill the gap between low output and full productive capacity?

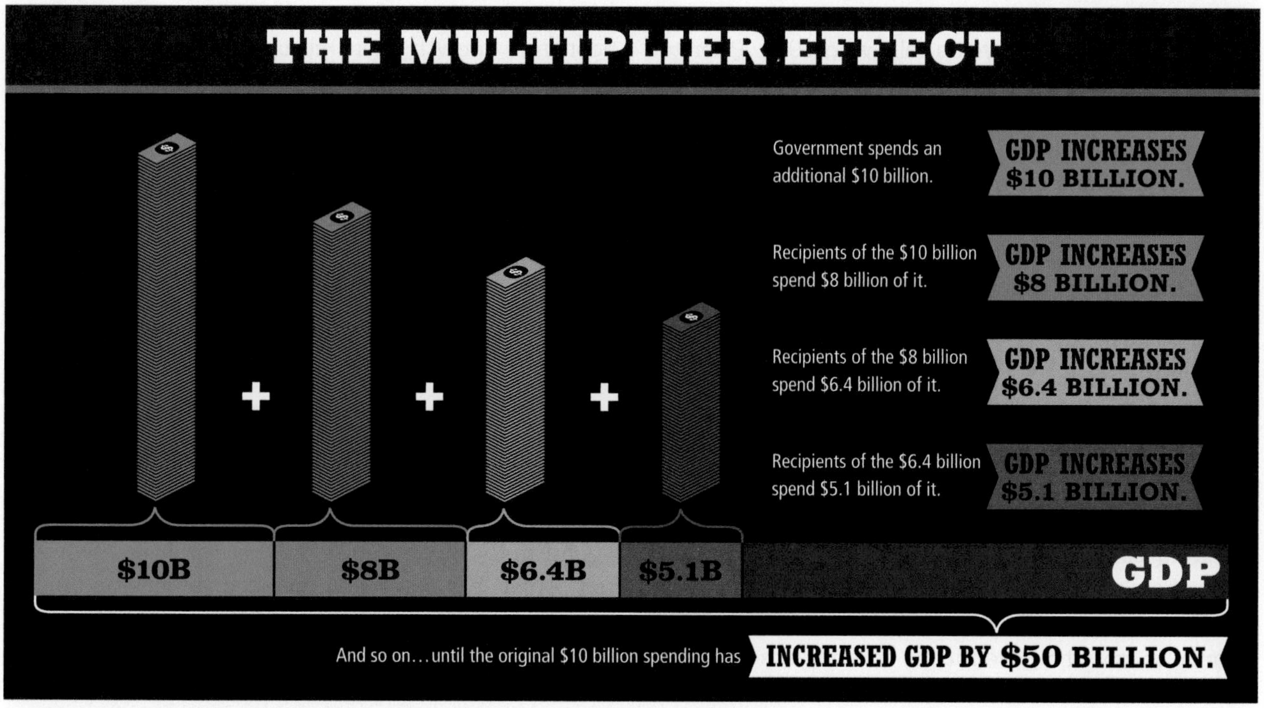

THE MULTIPLIER EFFECT

Government spends an additional $10 billion. → **GDP INCREASES $10 BILLION.**

Recipients of the $10 billion spend $8 billion of it. → **GDP INCREASES $8 BILLION.**

Recipients of the $8 billion spend $6.4 billion of it. → **GDP INCREASES $6.4 BILLION.**

Recipients of the $6.4 billion spend $5.1 billion of it. → **GDP INCREASES $5.1 BILLION.**

$10B + $8B + $6.4B + $5.1B = GDP

And so on…until the original $10 billion spending has **INCREASED GDP BY $50 BILLION.**

>> **Figure 9.11** The multiplier effect helps explain how government spending boosts the economy. **Synthesize** Explain how the multiplier effect supports Keynesian theory.

prevent inflation or reduce its severity. The government can reduce inflation either by increasing taxes or by reducing its own spending. Both of these actions decrease overall demand.

The Multiplier Effect Fiscal policy, although difficult to control, is a powerful tool. The key to its power is the multiplier effect. The **multiplier effect** in fiscal policy is the idea that each dollar spent or not taxed by government creates a change much greater than one dollar in the national income. In other words, the effects of changes in fiscal policy are multiplied.

Suppose the federal government finds that business investment is dropping. To prevent a recession, in the next budget the government decides to spend an extra $10 billion to stimulate the economy. How will this affect the economy?

With this government spending, demand, income, and GDP will increase by $10 billion. After all, if the government buys an extra $10 billion of goods and services, then an extra $10 billion of goods and services have been produced. However, the GDP could increase by more than $10 billion. Here's why:

The businesses that sold the $10 billion in goods and services to the government have earned an additional $10 billion. These businesses will spend their additional earnings on wages, raw materials, and investment, sending money to workers, other suppliers, and stockholders. What will the recipients do with this money? They will spend part of it. Suppose they spend 80 percent of it, or $8 billion. The businesses that benefit from this second round of spending will then pass it back to households and other businesses, who will again spend 80 percent of it, or $6.4 billion. The next round will add an additional $5.1 billion to the economy, and so on. This phenomenon is illustrated in **Figure 9.11**.

In this example, when all of the rounds of spending are added up, the initial spending of $10 billion adds about $50 billion to GDP. So, fiscal policy initiatives can have a bigger kick than the initial amount spent. Note, though, that not all spending multiplies at the same rate. For example, the multiplier effect on borrowed money may be greatly reduced.

The Role of Automatic Stabilizers Fiscal policy is used to achieve many economic goals. One of the most important things that fiscal policy can achieve is a more stable economy. A stable economy is one in which there are no rapid changes in economic indicators, which include stock prices, interest rates, and manufacturers' new orders of capital goods. What's more, set up properly, fiscal policy can come close to stabilizing the economy *automatically*.

Figure 9.12 shows how real GDP in the United States changed in the years following 1930. Prior to World War II, there were often large changes in GDP from year to year. Although GDP still fluctuates, these fluctuations have been smaller than they were before the war. Economic growth has been much more stable in the United States in the last 70 or so years.

Why did this happen? After the war, federal taxes and spending on transfer payments—two key tools of fiscal policy—increased sharply. National taxes and transfer payments, or transfers of cash from the government to consumers, stabilize economic growth. When national income is high, the government collects more in taxes and pays out less in transfer payments. Both of these actions take money away from consumers, and therefore reduce spending. This decrease in spending balances out the increase in spending that results from rising income in a healthy economy.

The opposite is also true. When income in the country is low, the government collects less in taxes and pays out more in transfer payments.

Both actions increase the amount of money held by consumers, and thus increase spending. This increase in spending balances out the decrease in spending resulting from decreased income. **Figure 9.13** shows the recent fluctuations in one type of transfer payment—food stamps.

Taxes and transfer payments do not eliminate changes in the rate of growth of GDP, but they do make these changes smaller. Because they help make economic growth more stable, they are known as stabilizers. Policymakers do not have to make changes in taxes and transfer payments for them to have their stabilizing effect. Taxes and most transfer payments are tied to the GDP and to personal income, so they change automatically. Thus, they are called **automatic stabilizers**—tools of fiscal policy that increase or decrease automatically depending on changes in GDP and personal income.

Some stabilizers are no longer automatic. The former Aid to Families with Dependent Children (AFDC), often called welfare, lost its entitlement status in 1996 and was renamed Temporary Assistance for Needy Families (TANF). Now the federal government gives the states a set amount of money each year to spend as they wish. However, the stabilizer effect was not completely lost. When the economy boomed in the late 1990s, state spending on TANF fell.

? **IDENTIFY MAIN IDEAS** How did Keynes propose to end the Great Depression?

Supply-Side Economics

Another school of economic thought promotes a different direction for fiscal policy. **Supply-side economics** is based on the idea that the supply of goods drives

Annual Change in GDP, 1930–2012

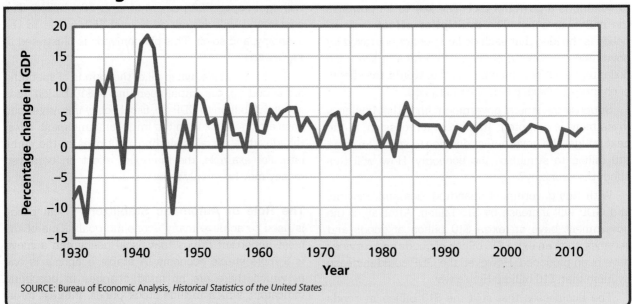

SOURCE: Bureau of Economic Analysis, *Historical Statistics of the United States*

>> **Figure 9.12** The U.S. economy has experienced regular ups and downs since 1930.
Analyze Graphs How do the years after World War II show the effect of automatic stabilizers?

Food Stamp Recipients, 1990–2012

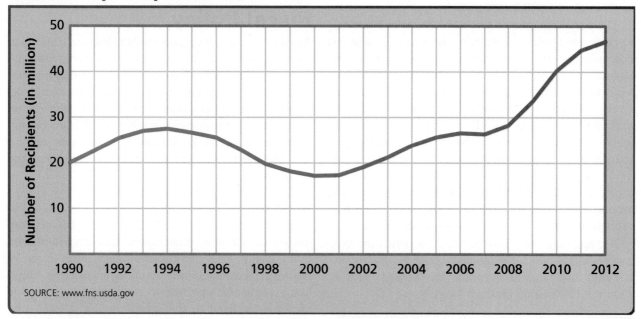

SOURCE: www.fns.usda.gov

>> **Figure 9.13** The number of food-stamp recipients fell during the economic growth of the mid-1990s and rose during a recession that began in 2007. **Analyze Graphs** How do macroeconomic developments affect the number of people requiring food-stamp assistance?

the economy. Whereas Keynesian economics tries to encourage economic growth by increasing aggregate demand, supply-side economics relies on increasing aggregate supply. It does this by focusing on taxes. In recent years, supply-side economics has had a significant impact on the U.S. economy and free enterprise system.

Analyzing the Laffer Curve Supply-side economists believe that taxes have a strong negative impact on economic output. They often use the Laffer curve, named after the economist **Arthur Laffer**, to illustrate the effects of taxes. The Laffer curve (**Figure 9.14**) presents a supply-side view of the relationship between the tax rate and the total tax revenue that the government collects. The total revenue depends on both the tax rate and the health of the economy. The Laffer curve suggests that high tax rates may not bring in much revenue if they cause economic activity to decrease.

Suppose the government imposes a tax on the wages of workers. If the tax rate is zero, as at point *a* on the graph, the government will collect no revenue, although the economy will benefit from the lack of taxes. As the government raises the tax rate, it starts to collect some revenue. You can see this change in **Figure 9.14**.

From a 0 percent tax rate (point *a*) to a 50 percent tax rate on the curve (point *b*), rising tax rates begin to discourage some people from working as many hours as they might, and hinder companies from investing and increasing production. The net effect of a higher tax rate and a slightly lower tax base is still an increase in revenue.

At tax rates higher than 50 percent, the decrease in workers' effort is so large that the higher tax rate actually decreases total tax revenue. In other words, high rates of taxation will eventually discourage so many people from working that tax revenues will fall. In the extreme case of a 100 percent tax rate, no one would want to work! In this case, shown at point *c* on the curve, the government would collect no revenue.

The Relationship Between Taxes and Output
The heart of the supply-side argument is that a tax cut increases total employment so much that the government actually collects more in taxes at the new, lower tax rate. Suppose the initial tax on labor is $3 an hour, and the typical worker works 30 hours per week, paying a total of $90 in taxes each week. If the government cuts the tax on labor to $2 an hour, and the worker responds by working 50 hours per week, the worker will pay $100 in taxes a week, an increase of $10. **Figure 9.15** shows the increase in government

revenues during a time when government was at least partly following supply-side policies.

The economic growth of the 1980s was impressive, but it is hard to pin down the role that U.S. supply-side economic policies played in this outcome. Some economists argue that although a tax cut encourages some workers to work more hours, the end result is a relatively small increase in the number of hours worked. Take the example of the worker above. These economists would say that if the tax cut increased the hours worked from 30 hours to 35 hours, the worker would pay only $70 in taxes ($2 per hour times 35 hours), down from $90 ($3 per hour times 30 hours). In general, these economists argue, taxpayers do not react strongly enough to tax cuts to increase tax revenue.

As you can see, there is much debate over the relationship between tax rates and output. In addition to being an economic question, this debate plays a major role in American politics today.

? CHECK UNDERSTANDING How does the supply-side economics theory link taxation to employment levels?

The Recent History of U.S. Fiscal Policy

As you recall, Keynes presented his ideas at a time when the world economy was engulfed in a severe economic downturn. President Herbert Hoover, a strong believer in classical economics, thought that the economy was basically sound and would return to equilibrium on its own, without government interference. His successor, President Franklin D. Roosevelt, was more willing to increase government spending to help boost the economy.

World War II Keynes's theory was fully tested in the United States during World War II. As the country geared up for war, government spending increased dramatically. The government spent large sums of money to feed soldiers and equip them with everything from warplanes to rifles to medical supplies. This money was given to the private sector in exchange for goods. Just as Keynesian economics predicted, the additional demand for goods and services moved the country sharply out of the Great Depression and toward full productive capacity.

The enormous government spending during the war boosted output and greatly reduced unemployment. But the benefits of this U.S. economic policy also had costs. Until the presidency of Franklin Roosevelt, the

Laffer Curve

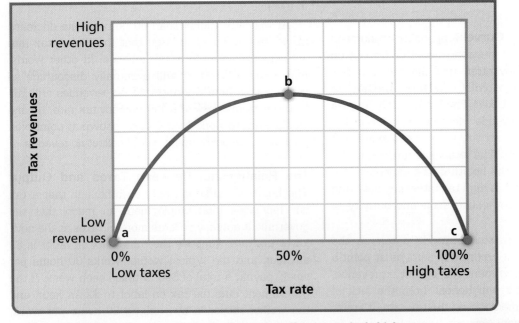

>> **Figure 9.14** The Laffer curve shows the theoretical effect increasingly higher tax rates have on tax revenues. **Analyze Graphs** According to the Laffer curve, what do both a very high and a very low tax rate produce?

Federal Revenue, 1975–1992

YEAR	REVENUE (IN BILLIONS OF DOLLARS)	YEAR	REVENUE (IN BILLIONS OF DOLLARS)
1975	279.09	1984	666.44
1976	298.06	1985	734.04
1977	355.56	1986	769.16
1978	399.56	1987	854.29
1979	463.30	1988	909.24
1980	517.11	1989	991.11
1981	599.27	1990	1,031.96
1982	617.77	1991	1,054.99
1983	600.56	1992	1,091.21

SOURCE: Office of Management and Budget

>> **Figure 9.15** Federal revenue clearly rose throughout the period shown, even though the 1980s was a decade of tax cuts. **Analyze Data** Do the data here support the idea of supply-side economics? Explain.

Interactive Chart

federal government had sought to balance its budget, spending no more than it received in revenue. During the New Deal and World War II, expenditures exceeded revenues, a situation known as **deficit spending**. To finance deficit spending, the government has to borrow money, for which it pays interest. This represents a financial cost as well as an opportunity cost—the money used to pay interest cannot be used for other purposes.

Postwar Keynesian Policy After World War II ended, Congress created the Council of Economic Advisers (CEA). Made up of three respected economists, the CEA advised the President on economic policy.

Between 1945 and 1960, the U.S. economy was generally healthy and growing, despite a few minor recessions. The last recession continued into the term of President John F. Kennedy, with unemployment reaching a level of 6.7 percent. Kennedy's chief financial policy adviser, chairperson of the CEA Walter Heller, thought that the economy was below its productive capacity. He convinced Kennedy that tax cuts would stimulate demand and bring the economy closer to full productive capacity.

As **Figure 9.16** shows, the highest marginal tax rate on individual income was about 90 percent in the early 1960s—compared with a top rate of 39.6 in 2013.

Kennedy proposed tax cuts, both because he agreed with Heller and because tax cuts are popular.

A version of Kennedy's tax cuts was enacted in 1964, under President Lyndon Johnson. At the same time, the Vietnam War raised government spending. Over two years, consumption and GDP increased by more than 4 percent a year. There is no way to prove that the tax cut caused this growth, but the result was generally what Keynesian economics predicted.

Keynesian economics was used often in the 1960s and 1970s. One Keynesian economist, **John Kenneth Galbraith,** greatly influenced national policies. Galbraith, a strong supporter of public spending, helped develop the far-reaching—and enormously costly—social welfare programs that lay at the heart of President Johnson's vision of a Great Society. (See **Figure 9.17**.)

Supply-Side Policy in the 1980s During the late 1970s, with Keynesian fiscal policy in place, unemployment and inflation rates soared. When Ronald Reagan became President in 1981, he vowed to cut taxes and spending. An "anti-Keynesian," Reagan did not believe that government should spend its way out of a recession:

Government spending has become
so extensive that it contributes to the

economic problems it was designed to cure. More government intervention in the economy cannot possibly be a solution to our economic problems.

—Ronald Reagan, White House Report on the Program for Economic Recovery, 1981

Reagan instituted policies based on supply-side economics, a theory promoted by economists such as George Gilder. Among Reagan's advisers was **Milton Friedman**, a former professor of economics. Friedman strongly supported individual freedom and pushed for more laissez-faire policies—hallmarks of classical and supply-side economics. He also supported a constitutional amendment to balance the federal budget. In 1981, Reagan proposed a tax cut that reduced taxes by 25 percent over three years. In a short time, the economy recovered and flourished. Still, tax cuts plus an expanded defense budget led to further deficit spending, just as following Keynesian policy would have done.

Under the next few Presidents, the federal government spent much more money than it took in. As you will read in the next lesson, this gap caused increasing concern among economists and policymakers.

A Return to Keynes In late 2008, the United States was hit with what many economists believed was the worst financial crisis since the Great Depression. A number of major financial institutions failed. Credit became harder to get, consumer spending dropped, and unemployment rose. The crisis occurred in the midst of what news commentators named the Great Recession, an economic downturn that had begun in December 2007.

In November 2008, voters elected a new President, Barack Obama. He promised to take firm action to stimulate the economy. Obama signed a stimulus bill in February 2009 that aimed to boost demand and create jobs. The $840 billion package included contracts, grants, and loans for education, transportation, and infrastructure projects. It also included a set of tax cuts and additional entitlement payments. To many observers, such proposals seemed to signal a shift back to a Keynesian fiscal policy, as in the New Deal.

Obama's economic stimulus program received mixed reviews. The economy emerged from the recession in June 2009, but growth remained unsteady into 2013. By the middle of that year, the unemployment rate had fallen to 7.4 percent from a high of 10 percent, but that left about 12 million Americans looking for work. Some of Obama's advisers, following Keynesian principles, insisted that the government should have injected much more money into the economy to encourage sustained growth. However, concerns

Top Marginal Tax Rate, 1925–Present

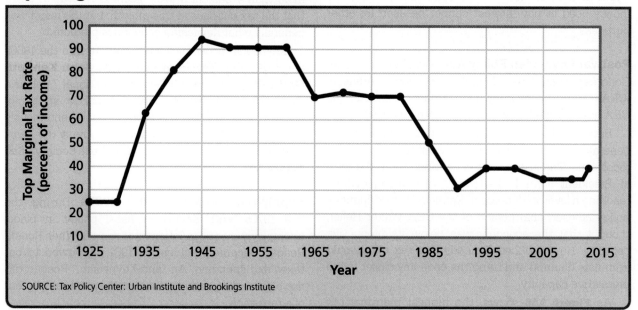

SOURCE: Tax Policy Center: Urban Institute and Brookings Institute

>> **Figure 9.16** The top marginal tax rates—rates affecting the highest incomes—have varied widely over the last century. **Analyze Graphs** What has been the general trend in the top marginal tax rate since 1945?

Great Society Programs

Community Action Program	Focused on helping the urban poor become self-sufficient	**Model Cities Program**	Funded urban redevelopment
Head Start	Gave underprivileged preschoolers the early learning necessary to be prepared for kindergarten	**National Endowment for the Arts and Humanities**	Funded artists and galleries for the cultural betterment of society
Job Corps	Provided vocational training to the underprivileged	**Neighborhood Youth Corps**	Gave poor urban youths work experience and encouraged continued education
Medicare	Ensured health care services to people age 65 and older and others with certain disabilities	**Upward Bound**	Helped poor high school students get a college education
Medicaid	Provided medical insurance for low-income people	**Volunteers in Service to America**	A domestic Peace Corps aimed at helping communities in the U.S.

SOURCE: www.ushistory.org

>> **Figure 9.17** Publicly funded Great Society programs served all age groups but focused mainly on the poor and underprivileged. **Predict Consequences** How do you think the Great Society affected the federal budget?

in Congress about the escalating deficit undercut arguments for pursuing further expansionary fiscal policies.

? IDENTIFY What Keynesian fiscal policy tool did President Kennedy use?

ASSESSMENT

1. **Interpret** When John Maynard Keynes said, "In the long run we are all dead," what problem of classical economics was he pointing out?

2. **Analyze Information** What might be one cost and one benefit of Keynesian economic policies?

3. **Identify Cause and Effect** Why might cutting taxes increase economic output and total employment?

4. **Support Ideas With Evidence** What ideas of Milton Friedman are reflected in the policies of Ronald Reagan?

5. **Draw Conclusions** Did Keynesian fiscal policy help end the Great Recession of 2007–2009? Explain your answer.

If you have used a credit card, you might have some idea how easy it is to spend money you don't have. If you fail to pay the credit card bill in full each month, the high interest rate may mean that the amount you owe just keeps increasing. Soon you may face a mountain of debt.

>> When this picture was taken in early 2013, the national debt was $16.5 trillion—on its way to topping $17 trillion by the end of the year.

Interactive Flipped Video

>> **Objectives**

Explain the importance of balancing the budget.

Analyze the impact of fiscal policy decisions on the nation's economy.

Summarize the way budget deficits add to the national debt.

Identify how political leaders have tried to control the deficit.

>> **Key Terms**

budget surplus
budget deficit
Treasury bill
Treasury note
Treasury bond
national debt
crowding-out effect

The National Debt and Deficits

Budget Surpluses and Deficits

The federal government is no stranger to spending more than it has. The government uses spending as a fiscal policy tool to improve the economy.

The basic tool of fiscal policy is the federal budget. It is made up of two fundamental parts: revenue (taxes) and expenditures (spending programs). When the federal government's revenues equal its expenditures in any particular fiscal year, the federal government has a balanced budget.

In reality, the federal budget is almost never balanced. Usually, it is either running a surplus or a deficit. A **budget surplus** occurs in any year when revenues exceed expenditures. In other words, there is more money going into the Treasury than coming out of it. A **budget deficit** occurs in any year when expenditures exceed revenues. In other words, there is more money coming out of the Treasury than going into it. Deficits have become a common characteristic of the economy in recent decades. **Figure 9.18** illustrates this development clearly.

Assume the federal government starts with a balanced budget. If the government decreases expenditures without changing anything else, it will run a budget surplus. Similarly, if it increases taxes—revenues—without changing anything else, it will run a surplus.

This analysis also explains budget deficits. If the government increases expenditures without changing anything else, it will run a deficit.

Similarly, if it decreases taxes without changing anything else, it will run a deficit. The deficit can grow or shrink because of forces beyond the government's control. Surpluses and deficits can be very large figures. The largest deficit, in 2009, was over $1.4 trillion.

Dealing With Deficits When the government runs a deficit, it is because it did not take in enough revenue to cover its expenses for the year. When this happens, the government must find a way to pay for the extra expenditures. There are two basic actions the government can take to do so.

Creating Money The government can create new money to pay salaries for its workers and benefits for citizens. Traditionally, governments simply printed the bills they needed. Today, the government can create money electronically by actions that effectively deposit money in people's bank accounts. The effect is the same. This approach works for relatively small deficits but can cause severe problems when there are large deficits. What are these problems?

When the government creates more money, it increases the amount of money in circulation. This increases the demand for goods and services and can increase output. But once the economy reaches full employment, output cannot increase. The increase in money will mean that there are more dollars but the same amount of goods and services. Prices will rise so that a greater amount of money will be needed to purchase the same amount of goods and services. In other words, prices go up, and the result is inflation.

Covering very large deficits by printing more money can cause hyperinflation. This happened in Germany and Russia after World War I, in Brazil and Argentina in the 1980s, and in Ukraine in the 1990s. If the United States experienced hyperinflation, a shirt that cost $30 in June might cost $50 in July, $80 in August, and $400 in December!

Borrowing Money The U.S. federal government usually does not resort to creating money to cover a budget deficit. Instead, it borrows money. The government commonly borrows money by selling bonds. A bond is a type of loan: a promise to repay money in the future, with interest. Consumers and businesses buy bonds from the government. The government thus has the money to cover its budget deficit. In return, the purchasers of the bonds earn interest on their investment over time.

Budget Surpluses and Deficits, 1950–2012

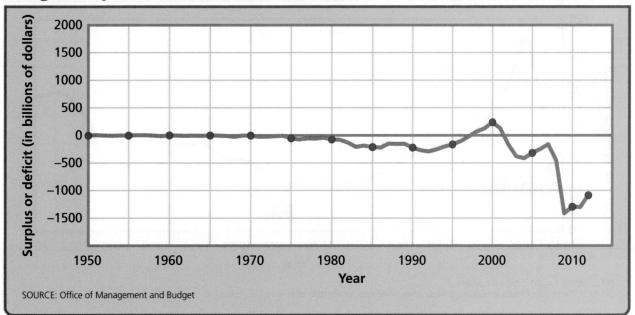

SOURCE: Office of Management and Budget

>> **Figure 9.18** Budgets that followed the gray horizontal line on this graph would be balanced. **Analyze Graphs** Write a brief summary of this graph and the story it tells about surpluses and deficits from 1950 to 2012.

United States Savings Bonds ("EE Bonds") allow millions of Americans to lend small amounts of money to the federal government. In return, they earn interest on the bonds for up to 30 years. Other common forms of government borrowing are Treasury bills, notes, and bonds. **Treasury bills** are short-term bonds that have maturity dates of 26 weeks or less. **Treasury notes** have terms of 2 to 10 years. **Treasury bonds** mature 30 years after issue.

Federal borrowing lets the government undertake more projects than it could otherwise afford. Wise borrowing allows the government to create more public goods and services. Federal borrowing, however, also has serious disadvantages.

? RECALL What is the most common method the federal government uses to pay for expenditures that exceed revenues?

Deficits and the National Debt

Like people, when the government borrows money, it goes into debt. The **national debt** is the total amount of money the federal government owes to bondholders. Every year that there is a budget deficit and the federal government borrows money to cover it, the national debt will grow.

The national debt is owed to investors who hold Treasury bonds, bills, and notes. These bonds are considered to be among the safest investments in the world. As such, they offer a secure investment for individuals and businesses. Because the United States is widely viewed as stable and trustworthy, the federal government can borrow money at a lower rate of interest than private citizens or corporations can. Lower interest rates benefit taxpayers by reducing the cost of government borrowing.

The Difference Between Deficit and Debt Many people are confused about the difference between the deficit and the debt. The deficit is the amount of money the government borrows for one budget, representing one fiscal year. The debt, on the other hand, is the sum of all the government borrowing before that time, minus the borrowings that have been repaid. Each deficit adds to the debt. Each surplus subtracts from it.

Measuring the National Debt In dollar terms, the size of the national debt is extremely large. By the end of 2013, it exceeded $17 trillion! Such a large number can best be analyzed in relation to the size of the economy as a whole. Therefore, let's look at the size of the debt as a percentage of gross domestic product (GDP) over

National Debt as a Percentage of GDP

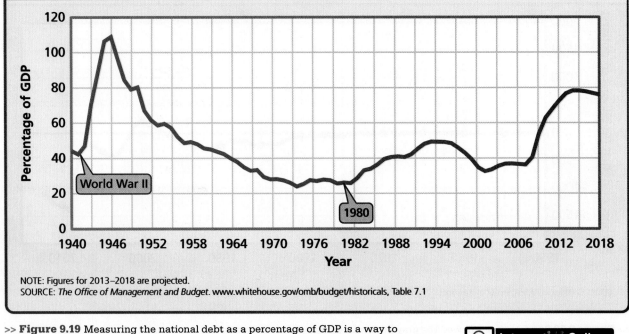

NOTE: Figures for 2013–2018 are projected.
SOURCE: *The Office of Management and Budget.* www.whitehouse.gov/omb/budget/historicals, Table 7.1

>> **Figure 9.19** Measuring the national debt as a percentage of GDP is a way to compare debt at different times in history. **Analyze Graphs** How would you describe today's debt in the context of the last 80 years?

▶ Interactive Gallery

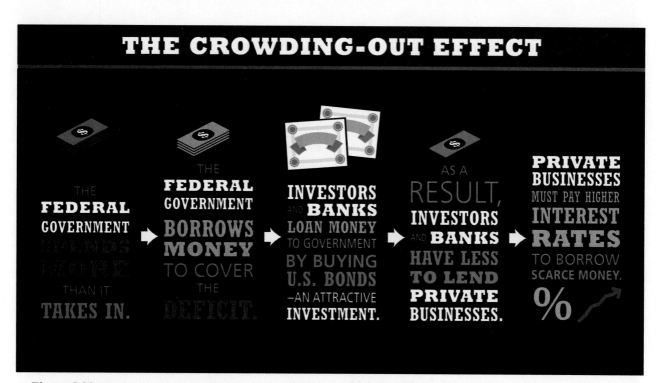

THE CROWDING-OUT EFFECT

THE **FEDERAL** GOVERNMENT SPENDS MORE THAN IT TAKES IN.

THE **FEDERAL** GOVERNMENT **BORROWS MONEY** TO COVER THE DEFICIT.

INVESTORS AND **BANKS** LOAN MONEY TO GOVERNMENT BY BUYING U.S. BONDS –AN ATTRACTIVE **INVESTMENT.**

AS A **RESULT,** INVESTORS AND **BANKS HAVE LESS TO LEND PRIVATE** BUSINESSES.

PRIVATE BUSINESSES MUST PAY HIGHER **INTEREST RATES** TO BORROW SCARCE MONEY. %

>> **Figure 9.20** This diagram shows one way excess spending can hurt the economy. **Analyze Charts** According to this diagram, what causes private businesses to be crowded out in the quest for investment?

time. This can be seen in **Figure 9.19**. Historically, debt as a percentage of GDP rises during wartime, when government spending increases faster than taxation, and it falls during peacetime.

Notice how this characteristic of the U.S. economy has changed in recent times. In the 1980s, the United States began to run a large debt, even though the country wasn't at war. The debt was in part a result of increases in spending during President Ronald Reagan's terms. In addition, the Reagan administration also cut taxes. The combined effect of higher spending and lower tax rates was several years of increased budget deficits. The impact of these fiscal policy decisions on the economy was significant. The government borrowed billions of dollars to cover the deficits, adding to the national debt. As a result, the ratio of debt to GDP grew very large for peacetime.

? **CHECK UNDERSTANDING** To whom does the government owe the national debt?

The Impact of Debt

The growth of the national debt during the Reagan administration led many to focus on the problems caused by a national debt. In general, three problems can arise from a national debt.

Problems of a National Debt The first problem with a national debt is that it reduces the funds available for businesses to invest. This is because in order to sell its bonds, the government must offer a higher interest rate. Individuals and businesses, attracted by the higher interest rates and the security of investing in the government, use their savings or profits to purchase government bonds.

Take a look at **Figure 9.20**. It explains how every dollar spent on a government bond is one fewer dollar that can be invested in private business. Less money is available for companies to expand their factories, conduct research, and develop new products, and so interest rates rise. This loss of funds for private investment caused by government borrowing is called the **crowding-out effect**.

Federal borrowing "crowds out" private borrowing by making it harder for private businesses to borrow. A national debt, then, can hurt investment and slow economic growth over the long run. In this way, fiscal policy decisions can have a significant impact on how the economy and the free enterprise system function.

The second problem with a high national debt is that the government must pay interest to bondholders. The more the government borrows, the more interest it has to pay. Paying the interest on the debt is sometimes called servicing the debt. Over time, the interest payments have become very large. About the year 2000, the federal government spent about $250 billion a year servicing the debt. Moreover, there is an opportunity cost—dollars spent servicing the debt cannot be spent on something else, such as defense, healthcare, or infrastructure.

A possible third problem involves foreign ownership of the national debt. The biggest holder of that debt is the United States government itself. The government uses bonds as a secure savings account for holding Social Security, Medicare, and other funds. But about a quarter of the debt is owned by foreign governments, including Japan, China, and the United Kingdom. Some critics of the debt fear that a country like China could use its large bond holdings as a tool to extract favors from the United States. Others disagree, arguing that foreign states own too little of the debt to cause any concern.

Other Views on the National Debt Some people insist that the national debt is not a big problem. (You can see an example of such a view in **Figure 9.21**.) Traditional Keynesian economists believe that fiscal policy is an important tool that can be used to help achieve full productive capacity. To these analysts, the benefits of a productive economy outweigh the costs of interest on national debt.

In the short term, deficit spending may help create jobs and encourage economic growth. However, a budget deficit can be an effective tool only if it is temporary. Most people agree that if the government runs large budget deficits year after year, the costs of the growing debt will eventually outweigh the benefits.

? **IDENTIFY** What are the problems of having a large national debt?

Measures to Control the Deficit

During the 1980s and the early 1990s, annual budget deficits added substantially to the national debt. Several factors frustrated lawmakers in their attempts to control the deficit. As we have seen, much of the budget consists of entitlement spending that is politically difficult to change. Another large part of the budget consists of interest that must be paid to bondholders. Finally, specific budget cuts are often opposed by interest groups.

Reducing Deficits Concerns about the budget deficits of the mid-1980s caused Congress to pass the Gramm-Rudman-Hollings Act. This law created automatic

OPPOSING VIEWS ON THE DANGER OF DEBT

"**Recent and projected growth in U.S. government debt poses a serious hazard to the nation.**

At a minimum, high levels of government debt mean substantial government resources must go toward servicing debt—to pay interest."

—J.D. Foster, Ph.D, The Heritage Foundation, June 18, 2013

"**With so many economic, political, and social problems facing us today, there is little point in focusing attention on something that is not one.**

The false fear of which I speak is the chance of US debt default."

—John T. Harvey, *Forbes*, September 10, 2012

>> **Figure 9.21** On the subject of the national debt, observers differ over the nature and extent of the threat. **Compare Points of View** Explain how these two viewpoints differ on the subject of the national debt.

across-the-board cuts in federal expenditures if the deficit exceeded a certain amount. The automatic nature of the cuts saved lawmakers from having to make difficult decisions about individual funding cuts. However, the act exempted significant portions of the budget (including interest payments and many entitlement programs such as Social Security) from the cuts.

The Supreme Court found that some parts of the Gramm-Rudman-Hollings Act were unconstitutional. Congress attempted to correct the flaws. In 1990, however, lawmakers realized that the deficit was going to be much larger than expected. Because Congress had exempted so many programs from automatic cuts, funding for nonexempt programs would be dramatically slashed.

To resolve the crisis, President George H. W. Bush and congressional leaders negotiated a new budget system that replaced Gramm-Rudman-Hollings. The 1990 Budget Enforcement Act created a "pay-as-you-go" system (also known as PAYGO). PAYGO required Congress to raise enough revenue to cover increases in direct spending that would otherwise contribute to the budget deficit. This law expired in 2002, but in 2007 the House and Senate restored PAYGO in the form of special budget rules.

At various times, citizens and politicians have suggested amending the Constitution to require a balanced budget. In 1995, a balanced budget amendment gained the two-thirds majority it needed to pass the House, but the next year it failed by a single vote in the Senate. Supporters argued that the amendment would force the federal government to be more disciplined about its spending. Opponents said that a constitutional amendment requiring a balanced budget would not give the government the flexibility it needed to deal with rapid changes in the economy.

The Surpluses of the Late 1990s The late 1990s brought a welcome reversal of fortune. For the first time in thirty years, the President and the Office of Management and Budget were able to announce that the federal government was running a surplus.

How did this happen? First, the new budget procedures begun under President Bush and extended under President Clinton helped Congress control the growth of government spending. Second, tax increases by President Clinton in 1993 resulted in more federal revenue. Finally, the strong economy and low unemployment meant that more individuals and corporations were earning more money—and thus paying more to the government in taxes.

>> This 1993 magazine reflected a booming market for personal computers—a boom that played a key role in the fast-growing economy of the 1990s.

A Return to Deficit Spending The changeover from deficits to surplus brought with it a different set of political concerns. Investors who had come to rely heavily upon Treasury bonds as the basic "safe" investment worried that the federal government would remove all bonds from the market as it repaid its debt.

Americans debated how to make best use of the budget surplus. As a presidential candidate in 2000, George W. Bush pledged to use the surplus to guarantee Social Security into the new century, provide additional medical benefits to older people, and reduce income taxes.

However, the surplus was short-lived. The end of the stock market boom, an economic slowdown, and a new federal income tax cut reduced federal revenues. The Islamist terrorist attacks of September 11, 2001, dealt a double blow to the federal budget by disrupting the economy and imposing a new set of defense costs. You can see how these costs affected government spending in **Figure 9.22**.

In response, the federal government returned to deficit spending. The federal budget continued to show a large deficit for the next several years, due in part to counterterrorism efforts and the very costly wars in Afghanistan and Iraq. In fiscal year 2008 alone, the President's funding requests for the war on terrorism approached $200 billion.

Federal Spending, 2000 and 2007

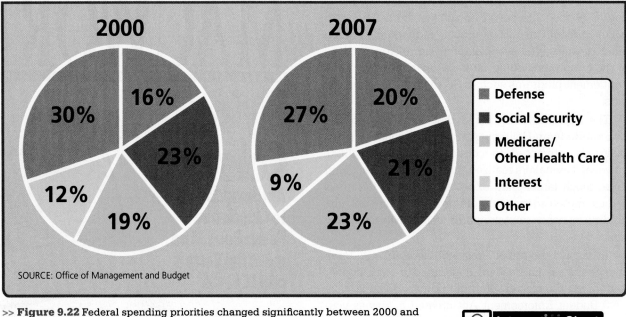

SOURCE: Office of Management and Budget

>> **Figure 9.22** Federal spending priorities changed significantly between 2000 and 2007. **Analyze Graphs** Which categories saw the greatest increase over this time period?

▶ **Interactive Chart**

The long-term outlook for the federal budget is uncertain. Funding for stimulus projects and new healthcare initiatives may cause long-term spending to increase. Social Security and Medicare are projected to rise sharply in the next 30 years as large numbers of baby boomers leave the job market and retire. Balancing the budget is expected to become even more difficult.

? **IDENTIFY** What factors contributed to the deficit spending of the 2000s?

ASSESSMENT

1. **Identify Cause and Effect** What is the impact of a budget deficit on the national debt?

2. **Check Understanding** Explain the crowding-out effect that results from national debt.

3. **Evaluate Arguments** Is creating money to cover a budget deficit a good or bad idea? Explain your answer.

4. **Draw Conclusions** Of the three possible problems that can arise from having a large national debt, which is the most serious? Explain.

5. **Predict Consequences** How could lowering income taxes during an economic downturn lead to increased national debt?

Suppose you have a checkbook that allows you to write as many checks as you wish for any amount you desire. You don't need to worry about the balance in your account, and the checks will always be cashed, no matter how much you spend. Of course, no person has an account like that. However, the Federal Reserve comes close. By using its monetary policy tools, the Federal Reserve System affects the nation's money supply. The Fed has the power to increase or decrease the amount of money in the United States. The Fed manipulates the money supply in order to stabilize the American economy.

>> Coins and paper bills are manufactured in facilities like this. But it is the Federal Reserve that puts money in circulation through the process of money creation.

▶ **Interactive Flipped Video**

Monetary Policy Options

Creating Money

Money Manufacture vs. Money Creation The U.S. Department of the Treasury is responsible for manufacturing money in the form of currency. The Federal Reserve is responsible for putting money into circulation. How does this money get into the economy?

The process is called **money creation**, and it is carried out by the Fed and by banks all around the country. This process is similar to the multiplier effect of government spending. The multiplier effect in fiscal policy holds that every one-dollar change in fiscal policy creates a change greater than one dollar in the economy. The process of money creation works in much the same way.

How Banks Create Money Money creation does not mean the printing of new bills. Banks create money not by printing it, but by simply going about their business.

For example, suppose you take out a loan of $1,000. You decide to deposit the money in a checking account. Once you have deposited the money, you now have a balance of $1,000. This money is a demand deposit that must be paid by the bank to you whenever you ask for it.

>> Objectives

Describe the process of money creation.

Analyze how the Federal Reserve uses reserve requirements to implement U.S. monetary policy.

Analyze the three primary tools the Federal Reserve uses to implement monetary policy, including open market operations.

Explain why the Federal Reserve prefers open market operations as a means to implementing monetary policy.

>> Key Terms

money creation
required reserve
 ratio
money multiplier
 formula
excess reserves
discount rate
federal funds rate
prime rate
open market
 operations
security

It is counted as part of what economists call M1—the total amount of money people can gain access to and spend readily. So, as a result of this loan and deposit, the money supply has increased by $1,000. The process of money creation begins here.

Banks make money by charging interest on loans. Your bank will lend part of the $1,000 that you deposited. The maximum amount that a bank can lend is determined by the **required reserve ratio** (RRR)—the fraction of deposits that banks are required to keep in reserve. This is calculated as the ratio of reserves to deposits. The RRR, which is established by the Federal Reserve, ensures that banks will have enough funds to supply customers' withdrawal needs.

Suppose in our example that the RRR is 0.1, or 10 percent. This means that the bank is required to keep 10 percent of your $1,000 demand deposit balance, or $100, in reserve. It is allowed to lend $900. Follow along in **Figure 9.23** to see what happens to this money next.

Let's say the bank lends that $900 to Kai, and he deposits it in his checking account. Kai now has $900 he didn't have before. Kai's $900 is now included in M1.

You still have your $1,000 in your account, on which you can write a check at any time. Thus, your initial deposit to the bank and the subsequent loan have caused the money supply to increase by $1,000 + $900 for a total of $1,900.

Now suppose that Kai uses the $900 to buy Lena's old car. Lena deposits the $900 from Kai into her checking account. Her bank keeps 10 percent of the deposit, or $90, as required reserves. It will lend the other $810 to its customers. So, Lena has a demand deposit balance of $900, which is included in the money supply, and the new borrowers get $810, which is also added to the money supply. This means that the money supply has now increased by $1,000 + $900 + $810 = $2,710—all because of your initial $1,000 deposit.

The Money Multiplier This money creation process will continue until the loan amount, and hence the amount of new money that can be created, becomes very small. To determine the total amount of new money that can be created and added to the money supply, economists use the **money multiplier formula**, which is calculated as 1 ÷ RRR. To apply the formula, they multiply the initial deposit by the money multiplier:

Increase in money supply = initial cash deposit × 1/RRR. In our example the RRR is 0.1, so the money multiplier is 1 ÷ 0.1 = 10. (See **Figure 9.24**.) This means that the deposit of $1,000 can lead to a $10,000 increase in the money supply.

As of 2012, banks in the United States had no reserve requirements on the first $12.4 million of

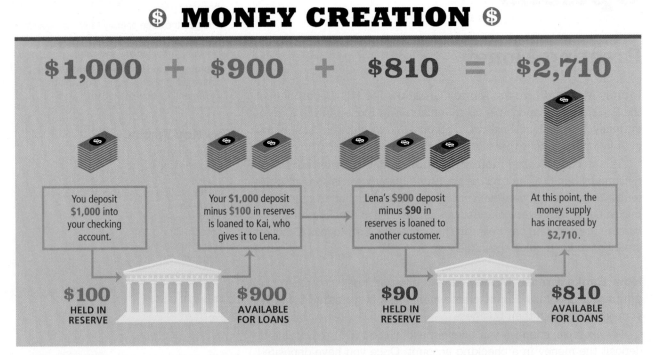

$ MONEY CREATION $

$1,000 + $900 + $810 = $2,710

| You deposit $1,000 into your checking account. | Your $1,000 deposit minus $100 in reserves is loaned to Kai, who gives it to Lena. | Lena's $900 deposit minus $90 in reserves is loaned to another customer. | At this point, the money supply has increased by $2,710. |

$100 HELD IN RESERVE $900 AVAILABLE FOR LOANS $90 HELD IN RESERVE $810 AVAILABLE FOR LOANS

>> **Figure 9.23** Money is created as banks loan out money not kept in reserve.
Analyze Charts How would an increase in the reserve requirement affect money creation in this example?

MONEY MULTIPLIER FORMULA

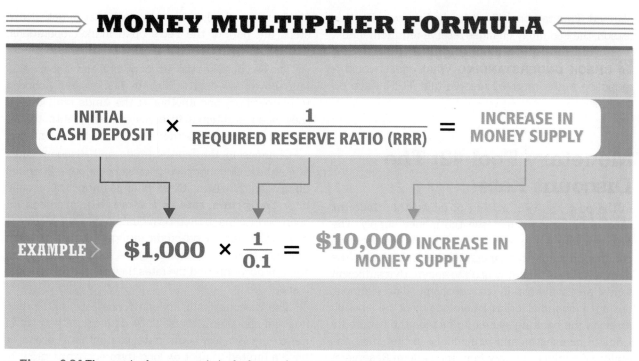

INITIAL CASH DEPOSIT $\times \dfrac{1}{\text{REQUIRED RESERVE RATIO (RRR)}} =$ INCREASE IN MONEY SUPPLY

EXAMPLE $\quad \$1{,}000 \times \dfrac{1}{0.1} = \$10{,}000$ INCREASE IN MONEY SUPPLY

>> **Figure 9.24** The required reserve ratio is the key to the money multiplier formula. **Analyze Charts** What would the increase in money supply be if the RRR in this example were 0.2?

demand deposit assets. They were required to hold 3 percent reserves on demand deposit assets between $12.4 and $79.5 million, and 10 percent on all demand deposit assets exceeding $79.5 million.

In the real world, however, people hold some cash outside of the banking system, meaning that some funds leak out of the money multiplier process. Also, banks sometimes hold **excess reserves**, which are reserves greater than the required amounts. These excess reserves ensure that banks will always be able to meet their customers' demands and the Fed's reserve requirements. The actual money multiplier effect in the United States is estimated to be between 2 and 3.

The Federal Reserve has three basic tools to implement U.S. monetary policy and adjust the amount of money in the economy. These tools for creating money (or destroying it, if need be) are reserve requirements, the discount rate, and open market operations.

? DESCRIBE How do banks create money by going about their ordinary business?

Monetary Tool #1: Reserve Requirements

The simplest way for the Fed to adjust the amount of reserves in the banking system is to change the required reserve ratio. (See **Figure 9.25**.) The Fed's Board of Governors has sole responsibility over changes in reserve requirements. However, changing the reserve requirement is not the Fed's preferred tool.

A reduction of the RRR frees up reserved money in banks, allowing them to make more loans. It also increases the money multiplier. Both effects will lead to a substantial expansion of the money supply.

The process also works in reverse. Even a slight increase in the RRR forces banks to hold more money in reserves. This causes a contraction in the money supply.

Although changing reserve requirements can be an effective means of changing the money supply, the Fed does not use this tool often because it is disruptive to the banking system. Even a small increase in the RRR would force banks to "call in" significant numbers of loans—that is, to require some borrowers to pay the entire outstanding balance of their loans sooner than planned. This can be difficult for the borrower. For this reason, the Fed rarely changes reserve requirements.

? CHECK UNDERSTANDING What effect would a reduction in the required reserve rate (RRR) have on banks?

Monetary Tool #2: The Discount Rate

In the past, the Fed lowered or raised the **discount rate** to increase or decrease the money supply. The discount rate is the interest rate the Federal Reserve charges on loans to financial institutions. Today, the discount rate is primarily used to ensure that sufficient funds are available in the economy. For example, during a financial crisis, there may not be enough funds in the banking system to provide the necessary loans to businesses and individuals. In that case, the ability of banks to borrow from the Federal Reserve at the discount rate provides a key safety net.

Today, to implement monetary policy, the Federal Reserve primarily adjusts the **federal funds rate**, which is the interest rate that banks charge one another for loans. It does not actually set a new federal funds rate, however. Instead, it decides on a "target" level for the rate and takes steps to reach that target. These steps are part of the Fed's open market operations, which you will read about shortly.

The Fed does set the discount rate, and it keeps this rate above the federal funds rate. Banks usually choose to borrow from one another at the funds rate. Only if they need additional reserves will they turn to the Federal Reserve and borrow at the higher discount rate.

Changes in the federal funds and discount rates affect the cost of borrowing for banks or other financial institutions. In turn, these changes affect the prime rate. The **prime rate** is the rate banks charge on short-term loans to their best customers—usually large companies with good credit ratings. Ultimately, other interest rates follow, including the rates banks pay on savings accounts and the rates they charge for personal loans.

The discount rate, federal funds rate, and prime rate are short-term rates. They determine the cost of borrowing for a few hours, days, or months, These rates have a limited impact on long-term economic growth. To influence long-term rates, the Fed must use other tools.

? IDENTIFY MAIN IDEAS What is the main tool that the Federal Reserve uses to adjust the money supply?

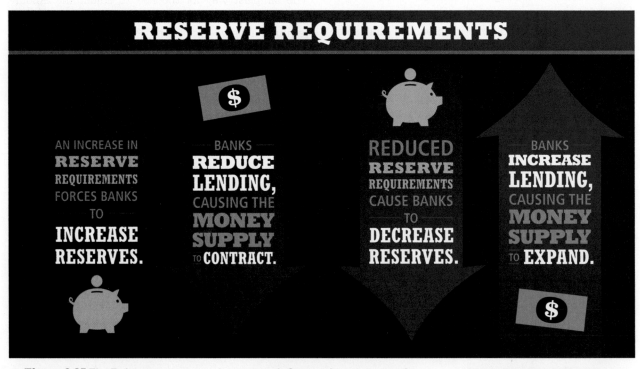

>> **Figure 9.25** The Fed uses reserve requirements to influence the money supply. **Express Ideas Clearly** Who or what is directly affected by a change in reserve requirements?

▶ Interactive Chart

OPEN MARKET OPERATIONS

WHEN THE FED **SELLS BONDS,** BOND BUYERS **REMOVE RESERVES** FROM BANKS.

BANKS **REDUCE LENDING,** CAUSING THE **MONEY SUPPLY** TO **CONTRACT.**

WHEN THE FED **PURCHASES BONDS,** BOND SELLERS **ADD RESERVES** TO BANKS.

BANKS **INCREASE LENDING,** CAUSING THE **MONEY SUPPLY** TO **EXPAND.**

>> **Figure 9.26** Open market operations involve the buying and selling of government securities. **Identify Steps in a Process** What steps would lead to a reduction in the money supply through open market operations?

▶ **Interactive Chart**

Monetary Tool #3: Open Market Operations

Open market operations are the buying and selling of government securities in order to alter the supply of money. (See **Figure 9.26**.) A **security** is a financial document, such as a stock certificate or bond, that represents ownership of corporate shares or the promise of repayment by a company or government. Today open market operations are by far the most important—and most often used—tool employed by the Fed to implement U.S. monetary policy.

Purchasing Government Securities When the Federal Open Market Committee (FOMC) chooses to increase the money supply, it orders the trading desk at the Federal Reserve Bank of New York to purchase a certain quantity of government securities on the open market. The Federal Reserve Bank buys these securities with checks drawn on Federal Reserve funds. The bond sellers then deposit the money from the bond sales into their banks. As the Federal Reserve Board explains:

[T]he bank now has more reserves than it wants. So the bank can lend these unwanted reserves to another bank in the federal funds market.

Thus, the Fed's open market purchase increases the supply of reserves to the banking system, and the federal funds rate falls.

—"What Are Open Market Operations?" Federal Reserve Bank of San Francisco

In this way, funds enter the banking system, setting in motion the money creation process described earlier.

Selling Government Securities If the FOMC chooses to decrease the money supply, it must make an open market bond sale. In this case, the Fed sells government securities back to bond dealers, receiving from them checks drawn on their own banks. After the Fed processes these checks, the money is out of circulation. This operation reduces reserves in the banking system. In order to keep their reserves at the required levels, banks reduce their outstanding loans. The money multiplier process then works in reverse, resulting in a decline in the money supply that is greater than the value of the initial securities purchase.

Targets To judge whether its open market operations are having the desired effect on the economy, the Fed periodically evaluates one or more economic targets. You have read about how the federal funds rate serves

>> The economic crisis that occurred from 2007 to 2009 shook financial markets and prompted the Fed to take action.

Today, the Fed does not change reserve requirements to conduct monetary policy. Changing reserve requirements would force banks to make drastic changes in their plans. Open market operations or changes in the discount rate do not disrupt financial institutions.

During the recent financial crisis of 2007–2009, the Fed took aggressive action to stabilize the financial system and promote economic growth. It used open market operations to lower the federal funds rate to nearly zero. The goal was to stimulate more lending and help boost economic activity, but it was still not enough to stem the crisis. So the Fed took an additional, unconventional step: It purchased longer-term securities from banks in the hope of bringing down long-term interest rates. This action pumped billions of dollars into the financial system and helped ease the crisis. But this action did come at a potential cost, as some economists worried that it would lead to inflation.

In setting its monetary policy goals, the Federal Reserve keeps a close eye on market forces, studying inflation and business cycles to determine its policy. As you just read, changes in the money supply affect interest rates. You will find out more about how this process works shortly.

? **IDENTIFY MAIN IDEAS** Why are open market operations the Fed's preferred monetary policy tool?

as the main target for interest rates. The Fed also keeps an eye on various measures of the money supply. Close analysis of these targets helps the Fed meet its goal of promoting a stable and prosperous economy.

? **RECALL** What action does the Federal Open Market Committee take if it wants to decrease the money supply?

Using Monetary Policy Tools

Open market operations are the most often used of the Federal Reserve's monetary policy tools. They can be conducted smoothly and on an ongoing basis to meet the Fed's goals. The Fed changes the discount rate less frequently. It usually follows a policy of keeping the discount rate in line with other interest rates in the economy in order to prevent excess borrowing by member banks from the Fed, which might threaten economic stability.

ASSESSMENT

1. **Check Understanding** What is money creation?

2. **Summarize** What are the three basic tools the Federal Reserve can use to affect the nation's money supply and implement monetary policy?

3. **Hypothesize** What would likely happen if the Fed changed reserve requirements?

4. **Analyze Information** Why do the discount rate, federal funds rate, and prime rate have a limited impact on the long-term growth of the economy?

5. **Synthesize** What was one benefit and one cost of the Fed's unusual step of buying long-term securities following the financial crisis of 2008–2009?

Have you ever asked a parent for money—a raise in your allowance, perhaps, or cash to buy concert tickets? If so, you know that timing is everything. If, for example, your parent has just paid a huge bill for home or car repairs, you know that's the wrong time to ask for spending money. Timing is also critical to the Fed. Proper timing can support the Fed's effort to achieve economic growth and stability. Bad timing can impede it.

>> A building project such as this takes months or years to plan and carry out. So, the monetary policy that influenced the decision to build may take even longer to have its full impact.

▶ **Interactive Flipped Video**

The Effects of Monetary Policy

The Basics of Monetary Policy

How, then, does monetary policy influence macroeconomic performance—that is, the functioning of the entire economy? Monetary policy alters the supply of money. The supply of money, in turn, affects interest rates. Interest rates affect the level of investment and spending in the economy. (See **Figure 9.27**.)

How Money Supply Impacts Interest Rates It is easy to see the cost of money if you are borrowing it. The cost—the price that you, as a borrower, pay—is the interest rate. Even if you spend your own money, the interest rate still affects you because you are giving up interest by not saving or investing.

The market for money is like any other market. If the supply is higher, the price—the interest rate—is lower. If the supply is lower, the price is higher. In other words, when the money supply is high, interest rates are low. When the money supply is low, interest rates are high.

How Interest Rates Affect Spending Recall that interest rates are important factors of spending in the economy. Lower interest rates encourage greater investment spending by business firms. This is

>> **Objectives**

Explain how monetary policy works.

Describe how the timing of monetary policy can impact business cycles and key economic indicators.

Analyze the costs and benefits of monetary policy in terms of economic growth.

Contrast two general approaches to monetary policy.

>> **Key Terms**

easy money policy
tight money policy
inside lag
outside lag
monetarism
Friedrich Hayek
(1899–1992)

because a firm's cost of borrowing, or of using its own funds, decreases as the interest rate decreases. Higher interest rates discourage business spending.

Firms find that lower interest rates give them more opportunities for profitable investment. If a firm has to pay 15 percent interest on its loans, it may find few profitable opportunities. If interest rates fall to 6 percent, however, the firm may find that some opportunities become profitable.

If the macroeconomy is experiencing a contraction—declining income—the Federal Reserve may try to stimulate, or expand, it. The Fed will follow an **easy money policy**. That is, it will increase the money supply. An increased money supply will lower interest rates, thus encouraging investment spending. Of course, such a policy comes with some risk. For example, it may encourage overborrowing and overinvestment, followed by layoffs and cutbacks.

If the economy is experiencing a rapid expansion that may cause high inflation, the Fed may introduce a **tight money policy**. That is, it will reduce the money supply. The Fed reduces the money supply to push interest rates upward. By raising interest rates, the Fed causes investment spending to decline. This brings real GDP down, too.

Even though it can only alter the money supply, the Fed can have a great impact on the economy. The money supply influences interest rates, and interest rates influence the level of aggregate demand. Recall that aggregate demand represents the relationship between price levels and quantity demanded in the overall economy. Thus, the level of aggregate demand helps determine the level of real GDP.

? IDENTIFY CAUSE AND EFFECT How are money supply and interest rates connected?

Timing Monetary Policy

Monetary policy, like fiscal policy, must be carefully timed if it is to help the macroeconomy. Properly handled, monetary policy can help the nation's economy grow at a steady, sustainable pace. If policies are enacted at the wrong time, they could actually intensify the business cycle rather than stabilize it.

The Results of Good Timing To see why, consider **Figure 9.28**. Graph A shows the business cycle with a properly timed stabilization policy. The purple curve, which shows greater fluctuations, represents a normal business cycle. The goal of stabilization policy is to smooth out those fluctuations—in other words, to make the peaks a little bit lower and the troughs not quite so deep. This will minimize inflation in the peaks and

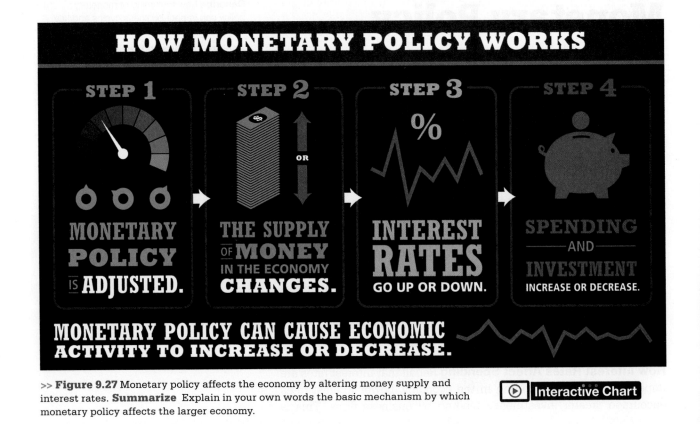

>> **Figure 9.27** Monetary policy affects the economy by altering money supply and interest rates. **Summarize** Explain in your own words the basic mechanism by which monetary policy affects the larger economy.

▶ **Interactive Chart**

Business Cycles and Stabilization Policy

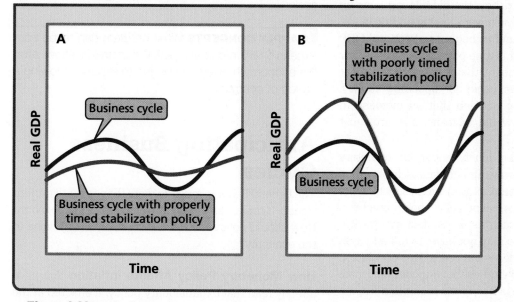

>> **Figure 9.28** Poorly timed policy can create more instability than the normal business cycle. **Analyze Graphs** Which scenario shown in these graphs represents the least stable economy?

the effects of recessions in the troughs. Properly timed stabilization policy smooths out the business cycle, as shown by the orange curve.

The Results of Bad Timing If stabilization policy is not timed properly, however, it can actually make the business cycle more extreme, not smoother. The orange line in Graph B in **Figure 9.28** shows the result of a poorly timed monetary policy, producing higher peaks and lower valleys than might otherwise occur. This can happen if, as GDP begins to fall from its peak, government economists fail to recognize that a contraction is occurring until the economy is already deeply into it.

By the time they enact expansionary policies and have those policies take effect, the economy might already be coming out of the recession on its own. In such a situation, the expansionary effects of an easy money policy would boost the economy while it is already expanding. This could result in a larger expansion—but also very high inflation.

Being late in implementing expansionary policies can have other effects, too. Suppose, for example, the economy has slowed down so much that businesses are reluctant to borrow at any rate for new investment. In that case, easy money would have little effect.

As you can see, properly timing monetary policy is important. It is also difficult. **Figure 9.29** shows some of many indicators economists study in their effort to understand the economy. There are two basic problems

in the timing of any macroeconomic policy. These are called policy lags.

Inside Lags The **inside lag** is the time it takes to implement monetary policy. Such lags, or delays, occur for two reasons. First, it takes time to identify a problem. Although economists have developed sophisticated computer models for predicting economic trends, they still cannot know for sure that the economy is headed into a new phase of the business cycle until it is already there. Statistics may conflict, and it can take up to a year to recognize a serious economic downturn.

A second reason for inside lags is that once a problem has been recognized, it can take additional time to enact policies. This problem is more severe for fiscal policy than for monetary policy. Fiscal policy, which includes changes in government spending and taxation, requires actions by Congress and the President. Since Congress must debate new plans and get the approval of the President, it takes time to get a new policy enacted. The enactment of monetary policy, on the other hand, is streamlined. The Federal Open Market Committee (FOMC) meets eight times per year to discuss monetary policy—more often if necessary. Once it has decided that changes are called for, the FOMC can enact policy almost immediately through open market operations or discount rate changes.

Outside Lags Once a new policy is determined, it takes time to become effective. This time period, known as the **outside lag**, also differs for monetary and fiscal policy. For fiscal policy, the outside lag lasts as long as is required for new government spending or tax policies to take effect and to begin to affect real GDP and the inflation rate. This time period can be relatively short, as with a tax rebate that returns government revenues to households eager for spending money. One statistical model concluded that an increase in government spending would increase GDP after just six months.

Outside lags can be much longer for monetary policy, since they primarily affect business investment plans. Firms may require months or even years to make large investment plans, especially those involving new physical capital, such as a new factory. Thus, a change in interest rates may not have its full effect on investment spending for several years. This conclusion is supported by several studies that suggest that more than two years may pass before the maximum impact of monetary policy is felt.

Given the longer inside lag for fiscal policy and the longer outside lag for monetary policy, it is difficult to know which policy has the shorter total lag. In practice, partisan politics and budgetary pressures often prevent the President and Congress from agreeing on fiscal policy. Because of the political difficulties of implementing fiscal policy, we rely to a greater extent on the Fed to use monetary policy to soften the business cycle.

? APPLY CONCEPTS What problem can result from expansionary monetary policy that takes effect after the economy has already begun to expand following a period of contraction?

Anticipating Business Cycles

The Federal Reserve must do more than react to current trends. It must also anticipate changes in the economy. How should policymakers decide when to intervene in the economy?

How Monetary Policy Affects Inflation You have already read that expansionary policy, if enacted at the wrong time, may push an economy into high inflation. This is the chief danger of using an easy money policy to get the economy out of a recession.

An inflationary economy can be tamed by a tight money policy, but the timing is again crucial. If the policy takes effect as the economy is already cooling off on its own, the tight money could turn a mild contraction into a full-blown recession.

Components of the Index of Leading Economic Indicators®

1	Average weekly hours, manufacturing
2	Average weekly initial claims for unemployment insurance
3	Manufacturers' new orders for consumer goods and materials
4	Manufacturers' new orders for nondefense capital goods excluding aircraft orders
5	Institute of Supply Management's Index of New Orders—another measure of manufacturing activity
6	Building permits, new private housing units
7	Stock prices, 500 common stocks
8	Leading Credit Index™, a measure of credit and lending
9	Interest rate spread between the 10-year Treasury bonds rate and the federal funds rate
10	Average consumer expectations for business conditions (measure of consumer confidence)

SOURCE: The Conference Board

>> **Figure 9.29** Monitoring the economy means watching developments in manufacturing, labor, housing, the stock market, credit markets, and more. **Identify Central Issues** What does this list suggest about the challenge of managing the economy?

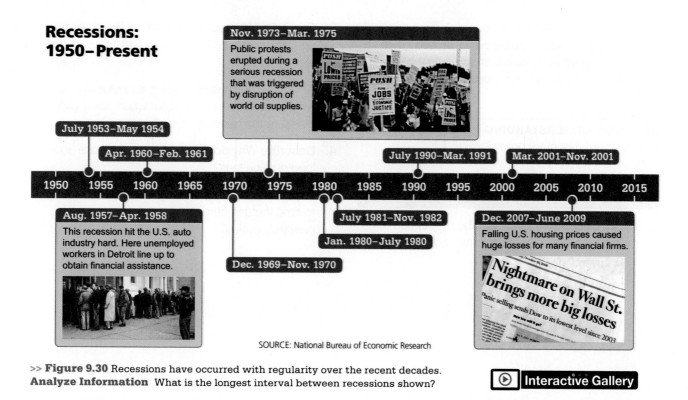

Recessions: 1950–Present

Nov. 1973–Mar. 1975
Public protests erupted during a serious recession that was triggered by disruption of world oil supplies.

July 1953–May 1954

Apr. 1960–Feb. 1961

July 1990–Mar. 1991

Mar. 2001–Nov. 2001

1950 1955 1960 1965 1970 1975 1980 1985 1990 1995 2000 2005 2010 2015

Aug. 1957–Apr. 1958
This recession hit the U.S. auto industry hard. Here unemployed workers in Detroit line up to obtain financial assistance.

July 1981–Nov. 1982

Jan. 1980–July 1980

Dec. 1969–Nov. 1970

Dec. 2007–June 2009
Falling U.S. housing prices caused huge losses for many financial firms.

Nightmare on Wall St. brings more big losses
Panic selling sends Dow to its lowest level since 2003

SOURCE: National Bureau of Economic Research

>> **Figure 9.30** Recessions have occurred with regularity over the recent decades. **Analyze Information** What is the longest interval between recessions shown?

▶ **Interactive Gallery**

The decision of whether to use monetary policy, then, must be based partly on expectations of the business cycle. Some recessions are mild and likely to end quickly even without any policy intervention. The same is true of some periods of inflation.

Given the timing problems of monetary policy, it may be wiser in some cases to allow the business cycle to correct itself rather than run the risk of an ill-timed policy change. If a recession is expected to turn into an expansion in a short time, the best course of action may be to let the economy correct itself. On the other hand, if we expect a recession to last several years, then most economists would recommend an active policy. So, the question most policymakers face is this: How long will this recessionary (or inflationary) period last?

How Quickly Do Economies Self-Correct?
Economists disagree on the answer to this question. Their estimates for the U.S. economy range from two to six years. **Figure 9.30** shows the timing and duration of the recessions in recent U.S. history. Since the economy may take quite a long time to recover on its own from an inflationary peak or a recessionary trough, policymakers have time to help the economy return to stable levels of output and prices.

? ANALYZE INFORMATION How would the Fed most likely respond if it predicted that a recession would soon turn into an expansion?

Debating Monetary Policy

In practice, the lags discussed here make monetary and fiscal policy difficult to apply. The lags and the general complexity of the national economy also make it difficult to sort out how different policies have affected the economy in the past. Economists have debated these matters for many years.

Some economists believe that governments should emphasize fiscal policy more than monetary policy. These economists are in the tradition of John Maynard Keynes. According to them, government spending should be used to smooth out the peaks and valleys of the business cycle.

Other economists are more in tune with the ideas of Milton Friedman. That is, they have greater faith in monetary policy. These proponents of **monetarism** believe that adjusting the money supply is the most useful tool to improve macroeconomic performance.

Other economists, such as **Friedrich Hayek**, have taken different views. Hayek questioned economists' ability to influence the economy effectively and had faith in a free economy's ability to self-adjust. Though Hayek died in 1992, his ideas continue to exert a strong influence. Like-minded economists today will usually recommend against enacting new policies, arguing that government intervention disrupts the proper functioning of a free market economy.

This debate over which approach to take with monetary policy will probably never be settled to the satisfaction of all economists. If you follow the news, you will hear politicians carrying on the debate nearly every day.

? CHECK UNDERSTANDING What do monetarists believe about monetary policy?

ASSESSMENT

1. **Apply Concepts** How might the proper use of monetary policy affect economic stability?

2. **Compare** Why would the Federal Reserve enact an easy money policy? Why would it enact a tight money policy?

3. **Analyze Information** What is an inside lag, and why does it sometimes occur when using GDP to measure the business cycle?

4. **Describe** Why does monetary policy have such long outside lags?

5. **Express Problems Clearly** Why is it difficult to time the use of monetary policy in controlling business cycles?

1. **Analyze the Importance of Economic Philosophers** Analyze the importance of Milton Friedman and his impact on the U.S. economy. Answer the following questions: What kinds of policies did Friedman advocate? Did the Reagan-era tax cuts reflect Friedman's economic views? Explain.

2. **Explain Federal Reserve Actions and Analyze the Impact of Fiscal Policy** Summarize summarizing the difficulties policy makers face in the timing of monetary and fiscal policy. Use economic-related terminology, including "inside lag" and "outside lag" correctly in your response.

3. **Analyze Changes** Analyze recent changes in the basic characteristics of the U.S. economy. Write a paragraph that answers the following questions: What policies did President Obama pursue in response to the country's economic situation when he first took office? How did these policies reflect a change in U.S. economic policy?

4. **Analyze Costs and Benefits** Describe government policies that aim to increase employment, the expected benefits of those policies, and the costs some economists associate with the policies. Use standard grammar, spelling, sentence structure, and punctuation in your response.

5. **Analyze U.S. Economic Policies and Analyze Information by Categorizing** Analyze the costs and benefits of U.S. economic policies related to the economic goal of stability. Categorize and explain different points of view in the current debate over the use of monetary policy to achieve stability in the economy.

6. **Describe the Role and the Changes Over Time** Describe the role of the government in the U.S. economy and explain how that role has changed over time. In your response, make reference to classical and Keynesian economics. Use standard grammar, spelling, sentence structure, and punctuation in your response.

7. **Analyze U.S. Economic Policies and Analyze and Evaluate Primary and Secondary Sources** Referring to the quotation, respond to the following question: To what benefits of investment does President Obama refer? How does he acknowledge the costs of such policies?

"By making investments in our people that we pay for responsibly, we will strengthen the middle class, make America a magnet for jobs and innovation, and grow our economy, which will in turn help us to reduce deficits."

—President Barack Obama, April 10, 2013

8. **Analyze Tools and Explain Actions** Analyze the three basic tools used to implement U.S. monetary policy, including reserve requirements, and explain how the actions of the Federal Reserve System affect the nation's money supply. Be sure to use economic-related terminology, such as "reserve requirements," "money supply," and "Federal Reserve," correctly in your response and answer the following questions: What are the three basic tools that the Federal Reserve uses to implement monetary policy? How does the Federal Reserve use reserve requirements to affect the money supply? What is the Federal Reserve trying to achieve in its adjustment of the money supply?

9. **Analyze Fiscal Policy Decisions** Analyze the impact of fiscal policy decisions on the economy. Be sure to use the economic-related terms "expansionary fiscal policy" and "contractionary fiscal policy" correctly in your response and answer the following questions: What is an expansionary fiscal policy and why would it be employed? What is a contractionary fiscal policy and why would it be employed?

10. **Analyze Fiscal Policy Decisions** Write a paragraph that answers the following questions: What is the government's basic tool in implementing fiscal policy? How can use of that tool lead to government debt? What are the positive and negative impacts of fiscal policy decisions that lead to government debt?

Annual Change in GDP, 1930–2012

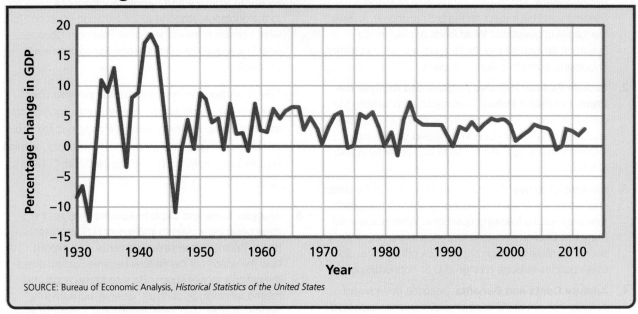

SOURCE: Bureau of Economic Analysis, *Historical Statistics of the United States*

11. **Interpret and Evaluate Economic Data** Referring to the graph, answer the following questions: What interpretations can you make about the U.S. economy using the gross domestic product data presented in the graph? How would you evaluate the data in terms of what the graph communicates about economic conditions for people in the United States?

12. **Describe the Role of Government in the Free Enterprise System and Analyze Information by Sequencing** Write a paragraph that describes the sequence of important developments in U.S. economic policy in the United States from the Great Depression to the present, including how the role of government in economic policy has changed over time.

13. **Explain How the Federal Reserve System Affects the Money Supply** Explain how the actions of the Federal Reserve System affect the nation's money supply. Be sure to use the economic-related terminology "easy money policy" and "tight money policy" correctly in your response and answer following questions: What is the difference between an easy money policy and a

tight money policy? In what ways do easy money and tight money policies affect the money supply and the broader economy? In what situations might each policy be employed?

14. **Analyze the Importance of Economic Philosophers** Analyze the importance of Friedrich Hayek and his impact on the U.S. free enterprise system. What was Hayek's basic thought concerning government activism in regard to the economy? What is an example of Hayek's influence on current economic policies?

15. **Explain How the Federal Reserve System Affects the Money Supply** Explain how the actions of the Federal Reserve System affect the nation's money supply. Write a paragraph that answers the following questions: How does the money supply affect interest rates? How do interest rates affect economic activity?

16. **Analyze Information and Explain Actions** Write a paragraph describing the cause-and-effect relationships involved in monetary policies the Federal Reserve might implement to improve a stagnant economy.

Components of the Index of Leading Economic Indicators®

1	Average weekly hours, manufacturing
2	Average weekly initial claims for unemployment insurance
3	Manufacturers' new orders for consumer goods and materials
4	Manufacturers' new orders for nondefense capital goods excluding aircraft orders
5	Institute of Supply Management's Index of New Orders—another measure of manufacturing activity
6	Building permits, new private housing units
7	Stock prices, 500 common stocks
8	Leading Credit Index™, a measure of credit and lending
9	Interest rate spread between the 10-year Treasury bonds rate and the federal funds rate
10	Average consumer expectations for business conditions (measure of consumer confidence)

SOURCE: The Conference Board

17. **Analyze Business Cycles** Analyze business cycles using key economic indicators. Using the table, write a paragraph that answers the following questions: What, in terms of economic activity, is revealed by key economic indicators? Why do key economic indicators include a wide variety of information?

18. **Analyze Tools and Explain Actions** Analyze the three basic tools used to implement U.S. monetary policy, including open-market operations, and explain how the actions of the Federal Reserve System affect the nation's money supply. Be sure to use economic-related terminology, such as "open market operations" and "money supply," correctly in your response and answer the following questions: What are open market operations? How do open market operations work in practice to affect the money supply?

19. **Explain Actions and Analyze Tools** Explain how the actions of the Federal Reserve System affect the nation's money supply and analyze the three basic tools used to implement U.S. monetary policy. Be sure to use economic-related terminology, such as "money supply,"

"reserve requirements," and "open market operations," correctly in your response and answer the following questions: What are the three tools the Federal Reserve uses to affect the nation's money supply, and how do these tools do so? What effects do increasing and decreasing the money supply have on the economy?

20. **Analyze Changes in Characteristics** How has the national debt as a basic characteristic of the U.S. economy changed in recent times? What effect does the change in national debt have on the federal budget?

21. **Identify the Economic Importance of Taxes** Identify the economic importance of types of national taxes by answering the following questions: What are marginal taxes? What has been the general tax policy of the United States concerning marginal rates since 1925? What belief about taxes explains tax policy since?

22. **Write About the Essential Question** Write an essay on the Essential Question: **What is the proper role of government in the economy?** Use evidence from your study of this Topic to support your answer.

[**ESSENTIAL QUESTION**] How might scarcity divide our world or bring it together?

10 **Trade, Development, and Globalization**

>> Cranes and freight containers move huge amounts of goods in today's globalized economy.

Enduring Understandings

- As global trade increases, nations have become economically interdependent.

- Nations use trade barriers and agreements to protect their economic interests.

- Nations use economic data such as exchange rates to guide decision making.

- The level of economic development affects every nation's standard of living, as measured by such standards as the adequacy of diet and shelter.

- In recent decades, the economies of many countries have been growing and changing in critical ways.

- Globalization presents opportunities for economic growth around the world, but it also presents social and economic challenges.

Watch the My Story Video to compare market and command economies in action.

PEARSON
realize™
www.PearsonRealize.com

Access your digital lessons including:
Topic Inquiry • Interactive Reading Notepad • Interactivities • Assessments

>> The United States is a major exporter of crops. The use of labor-saving machines and sophisticated technology combine with good soil and climate to make American farms among the world's most productive.

▶ **Interactive Flipped Video**

(10.1) Have you used a computer or bought a pair of jeans lately? The chances are good that the computer and the jeans were made outside the United States. But why do Americans buy so many goods from overseas? Wouldn't it make a lot more sense for us to produce everything we need ourselves?

>> Objectives

Evaluate the impact of the unequal distribution of resources.

Analyze the concepts of specialization and comparative advantage to explain why nations trade.

Summarize the position of the United States in world trade.

Describe the effects of trade on employment.

>> Key Terms

export
import
absolute advantage
comparative
   advantage
law of comparative
   advantage
interdependence

Why Nations Trade

Resource Distribution and Specialization

The answer to these questions lies in two economic ideas you already know about: factors of production and scarcity. By looking at two odd products—birdhouses and T-shirts—you can better understand why nations trade.

As you learned earlier, the resources that are used to make goods and services are called the factors of production. They include land (natural resources), labor, and capital (both physical and human). Because these resources are scarce, countries have to choose how to use their factors of production to produce particular goods.

Because they cannot produce all goods with their scarce resources, they need to obtain those they do not produce somehow. Trade is how countries obtain those goods they do not produce.

Natural Resources Natural resources, along with climate and geographic location, help determine what goods and services an economy produces. Fertile soil and a good growing climate allowed the central United States to develop an economy based on agriculture. Much of Southwest Asia—with scarce farmland and water but large reserves of oil and natural gas—has an economy based on extracting and selling these energy resources.

Capital and Labor Capital and labor also shape a region's economy. Physical capital includes the things that people make in order to produce final goods and services. Machinery, tractors, computers, and factories are examples of physical capital, as are the transportation and communication networks that allow the flow of goods and information. Capital also includes the money needed to invest in businesses and use natural resources.

Human capital differs from labor. Labor refers to the size of a nation's workforce. Human capital is the knowledge and skills a worker gains through education and experience. Every job requires human capital. A surgeon must learn anatomy and how to use a scalpel. A taxi driver must memorize the layout of a city's streets.

One way to measure a nation's human capital is to look at the general educational level of the populace. A country whose citizens have more schooling than those of another country has more human capital.

Unequal Resource Distribution As **Figure 10.1** shows, the availability of resources differs greatly from one country to another. For example, Nigeria has less than three quarters the land area of Peru but more than ten times the arable land and six times the population. This suggests that Nigeria has more human capital and land that can be farmed than Peru does.

A nation's ability to exploit, or use, its physical resources is affected by culture and history. For example, prolonged warfare may severely damage a nation's farms, forests, and transportation systems. History and culture affect human resources as well. In colonial America, a labor shortage led to the establishment of slavery. Today, a culture that bans education of women wastes much of its potential human capital.

Specialization and Trade Unequal distribution of resources creates a need for specialization. (As you have read, specialization occurs when individuals, businesses, or nations produce only certain goods and services.) In the United States, we grow wheat, corn, and other crops for which we have suitable soil and climate conditions. However, we cannot grow large quantities of coffee or bananas.

When nations specialize in certain goods, they obtain the goods they do not or cannot produce through importing and exporting. An **export** is a good or service sent to another country for sale.

An **import** is a good or service brought in from another country for sale. For example, Costa Rica specializes in growing and exporting coffee. The nation uses the money earned from selling coffee to import goods that it does not produce.

In some cases, more than 70 percent of a nation's export trade depends upon a single resource. Examples

Resource Distribution

	INDIA	NIGERIA	PERU	UNITED STATES
Total area (sq km)	3,287,263 sq km	923,768 sq km	1,285,216 sq km	9,826,675 sq km
Arable land (%)	47.9%	39.0%	2.8%	16.3%
Natural resources	coal, iron ore, manganese, mica, bauxite, rare earth elements, titanium ore, chromite, natural gas, diamonds, petroleum, limestone, arable land	natural gas, petroleum, tin, iron ore, coal, limestone, niobium, lead, zinc, arable land	copper, silver, gold, petroleum, timber, fish, iron ore, coal, phosphate, potash, hydropower, natural gas	coal, copper, lead, molybdenum, phosphates, rare earth elements, uranium, bauxite, gold, iron, mercury, nickel, potash, silver, tungsten, zinc, petroleum, natural gas, timber
Population	1,220.8 million	174.5 million	29.8 million	316.4 million
Labor force	486.6 million	51.53 million	16.2 million	155 million
Literacy rate	62.8%	61.3%	89.6%	99%
Telephones	Main: 31.1 million Cellular: 893.9 million	Main: 418,200 Cellular: 112.8 million	Main: 3.4 million Cellular: 29.4 million	Main: 139 million Cellular: 310 million
Airports	346	54	191	13,513

SOURCE: *CIA World Factbook*

>> **Figure 10.1 Analyze Charts** Which factors of production does India have in abundance? Which factors of production does it lack in comparison to the United States?

▶ **Interactive Gallery**

include Kuwait (petroleum and natural gas), Guinea-Bissau (cashews), and the Marshall Islands (fish).

? **SUMMARIZE** Why are scarcity and choice basic economic problems faced by every country?

Absolute and Comparative Advantage

Suppose a nation enjoys an abundance of resources, including a rich natural environment, an educated workforce, and the latest technologies. In theory, such a nation could be self-sufficient, producing almost all that it needs by itself. Why, then, would it choose to engage in foreign trade?

Although self-sufficiency may sound appealing, it is actually better for countries to specialize in some products and trade for others. To see why, you need to look at two related concepts—absolute advantage and comparative advantage. A person or nation has an **absolute advantage** when it can produce more of a given product than another person or nation using a given amount of resources.

Explaining Absolute Advantage A simple example can illustrate the idea of absolute advantage. Suppose that two people, Jenny and Carlos, work at making both birdhouses and printed T-shirts. In one hour, Carlos can either print six T-shirts or make two birdhouses. (See **Figure 10.2.**) Jenny can print one T-shirt or make one birdhouse per hour. In other words, Carlos is more productive than Jenny in making both T-shirts and birdhouses. In economic terms, Carlos has an absolute advantage over Jenny in producing both goods.

Productivity and Opportunity Cost

	CARLOS	JENNY
T-shirts per hour	6	1
Birdhouses per hour	2	1
Opportunity cost of one T-shirt	$\frac{1}{3}$ birdhouse	1 birdhouse
Opportunity cost of one birdhouse	3 T-shirts	1 T-shirt

>> **Figure 10.2 Analyze Charts** How many T-shirts can Carlos make in the time it takes Jenny to make five T-shirts?

Because Carlos enjoys an absolute advantage in both goods, should he remain self-sufficient? Or would he be better off specializing in either T-shirts or birdhouses? What about Jenny? Should she make T-shirts, birdhouses, or both?

Countries have to face the same sorts of questions. Should a wealthy country with many resources be self-sufficient, or should it specialize in producing a few products and trade for the others? How does a poorer nation decide what to produce? The answers to these questions lie with the concept of comparative advantage.

Explaining Comparative Advantage Early in the nineteenth century, British economist David Ricardo argued that the key to determining which country should produce which goods is opportunity cost. Remember that opportunity cost is what you give up in order to produce a certain product.

A country has a **comparative advantage** in the product that it can produce most efficiently given all the products it could choose to produce. It is the nation with the comparative advantage—not necessarily the one with the absolute advantage—that should specialize in producing that good.

According to the **law of comparative advantage,** a nation is better off when it produces goods and services for which it has a comparative advantage. Each nation can then use the money it earns selling those goods and services to buy those that it cannot produce as efficiently.

Opportunity Cost and Comparative Advantage To see how comparative advantage works, look again at **Figure 10.2.** It shows the opportunity costs of producing T-shirts and birdhouses for both Carlos and Jenny.

- *Carlos's opportunity costs* In an hour, Carlos can make either six T-shirts or two birdhouses. He therefore sacrifices three T-shirts for every birdhouse he produces. In terms of opportunity cost, the opportunity cost of a birdhouse is the three T-shirts he could have produced instead. The opportunity cost of a T-shirt is one third of a birdhouse.

- *Jenny's opportunity costs* In an hour, Jenny can make either one T-shirt or one birdhouse. Therefore, her opportunity cost for one birdhouse is one T-shirt, and her opportunity cost for one T-shirt is one birdhouse.

According to the law of comparative advantage, each person should produce the good for which he or she has a lower opportunity cost than other producers. Carlos's opportunity cost for producing a T-shirt (one third of a birdhouse) is lower than Jenny's (one birdhouse), so

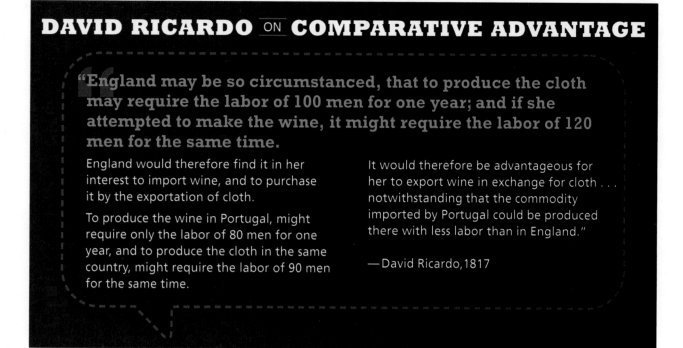

DAVID RICARDO ON COMPARATIVE ADVANTAGE

"**England may be so circumstanced, that to produce the cloth may require the labor of 100 men for one year; and if she attempted to make the wine, it might require the labor of 120 men for the same time.**

England would therefore find it in her interest to import wine, and to purchase it by the exportation of cloth.

To produce the wine in Portugal, might require only the labor of 80 men for one year, and to produce the cloth in the same country, might require the labor of 90 men for the same time.

It would therefore be advantageous for her to export wine in exchange for cloth . . . notwithstanding that the commodity imported by Portugal could be produced there with less labor than in England."

—David Ricardo, 1817

>> **Analyze Information** Why does Ricardo think Portugal should import cloth from England and produce wine rather than producing both?

it is sensible for Carlos to produce T-shirts. Jenny's opportunity cost for producing a birdhouse (one T-shirt) is lower than Carlos's (three T-shirts), so Jenny should produce birdhouses.

The Mutual Benefits of Specialization If Carlos wants a birdhouse, he can either make it himself or make T-shirts and trade some of them to Jenny for a birdhouse. Suppose Carlos and Jenny agree to trade two T-shirts for one birdhouse. In this case, Carlos is clearly better off producing T-shirts and trading for a birdhouse. After all, in the time he would have used to make his own birdhouse, he can make three T-shirts. Since he pays Jenny only two T-shirts for a birdhouse, he has a T-shirt left over. Trade makes Carlos better off by one T-shirt.

Jenny is also better off as a result of trade. She can make two birdhouses in the time she would need to produce two T-shirts for herself. Since she only pays one birdhouse to Carlos for the two T-shirts, she will still have one birdhouse left over. Trade makes her better off by one birdhouse.

Carlos and Jenny both benefit from trade. Each person specializes in producing the good for which he or she has a comparative advantage. Since both producers are operating at greater efficiency, more total goods are produced overall. After the trade, each of them is left with an extra unit of the good originally produced, which can be used to trade for other goods.

? APPLY CONCEPTS How is opportunity cost related to comparative advantage?

Comparative Advantage and World Trade

The lessons from the example of Carlos and Jenny also apply to trade between nations. As you read, David Ricardo argued that the nation having the lower opportunity cost in producing a good has a comparative advantage in producing that good. It is the nation with the comparative advantage in producing a good—not necessarily the absolute advantage—that should specialize in producing that good. It carries out that trade by shipping its goods to other countries and allowing them to ship goods to it.

Comparative Advantage in Action Suppose two countries, A and B, are capable of producing both bananas and sugar. However, Country A's climate and land are somewhat more suitable for growing bananas. For Country A, the opportunity cost of a ton of bananas is two tons of sugar.

For Country B, the opportunity cost of a ton of bananas is three tons of sugar. Since Country A has a lower opportunity cost than does Country B, Country A has a comparative advantage in producing bananas. It should therefore specialize in growing bananas and exporting them to the world market. Trade allows countries to obtain goods for which they might have a high opportunity cost. Thus, Country A can use the money it earns from exporting bananas to import other goods and services that it cannot produce for itself as efficiently as other countries. If a country focuses its resources on producing certain goods, it can make more of them. This is one way that trade causes economic growth.

Growing Interdependence The growth of international trade has led to greater economic interdependence among nations. **Interdependence** is the shared need of countries for the resources, goods, services, labor, and knowledge supplied by other countries.

Because countries are interdependent, changes in one country's economy influence other economies. For example, a drought in Brazil would hurt that country's coffee growers. Coffee growers in Costa Rica or

Colombia may benefit, though, because they would be able to sell more of their product on the world market.

Another example of interdependence can be seen when one country experiences economic growth. Suppose that Mexico's economy grows, resulting in more jobs and higher wages for Mexican workers. With more income, these workers are likely to have greater demand for goods. By buying some of those goods from other countries, Mexico would be helping the economies of its trading partners to grow.

? IDENTIFY CENTRAL ISSUES How does comparative advantage explain why countries trade?

The United States and Its Trading Partners

The United States enjoys a comparative advantage in producing many goods and services. What, then, is its position as an importer and exporter, and what is the impact of that trade?

The Impact of U.S. Exports The United States exports more goods than any other country except China. (The 28-nation European Union exports more than the United States, but less than China.) One reason is the wide range of its export products, from soybeans to telecommunications equipment. Another reason is that the United States excels in technologically sophisticated goods such as software, chemicals, and medical testing supplies.

Goods make up the bulk of international trade, but the United States is also the world's leading exporter of services. These include education, computer and data processing, financial services, and medical care. Exports of services have grown rapidly in recent decades. U.S. cultural exports such as movies, television shows, and popular music have an economic impact. American movies capture about two thirds of ticket sales in Western Europe, creating difficulties for domestic production companies. These pop culture exports also have a cultural impact. They can convey particular images of the American lifestyle and values, introducing new ideas to people of other cultures.

The leading trading partners for U.S. exports are Canada, Mexico, China, and Japan. Nearly half of all exports are capital goods—transistors, aircraft, motor vehicle parts, computers, and telecommunications equipment. Another quarter are industrial supplies, with the remainder coming from consumer goods and agricultural products. Sometimes these exports provide goods that the country could not produce on its own. Sometimes, though, U.S. products compete with

>> Cities, as well as countries, produce goods in which they have a comparative advantage. The skilled weavers in Cuenca, Ecuador, make Panama hats that sell for hundreds of dollars overseas.

Top U.S. Exports

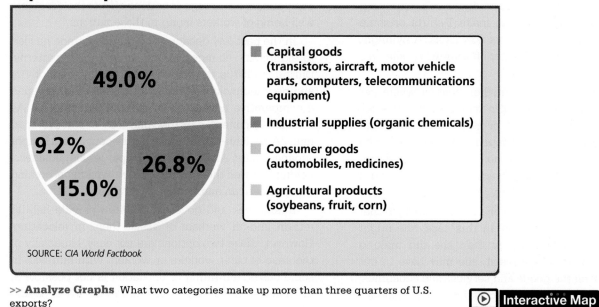

■	**Capital goods** (transistors, aircraft, motor vehicle parts, computers, telecommunications equipment)
■	**Industrial supplies (organic chemicals)**
■	**Consumer goods** (automobiles, medicines)
■	**Agricultural products** (soybeans, fruit, corn)

49.0%

9.2%

26.8%

15.0%

SOURCE: *CIA World Factbook*

>> **Analyze Graphs** What two categories make up more than three quarters of U.S. exports?

▶ Interactive Map

locally produced goods, and low-cost U.S. products have an impact on local suppliers. For instance, U.S. exports of corn to Mexico have surged in recent years. Competition from these products has cut the income of as many as 3 million Mexican farmers, according to some estimates.

The Impact of U.S. Imports The United States is also the world's top importing country—by a significant amount. U.S. imports total nearly $2.3 trillion, $600 billion more than China, the next biggest importer. (The multinational EU imports more than any single country.)

Where do most goods imported into the United States come from? As you might expect, Canada and Mexico provide a significant share of U.S. imports, at 14.1 and 12 percent of all imports, respectively. These neighbors and trading partners have a significant impact on the U.S. economy, literally helping to fuel it. Canada and Mexico are the second and third leading suppliers of energy to the United States, after Saudi Arabia.

While Canada and Mexico account for a quarter of U.S. imports, China has become a major source of U.S. imports and occupies the top position at 19 percent. The leading commodities imported from China are computer equipment, communications devices, consumer manufactured goods (including toys and games), clothing, and electronic parts. These imports give consumers access to goods they want at lower prices than they would have to pay if imported from

another source. Rising U.S. imports from China have also helped fuel China's economic growth.

❓ **CONNECT** What impact do you think the United States has had on China's manufacturing sector? Why?

The Impact of Trade on Jobs

Trade allows nations to specialize in producing a limited number of goods while consuming a greater variety of goods. However, specialization can also dramatically affect a nation's employment patterns. The impact may be negative (loss of jobs) or positive (creation of new job opportunities)—or both.

Specialization and Job Loss To help you better understand the effects of international trade on employment, think back to the example of Carlos and Jenny. Remember that Carlos can make six T-shirts or two birdhouses by himself in an hour. Suppose he hires Amy to help him build birdhouses. He later realizes that he should specialize only in T-shirts since that is where his comparative advantage lies. Since he no longer needs Amy to help him make birdhouses, he fires her.

Up to this point, Amy has specialized in the skills needed to make birdhouses. These skills are no longer in demand where she lives.

- Amy can gain new job skills that are more in demand. She might find a job retraining program and learn to make T-shirts or some other product. With her new skills, Amy might even find herself better off than when she was making birdhouses.

- Amy can move to another location where her existing skills are still in demand. If she chooses to relocate, she may or may not be better off. How well she does depends on the wages she earns from her new job, housing prices in her new location, the impact on her family, and a variety of other factors.

- Amy can stay where she is and take a job that calls for lesser skills. In this case, she might well earn less money than she did making birdhouses. As a result, she may have to cut back on the goods and services she consumes, or take a second job to maintain her standard of living.

- If Amy takes none of these three options, she will be unemployed.

Trade and Employment in the United States

Carlos's decision to focus on his comparative advantage and specialize in making T-shirts had an impact on Amy's economic well-being. In the same way, the comparative advantage of nations affects the economic well-being of workers living in those nations.

In the past few decades, international trade has led to significant changes in U.S. employment patterns. During the 1970s, for example, high worker productivity and new technologies like robotics helped give Japan a comparative advantage in making automobiles. As a result, Japanese cars became less expensive than many American-made cars. As more consumers bought Japanese cars, American car companies lost business. Falling sales led them to reduce their workforce, costing many American autoworkers their jobs.

Businesses and government often provide help to retrain laid-off workers or assist them in relocating. However, these two options are not easy, especially in the case of older workers or workers with families. In some cases, retraining or relocation is not possible at all. Some workers may be forced to take lower-paying jobs or face prolonged unemployment.

Trade can also result in the creation of new jobs. If American exports grow, there will be more demand for workers to make those products. President Obama said in his 2010 State of the Union Address:

> The more products we make and sell to other countries, the more jobs we support right here in America. So tonight, we set a new goal: We will double our exports over the next five years, an increase that will support two million jobs in America.
>
> —President Barack Obama

In 2013, the government reported that 1.3 million American jobs had been added as a result of increased exports. Workers who lost jobs because they were on the negative end of comparative advantage may find work in those growing industries. To do so, they may have to retrain to gain the needed skills.

? SYNTHESIZE What advantages does a person who is retrained for a new industry have versus a person who relocates to get a job?

>> Governments fund retraining programs to help workers laid off from struggling industries prepare for careers that require new sets of skills and knowledge.

ASSESSMENT

1. **Apply Concepts** How does the unequal distribution of resources help explain why nations specialize in producing certain goods?

2. **Contrast** How does comparative advantage contrast with absolute advantage?

3. **Make Generalizations** Why do countries trade, and what determines what they trade?

4. **Identify Central Ideas** What is the impact of U.S. exports on the United States and its trading partners?

5. **Identify Central Ideas** What is the impact of U.S. imports on the United States and its trading partners?

>> In 2013 demonstrators in Thailand protested talks on a free trade agreement between Thailand and the European Union. Farmers feared that extended patents on plant varieties would force them to pay more for seeds.

▶ **Interactive Flipped Video**

Would you take part in marches and strikes to protest against a trade policy? That's what more than 200,000 citizens of Colombia did in a nationwide strike in August 2013. Blocking roads, the marchers voiced opposition to the U.S.–Colombia Trade Promotion Agreement. To these protesters, trade policy was not just an economic idea; it had a major impact on their lives. And the same is true of you—whether you know it or not.

>> Objectives

Describe the policies nations use to control or direct international trade.

Analyze the effects of international trade agreements.

Summarize the arguments for and against free international trade.

Explain the role of multinational corporations in the process of globalization.

>> Key Terms

trade barrier
tariff
import quota
sanctions
embargo
trade war
protectionism
infant industry
free trade
free trade zone
World Trade
    Organization

Trade Barriers and Agreements

Free Trade and Trade Barriers

Today, many people favor increased foreign trade, while others fear its effects. To understand why, you need to understand the kinds of barriers that nations sometimes erect to trade. In this section, you will also see how trade policies may affect what you pay for dozens of products, from chocolate to cars.

A **trade barrier,** or trade restriction, is a means of preventing a foreign product or service from freely entering a nation's territory. Trade barriers take several forms and may be used for various purposes.

Tariffs One common trade barrier is a **tariff,** or a tax on imported goods. Until the early 1900s, tariffs were a major tool of fiscal policy in the United States and the main source of revenue for the federal government. As you can see from **Figure 10.3,** however, tariffs today are much lower. Still, the United States continues to collect tariffs on steel, foreign-made cars, and many other products.

If you have traveled abroad, you may have had to pay a tax on foreign goods you brought back to the United States. These customs duties are another form of tariff.

Quotas and VERs Another kind of barrier is an import quota. **Import quotas** place a limit on the amount of a good that can be imported. For example, the United States limits the annual amount of raw cotton coming into the country from other nations. Many import quotas are now illegal under international trade laws.

Tariffs and quotas are laws set by the importing country. By contrast, a voluntary export restraint (VER) is a voluntary limit set by the exporting country, restricting the quantity of a product it will sell to another country. A nation that adopts a VER seeks to reduce the risk that the importing country will impose damaging trade barriers itself.

Other Barriers to Trade Other government actions may also create trade barriers. For example, a government may require foreign companies to obtain a license to sell goods in that country. High licensing fees and slow licensing processes act as informal trade barriers.

Health, safety, or environmental regulations can also act as trade barriers. Suppose a nation treats the fruit it grows with a particular insecticide. Another nation might ban any fruit treated with that insecticide in order to discourage imports of foreign fruit. The U.S. antipollution standard that requires cars to be equipped with catalytic converters is another example. Cars that do not meet this requirement cannot be exported to the United States.

Finally, a nation may impose trade barriers and other economic sanctions for political reasons. **Sanctions** are actions a nation or group of nations takes in order to punish or put pressure on another nation. For example, in the 1960s, the United States banned all trade with Cuba. The purpose of this trade **embargo** was to cause economic strain that might weaken Cuba's communist dictatorship. An embargo is an official ban on trade or other commercial activity with a country.

? **COMPARE AND CONTRAST** How are voluntary export restraints and import quotas different?

Effects of Trade Barriers

By limiting supply, trade barriers can have very different effects on domestic producers and consumers. Trade barriers may also create tense relations between importing and exporting countries.

Higher Prices for Foreign Goods Trade barriers can help domestic producers compete with foreign firms. By limiting imports from those firms, or by making the prices of those imports higher, trade barriers give a competitive advantage to domestic companies.

Although domestic producers may benefit, consumers can lose out. Restrictions on imports result in higher prices. For example, suppose the market price of an imported car is $20,000. If the government places

Average Tariff Rates, 1900–2010

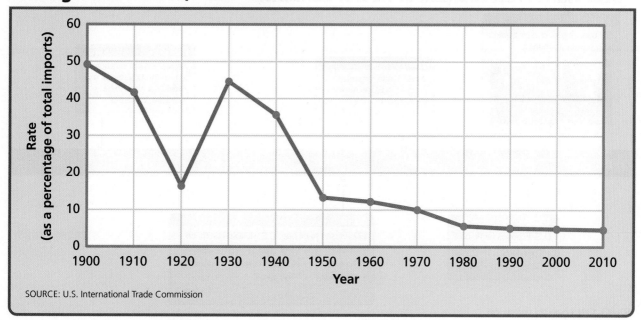

SOURCE: U.S. International Trade Commission

>> **Figure 10.3 Analyze Graphs** Describe what has happened to tariff rates since 1950 versus the period from 1900 to 1950.

a 10-percent tariff on all imported foreign cars, the price of the average imported car would increase from $20,000 to $22,000. Consumers who bought such a vehicle would be paying a higher price than if there had been no tariff. Also, with foreign competition limited, domestic carmakers would have no incentive to keep prices low.

Trade Wars Trade barriers may also fuel international conflict. When one country restricts imports, its trading partner may retaliate by placing its own restrictions on imports. If the first country responds with further trade limits, the result is a **trade war,** a cycle of escalating trade barriers. Trade wars often cause economic hardship for both sides.

Probably the most damaging trade war in American history began during the Great Depression. In 1930, Congress passed the Smoot-Hawley Act, raising average tariff rates on all imports to 50 percent. Congress hoped the tariff would protect American workers and businesses from foreign competition and help the economy rebound.

The reverse effect took place, though. Other countries responded by raising tariffs on American-made goods. The resulting trade war decreased international trade and deepened the worldwide depression. Most economists blame the Smoot-Hawley tariff for increasing American unemployment.

Trade wars still occur, but they usually involve a few products rather than all imports. In 2002, the United States placed temporary tariffs on imported steel to help American steelmakers recover from bankruptcy. European nations threatened to retaliate. This "steel war" ended when an international panel ruled that the tariffs were illegal.

❓ **IDENTIFY CAUSE AND EFFECT** Why are trade wars harmful?

Arguments for Protectionism

Why does a nation impose trade barriers? One reason is **protectionism,** the use of trade barriers to shield domestic industries from foreign competition. Protectionists have generally used three main arguments to support their view: saving jobs, protecting infant industries, and safeguarding national security.

Protecting Jobs One argument for protectionism is that it shelters workers in industries that may be hurt by foreign competition. Suppose that certain East Asian nations had a comparative advantage in producing textiles. If the United States cut tariffs on textile imports, domestic manufacturers might find it

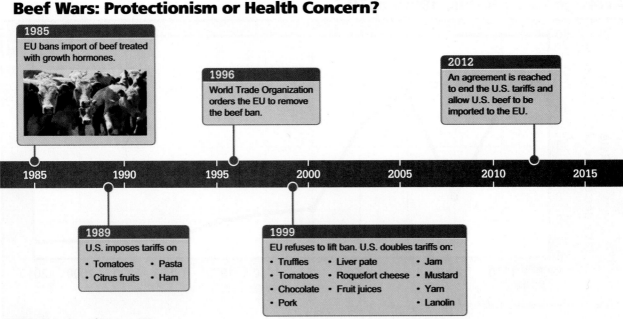

Beef Wars: Protectionism or Health Concern?

1985
EU bans import of beef treated with growth hormones.

1996
World Trade Organization orders the EU to remove the beef ban.

2012
An agreement is reached to end the U.S. tariffs and allow U.S. beef to be imported to the EU.

1985   1990   1995   2000   2005   2010   2015

1989
U.S. imposes tariffs on
- Tomatoes
- Pasta
- Citrus fruits
- Ham

1999
EU refuses to lift ban. U.S. doubles tariffs on:
- Truffles
- Liver pate
- Jam
- Tomatoes
- Roquefort cheese
- Mustard
- Chocolate
- Fruit juices
- Yarn
- Pork
- Lanolin

SOURCE: CNN, Library of Congress, BBC

>> **Analyze Charts** How long did the Beef Wars last? Who do you think won the wars?

hard to compete with imports from East Asia. They would have to close their factories and lay off workers.

Ideally, the laid-off workers would take new jobs in other industries. In practice, however, many of these workers would find retraining or relocation difficult. In addition, few industry or political leaders want to see existing industries shut down or large numbers of people lose their jobs. For this reason, public officials might favor protectionism to keep companies alive and people working.

Protecting Infant Industries Another argument for protectionism is that industries in the early stages of development need time and experience to become efficient producers. Tariffs that raise the price of imported goods provide a period of time for these **infant industries** to become more competitive. Once that happens, the tariff can be eliminated.

In the early years of the United States, Alexander Hamilton favored using tariffs to protect young American industries from European competition. Today, many developing nations adopt protectionist policies for similar reasons:

> Global economic competition is a game of unequal players. It pits against each other countries that range from Switzerland to Swaziland. . . . It is only fair that we 'tilt the playing field' in favor of the weaker countries. In practice, this means allowing them to protect . . . their producers more vigorously.
>
> —Ha-Joon Chang, "Protecting the Global Poor"

Three problems may arise with such protective tariffs, however. First, a protected infant industry may lack the incentive to "grow up," that is, to become more efficient and competitive. Second, once an industry has been given tariff protection, lawmakers may find it difficult for political reasons to take the protections away. Third, a protected industry can keep its prices relatively high, increasing costs to consumers.

Safeguarding National Security Certain industries may require protection because their products are essential to defending the country. In the event of a war, the United States would need an uninterrupted supply of steel, energy, and advanced technologies. For this reason, the government wants to ensure that such domestic industries remain active.

>> The slogan "Buy American" is used to encourage Americans to spend their money on products made in the U.S. This more directly supports American industries and workers.

>> **Analyze Political Cartoons** What do the size and the attitude of the baby tell about the pitfalls of protecting infant industries?

Foes of trade barriers agree that protecting defense industries is important. They argue, however, that some industries that seek protection are not really essential to national security.

❓ SUPPORT A POINT OF VIEW WITH EVIDENCE
What are the three arguments given for protectionism?

Trade Agreements

In opposition to protectionism is the principle of free trade. **Free trade** involves the lowering or elimination of protective tariffs and other trade barriers between two or more nations. Supporters argue that free trade is the best way to pursue comparative advantage, raise living standards, and further cooperative relationships among nations.

To encourage free trade, a number of countries in recent decades have signed international free trade agreements. Some of these pacts involve dozens of nations.

Roots of Free Trade Today's free trade movement began in the 1930s. The Smoot-Hawley Act caused a rapid decline in international trade. To encourage trade, Congress passed the Reciprocal Trade Agreements Act of 1934. It gave the president the power to reduce tariffs by as much as 50 percent.

That law also allowed Congress to grant most-favored nation (MFN) status to U.S. trading partners. Today, MFN status is called normal trade relations status, or NTR. All countries with NTR status pay the same tariffs, though imports from non-NTR nations may be taxed at a higher rate.

In 1948, after World War II had disrupted world trade, many nations reached an agreement called the General Agreement on Tariffs and Trade (GATT). Its goal was to reduce tariffs and stabilize world trade.

World Trade Organization In 1995, the **World Trade Organization** (WTO) was founded with the goal of making global trade more free. The WTO works to ensure that countries comply with GATT, to negotiate new trade agreements, and to resolve trade disputes. Various conferences, or rounds, of tariff negotiations have advanced the goals of GATT and the WTO. For example, the Uruguay round of negotiations, completed in 1994, decreased average global tariffs by about a third.

Today, the World Trade Organization also acts as a referee, enforcing the rules agreed upon by the member countries. WTO decisions resolved the beef war and

OPPOSING VIEWS ON TRADE

For Trade Barriers

- **Jobs:** Trade barriers protect jobs from going to other countries

- **Industries:** Trade barriers protect domestic industries from competition

- **Security:** Trade barriers protect industries essential to national security

- **Multinationals:** Trade barriers limit the political power of multinationals in host nations

For Trade Agreements

- **Competition:** Trade agreements allow and enhance competition

- **Prices:** Trade agreements lower prices for foreign goods

- **Efficiency:** Free trade is the best way to pursue comparative advantage

- **Risk:** Trade agreements lessen risk of trade wars

>> **Analyze Charts** Using the chart, name one way trade barriers benefit workers and one way trade agreements benefit consumers.

the steel tariff disputes between the United States and the European Union.

❓ IDENTIFY CAUSE AND EFFECT What effect does a free trade agreement have on the countries that sign it?

Regional Trade Organizations

In addition to the WTO, there are smaller regional trade organizations, often made up of several countries in the same general geographic area. These trade organizations seek to enhance free trade among member nations.

The European Union In recent years, many countries have signed agreements to abolish tariffs and trade restrictions among member nations and adopt uniform tariffs for all countries that are not members. One example is the European Union (EU).

The European Union developed slowly over several decades. In 1957, six western European nations set up the Common Market to coordinate economic and trade policies. In the years that followed, more countries joined the Common Market. In 1986, the member nations agreed to eliminate tariffs on one another's exports. They created a single market, called the European Economic Community (EEC).

In 1993, the EEC nations formed the European Union. This new organization became the largest trading bloc in the world. By 2013, the EU included 28 countries—almost all of Europe. This includes Poland, Hungary, Romania, and other former Soviet bloc nations that had once been forbidden to trade with the rest of Europe.

The EU adopted various policies to strengthen member economies, such as using agricultural subsidies and tariffs to keep farm prices high. Some member nations signed the European Monetary Union, agreeing to adopt a single currency and monetary system. In 2002, 12 member nations replaced their individual currencies with a single currency called the euro. As of 2013, 18 countries used the euro. The EU also adopted political ties, forming a parliament and council that make laws all member nations must follow. Still, many Europeans feared such measures threatened each nation's right to make decisions in its own interest.

NAFTA Other nations have created **free trade zones,** where a group of countries agrees to reduce or eliminate trade barriers. One such pact, the North American Free

"You drive a Japanese car, drink French wine, eat Chinese food, own an American computer, buy Canadian lumber and vacation in Mexico. How can you be AGAINST free trade?!"

>> Analyze Political Cartoons Americans use imported products every day. What products do you use that you could add to the cartoon caption?

>> Secretary of State John Kerry and German Foreign Minister Guido Westerwelle met in 2013 to discuss a free trade agreement between the U.S. and the EU. This would create the largest free trade zone in the world.

"They moved our industry across the Mexican border, and all we get is the smoke!"

>> **Analyze Political Cartoons** NAFTA has both benefits and drawbacks. How do the workers in the cartoon feel about NAFTA? Why?

>> Electronics are a major export from the United States to Mexico. This computer is being assembled in Texas to be sold in Mexico.

▶ **Interactive Map**

Trade Agreement (NAFTA), created a free trade zone linking the United States, Canada, and Mexico.

NAFTA aroused controversy in the United States. Opponents worried that American companies would move factories to Mexico, where wages were lower and environmental regulations were less strict. As a result, they said, American workers would lose jobs. Supporters of NAFTA claimed that the measure would instead create more jobs in the United States, because it would increase exports to Mexico and Canada.

After a spirited debate, the Senate ratified NAFTA in 1993. Major provisions include:

- Tariffs on all farm products and on some 10,000 other goods were eliminated over 15 years.

- Some auto tariffs were eliminated immediately while others were phased out in periods of five to ten years.

- Trucks were to have free access across borders and throughout the three member countries.

- Special judges were given authority to resolve trade disputes.

- The agreement could not be used to override national and state environmental, health, or safety laws.

More than 20 years after it went into effect, the agreement has remained controversial. Many studies suggest that NAFTA has had its intended economic benefits. Yet, other studies suggest these benefits have come at a cost to U.S. workers. It is difficult to measure the overall effects of the agreement, because some effects may be due to causes other than NAFTA.

What is clear is that trade between the member nations has increased. U.S. trade with Canada and Mexico has tripled since 1993. All in all, NAFTA is estimated to have had a small but positive effect on the U.S. economy.

CAFTA-DR and FTAA In 2003, the United States government reached a free trade agreement with five nations of Central America. At the time, the deal was called the Central American Free Trade Agreement (CAFTA). The next year, when the Dominican Republic joined the pact, the name was changed to CAFTA-DR. Congress approved the agreement in July 2005, and the other nations formally approved it as well. Costa Rica formally accepted CAFTA-DR in late 2007.

Free trade hit a roadblock with the failure of the Free Trade Area of the Americas (FTAA). This trade deal would have opened trade among 34 nations of North and South America. However, after more than a decade of negotiations, the proposal was rejected by several key South American nations in 2005.

KEY
- EU
- CARICOM
- MERCOSUR
- APEC
- ASEAN
- NAFTA

>> **Analyze Maps** What geographic feature do the nations belonging to APEC have in common? What advantage might that feature give to trade among those nations?

Other Regional Trade Agreements About 100 regional trading organizations operate in the world today. They include the following:

APEC The Asia-Pacific Economic Cooperation is an economic forum that includes 21 countries along the Pacific Rim, including the United States. They have signed a nonbinding agreement to reduce trade barriers.

MERCOSUR The Southern Common Market is similar to the EU in its goals. Its members are the South American nations of Brazil, Paraguay, Uruguay, Argentina, and Venezuela.

CARICOM The Caribbean Community and Common Market includes countries from South America and the Caribbean.

ASEAN The ten-member Association of Southeast Asian Nations has taken steps to establish a free trade zone similar to the EU.

The Debate Over Free Trade While the world's economies have moved toward free trade, controversy on trade continues. Debates over the impact of NAFTA became a campaign issue in the American presidential election of 2008. As you saw, protests across the Americas slowed negotiations on the FTAA.

Meetings of the World Trade Organization have also spurred large protests. A 1999 WTO meeting in Seattle, Washington, drew as many as 50,000 angry demonstrators. Not all of these protesters were opposed to free trade. Rather, they were concerned that current free trade agreements gave too much economic power to large multinational corporations.

? SUPPORT A POINT OF VIEW WITH EVIDENCE Why do you think NAFTA stirred such debate in the United States?

The Role of Multinationals

As you read earlier, a corporation is a legal entity that is owned by shareholders and run by managers. Its stockholders have limited liability. A corporation can grow very large and merge with other corporations. A large corporation that sells goods and services throughout the world is a multinational. For example, an automobile company might design its cars in the United States and import parts made in Asia to an assembly plant in Canada. Even if you purchase the car from an American company, it is not a purely domestic product.

Many goods besides cars are produced globally. Some brands of athletic shoes are designed in the United States but are produced in East Asia. Some personal computers are designed in the United States and assembled abroad with parts and components from the United States.

Multinationals with Largest Foreign Assets, 2011

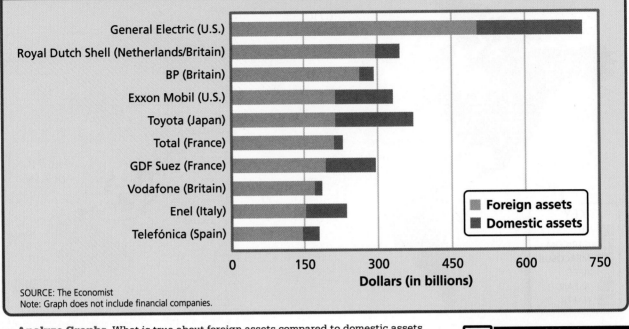

SOURCE: The Economist
Note: Graph does not include financial companies.

>> **Analyze Graphs** What is true about foreign assets compared to domestic assets for each of the multinationals on the graph?

▶ **Interactive Illustration**

The decision to build production facilities in a foreign country benefits both the multinational and the host nation. By locating abroad, the corporation avoids some shipping fees and tariffs. It may also benefit from cheaper labor. The host nation benefits by gaining jobs and tax revenue.

Still, host nations worry about the effect of multinationals on their countries. In a small country with a fragile economy, multinationals can gain excessive political power. In addition, host nations fear that multinationals could drive out domestic industries and exploit local workers. To protect domestic industries, some host nations have created rules requiring multinationals to export a certain percentage of their products.

? **IDENTIFY CENTRAL ISSUES** Why are some nations concerned about the negative effects of multinationals?

ASSESSMENT

1. **Support a Point of View With Evidence** Describe a way that trade barriers can affect you as a consumer.

2. **Identify Cause and Effect** What is the difference between an import quota and a tariff?

3. **Categorize** What are the positive effects of international trade agreements?

4. **Express Problems Clearly** What is one negative effect of participating in free trade agreements?

5. **Summarize** Who owns multinational corporations?

It's happened to everyone. You buy something in a store. You hand over a couple of bills. The clerk hands you your change. When you get outside, you notice something funny about one of the quarters. Instead of the familiar profile of George Washington, you see a caribou with a large pair of antlers. You've been given a Canadian quarter.

>> A depreciating dollar makes American goods less expensive for tourists visiting the United States, such as these visitors to Miami.

▶ **Interactive Flipped Video**

Exchange Rates and Trade

Foreign Exchange and Currencies

Maybe you feel cheated. But should you? Is this Canadian quarter worth less than a U.S. quarter—or more? How would you find out? These questions may seem unimportant when you're dealing with just a single quarter. But if you were dealing with hundreds or thousands of dollars, the questions might be very important indeed!

The difference in value between an American dollar and a Canadian dollar—or a British pound or a Japanese yen or a Saudi Arabian riyal—does not stay the same from day to day. In this text, you will see how these fluctuations have a huge impact on imports and exports. Nevertheless, currency is a good means for trading between countries.

International trade is more complex than buying and selling within one country because of the world's many currencies and their changing values. If you want to buy a newspaper in Beijing, you will need to change your American dollars for Chinese yuan. If a Mexican family visiting New York wants to buy lunch, they must change their pesos to dollars.

>> **Objectives**

Analyze the effects of changes in exchange rates on world trade.

Define *balance of trade.*

Summarize the effects of international trade on the United States and its trading partners.

Analyze the role of the United States in international trade.

>> **Key Terms**

exchange rate
appreciation
depreciation
foreign exchange
  market
fixed exchange-rate
  system
flexible exchange-
  rate system
balance of trade
trade surplus
trade deficit
balance of payments

Exchange Rates Changing money from one nation's currency to another's is never a simple matter of exchanging, say, one yuan or one peso for one American dollar. A dollar might be worth 8 yuan or 11 pesos. The value of a nation's currency in relation to a foreign currency is called the **exchange rate.** Understanding how exchange rates work enables you to convert prices in one currency to prices in another currency.

Daily exchange rates are listed in major newspapers and on the Internet. **Figure 10.4** shows a sample table of exchange rates. If you read down the first column, you will see that one U.S. dollar can be exchanged for more than one (1.10) Australian dollar, for less than one (0.74) euro, and so forth.

An exchange-rate table shows what one U.S. dollar is worth on one particular day. Remember, the rates change daily, so it is important to keep checking, especially if you are visiting a foreign country or doing business overseas.

Converting Prices A simple formula allows you to convert the price of an item from foreign currency to American dollars. Just divide the price by the value of the currency per one dollar according to the exchange rate.

Look at the following example:

Suppose your family is planning a trip to Mexico and that the exchange rate is as shown in **Figure 10.4.**

If a hotel room in Mexico costs 500 pesos per night, the price in U.S. dollars is $38.20.

500 pesos ÷ 13.09 pesos/dollar = $38.20. Now suppose your family decides to go to Mexico next year instead, and the exchange rate has risen to 15.0 pesos per dollar. Assuming that the room rate is still 500 pesos, the hotel room will cost only $33.33 per night:

500 pesos ÷ 15.0 pesos/dollar = $33.33

Appreciating Currency You have probably heard newscasters talk about a "strong" or "weak" dollar or a currency like the Japanese yen "rising" or "falling." What do these terms mean? Do they indicate good news or bad news for the United States economy?

An increase in the value of a currency is called **appreciation.** When a currency appreciates, it becomes "stronger."

If the exchange rate between the dollar and the yen increases from 100 yen per dollar to 120 yen per dollar, each dollar can buy more yen. Since the dollar has increased in value, we say that the dollar has appreciated against the yen. This appreciation means that people in Japan will have to spend more yen to purchase a dollar's worth of goods from the United States. On the other hand, Americans who travel to Japan can buy more goods and services for the same amount of money than they could before the dollar appreciated.

Foreign Exchange Rates

	U.S. $	AUST. $	CANADIAN $	U.K. £	JAPANESE ¥EN	€URO	MEXICAN PESO	CHINESE YUAN
U.S. $	1	.91	.95	1.62	.010	1.35	.08	.16
Aust. $	1.10	1	1.04	1.77	.011	1.49	.08	.18
Canadian $	1.05	.96	1	1.70	.010	1.43	.08	.17
U.K. £	.62	.56	.59	1	.006	.84	.05	.10
Japanese ¥en	101.42	92.46	96.31	163.98	1	137.40	7.75	16.64
€uro	.74	.67	.70	1.19	.007	1	.06	.12
Mexican peso	13.09	11.93	12.43	21.16	.129	17.73	1	2.14
Chinese yuan	6.09	5.55	5.79	9.85	.060	8.25	.47	1

SOURCE: x-rates.com accessed on Tuesday, November 26, 2013. Note: These data are highly time sensitive and can change hourly.

>> **Figure 10.4** This chart shows exchange rates on a single day. **Analyze Charts** If you had 100 euros, would it buy more Australian or U.S. dollars?

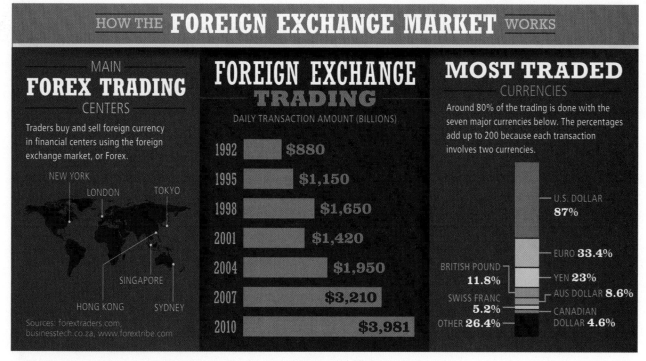

HOW THE FOREIGN EXCHANGE MARKET WORKS

MAIN FOREX TRADING CENTERS

Traders buy and sell foreign currency in financial centers using the foreign exchange market, or Forex.

NEW YORK
LONDON
TOKYO
SINGAPORE
HONG KONG
SYDNEY

Sources: forextraders.com, businesstech.co.za, www.forextribe.com

FOREIGN EXCHANGE TRADING

DAILY TRANSACTION AMOUNT (BILLIONS)

Year	Amount
1992	$880
1995	$1,150
1998	$1,650
2001	$1,420
2004	$1,950
2007	$3,210
2010	$3,981

MOST TRADED CURRENCIES

Around 80% of the trading is done with the seven major currencies below. The percentages add up to 200 because each transaction involves two currencies.

- U.S. DOLLAR 87%
- EURO 33.4%
- YEN 23%
- AUS DOLLAR 8.6%
- CANADIAN DOLLAR 4.6%
- BRITISH POUND 11.8%
- SWISS FRANC 5.2%
- OTHER 26.4%

>> The foreign exchange market assists international trade by converting currencies.
Analyze Charts Which two currencies are the most frequently traded? Why do you think this is so?

When a nation's currency appreciates, its products become more expensive in other countries. For example, a strong dollar makes American goods and services more expensive for Japanese consumers. Japan will therefore probably import fewer products from the United States. As a result, total United States exports to Japan will likely decline. On the other hand, a strong dollar makes foreign products less expensive for consumers in the United States. A strong dollar is therefore likely to lead consumers in the United States to purchase more imported goods.

Depreciating Currency A decrease in the value of a currency is called **depreciation.** You might also hear depreciation referred to as "weakening." If the dollar exchange rate fell to 80 yen per dollar, you would get fewer yen for each dollar. In other words, the dollar has depreciated against the yen.

When a nation's currency depreciates, its products become cheaper to other nations. A depreciated, or weak, dollar means that foreign consumers will be able to better afford products made in the United States. A weakened dollar probably results in increased exports. At the same time, other nations' products become more expensive for consumers in the United States, so they will buy fewer imports.

Exchanging Currency Suppose that a company in the United States sells computers in Japan. That company is paid in yen. It must, however, pay its workers and suppliers back in the United States in dollars. The company must therefore exchange its yen for U.S. dollars. This exchange takes place on the foreign exchange market. International trade would not be possible without this market.

The **foreign exchange market** consists of about 2,000 banks and other financial institutions that facilitate the buying and selling of foreign currencies. These banks are located in various financial centers around the world, including such cities as New York, London, Paris, Singapore, and Tokyo. These banks maintain close links to one another through telephones and computers. This technology allows for the instantaneous transmission of market information and rapid financial transactions.

? CHECK UNDERSTANDING What are the likely effects of the dollar becoming stronger?

Determining the Value of Currency

As you read earlier, currencies varied in value from state to state in early America. In the United States today, of course, it doesn't matter which state you live in. All prices are in dollars, and all dollars have the same value.

Think how much more complicated it would be to do business if each state still had its own currency. To buy goods from a mail-order company in Indiana, for instance, someone in Texas would have to find out the exchange rate between a Texas dollar and an Indiana dollar. The economy would become less efficient as individuals and businesses spent time keeping track of exchange rates.

Such complications do not exist within the United States. They do, however, apply to international trade.

Fixed Exchange-Rate Systems Of course, it would be simpler if all countries either used the same currency or kept their exchange rates constant. Then no one would have to worry about rate shifts. A system in which governments try to keep the values of their currencies constant against one another is called a **fixed exchange-rate system.**

In a typical fixed exchange-rate system, one country with a stable currency is at the center. Other countries fix, or peg, their exchange rates to this currency.

Normally, the fixed exchange-rate is not a single value, but is kept within a certain specified range (for example, plus or minus 2 percent). If the exchange rate moves outside of this range, governments usually intervene to maintain the rate.

How do governments intervene to maintain an exchange rate? The exchange rate is essentially the price of a currency. Like the price of any product or service, the exchange rate relies on supply and demand.

To preserve its exchange rate, a government may buy or sell foreign currency in order to affect a currency's supply and demand. It will follow this course of action until the exchange rate is back within the specified limits.

The Bretton Woods Conference In 1944, as World War II was drawing to a close, representatives from 44 countries met in Bretton Woods, New Hampshire. Their purpose was to make financial arrangements for the postwar world.

The Bretton Woods conference resulted in the creation of a fixed exchange-rate system for the United States and much of western Europe. Because the United States had the strongest economy and most stable currency, conference participants agreed to peg their currencies to the United States dollar.

To make the new system work, the Bretton Woods conference established the International Monetary

Fixed Exchange Rates, Selected Countries

COUNTRY	REGION	CURRENCY NAME	PEG CURRENCY	PEG RATE	RATE SINCE
Benin	Africa	West African CFA Franc	Euro	655.957	1999
Cameroon	Africa	Central African CFA Franc	Euro	655.957	1999
Hong Kong	Asia	Dollar	US Dollar	7.75–7.85	1998
Cuba	Central America	Convertible Peso	US Dollar	1	2011
Panama	Central America	Balboa	US Dollar	1	1904
Latvia	Europe	Lats	Euro	0.702804	2004
Denmark	Europe	Krone	Euro	7.46038	1999
Jordan	Middle East	Dinar	US Dollar	0.709	1995
Saudi Arabia	Middle East	Riyal	US Dollar	3.75	2003
Venezuela	South America	Bolivar	US Dollar	6.3	2013

SOURCE: www.investmentfrontier.com

>> These countries have adopted the fixed-exchange rate system to ensure stability.
Analyze Charts Which country in the chart has had the same pegged currency rate the longest?

Fund (IMF). Today, the IMF promotes international monetary cooperation, currency stabilization, and trade.

Flexible Exchange-Rate Systems Although fixed exchange-rate systems make trade easier, they depend on countries maintaining similar economic policies as well as similar inflation and interest rates. By the late 1960s, worldwide trade was growing and changing rapidly. At the same time, the war in Vietnam was causing inflation in the United States. These factors made it increasingly difficult for many countries to rely on a fixed exchange rate.

In 1971, the Netherlands and West Germany abandoned the fixed exchange-rate system. Other countries followed. By 1973, even the United States had adopted a system based on flexible exchange rates. Under a **flexible exchange-rate system,** the exchange rate is determined by supply and demand rather than according to any preset range.

Today, the countries of the world use a mixture of fixed and flexible exchange rates. Most major currencies—including the U.S. dollar and the Japanese yen—use the flexible exchange-rate system. This system accounts for the day-to-day changes in currency values that you read about earlier in this section.

When the current flexible exchange-rate system was first adopted, some economists worried that changes in the exchange rate might interrupt the flow of world trade. In actual fact, trade has grown rapidly since the flexible exchange-rate system was adopted. Today, more nations trade than ever before.

The Euro Although the flexible exchange-rate system works well, some countries whose economies are closely tied together want the advantages of fixed rates. One way to enjoy the advantages but avoid some of the difficulties of fixed exchange rates is to abolish individual currencies and establish a single currency.

This is what 11 countries of the European Union did by adopting the euro. Use of this common currency requires countries to coordinate their economic policies, but it also simplifies trade. People traveling from, say, Germany to France do not need to exchange marks for francs at the border. They simply use their euros. However, having one currency has had its disadvantages. During the financial crisis that started in 2007, a number of countries, including Greece, Spain, and Italy, faced economic difficulties and became less competitive on world markets.

Because they were part of the single currency block, they could not depreciate their own currency or use monetary policy to help alleviate their economic problems. Instead, they were forced to suffer through

>> Global leaders met at the Mount Washington Hotel in Bretton Woods, NH, to stabilize the world's financial system. They instituted policies that were designed to prevent practices that could lead to severe economic downturns.

a deep and prolonged recession to reduce their wages and prices in order to restore their competitiveness. These adjustments not only caused economic strife for those countries, but also created tensions within the entire group of nations using the euro.

? IDENTIFY CAUSE AND EFFECT Has the flexible exchange-rate system prevented or enabled an increase in world trade?

Balance of Trade

The value of a nation's currency is affected by the overall flow of goods and services into and out of the country. In turn, exchange rates can affect a nation's **balance of trade,** the relationship between the value of its exports and the value of its imports.

Surpluses and Deficits The importing and exporting of goods and services can have a significant impact on the United States and its trading partners. A trade imbalance, which occurs when a large difference between a nation's imports and exports arises, is one example. A nation that exports more goods and services than it imports has a positive trade balance, or a **trade surplus.** A nation that imports more goods and services than it exports has a negative trade balance, or a **trade deficit.**

Nations seek to maintain a balance of trade. That is, they hope the value of imports is roughly equal to the value of exports.

By balancing trade, a nation can protect the value of its currency on the international market. When a country has a continuing negative balance of trade, importing more than it is exporting over an extended period of time, the value of its currency falls.

For example, in the 1980s, the United States imported considerably more than it exported. As a result of this trade imbalance, the foreign exchange market was glutted with U.S. dollars. Because the supply of dollars was so high, the value of the dollar fell. The prices of imports increased, and American consumers had to pay more for imported goods.

A negative balance of trade can be corrected either by limiting imports or by increasing the number or value of exports. Both of these actions affect trading partners, of course, who may then retaliate by raising tariffs. Maintaining a balance of trade thus requires international cooperation and fair trade practices.

Balance of Payments and Circular Flow Model
Balance of trade measures the flow of goods and services among nations. Economists get a more complex picture of international trade by looking at the balance of payments. **Balance of payments** is the value of all monetary transactions between all sectors of a country's economy—households, firms, and government—and the rest of the world.

Look again at the circular flow model of a mixed economy (**Figure 2.10**) that you saw earlier. It shows the movement of money and goods within a single economy. Now suppose you had to add in the international sector as well. Foreign transactions would enter into every stage. For example, if an American invested in a foreign company, the capital he or she invested would be part of the monetary flow going overseas. Any returns from the investment would be part of the monetary flow coming into the country. Income from foreign companies, government aid to foreign countries, borrowing from foreign banks, exchange rates—all of these must be factored into the balance of payments.

❓ **IDENTIFY CENTRAL IDEAS** What impact did the United States trade imbalance in the 1980s have on the cost of imported goods?

A Growing Trade Deficit

Although the United States sells many goods abroad, it generally imports more than it exports. As a result, the United States currently runs a trade deficit. (See **Figure 10.5**)

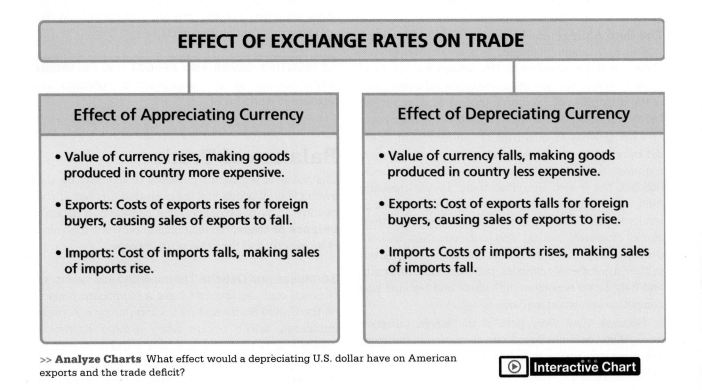

EFFECT OF EXCHANGE RATES ON TRADE

Effect of Appreciating Currency

- Value of currency rises, making goods produced in country more expensive.

- Exports: Costs of exports rises for foreign buyers, causing sales of exports to fall.

- Imports: Cost of imports falls, making sales of imports rise.

Effect of Depreciating Currency

- Value of currency falls, making goods produced in country less expensive.

- Exports: Cost of exports falls for foreign buyers, causing sales of exports to rise.

- Imports Costs of imports rises, making sales of imports fall.

>> **Analyze Charts** What effect would a depreciating U.S. dollar have on American exports and the trade deficit?

▶ **Interactive Chart**

U.S. Balance of Trade, 1965–2012

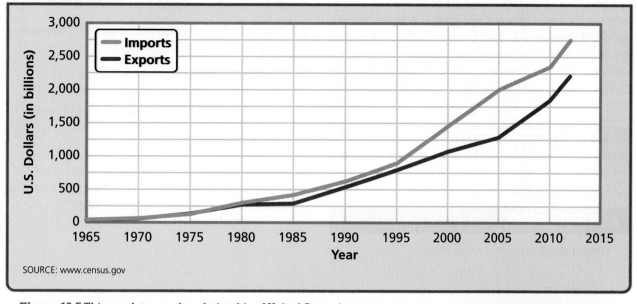

SOURCE: www.census.gov

>> **Figure 10.5** This graph traces the relationship of United States imports to exports for over four decades. **Analyze Graphs** In which year was the trade deficit greatest?

▶ Interactive Chart

Causes of the Trade Deficit The U.S. trade deficit began to take shape in the 1970s, when the Organization of Petroleum Exporting Countries (OPEC) dramatically raised the price of oil. The United States, which depends heavily on foreign oil, thus had to increase the money spent on this vital resource. As a result, the total cost of imports to the United States began to exceed the income from its exports.

The United States suffered record trade deficits in 1986 and 1987. In the early 1990s, the trade deficit began to fall. By the late 1990s, however, the deficit had skyrocketed to record levels, largely as a result of a new increase in oil prices and an economic boom that fueled consumer buying of imported goods.

In 2012, the trade deficit totaled over $530 billion, with the largest amounts owed to China, the European Union, Japan, Germany, Mexico, Canada, and oil exporting nations such as Venezuela. Energy imports, including petroleum, accounted for 40 percent of the deficit.

Effects of the Trade Deficit When Americans import more than they export, more dollars end up in the hands of foreigners. They can then use these extra dollars to purchase American land, stocks, bonds, and other assets. As a result of America's trade deficits, people from other countries now own a large piece of the U.S. economy. Many people fear this trend threatens national independence and even national security.

Some economists worry that foreign financial investment might not always support the trade deficit. They worry that, with U.S. imports on the rise and American foreign debt growing, overseas investors might become reluctant to purchase American assets.

As a result, that monetary flow into the United States would slow down. In 2000, a federal commission formed to study the deficit concluded that "maintaining large and growing trade deficits is neither desirable nor likely to be sustainable for the extended future."

Can Balance of Trade Be Restored? To reduce the trade deficit, the government could depreciate the exchange rate. As you saw, when the dollar is weak, American products become cheaper to buy on the world market, and other countries' goods become correspondingly more expensive. As a result, exports rise and imports fall. The head of the nation's largest steelmaker noted this process at work in 2008:

> The opportunities for exporting are definitely greater than they were a year or two years ago. We have folks who were bringing in steel for decades coming to us and saying we'd like to talk to you about exporting. That is a huge change. It's because of the dollar.

> —Dan DiMicco, interview

The federal government could also cut back spending by adjusting its monetary or fiscal policy. Individuals could voluntarily purchase fewer foreign goods, despite the higher price of certain domestic items. Or American companies could try to sell more domestic products overseas. All of these approaches involve sacrifices or risk, but they would result in fewer surplus dollars ending up in foreign hands.

? **MAKE GENERALIZATIONS** What has been the trend of the United States balance of trade in recent decades?

ASSESSMENT

1. **Recall** What is an exchange rate?

2. **Explain** How do a fixed exchange-rate system and a flexible exchange-rate system differ?

3. **Distinguish** How does the balance of payments differ from the balance of trade?

4. **Predict Consequences** How do you think a nation's balance of trade might be affected if its government instituted policies to support science education and give tax breaks to high-tech industries?

5. **Identify Cause and Effect** What effect does a decrease in demand for goods exported from the United States have on the trade deficit?

Have you ever given money for world famine relief? Or taken part in a fund-raising drive to build a school in a foreign country? Each year, Americans of all ages donate money and time to such efforts. And the need is very real. About 1.2 billion people around the world live in extreme poverty. More than a third of them are children under the age of 13.

>> Volunteers and interns work with students at NairobiBits, a youth-based organization in Kenya that teaches Information Communication Technology (ICT) skills to children who have little access to education.

▶ **Interactive Flipped Video**

Development

Development Around the World

There are vast differences between prosperous nations—such as the United States or Canada—and poorer nations such as Ethiopia or El Salvador. In this Lesson, you will examine what some of these differences are and why they exist.

Economists divide the world's nations into different categories according to their level of development. **Development** is the process by which a nation improves the economic, political, and social well-being of its people. It is important to remember that development refers to a nation's material well-being. It is not a judgment of the worth of a nation or its people. The level of development does not indicate cultural superiority or inferiority. It simply indicates how well a nation is able to feed, clothe, and shelter its people.

Nations with a relatively high average of material well-being are called **developed nations.** The United States, Canada, Japan, Australia, New Zealand, and the nations of Western Europe fall into this category.

Most nations, however, have relatively low levels of material well-being. These **less developed countries** (LDCs) include the world's poorest countries, such as Bangladesh, Nepal, Albania, and nations of central and southern Africa.

One group of LDCs has made great progress toward developing their economies. These **newly industrialized countries** (NICs)

>> **Objectives**

Summarize the concept of economic development.

Identify the characteristics of developed and less developed countries.

Explain the use of GDP and other measurements of economic development.

>> **Key Terms**

development
developed nation
less developed
   country
newly industrialized
   country
per capita GDP
industrialization
literacy rate
life expectancy
infant mortality rate
subsistence
   agriculture

include Mexico, Brazil, Saudi Arabia, South Korea, and several countries in Eastern Europe. Some NICs are rich in resources, especially oil. Saudi Arabia, for example, has made a great deal of money from selling oil and oil products. Others have turned to manufacturing. Although the NICs have pulled ahead of the poorer LDCs, they have yet to achieve the high standard of living of developed nations.

❓ CONTRAST How do NICs differ from both developed nations and LDCs?

Indicators of Development

Economists use many different factors to measure a nation's level of development. These economic indicators include production of goods and services, energy consumption, distribution of the workforce, availability of consumer goods, and social conditions.

Per Capita GDP As you read earlier, gross domestic product (GDP) is the total value of all final goods and services produced within an economy in a year. GDP alone, however, is not adequate to compare the living standards of nations. Instead, economists use **per capita GDP,** a nation's GDP divided by its population. As **Figure 10.6** shows, per capita GDP can vary widely from nation to nation.

Why is per capita GDP considered to be a more accurate measure of development than GDP by itself? Look at two nations, Spain and India.

Both have high GDPs—about $1.32 trillion for Spain and about $1.84 trillion for India. Yet Spain enjoys a high standard of living, while India is relatively poor.

The reason for this discrepancy is population size. Spain's $1.32 trillion is shared by more than 46.2 million people. Thus, its per capita GDP is around $28,751. India's $1.84 trillion is shared by about 1.2 billion people, so its per capita GDP is only around $1,530. These figures indicate that the average person in Spain is better off, in material terms, than the average person in India.

Of course, per capita GDP does not take into account distribution of income. Within every nation, some people are wealthier than most, while others are poorer than most. In many LDCs, the gap between rich and poor is especially wide.

The World Bank, an international economic organization that studies development, uses a similar measure called per capita gross national income (GNI). Using this yardstick, the World Bank classifies nations as *high income, middle income,* and *low income.*

Energy Use Energy use is another good way to measure development. The amount of energy that a nation consumes is closely linked to its level of

Per Capita GDP of Selected Nations, 2012

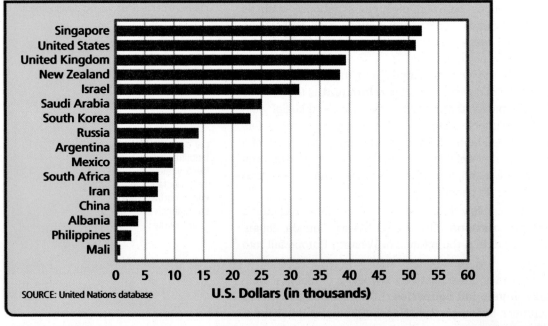

SOURCE: United Nations database

>> **Figure 10.6** Economists use per capita GDP as a measure of development. **Analyze Graphs** What does this graph show about the material well-being of people in Israel as compared with people in Albania?

▶ Interactive Gallery

Per Capita GNI of Selected Countries, 2004–2012

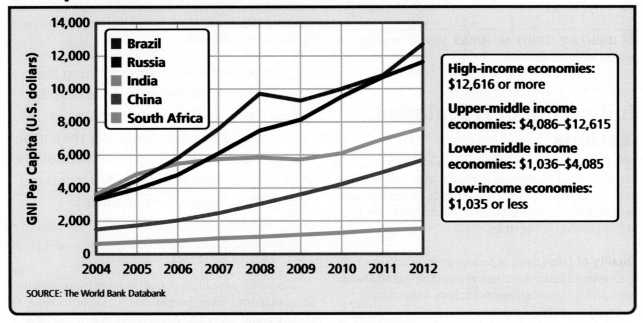

GNI Per Capita (U.S. dollars)

Legend:
- Brazil
- Russia
- India
- China
- South Africa

High-income economies: $12,616 or more

Upper-middle income economies: $4,086–$12,615

Lower-middle income economies: $1,036–$4,085

Low-income economies: $1,035 or less

SOURCE: The World Bank Databank

>> These fast-growing LDCs are known as the BRICS, from the first letter of each country's name. **Analyze Graphs** Which one reached the "high-income economy" level during this period?

industrialization. **Industrialization** is the organization of an economy for the purpose of manufacture. Because industrial processes generally require large amounts of energy, high levels of energy use tend to indicate high levels of industrial activity. They also indicate a high level of development.

Conversely, a low level of energy consumption tends to indicate that a nation has a low level of industrial activity. Most of the people work with simple tools rather than machines.

Workforce Another sign of low-level development is that a large share of the population works in agriculture. Why is that the case?

If most people are raising food just for themselves, few are available to work in industry. As a result, there is little opportunity for workers to specialize. As you read earlier, specialization makes an economy more efficient and productive. It also allows workers to focus on particular jobs, which enables them to earn cash income.

Consumer Goods The quantity of consumer goods a nation produces per capita also indicates its level of development. Availability of a large number of consumer goods indicates that people have enough

money to meet their basic needs and still have enough left over to buy nonessential goods. Thus, economists measure how many people in a country own products such as computers, automobiles, washing machines, or telephones.

Social Indicators Three social indicators also measure a nation's level of development. The first is **literacy rate,** the proportion of the population over age 15 who can read and write. In general, a high percentage of people attending school suggests a high level of development. An educated population has the potential to be more productive and to use or produce advanced technology.

Another indicator is **life expectancy,** the average expected life span of an individual. It indicates how well an economic system supports life. People who are well nourished and housed and have access to medical care live longer. A population that lacks food and adequate housing and is exposed to poor sanitation and disease will have a shorter life expectancy.

A country's **infant mortality rate** indicates the number of deaths that occur in the first year of life per 1,000 live births. For example, in the United States, out of every 1,000 infants born alive in a given year, 5.9 of them die before they reach their first birthdays. This means that the United States has an infant mortality rate of 5.9. Generally speaking, the lower a nation's infant mortality rate, the higher its level of development.

? IDENTIFY CENTRAL IDEAS How is energy use related to development?

Indicators of Developed Nations

Developed nations have high per capita GDPs, and the majority of the population is neither very rich nor very poor. In general, people in these nations enjoy a greater degree of economic and political freedom than do those in less developed countries.

Quality of Life Levels of consumer spending are high in developed nations. For example, in the United States, almost 75 percent of households have computers.

The populations of developed nations are generally healthy, with low infant mortality rates and high life expectancy. Literacy rates are high as well. People tend to receive schooling well into their teens, and many go on to college.

High Productivity In most developed nations, agricultural output is high, but relatively few people work on farms. For example, with the equipment available today, a single farmer in the United States can feed 155 people. Agriculture has largely become a high-tech big business:

> New technologies are making the profession of farming more efficient, less risky, and less labor-intensive. . . . [Big farmers] are automating the entire farming process using GPS technology, genetically modified crops, automated irrigation systems, specialized fertilizers.
>
> —Bob Baddeley, "Farm Technology: Applying High Tech for High Yields"

Since only a small portion of the labor force is needed in agriculture, more people are available to work in industry and services. Widespread use of technology increases the productivity of this workforce, too.

Urbanization and Infrastructure Developed nations tend to be urban rather than rural. Most of their populations live in cities and towns and have done so for many years. Major cities such as New York, London, and Tokyo are centers of finance and trade.

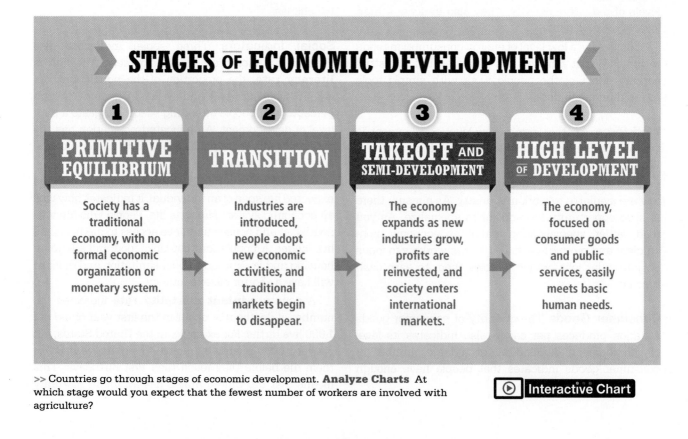

STAGES OF ECONOMIC DEVELOPMENT

1 PRIMITIVE EQUILIBRIUM
Society has a traditional economy, with no formal economic organization or monetary system.

2 TRANSITION
Industries are introduced, people adopt new economic activities, and traditional markets begin to disappear.

3 TAKEOFF AND SEMI-DEVELOPMENT
The economy expands as new industries grow, profits are reinvested, and society enters international markets.

4 HIGH LEVEL OF DEVELOPMENT
The economy, focused on consumer goods and public services, easily meets basic human needs.

>> Countries go through stages of economic development. **Analyze Charts** At which stage would you expect that the fewest number of workers are involved with agriculture?

▶ **Interactive Chart**

Hand-in-hand with urbanization goes a solid infrastructure. Power plants enhance a nation's capacity to produce goods. Transportation and communication systems allow easier transfer of products, services, people, and ideas. Schools increase a nation's literacy rate and productive capacity. Banks allow for secure transfer of financial assets.

? SUPPORT IDEAS WITH EXAMPLES What forms of infrastructure support urbanization?

Indicators of Less Developed Nations

Less developed countries generally have low per capita GDPs. Their per capita energy consumption is also low, which is an indicator of their limited level of industrialization. These characteristics affect LDCs' ability to produce goods efficiently and to provide their citizens with a satisfactory standard of living.

Low Productivity Many people in LDCs engage in **subsistence agriculture,** raising only enough food to feed themselves and their families. Subsistence agriculture requires heavy labor, leaving fewer workers available for industry or services.

Unemployment rates are high in less developed countries, often around 20 percent. In addition, much of the labor force in these nations is underemployed. Often people who are underemployed have work, but not enough to support themselves or their families because they work less than full time.

Quality of Life Even if an LDC could produce a large quantity of consumer goods—which they generally do not—most of the population would be unable to buy them. Subsistence-level agriculture and underemployment do not provide families with enough income to buy these goods. Consumer goods that are produced are often shipped out of the country and sold in more developed nations.

A less developed country has trouble educating its populace. Resources for schools are limited. In addition, children are often needed to work on the family farm, limiting the amount of time they can spend in school. As a result, literacy rates in LDCs are very low. In Afghanistan, for example, only about 28 percent of the people over 15 years old can read and write. Compare this figure with the United States, where the literacy rate is nearly 100 percent.

In the world's poorest countries, housing and diet are of poor quality. Along with limited access to healthcare, these factors lead to high infant mortality rates and short life expectancy.

There are additional characteristics common to most LDCs. In the next Lesson, you will read about some of the difficult issues challenging less developed countries.

? INFER Why do most people in LDCs have few consumer goods?

ASSESSMENT

1. **Make Generalizations** What are some characteristics of the newly industrializing countries (NICs)?

2. **Apply Concepts** Why can two countries with similar GDPs have greatly differing average levels of material well-being?

3. **Draw Conclusions** What social indicator would you expect to be low in a country with poor nutrition and a lack of clean water?

4. **Support Ideas With Evidence** Explain how literacy, human capital, and economic development are interrelated.

5. **Support Ideas With Examples** Why would establishing an agricultural college be a way to enhance a country's rate of development?

>> A growing number of Bolivia's women are exercising their voting rights and participating in politics because of funding from the United Nations Development Programme.

▶ **Interactive Flipped Video**

(10.5) Even in a developed nation like ours, there are people who can't read or don't eat a healthy diet. But imagine that you never even had a *chance* to go to school. Imagine that a severe shortage of food reduced your chances of living to adulthood. For many people your age, such conditions are a grim reality.

>> **Objectives**

Summarize major issues that affect international economic development.

Describe the role of government in promoting or hindering national economic development.

Summarize the role of international investment and foreign aid in economic development.

Analyze the functions of international economic institutions in the global economy.

>> **Key Terms**

population growth
   rate
malnutrition
internal financing
foreign investment
foreign direct
   investment
foreign portfolio
   investment
debt rescheduling
stabilization program
nongovernmental
   organizations

Growth, Resources, and Development

A Growing Population

Illiteracy and poor nutrition are just two of the factors that hinder development. In this section, you will see what LDCs and the world community are doing to combat these conditions and encourage economic growth.

As long ago as 1798, the English economist Thomas Malthus predicted that rapid population growth would become a serious problem:

> The power of population is indefinitely greater than the power in the earth to produce subsistence for man . . . . The food therefore which before supported seven millions, must now be divided among seven millions and a half or eight millions. The poor consequently must live much worse, and many of them be reduced to severe distress.

— Thomas Malthus, *Essay on Population*

Thanks to modern technology, the earth now produces more food than Malthus could have imagined. Still, rapid population growth remains one of the most pressing issues facing many less developed countries. The already poor economies of many LDCs have trouble meeting the needs of their rapidly growing populations.

Measuring Population Growth The **population growth rate** is a measure of how rapidly a country's population increases in a given year. It is expressed as a percentage of the population figure at the start of the year. The population growth rate takes into account the number of babies born, the number of people who died, and the number of people who migrated to or from a country.

Compare the growth rates shown in **Figure 10.7.** Average population growth of less developed countries is estimated to be around 1.8 percent. This may sound low to you, but at this rate the population of LDCs will increase by nearly two thirds from 2007 to 2050. That is more than 20 times the population growth of developed nations during the same period.

Causes of Rapid Population Growth Rapid population growth has several causes. Many LDCs are experiencing increased life expectancy. While people are living longer, birth rates in some LDCs have not decreased. When births far outpace deaths, the population grows.

Age structure also contributes to rapid population growth. In many LDCs, a high proportion of the population is of childbearing age. As these younger adults have children, the population continues to grow. The question for the future is whether these families will choose to have as many children as their parents did. Birth rates have been declining in parts of the world, which may signal a new trend. In developed nations, a larger segment of the population is older, so population increases at a much slower rate.

Population Growth Challenges As its population grows, a country must expand employment opportunities, healthcare, education, and infrastructure just to maintain its existing standard of living. To actually improve the lives of its people, a nation has to generate a higher per capita GDP. Economic output must grow faster than the population grows.

In a less developed country with a high population growth rate, such accelerated economic growth is a daunting task. A primary reason is that these LDCs lack various factors of production.

? **DETERMINE POINT OF VIEW** What did English economist Thomas Malthus predict in 1798, and what influenced his prediction?

Population Growth Rates of Selected Nations, 2012

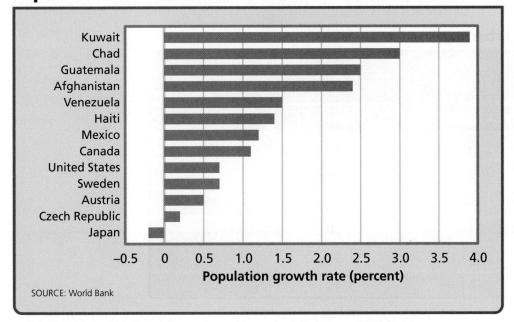

SOURCE: World Bank

>> **Figure 10.7 Analyze Graphs** Which of the selected countries have a population growth rate higher than the average 1.8 percent for less developed countries?

Obstacles to Development

In parts of Africa, Asia, and Latin America, physical geography is a serious obstacle to development. Natural resources are not evenly distributed throughout the world. Some nations lack mineral resources or fertile farmland. Harsh temperatures, uncertain rainfall, and vulnerability to natural disasters such as floods or earthquakes also contribute to the economic problems of some LDCs.

The problem is not always lack of resources. Rather, less developed countries often lack the means to use their resources efficiently. Technology can help LDCs develop the resources they do have. Technology, however, is costly and requires much capital. The formation of capital is another important obstacle to development.

Physical Capital The low productivity typical of LDCs is due in part to lack of physical capital. Without capital, industry cannot grow, and farm output remains low. Also, subsistence agriculture does not give farmers the opportunity to save. As a result, they do not have the cash to purchase capital that would make their farm work more productive or to pay for goods and services that would improve their lives.

Educating and Training Growing Populations Lack of human capital also hinders development. To be able to move beyond mere subsistence, a nation needs an educated workforce. Education and training allow people to develop new skills and adapt to new technologies and processes. As you have read, however, many less developed countries have low literacy rates. **Figure 10.8** compares figures for education and literacy in the United States and several other countries.

Two factors combine to lower literacy rates in these countries. First, only three out of four children in LDCs who begin primary school are still in school four years later. Many children are forced to leave school because they are needed at home to work on family farms.

Second, in many LDCs, the literacy rate for women lags far behind that for men. Many women in these countries begin raising children at an early age. Those who do work have limited job opportunities and earn low wages. In addition, some cultures devalue women. Due to all these factors, a large part of a country's population lacks the training needed to be highly productive.

Nutrition and Health Poor nutrition and health also impede the development of human capital. Many people in less developed countries suffer from **malnutrition,** or consistently inadequate nutrition. (A worldwide increase in food prices in 2008 through 2011 aggravated the situation.) Malnutrition lowers the energy of adults and makes them more vulnerable to disease. Both results can reduce worker productivity. Malnutrition also slows the physical and mental development of children, hurting their chances of being productive workers once they become adults.

In many LDCs, poor sanitation leads to the spread of disease. In addition, many poorer countries have high rates of infection by HIV, the virus that causes AIDS.

Education and Literacy

COUNTRY	PRIMARY SCHOOL ENROLLMENT (PERCENTAGE)	LITERACY RATE (PERCENTAGE)	
		FEMALE	MALE
United States	95.7	99	99
Indonesia	99	90	96
Peru	97.1	85	95
Nigeria	57.6	50	72
Italy	99.1	99	99
Niger	63.7	15	43

SOURCE: United Nations, World Bank

>> **Figure 10.8 Analyze Charts** Which country has the highest primary school enrollment?

Food Price Index

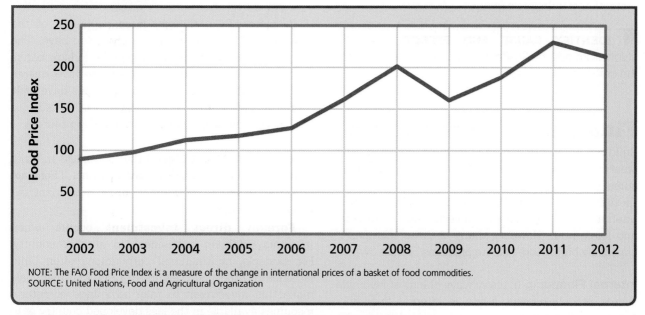

NOTE: The FAO Food Price Index is a measure of the change in international prices of a basket of food commodities.
SOURCE: United Nations, Food and Agricultural Organization

>> **Analyze Graphs** From 2004 to 2011, the food price index doubled. How many years was that, and what effect would the steep increase have had on people in LDCs?

This epidemic removes large numbers of workers from the workforces of these countries. In addition, caring for these people and their families puts a strain on the resources of many LDCs. Money that could be spent on schools or infrastructure has to be devoted to healthcare or providing for orphaned children.

? **DRAW CONCLUSIONS** Why is lack of physical capital, such as farm machinery, an obstacle to development?

Political Barriers to Growth

Political factors may also limit or even reverse a nation's development. Many LDCs are former colonies of European powers. Colonies had to supply the ruling powers with resources and rely on them for manufactured goods. This dependency prevented the development of industry.

In the decades after World War II, these colonies won independence. Many then turned to central planning, rather than free enterprise, as the way to modernize their economies quickly. These nations made some gains at first, but in the long run, central planning hindered their economic growth. Many are now making the transition to free enterprise systems.

Government corruption has also held back development in many LDCs. Some leaders have

funneled huge sums of money into private accounts, allowing them to live luxurious lives while large numbers of their people remain poor.

Civil war and social unrest have plagued many countries, including El Salvador and, more recently, the Central African Republic, Syria, and Nigeria. Years of fighting may leave millions dead and millions more as refugees. Loss of workers, as well as damage to resources and infrastructure, can throw a nation's economy into chaos.

Finally, economic policies in many LDCs have favored small minorities. In some countries, policies benefit city dwellers and not the rural majority. In some, leaders favor only one ethnic group—typically their own. In extreme cases, governments practice policies of genocide—the attempted extermination of an entire ethnic or religious group.

International organizations like the World Bank work with developing countries to help them fight corruption and develop into free enterprise systems. In Burundi, for example, the organization is helping the government protect and consolidate the country's transition from an economy torn by conflict to a more stable economy. The Bank is working with Burundi to strengthen public finance management, promote private-sector development and economic diversification, and improve protection of vulnerable groups.

? **IDENTIFY CAUSE AND EFFECT** How did colonialism adversely affect economic development in the colonized countries?

Finance and Development

Building an infrastructure, providing services, and creating technology and industry all require large sums of money. A developing country can acquire these funds through a variety of means. These include internal financing, foreign investment, borrowing, and foreign aid. However, many of these solutions—especially borrowing—create problems of their own.

Internal Financing In many ways, the most favorable source of development funds is internal financing. **Internal financing** is capital derived from the savings of a country's own citizens. As you read earlier, when savers deposit money in banks or other financial institutions, some of the money is used to make loans to firms. Firms invest in physical and human capital so they can expand, creating new jobs. Job growth enables workers to improve their standard of living. They buy more goods and services, which encourages businesses to expand further. As a result, the entire economy grows.

In most LDCs, though, large segments of the population do not have enough money to save. The wealthy few often keep their money in foreign banks or invest in foreign firms because these investments are safer. As a result, most poor countries have little capital available from internal financing. In order to fund development, they must turn to foreign sources.

Foreign Investment Capital that originates in other countries is called **foreign investment.** There are two types of foreign investment: direct investment and portfolio investment.

Foreign direct investment occurs when investors establish a business in another country. For example, multinational corporations often build factories or other facilities in an LDC. Multinationals make this investment to take advantage of natural resources available in the less developed country or to tap into the large and cheap labor force.

As you have seen, multinationals are controversial. Some economists say that the people of the LDC who work for the foreign corporation are better off than they would be doing other work. Their wages give them cash they can use to buy goods, which can help stimulate their country's economy. Critics say that multinationals

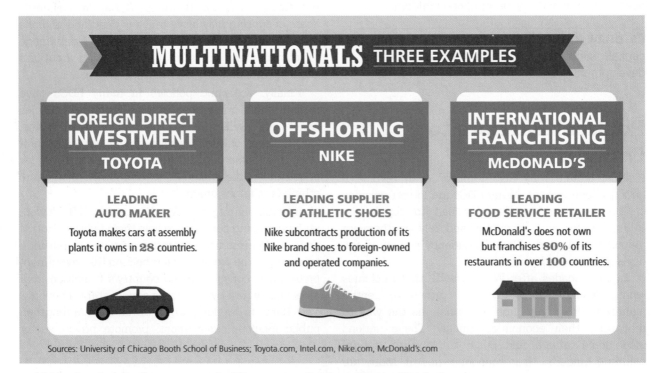

Sources: University of Chicago Booth School of Business; Toyota.com, Intel.com, Nike.com, McDonald's.com

>> Multinationals do business overseas in different ways. **Analyze Charts** Which of the examples above describes a multinational that builds a plant in a foreign country to test computer parts?

U.S. Foreign Aid, 2013

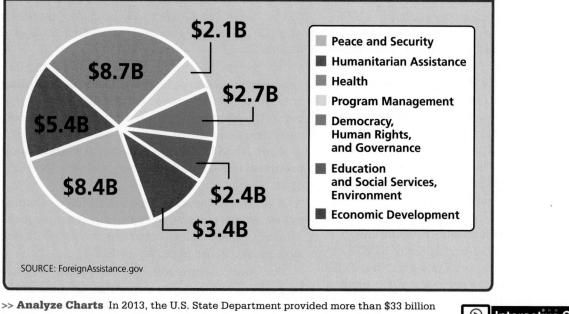

$2.1B
$8.7B
$2.7B
$5.4B
$8.4B
$2.4B
$3.4B

Peace and Security
Humanitarian Assistance
Health
Program Management
Democracy, Human Rights, and Governance
Education and Social Services, Environment
Economic Development

SOURCE: ForeignAssistance.gov

>> **Analyze Charts** In 2013, the U.S. State Department provided more than $33 billion in aid to foreign countries. What are the two largest categories of spending?

⊙ **Interactive Chart**

exploit workers by paying them less than they would pay workers in developed nations. Critics also charge that multinationals can hurt a nation's economic growth by taking profits out of the country.

Instead of building businesses, foreign investors can make purchases in another country's financial markets. This is known as **foreign portfolio investment.** For example, an American investor might buy shares in a mutual fund. The mutual fund then buys stock in a foreign company. That company can use the funds to build another plant or to pay for research and development. Still, portfolio investment does present some problems. Since the investors live in another country, some or all of the company's profits may be drained away from the LDC.

Borrowing and Debt In the 1970s and 1980s, many less developed countries acquired loans from foreign governments and private banks to finance development. Some of that money was misspent because of inexperience or political corruption.

Changes in the world economy also caused problems for the LDCs. As oil prices rose, they borrowed more money to buy needed fuel. Also, many of the loans were issued in—and had to be repaid in—U.S. dollars. When the value of the dollar increased in the 1980s, many LDCs found it impossible to repay their loans. Once again, many were forced to borrow even more funds. As a result, the foreign debt in some countries grew to be greater than their annual GDP. As you will see, the

world financial community has sought ways to relieve this severe debt crunch.

Foreign Aid Sometimes, rather than making loans to developing nations, foreign governments give money and other forms of aid. For instance, many developed nations provide cash payments for building schools, sanitation systems, roads, and other infrastructure. These foreign aid grants do not need to be repaid.

Foreign aid can be motivated by humanitarian concerns. At the same time, developed nations have military, political, economic, and cultural reasons to extend aid to LDCs. In the years following World War II, for instance, American officials gave aid to countries in Africa, Asia, and Latin America to try to block the influence of the Soviet Union in those areas. In the early 2000s, the United States provided money to Iraq and Afghanistan. American leaders hoped to fight international terrorism by building stable democracies in those countries.

? **CATEGORIZE** How is a foreign aid grant different from making a loan to a developing nation?

Promoting Development

Several international economic organizations promote development. The most prominent institutions are the World Bank, the United Nations Development

Programme, and the International Monetary Fund. In addition, privately run aid groups give economic help and advice in some less developed countries.

World Bank The largest provider of development assistance is the World Bank, founded in 1944. As discussed earlier, the World Bank raises money on world financial markets and also accepts contributions from the wealthier member nations. The World Bank uses these funds to offer loans and other resources to more than 100 less developed countries. The World Bank also coordinates with other organizations to promote development throughout the world and provides advice to LDCs on how to build their economies.

United Nations Development Programme The United Nations Development Programme (UNDP) is dedicated to the elimination of poverty. The UNDP is one of the world's largest sources of grant funding for economic and social development. It assists over 177 countries and territories, in which the majority of the world's poorest people live. The UNDP is funded by voluntary contributions made by United Nations member states and agencies.

International Monetary Fund As you already learned, the International Monetary Fund was founded in 1946 to stabilize international exchange rates. Today,

the IMF has expanded its role in the world economy. It promotes development by offering policy advice and technical assistance to LDCs. It also intervenes when LDCs need help in financing their international transactions.

If a country has trouble repaying a debt, the IMF may arrange a rescheduling plan. **Debt rescheduling** is an agreement between a lending nation and a debtor nation.The lending nation lengthens the time of debt repayment and forgives, or dismisses, part of the loan. In return, the LDC agrees to accept a **stabilization program,** changing its economic policies to meet IMF goals.

A typical stabilization program involves providing incentives that will lead to higher export earnings and to fewer imports. By increasing exports, the LDC earns more foreign money to pay off its debt.

Stabilization programs are controversial because they can have a negative impact on the poor in the short term. They often require the LDC to lift wage and price controls. As wages drop and prices rise, the poor suffer. Stabilization may also force a government to cut spending on health, food, and education. Negative experiences in East Asia and Argentina have led some critics to question whether IMF policies are the most effective way to repair a troubled economy.

The World Bank, UN Development Program, and IMF

	WORLD BANK	UNDP	IMF
Founding	1944	1965	1944
Purpose	The World Bank gives financial and technical assistance to developing countries. Its mission is to end extreme poverty and boost shared prosperity.	The UNDP implements programs that focus on four main sectors: • Crisis Prevention and Recovery • Democracy/Good Governance • Poverty Reduction • Energy and Environment	The IMF promotes the stability of the international monetary system by overseeing exchange rates and international payments. Its purpose is to facilitate economic growth and reduce poverty.
Recent Programs	• Providing microcredit in Bosnia and Herzegovina • Supporting education of girls in Bangladesh • Improving health care delivery in Mexico	• Helping women in Yemen acquire job skills • Supporting mobile courts to bring justice in rural Pakistan • Providing water to communities in Myanmar	• Committing more than $300 billion to crisis-hit countries such as Greece, Ireland, and Portugal • Setting a goal of $750 billion in lendable resources

SOURCES: World Bank, UNDP, IMF

>> **Analyze Charts** The World Bank, UNDP, and IMF are international economic organizations. What goal do these three organizations share, as described in the purpose section of the chart?

▶ **Interactive Gallery**

Nongovernmental Organizations Some private aid groups also work to help LDCs build their economies. **Nongovernmental organizations**(NGOs) are independent groups that raise money to fund aid and development programs. Examples include the Red Cross, CARE, and the World Wildlife Fund.

Some NGOs focus on providing food or medical help when natural disasters or wars cause problems. For instance, Oxfam International provides food to poor countries when they face extreme needs. Others try to promote development. For example, Heifer International gives animals to families in less developed countries. Families use these animals to produce and sell products such as wool, milk, or honey.

In 1976, Muhammad Yunus of Bangladesh founded the Grameen Bank. Since then, the bank has extended its operations to nearly every continent. The bank makes small loans—often, as little as a few dollars—to poor people. Many of the borrowers are women in rural villages. They use the loans to start their own businesses and lift their families out of poverty.

? CHECK UNDERSTANDING What do nongovernmental organizations (NGOs) do?

>> During the civil war in Syria, the Red Cross and the Syrian Arab Red Crescent helped Syrians who fled the country as well as those who faced extremely difficult wartime conditions at home.

ASSESSMENT

1. **Identify Cause and Effect** How do limited natural resources adversely affect many LDCs?

2. **Classify**What is the term used to describe capital derived from the savings of a country's own citizens?

3. **Contrast**Distinguish between foreign direct investment and foreign portfolio investment.

4. **Identify Steps in a Process** What does the Grameen Bank do to promote free enterprise in a country?

5. **Support a Point of View With Evidence** Do you think it would be more beneficial for a country to take a loan to fund new development or to invite in foreign investors?

>> Shanghai's skyscrapers are a symbol of China's rapid economic growth. The country has set up a free trade zone in Shanghai to allow foreign competition.

 Interactive Flipped Video

Change is always challenging. Suppose that suddenly no American could attend high school without paying tuition. It is easy to imagine the hardships this might cause. But if somebody gave you a million dollars, you might face different sorts of problems. Would you be tempted to spend the money on the wrong things? What new demands might friends and family make of you?

>> Objectives

Identify the characteristics of economic transition.

Summarize the political and economic changes experienced by Russia since the fall of communism.

Analyze the reasons for economic growth in China and India in recent years.

Identify the economic challenges faced by developing nations in Africa and Latin America.

>> Key Terms

privatization
special economic
  zones

Changing Economies

Moving Toward a Market Economy

The same is true of nations. Economic change—even change for the better—always brings new challenges.

Today, many countries are undergoing economic transition. Some are enjoying rapid growth, while others are changing their entire economic systems. In this Lesson, you will look at the changing economies of Russia, China, India, and the countries of Africa and Latin America.

For many nations, economic transition has meant moving from central planning to a market-based economy. In a command economy, the government owns and controls the factors of production. By contrast, in a market-based economy, the factors of production are owned and controlled by individuals. One of the first steps, then, in moving to a market economy is to sell or transfer government-owned businesses to individuals. This process is called **privatization.**

Privatizing Business A government can privatize businesses in several ways. It could simply sell the business to one owner. It could also sell shares to investors. A third option is to give every citizen a voucher that can be used to purchase shares in whatever businesses they wish, once those businesses are privatized.

Privatization can be a painful process. Only profitable enterprises will survive in a free market. No one will want to buy unprofitable ones, so many people will lose their jobs. Other job opportunities will eventually appear as the economy grows. However, the initial transition can be difficult for workers accustomed to jobs guaranteed by the government.

Another concern is corruption. Government leaders might make it easier for their own friends and associates to gain control of businesses. The result is an unfair distribution of ownership.

Protecting Property Rights Moving to a market economy also requires changes in the legal system. Centrally planned economies have no need to protect private property rights. A free market economy, however, cannot function without such protections. As a result, the government must create new laws that ensure a person's right to own and transfer property. Such a basic overhaul of the legal system takes time.

Work Ethic and Attitudes In a planned economy, workers grow used to security. Many have guaranteed jobs in which their only concern is to meet government quotas. In the free market, such guarantees do not exist. Incentives, not quotas, motivate people's labor. As a result, workers in a transitioning economy need to learn a new work ethic.

Not surprisingly, people accustomed to central planning often worry about how change will affect them. They might resist the shift to the free market out of fear and uncertainty.

❓ APPLY CONCEPTS Why does moving to a market economy require changes in the legal system?

Changes in Russia

Russia has faced all of the challenges described above. It was once part of the Soviet Union, the world's most powerful communist nation. But in 1991, Soviet communism—and the Soviet Union itself— collapsed. Russia and the other former Soviet republics began the difficult transition toward a free market economy.

The End of Soviet Communism Under communism, government planners directed the Soviet economy. The nation became an industrial giant and a military superpower. The Soviet Union was enormous and rich in many resources, but in the long run, its economy was unable to use those resources to provide for its people. Citizens faced frequent shortages of consumer goods, and the goods they did get were often of poor quality.

In the late 1980s, a new Soviet leader named Mikhail Gorbachev began a series of dramatic political and economic changes to revive the country's stagnant

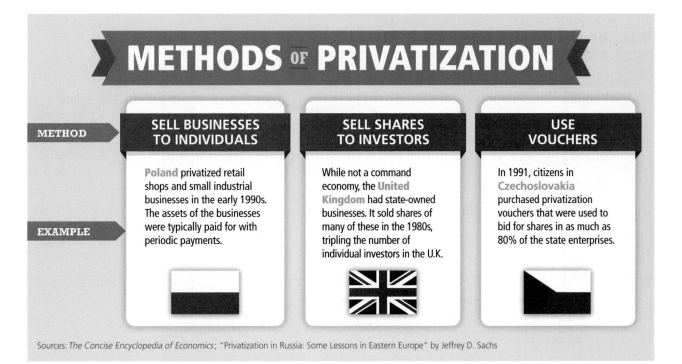

Sources: *The Concise Encyclopedia of Economics*; "Privatization in Russia: Some Lessons in Eastern Europe" by Jeffrey D. Sachs

>> **Analyze Charts** What is the difference between the privatization method Czechoslovakia used and the method Poland chose?

economy. Gorbachev did not want to overturn the communist economic and political system. Rather, he hoped to incorporate the use of markets and incentives into the existing structure of communism.

The transition to free market economics created problems, however. Economic reform produced some initial hardships. People lost secure government jobs, benefits, and pensions. Many people, especially the elderly, were hurt financially. Some Russians did begin to make the new system work for them, starting their own businesses and prospering. Still, unrest grew.

At the same time, some officials and army officers feared that the central government was becoming weak. In 1991, they tried to restore old-style communism. The attempt backfired. One by one, the 15 Soviet republics declared their independence. The largest of the new nations was the Russian Republic.

A Hard Transition Russia's new president, Boris Yeltsin, promised rapid progress toward a market economy. Despite some improvements, hardships continued. When Yeltsin lifted price controls in 1992, prices skyrocketed. People on fixed incomes, such as retirees living on government pensions, could not afford to buy basics like food and clothing.

In the new Russia, wealth tended to become concentrated in cities such as Moscow. The uneven distribution of income led many to call for additional change. It also led to extensive corruption and widespread organized crime.

Billions of dollars in financial aid flooded into the country from the World Bank, the IMF, and independent investors. However, due to mismanagement and corruption, these funds were not used efficiently. By 1998, the Russian economy was in a shambles. Debt was high, investor confidence was low, and the nation was in the midst of an economic crisis.

Russia in the 21st Century Tight controls from the central government, combined with rising prices for Russian oil, allowed Russian leaders to stem the crisis and repay foreign debt. According to the World Bank, Russia had the world's sixth-largest GDP in 2012, due to its oil- and export-driven economy. Economic growth has fed growing consumer demand. New laws protect investments, encouraging foreign investors to supply capital to launch new businesses.

Still, problems persist. Russia's economy relies too much on the export of natural resources. If the prices of these goods drop, export income will fall, as happened in the economic crisis of 2008. Russia, however, has other goods and services it can develop. It joined the World Trade Organization in 2012, which will reduce trade barriers for Russian imports and help open foreign markets. The future holds challenges—a shrinking workforce, corruption, and lack of investment in infrastructure—but economic integration with the

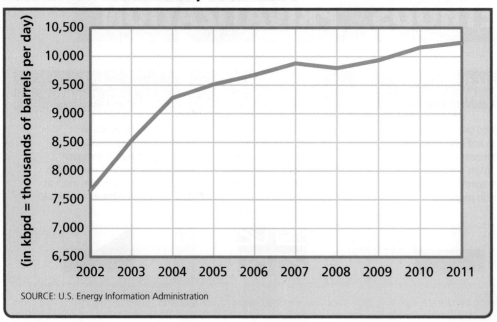

Russian Oil Production, 2002–2011

SOURCE: U.S. Energy Information Administration

>> **Analyze Graphs** In what year was Russia's peak oil production? Which years showed the steepest rise in oil production?

▶ **Interactive Timeline**

Trade Growth in China

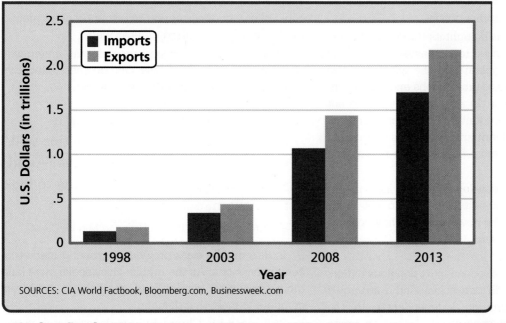

SOURCES: CIA World Factbook, Bloomberg.com, Businessweek.com

>> **Analyze Graphs** Which grew more rapidly between 1998 and 2013, imports or exports? How do you think that helped the Chinese economy?

▶ **Interactive Chart**

rest of the world is likely to keep the Russian economy within the free market.

❓ **SUPPORT IDEAS WITH EXAMPLES** Name one economic problem Russia faced before the transition to a free market economy and one problem after the transition.

Growth in Asia Through Trade

Asia, the world's largest continent, is home to more than 4 billion people—over 60 percent of the world's total population. These people provide a huge workforce and a huge market for goods and services. In recent decades, Asia has become one of the most dynamic players in the global economy. Nations such as Singapore, South Korea, and Taiwan have incomes comparable to highly developed nations in the rest of the world.

China is a major exporter of goods and a key trading partner of the United States. India, too, has experienced rapid economic growth. How did these two nations, once among the world's poorest, advance so far, so rapidly?

China In 1949, after a long civil war, communists led by Mao Zedong took power in China. They quickly put

in place communist policies, giving the government ownership of all land, resources, and enterprises. Government planners made all key decisions about the economy.

After Mao died in 1976, Deng Xiaoping became China's new leader. Deng soon began using the tools of the free market to increase productivity. He gave farmers and factory managers more freedom to make decisions about what to produce and how much to charge for it. He also rewarded farmers, managers, and workers who increased output. With such incentives, production increased.

Deng also set up four free market centers along China's east coast. Foreign businesses could operate, and local governments were allowed to offer tax incentives to foreign investors in these **special economic zones.** Chinese businesses could operate freely as well, with managers making most of their own investment and production decisions. This approach proved so successful that China now has hundreds of these zones.

Deng's successors have continued his policies. The economic changes, especially increased trade, have led to huge economic growth. Where the country once lagged far behind most nations of Europe and North America, China in 2013 had the world's second most productive economy, after the United States. In 2009, China became the world's largest exporter of goods. Since 2011, consumer spending by Chinese citizens has been a bigger driver of growth than investment. Chinese cities are now full of people who enjoy access to a wide variety of consumer goods.

Still, development has brought its share of problems. Rapid urban growth has led to increases in crime and pollution. The poor complain that the government is abandoning its promise to provide jobs and healthcare for all the nation's people. In addition, growth has not reached all parts of the country. The government has announced that it is planning to focus less on trade in the coming years and more on economic reform and education.

Finally, economic development has not meant political liberty. Chinese citizens still do not enjoy many political rights. The government tightly controls the press and stifles dissent.

India India is the world's second most populous nation, after China. A former British colony, India struggled economically after winning independence. In the 1990s, though, India's government began to invite foreign investment and promote other free market practices.

New policies encouraged Indian companies to expand. One area of significant growth was in high-technology industries. Many software companies opened new facilities in India, where educated workers could offer technical support to computer users around the world. Manufacturing grew as well.

Economic growth helped promote the emergence of a much larger middle class. One business executive noted the significance of this development:

> When half the population in a society is middle class, its politics will change . . . its poor will be fewer—and society will have greater means to look after them.
>
> —Gurcharan Das, "India's Growing Middle Class"

India's middle class provides a growing market for consumer goods. As the middle class seeks more (and more expensive) goods, local and foreign producers compete to meet that demand.

Still, as with China, India's development is not complete. Over half of the labor force farms, and only 19 percent is employed in industry. The result is a growing gap between the richest and poorest citizens. In fact, this is true of virtually all nations with developing economies. Urban dwellers with education and skills benefit the most from growth. Uneducated people in poor rural areas struggle with poverty and continue to rely on subsistence farming.

? **IDENTIFY SUPPORTING DETAILS** Name two areas of growth in India's economy.

Growth and Challenges in Africa and Latin America

Like Asia, Africa and Latin America are home to many poor countries. Some nations in these two regions have seen great economic growth in recent years. Others continue to struggle.

Continuing Poverty in Africa Some North African nations have built productive economies. This success is mainly due to large reserves of oil. South of the Sahara, however, most nations face the obstacles common to all less developed countries. Economies are largely based on subsistence farming. Low literacy rates, inadequate healthcare and nutrition, high rates of HIV infection, and mounting debt hinder development efforts. Some nations are also plagued by years of civil war or ethnic conflict. Only two African nations south of the Sahara have sizable economies—South Africa and Nigeria.

>> Rapid industrialization without government regulation has caused damage to the environment in China. Heavy pollution is an ongoing problem, and it is common for people to wear face masks outside, as these Beijing pedestrians are doing.

Brazil's Major Exports, 2010

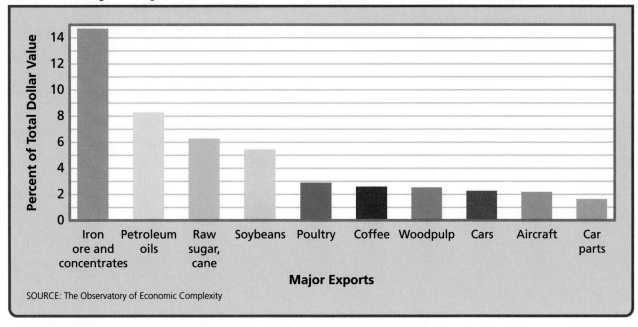

SOURCE: The Observatory of Economic Complexity

>> **Analyze Graphs** How much more valuable is Brazil's export of petroleum oils than its export of cars? Do you think that ratio will change in the future? Why or why not?

Nigeria benefits from large reserves of oil. Yet over-dependence on oil has slowed growth in other areas. Nigeria also suffers from widespread political corruption and ethnic conflict. However, President Goodluck Jonathan, who became president in 2010, promised to reform the country's electoral process, tackle corruption, and resolve Nigeria's energy problems.

In the 1990s, South Africa shifted from longtime rule by its white minority to black majority rule. Problems in this political transition, along with high rates of HIV infection, slowed economic growth. Unemployment remains high, and poverty remains a problem. Still, South Africa has one of the 25 highest GDPs in the world. It benefits from a rich array of natural resources and a strong manufacturing base.

Different Paths in Latin America In Latin America, the two biggest success stories are Brazil and Mexico. Both countries have abundant resources. Both have also taken steps to make their economies more diverse.

Brazil exports iron ore and timber, and its land and climate are highly suitable for growing coffee and soybeans. The discovery of large offshore oil reserves in late 2007 promises to turn Brazil into a major oil-exporting power. Oil production grew from around 2,300 barrels a day in 2007 to 2,600 barrels a day in 2012. Brazil has become a strong manufacturing power, producing everything from vehicles to shoes. It has also adapted its sugar industry to produce ethanol. Brazil builds cars that can run on either gasoline or ethanol. More than 40 percent of the fuel that powers Brazilian cars comes from ethanol derived from sugar cane.

Mexico has reserves of oil and silver and produces rich crops of cotton and coffee. Like Brazil, Mexico has diversified its economy by promoting its tourism industry and building factories, and this increased trade has led to growth.

By diversifying their economies, Mexico and Brazil have freed 80 percent or more of their labor forces from farm work. Employment in manufacturing and service industries has helped these two economies grow.

Venezuela also has large reserves of oil. Its leadership turned in a different direction, though. President Hugo Chávez shifted the economy away from the market system to socialism. In addition to the oil industry, Chávez nationalized agricultural, financial, telecommunications, construction, and steel companies. He promised to use money derived from the sale of oil and gas to eliminate poverty and improve health and education. These advances have yet to be seen, however. The successor to Chávez, President Nicolás Maduro, is expected to continue along the same political path.

? **SUPPORT IDEAS WITH EXAMPLES** What do Brazil and Mexico have in common that has made these countries economic success stories?

ASSESSMENT

1. **Identify Central Issues** Identify three challenges in moving to a free market economy.

2. **Summarize** How did communism end in the Soviet Union?

3. **Summarize** What free market reforms did Deng Xiaoping introduce in China?

4. **Distinguish** Which countries in Latin America have built the strongest economies?

5. **Identify Cause and Effect** What caused Venezuela to take a different economic path from Mexico and Brazil?

By now, you have seen many examples of how the world's economies are interconnected. You pick up the telephone to get tech support for your computer, and the call is answered in India. You eat a banana that was grown in Costa Rica and fill your car with gas made from petroleum that originally came out of the ground in Saudi Arabia. The value of the dollar goes down, and the cost of a vacation goes up. The list goes on and on.

>> These workers in Indonesia are assembling motorcycles for a multinational company with headquarters in Japan.

Interactive Flipped Video

Globalization

What Causes Globalization?

The economies of the world's nations are interconnected in deep and complex ways—and they will remain interconnected. The global economy creates new issues that business managers, workers, and government leaders must take into account. In this lesson, you will look at many of these issues, from impact on the environment to increased competition for American businesses.

The increasingly tight interconnection of producers, consumers, and financial systems around the world is known as **globalization.** Such connections are not a new phenomenon. In the Middle Ages, the Asian spice trade connected Europe, Asia, and Africa. The voyages of Columbus led to the colonization of the Americas by European sea powers and to the development of the African slave trade. The Age of Imperialism that began in the late 1800s forged even closer links between the economies of Europe and the United States and those of Africa and Asia.

Still, globalization today is taking place at a much faster pace than in the past. Several factors contribute to the ever-tightening links between economies around the world. They include the development of faster methods of communication and transportation, the widespread adoption of elements of the free enterprise system, and the growth of international trade agreements.

>> **Objectives**

Define *globalization,* and summarize the factors that have led to its spread.

Identify challenges created by globalization.

Analyze the benefits of globalization.

Summarize the effects of globalization on the U.S. economy.

>> **Key Terms**

globalization
offshoring
remittances
"brain drain"
sustainable
   development
deforestation

PEARSON realize www.PearsonRealize.com
Access your Digital Lesson.

Transportation and Communication What do the domestication of the camel, the invention of the compass, and the creation of the Internet have in common? All these innovations allowed greater movement of products, people, and ideas. Today, as in the past, globalization depends on breaking through barriers of time and space.

In the past, camels and ships made it possible to trade across vast deserts and oceans. Today, jet airplanes allow producers to sell goods in distant markets that would have been impossible to reach quickly in the past. For example, flower growers in the Netherlands or Colombia can send fresh flowers for sale in the United States.

Today's communications revolution has also sped up the pace of globalization. Thanks to satellite communications, customers and suppliers on opposite sides of the world can talk quickly and clearly. Computers give people greater access to information about the availability and prices of products in distant countries. Investors in one country can get up-to-date information and use it to buy stocks on financial markets anywhere.

Expansion of the Free Market As you read earlier, many nations have moved away from central planning. Even some communist governments have chosen to pursue free market policies. As a result, the proportion of the world that practices free market economics has more than tripled. At the same time, the fall of communism in the Soviet Union and Eastern Europe has allowed nations that had once been locked out of world trade to enter the global marketplace.

The new free market economies are more open to foreign investment. In 1975, the value of foreign direct investment worldwide totaled only about $23 billion. By 2012, the total had grown to $1.4 trillion. The opening of new markets has created new investment opportunities as countries across the globe learn the benefits of a free enterprise system. It has also created new global economic ties.

Trade Agreements Earlier, you read that many nations have signed regional trade agreements. This is another example of the role of government in economic systems. Some trade agreements, such as the Trans-Pacific Partnership under consideration in 2014, must pass both houses of Congress to become law.

The United States is the world's most productive single economy, with output far exceeding that of any single nation in Europe. However, the *combined* output of the 28 nations that make up the European Union (EU) is competitive with that of the United States. The democratically elected governments of the EU recognize the benefits of free enterprise and of trading blocs. People, goods, and services can flow freely

Foreign Direct Investment in Latvia

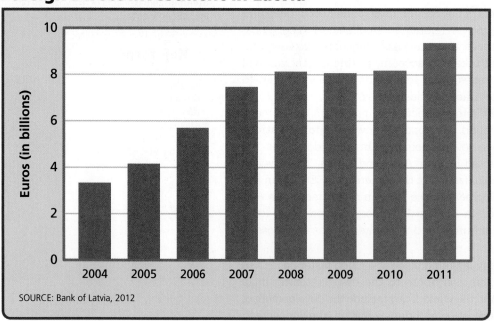

SOURCE: Bank of Latvia, 2012

>> Latvia, once part of the Soviet Union, now practices free market economics.
Analyze Graphs What does this graph indicate about the health of Latvia's economy? Explain.

among members of the EU, making it almost like a single economy.

Concern about competition from the EU was one of the factors that spurred the United States, Canada, and Mexico to sign the North American Free Trade Agreement (NAFTA). With the passage of NAFTA and the lowering of trade barriers, businesses had increased incentives to take part in regional trade.

Trading blocs do not remain fixed. The EU has repeatedly expanded to include more nations. It is also working to forge trade ties with other regions. All of this activity has added to the tighter globalization of the world economy.

IDENTIFY CENTRAL IDEAS How have modern communications contributed to globalization?

Challenges of Globalization

"Arguing against globalization," said former UN Secretary General Kofi Annan, "is like arguing against the laws of gravity." While globalization is a fact of modern economic life, it has also created challenges.

Closely Linked Financial Markets In 2007 and 2008, many American financial firms lost money—or went out of business—as a result of making too many risky home mortgage loans. Worried that the crisis would cause a downturn in the economy, investors sold stocks. Heavy losses on the New York Stock Exchange raised concerns among investors elsewhere in the world. They, in turn, sold stocks on European and Asian exchanges.

The ripple effect caused by this American financial crisis is not unique. In recent decades, economic problems in Mexico, Japan, Russia, and Argentina had a similar impact on world financial markets.

Why do financial problems in one country affect people in another? The reason is that world financial markets are closely connected. Computerization has allowed investors around the world to watch the values of stocks in many different markets. They move quickly to buy the stock of promising companies in whatever country they find them—and sell just as quickly at any sign of trouble.

Another reason for the widespread impact of these financial crises is the booming trade in currencies on foreign exchange markets. As you read earlier, most of the world now follows a flexible exchange-rate system. The values of various national currencies go up or down every day. Investors holding money in a particular currency sell it off if the value of that currency declines.

>> South Korean shoppers line up to buy beef imported from the United States. The U.S.–Korea Free Trade Agreement of 2012 gives new opportunities for U.S. exporters.

>> The sharp drop in the U.S. stock market during the 2008 financial crisis negatively affected foreign stock markets, as this display of stock prices in Tokyo, Japan, reveals.

▶ **Interactive Chart**

As sales of a country's currency mount, its economy will suffer.

These effects do not just hurt investors who risk their money in the hope of making profits. They have an impact on ordinary people as well. Banks buy assets in other countries. If the value of those assets falls, the banks have less capital available to make loans to people in their own countries.

Multinational Corporations As you read in an earlier Lesson, the expansion of multinational corporations has sparked controversy. Some economists argue that these companies have a beneficial impact on the countries in which they set up operations. For example, multinationals have been credited with much of the development of Eastern Europe after the fall of communism:

> [Multinationals] brought countless benefits. These include . . . improving the environment; rescuing collapsing factories and rotting company towns; establishing new industries; laying new telecommunications networks;

stabilizing banking systems . . . and facing down corrupt vested interests in governments that in too many cases had plundered their own countries.

—Paul Lewis, "Harnessing the Power of the Multinationals"

Multinationals have the capital to introduce technology to developing countries, offer jobs, train the labor force, and provide the opportunity for related services and industries to develop.

Critics, however, claim that multinationals do little to aid less developed countries. Some point out that most of the profits go not to the host LDC, but to the foreign owners of the corporation. Others say that multinationals create far fewer job opportunities than they claim. Many of the industries are highly mechanized, allowing high productivity with little labor. Thus, they provide few jobs relative to the massive size of the labor pool and may even drive traditional craftworkers out of business.

Another area of controversy is wages. Generally, wages in less developed countries are very low compared with wages in industrialized nations. Supporters argue that the lower wages are justified since the cost of living in LDCs is also relatively low. In addition, many of the people employed by multinationals might not have jobs otherwise. Critics argue that multinationals benefit unfairly from the low wages. Also, many LDCs do not require companies to provide the same high standard of working conditions that industrialized countries require.

Loss of Jobs Much of the debate over multinationals and globalization focuses on the impact on less developed countries. However, people in developed nations are equally concerned about a related issue— the loss of jobs.

In the global economy, companies may move parts of their operations to other countries. This practice is known as **offshoring.** Offshoring may involve a single process, as when an American bank hires a call center in India or Kenya to handle its telemarketing. Or it can be total, as when a multinational manufacturer closes a plant in the United States to build one in another country, where labor is cheaper. In either case, the result is job loss. As you learned earlier, movement of jobs overseas is one of the key causes of structural unemployment.

>> Hyundai Motor Company is a Korean multinational with automobile factories and showrooms in the United States and other nations around the world, including the Czech Republic and Russia.

❓ IDENTIFY CAUSE AND EFFECT What problems can result when financial markets are interconnected?

Migration

People have always moved from place to place in hopes of building a better life. Globalization and development have accelerated these population shifts.

Domestic Migration Much of this migration takes place domestically, within a nation's borders. In many less developed countries, cities offer more job opportunities than rural areas. As a result, large numbers of people in villages are streaming into cities. By 2012, more than 40 percent of the people in Africa and Asia lived in cities. Today, 22 of the world's 30 largest cities are located in less developed countries. Each of them has more than 10 million people.

Rapid urbanization has caused several problems. Cities have grown so fast that they cannot provide enough housing, schools, or sanitation for all of their inhabitants. Poverty, crime, and disease are widespread.

International Migration Each year, millions of workers leave less developed countries in the hopes of finding jobs in developed nations. This international migration has an economic impact on both the source country and the destination country.

Most immigrants come legally, with proper visas and proof that they have jobs waiting for them. Although their labor contributes to a country's GDP, they may face resentment from native-born workers who view the newcomers as competition for jobs. Other people come without legal authorization. Illegal immigration raises security concerns and puts a strain on public resources.

Migration also affects the source country. Once they find work, many immigrants send regular cash payments to their families back home. These **remittances** provide an important source of income. The World Bank estimated that, in 2013 alone, the value of remittances to LDCs totaled $410 billion.

At the same time, many well-trained and educated people also leave LDCs for well-paying jobs in developed nations. This **"brain drain"** may hurt development by siphoning off vital human capital.

? **IDENTIFY CAUSE AND EFFECT** How does migration affect less developed countries?

Ongoing Issues

Globalization has created new opportunities but also new challenges for the world's economies. Some of these challenges have become sources of tension between the developed world and the developing world.

>> Rapid urbanization has led to the development of densely populated slums in some cities, including São Paulo, Brazil's largest city.

>> When scientists or other professionals emigrate, their home country is hurt in two ways. Expertise in their field is lost, along with the consumer spending that accompanies high salaries.

▶ **Interactive Gallery**

>> The views expressed by this protester at a 2013 meeting of the G8, a group of eight industrial democracies, reflect some of the criticisms made about the developed world.

>> More than half of the world's rain forests, including huge areas of Brazil's Amazon, have been cut or burned to meet the demand for arable land and wood. Scientists believe that rain forest destruction can cause environmental problems on a global level.

Issues related to equal treatment and the environment are key causes of conflict, as is competition for scarce resources.

A Greater Voice for the Developing World
Leaders in less developed countries—and even newly industrialized countries—argue that international trade and financial policies favor the wealthier nations. They charge that the trade rules set by the World Trade Organization give preference to developed nations at their expense. They also claim that the financial demands made by the International Monetary Fund make lives more difficult for poor people in their countries.

In an effort to give emerging economies a greater voice, 19 countries plus the European Union have formed an organization called the Group of 20. The G20 includes finance ministers and central bank governors from growing nations such as China, South Korea, Russia, India, South Africa, Brazil, and Mexico, as well as from the United States and Europe. The G20 has discussed such issues as promoting growth and combating the financing of terrorist operations.

Environment Versus Development The environment can be another source of tension. Environmental scientists—mostly based in developed nations—worry that rapid development can cause environmental damage. They seek to promote **sustainable development,** that is, the goal of meeting current development needs without using up the resources needed by future generations.

On the other hand, government leaders in many less developed nations see an urgent need to exploit their resources *now.* They view combating poverty and creating modern economies as a higher priority than protecting the environment. Developed nations, they argue, were able to use resources such as oil without restriction. LDCs now seek the same opportunity.

One major issue is **deforestation,** or large-scale destruction of forests. Many developing nations are cutting down forests at a rapid rate. Cleared land is used for farming and industry, while timber sales fund other projects that create jobs. Environmentalists warn that deforestation contributes to global warming and destroys rare animal and plant species. To such concerns, a past president of Brazil replied:

There are meddlers who have no political authority, who emit carbon dioxide like nobody else, who destroy everything they have, and who put forth opinions about what we should do. . . . We can't allow people to dictate rules to us about what we should do in the Amazon.

—Luiz Inácio Lula da Silva, quoted in *Terra Daily,* June 5, 2008

Competition for Resources A related challenge is competition for scarce resources. In some regions, it is increasingly difficult to find enough clean water to meet the needs of a growing population.

In China, for example, rapid population growth and economic growth have led to serious contamination of an already uncertain water supply. Some experts warn that reserves of oil and gas are dwindling as well. They fear that unless new sources of these fuels—or different sources of energy—are found, the world's economies may grind to a halt.

Even if resources do not run out, the cost of scarce water and fuel causes problems. In 2008, world oil prices skyrocketed. Even in developed nations, this inflation strained the financial resources of businesses and consumers. In less developed countries, the impact was even more severe. Inflation, caused by competition for resources, made it harder for LDCs to channel resources to development.

⁇ SUPPORT A POINT OF VIEW WITH EVIDENCE How might environmental protection conflict with economic development?

>> A technician tests the quality of the water in a newly drilled well in Pakistan, as a local farmer watches. Dozens of international nongovernmental organizations are working to increase access to clean water.

The United States and the Global Economy

Globalization poses challenges even for the world's most successful economy—our own. For the United States to compete in global markets, American workers must be ready to respond to changes in the workplace. And American companies must continue their long tradition of innovation.

A Changing Workplace The workplace is not what it used to be. Manufacturing is still important, but information now drives the economy of the United States and the world. Workers need to gain the technical skills that are necessary to access, understand, and use all sorts of information. Getting as much education as possible is a good first step.

The need for education does not end when people find jobs. Skilled workers must keep up-to-date with new technology so that they can remain productive in their current jobs. Others must learn completely new skills when they find that their existing jobs no

>> This student is applying technical skills by using diagnostic equipment to test a vehicle's performance.

longer pay a good wage—or when jobs are lost due to offshoring.

As you read earlier, some companies provide the retraining that their workers need. When that is not the case, though, workers must take responsibility to learn needed skills. If they fail to do so, they risk being left behind as work moves in a new direction.

Another feature of the changing American workplace is greater diversity. Generations of African Americans, Asian Americans, and Latinos have made major contributions to the culture and the economy of the nation. As a result of immigration, a growing percentage of American workers are foreign-born.

The Pressure to Compete Globalization has made economic competition more intense. Consumers in developing nations are demanding a greater variety of products and services.

As you have read, the growth of India's middle class has led to a boom in shopping malls. In Africa, the number of cellular phone subscriptions rose from only 2 million in 1998 to more than 700 million in 2013. At the same time, more countries are competing to meet this growing demand.

Competition affects business relationships as well. One firm might have a long relationship with a local supplier. Yet, if a different supplier can offer lower prices or better service, the firm will make a deal with that supplier—even when that supplier is located on the other side of the world.

For all these reasons, American companies need to stay competitive. Business managers face constant pressure to cut costs and increase profits. They must ensure high productivity to avoid wasting money and work. They need to be constantly on the lookout for better ways to respond to customer needs. Only by staying competitive can American companies thrive.

The Need to Innovate As in the past, growing competition spurs innovation. The companies that develop new products or processes can quickly gain a large share of the world market. For example, in 1996, two young American entrepreneurs began work on the Internet search engine company that became Google. Ten years later, the company had worldwide sales of $10.6 billion. By 2013, Google's sales had climbed to around $50 billion.

Still, introducing an innovative product and enjoying its success is not the end of the story. Any new good or service can quickly be replaced by a newer one, developed by another entrepreneur hungry to succeed.

Writer Thomas Friedman, who has studied globalization, says that the new economic world is like a sprint that competitors must run over and over

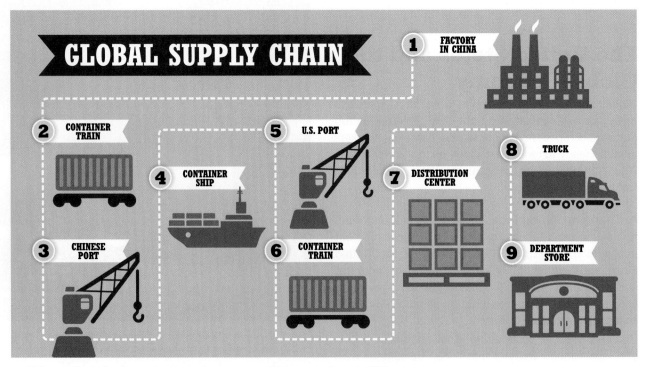

>> This supply chain shows the steps that get a good from a producer in China to a consumer in the U.S. **Analyze Charts** Tell which steps will cost more if the price of fuel rises. Explain why.

again. Anyone who wins one race cannot guarantee winning a later one. The only solution is to go back to the starting line and—with fresh innovations to help—run as fast as possible, again and again.

? **APPLY CONCEPTS** How can American workers help companies stay competitive?

ASSESSMENT

1. **Generate Explanations** How did the spread of free market economies help promote globalization?

2. **Hypothesize** What is it about the free enterprise system that has caused many communist and formerly communist nations to adopt free market economic policies?

3. **Evaluate Arguments** Present arguments about whether or not the wages that multinationals pay workers in LDCs are acceptable.

4. **Draw Conclusions** How can governments, such as those in the G20, encourage economic progress in less developed countries?

5. **Generate Explanations** How can globalization and increased competition lead firms to sever ties with longtime suppliers?

Resource Distribution

	INDIA	NIGERIA	PERU	UNITED STATES
Total area (sq km)	3,287,263 sq km	923,768 sq km	1,285,216 sq km	9,826,675 sq km
Arable land (%)	47.9%	39.0%	2.8%	16.3%
Natural resources	coal, iron ore, manganese, mica, bauxite, rare earth elements, titanium ore, chromite, natural gas, diamonds, petroleum, limestone, arable land	natural gas, petroleum, tin, iron ore, coal, limestone, niobium, lead, zinc, arable land	copper, silver, gold, petroleum, timber, fish, iron ore, coal, phosphate, potash, hydropower, natural gas	coal, copper, lead, molybdenum, phosphates, rare earth elements, uranium, bauxite, gold, iron, mercury, nickel, potash, silver, tungsten, zinc, petroleum, natural gas, timber
Population	1,220.8 million	174.5 million	29.8 million	316.4 million
Labor force	486.6 million	51.53 million	16.2 million	155 million
Literacy rate	62.8%	61.3%	89.6%	99%
Telephones	Main: 31.1 million Cellular: 893.9 million	Main: 418,200 Cellular: 112.8 million	Main: 3.4 million Cellular: 29.4 million	Main: 139 million Cellular: 310 million
Airports	346	54	191	13,513

SOURCE: *CIA World Factbook*

1. **Describe and Explain Economic Factors** Using an example from the table, write a paragraph in which you describe the way economic factors of production are scarce and force one country to make choices about the way it uses its resources. Consider such things as the following: What are the economic factors of production? How is scarcity related to factors of production? How do the choices about what to produce relate to scarcity?

2. **Explain Concepts** Using the table provided, explain the opportunity costs faced by Carlos in deciding what combination of the two goods to produce. Consider such things as the following: What is opportunity cost? What are the two goods being produced? What is the opportunity cost of producing one T-shirt for Carlos? What is the opportunity cost of producing one birdhouse for Carlos?

	CARLOS	JENNY
T-shirts per hour	6	1
Birdhouses per hour	2	1

3. **Apply Concepts** Write a paragraph that applies the concept of comparative advantage to explain why countries trade. Consider such things as the following: What is comparative advantage? How does producing goods efficiently affect the overall economy? Why does comparative advantage provide an incentive for nations to trade?

4. **Explain Concepts** Using the table provided, explain which individual has the comparative advantage in producing which product. Consider such things as the following: What is comparative advantage? What goods are being produced? For which of the goods does Jenny have a comparative advantage over Carlos? How does the concept of opportunity cost affect which good Jenny has a comparative advantage for?

Productivity and Opportunity Cost

	CARLOS	JENNY
T-shirts per hour	6	1
Birdhouses per hour	2	1
Opportunity cost of one T-shirt	$\frac{1}{3}$ birdhouse	1 birdhouse
Opportunity cost of one birdhouse	3 T-shirts	1 T-shirt

EFFECT OF EXCHANGE RATES ON TRADE

Effect of Appreciating Currency

- Value of currency rises, making goods produced in country more expensive.

- Exports: Costs of exports rises for foreign buyers, causing sales of exports to fall.

- Imports: Cost of imports falls, making sales of imports rise.

Effect of Depreciating Currency

- Value of currency falls, making goods produced in country less expensive.

- Exports: Cost of exports falls for foreign buyers, causing sales of exports to rise.

- Imports Costs of imports rises, making sales of imports fall.

---

5. **Examine and Analyze Currency** Using the graphic organizer, examine positive and negative aspects of currency. Consider such things as the following: How does the function of currency as a unit of account affect a nation's economy positively? How might the function of currency as a store of value affect a nation's economy negatively? Based on the chart, what do some nations do to protect against the potentially negative aspects of currency? How could a change to a flexible exchange rate potentially affect a nation's economy negatively?

6. **Apply Concepts** Using the quotation provided, apply the concept of comparative advantage to explain how two countries trade. Consider such things as the following: What is comparative advantage? How is opportunity cost related to the decision to produce goods one has a comparative advantage in? According to the theory of comparative advantage, how will Country A trade with Country B?

"For Country A, the opportunity cost of a ton of bananas is two tons of sugar. For Country B, the opportunity cost of a ton of bananas is three tons of sugar."

7. **Compare Effects of Trade** Compare the effects of free trade to those of trade barriers on overall economic activity. Consider such things as the following: What is free trade? What are trade barriers? How do free trade and trade barriers affect overall economic activity? How does any change in overall economic activity affect people?

8. **Analyze Impacts** Referring to the quotation provided, analyze the impact of U.S. imports on the United States and its trading partners. Consider such things as the following: What are three examples of goods the United States imports? How does the United States benefit from importing these goods? How do other nations benefit from importing goods into the United States?

". . . access to goods they want at lower prices than they would have to pay . . ."

9. **Evaluate Free-Trade** Evaluate the benefits and costs of participation in international free-trade agreements. Consider such things as the following: How can free trade benefit an economy? How can free trade cost an economy? What might lead a nation to sign a free-trade agreement? Why might a nation refuse to sign a free-trade agreement?

10. **Analyze Exchange Rates** Analyze the effects of changes in exchange rates on imports when the domestic currency is depreciating. Consider such things as the following: What causes exchange rates to depreciate? How does depreciation of the domestic currency affect the level and price of imports?

11. **Analyze Exchange Rates** Analyze the effects of changes in exchange rates on exports when the domestic currency appreciates and depreciates. Consider such things as the following: How does the depreciation of a domestic currency affect its value in relation to other currencies? How does the depreciation of a domestic currency affect the level and price of that country's exports?

12. **Explain the Circular-Flow Model** Explain how the circular-flow model is affected by the rest of the world. Consider such things as the following: How does the possibility of interacting with foreign economies affect the flow of money in the circular-flow model? How does the possibility of interacting with foreign economies affect the flow of goods in the circular-flow model?

13. **Examine Free Enterprise and Explain Corporations** Examine current examples of transitioning to a free enterprise system in Benin and explain the place of corporations in Benin as the country changes. Consider such things as the following: What type of economy is Benin transitioning from? What is involved in the transition to a free enterprise economic system in Benin? What characteristic of corporations will likely be strengthened by the transition to free enterprise economic system in Benin?

14. **Analyze Trade** Referring to the quotation, analyze how trade relates to growth. Consider the following questions: What purpose for trade is implied in the quotation? How can trade enable nations to grow faster than they would have without trade?

"Because they cannot produce all goods with their scarce resources, they need to obtain those they do not produce somehow."

15. **Write About the Essential Question** **Write an essay on the Essential Question: How might scarcity divide our world or bring it together?** Use evidence from your study of this Topic to support your answer.

Go online to PearsonRealize.com and use the texts, quizzes, interactivities, Interactive Reading Notepads, Flipped Videos, and other resources from this Topic to prepare for the Topic Test.

Texts

Quizzes

Interactivities

Interactive Reading Notepads

Flipped Videos

While online you can also check the progress you've made learning the topic and course content by viewing your grades, test scores, and assignment status.

Stock Connection Blue/Alamy

Constitution Quick Study Guide

Preamble

Amendments

1st Amendment: Freedom of Religion, Speech, Press, Assembly, and Petition

2nd Amendment: Right to Keep, Bear Arms

3rd Amendment: Lodging Troops in Private Homes

4th Amendment: Search, Seizures, Proper Warrants

5th Amendment: Criminal Proceedings, Due Process, Eminent Domain

6th Amendment: Criminal Proceedings

7th Amendment: Jury Trials in Civil Cases

8th Amendment: Bail; Cruel, Unusual Punishment

9th Amendment: Unenumerated Rights

10th Amendment: Powers Reserved to the States

11th Amendment: Suits Against the States

12th Amendment: Election of President and Vice President

13th Amendment: Slavery and Involuntary Servitude

Section 1.	Slavery and Involuntary Servitude Prohibited
Section 2.	Power of Congress

14th Amendment: Rights of Citizens

Section 1.	Citizenship; Privileges and Immunities; Due Process; Equal Protection
Section 2.	Apportionment of Representation
Section 3.	Disqualification of Officers
Section 4.	Public Debt
Section 5.	Powers of Congress

15th Amendment: Right to Vote—Race, Color, Servitude

Section 1.	Suffrage Not to Be Abridged
Section 2.	Power of Congress

16th Amendment: Income Tax

17th Amendment: Popular Election of Senators

Section 1.	Popular Election of Senators
Section 2.	Senate Vacancies
Section 3.	Inapplicable to Senators Previously Chosen

18th Amendment: Prohibition of Intoxicating Liquors

Section 1.	Intoxicating Liquors Prohibited
Section 2.	Concurrent Power to Enforce
Section 3.	Time Limit on Ratification

19th Amendment: Equal Suffrage—Sex

Section 1.	Suffrage Not to Be Abridged
Section 2.	Power of Congress

20th Amendment: Commencement of Terms; Sessions of Congress; Death or Disqualification of President-Elect

Section 1.	Terms of President, Vice President, members of Congress
Section 2.	Sessions of Congress
Section 3.	Death or Disqualification of President-Elect
Section 4.	Congress to Provide for Certain Successors
Section 5.	Effective Date
Section 6.	Time Limit on Ratification

21st Amendment: Repeal of 18th Amendment

Section 1.	Repeal of Prohibition
Section 2.	Transportation, Importation of Intoxicating Liquors
Section 3.	Time Limit on Ratification

22nd Amendment: Presidential Tenure

Section 1.	Restriction on Number of Terms
Section 2.	Time Limit on Ratification

23rd Amendment: Inclusion of District of Columbia in Presidential Election Systems

Section 1.	Presidential Electors for District
Section 2.	Power of Congress

24th Amendment: Right to Vote in Federal Elections—Tax Payment

Section 1.	Suffrage Not to Be Abridged
Section 2.	Power of Congress

25th Amendment: Presidential Succession; Vice Presidential Vacancy; Presidential Inability

Section 1.	Presidential Succession
Section 2.	Vice Presidential Vacancy
Section 3.	Presidential Inability

26th Amendment: Right to Vote—Age

Section 1.	Suffrage Not to Be Abridged
Section 2.	Power of Congress

27th Amendment: Congressional Pay

The Preamble states the broad purposes the Constitution is intended to serve—to establish a government that provides for greater cooperation among the States, ensures justice and peace, provides for defense against foreign enemies, promotes the general well-being of the people, and secures liberty now and in the future. The phrase We the People emphasizes the twin concepts of popular sovereignty and of representative government.

Legislative Department

Section 1. Legislative power; Congress

Congress, the nation's lawmaking body, is bicameral in form; that is, it is composed of two houses: the Senate and the House of Representatives. The Framers of the Constitution purposely separated the lawmaking power from the power to enforce the laws (Article II, the Executive Branch) and the power to interpret them (Article III, the Judicial Branch). This system of separation of powers is supplemented by a system of checks and balances; that is, in several provisions the Constitution gives to each of the three branches various powers with which it may restrain the actions of the other two branches.

Section 2. House of Representatives

▶ **Clause 1. Election** Electors means voters. Members of the House of Representatives are elected every two years. Each State must permit the same persons to vote for United States representatives as it permits to vote for the members of the larger house of its own legislature. The 17th Amendment (1913) extends this requirement to the qualification of voters for United States senators.

▶ **Clause 2. Qualifications** A member of the House of Representatives must be at least 25 years old, an American citizen for seven years, and a resident of the State he or she represents. In addition, political custom requires that a representative also reside in the district from which he or she is elected.

▶ **Clause 3. Apportionment** The number of representatives each State is entitled to is based on its population, which is counted every 10 years in the census. Congress reapportions the seats among the States after each census. In the Reapportionment Act of 1929, Congress fixed the permanent size of the House at 435 members with each State having at least one representative. Today there is one House seat for approximately every 700,000 persons in the population.

The words "three-fifths of all other persons" referred to slaves and reflected the Three-Fifths Compromise reached by the Framers at Philadelphia in 1787; the phrase was made obsolete, was in effect repealed, by the 13th Amendment in 1865.

---

*   The gray words indicate portions of the Constitution altered by subsequent amendments to the document.

▶ **Clause 4. Vacancies** The executive authority refers to the governor of a State. If a member leaves office or dies before the expiration of his or her term, the governor is to call a special election to fill the vacancy.

PREAMBLE

We the People of the United States, in Order to form a more perfect Union, establish Justice, insure domestic Tranquility, provide for the common defence, promote the general Welfare, and secure the Blessings of Liberty to ourselves and our Posterity, do ordain and establish this Constitution for the United States of America.

Article I.

Section 1.

All legislative Powers herein granted shall be vested in a Congress of the United States, which shall consist of a Senate and House of Representatives.

Section 2.

▶ 1. The House of Representatives shall be composed of Members chosen every second Year by the People of the several States, and the Electors in each State shall have the Qualifications requisite for Electors of the most numerous Branch of the State Legislature.

▶ 2. No Person shall be a Representative who shall not have attained to the age of twenty-five Years, and been seven Years a Citizen of the United States, and who shall not, when elected, be an Inhabitant of that State in which he shall be chosen.

▶ 3. Representatives and direct Taxes* shall be apportioned among the several States which may be included within this Union, according to their respective Numbers, which shall be determined by adding to the whole Number of free Persons, including those bound to Service for a Term of Years and excluding Indians not taxed, three fifths of all other Persons. The actual Enumeration shall be made within three Years after the first Meeting of the Congress of the United States, and within every subsequent term of ten Years, in such Manner as they shall by Law direct. The Number of Representatives shall not exceed one for every thirty Thousand, but each State shall have at Least one Representative; and, until such enumeration shall be made, the State of New Hampshire shall be entitled to choose three, Massachusetts eight, Rhode Island and Providence Plantations one, Connecticut five, New York six, New Jersey four, Pennsylvania eight, Delaware one, Maryland six, Virginia ten, North Carolina five, South Carolina five, and Georgia three.

▶ 4. When vacancies happen in the Representation from any State, the Executive Authority thereof shall issue Writs of Election to fill such Vacancies.

5. The House of Representatives shall choose their Speaker and other Officers; and shall have the sole Power of Impeachment.

> **Clause 5. Officers; impeachment** The House elects a Speaker, customarily chosen from the majority party in the House. Impeachment means accusation. The House has the exclusive power to impeach, or accuse, civil officers; the Senate (Article I, Section 3, Clause 6) has the exclusive power to try those impeached by the House.

Section 3.

1. The Senate of the United States shall be composed of two Senators from each State chosen by the Legislature thereof for six Years; and each Senator shall have one Vote.

2. Immediately after they shall be assembled in Consequences of the first Election, they shall be divided, as equally as may be, into three Classes. The Seats of the Senators of the first Class shall be vacated at the Expiration of the second Year; of the second Class, at the Expiration of the fourth Year; and of the third Class, at the Expiration of the sixth Year; so that one-third may be chosen every second Year; and if Vacancies happen by Resignation, or otherwise, during the Recess of the Legislature of any State, the Executive thereof may make temporary Appointments until the next Meeting of the Legislature, which shall then fill such Vacancies.

3. No Person shall be a Senator who shall not have attained to the Age of thirty Years, and been nine Years a Citizen of the United States, and who shall not, when elected, be an Inhabitant of that State for which he shall be chosen.

4. The Vice President of the United States shall be President of the Senate but shall have no Vote, unless they be equally divided.

5. The Senate shall choose their other Officers, and also a President pro tempore, in the Absence of the Vice President, or when he shall exercise the Office of President of the United States.

6. The Senate shall have the sole Power to try all Impeachments. When sitting for that Purpose, they shall be on Oath or Affirmation. When the President of the United States is tried, the Chief Justice shall preside: And no Person shall be convicted without the Concurrence of two thirds of the Members present.

7. Judgment in Cases of Impeachment shall not extend further than to removal from Office, and disqualification to hold and enjoy any Office of honor, Trust, or Profit under the United States: but the Party convicted shall nevertheless be liable and subject to Indictment, Trial, Judgment and Punishment, according to Law.

Section 3. Senate

> **Clause 1. Composition, election, term** Each State has two senators. Each serves for six years and has one vote. Originally, senators were not elected directly by the people, but by each State's legislature. The 17th Amendment, added in 1913, provides for the popular election of senators.

> **Clause 2. Classification** The senators elected in 1788 were divided into three groups so that the Senate could become a "continuing body." One-third of the Senate's seats are up for election every two years.
>
> The 17th Amendment provides that a Senate vacancy is to be filled at a special election called by the governor; State law may also permit the governor to appoint a successor to serve until that election is held.

> **Clause 3. Qualifications** A senator must be at least 30 years old, a citizen for at least nine years, and must live in the State from which elected.

> **Clause 4. Presiding officer** The Vice President presides over the Senate, but may vote only to break a tie.

> **Clause 5. Other officers** The Senate chooses its own officers, including a president pro tempore to preside when the Vice President is not there.

> **Clause 6. Impeachment trials** The Senate conducts the trials of those officials impeached by the House. The Vice President presides unless the President is on trial, in which case the Chief Justice of the United States does so. A conviction requires the votes of two-thirds of the senators present.
>
> No President has ever been convicted. In 1868 the House voted eleven articles of impeachment against President Andrew Johnson, but the Senate fell one vote short of convicting him. In 1974 President Richard M. Nixon resigned the presidency in the face of almost certain impeachment by the House. The House brought two articles of impeachment against President Bill Clinton in late 1998. Neither charge was supported by even a simple majority vote in the Senate, on February 12, 1999.

> **Clause 7. Penalty on conviction** The punishment of an official convicted in an impeachment case has always been removal from office. The Senate can also bar a convicted person from ever holding any federal office, but it is not required to do so. A convicted person can also be tried and punished in a regular court for any crime involved in the impeachment case.

Section 4. Elections and Meetings

▶ **Clause 1. Election In 1842** Congress required that representatives be elected from districts within each State with more than one seat in the House. The districts in each State are drawn by that State's legislature. Seven States now have only one seat in the House: Alaska, Delaware, Montana, North Dakota, South Dakota, Vermont, and Wyoming. The 1842 law also directed that representatives be elected in each State on the same day: the Tuesday after the first Monday in November of every even-numbered year. In 1914 Congress also set that same date for the election of senators.

▶ **Clause 2. Sessions Congress** must meet at least once a year. The 20th Amendment (1933) changed the opening date to January 3.

Section 5. Legislative Proceedings

▶ **Clause 1. Admission of members; quorum** In 1969 the Supreme Court held that the House cannot exclude any member-elect who satisfies the qualifications set out in Article I, Section 2, Clause 2.

A majority in the House (218 members) or Senate (51) constitutes a quorum. In practice, both houses often proceed with less than a quorum present. However, any member may raise a point of order (demand a "quorum call"). If a roll call then reveals less than a majority of the members present, that chamber must either adjourn or the sergeant at arms must be ordered to round up absent members.

▶ **Clause 2. Rules** Each house has adopted detailed rules to guide its proceedings. Each house may discipline members for unacceptable conduct; expulsion requires a two-thirds vote.

▶ **Clause 3. Record** Each house must keep and publish a record of its meetings. The Congressional Record is published for every day that either house of Congress is in session, and provides a written record of all that is said and done on the floor of each house each session.

▶ **Clause 4. Adjournment** Once in session, neither house may suspend (recess) its work for more than three days without the approval of the other house. Both houses must always meet in the same location.

Section 4.

▶ 1. The Times, Places and Manner of holding Elections for Senators and Representatives, shall be prescribed in each State by the Legislature thereof; but the Congress may at any time by law make or alter such Regulations, except as to the Places of choosing Senators.

▶ 2. The Congress shall assemble at least once in every Year, and such Meeting shall be on the first Monday in December, unless they shall by Law appoint a different Day.

Section 5.

▶ 1. Each House shall be the Judge of the Elections, Returns and Qualifications of its own Members, and a Majority of each shall constitute a Quorum to do Business; but a smaller Number may adjourn from day to day, and may be authorized to compel the Attendance of absent Members, in such Manner, and under such Penalties, as each House may provide.

▶ 2. Each House may determine the Rules of its Proceedings, punish its Members for disorderly Behavior, and, with the Concurrence of two thirds, expel a Member.

▶ 3. Each House shall keep a Journal of its Proceedings, and from time to time publish the same, excepting such Parts as may in their Judgment require Secrecy; and the Yeas and Nays of the Members of either House on any question shall, at the Desire of one fifth of those Present, be entered on the Journal.

▶ 4. Neither House, during the Session of Congress, shall, without the Consent of the other, adjourn for more than three days, nor to any other Place than that in which the two Houses shall be sitting.

Section 6.

▶ 1. The Senators and Representatives shall receive a Compensation for their Services, to be ascertained by Law, and paid out of the Treasury of the United States. They shall in all Cases, except Treason, Felony, and Breach of the Peace, be privileged from Arrest during their Attendance at the Session of their respective Houses, and in going to and returning from the same; and for any Speech or Debate in either House, they shall not be questioned in any other Place.

▶ 2. No Senator or Representative shall, during the Time for which he was elected, be appointed to any civil Office under the Authority of the United States, which shall have been created, or the Emoluments whereof shall have been increased during such time; and no Person holding any Office under the United States, shall be a Member of either House during his Continuance in Office.

Section 7.

▶ 1. All Bills for raising Revenue shall originate in the House of Representatives; but the Senate may propose or concur with amendments as on other Bills.

▶ 2. Every Bill which shall have passed the House of Representatives and the Senate, shall, before it become a law, be presented to the President of the United States: If he approve, he shall sign it, but if not he shall return it, with his Objections to that House in which it shall have originated, who shall enter the Objections at large on their Journal, and proceed to reconsider it. If after such Reconsideration two thirds of the House shall agree to pass the Bill, it shall be sent, together with the Objections, to the other House, by which it shall likewise be reconsidered, and if approved by two thirds of that House, it shall become a Law. But in all such Cases the Votes of both Houses shall be determined by Yeas and Nays, and the Names of the Persons voting for and against the Bill shall be entered on the Journal of each House respectively. If any Bill shall not be returned by the President within ten Days (Sunday excepted) after it shall have been presented to him, the Same shall be a law, in like Manner as if he had signed it, unless the Congress by their Adjournment, prevent its Return, in which Case it shall not be a Law.

▶ 3. Every Order, Resolution, or Vote to which the Concurrence of the Senate and House of Representatives may be necessary (except on a question of adjournment) shall be presented to the President of the United States; and before the Same shall take Effect, shall be approved by him, or, being disapproved by him, shall be repassed by two thirds of the Senate and House of Representatives, according to the Rules and Limitations prescribed in the Case of a Bill.

Section 6. Compensation, Immunities, and Disabilities of Members

▶ **Clause 1. Salaries; immunities** Each house sets its members' salaries, paid by the United States; the 27th Amendment (1992) modified this pay-setting power. This provision establishes "legislative immunity." The purpose of this immunity is to allow members to speak and debate freely in Congress itself. Treason is strictly defined in Article III, Section 3. A felony is any serious crime. A breach of the peace is any indictable offense less than treason or a felony; this exemption from arrest is of little real importance today.

▶ **Clause 2. Restrictions on office holding** No sitting member of either house may be appointed to an office in the executive or in the judicial branch if that position was created or its salary was increased during that member's current elected term. The second part of this clause—forbidding any person serving in either the executive or the judicial branch from also serving in Congress—reinforces the principle of separation of powers.

Section 7. Revenue Bills, President's Veto

▶ **Clause 1. Revenue bills** All bills that raise money must originate in the House. However, the Senate has the power to amend any revenue bill sent to it from the lower house.

▶ **Clause 2. Enactment of laws; veto** Once both houses have passed a bill, it must be sent to the President. The President may (1) sign the bill, thus making it law; (2) veto the bill, whereupon it must be returned to the house in which it originated; or (3) allow the bill to become law without signature, by not acting upon it within 10 days of its receipt from Congress, not counting Sundays. The President has a fourth option at the end of a congressional session: If he does not act on a measure within 10 days, and Congress adjourns during that period, the bill dies; the "pocket veto" has been applied to it. A presidential veto may be overridden by a two-thirds vote in each house.

▶ **Clause 3. Other measures** This clause refers to joint resolutions, measures Congress often passes to deal with unusual, temporary, or ceremonial matters. A joint resolution passed by Congress and signed by the President has the force of law, just as a bill does. As a matter of custom, a joint resolution proposing an amendment to the Constitution is not submitted to the President for signature or veto. Concurrent and simple resolutions do not have the force of law and, therefore, are not submitted to the President.

Section 8. Powers of Congress

▶ **Clause 1.** The 18 separate clauses in this section set out 27 of the many expressed powers the Constitution grants to Congress. In this clause Congress is given the power to levy and provide for the collection of various kinds of taxes, in order to finance the operations of the government. All federal taxes must be levied at the same rates throughout the country.

▶ **Clause 2.** Congress has power to borrow money to help finance the government. Federal borrowing is most often done through the sale of bonds on which interest is paid. The Constitution does not limit the amount the government may borrow.

▶ **Clause 3.** This clause, the Commerce Clause, gives Congress the power to regulate both foreign and interstate trade. Much of what Congress does, it does on the basis of its commerce power.

▶ **Clause 4.** Congress has the exclusive power to determine how aliens may become citizens of the United States. Congress may also pass laws relating to bankruptcy.

▶ **Clause 5.** has the power to establish and require the use of uniform gauges of time, distance, weight, volume, area, and the like.

▶ **Clause 6.** Congress has the power to make it a federal crime to falsify the coins, paper money, bonds, stamps, and the like of the United States.

▶ **Clause 7.** Congress has the power to provide for and regulate the transportation and delivery of mail; "post offices" are those buildings and other places where mail is deposited for dispatch; "post roads" include all routes over or upon which mail is carried.

▶ **Clause 8.** Congress has the power to provide for copyrights and patents. A copyright gives an author or composer the exclusive right to control the reproduction, publication, and sale of literary, musical, or other creative work. A patent gives a person the exclusive right to control the manufacture or sale of his or her invention.

▶ **Clause 9.** Congress has the power to create the lower federal courts, all of the several federal courts that function beneath the Supreme Court.

▶ **Clause 10.** Congress has the power to prohibit, as a federal crime: (1) certain acts committed outside the territorial jurisdiction of the United States, and (2) the commission within the United States of any wrong against any nation with which we are at peace.

Section 8.

The Congress shall have Power

▶ 1. To lay and collect Taxes, Duties, Imposts and Excises to pay the Debts and provide for the common Defence and general Welfare of the United States; but all Duties, Imposts and Excises, shall be uniform throughout the United States;

▶ 2. To borrow Money on the credit of the United States;

▶ 3. To regulate Commerce with foreign Nations, and among the several States, and with the Indian Tribes;

▶ 4. To establish an uniform Rule of Naturalization, and uniform Laws on the subject of Bankruptcies throughout the United States;

▶ 5. To coin Money, regulate the Value thereof, and of foreign Coin, and fix the Standard of Weights and Measures;

▶ 6. To provide for the Punishment of counterfeiting the Securities and current Coin of the United States;

▶ 7. To establish Post Offices and post Roads;

▶ 8. To promote the Progress of Science and useful Arts, by securing, for limited Times to Authors and Inventors the exclusive Right to their respective Writings and Discoveries;

▶ 9. To constitute Tribunals inferior to the supreme Court;

▶ 10. To define and punish Piracies and Felonies committed on the high Seas, and Offences against the Law of nations;

11. To declare War, grant Letters of Marque and Reprisal, and make Rules concerning Captures on Land and Water;

12. To raise and support Armies; but no Appropriation of Money to that Use shall be for a longer Term than two Years;
13. To provide and maintain a Navy;

14. To make Rules for the Government and Regulation of the land and naval Forces;

15. To provide for calling forth the Militia to execute the Laws of the Union, suppress Insurrections and repel Invasions;
16. To provide for organizing, arming, and disciplining the Militia, and for governing such Part of them as may be employed in the Service of the United States, reserving to the States respectively the Appointment of the Officers, and the Authority of training the Militia according to the discipline prescribed by Congress;

17. To exercise exclusive Legislation in all Cases whatsoever, over such District (not exceeding ten Miles square) as may, by Cession of Particular States, and the Acceptance of Congress, become the Seat of the Government of the United States, and to exercise like Authority over all Places purchased by the Consent of the Legislature of the State in which the Same shall be, for the Erection of Forts, Magazines, Arsenals, Dockyards and other needful Buildings;—And

18. To make all Laws which shall be necessary and proper for carrying into Execution the foregoing Powers and all other Powers vested by this Constitution in the Government of the United States, or in any Department or Officer thereof.

Section 9.

1. The Migration or Importation of such Persons as any of the States now existing shall think proper to admit, shall not be prohibited by the Congress prior to the Year one thousand eight hundred and eight, but a Tax or duty may be imposed on such Importation, not exceeding ten dollars for each Person.

▶ **Clause 11.** Only Congress can declare war. However, the President, as commander in chief of the armed forces (Article II, Section 2, Clause 1), can make war without such a formal declaration. Letters of marque and reprisal are commissions authorizing private persons to outfit vessels (privateers) to capture and destroy enemy ships in time of war; they were forbidden in international law by the Declaration of Paris of 1856, and the United States has honored the ban since the Civil War.

▶ **Clauses 12 and 13.** Congress has the power to provide for and maintain the nation's armed forces. It established the air force as an independent element of the armed forces in 1947, an exercise of its inherent powers in foreign relations and national defense. The two-year limit on spending for the army insures civilian control of the military.

▶ **Clause 14.** Today these rules are set out in three principle statutes: the Uniform Code of Military Justice, passed by Congress in 1950, and the Military Justice Acts of 1958 and 1983.

▶ **Clauses 15 and 16.** In the National Defense Act of 1916, Congress made each State's militia (volunteer army) a part of the National Guard. Today, Congress and the States cooperate in its maintenance. Ordinarily, each State's National Guard is under the command of that State's governor; but Congress has given the President the power to call any or all of those units into federal service when necessary.

▶ **Clause 17.** In 1791 Congress accepted land grants from Maryland and Virginia and established the District of Columbia for the nation's capital. Assuming Virginia's grant would never be needed, Congress returned it in 1846. Today, the elected government of the District's 69 square miles operates under the authority of Congress. Congress also has the power to acquire other lands from the States for various federal purposes.

▶ **Clause 18.** This is the Necessary and Proper Clause, also often called the Elastic Clause. It is the constitutional basis for the many and far-reaching implied powers of the Federal Government.

Section 9. Powers Denied to Congress

▶ **Clause 1.** The phrase "such persons" referred to slaves. This provision was part of the Commerce Compromise, one of the bargains struck in the writing of the Constitution. Congress outlawed the slave trade in 1808.

Clause 2. A writ of habeas corpus, the "great writ of liberty," is a court order directing a sheriff, warden, or other public officer, or a private person, who is detaining another to "produce the body" of the one being held in order that the legality of the detention may be determined by the court.

Clause 3. A bill of attainder is a legislative act that inflicts punishment without a judicial trial. See Article I, Section 10, and Article III, Section 3, Clause 2. An ex post facto law is any criminal law that operates retroactively to the disadvantage of the accused. See Article I, Section 10.

Clause 4. A capitation tax is literally a "head tax," a tax levied on each person in the population. A direct tax is one paid directly to the government by the taxpayer—for example, an income or a property tax; an indirect tax is one paid to another private party who then pays it to the government—for example, a sales tax. This provision was modified by the 16th Amendment (1913), giving Congress the power to levy "taxes on incomes, from whatever source derived."

Clause 5. This provision was a part of the Commerce Compromise made by the Framers in 1787. Congress has the power to tax imported goods, however.

Clause 6. All ports within the United States must be treated alike by Congress as it exercises its taxing and commerce powers. Congress cannot tax goods sent by water from one State to another, nor may it give the ports of one State any legal advantage over those of another.

Clause 7. This clause gives Congress its vastly important "power of the purse," a major check on presidential power. Federal money can be spent only in those amounts and for those purposes expressly authorized by an act of Congress. All federal income and spending must be accounted for, regularly and publicly.

Clause 8. This provision, preventing the establishment of a nobility, reflects the principle that "all men are created equal." It was also intended to discourage foreign attempts to bribe or otherwise corrupt officers of the government.

Section 10. Powers Denied to the States

Clause 1. The States are not sovereign governments and so cannot make agreements or otherwise negotiate with foreign states; the power to conduct foreign relations is an exclusive power of the National Government. The power to coin money is also an exclusive power of the National Government. Several powers forbidden to the National Government are here also forbidden to the States.

Clause 2. This provision relates to foreign, not interstate, commerce. Only Congress, not the States, can tax imports; and the States are, like Congress, forbidden the power to tax exports.

▶ 2. The Privilege of the Writ of Habeas Corpus shall not be suspended, unless when in Cases of Rebellion or Invasion the public safety may require it.

▶ 3. No Bill of Attainder or ex post facto Law shall be passed.

▶ 4. No Capitation, or other direct, Tax shall be laid, unless in Proportion to the Census of Enumeration hereinbefore directed to be taken.

▶ 5. No Tax or Duty shall be laid on Articles exported from any State.

▶ 6. No Preference shall be given by any Regulation of Commerce or Revenue to the Ports of one State over those of another: nor shall Vessels bound to, or from, one State, be obliged to enter, clear or pay Duties in another.

▶ 7. No Money shall be drawn from the Treasury, but in Consequence of Appropriations made by Law; and a regular Statement and Account of the Receipts and Expenditures of all public Money shall be published from time to time.

▶ 8. No Title of Nobility shall be granted by the United States: And no Person holding any Office of Profit or Trust under them, shall, without the Consent of the Congress, accept of any present, Emolument, Office, or Title, of any kind whatever, from any King, Prince, or foreign State.

Section 10.

▶ 1. No State shall enter into any Treaty, Alliance, or Confederation; grant Letters of Marque and Reprisal; coin Money; emit Bills of Credit; make any Thing but gold and silver Coin a Tender in Payment of Debts; pass any Bill of Attainder, ex post facto Law, or Law impairing the Obligation of Contracts, or grant any Title of Nobility.

▶ 2. No State shall, without the Consent of the Congress, lay any Imposts or Duties on Imports or Exports, except what may be absolutely necessary for executing its inspection Laws; and the net Produce of all Duties and Imposts, laid by any State on Imports or Exports, shall be for the Use of the Treasury of the United States; and all such Laws shall be subject to the Revision and Control of the Congress.

3. No State shall, without the Consent of Congress, lay any Duty of Tonnage, keep Troops, or Ships of War in time of Peace, enter into any Agreement or Compact with another State, or with a foreign Power, or engage in War, unless actually invaded, or in such imminent Danger as will not admit of delay.

> **Clause 3.** A duty of tonnage is a tax laid on ships according to their cargo capacity. Each State has a constitutional right to provide for and maintain a militia; but no State may keep a standing army or navy. The several restrictions here prevent the States from assuming powers that the Constitution elsewhere grants to the National Government.

Article II
Section 1.

1. The executive Power shall be vested in a President of the United States of America. He shall hold his Office during the Term of four Years, and, together with the Vice President, chosen for the same Term, be elected as follows:

2. Each State shall appoint, in such Manner as the Legislature thereof may direct, a Number of Electors, equal to the whole Number of Senators and Representatives to which the State may be entitled in the Congress: but no Senator or Representative, or Person holding an Office of Trust or Profit, under the United States, shall be appointed an Elector.

3. The Electors shall meet in their respective States, and vote by Ballot for two Persons, of whom one at least shall not be an Inhabitant of the same State with themselves. And they shall make a List of all the Persons voted for, and of the Number of Votes for each; which List they shall sign and certify, and transmit sealed to the Seat of the Government of the United States, directed to the President of the Senate. The President of the Senate shall, in the Presence of the Senate and House of Representatives, open all the Certificates, and the Votes shall then be counted. The Person having the greatest Number of Votes shall be the President, if such Number be a majority of the whole Number of Electors appointed; and if there be more than one who have such Majority, and have an equal Number of Votes, then, the House of Representatives shall immediately choose by Ballot one of them for President; and if no Person have a Majority, then from the five highest on the List the said House shall in like Manner choose the President. But in choosing the President, the Votes shall be taken by States, the Representatives from each State having one Vote; a quorum for this Purpose shall consist of a Member or Members from two thirds of the States, and a Majority of all the States shall be necessary to a Choice. In every Case, after the Choice of the President, the Person having the greatest Number of Votes of the Electors shall be the Vice President. But if there should remain two or more who have equal Votes, the Senate shall choose from them by Ballot the Vice President.

Executive Department
Section 1. President and Vice President

> **Clause 1. Executive power, term** This clause gives to the President the very broad "executive power," the power to enforce the laws and otherwise administer the public policies of the United States. It also sets the length of the presidential (and vice-presidential) term of office; see the 22nd Amendment (1951), which places a limit on presidential (but not vice-presidential) tenure.

> **Clause 2. Electoral college** This clause establishes the "electoral college," although the Constitution does not use that term. It is a body of presidential electors chosen in each State, and it selects the President and Vice President every four years. The number of electors chosen in each State equals the number of senators and representatives that State has in Congress.

> **Clause 3. Election of President and Vice President** This clause was replaced by the 12th Amendment in 1804.

Clause 4. Date Congress has set the date for the choosing of electors as the Tuesday after the first Monday in November every fourth year, and for the casting of electoral votes as the Monday after the second Wednesday in December of that year.

Clause 5. Qualifications The President must have been born a citizen of the United States, be at least 35 years old, and have been a resident of the United States for at least 14 years.

Clause 6. Vacancy This clause was modified by the 25th Amendment (1967), which provides expressly for the succession of the Vice President, for the filling of a vacancy in the Vice Presidency, and for the determination of presidential inability.

Clause 7. Compensation The President now receives a salary of $400,000 and a taxable expense account of $50,000 a year. Those amounts cannot be changed during a presidential term; thus, Congress cannot use the President's compensation as a bargaining tool to influence executive decisions. The phrase "any other emolument" means, in effect, any valuable gift; it does not mean that the President cannot be provided with such benefits of office as the White House, extensive staff assistance, and much else.

Clause 8. Oath of office The Chief Justice of the United States regularly administers this oath or affirmation, but any judicial officer may do so. Thus, Calvin Coolidge was sworn into office in 1923 by his father, a justice of the peace in Vermont.

Section 2. President's Powers and Duties

Clause 1. Military, civil powers The President, a civilian, heads the nation's armed forces, a key element in the Constitution's insistence on civilian control of the military. The President's power to "require the opinion, in writing" provides the constitutional basis for the Cabinet. The President's power to grant reprieves and pardons, the power of clemency, extends only to federal cases.

▶4. The Congress may determine the Time of choosing the Electors, and the Day on which they shall give their Votes; which Day shall be the same throughout the United States.

▶5. No Person except a natural born Citizen, or a Citizen of the United States, at the time of the Adoption of this Constitution, shall be eligible to the Office of President; neither shall any person be eligible to that Office who shall not have attained to the Age of thirty-five Years, and been fourteen Years a Resident within the United States.

▶6. In Case of the Removal of the President from Office, or of his Death, Resignation, or Inability to discharge the Powers and Duties of the said Office, the Same shall devolve on the Vice President, and the Congress may by Law provide for the Case of Removal, Death, Resignation or Inability, both of the President and Vice President, declaring what Officer shall then act as President, and such Officer shall act accordingly, until the Disability be removed, or a President shall be elected.

▶7. The President shall, at stated Times, receive for his Services, a Compensation, which shall neither be increased nor diminished during the Period for which he shall have been elected, and he shall not receive within that Period any other Emolument from the United States, or any of them.

▶8. Before he enter on the Execution of his Office, he shall take the following Oath or Affirmation:
"I do solemnly swear (or affirm) that I will faithfully execute the Office of President of the United States, and will to the best of my Ability, preserve, protect and defend the Constitution of the United States."

Section 2.

▶1. The President shall be Commander in Chief of the Army and Navy of the United States, and of the Militia of the several States, when called into the actual Service of the United States; he may require the Opinion, in writing, of the principal Officer in each of the executive Departments, upon any Subject relating to the Duties of their respective Offices, and he shall have Power to Grant Reprieves and Pardons for Offences against the United States, except in Cases of Impeachment.

2. He shall have Power, by and with the Advice and Consent of the Senate, to make Treaties, provided two thirds of the Senators present concur; and he shall nominate, and by and with the Advice and Consent of the Senate, shall appoint Ambassadors, other public Ministers and Consuls, Judges of the supreme Court, and all other Officers of the United States, whose Appointments are not herein otherwise provided for, and which shall be established by Law: but the Congress may by Law vest the Appointment of such inferior Officers, as they think proper, in the President alone, in the Courts of Law, or in the Heads of Departments.

▶ **Clause 2. Treaties, appointments** The President has the sole power to make treaties; to become effective, a treaty must be approved by a two-thirds vote in the Senate. In practice, the President can also make executive agreements with foreign governments; these pacts, which are frequently made and usually deal with routine matters, do not require Senate consent. The President appoints the principal officers of the executive branch and all federal judges; the "inferior officers" are those who hold lesser posts.

3. The President shall have Power to fill up all Vacancies that may happen during the Recess of the Senate, by granting Commissions which shall expire at the End of their next Session.

▶ **Clause 3. Recess appointments** When the Senate is not in session, appointments that require Senate consent can be made by the President on a temporary basis, as "recess appointments." Recess appointments are valid only to the end of the congressional term in which they are made.

Section 3.

He shall from time to time give to the Congress Information of the State of the Union, and recommend to their Consideration such Measures as he shall judge necessary and expedient; he may, on extraordinary Occasions, convene both Houses, or either of them, and in Case of Disagreement between them, with Respect to the Time of Adjournment, he may adjourn them to such Time as he shall think proper; he shall receive Ambassadors and other public Ministers; he shall take Care that the Laws be faithfully executed, and shall Commission all the Officers of the United States.

Section 3. President's Powers and Duties

The President delivers a State of the Union Message to Congress soon after that body convenes each year. That message is delivered to the nation's lawmakers and, importantly, to the American people, as well. It is shortly followed by the proposed federal budget and an economic report; and the President may send special messages to Congress at any time. In all of these communications, Congress is urged to take those actions the Chief Executive finds to be in the national interest. The President also has the power: to call special sessions of Congress; to adjourn Congress if its two houses cannot agree for that purpose; to receive the diplomatic representatives of other governments; to insure the proper execution of all federal laws; and to empower federal officers to hold their posts and perform their duties.

Section 4.

The President, Vice President and all Civil Officers of the United States, shall be removed from Office on Impeachment for and Conviction of, Treason, Bribery, or other high Crimes and Misdemeanors.

Section 4. Impeachment

The Constitution outlines the impeachment process in Article I, Section 2, Clause 5 and in Section 3, Clauses 6 and 7.

Article III
Section 1.

The judicial Power of the United States, shall be vested in one supreme Court, and in such inferior Courts as the Congress may from time to time ordain and establish. The Judges, both of the supreme and inferior Courts, shall hold their Offices during good Behaviour, and shall, at stated Times, receive for their Services, a Compensation, which shall not be diminished during their Continuance in Office.

Judicial Department
Section 1. Judicial Power, Courts, Terms of Office

The judicial power conferred here is the power of federal courts to hear and decide cases, disputes between the government and individuals and between private persons (parties). The Constitution creates only the Supreme Court of the United States; it gives to Congress the power to establish other, lower federal courts (Article I, Section 8, Clause 9) and to fix the size of the Supreme Court. The words "during good Behaviour" mean, in effect, for life.

Section 2. Jurisdiction

▶ **Clause 1. Cases to be heard** This clause sets out the jurisdiction of the federal courts; that is, it identifies those cases that may be tried in those courts. The federal courts can hear and decide—have jurisdiction over—a case depending on either the subject matter or the parties involved in that case. The jurisdiction of the federal courts in cases involving States was substantially restricted by the 11th Amendment in 1795.

▶ **Clause 2. Supreme Court jurisdiction** Original jurisdiction refers to the power of a court to hear a case in the first instance, not on appeal from a lower court. Appellate jurisdiction refers to a court's power to hear a case on appeal from a lower court, from the court in which the case was originally tried. This clause gives the Supreme Court both original and appellate jurisdiction. However, nearly all of the cases the High Court hears are brought to it on appeal from the lower federal courts and the highest State courts.

▶ **Clause 3. Jury trial in criminal cases** A person accused of a federal crime is guaranteed the right to trial by jury in a federal court in the State where the crime was committed; see the 5th and 6th amendments. The right to trial by jury in serious criminal cases in the State courts is guaranteed by the 6th and 14th amendments.

Section 3. Treason

▶ **Clause 1. Definition** Treason is the only crime defined in the Constitution. The Framers intended the very specific definition here to prevent the loose use of the charge of treason—for example, against persons who criticize the government. Treason can be committed only in time of war and only by a citizen or a resident alien.

▶ **Clause 2. Punishment** Congress has provided that the punishment that a federal court may impose on a convicted traitor may range from a minimum of five years in prison and/or a $10,000 fine to a maximum of death; no person convicted of treason has ever been executed by the United States. No legal punishment can be imposed on the family or descendants of a convicted traitor. Congress has also made it a crime for any person (in either peace or wartime) to commit espionage or sabotage, to attempt to overthrow the government by force, or to conspire to do any of these things.

Section 2.

▶ 1. The judicial Power shall extend to all Cases, in Law and Equity, arising under this Constitution, the Laws of the United States, and Treaties made, or which shall be made, under their Authority;— to all Cases affecting Ambassadors, other public ministers, and Consuls;— to all Cases of Admiralty and maritime Jurisdiction;— to Controversies to which the United States shall be a Party;— to Controversies between two or more States;— between a State and Citizens of another State;— between Citizens of different States;— between Citizens of the same State claiming Lands under Grants of different States, and between a State, or the Citizens thereof, and foreign States, Citizens, or Subjects.

▶ 2. In all Cases affecting Ambassadors, other public Ministers and Consuls, and those in which a State shall be a Party, the supreme Court shall have original Jurisdiction. In all the other Cases before mentioned, the supreme Court shall have appellate Jurisdiction, both as to Law and Fact, with such Exceptions, and under such Regulations as the Congress shall make.

▶ 3. The trial of all Crimes, except in Cases of Impeachment, shall be by Jury; and such Trial shall be held in the State where the said Crimes shall have been committed; but when not committed within any State, the Trial shall be at such Place or Places as the Congress may by Law have directed.

Section 3.

▶ 1. Treason against the United States shall consist only in levying War against them, or in adhering to their Enemies, giving them Aid and Comfort. No Person shall be convicted of Treason unless on the Testimony of two Witnesses to the same overt Act, or on Confession in open Court.

▶ 2. The Congress shall have Power to declare the Punishment of Treason, but no Attainder of Treason shall work Corruption of Blood, or Forfeiture except during the Life of the Person attainted.

Article IV

Section 1.

Full Faith and Credit shall be given in each State to the public Acts, Records, and judicial Proceedings of every other State. And the Congress may by general Laws prescribe the Manner in which such Acts, Records and Proceedings shall be proved, and the Effect thereof.

Section 2.

▶ 1. The Citizens of each State shall be entitled to all Privileges and Immunities of Citizens in the several States.

▶ 2. A Person charged in any State with Treason, Felony, or other Crime, who shall flee from justice, and be found in another State, shall on Demand of the executive Authority of the State from which he fled, be delivered up, to be removed to the State having Jurisdiction of the Crime.

▶ 3. No Person held to Service or Labor in one State, under the Laws thereof, escaping into another, shall, in Consequence of any Law or Regulation therein, be discharged from Service or Labor, but shall be delivered up on Claim of the Party to whom such Service or Labor may be due.

Section 3.

▶ 1. New States may be admitted by the Congress into this Union; but no new State shall be formed or erected within the Jurisdiction of any other State; nor any State be formed by the Junction of two or more States, or Parts of States, without the Consent of the Legislatures of the States concerned as well as of the Congress.

▶ 2. The Congress shall have Power to dispose of and make all needful Rules and Regulations respecting the Territory or other Property belonging to the United States; and nothing in this Constitution shall be so construed as to Prejudice any Claims of the United States, or of any particular State.

Section 4.

The United States shall guarantee to every State in this Union a Republican Form of Government, and shall protect each of them against Invasion; and on Application of the Legislature, or of the Executive (when the Legislature cannot be convened) against domestic Violence.

Relations Among States

Section 1. Full Faith and Credit

Each State must recognize the validity of the laws, public records, and court decisions of every other State.

Section 2. Privileges and Immunities of Citizens

▶ **Clause 1. Residents of other States** In effect, this clause means that no State may discriminate against the residents of other States; that is, a State's laws cannot draw unreasonable distinctions between its own residents and those of any of the other States. See Section 1 of the 14th Amendment.

▶ **Clause 2. Extradition** The process of returning a fugitive to another State is known as "interstate rendition" or, more commonly, "extradition." Usually, that process works routinely; some extradition requests are contested however—especially in cases with racial or political overtones. A governor may refuse to extradite a fugitive; but the federal courts can compel an unwilling governor to obey this constitutional command.

▶ **Clause 3. Fugitive slaves** This clause was nullified by the 13th Amendment, which abolished slavery in 1865.

Section 3. New States; Territories

▶ **Clause 1. New States** Only Congress can admit new States to the Union. A new State may not be created by taking territory from an existing State without the consent of that State's legislature. Congress has admitted 37 States since the original 13 formed the Union. Five States—Vermont, Kentucky, Tennessee, Maine, and West Virginia—were created from parts of existing States. Texas was an independent republic before admission. California was admitted after being ceded to the United States by Mexico. Each of the other 30 States entered the Union only after a period of time as an organized territory of the United States.

▶ **Clause 2. Territory, property** Congress has the power to make laws concerning the territories, other public lands, and all other property of the United States.

Section 4. Protection Afforded to States by the Nation

The Constitution does not define "a republican form of government," but the phrase is generally understood to mean a representative government. The Federal Government must also defend each State against attacks from outside its border and, at the request of a State's legislature or its governor, aid its efforts to put down internal disorders.

Provisions for Amendment

This section provides for the methods by which formal changes can be made in the Constitution. An amendment may be proposed in one of two ways: by a two-thirds vote in each house of Congress, or by a national convention called by Congress at the request of two-thirds of the State legislatures. A proposed amendment may be ratified in one of two ways: by three-fourths of the State legislatures, or by three-fourths of the States in conventions called for that purpose. Congress has the power to determine the method by which a proposed amendment may be ratified. The amendment process cannot be used to deny any State its equal representation in the United States Senate. To this point, 27 amendments have been adopted. To date, all of the amendments except the 21st Amendment were proposed by Congress and ratified by the State legislatures. Only the 21st Amendment was ratified by the convention method.

National Debts, Supremacy of National Law, Oath

Section 1. Validity of Debts

Congress had borrowed large sums of money during the Revolution and later during the Critical Period of the 1780s. This provision, a pledge that the new government would honor those debts, did much to create confidence in that government.

Section 2. Supremacy of National Law

This section sets out the Supremacy Clause, a specific declaration of the supremacy of federal law over any and all forms of State law. No State, including its local governments, may make or enforce any law that conflicts with any provision in the Constitution, an act of Congress, a treaty, or an order, rule, or regulation properly issued by the President or his subordinates in the executive branch.

Section 3. Oaths of Office

This provision reinforces the Supremacy Clause; all public officers, at every level in the United States, owe their first allegiance to the Constitution of the United States. No religious qualification can be imposed as a condition for holding any public office.

Ratification of Constitution

The proposed Constitution was signed by George Washington and 37 of his fellow Framers on September 17, 1787. (George Read of Delaware signed for himself and also for his absent colleague, John Dickinson.)

Article V

The Congress, whenever two thirds of both Houses shall deem it necessary, shall propose Amendments to this Constitution, or, on the Application of the Legislatures of two thirds of the several States, shall call a Convention for proposing Amendments, which, in either Case, shall be valid to all Intents and Purposes, as Part of this Constitution, when ratified by the Legislatures of three fourths of the several States, or by Conventions in three fourths thereof, as the one or the other Mode of Ratification may be proposed by the Congress; Provided that no Amendment which may be made prior to the Year One thousand eight hundred and eight shall in any Manner affect the first and fourth Clauses in the Ninth section of the first Article; and that no State, without its Consent, shall be deprived of its equal Suffrage in the Senate.

Article VI

Section 1.

All Debts contracted and Engagements entered into, before the Adoption of this Constitution, shall be as valid against the United States under this Constitution, as under the Confederation.

Section 2.

This Constitution, and the Laws of the United States which shall be made in Pursuance thereof; and all Treaties made, or which shall be made, under the Authority of the United States, shall be the supreme Law of the Land; and the Judges in every State shall be bound thereby, anything in the constitution or Laws of any State to the Contrary notwithstanding.

Section 3.

The Senators and Representatives before mentioned, and the Members of the several State legislatures, and all executive and judicial Officers, both of the United States and of the several States, shall be bound by Oath or Affirmation, to support this Constitution; but no religious Test shall ever be required as a Qualification to any Office or public Trust under the United States.

Article VII

The ratification of the Conventions of nine States, shall be sufficient for the Establishment of this Constitution between the States so ratifying the same.

Done in Convention by the Unanimous Consent of the States present the Seventeenth Day of September in the Year of our Lord one thousand seven hundred and Eighty-seven and of the Independence of the United States of America the twelfth. In witness whereof We have hereunto subscribed our Names.

Attest:
William Jackson,
Secretary
George Washington,
President and Deputy from Virginia

New Hampshire
John Langdon
Nicholas Gilman

Massachusetts
Nathaniel Gorham
Rufus King

Connecticut
William Samuel Johnson
Roger Sherman

New York
Alexander Hamilton

New Jersey
William Livingston
David Brearley
William Paterson
Jonathan Dayton

Pennsylvania
Benjamin Franklin
Thomas Mifflin
Robert Morris
George Clymer
Thomas Fitzsimons
Jared Ingersoll
James Wilson
Gouverneur Morris

Delaware
George Read
Gunning Bedford, Jr.
John Dickinson
Richard Bassett
Jacob Broom

Maryland
James McHenry
Dan of St. Thomas Jennifer
Daniel Carroll

Virginia
John Blair
James Madison, Jr.

North Carolina
William Blount
Richard Dobbs Spaight
Hugh Williamson

South Carolina
John Rutledge
Charles Cotesworth
   Pinckney
Charles Pinckney
Pierce Butler

Georgia
William Few
   Abraham Baldwin

The first 10 amendments, the Bill of Rights, were each proposed by Congress on September 25, 1789, and ratified by the necessary three-fourths of the States on December 15, 1791. These amendments were originally intended to restrict the National Government—not the States. However, the Supreme Court has several times held that most of their provisions also apply to the States, through the 14th Amendment's Due Process Clause.

1st Amendment. Freedom of Religion, Speech, Press, Assembly, and Petition

The 1st Amendment sets out five basic liberties: The guarantee of freedom of religion is both a protection of religious thought and practice and a command of separation of church and state. The guarantees of freedom of speech and press assure to all persons a right to speak, publish, and otherwise express their views. The guarantees of the rights of assembly and petition protect the right to join with others in public meetings, political parties, interest groups, and other associations to discuss public affairs and influence public policy. None of these rights is guaranteed in absolute terms, however; like all other civil rights guarantees, each of them may be exercised only with regard to the rights of all other persons.

2nd Amendment. Bearing Arms

The right of the people to keep and bear arms was insured by the 2nd Amendment.

3rd Amendment. Quartering of Troops

This amendment was intended to prevent what had been common British practice in the colonial period; see the Declaration of Independence. This provision is of virtually no importance today.

4th Amendment. Searches and Seizures

The basic rule laid down by the 4th Amendment is this: Police officers have no general right to search for or seize evidence or seize (arrest) persons. Except in particular circumstances, they must have a proper warrant (a court order) obtained with probable cause (on reasonable grounds). This guarantee is reinforced by the exclusionary rule, developed by the Supreme Court: Evidence gained as the result of an unlawful search or seizure cannot be used at the court trial of the person from whom it was seized.

5th Amendment. Criminal Proceedings; Due Process; Eminent Domain

A person can be tried for a serious federal crime only if he or she has been indicted (charged, accused of that crime) by a grand jury. No one may be subjected to double jeopardy—that is, tried twice for the same crime. All persons are protected against self-incrimination; no person can be legally compelled to answer any question in any governmental proceeding if that answer could lead to that person's prosecution. The 5th Amendment's Due Process Clause prohibits unfair, arbitrary actions by the Federal Government; a like prohibition is set out against the States in the 14th Amendment. Government may take private property for a legitimate public purpose; but when it exercises that power of eminent domain, it must pay a fair price for the property seized.

1st Amendment

Congress shall make no law respecting an establishment of religion, or prohibiting the free exercise thereof, or abridging the freedom of speech, or of the press; or the right of the people peaceably to assemble, and to petition the Government for a redress of grievances.

2nd Amendment

A well-regulated Militia being necessary to the security of a free State, the right of the people to keep and bear Arms, shall not be infringed.

3rd Amendment.

No Soldier shall, in time of peace be quartered in any house, without the consent of the Owner, nor, in time of war, but in a manner to be prescribed by law.

4th Amendment.

The right of the people to be secure in their persons, houses, papers, and effects, against unreasonable searches and seizures, shall not be violated, and no Warrants shall issue, but upon probable cause, supported by Oath or affirmation, and particularly describing the place to be searched, and the persons or things to be seized.

5th Amendment.

No person shall be held to answer for a capital, or otherwise infamous crime, unless on a presentment or indictment of a Grand Jury, except in cases arising in the land or naval forces, or in the Militia, when in actual service in time of War, or public danger; nor shall any person be subject for the same offence to be twice put in jeopardy of life or limb; nor shall be compelled in any criminal case to be a witness against himself, nor be deprived of life, liberty, or property, without due process of law; nor shall private property be taken for public use, without just compensation.

6th Amendment

In all criminal prosecutions, the accused shall enjoy the right to a speedy and public trial, by an impartial jury of the State and district wherein the crime shall have been committed, which district shall have been previously ascertained by law, and to be informed of the nature and cause of the accusation; to be confronted with the witnesses against him; to have compulsory process for obtaining witnesses in his favor, and to have the Assistance of Counsel for his defence.

7th Amendment

In Suits at common law, where the value in controversy shall exceed twenty dollars, the right of trial by jury shall be preserved, and no fact tried by a jury, shall be otherwise re-examined in any Court of the United States, than according to the rules of the common law.

8th Amendment

Excessive bail shall not be required, nor excessive fines imposed, nor cruel and unusual punishment inflicted.

9th Amendment

The enumeration in the Constitution, of certain rights, shall not be construed to deny or disparage others retained by the people.

10th Amendment

The powers not delegated to the United States by the Constitution, nor prohibited by it to the States, are reserved to the States respectively, or to the people.

6th Amendment. Criminal Proceedings

A person accused of crime has the right to be tried in court without undue delay and by an impartial jury; see Article III, Section 2, Clause 3. The defendant must be informed of the charge upon which he or she is to be tried, has the right to cross-examine hostile witnesses, and has the right to require the testimony of favorable witnesses. The defendant also has the right to be represented by an attorney at every stage in the criminal process.

7th Amendment. Civil Trials

This amendment applies only to civil cases heard in federal courts. A civil case does not involve criminal matters; it is a dispute between private parties or between the government and a private party. The right to trial by jury is guaranteed in any civil case in a federal court if the amount of money involved in that case exceeds $20 (most cases today involve a much larger sum); that right may be waived (relinquished, put aside) if both parties agree to a bench trial (a trial by a judge, without a jury).

8th Amendment. Punishment for Crimes

Bail is the sum of money that a person accused of crime may be required to post (deposit with the court) as a guarantee that he or she will appear in court at the proper time. The amount of bail required and/or a fine imposed as punishment must bear a reasonable relationship to the seriousness of the crime involved in the case. The prohibition of cruel and unusual punishment forbids any punishment judged to be too harsh, too severe for the crime for which it is imposed.

9th Amendment. Unenumerated Rights

The fact that the Constitution sets out many civil rights guarantees, expressly provides for many protections against government, does not mean that there are not other rights also held by the people.

10th Amendment. Powers Reserved to the States

This amendment identifies the area of power that may be exercised by the States. All of those powers the Constitution does not grant to the National Government, and at the same time does not forbid to the States, belong to each of the States, or to the people of each State.

11th Amendment. Suits Against States

Proposed by Congress March 4, 1794; ratified February 7, 1795, but official announcement of the ratification was delayed until January 8, 1798. This amendment repealed part of Article III, Section 2, Clause 1. No State may be sued in a federal court by a resident of another State or of a foreign country; the Supreme Court has long held that this provision also means that a State cannot be sued in a federal court by a foreign country or, more importantly, even by one of its own residents.

12th Amendment. Election of President and Vice President

Proposed by Congress December 9, 1803; ratified June 15, 1804. This amendment replaced Article II, Section 1, Clause 3. Originally, each elector cast two ballots, each for a different person for President. The person with the largest number of electoral votes, provided that number was a majority of the electors, was to become President; the person with the second highest number was to become Vice President. This arrangement produced an electoral vote tie between Thomas Jefferson and Aaron Burr in 1800; the House finally chose Jefferson as President in 1801. The 12th Amendment separated the balloting for President and Vice President; each elector now casts one ballot for someone as President and a second ballot for another person as Vice President. Note that the 20th Amendment changed the date set here (March 4) to January 20, and that the 23rd Amendment (1961) provides for electors from the District of Columbia. This amendment also provides that the Vice President must meet the same qualifications as those set out for the President in Article II, Section 1, Clause 5.

13th Amendment. Slavery and Involuntary Servitude

Proposed by Congress January 31, 1865; ratified December 6, 1865. This amendment forbids slavery in the United States and in any area under its control. It also forbids other forms of forced labor, except punishments for crime; but some forms of compulsory service are not prohibited—for example, service on juries or in the armed forces. Section 2 gives to Congress the power to carry out the provisions of Section 1 of this amendment.

11th Amendment

The Judicial power of the United States shall not be construed to extend to any suit in law or equity, commenced or prosecuted against one of the United States by Citizens of another State, or by Citizens or Subjects of any Foreign State.

12th Amendment

The Electors shall meet in their respective States and vote by ballot for President and Vice President, one of whom, at least, shall not be an inhabitant of the same State with themselves; they shall name in their ballots the person voted for as President, and in distinct ballots the person voted for as Vice President, and they shall make distinct lists of all persons voted for as President, and of all persons voted for as Vice President, and of the number of votes for each, which lists they shall sign and certify, and transmit sealed to the seat of the government of the United States, directed to the President of the Senate;— The President of the Senate shall, in the presence of the Senate and the House of Representatives, open all the certificates and the votes shall then be counted;— the person having the greatest Number of votes for President shall be the President, if such number be a majority of the whole number of Electors appointed; and if no person have such a majority, then, from the persons having the highest numbers not exceeding three on the list of those voted for as President, the House of Representatives shall choose immediately, by ballot, the President. But in choosing the President, the votes shall be taken by States, the representation from each State having one vote; a quorum for this purpose shall consist of a member or members from two thirds of the States, and a majority of all the States shall be necessary to a choice. And if the House of Representatives shall not choose a President whenever the right of choice shall devolve upon them, before the fourth day of March next following, then the Vice President shall act as President, as in case of death or other constitutional disability of the President. The person having the greatest number of votes as Vice President, shall be the Vice President, if such number be a majority of the whole number of Electors appointed, and if no person have a majority, then from the two highest numbers on the list, the Senate shall choose the Vice President; a quorum for the purpose shall consist of two thirds of the whole number of Senators, a majority of the whole number shall be necessary to a choice. But no person constitutionally ineligible to the office of President shall be eligible to that of Vice-President of the United States.

13th Amendment

Section 1. Neither slavery nor involuntary servitude, except as a punishment for crime whereof the party shall have been duly convicted, shall exist within the United States, or any place subject to their jurisdiction.

Section 2. Congress shall have power to enforce this article by appropriate legislation.

14th Amendment

Section 1. All persons born or naturalized in the United States and subject to the jurisdiction thereof, are citizens of the United States and of the State wherein they reside. No State shall make or enforce any law which shall abridge the privileges or immunities of citizens of the United States; nor shall any State deprive any person of life, liberty, or property, without due process of law; nor deny to any person within its jurisdiction the equal protection of the laws.

Section 2. Representatives shall be apportioned among the several States according to their respective numbers, counting the whole number of persons in each State, excluding Indians not taxed. But when the right to vote at any election for the choice of electors for President and Vice President of the United States, Representatives in Congress, the Executive and Judicial officers of a State, or the members of the Legislature thereof, is denied to any of the male inhabitants of such State, being twenty-one years of age and citizens of the United States, or in any way abridged, except for participation in rebellion, or other crime, the basis of representation therein shall be reduced in the proportion which the number of such male citizens shall bear to the whole number of male citizens twenty-one years of age in such State.

Section 3. No person shall be a Senator or Representative in Congress, or elector of President and Vice President, or hold any office, civil or military, under the United States, or under any State, who, having previously taken an oath, as a member of Congress, or as an officer of the United States, or as a member of any State legislature, or as an executive or judicial officer of any State, to support the Constitution of the United States, shall have engaged in insurrection or rebellion against the same, or given aid or comfort to the enemies thereof. But Congress may, by a vote of two thirds of each House, remove such disability.

Section 4. The validity of the public debt of the United States, authorized by law, including debts incurred for payment of pensions and bounties for services in suppressing insurrection or rebellion, shall not be questioned. But neither the United States nor any State shall assume or pay any debt or obligation incurred in aid of insurrection or rebellion against the United States, or any claim for the loss or emancipation of any slave; but all such debts, obligations and claims shall be held illegal and void.

Section 5. The Congress shall have power to enforce, by appropriate legislation, the provisions of this article.

14th Amendment. Rights of Citizens

Proposed by Congress June 13, 1866; ratified July 9, 1868. Section 1 defines citizenship. It provides for the acquisition of United States citizenship by birth or by naturalization. Citizenship at birth is determined according to the principle of jus soli—"the law of the soil," where born; naturalization is the legal process by which one acquires a new citizenship at some time after birth. Under certain circumstances, citizenship can also be gained at birth abroad, according to the principle of jus sanguinis—"the law of the blood," to whom born. This section also contains two major civil rights provisions: the Due Process Clause forbids a State (and its local governments) to act in any unfair or arbitrary way; the Equal Protection Clause forbids a State (and its local governments) to discriminate against, draw unreasonable distinctions between, persons.

Most of the rights set out against the National Government in the first eight amendments have been extended against the States (and their local governments) through Supreme Court decisions involving the 14th Amendment's Due Process Clause.

The first sentence here replaced Article I, Section 2, Clause 3, the Three-Fifths Compromise provision. Essentially, all persons in the United States are counted in each decennial census, the basis for the distribution of House seats. The balance of this section has never been enforced and is generally thought to be obsolete.

This section limited the President's power to pardon those persons who had led the Confederacy during the Civil War. Congress finally removed this disability in 1898.

Section 4 also dealt with matters directly related to the Civil War. It reaffirmed the public debt of the United States; but it invalidated, prohibited payment of, any debt contracted by the Confederate States and also prohibited any compensation of former slave owners.

15th Amendment. **Right to Vote— Race, Color, Servitude**

Proposed by Congress February 26, 1869; ratified February 3, 1870. The phrase "previous condition of servitude" refers to slavery. Note that this amendment does not guarantee the right to vote to African Americans, or to anyone else. Instead, it forbids the States from discriminating against any person on the grounds of his "race, color, or previous condition of servitude" in the setting of suffrage qualifications.

16th Amendment. **Income Tax**

Proposed by Congress July 12, 1909; ratified February 3, 1913. This amendment modified two provisions in Article I, Section 2, Clause 3, and Section 9, Clause 4. It gives to Congress the power to levy an income tax, a direct tax, without regard to the populations of any of the States.

17th Amendment. **Popular Election of Senators**

Proposed by Congress May 13, 1912; ratified April 8, 1913. This amendment repealed those portions of Article I, Section 3, Clauses 1 and 2 relating to the election of senators. Senators are now elected by the voters in each State. If a vacancy occurs, the governor of the State involved must call an election to fill the seat; the governor may appoint a senator to serve until the next election, if the State's legislature has authorized that step.

18th Amendment. **Prohibition of Intoxicating Liquors**

Proposed by Congress December 18, 1917; ratified January 16, 1919. This amendment outlawed the making, selling, transporting, importing, or exporting of alcoholic beverages in the United States. It was repealed in its entirety by the 21st Amendment in 1933.

19th Amendment. **Equal Suffrage—Sex**

Proposed by Congress June 4, 1919; ratified August 18, 1920. No person can be denied the right to vote in any election in the United States on account of his or her sex.

15th Amendment

Section 1. The right of citizens of the United States to vote shall not be denied or abridged by the United States or by any State on account of race, color, or previous condition of servitude.

Section 2. The Congress shall have power to enforce this article by appropriate legislation.

16th Amendment

The Congress shall have power to lay and collect taxes on incomes, from whatever source derived, without apportionment among the several States, and without regard to any census or enumeration.

17th Amendment

The Senate of the United States shall be composed of two Senators from each State, elected by the people thereof, for six years; and each Senator shall have one vote. The electors in each State shall have the qualifications requisite for electors of the most numerous branch of the State legislatures.

When vacancies happen in the representation of any State in the Senate, the executive authority of such State shall issue writs of election to fill such vacancies: Provided, That the legislature of any State may empower the executive thereof to make temporary appointments until the people fill the vacancies by election as the legislature may direct.

This amendment shall not be so construed as to affect the election or term of any Senator chosen before it becomes valid as part of the Constitution.

18th Amendment.

Section 1. After one year from the ratification of this article the manufacture, sale, or transportation of intoxicating liquors within, the importation thereof into, or the exportation thereof from the United States and all territory subject to the jurisdiction thereof for beverage purposes is hereby prohibited.

Section 2. The Congress and the several States shall have concurrent power to enforce this article by appropriate legislation.

Section 3. This article shall be inoperative unless it shall have been ratified as an amendment to the Constitution by the legislatures of the several States, as provided in the Constitution, within seven years of the date of the submission hereof to the States by Congress.

19th Amendment

The right of citizens of the United States to vote shall not be denied or abridged by the United States or by any State on account of sex.

Congress shall have power to enforce this article by appropriate legislation.

20th Amendment

Section 1. The terms of the President and Vice President shall end at noon on the 20th day of January, and the terms of Senators and Representatives at noon on the 3d day of January, of the years in which such terms would have ended if this article had not been ratified; and the terms of their successors shall then begin.

Section 2. The Congress shall assemble at least once in every year, and such meeting shall begin at noon on the 3d day of January, unless they shall by law appoint a different day.

Section 3. If, at the time fixed for the beginning of the term of the President, the President elect shall have died, the Vice President elect shall become President. If a President shall not have been chosen before the time fixed for the beginning of his term, or if the President-elect shall have failed to qualify, then the Vice President elect shall act as President until a President shall have qualified; and the Congress may by law provide for the case wherein neither a President elect nor a Vice President elect shall have qualified, declaring who shall then act as President, or the manner in which one who is to act shall be selected, and such person shall act accordingly until a President or Vice President shall have qualified.

Section 4. The Congress may by law provide for the case of the death of any of the persons from whom the House of Representatives may choose a President whenever the right of choice shall have devolved upon them, and for the case of the death of any of the persons from whom the Senate may choose a Vice President whenever the right of choice shall have devolved upon them.

Section 5. Sections 1 and 2 shall take effect on the 15th day of October following the ratification of this article.

Section 6. This article shall be inoperative unless it shall have been ratified as an amendment to the Constitution by the legislatures of three fourths of the several States within seven years from the date of its submission.

21st Amendment

Section 1. The eighteenth article of amendment to the Constitution of the United States is hereby repealed.

Section 2. The transportation or importation into any State, Territory, or possession of the United States for delivery or use therein of intoxicating liquors, in violation of the laws thereof, is hereby prohibited.

Section 3. This article shall be inoperative unless it shall have been ratified as an amendment to the Constitution by conventions in the several States, as provided in the Constitution, within seven years from the date of the submission hereof to the States by the Congress.

20th Amendment. Commencement of Terms; Sessions of Congress; Death or Disqualification of President-Elect

Proposed by Congress March 2, 1932; ratified January 23, 1933. The provisions of Sections 1 and 2 relating to Congress modified Article I, Section 4, Clause 2, and those provisions relating to the President, the 12th Amendment. The date on which the President and Vice President now take office was moved from March 4 to January 20. Similarly, the members of Congress now begin their terms on January 3. The 20th Amendment is sometimes called the "Lame Duck Amendment" because it shortened the period of time a member of Congress who was defeated for reelection (a "lame duck") remains in office.

This section deals with certain possibilities that were not covered by the presidential selection provisions of either Article II or the 12th Amendment. To this point, none of these situations has occurred. Note that there is neither a President-elect nor a Vice President-elect until the electoral votes have been counted by Congress, or, if the electoral college cannot decide the matter, the House has chosen a President or the Senate has chosen a Vice President.

Congress has not in fact ever passed such a law. See Section 2 of the 25th Amendment, regarding a vacancy in the vice presidency; that provision could some day have an impact here.

Section 5 set the date on which this amendment came into force.

Section 6 placed a time limit on the ratification process; note that a similar provision was written into the 18th, 21st, and 22nd amendments.

21st Amendment. Repeal of 18th Amendment

Proposed by Congress February 20, 1933; ratified December 5, 1933. This amendment repealed all of the 18th Amendment. Section 2 modifies the scope of the Federal Government's commerce power set out in Article I, Section 8, Clause 3; it gives to each State the power to regulate the transportation or importation and the distribution or use of intoxicating liquors in ways that would be unconstitutional in the case of any other commodity. The 21st Amendment is the only amendment Congress has thus far submitted to the States for ratification by conventions.

22nd Amendment. **Presidential Tenure**

Proposed by Congress March 21, 1947; ratified February 27, 1951. This amendment modified Article II, Section I, Clause 1. It stipulates that no President may serve more than two elected terms. But a President who has succeeded to the office beyond the midpoint in a term to which another President was originally elected may serve for more than eight years. In any case, however, a President may not serve more than 10 years. Prior to Franklin Roosevelt, who was elected to four terms, no President had served more than two full terms in office.

23rd Amendment. **Presidential Electors for the District of Columbia**

Proposed by Congress June 16, 1960; ratified March 29, 1961. This amendment modified Article II, Section I, Clause 2 and the 12th Amendment. It included the voters of the District of Columbia in the presidential electorate; and provides that the District is to have the same number of electors as the least populous State—three electors—but no more than that number.

24th Amendment. **Right to Vote in Federal Elections—Tax Payment**

Proposed by Congress August 27, 1962; ratified January 23, 1964. This amendment outlawed the payment of any tax as a condition for taking part in the nomination or election of any federal officeholder.

25th Amendment. **Presidential Succession, Vice Presidential Vacancy, Presidential Inability**

Proposed by Congress July 6, 1965; ratified February 10, 1967. Section 1 revised the imprecise provision on presidential succession in Article II, Section 1, Clause 6. It affirmed the precedent set by Vice President John Tyler, who became President on the death of William Henry Harrison in 1841. Section 2 provides for the filling of a vacancy in the office of Vice President. The office had been vacant on 16 occasions and remained unfilled for the rest of each term involved. When Spiro Agnew resigned the office in 1973, President Nixon selected Gerald Ford per this provision; and, when President Nixon resigned in 1974, Gerald Ford became President and chose Nelson Rockefeller as Vice President.

22nd Amendment

Section 1. No person shall be elected to the office of the President more than twice, and no person who has held the office of President, or acted as President, for more than two years of a term to which some other person was elected President shall be elected to the office of the President more than once. But this Article shall not apply to any person holding the office of President, when this Article was proposed by the Congress, and shall not prevent any person who may be holding the office of President, or acting as President, during the term within which this Article becomes operative from holding the office of President or acting as President during the remainder of such term.

Section 2. This article shall be inoperative unless it shall have been ratified as an amendment to the Constitution by the legislatures of three fourths of the several states within seven years from the date of its submission to the States by the Congress.

23rd Amendment.

Section 1. The District constituting the seat of Government of the United States shall appoint in such manner as the Congress may direct:

A number of electors of President and Vice President equal to the whole number of Senators and Representatives in Congress to which the District would be entitled if it were a State, but in no event more than the least populous State; they shall be in addition to those appointed by the States, they shall be considered, for the purposes of the election of President and Vice President, to be electors appointed by a State; and they shall meet in the District and perform such duties as provided by the twelfth article of amendment.

24th Amendment.

Section 1. The right of citizens of the United States to vote in any primary or other election for President or Vice President, for electors for President or Vice President, or for Senator or Representative in Congress, shall not be denied or abridged by the United States or any State by reason of failure to pay any poll tax or other tax.

Section 2. The Congress shall have power to enforce this article by appropriate legislation.

25th Amendment.

Section 1. In case of the removal of the President from office or of his death or resignation, the Vice President shall become President.

Section 2. Whenever there is a vacancy in the office of the Vice President, the President shall nominate a Vice President who shall take office upon confirmation by a majority vote of both Houses of Congress.

Section 3. Whenever the President transmits to the President pro tempore of the Senate and the Speaker of the House of Representatives his written declaration that he is unable to discharge the powers and duties of his office, and until he transmits to them a written declaration to the contrary, such powers and duties shall be discharged by the Vice President as Acting President.

Section 4. Whenever the Vice President and a majority of either the principal officers of the executive departments or of such other body as Congress may by law provide, transmit to the President pro tempore of the Senate and the Speaker of the House of Representatives their written declaration that the President is unable to discharge the powers and duties of his office, the Vice President shall immediately assume the powers and duties of the office as Acting President.

Thereafter, when the President transmits to the President pro tempore of the Senate and the Speaker of the House of Representatives his written declaration that no inability exists, he shall resume the powers and duties of his office unless the Vice President and a majority of either the principal officers of the executive department or of such other body as Congress may by law provide, transmit within four days to the President pro tempore of the Senate and the Speaker of the House of Representatives their written declaration that the President is unable to discharge the powers and duties of his office. Thereupon Congress shall decide the issue, assembling within forty-eight hours for that purpose if not in session. If the Congress, within twenty-one days after receipt of the latter written declaration, or, if Congress is not in session, within twenty-one days after Congress is required to assemble, determines by two-thirds vote of both Houses that the President is unable to discharge the powers and duties of his office, the Vice President shall continue to discharge the same as Acting President; otherwise, the President shall resume the powers and duties of his office.

This section created a procedure for determining if a President is so incapacitated that he cannot perform the powers and duties of his office.

Section 4 deals with the circumstance in which a President will not be able to determine the fact of incapacity. To this point, Congress has not established the "such other body" referred to here. This section contains the only typographical error in the Constitution; in its second paragraph, the word "department" should in fact read "departments."

26th Amendment.

Section 1. The right of citizens of the United States, who are eighteen years of age or older, to vote shall not be denied or abridged by the United States or by any State on account of age.

Section 2. The Congress shall have the power to enforce this article by appropriate legislation.

26th Amendment. **Right to Vote—Age**

Proposed by Congress March 23, 1971; ratified July 1, 1971. This amendment provides that the minimum age for voting in any election in the United States cannot be more than 18 years. (A State may set a minimum voting age of less than 18, however.)

27th Amendment.

No law varying the compensation for the services of the Senators and Representatives, shall take effect, until an election of Representatives shall have intervened.

27th Amendment. **Congressional Pay**

Proposed by Congress September 25, 1789; ratified May 7, 1992. This amendment modified Article I, Section 6, Clause 1. It limits Congress's power to fix the salaries of its members—by delaying the effectiveness of any increase in that pay until after the next regular congressional election.

[Declaration of Independence]

Introduction

By signing the Declaration of Independence, members of the Continental Congress sent a clear message to Britain that the American colonies were free and independent states. Starting with its preamble, the document spells out all the reasons the people of the United States have the right to break away from Britain.

Primary Source

The Unanimous Declaration of the Thirteen United States of America

When in the Course of human events, it becomes necessary for one people to dissolve the political bands which have connected them with another, and to assume among the powers of the earth, the separate and equal station to which the Laws of Nature and of Nature's God entitle them, a decent respect to the opinions of mankind requires that they should declare the causes which impel [force] them to the separation. We hold these truths to be self-evident, that all men are created equal, that they are endowed [gifted] by their Creator with certain unalienable [cannot be taken away] Rights, that among these are Life, Liberty and the pursuit of Happiness. That to secure these rights, Governments are instituted among Men, deriving their just powers from the consent of the governed. That whenever any Form of Government becomes destructive of these ends, it is the Right of the People to alter or to abolish it, and to institute new Government, laying its foundation on such principles and organizing its powers in such form, as to them shall seem most likely to effect their Safety and Happiness. Prudence [cautiousness], indeed, will dictate that Governments long established should not be changed for light and transient causes; and accordingly all experience hath shown that mankind are more disposed to suffer, while evils are sufferable, than to right themselves by abolishing the forms to which they are accustomed. But when a long train of abuses and usurpations [unjust uses of power], pursuing invariably the same Object evinces a design to reduce them under absolute Despotism [rule of absolute power], it is their right, it is their duty, to throw off such Government, and to provide new Guards for their future security.

Such has been the patient sufferance of these Colonies; and such is now the necessity which constrains them to alter their former Systems of Government. The history of the present King of Great Britain is a history of repeated injuries and usurpations, all having in direct object the establishment of an absolute Tyranny over these States. To prove this, let Facts be submitted to a candid world.

He has refused his Assent to Laws, the most wholesome and necessary for the public good.

He has forbidden his Governors to pass Laws of immediate and pressing importance, unless suspended in their operation till his Assent should be obtained; and when so suspended, he has utterly neglected to attend to them.

He has refused to pass other Laws for the accommodation of large districts of people, unless those people would relinquish [give up] the right of Representation in the Legislature, a right inestimable [priceless] to them and formidable to tyrants only.

He has called together legislative bodies at places unusual, uncomfortable, and distant from the depository of their public Records, for the sole purpose of fatiguing them into compliance with his measures.

He has dissolved Representative Houses repeatedly, for opposing with manly firmness his invasions on the rights of the people.

He has refused for a long time, after such dissolutions [closing down], to cause others to be elected; whereby the Legislative powers, incapable of Annihilation, have returned to the People at large for their exercise; the State remaining in the mean time exposed to all the dangers of invasion from without, and convulsions [riots] within.

He has endeavoured to prevent the population of these States; for that purpose obstructing the Laws for Naturalization of Foreigners; refusing to pass others to encourage their migrations hither, and raising the conditions of new Appropriations of Lands.

He has obstructed the Administration of Justice by refusing his Assent to Laws for establishing Judiciary powers.

He has made Judges dependent on his Will alone, for the tenure [term] of their offices, and the amount and payment of their salaries.

He has erected a multitude of New Offices, and sent hither swarms of Officers to harass our people, and eat out their substance.

He has kept among us, in times of peace, Standing Armies without the Consent of our legislatures.

He has affected to render the Military independent of and superior to the Civil power.

He has combined with others to subject us to a jurisdiction foreign to our constitution, and unacknowledged by our laws; giving his Assent to their Acts of pretended Legislation:

For quartering [lodging] large bodies of armed troops among us:

For protecting them, by a mock Trial, from punishment for any Murders which they should commit on the Inhabitants of these States:

For cutting off our Trade with all parts of the world:

For imposing Taxes on us without our Consent:

For depriving us in many cases, of the benefits of Trial by Jury: For transporting us beyond Seas to be tried for pretended offences:

For abolishing the free System of English Laws in a neighbouring Province, establishing therein an Arbitrary government, and enlarging its Boundaries so as to render it at once an example and fit instrument for introducing the same absolute rule into these Colonies:

For taking away our Charters, abolishing our most valuable Laws, and altering fundamentally the Forms of our Governments:

For suspending our own Legislatures, and declaring themselves invested with power to legislate for us in all cases whatsoever.

He has abdicated Government here, by declaring us out of his Protection and waging War against us.

He has plundered our seas, ravaged our Coasts, burnt our towns, and destroyed the lives of our people.

He is at this time transporting large Armies of foreign Mercenaries [soldiers] to complete the works of death, desolation, and tyranny, already begun with circumstances of Cruelty and perfidy [dishonesty] scarcely paralleled in the most barbarous ages, and totally unworthy the Head of a civilized nation.

He has constrained our fellow Citizens taken Captive on the high Seas to bear Arms against their Country, to become the executioners of their friends and Brethren, or to fall themselves by their Hands.

He has excited domestic insurrections amongst us, and has endeavoured to bring on the inhabitants of our frontiers, the merciless Indian Savages whose known rule of warfare, is an undistinguished destruction of all ages, sexes and conditions.

In every stage of these Oppressions We have Petitioned for Redress [correction of wrongs] in the most humble terms: Our repeated Petitions have been answered only by repeated injury. A Prince, whose character is thus marked by every act which may define a Tyrant, is unfit to be the ruler of a free people.

Nor have We been wanting in attentions to our British brethren. We have warned them from time to time of attempts by their legislature to extend an unwarrantable jurisdiction over us. We have reminded them of the circumstances of our emigration and settlement here. We have appealed to their native justice and magnanimity [generosity], and we have conjured [begged] them by the ties of our common kindred, to disavow these usurpations, which would inevitably interrupt our connections and correspondence. They too have been deaf to the voice of justice and of consanguinity [relation by blood]. We must, therefore, acquiesce in the necessity, which denounces our Separation, and hold them, as we hold the rest of mankind, Enemies in War, in Peace Friends.

We, therefore, the Representatives of the United States of America, in General Congress, Assembled, appealing to the Supreme Judge of the world for the rectitude [justness] of our intentions, do, in the Name, and by Authority of the good People of these Colonies, solemnly publish and declare, That these United Colonies are, and of Right ought to be Free and Independent States; that they are Absolved from all Allegiance to the British Crown, and that all political connection between them and the State of Great Britain, is and ought to be totally dissolved; and that as Free and Independent States, they have full Power to levy War, conclude Peace, contract Alliances, establish Commerce, and to do all other Acts and Things which Independent States may of right do. And for the support of this Declaration, with a firm reliance on the protection of Divine Providence, we mutually pledge to each other our Lives, our Fortunes and our sacred Honor.

ASSESSMENT

1. **Identify Cause and Effect** How might the ideas about equality expressed in the Declaration of Independence have influenced later historical movements, such as the abolitionist movement and the women's suffrage movement?

2. **Identify Key Steps in a Process** Why was the Declaration of Independence a necessary document for the founding of the new nation?

3. **Draw Inferences** English philosopher John Locke wrote that government should protect "life, liberty, and estate." How do you think Locke's writing influenced ideas about government put forth in the Declaration of Independence?

4. **Analyze Structure** How does the Declaration organize its key points from beginning to end?

Your Fiscal Fitness: An Introduction

Think Long-Term If you start investing $40 a week at a 5 percent rate of return, in 20 years you will have accumulated $17,800. If you get a higher return, say 7 percent, then by the time you retire in 45 years, you would have $163,688.

"Whoa! Slow down! 20 years? Retirement? I'm still living at home! I don't even own my first car yet! Who do you think you are—my parents?"

If that's your reaction, you're not alone. A great many high school students do not think much about their financial future. They also don't like to get stern lectures from Mom or Dad—whether it's about financial planning or about those 5,000 extra text messages that appeared on last month's cellphone bill.

But let's face it: free room and board doesn't last forever. And often, it comes to an end soon after you get handed a diploma. At some point in the not-too-distant future, the bills in the mail will be yours.

The fact is that responsible financial citizens were not born that way. Even your parents had to learn how to comparison shop, avoid impulse buying, and put money aside that they would much rather spend on fun. Chances are they made mistakes along the way. And they wish you could avoid all the same pitfalls.

Take a Checkup Start by taking a good look at your own money habits. Are you a big spender? Moderate saver? Do you save anything at all? The answer is pretty easy to figure out. If you have an unexpected windfall, a bigger than expected birthday check, or an opportunity to earn extra money, what do you do with the money? Save it all? Save half? Look to see what you can buy now?

Skip the Fats, Go for the Protein! It comes down to fiscal fitness. Developing a solid, fiscal muscle also involves training or budgeting, short- and long-term goal setting, and most of all, patience. Personal finance, like athletics, requires discipline.

<< One way to be financially responsible is to look for sales. Comparison shopping can help people find the best deals and work towards meeting a budget.

Preparing for a long race often involves delayed gratification. An athlete will sacrifice fast-food because it's bad for his health, and healthy eating will pay off in the long run. The same is true of investing in your future. It may mean putting off purchases today for financial security sometime later on.

That's easy to say but hard to do, especially if you want to keep up with your peers. You and your dollars are the target of marketers and advertisers. According to a national survey, teenagers are rabid consumers of high-tech products. About 75 percent of U.S. teenagers own a cellphone, 60 percent have an MP3 player, and 43 percent have a car.

The Long Race The spirit is willing but the flesh is weak. The impulse to get what we want now is far stronger than the motivation to save for something that is months or even years down the road. You may have to trick yourself into saving by promising yourself a reward when you have met certain goals.

Obstacles What could slow down your progress? One outstanding speed bump is credit card abuse. You don't want to join the ranks of those who struggle to pay their credit card balance in full every month. They let matters slide—failing to balance their checkbooks, check their credit card statements, or keep an eye on bank fees and interest rates. You want to develop the fiscal awareness that will keep you out of trouble.

Grow Your Money Despite the difficulty of thinking long-term, 65 percent of teens actually admit that they want to learn how to grow their money. This is good news. Even better, 84 percent of teens have savings, with an average amount of $1,044. Fueling those savings is their attitude that the future is now.

Savings could translate into a car and college in the short run and a secure life and retirement in the years to come. With the right attitude, you're ready for basic training.

In no time at all, the following words will be part of your conversation. *Budgeting*—how to spend your income in such a way that there's something left over to invest. *Compounding*—how saving a little now can translate into big money later on in life. *Investing*—why the stock market can be both friend and foe. (Over the last 50 years or more, the stock market has averaged a higher return than bank accounts or bonds.) Ready, set, grow.

Weekly Savings

AGE	$10	$25	$50	$100
20	$228,563	$571,408	$1,142,817	$2,285,634
25	$151,277	$378,193	$756,385	$1,512,770
30	$99,402	$248,504	$497,008	$994,016
35	$64,582	$161,456	$322,911	$645,822
40	$41,211	$103,028	$206,056	$412,111
45	$25,524	$63,811	$127,621	$255,242
50	$14,995	$37,487	$74,975	$149,950
55	$7,928	$19,819	$39,638	$79,277

>> Starting a savings plan early in life can result in a substantial amount of money at retirement age. This chart indicates how much money a saver will have at the age of 65 (with an annual rate of return of 8 percent) if he or she saves certain amounts each week and starts saving at a certain age.

SOURCE: www.osu-tulsa.okstate.edu/financialaid, Savings Growth Chart

Budgeting

Budgeting 101 A **budget** is simply a plan for spending and saving. The word may conjure up images of driving a junk car or eating canned spaghetti every night. But the reality can be just the opposite. In fact, most millionaires use a budget to manage their money. And most of them started early.

Average American Family Budget

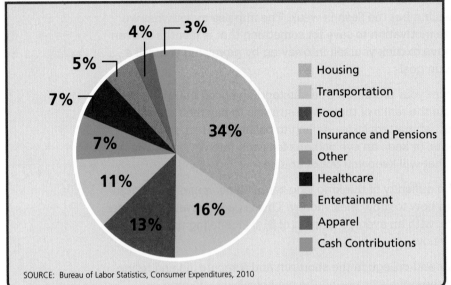

- Housing
- Transportation
- Food
- Insurance and Pensions
- Other
- Healthcare
- Entertainment
- Apparel
- Cash Contributions

34%
16%
13%
11%
7%
7%
5%
4%
3%

SOURCE: Bureau of Labor Statistics, Consumer Expenditures, 2010

<< Budgets can vary based on lifestyle and income. Developing a budget that includes all of the categories of spending will help determine how much money to set aside for each category.

Spending Awareness Surveys show that almost one half of Americans between the ages of 13 and 18 know how to budget their money. That's the good news. The bad news is more than half don't. Which group do you fall into? Take this quick quiz:

- How much money did you spend on beverages—from coffee or water to energy drinks—last week?
- How much money will you spend on gas next week?
- How long will it take you to save up for the most expensive thing you'd like to buy?

If you answered these questions without much trouble, you've already taken the first steps to good money management. If you don't have a clue, maybe it's time to think about making a budget.

Good Habits Start Early Now here's another question. Did you ever ask for money to spend on concert tickets—or a piece of jewelry, or a ski trip—only to hear *"You don't need it, and we can't afford it"*? Odds are you didn't think of it as an economics lesson. But according to surveys, students who learned about money management at home scored higher than those who learned about it only in school.

Budget Boosters

Record spending	Keep a spending journal for one week: Include every latte, vending-machine snack and music download.
Identify needs	Identify needs: bills, car payment, etc.
Spend wisely	Downsize or eliminate impulse buys such as coffee and soda.
Prioritize saving	Make saving a priority and a habit.
Save weekly	Add to your savings weekly, even if just a small amount.
Plan for the long-term	Identify a long-term want and start saving for it. (You'll be surprised how fast those fast-food outings diminish when you set your mind on something.)
Pay down debt	Prioritize and pay down any outstanding debt—including that $5 you owe your sister.
Use cash	Use cash for daily spending.
Work more	During vacations or the summer, pick up some extra hours at work.
Spend less	Live within your means. Spend less than you make.

>> Be budget smart! Follow these tips to stay on track with your spending and saving.

Income and Expenses Budgeting is a balancing act between income and expenses. It also means weighing your needs against your wants. To begin creating a budget, follow these steps in order.

- Make a list of your earnings per month from all sources. Add these up to calculate your expected monthly income.
- For one month, keep a record of everything you spend, from chewing gum to car payments. Collect receipts or write everything in a notebook. Make sure you don't leave anything out. (And that includes savings!)
- At the end of the month, organize your spending into categories such as food, entertainment, and car payments. Total the amount in each category.
- On a sheet of paper, list your income and expenses.

If your total expenses are less than your total income, you're doing fine. If not, you need to take a hard look at where your money is going.

Needs and Wants Right now, many of your basic needs are probably part of the household budget. Still, some of your personal funds may be going toward needs such as car insurance, lunches, or college savings. So, if you are looking to cut down expenses, you should focus first on the wants.

Consider the example of Michelle, a high school senior. She works 20 hours a week at a department store, where she earns $10.00 an hour. Her net income—that is, her take-home pay after taxes—is $150. Her monthly necessities include $40 for her cellphone bill, $60 on average for gas, and $65 a month on car insurance. Michelle has already set aside $300 a month for her prom and hopes to have $500 by the time prom rolls around. To stay within her budget, she gives up her daily soda habit, saving almost $30 a month. She and her friends also decide to watch movies at home rather than go out. This trade-off will allow them to rent a limousine to go to their prom. Michelle has planned for a long-term goal and budgeted correctly. She has drawn a fine line between needs and wants.

If you find you're have a difficult time staying within your budget, enlist a friend or family member to review your expenditures each week to help keep you on track. Try not to rationalize impulse buys. Consider them your sworn budget enemies!

Long-Term Rewards Err on the side of thrift and responsibility. Live within your means and try to save a set percentage of your income. Some budget counselors suggest allotting 80 percent for needs, 10 percent for wants, and 10 percent for savings. Do that and you might find yourself with a tidy savings within a few short years.

Spend without a plan and you might end up like many Americans: deep in debt. In fact, U.S. consumer debt topped an estimated 11.52 trillion dollars in 2013. About $820 billion, or 7.1 percent of outstanding debt is in some stage of delinquency, or late payment, with $580 billion over 90 days late in payment. The 90-day delinquency rate on credit card balances was 9.5 percent of the total credit card debt in 2013, while 11.5 percent of student loans in 2013 were in 90-day delinquency or in **default.** Learning to budget now may spare you from being part of this grim statistic later.

Checking

The Right Bank Banks are everywhere. Often they face each other at busy intersections in a community or are tucked in the corner of a supermarket. Every bank is vying for your business. How do you choose among them?

You want to use a bank that is insured by the **Federal Deposit Insurance Corporation (FDIC).** The FDIC protects your money and the interest it has earned—up to the insurance limit—in the event that your bank fails. For an account held by a single individual, the limit was raised to $250,000 in 2008. Banks are generally considered to be financially sound, but failures do occur.

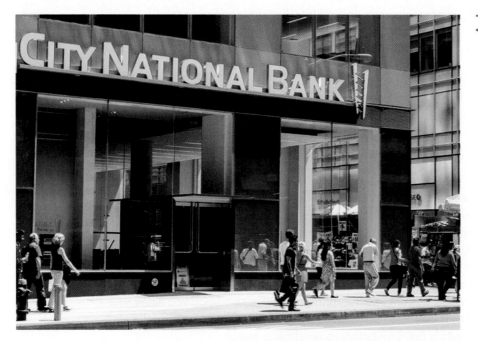

<< Banks offer FDIC services.

Endless Variety It may be impossible for you to believe, but not so very long ago even the biggest cities offered only ten different television stations. That was it for choices. The services offered by banks have grown in a similar way to the expansion of TV entertainment options. Although banks may look very similar, their services are not one-size-fits-all. The bank that is most convenient for you meets your needs. First, you have to figure out what you want and then figure out where to get it.

Checking Accounts One universal need is convenient and safe access to your money. Checking accounts and debit cards have made both readily available. To open a checking account you will need identification, such as a birth certificate or a driver's license and a Social Security number. You will also need money to **deposit.**

Which checking account meets your needs?

Basic checking: Best bet for customers who use a checking account to pay some bills and use a debit card for some daily expenses. *Drawback:* Monthly maintenance fees may apply unless you retain a minimum balance or enroll in direct deposit. Some banks may limit the number of checks you can write each month and charge you a per-item fee if you exceed the limit.

Free checking: The operative word here is "free," meaning a no-strings attached account with no monthly service charges or per-item fees, regardless of the balance or activity. *Drawback:* These are harder to find and the "free" part may be an introductory offer that expires in six months or a year.

Checking with overdraft protection: In effect, if you write checks for more than the balance of your deposits, the bank will honor the check by lending you the money you need, up to a preset limit. *Drawback:* This service comes with hefty fees.

Use words to write the payment amount.

Write the name of the payee.

Write the current date.

Use numerals to enter the payment amount.

Tomás Q. Public
123 Main Street
Anywhere, USA 45678

1027

October 14, 2014 DATE

$ 25.99

PAY TO THE ORDER OF GameOh!

Twenty-five and 99/100 ———————— DOLLARS

Security Features Details on Back.

Main Street Bank
321 Main Street
Anywhere, USA 45678

FOR game rental

Tomás Q. Public

⑆ 22222222 ⑆ 000 111 555⑈ 1027

Write additional information about the payment or payee, such as a reason or an account number.

Sign your check.

>> To avoid problems with checks: 1. Write clearly. 2. Do not cross out or write over a mistake. 3. Tear a check with any errors into small pieces and write "Void" next to the check number in your check register. 4. NEVER write a check for more than your account balance.

The Debit Card Most banks offer you a debit card with a checking account. With a credit card logo, it has the look and feel of a credit card, but there is a major difference. The money you spend is deducted from your checking account balance. Debit cards are also used to withdraw money from ATMs, giving you access to your money 24/7. If you use an ATM from a bank other than your own, you will likely be charged a fee. You could pay $2 to get access to your own $20. Debit cards are convenient, but convenience comes with a price.

Direct Deposit Banks and employers encourage people to take advantage of direct deposit. A win-win for you and the environment, the paperless transaction enlists your employer to deposit your paycheck directly into your bank account. An employer may ask for your Social Security number, a voided check containing your bank's routing number, and your account number.

Keeping Track When you open a checking account, you will receive a checkbook that includes sequentially numbered checks and a check register, or a booklet in which you'll record your account transactions. Every time you write a check, make a deposit, or use an ATM, you should take a few seconds to write it down. It is also important to hold onto your ATM receipts. They are the only proof that you withdrew $40, not $400.

Each month the bank will send you a statement of the activity on your account. If you opt to do your banking online, you can access your statement electronically. Your statement lists deposits, withdrawals, ATM transactions, interest paid, and fees charged. You will get a photocopy of any checks that were cashed during that month. Reconcile your bank statement by comparing the transactions on the bank statement to your own records to make sure they agree.

By taking a little time to be a good record keeper, you will make life a lot easier and protect yourself from mistakes and fraud. For more banking tips, check out fdic.gov.

Online Banking Once upon a time, people had to go to the bank to deposit money, to transfer money from one account to another, or to withdraw money from an account. They had to write a check or use cash to pay bills. This has become ancient history. The online bank is growing fast in popularity. An online bank can be a virtual extension of a brick-and-mortar bank or can exist solely in cyberspace. As long as a bank is insured by the FDIC, deposits are safe up to $250,000.

Online Banking Tips

1. Make sure your computer is protected with the latest versions of antivirus and antispyware software.

2. When banking online, ALWAYS double-check the Web site.

3. When creating a password, avoid the obvious, including first names, birthdays, anniversaries, or Social Security numbers.

4. Use Paypal. If your bank doesn't offer online bill pay, this online escrow service distributes your money fee-free to registered clients.

5. Exit a banking site after completing your online transactions and empty your computer's cache.

6. Make sure all other browser windows are closed during your transaction.

7. Visit the U.S. government's site onguardonline.gov for further tips to protect yourself against online fraud.

8. Change passwords on a routine basis.

>> Follow these tips to develop good habits that will help keep you protected when banking online. Online transactions offer layers of encrypted protection to safeguard your transaction and privacy.

Online Benefits As an online banking customer, you can access your accounts, pay your bills, and transfer funds from one account to another twenty-four hours a day. Internet banks also offer the environmentally friendly option to stop paper records, allowing you to access your statements, canceled checks, and notices online only. Your can even arrange **automatic bill payment.** Although you receive a bill in the mail or in your e-mail, the amount you owe is automatically deducted from your bank account on a predetermined date. You save time, postage, and the possibility of missing a payment and incurring late fees.

There can be other financial advantages to using online banks. Internet bank fees can be as much as 80 percent less than those charged by traditional banks. They may also offer checking, savings, or money market and CD accounts that yield higher interest rates than those offered by traditional banks.

A major benefit to the consumer is the ability to find these good deals by comparison shopping online. In the wise words of Benjamin Franklin, "A penny saved is a penny earned." By getting in the habit of looking for the lowest interest rates on loans and the highest interest rates on savings, the wise consumer will slowly pull ahead of the pack. Add a little compound interest into the mix and the pace of progress will pick up.

>> Depositing checks into a savings or checking account using a mobile device is a beneficial service that many people prefer.

Be Responsible Even though you may choose to bank online, every month you will get a statement in the mail from your financial institution. It is your responsibility to check this against your online transactions and report any discrepancies to your bank. Laws regulating an **Electronic Funds Transfer (EFT),** a system for transferring money from one bank to another, protect you in the case of fraud. You, however, have to do your part. In order to be protected by the law, you must report any errors in transactions within 60 days of the receipt of your bank statement. No matter how careful banks are not to make errors, no one is perfect.

If you use automatic bill pay, it is your responsibility to have sufficient funds in the account to cover the transaction. Some procedures of online banking are still affected by the business hours of the bank. If you are transferring funds to cover your bills, the money may not show up in your account unless you have made the transfer the previous day before a specific cutoff time. A deposit made at 1 a.m. may not show up on your account until the next business day. Plan your transactions accordingly, particularly if you wait until the last moment to pay your bills.

Gone Phishing Phishing is a scam in which a fraudulent Web site is used to gain personal and financial data to commit fraud. It's good to examine the risks of using a computer to maintain accounts at financial institutions.

There are several steps you can take to protect yourself.

- Online banking transactions should be done through the bank's Web site only.
- Never respond to e-mails from your "alleged" bank that request sensitive personal or financial information.
- If you suspect fraud, contact your bank by phone to determine if it's a legitimate communication from the bank. If not, alert them to the scam.

If you think you can't be fooled, think again. Phishing techniques can be highly elaborate. Many even set up mirror Web pages intended to look like your financial institution's Web site to earn your trust.

Traditional Banking In the balance, why would anyone still use a brick-and-mortar bank? There are a number of reasons that make some consumers reluctant to drop traditional banking altogether.

While Internet-only banks receive high marks for convenience, they also can be inconvenient.

- To fund an account, you will have to mail in a check, arrange for direct deposit, or make a transfer from another bank. This is not a problem, of course, with banks that also operate a physical branch.
- Not having the option of being able to speak with someone face-to-face is another inconvenience. Some customers prefer to interact with people who know them personally. Making a phone call or communicating by e-mail is not to everyone's liking.
- Another drawback is the difficulty of finding fee-free ATMs, although online banks often have ATM networks for their customers to use at minimal cost.

<< ATM machines are a banking convenience that usually charge a small transaction fee.

- Lack of paper checks is a fourth issue. Instead, Internet-only banks offer a bill-pay service. But payments have to be scheduled ahead of time and take several days to process. As a result, you have to keep close tabs on your account to ensure that you have money to cover the payments.

Investments

Self-Made Success Look in the mirror and the face of a future millionaire may be staring back at you. More than 80 percent of millionaires are self-made, first-generation rich. But forget the lottery and other get-rich-quick schemes. You have to set your own goals and work toward them.

Pay Yourself First In order to get started on your road to wealth, you have to remember one simple rule: Pay yourself first. A good rule of thumb is to set aside 10 to 15 percent of your income. We will talk later about how to achieve this goal, but for the time being, accept the fact. The lifestyle you choose to live now will determine the lifestyle you will be able to have in the future. But, don't forget others, as well. Charitable giving to organizations working to help the less fortunate are good investments in everyone's future.

Get Help From Interest Let's assume that you have made the decision to save. The positive news is that your savings will work for you. Banks pay you interest for using your money. Interest rates are expressed as percentages and indicate how much money an account will earn on funds deposited for a full year. Interest is compounded when it is added to your principal and you earn interest on both amounts. In effect, compound interest is interest on interest.

Most first-generation millionaires acquire their wealth over a lifetime. Their road to riches has more to do with budgeting, compound interest, and careful investing than with salary and inheritances.

Basic Investing Putting money in a savings account is very safe. The only danger to money in a savings account is that the rate of inflation will be greater than the interest rate. Over time, the money in your savings account could lose value—it will buy less and less. But you will never lose your principal, the amount of money you put in the account.

Investing money is not the same as "saving" money. Investors take more risk—even possibly losing money—in the hopes of getting a higher return on their money.

Investing your money can give your dollars a greater opportunity to grow. Bonds, stocks, and mutual funds are among the many investment choices that you have. Of course, with the possibility of greater growth comes the possibility of greater loss. If you invest in a corporate bond, stock, or mutual fund, you stand the risk of losing some or all of the money you invested. This risk is offset by the possibility of greater gain, allowing your money to grow at a faster rate than the rate of inflation.

The Name Is Bond A **bond** is an IOU issued by a corporation or by some level of government. When you buy a bond, you are lending money in return for a guaranteed payout at some later date. The safest bonds to buy are government-issued bonds because it is unlikely that a government will go bankrupt.

You can get U.S. government bonds through your bank, and they can be bought in small denominations. Many corporate bonds carry a low-to-moderate risk to investors and take anywhere from 5 to 30 years to mature.

The value of some bonds varies. For example, if you buy a bond when interest rates are 6 percent but you want to sell it before it matures, then the bond's value will be affected by current interest rates. If rates have gone up since you bought the bond, then you will have to discount the price to sell it. Why else would anyone want it, if they could get a higher rate of interest elsewhere? But, if interest rates have gone down, then that 6 percent rate will seem much more inviting. In this case, you could sell the bond for more than you paid for it.

Because the value of bonds is relatively stable, they are a good investment for people who cannot tolerate much risk. Families saving to send children to college may find bonds attractive because they generally earn higher interest than a savings account and aren't likely to fall sharply in value the way stocks can.

Stock Up **Stocks** represent ownership in a public company. If you buy shares in a corporation, you become a part owner. You will make money if the price of the stock goes up and if you receive dividends, which are a portion of the profits paid to the owners. There are two kinds of stock, preferred stock and common stock. Preferred stock holders get a set dividend and are paid from the corporate profits before the common stock holders.

Stocks are generally a riskier investment than bonds. Historically, however, stocks have rewarded their owners with higher returns than bonds or savings accounts. By knowing about the types of stocks, understanding how returns are generated, and weighing the risk factors, you can assess ways to be a wise investor in the stock market.

Five-Year Rate of Return

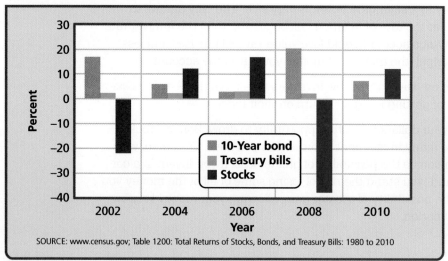

SOURCE: www.census.gov; Table 1200: Total Returns of Stocks, Bonds, and Treasury Bills: 1980 to 2010

>> The rate of return (profit and loss) on investments changes over time. Historically, stocks have provided investors with the greatest potential for profit. But they can also be riskier than other types of investments.

What About Mutual Funds? A mutual fund is an investment in a company that buys and sells stocks and bonds in other companies. By combining your money with that of other investors, the managers of the mutual fund can buy a wide variety of stocks and bonds.

When you buy a mutual fund, you are buying a part ownership of the stocks or bonds owned by the investment company. The biggest advantage of investing in this way is that you instantly have a diversified portfolio. Your risk is spread out.

Three kinds of mutual funds have three levels of risk.

- Money market funds, which are not the same as money market accounts, are short-term, low-risk investments. The money you invest is used to make short-term loans to businesses or governments.
- Bond funds are investments in bonds. Though riskier than money market funds, they have a higher potential return.
- Stock funds are made up of a variety of stocks. Over the long term, they have provided higher returns than either market funds or bond funds.

Mutual fund companies are required by law to register reports and statements with the U.S. Securities and Exchange Commission. You can check up on them through the SEC's database at www.sec.gov/edgar/searchedgar/mutualsearch.htm. Morningstar and Standard and Poors are two companies that rate mutual funds, stocks, bonds, and other investments.

Investment Strategy Many first-time investors think that the way to make money is to buy low and sell high. But, trying to time the stock market has proven elusive to even the most savvy investor. When all is said and done, it's best to use common sense. Dollar cost averaging is one simple investment strategy that rewards the patient investor.

Tale of Two Search Engines

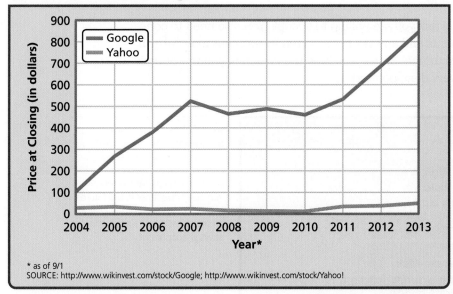

* as of 9/1
SOURCE: http://www.wikinvest.com/stock/Google; http://www.wikinvest.com/stock/Yahoo!

>> Since 2007, Google's stock has soared to over $1,000 a share. Meanwhile Yahoo stock has leveled off at a low price. As much as they try, it is not possible for investors to predict a sure thing.

Dollar Cost Averaging **Dollar cost averaging** is the strategy of investing on a regular schedule over a period of time. In this way, you capture both the lower and higher prices as prices rise and fall. In the long run, you hope to get a better average price for the purchase or sale of stocks and mutual funds.

People use dollar cost averaging because they know they can't predict the market. It is especially useful for common stocks, which can be very volatile—that is, the price can swing far above and below the average price. Dollar cost averaging is an attempt to hedge against the ups and downs of the stock market. It does not guarantee gains or eliminate all possible losses, but it improves your odds of coming out ahead.

The Case for Dollar Cost Averaging

MONTH	PRICE PER SHARE	SHARES YOU BUY
January	$10	50
February	8	62.5
March	6	83.3
April	8	62.5
May	10	50
TOTAL		**308.3**

>> Let's say you put $500 a month into a mutual fund each month for 5 months. The price of a share goes from $5 to $10. You own 308.3 shares, worth $3,083. You invested $2,500 over 5 months. You made $583 at an average price per share of $8.40.

Other Options The risk and payout on investments covers a range from the most secure to the very, very risky. Junk bonds didn't get their name because they were a secure place to park money. Some people invest in collectibles—fine art, baseball cards, Civil War memorabilia. If the market remains strong, people who can part with what they have bought stand to make a lot of money. But, if no one is interested in your stamp collection, you may end up using it for postage.

What you choose depends on the risk you are willing to accept. You also need to consider the length of your investments and any tax burdens the investment may carry. If your scheme is to count on "sure things" or use tips from the cousin of your neighbor's son-in-law, you are likely to be very disappointed.

The Risk Pyramid

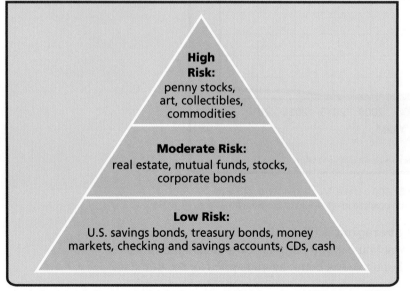

High Risk:
penny stocks, art, collectibles, commodities

Moderate Risk:
real estate, mutual funds, stocks, corporate bonds

Low Risk:
U.S. savings bonds, treasury bonds, money markets, checking and savings accounts, CDs, cash

>> "Risk" means the danger that an investment will disappoint you. A pyramid is sometimes used to demonstrate the riskiness of various investments. At the top are very risky investments like futures in precious metals. At the bottom are the least risky investments like savings accounts.

The Final Word The federal government encourages investment. Even though the government taxes interest and dividends at the same rate as earned income, the profits from the sale of stocks or property are capital gains. In recent years, the taxes on long-term capital gains have been lower than the tax rate on the interest from bonds and savings accounts. As an added bonus, interest earned on U.S. government bonds is exempt from state and local taxes. What it comes down to in the end is that informed decisions and careful planning are your best strategies for successful investment.

Portfolios: Where do you stand?

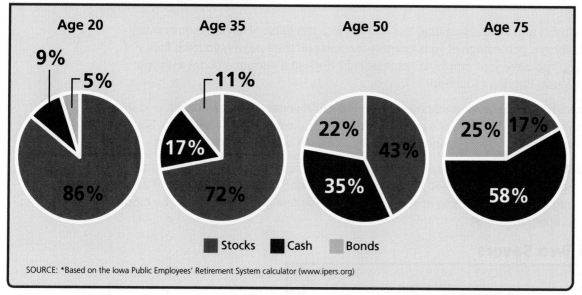

SOURCE: *Based on the Iowa Public Employees' Retirement System calculator (www.ipers.org)

>> No government agency provides a standard model for how to invest money. Experience suggests a good strategy is focused on a mix of assets. The allocations should change as a person's circumstances change. This is one widely accepted model of such allocations.

Savings and Retirement

Pay Yourself First You already know about the advantages of making a budget. Spending less than you earn is a critical step to financial freedom. But it's only the beginning.

Meet Ricky. Ricky is a recent college graduate with a decent entry-level job. He's developed good financial habits. He got through college without building up a huge credit card debt. He budgets carefully—so much for rent, so much for food, so much for car insurance. Only after he has paid all necessary expenses does Ricky use what's left over for the things he enjoys, such as a trip or a new jacket. This may seem like a good plan—*UNTIL*

- he decides to buy a house.
- he starts a family.
- he loses his job.
- he gets hit with a long-term illness.
- he retires.

Ricky's habit of living within his budget month to month does not allow for life changes and emergencies. On his list of people to pay, Ricky has left someone out. He has forgotten to pay himself.

Get in the Habit What does it mean to pay yourself first? It simply means to make personal savings a regular part of your budget, just like rent and food. Everyone has the potential to save, even if it means sacrificing a few immediate wants. You'd be surprised where the savings can come from. Cut out the daily $2.00 for soft drinks at the vending machine, and you've just saved $14 a week. Multiply that by 52, and you've pocketed a tidy sum in just one year.

Saving is a habit and takes discipline. You can get into the habit of saving money every month by taking a percentage of your monthly income and then paying yourself first. For example, you can have your employer automatically deposit a certain amount into your savings account. But don't touch it!

People who have trouble saving manage their money in reverse. They spend first, and then save what is left. But what if there's nothing left? Then there's nothing left to save. Saving doesn't mean you don't get to spend your money. It means you get to spend it later.

Why Save? Not many young people think about saving for retirement. ("Retirement? I haven't even started working!") Yet, when it comes to saving, time is money. There are at least three big benefits to thinking *now* about the day you finally stop working. The biggest benefit is compound interest.

Tale of Two Savers

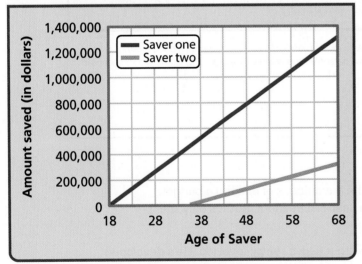

<< Both savers start with $200 and put away $200 a month. Both earn 8 percent interest compounded annually. Saver 1 starts at age 18. Saver 2 starts at age 36. The difference in the amount they have at retirement is more than $1 million!

The Magic of Compound Interest The earlier you start saving, the faster your money will grow. The reason: compound interest. **Compound interest** is interest you earn, not only on the money you put into an account, but also on all the interest you have previously built up. Today's interest earnings will start earning interest tomorrow. The more you save today, the more interest you will gain tomorrow. And that savings will add up at a faster rate. For every year that you put off saving, you could lose thousands of dollars in the long haul.

Other Benefits There are also big tax benefits when you stash money away for retirement. If you put funds into an **Individual Retirement Account (IRA),** the money may escape taxation until you retire—or at least until you reach age 59 1/2. That cuts your tax bill NOW. Even better, when you withdraw your money from a special IRA (called a Roth IRA), the money you make—the appreciation—may not be taxed at all.

Finally, putting money away now allows you to have a cushion in case of emergencies. There are even circumstances in which—despite the government's restrictions—you can dip into a retirement fund to pay for other expenses. For example, you can access some retirement accounts to buy your first house or to cover high medical expenses.

Whether your dream is a comfortable retirement, a nice home, or foreign travel, you're going to need a savings plan to make it come true. As you'll see, there are many options to choose from. But it all starts with developing a saving habit—with paying yourself first.

<< Planning for retirement in your early years of employment can provide tax breaks and retirement security.

Three Savers Okay, so you've decided to take a portion of your income every week and put it towards your financial future. Your goal is to achieve financial freedom, meet emergencies, and have a comfortable retirement—maybe even to "get rich." But not all paths are equal.

Different "Plans" Let's look at three young adults: Amanda, Tyler, and A.J. Each of them is making about the same amount of money. Each of them decides to take $10 per week and dedicate it to their financial future.

Amanda takes her $10 and puts it in a shoebox under her bed. Tyler takes his $10 and puts it in a simple savings account paying 3.6 percent interest. A.J. takes his $10 and invests in lottery tickets in the hopes of winning a million dollars.

Different Results Each of the three keeps this up regularly for 20 years. Each of them would say, "I'm paying myself first." But see how different the results are:

- Amanda has paid herself a total of $10,400. She now has $10,400.
- Tyler has paid himself a total of $10,400. He now has $15,392.
- A.J. has paid himself a total of $10,400. He now has $0.

The fact is, the odds of winning a state lottery are something like one in 18 million. So what sounds better to you? A 100 percent chance of increasing your savings by nearly $5,000 ... or a 99.99999995 percent chance of losing it all? That's a no-brainer. Tyler's savings account is also clearly more profitable than Amanda's shoebox. But even the savings account may not be the best option of all.

Park Your Savings In making a personal savings plan, the first question you have to ask yourself is: How much can I save? You've seen how putting aside even a small amount can build up as long as you do it regularly. The amount you save per week should be one that you can reasonably commit to for a year. The key to success is that you must do this even if you cannot afford it. Then, pay your other bills as usual.

Savings Account Usually, saving starts with setting up a basic savings account carrying no monthly fee. But when choosing a place to park your savings, *shop around*. Make sure the bank is FDIC insured. Some banks will charge you excessive fees just for the privilege of having your money. Web sites such as bankrate.com show you what interest rate different banks are currently paying for checking accounts.

CDs Once you start making more money, think about moving some cash into a **certificate of deposit,** or CD. Like a savings account, a CD is insured and therefore very low-risk. But CDs generally offer higher interest than a savings account. The catch is, once you put your money in, you can't take it out for a fixed period of time. Depending on the length of the CD, you would have to part company with your money for as little as three months or as long as five years. There are penalty fees for early withdrawal.

As with savings accounts, you can compare CD rates online. You might even opt for an online bank that offers even higher interest rates than traditional brick-and-mortar banks. Here are the details for one available CD:

- Initial Deposit: $1,000
- Length of CD: 1 year, 6 months (18 months)
- Interest Rate: 4% compounded daily
- Annual Percentage Yield (APY): 4.081%
- Ending Balance: $1,061.83

Money Markets What if you want a higher yield than a regular savings account without tying up your money? You might open a **money market account.** This is a type of savings account with a high yield that allows you to write checks as long as you maintain a high balance in the account.

So which is the best plan? It all depends on how much you can afford to put aside, and whether high yield is more important to you than easy access to your money. Your early savings plan may involve a combination of options. As you get nearer to retirement, your options change and multiply.

Retire in Style Prom, graduation, car, college. With so much on your mind now, why would you even think about retirement? The answer is simple. You will have to live later with the consequences of your decisions now. Most people on the brink of retirement today will tell you that they wished they had known then what they know now.

It is never too early to plan for retirement. The longer you wait to save, the less time your money has to work for you. If you have a job now, you're already putting some money away for retirement. The government takes money from your paycheck to save for your future in the form of the FICA tax, or Social Security tax. But experts generally agree that Social Security payments alone will not fund a comfortable retirement.

How Much Will You Need? How much money will you need in retirement? That depends on mountains of variables—your health, your lifestyle, where you live. Everybody has different needs. Let's look at some current, general estimates.

Many financial advisers estimate that you will need 70 percent of your pre-retirement income in order to retire comfortably. By comfortably they mean you will be able to keep up your pre-retirement lifestyle. Your needs are lower because you do not have to buy clothes for work or pay for commuting and eating out. You also won't have to put as much money into your retirement investments. It is time for them to pay you.

No one is average, however. Some people spend more money when they first retire because they have more time for travel and entertainment. As they age, they travel less, and those costs go down. But, in many cases the cost of healthcare goes up.

Where Does the Money Come From? The first source is Social Security. You might also have a defined pension, a set amount of money paid by your employer based on your wages and length of employment. Defined pensions, however, are disappearing in private industry. The rest of your retirement income depends on you: a 401(k), Individual Retirement Accounts (IRAs), investments, and savings.

Social Security Each year the Social Security Administration sets the minimum amount of earnings you need to have to be entitled to Social Security benefits. You can begin to collect reduced benefits at age 62 and full benefits at age 67 for people born after 1959. As the population ages, the point will come when Social Security will pay out more in benefits than it collects each year in payroll taxes. There is a lively debate in progress about how long Social Security will last and what it will provide in the future. The message here is that you have to prepare to take care of yourself.

<< Social Security can offer funds to help with expenses for seniors.

401(k) This leads us to the 401(k). You want to pay attention to this retirement plan. The law allows you to set aside a portion of your pay before taxes are withheld. Rent, credit cards, and student loans may limit what you can contribute to your 401(k), but the returns are worth the sacrifice. Some employers match every dollar you save up to three percent of your salary. Others may choose to contribute 50 cents per dollar you save, up to six percent of your salary. Either way, you get an immediate return on your money and you don't pay taxes on any of it until you withdraw it years later.

Employers have come to realize that many people do not have a clue how to invest the money in their 401(k) accounts. More and more employers are providing sources of investment advice to their employees to help them make the most of their money.

Other Accounts The federal government also encourages you to save for retirement by providing special tax advantages for other retirement accounts. You can open up a traditional Individual Retirement Account (IRA) at a bank and contribute $5,000 per year. Depending on your income, this money may be tax deductible.

You have to be ready to leave this money alone. Tapping an IRA prior to age 59 1/2 will cost you dual penalties. You will forfeit 10 percent of your interest, plus pay taxes on what you have withdrawn as though it were added income. The 10 percent penalty is waived if the money is used for higher education or first-time home ownership.

In a **ROTH IRA,** contributions are taxed prior to investing but withdrawals after age 59 1/2 are tax free, meaning you never pay taxes on the interest or dividends that have accumulated over the years. Roth IRA money may be withdrawn for first-time homeowners or higher education on the condition that the account has been open for 5 years. Early withdrawals will be subject to the 10 percent penalty.

Federal regulations regarding these kinds of accounts are subject to change by Congress. In recent years, Congress has raised the savings limits to encourage people to save more for retirement. Examine all investment options available in a personal retirement plan when planning for your financial future.

Credit and Debt

Establishing Your Credit Congratulations! You got great grades. You're one step closer to the college of your choice and maybe even lower car insurance costs—all for being responsible. Believe it or not, your credit history will have a similar impact.

As a first-time borrower, you may find it tough to get a credit card or a car loan on your own. Without a credit history to check, lenders often will require a co-signer to guarantee that the loan will be repaid if you fail to repay. This person could be your parent or another relative with a good credit history.

The rest is up to you. How can you prove to future lenders that you are a good credit risk? The most important step is simple: Pay your bills on time to eliminate credit card debt and strengthen your credit report. Every late or missed payment will end up on your credit report.

Are You a Good Credit Risk?

Capacity	Your expenses, your job, and how long you have had it
Character	Financial history and payment record
Capital	What assets you have to back up a loan, like a savings account, property, investments

<< Whether or not you are judged to be a good credit risk depends on the three C's.

Your Credit Report Your **credit report** is your financial report card. In addition to your payment history, it includes the details of your bank and credit card accounts. Lenders can see how much debt you are already carrying. They can also see if you have had any bankruptcies or judgments against you or if you owe back taxes.

National credit reporting agencies create a **FICO score** based on your credit history. The score falls in a range from about 300 to 900. Usually, a score of at least 700 gives you access to reasonable credit. For a fee, you can find out your credit score at MyFico.com.

A bad credit report can sink more than a loan. It also affects your chances of getting insurance, an apartment, a mortgage—even a job. Like lenders, many landlords and employers check credit histories. They see on-time bill paying as an indication of whether you will be a responsible tenant or worker. The **Fair Credit Reporting Act** sets the terms by which credit information about you can be gathered and used.

Protecting Your Credit Suppose there are mistakes in your credit report or you have made poor credit choices. What can you do?

Free credit reports are available once per year from each of the three national credit-reporting agencies: Experian, TransUnion, and Equifax. Sample credit reports can be found on their Web sites. To get a free credit report go online: www.annualcreditreport.com; call

(877) 322-8228; or mail: Annual Credit Report Request Service, P.O. Box 105281, Atlanta, GA, 30348. A credit report is not the same as a credit score.

How much information is gathered for a credit report? Take a look at the sample reports available on the Web sites of the credit-reporting agencies. Review your credit report for errors, such as the number of late payments, and for possible fraud.

If you find an error in your credit report, send a separate letter to each agency where the mistake is found as soon as possible. Include a copy of the credit report with the misinformation highlighted. The credit reporting agency is required by law to investigate with the creditor in question. It should remove from your credit report any mistakes a creditor admits. The **Fair Credit Billing Act** requires creditors to correct errors without lowering your credit rating.

How Do You Score?

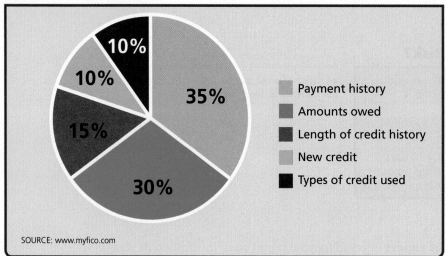

SOURCE: www.myfico.com

Legend:
- Payment history — 35%
- Amounts owed — 30%
- Length of credit history — 15%
- New credit — 10%
- Types of credit used — 10%

>> The chart shows the factors in your credit report that are used to create your credit score. Paying your bills on time has the greatest influence.

Clean It Up No matter how careful you might be with your finances, circumstances may get the better of you. The loss of a job or a medical emergency could leave you in a world of financial difficulty. Here are some steps to take if you have trouble paying your bills on time.

- Reassess your needs and wants. Be prepared to make hard choices.
- Stop using credit until you are out of trouble.
- Contact your lenders to negotiate a different payment schedule or interest rate.

Contact nonprofit credit counseling organizations who, for a small fee, can provide debt-management assistance and intervene with card issuers. Make sure the service is affiliated with a third party such as the Association of Independent Consumer Credit Counseling Agencies or National Foundation of Credit Counseling.

The Lure of Credit "Buy now—pay later." Those four words sum up the attraction of **credit,** or deferred payment. Credit comes in many forms, from car loans to mortgages—and most popular of all, the credit card.

Credit Convenience Credit cards make buying easy. With a piece of plastic, you can walk into nearly any store and walk out with merchandise. As for buying online, it would be almost unthinkable without credit cards.

No wonder credit card use by Americans has skyrocketed. And no wonder the companies that issue credit cards enjoy tremendous profits.

Teens and Credit Americans under 21 can have a credit card if a parent or other individual over 21 co-signs the account or if they can prove that they have the income to make the monthly payments. About one third of all high school students use cards linked to the account of a parent or relative. Credit card companies eager to issue young people their first card used to give out freebies such as t-shirts, but reforms in 2009 made this illegal.

Why do they want your business? The answer is simple: *teens spend*. Each year, consumers between the ages of 12 and 19 spend well over $100 billion of their own and their parents' money. Credit card companies want to tap into this spending power.

Credit Traps and Tips So there you are, card in hand and a world of things to buy. Unless you learn how to use credit responsibly, you could find yourself in a deep hole. You won't be there alone. It is estimated a majority of Americans between the ages of 18 and 24 spend nearly 30 percent of their monthly income on debt repayment.

Ideally, you'll want to pay off your credit card balance in full every month. True, you are *required* to make only a small minimum payment. But for every dollar you don't pay this month, you'll pay interest next month. Worse, first-time cardholders without an established credit rating are often subject to a higher-than-normal **annual percentage rate** (APR).

What if you pay late or miss a payment entirely? You'll be subject to a late penalty. The finance charges, which include the APR and any related fees, can quickly add up to more than your initial purchase.

Suppose a credit card company requires a $10 minimum payment on a $290 outfit. If your payment is late by even one day, you'll get hit with a late fee and more than likely a significantly higher APR. And if your balance goes over the credit limit set by the issuer, there's a charge for that, too. Suddenly, the $290 "bargain" can turn into a $600 headache.

Repayment Schedule on a $2,000 Credit Card Loan at 19 Percent Interest

MINIMUM PAYMENT AMOUNT	NUMBER OF MONTHS TO PAY	TOTAL INTEREST PAYMENT
$40	100	$1,994
$50	64	$1,193
$75	35	$619
$100	25	$424

SOURCE: Government Accounting Office: "College Students and Credit Cards"

>> This table shows the cumulative effect of a 19 percent interest rate on a $2,000 credit card debt. A person paying only $40 a month would incur $1,994 in interest charges by the time the loan was repaid—paying nearly double the amount of the original debt.

The Cost of Cash Fees mount up even faster if you use your credit card to get cash. A cash advance carries an up-front fee of 2 percent to 4 percent, plus a higher interest rate than the regular card. And the charges start the second the ATM coughs out the cash.

Read the Fine Print The importance of reading the fine print of a credit card's terms of agreement should not be lost on any cardholder. The **Truth in Lending Act** requires banks to provide complete information on the APR, fees, and surcharges. New regulations require credit card companies to tell you how long it will take to pay off your balance if you make only minimum payments. Companies must also notify customers before interest rates increase or terms change. You can opt out of the changes, which will close the account. You can then pay off the balance under the old terms. The time it takes to review these terms could save you headaches and money.

Credit or Debit? The surest way to avoid the debt trap is to keep credit card use to a minimum. For lower-cost purchases, you are better off using a debit card, a check, or cash. A **debit card** offers the same convenience as a credit card. But because the money comes straight out of your bank account, there is no interest rate and no risk of going over your limit. The danger of debit cards is that they are so easy to use, you may lose track of your spending. For online purchases, however, it's wisest to use a credit card. It offers greater security.

Getting Into Debt With today's world of easy credit, it is not hard to find yourself in debt over your head. Using credit cards or borrowing money is not necessarily bad. You get into trouble when you go overboard.

<< Credit cards offer advantages, but remember to use them wisely to avoid the dangers of debt!

Types of Loans Loans come in several forms. Single-payment loans are short-term loans paid off in one lump sum. **Installment loans,** such as home mortgages or auto loans, are repaid at regularly scheduled intervals. Each payment is divided between principal, or the amount borrowed, and interest. (The earlier you are in the life of the loan, the higher the proportion of each payment goes toward interest.) A third kind of debt is revolving credit, where the amount borrowed and paid changes each month. The best example is a credit card.

How Much is Too Much? Carrying some debt is not a problem—almost everybody does it. But you need to stay within safe limits and you need to keep in mind your obligation to repay borrowed money. A general rule is that your debt payments, including a mortgage, should not be more than 36 percent of your gross income (income before taxes and deductions). You can estimate your own debt-to-income ratio by dividing the amount of money that you owe by the amount of money that you earn. If the result is higher than 36 percent, you probably owe too much money.

Here are some warning signs:

- Inability to make minimum payments
- Relying on credit cards out of necessity and not convenience
- Borrowing from one credit card in order to pay another
- Tapping retirement savings or other investments to pay loans

Getting Out One reason people take on too much debt is that they want stuff NOW and ignore the fact that credit is a promise to pay later. They don't adequately plan for the fact that the repayment of principal and interest begins to eat into money needed for necessities.

Caught in the Debt Spiral Take Andy. His entry-level job had an entry-level salary. The debt he ran up in college soared as he depended more and more on "plastic" to cover the basics. Paying just the minimum spared his credit temporarily, but he was racking up high finance charges. Once he started missing payments, creditors began calling. Now what?

Credit Counseling Andy hated to admit it, but he needed help. He tried credit counseling. A credit counseling agency will negotiate on your behalf with the creditors, trying to get you an extension of time and lower interest rates. For a small service fee, it will take over your monthly payments. Andy checked with the National Foundation for Credit Counseling and the Association of Independent Consumer Credit Counseling Agencies to find a reputable agency. He now writes one check per month to the agency, instead of three to his creditors.

Other Options If you find yourself in Andy's shoes, there are other options to consider—with caution. You could swallow your pride and ask a relative or friend for a loan. If you go this route, though, make sure that you have a written repayment plan and offer to pay interest.

You could also try taking out a loan from a credit union. Credit unions usually offer more lenient credit terms than banks. You may, however, need a co-signer.

Bankruptcy: The Last Resort Bankruptcy is truly your last option. Common reasons for bankruptcy are large hospital and medical bills, uninsured losses, or high credit card bills. Some of these are unavoidable, but many people get into serious debt because of poor decisions and lack of foresight.

Once you declare bankruptcy it will be harder for you to obtain credit. Nearly every credit application asks: *Have you ever declared bankruptcy?* So take this step only with the help of a lawyer who specializes in bankruptcy and can explain the options and consequences.

One option is known as Chapter 7, or liquidation. You give up your assets in exchange for your debts. The cash value of your assets is paid to the creditors.

To reduce fraud and make it harder to declare bankruptcy, the federal government passed the **Bankruptcy Abuse Prevention and Consumer Protection Act** of 2005. Debtors must prove that their income is below their state's median income and complete financial counseling and financial management education. Also, the government randomly audits debtors to check up on the accuracy of the bankruptcy documents.

A second option is known as Chapter 13, or debt adjustment, which involves temporarily suspending foreclosures and collection actions while you draft and execute a plan to repay some or all of the debts in three to five years. The amount to be repaid depends on how much you have versus how much you owe. Any form of bankruptcy will make it far more difficult to rebuild a secure financial future.

Risk Management

Insuring the Future You just got ticketed for sailing past a stop sign. You got distracted while you were changing a CD. Your parents are using the word *grounded* a lot—and also the word *insurance*. Sure, they have you covered on their policy, but a moving violation could raise their rates—and yours—through the roof.

What Is Insurance? The road of life is peppered with the unexpected. Chances are you'll hit a few bumps along the way. Insurance is part of a **risk management plan** that will protect you against financial losses. Basically, insurance is a bet between you and your insurer. You are betting that something bad will happen to you, such as illness or a car accident. The company is betting against it.

Types of Insurance There are four basic types of insurance coverage most adults should have. Your age, family situation, and income are some major factors to consider when deciding the type and amount of coverage you should get.
- Auto: Protects you and other drivers in case of an accident that results in damage and injury. It also protects you in case of theft, vandalism, and natural disasters. Most states require you to have your own auto insurance or to be listed as a driver on someone else's policy.
- Health: Protects you in case of illness or injury. It also covers the cost of routine medical and preventive care, prescriptions, and in some cases dental care. Even if you're healthy, having health insurance is a very good idea.
- Property: Protects your home or apartment in case of damage or loss of belongings due to water, fire, or wind. It can cover your liability if someone is injured in your home and sues you for damages. Most policies do not, however, protect against flood damage. You must buy that coverage separately.

<< Health insurance is an important type of insurance to have when medical needs arise.

- Life: Pays a set amount to your **beneficiary** in case of your death. The beneficiary is the person or entity, such as a charity, that you name as the recipient of the death benefit of your life insurance policy.

The two most common types of life insurance are *term,* or temporary, insurance and *whole life* insurance. Rates for term insurance increase over time. The only way to collect from a term policy is to die during the term. Whole life insurance remains in effect for one's entire lifetime at a set rate. It builds cash value. The insured can borrow against the policy.

What It Costs The payment you make to an insurance company is called a premium. The cost of insurance is high and getting higher. So does it pay to buy it? Absolutely. You may never have an accident and file a claim. But if you do, the amount you collect could be many times what you paid in premiums. Even a brief stay in a hospital, for example, can run up a bill of hundreds of thousands of dollars.

Besides, in many cases, insurance is not optional. You can't even register a car without proof of auto insurance. Nor can you get a mortgage without homeowner coverage.

Deductibles Insurance companies spread out their risk by collecting premiums from a lot of customers. They also reduce their costs by requiring co-pays and deductibles.

A **deductible** is an amount you have to pay before your coverage kicks in. For example, if your car insurance policy has a $1,000 deductible, and you have an accident, you'll have to pay the first $1,000 in damages. The company pays the rest. The higher the deductible, the lower the premium.

Co-pays If you have a **co-pay,** you are responsible for a small portion of the total cost of a service covered by your insurance policy. Every time you go to a doctor, you might have to pay a relatively small amount of the bill and your insurance company pays the rest. Generally, you can keep co-pays to a minimum if your medical provider—a doctor, hospital, or specialist—is part of your insurance company's healthcare network.

Changing Needs As you get older, acquire more possessions, and expand your family, you have more to replace and more to protect.

Coreen at 18–25 Coreen is three months into her first full-time job. Finally eligible for employee health benefits, she lets her parents know that they can remove her from their policy. She also finds an apartment and gets rental insurance to protect her possessions from damage or theft. With no dependents, Coreen leads a relatively carefree existence. She can probably get by with basic auto, rental and health coverage—for now.

Karen and Bill at 25–54 Coreen's sister Karen and her husband Bill have purchased their first home. They are also expecting their second child. With a new home, children, and two cars, their insurance needs are due for a tune-up.

Karen and Bill now need a medical policy that covers more checkups for the children. They also can't risk having to pay for a new car if they have an accident. With lives and assets to protect, this young family will focus on adding collision insurance to their auto policy and purchasing home, mortgage, and life insurance coverage.

Alex and Isabel, Over 54 Coreen's parents, Isabel and Alex, decide to revisit their insurance needs as well. Free of dependents, they are less concerned about term or whole life insurance coverage. They are far more concerned about the cost of long-term healthcare.

Once again, insurance needs change according to age and life circumstances. Because Alex and Isabel are in their 50s, they can expect to pay more for their coverage, perhaps as much as hundreds of dollars a month. Their problem will be trying to find the right coverage at an affordable price. To find the best rates, they will want to get group coverage through an employer or a large organization.

Insurance Is an Investment You wind up in the hospital for an emergency appendectomy. Your house is robbed. An uninsured driver hits you from behind. You get to pick up the pieces—and, unless you're insured, the bill.

It's All About Risk Insurance is all about avoiding risk. For you, that means paying now to avoid a gigantic cost later. For the insurance company, it means identifying people who are likely to cost them a bundle.

Insurers set rates based on **risk factors,** hard statistics that predict whether someone is likely to be a bad risk. Do you plan to become a pilot or take up mountain climbing? That will make you a higher risk than a lawyer who spends leisure time doing crossword puzzles. A smoker must pay higher health insurance premiums than a nonsmoker. In the worst case, a risky lifestyle may make you uninsurable.

Who's Got You Covered? Right now, insurance costs are probably not your concern. Most teens are covered for pretty much everything—life, health, property—by a parent or guardian. However, some teens must foot their own auto insurance bill. And that's expensive. Statistically, new drivers are high-risk. But if you want wheels, you have no choice.

<< Blue Cross Blue Shield is one insurance company that provides coverage plans to individuals, families, and companies.

Health Insurance No matter how healthy your lifestyle is, you are going to face illness or accident. A bout of pneumonia or a broken leg may cost hundreds, even thousands. Even with health insurance, you'll have to pay something. But it's better than paying it all.

Employer Plans Most young people are covered under parents' health insurance whether they are in school or not—up to age 26. Once you enter the working world, it's up to you.

If you work for a company that offers health insurance, you can usually choose from a variety of group plans. Some cover you from day one. More often, there is a waiting period. Your share of the premium is deducted from your paycheck each pay period. The higher the deductible, the lower the premium.

The least expensive health insurance plan is generally a **Health Maintenance Organization (HMO).** An HMO allows you to pick a primary care physician, to whom you pay a co-pay. If you need to see a specialist, your primary doctor will refer you to an in-network doctor. This is a doctor who has agreed to accept the payment level paid by the insurance company.

Get Insured Can't get insurance through your job or your parents? As of 2014, you can purchase private health insurance from an exchange in your state. The healthcare reform law passed in 2010 also prevents insurance companies from denying you coverage for pre-existing conditions.

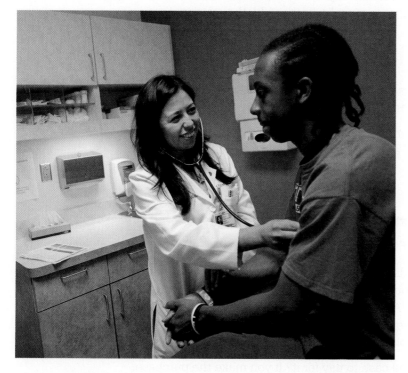

<< Insurance plans help people get the medical care they need, whether it's a basic check up or special treatment related to an illness or accident.

Cut Your Costs The rising number of claims, plus increasing cases of fraud, have caused insurance premiums to skyrocket. But there are a number of steps you can take to get the best coverage for your buck.

Comparison shop. Compare the rates of different companies. Check with the local Better Business Bureau. And don't forget word of mouth. For example, if you're shopping for auto insurance, talk to people with similar driving records. Don't just ask about premium costs. Ask about customer service as well. Low price is no bargain if an insurer takes forever to service your claim.

Make yourself a better risk. If you smoke—or collect speeding tickets like they were trading cards—it's going to cost you. But insurers also reward behavior that lowers risk. A healthy lifestyle and a good driving record can keep costs in check. And while good grades won't reduce health or life insurance premiums, they might get you a discount on car insurance.

Cover yourself. You and your insurer may not always see eye to eye on a claim. It's up to you to provide evidence of loss. Take pictures of that busted headlamp. And keep receipts. That way, you'll be more likely to be covered for everything you've paid.

Know your policy. Being smart about insurance involves keeping your policy updated. Talk to your insurer to make sure you have the coverage you need. Review your coverage before filing a claim. You'll avoid nasty surprises that way.

Should I Use an Agent? Nowadays, you can often buy insurance online. Still, it might pay for you to use a licensed agent. It all depends on your needs.

There are two kinds of insurance agents: captive and independent. Captive agents represent a single insurance company. Independent agents offer policies from many different companies. Both types of agents must be licensed by the state in which they sell.

For most purposes, buying directly with a company or its agents works out just fine. But if you are difficult to insure—for example, if you have a bad driving record—an independent agent might be the way to go. With access to many different companies, the independent agent can help you find a company that can meet your special needs.

A good agent also helps you through the process of filing a claim and acts on your behalf in dealing with the provider. Many agents are also certified to help you with other kinds of financial planning.

Consumer Smarts

A trip to the local mall is filled with all kinds of purchase temptations. There's that new pair of shoes and the latest video game that you just have to have. Or do you? Before you pull out that credit card, think before you buy. Analyze the costs and benefits of the purchase. The benefits seem obvious. You have something you didn't have before that you like. The purchase may also be something you absolutely need.

But, are the costs worth it? Do you have the cash to pay for it? If you make the purchase, will it keep you from purchasing something that you really need? How will you use what you are purchasing? Will something else already fill that desire or need? What will the purchase do to your future buying power? Can the purchase wait?

Another thing to consider is what happens to the purchase after it has exhausted its usefulness? How will you dispose of what you have? Many items, such as electronics, no longer can just be tossed away. Laws protecting the environment govern the disposal of many products. For example, perhaps you purchase the newest cellphone on the market. What happens to the phone when you want to replace it? Will it cost you again to dispose of it? How long do you have to keep it before you dispose of it? Analyzing the costs and benefits of the disposal of personal property, including your responsibility for proper disposal, is always part of a purchase decision.

A Major Purchase A major purchase is one that will use up a large chunk of your available cash or credit limit. Buying a home is an example of a major purchase. For most individuals, buying a home means many years of budgeting for repayment of a home loan. Before buying a home, people analyze the costs and benefits of home ownership.

<< Purchasing a new car involves finding the right car for the amount of money you can spend.

When looking to improve or expand, business owners may make major purchases, such as a building or piece of new equipment. Business owners must analyze the costs and benefits of the purchase and how best it will be used. Likewise, businesses must determine how they might dispose of what was purchased after it no longer is needed. Will the purchase truly benefit the business and help it grow or create greater costs that will hurt business growth?

Like most young people, your first major purchase may be a car. Having your own car gives you the freedom to make decisions on where and when you'd like to travel. It also provides a sense of pride in ownership. But, you need to do your homework and spend some time and effort to get a good deal.

The Costs of Ownership Step one is to determine what kind of car you can afford to buy and adequately insure and maintain. There are many money issues to consider:

- how much you can put down
- how much you need to borrow
- what your monthly payment will be
- how much your insurance premiums will be
- how much car maintenance will cost
- what gasoline, parking, and tolls will do to your budget

Since you have no credit history, you may have to search around for a bank or credit union that will lend you money. To get a vehicle loan, a bank may require you to have a co-signer, a person who is responsible for paying the loan if you default.

New or Used If you are going to buy a new car, you want to determine the invoice price of the model you want, and then get at least five competitive bids from dealers. Request bids in writing and then try to negotiate. Will the dealer closest to you match the price of the dealer who is less conveniently located? You can use Web sites such as cars.com, yahoo!autos, and myride.com as online resources for researching and getting bids.

Perhaps you have a car you would like to sell before getting another one. This will give you some additional money to use for your new purchase. It also means additional responsibilities to dispose of your personal property. If the car is in good working order, then selling the car may not pose a problem and you'll have cash in hand for your new purchase. But, what if the car you want to sell has some significant mechanical problems?

For example, perhaps the engine of the car cannot be repaired. Rather than sell the entire car, you decide instead to sell parts of the car. All good. What about the parts of the car you can't sell, such as a used battery? How will you properly dispose of the battery? What do the laws say about where and how you can responsibly dispose of other parts of the car that cannot be sold? How will the cost of disposal impact the amount of money you have to purchase another car?

If you're buying used, get a history of the **Vehicle Identification Number (VIN)** and have a mechanic inspect the car. That way you can determine how well the car has been cared for. There are also online sites that deal with buying used cars. They offer reviews of online used car classifieds, how to buy a used car from dealers or private sellers, how to negotiate with tough sellers, scams to avoid, and a list of questions for you to print out to ask the seller.

New automobiles **depreciate,** or lose value, quickly. A new car loses half its value in the first three years. But buying a new car can make sense if you plan to keep the car for a long time. You have to carry collision insurance if you have a car loan. Used cars are less expensive to buy and insure, but maintenance costs will likely be higher. Budget accordingly.

Making A Decision

Two things will have a major affect on what car you choose: what you like and what you can afford based on your savings and income. If you are still in school, you will have fewer options than a well-paid professional has.

To get a taste of what it is like to plan for a major purchase, choose two differently priced cars from ads in the newspaper or online. Go to a website with a loan calculator, like Bankrate.com, and estimate how much you would have to pay per month with various down payments, interest rates, and loan payment plans. How much income would you need in order to buy the car of your choice?

Points to Remember

- Taxes and fees will be lower on a less expensive car.
- You can lower your monthly payment by putting more money down.
- A lower interest rate will mean you pay less over the life of the loan.

>> Put some time and thought into making a decision that best meets your needs based on your available resources.

Leasing Leasing is primarily used by businesses or by those who don't plan on driving many miles. If you go over the mileage allowed for the term of the **auto lease,** generally 12,000 miles per year, you have to pay a substantial fee for each additional mile. If you have a long drive to college or a job, the commute could eat up the mileage limit in no time.

Dealing With Dealers You might want to consider taking a more experienced person along with you when you buy your first car. It pays to have an ally. People in business have experience with purchasing, using, and disposing of business property. Their advice may prove to be very helpful to you in making your purchase.

In many cases, salespeople hold the upper hand when it comes to negotiating car prices. You can take a few steps, however, to level the buying field and avoid being pressured into spending more money than you want or can afford.

- Be prepared. Know what you want, and get bids based on the invoice price.
- Don't be talked into unnecessary options.
- Don't ever discuss trade-in until after you've settled on a sale price. A dealer might want to consider the trade-in vehicle as a reduction to the sticker price. In fact, any trade-in should have nothing to do with the price of the new car.
- Don't be pushed into a quick decision, no matter what one-day specials are dangled before you.
- Get the sale offers in writing. If a dealer is not willing to put all agreements in writing, walk away.

Warranties Dealers are required by federal law to post a Buyer's Guide on the used cars they offer for sale. This guide must specify whether the vehicle is being sold "as is" or with a **warranty,** and what percentage of the repair costs the dealer will pay. Most new and some used cars come with a manufacturer's warranty that covers certain repairs for a set period of time or up to a certain mileage limit. Extended warranties increase the amount of time or mileage that repairs will be covered. No warranty covers basic maintenance, like oil changes or new tires.

If you do happen to buy a car and the next day the engine falls out, you're protected by federal and state "lemon laws." First, however, you should go back to the dealer if you think you've bought a lemon. If you cannot reach an agreement, check the law to see what recourse you have.

Can I Afford It? You've dreamed of this day of living under your roof and by your own rules. Independence. Rent. Bills. Cooking and cleaning. Yes, life is full of both ups and downs.

The first reality check is figuring out what you can afford. A general rule of thumb is that your rent and utility payments should not cost more than one week's take-home pay. How can you figure the average monthly cost of utilities? Ask the landlord or the previous tenant.

You will have to plan ahead. Many landlords require that you pay the first and last month's rent up front. In addition, you may have to pay a **security deposit.** This money is set aside for repairs of any damage you may do to the apartment beyond normal wear and tear.

Finding the Right Place Finding the right apartment or rental home takes more than a little time, effort, and money. It also takes evaluating the costs and benefits of any rental option. The federal government has stepped in to level the playing field. The **Federal Fair Housing Act of 1968** makes it illegal for a landlord to discriminate against a potential tenant because of that person's race, sex, national origin, or religion.

Annual Living Expenses in Select U.S. Metropolitan Areas

METRO AREA	ELECTRICITY	FOOD AND BEVERAGES	TRANSPORTATION
Los Angeles, CA	$3,257	$7,531	$8,784
Miami, FL	3,740	5,803	8,427
Chicago, IL	4,052	7,037	8,840
New York, NY	4,309	7,420	8,495
Boston, MA	4,248	8,167	8,591
Houston, TX	4,505	7,009	10,843

SOURCE: www.census.gov; Table 684: Average Annual Expenditures of All Consumer Units by Selected Major Types of Expenditure: 1990 to 2009

>> Geography has an impact on living expenses. In cities like New York, Boston, or Los Angeles, living expenses will be much higher than those in smaller cities or rural areas.

You can make the rental process easier by defining your needs and wants. Usually to rent an apartment, you have to make a commitment of at least six months. So while the cheap one-bedroom with high ceilings and walk-in closets may seem like a steal, the fact that it's near the firehouse could make it a case of home, sleepless home.

Online Web sites are a good place to begin your apartment hunting. You can also look for apartments in the real estate section of a local newspaper. And if you're hiring a realtor to search on your behalf, keep in mind that they will charge you a fee based on the rental price. So do your homework, and make a list of priorities for both what you want and do not want in your new apartment. What if the ideal apartment is beyond your means? That might be the time to consider getting a roommate to share the cost.

Key Questions for Renters

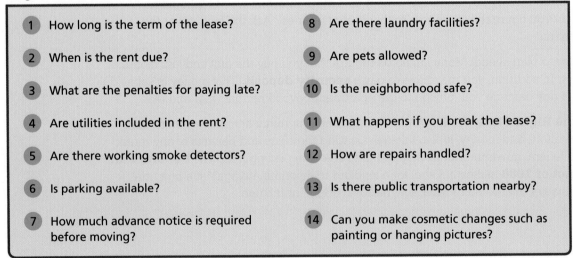

1. How long is the term of the lease?
2. When is the rent due?
3. What are the penalties for paying late?
4. Are utilities included in the rent?
5. Are there working smoke detectors?
6. Is parking available?
7. How much advance notice is required before moving?
8. Are there laundry facilities?
9. Are pets allowed?
10. Is the neighborhood safe?
11. What happens if you break the lease?
12. How are repairs handled?
13. Is there public transportation nearby?
14. Can you make cosmetic changes such as painting or hanging pictures?

>> Finding the right apartment can be hard. Before you sign a lease, be sure you get the answers to these questions.

Roommates Can two live more cheaply than one? More often than not, a two-bedroom apartment in many locales is not much more expensive than a one-bedroom place. Plus, you can split the utilities and rent. The sources for finding a roommate are the same as those for finding an apartment—Web sites like roommates.com, newspaper classifieds, and word of mouth. You want someone who has a compatible lifestyle and who can pay their share of the bills on time. Your search for the right roommate is just as important as your search for the right place to live.

Furnishings If you have decided to rent an unfurnished apartment, you will need to be resourceful to avoid major expenses. After you have tapped family and friends, yard sales and thrift shops are potential gold mines. An unfurnished apartment is not only empty, it will probably also be bare, right down to the windows and shower—not to mention the cupboards.

Protect Yourself Learn from others' mistakes. Many apartment complex Web sites are chock-full of comments posted by current or previous tenants. You might even ask a pass-erby in the parking lot. To protect yourself from being charged for pre-existing conditions, assess and photograph any existing damage before you sign a lease.

The Lease You, as **tenant** or "lessee," and the property owner, as "landlord" or "**lessor,**" enter into a contract called the lease or rental agreement.

Here are some tips to make it a positive experience.

- Be prepared with the documents you will need to provide. These items include proof of income and identity, letters of reference, and a check for any required deposit.
- Get the lease in writing! Never take an apartment on the basis of a handshake with the landlord.
- If you don't understand something, don't sign the lease!

<< Read the entire lease before signing a lease agreement.

Renter's Insurance Even if you furnish with hand-me-downs or thrift-store treasures, be sure to consider renter's insurance. Maybe your roommate comes fully loaded with a flat-screen television. Should it disappear, you'd be left footing the bill. The benefits can far outweigh the costs.

Rights and Responsibilities This is your money and your home, and you have rights. For example, you have the right to privacy. A landlord or maintenance worker is prohibited from entering your apartment without your permission. Renter's rights and responsibilities vary according to location, but most states provide a tenant-landlord bill of rights. Check with your local housing or consumer affairs office for specific information.

Tenants also have responsibilities, such as paying the rent on time and keeping the apartment clean. There may also be quiet hours, a policy imposed on most apartment dwellers. As always, a tenant's rights come with certain responsibilities.

Home Ownership Some individuals may wish to transition from renting to home ownership. Assess the financial aspects of home ownership before considering the transition. Evaluate the costs and benefits of buying a home. Owning a home usually means having a lot more space and privacy. Home ownership is an investment. You may make a substantial amount of money when you sell your home.

Home ownership also means monthly mortgage payments, property insurance, and money spent for upkeep and repair. It can limit your ability to move whenever you'd like, since it can take a while to sell a house. Unexpected loss of income can create difficulties in making monthly mortgage payments with the risk of **foreclosure.**

There is a lot to know before making the transition from renting to home ownership. Ask good questions. Will you be able to make the monthly mortgage payment? How will home ownership impact your ability to change jobs or locations? Do you have the time and financial resources to take care of needed upkeep and repair, such as a new roof or furnace? Will the costs of owning a home outweigh the benefits?

Assess all of the financial aspects of making the transition from renting to home ownership. Talk to a professional in real estate and banking.

There are different types of home loans available to consumers. Some individuals choose a fixed-rate mortgage. In this type of loan the interest rate stays the same over the life of the mortgage, which could be up to 30 years. Some home buyers opt for a variable rate. In this case the interest rate may change over the life of the loan. A rise in interest rate means a rise in the monthly loan payment. A balloon mortgage usually comes with an initial low interest rate, but the loan balance is due within a short time, perhaps at the end of five years. Some loans only require payment of interest. In this case money is not paid toward the **principle.** Other loans, such as VA (Veterans Administration) loans, FHA (Federal Housing Administration) loans, or reverse mortgages, are special types of home ownership options available to individuals who qualify. It is good to analyze all options before securing a home or other consumer loan.

A Growing Crime An estimated 9 million Americans have their identities stolen every year. Chances are you know someone who has been victimized. You may be a victim yourself—without even knowing it.

It Can Happen Anywhere Question: What do going to the beach . . . taking out the garbage . . . and answering your e-mail have in common?

Answer: They can all leave you vulnerable to identity theft.

A thief can raid your wallet while you're splashing in the water. A dumpster diver can retrieve old bank statements. Or an innocent-looking e-mail could be a phishing scam to get your personal info. Most people don't realize they've been victimized until it's too late. You might not find out until you're denied a student loan because you've missed several car payments—and you don't even own a car.

Identity Theft Complaints by Victims' Ages, 2012

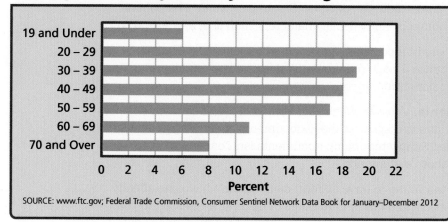

SOURCE: www.ftc.gov; Federal Trade Commission, Consumer Sentinel Network Data Book for January–December 2012

<< In 2012, the Federal Trade Commission received almost 300,000 complaints of identity theft. Nearly 30 percent fell into the under-30 age bracket. One reason for this trend could be that younger people tend to spend more time on the Internet, where much identity theft occurs.

The Cost of Theft Once they have your ID, thieves can use it to commit a wide variety of fraud, such as obtaining credit cards or even a mortgage in your name. Worse, if the crook who stole your identity gets arrested for *any* crime, you could get stuck with the criminal record.

In too many cases, the burden of proof is on the victim. According to the Identity Theft Resource Center, it can take 600 hours to repair the damage. Some victims need up to 10 years to fully clear their records. If your identity is stolen, you could face higher insurance costs, credit card fees, and interest rates for loans—or may even have trouble finding a job.

Prime Target: You So should you be worried? **Identity theft** topped the list of all complaints filed with the U.S. Federal Trade Commission (FTC) in 2012, with more than 369,000 complaints. About one in every 40 households experienced identity theft of a minor. About 27 percent of child ID theft cases are caused by individuals known to the minor. Child ID theft is difficult to resolve. It is important to always keep information about a child's identity in a safe place. This includes a child's Social Security number.

Why Me? Why are young people so vulnerable? One reason is that most teens have not established credit records that can be monitored. In addition, studies show that teens—

- are less likely than adults to check their credit card records.
- are more likely than adults to frequent the Internet and provide personal information.
- take greater risks relative to older age groups.
- often have an "it can't happen to me" attitude.

Finally, many Americans do not use their Social Security number until around the age of 15, when they apply for driver permits or first jobs. As a result, identity thefts against them may go unnoticed for years. There have even been babies that were the victims of identity theft!

At College Over half of all personal information security breaches take place at universities, experts say. Part of the reason may be that nearly half of all college students have had their grades posted by using a Social Security number. It's within your rights to tell a college administrator not to post your personal information.

Lower Your Risk Although there is no foolproof way to safeguard your identity, there are a number of common-sense steps you can take to protect yourself against fraud.

Be alert online. Think twice before sharing personal information. Users on social networking sites like Facebook often post personal statuses, favorite music, addresses, cellphone numbers, and former employers. All of this information could be used to create a credit account or take out a loan in your name.

Use passwords. Always use a password to protect your cellphone, laptop, and PDA. Do not store personal information on these electronic devices. Create passwords that contain uppercase and lowercase letters, numbers, and special characters such as !, $, *, #, and &.

Check your credit. Check your credit report with a major credit agency like Equifax, Experian, and TransUnion at least once a year. You are entitled to one free report yearly. You can find them online at www.annualcreditreport.com.

Check and shred your statements. Always check your bank and credit card statements for anything unusual. Then make sure to dispose of those documents containing personal information using a paper shredder. Simply tearing up documents isn't enough to keep thieves from easily reassembling those statements.

Watch your mailbox. If you're too young to have a credit card, or don't have one already, you should be suspicious of any unsolicited credit-card offers in the mail addressed to you. For more information on identity theft and what you can do to protect yourself, check out the government's Web site www.ftc.gov/bcp/edu/microsites/idtheft.

Protect your reputation. Loss of one's reputation could be worse than loss of one's identity. Be careful what you write and say online about others and check what is posted about you. Online postings are testing the limits of libel and slander laws.

Buying Online Online shopping may already be a regular part of your life. You don't have to drive anywhere, stand in line, or haul the stuff home. A few clicks will do it all. And you can shop 24/7.

If you have ever gone from store to store looking for a hard-to-find item, you will appreciate the ease of shopping online. Who has the item in stock? Who has the lowest price? Free shipping? Quickest delivery? You can get the answers to all these questions with a click of your mouse. For starters, you can check price comparison sites such as bizrate.com, mysimon.com or pricegrabber.com.

Online Shopping Tips

1. Check out the reviews written by other buyers.
2. Look for a padlock icon in the browser and "https" for security.
3. Check for endorsements from rating agencies, such as the Better Business Bureau (BBB).
4. Steer clear of sellers who offer low prices only to squeeze you on shipping costs.
5. Use a credit card as it offers the best safeguard against fraud, but never e-mail a credit card number, bank account information, password, or PIN number.

<< These five online shopping tips provide advice on making sure the sites you use are secure and reputable.

Read the Reviews All right, so you can't try on shoes or a shirt online. Online buyers trade that advantage for online customer reviews. A recent study of online buyers shows that 9 out of 10 Americans read reviews posted by other customers online before they make a purchase. You can access detailed customer-driven product reviews for almost any product. Love the product, and you can let the world know. Hate it, and you can warn others as well.

E-Buyer Be Aware Along with its unique benefits, online shopping includes some unique challenges. How do you really know if the online retailer you're dealing with is reputable and your information will be secure? For the most part, you have a higher degree of confidence if there is a brick-and-mortar backup to the online stores. Major retailers devote a lot of resources to ensuring that their customers have a satisfying and secure online shopping experience.

That does not mean that you should not deal with online-only vendors. You just need to be sure the sites you use are secure and reputable.

Bidding Online Comfortable online? The biggest and best deals often exist beyond the big stores. Two of the most-widely used alternatives are the relatively free classifieds and auction sites, such as eBay. These offer shopping alternatives that come with a different set of rules tailored for the online marketplace.

Local appeal can be a major advantage. Online classifieds provide access to backyard buyers and sellers at relatively no cost. Your next entertainment center might very well be three towns or three blocks away.

In its attempt to keep you scam- and worry-free, these services encourage buyers to deal locally with folks you can meet in person. The site also includes detailed safety guidelines. On Internet auctions, buyers can quickly and easily comparison shop for just about anything, from used cars and leather bomber jackets to concert tickets and even private jets. In this auction format, shoppers can engage in competitive bidding wars.

So how are buyers and sellers protected? Buyers rate the reliability and service provided by sellers and eBay makes these ratings available to you. However, if you win a bid and do not go through with the purchase, you are stuck with a negative rating for the rest of your eBay life. There are also services that make it possible for you to pay an individual seller using your credit card.

Fighting Fraud There is a new charge on your credit card bill! But where is the merchandise? You never got it, or even worse, you never ordered it. Many credit card companies will investigate suspected cases of fraud on your behalf, limiting your liability to $50. Also, the Fair Credit Billing Act allows you to withhold payment if you believe that someone has stolen your card number.

You also have the option of filing complaints with the Federal Trade Commission (FTC) at www.ftc.gov. The FTC offers you advice on how to protect against fraud, identity theft, and questionable business practices. The site guides you step-by-step through the process of filing a consumer complaint.

After High School

Almost Priceless It's hard to put a price on a college education. The personal and career rewards last a lifetime. Unfortunately, paying off the costs of a four-year degree can seem almost as long. The hard facts about paying for college are these: In constant dollars, the average cost of **tuition** and fees at two-year public colleges increased by 3 percent each year from 2003 to 2013. During the same time period, tuition and fees at four-year institutions increased 4.2 percent each year. The good news is that increases posted for the 2013–2014 tuition year were below the average rate increase for the preceding decade.

Choose Carefully If rapidly rising costs continue, in 2020 a four-year public education will cost over $158,510 (in constant dollars) for incoming freshman. This includes tuition, fees, room and board, supplies, transportation, and other personal expenses. By 2025 the projected cost is $212,123. The cost at a private university will be approximately twice that amount. For most students, those are pretty scary numbers.

Average Undergraduate Tuition, Fees, Room, and Board for Full-Time Students

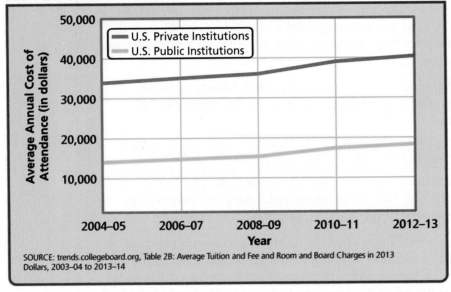

<< Between 2004 and 2013, costs of undergraduate tuition, room, and board rose for private and public institutions. Though these costs continue to rise, a college education greatly increases earning potential over a lifetime.

SOURCE: trends.collegeboard.org, Table 2B: Average Tuition and Fee and Room and Board Charges in 2013 Dollars, 2003–04 to 2013–14

Here are a few questions to consider:

- **What school do you want to attend, and why?** Examine your goals. Look for the educational resources you need at less-expensive public schools. Private schools generally are more costly, but can be more generous with their financial aid offers.
- **Does location matter?** Tuition costs vary considerably from region to region.
- **How much debt can you tolerate?** If your career goal is to be a freelance artist rather than a brain surgeon, you might want to choose the less-expensive college to cut down on your post-graduation debt.

Financial Aid Basics The thought of paying for college might send you into panic mode. But there is help. It comes in three forms: (a) grants and scholarships; (b) work-study programs; and (c) loans. The idea is to reduce the amount you're going to owe by applying for as many sources of aid as possible.

If you're like most students, you will qualify for some type of assistance. The biggest financial aid error is not to apply at all. Many colleges are substituting loans for grants and some are experimenting by waiving tuition for certain income levels altogether.

Types of Lenders Financial aid comes in many packages and, regardless of income, you can qualify for a government loan. Carefully analyze and compare student loan options, whether the loans are offered by the private sector or federal government. Determine what the interest rate is, when the loan needs to be repaid, and whether there are any other obligations associated with the loan. For example, you may need to have your parents co-sign for a student loan.

Federal Government When it comes to government aid, the Department of Education offers three basic loans: Direct Loans, Stafford Loans for parents or students, and the Parent Loan for Undergraduate Students (PLUS).

For those in financial need, there is the Federal Perkins Loan. These loans have a fixed interest rate and are made available through the college. Students who go on to take teaching jobs in certain areas or who volunteer in the Americorps, Peace Corps, or VISTA programs may be eligible to have their federal loans partially repaid or even canceled. To help qualifying graduates, the government limits loan payments to 10% of their discretionary income. Any person who makes their payment on time will have the balance forgiven after 20 years.

Private Sources If money from government loans does not cover all your college expenses, private lending sources could fill the gap. Compared to government loans, regular commercial loans typically have higher interest rates, fees, and credit requirements. Trade organizations and educational institutions also offer lending aid. Check with your guidance counselor to find out more information.

Other Sources There are other ways to obtain financial aid without taking out loans. All kinds of students can qualify for financial aid that does not have to be repaid. You need not be valedictorian or an all-state basketball star. Other sources of financial aid include grants, scholarships, and work study.

Grants A no-strings-attached grant is a no-brainer to consider when applying for financial aid. Available from the federal government, state governments, and higher education institutions, grants are usually awarded according to financial need and tuition rates. Analyze and compare each grant option to see which one is best for you.

There are wide varieties of grants out there. Evaluate grant opportunities before applying for a grant. Some grants may be specific to a particular area of study. Others may be specific to an affiliation with a business, or you may need a history of community work in order to qualify.

Don't forget FAFSA, also known as the Free Application for Federal Student Aid, available at www.fafsa.ed.gov. All students should complete the FAFSA, even if they believe they will not qualify for aid. There is always a chance that family circumstances will change. You need to complete this form if you want to be considered for federal aid, such as the Pell Grant and Supplemental Educational Opportunity Grant. These grants are given to students with "exceptional financial need."

You will need some basic information in order to complete the FAFSA. This includes your date of birth, income information for yourself and possibly for your parent(s), and basic information on available assets that could be used to pay for college. It's good to work with someone who is familiar with the FAFSA before completing the application, in order to learn more about the process. Find out more by checking out the U.S. Department of Education Web sites www.federalstudentaid.ed.gov or www.students.gov, your state education agency, or your high school guidance office.

Scholarships and Work Study Schools offer various scholarship opportunities. Besides aid from the school itself, there are scholarships available from individuals, local community initiatives, and civic groups. Check with local organizations such as the Kiwanis and Lions Clubs. Some companies also offer scholarships to children of their employees. Likewise, you might evaluate scholarship opportunities offered by state governments. Take time to research and evaluate scholarships offered by professional organizations, state governments, individuals, and from the schools you would like to attend.

Work-study programs are a win-win situation for the student, college, and community. This type of aid allows students to earn money to offset their educational expenses. Contact the schools you are interested in attending. Ask about the types of work-study opportunities offered by the school. Researching and evaluating work-study and scholarship opportunities will help in determining constructive ways to fund your college education.

In addition, investigate nontraditional methods of paying for college or post-secondary education and training, such as becoming a resident assistant who offers tutoring services to younger students. Some individuals set up a special investment fund called Plan 529 for children while they are in their early years. The money can later be used for education. Time spent in comparing and contrasting other sources of funding may lead you to some excellent possibilities to help pay for your college education.

Getting a Job You may already have had your first job—after school, weekends, or summers. But for most of us, finding a full-time, long-term job doesn't come until after we graduate from high school or college.

Your Resumé The first step is to prepare a **resumé,** a written summary of your educational and work experience. Think of it as an advertisement to market yourself to an employer.

You might be thinking, "That's fine if I have a lot of experience to list. But this is my first real job." True, but that doesn't mean you don't have qualities that employers are interested in. For example, suppose you worked the same job every summer for three years running. That shows that somebody liked you enough to keep hiring you back. Your service in school clubs or volunteer organizations could indicate qualities such as leadership, planning abilities, and a strong work ethic. Academic honors can count for a lot, too. Be sure to organize your resumé in a neat, readable fashion—no fancy type.

Job Application

Name*
First   Last

Email*   Phone*

How do you prefer to submit your resume?*

● Upload file   ○ Provide URL

Upload your resume   [Upload]

<< Today, many job hunts begin with completing an online application form.

References Some employers may ask for references. If you've been applying to colleges, you know the drill. Pick people—other than family—who can tell potential employers about your character and work ethic: a former boss, a colleague from an internship, a professor or advisor. Be sure to check with potential choices in advance to be sure they are willing to serve as your reference. Be ready with names, home or business addresses, e-mail addresses, and phone numbers.

Know Where to Look So you're ready to look for a job. Where should you start? Make a list of places that seem most promising. And try to find out something about a company before you apply there. It's all just part of being prepared.

The Interview That very first job interview can be an exciting but nerve-wracking experience. But you can prepare for it. Hold a mock interview with family members or friends. Have them ask you possible questions and then critique your responses and your delivery.

Make a Good Impression The minute you step into a potential employer's office, you are being judged. Don't blow it before you open your mouth. Posture, eye contact, and a firm handshake go a long way to making a positive impression.

> You never get a second chance to make a first impression.
>
> —Maxim attributed to 20th century Dutch author William Triesthof

Believe it or not, dressing the wrong way can be a deal-breaker. What works on the beach or in a dance club won't cut it in the office. Even a company that allows "casual" dress on the job doesn't want to see you in tank tops, cutoffs, or flip-flops. Be safe. Think conservative and professional. Yes, that may mean a suit or a dress. Let them tell you that you don't have to dress that way—after you get the job.

Turn Off That Cellphone The person interviewing you may have to interrupt to take a phone call. But you do not get the same privilege. Before you step in that office, make sure your cellphone is switched off. Nothing will ruin a good interview faster than a ringing cellphone.

Ask the Right Questions Where do you see yourself in five years? Why did you choose your particular college major? Why are you the best candidate for this position? Expect to be peppered with questions. But be equally as prepared to ask them. Questions like these show you're interested in the job:

- What are the company's goals for the next year or so?
- How does this job fit in with the company's goals?
- Describe a typical day here in this department.

Steer clear of questions about pay, benefits, hours, and vacation time. All of that will be covered if you are asked back for a second interview.

Benefits Paid by Private Companies

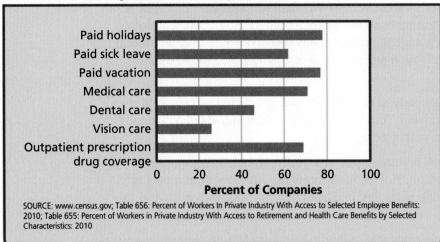

SOURCE: www.census.gov; Table 656: Percent of Workers In Private Industry With Access to Selected Employee Benefits: 2010; Table 655: Percent of Workers in Private Industry With Access to Retirement and Health Care Benefits by Selected Characteristics: 2010

<< Not all benefit packages are created equal. This chart shows that the types of benefits private companies offer can vary greatly.

After the Interview Follow up with a handwritten or e-mailed thank-you note. This reaffirms your interest and makes a lasting impression. If you're rejected, try not to get discouraged. It's part of the interview process. And remember: rejection can work either way. You're under no obligation to accept the first offer that comes along. Factor in benefits, commuting costs, work environment, and the possibility of career advancement. Look for the best fit for you.

Taxes and Income

What's in a Paycheck? You've got your first job—and your first paycheck. Attached to your check is a pay stub, also known as an earnings statement, which includes your identification information and the pay period you worked. But there's a lot more to it than that.

Salary and Wages It all begins with your wages or salary. Wages refer to hourly pay and can change based on how much time you worked. Salary is monthly or yearly pay, which is not dependent on the number of hours worked.

Average Salaries by Discipline, 2012

JOB CATEGORY	ENTRY-LEVEL PAY
Business	$51,541
Communications	$42,286
Computer Science	$60,038
Education	$39,080
Engineering	$60,639
Health Science	$46,567
Humanities & Social Sciences	$36,824
Math & Sciences	$42,355

<< Level of education, skill, and supply and demand are factors that determine entry-level pay. Typically, college graduates with technical, medical, or business degrees will command higher salaries.

SOURCE: www.naceweb.org: National Association of Colleges and Employers, NACE Salary Survey, September 2012 Executive Summary

Your pay stub shows your **gross pay,** the total amount of income you earned during the pay period. If you are paid hourly, it should be equal to the number of hours you worked times your hourly wage. (It will also show if you worked overtime at a higher rate.) If you are on an annual salary, it's your salary divided by the number of pay periods in the year.

Withholdings You will immediately notice that your **net pay**—the amount the check is made out for—is far less than your gross pay. Where did the rest of the money go?

Your stub lists all your **payroll withholdings,** the earnings that come out of your check before you get it. Some of these withholdings are voluntary. For example, if you join a company medical or insurance plan, your share of these benefits comes out of your check. Other withholdings, however, go into taxes to the state and federal government.

Federal and State Deductions Most workers have federal and state taxes deducted from their earnings. Your employer is also required to pay the federal government a certain percentage of your earnings.

A **Year-to-date**
(for pay and deductions)
The year-to-date shows the total amount withheld for a particular deduction at any point in the calendar year.

Earnings Statement

Period ending: 00/00/0000
Pay date: 00/00/0000

XYZ Corporation
100 Corporation Crt.
New Town, NY 10000

C **Leave Time**
Includes vacation hours or sick hours. Many employers will detail how many hours have been used to date, and how many hours are remaining for the calendar year.

B **Gross Pay**
The total amount of income that you earned during the pay period.

Social Security Number: 999-99-9999
Taxable Marital Status: Single
Exemptions/Allowances:
  Federal: 1
  State: 1
  Local: 1

TOMÁS Q. PUBLIC
123 MAIN STREET
ANYWHERE, USA 12345

Earnings	rate	hours	this period	year to date
Regular	20.00	40.00	800.00	16,640.00
Overtime	30.00	1.00	30.00	780.00 **A**
Holiday	30.00	8.00	240.00	1,200.00 **A**
B **Gross Pay**			**$ 1,070.00**	18,620.00

Other Benefits and Information	this period	year-to-date
Vac Hrs Left		40.00 **C**
Sick Hrs Left		16.00

>> Earnings statements show figures such as pay rate, gross pay, net pay, and deductions for insurance and other benefits. This portion of a sample earnings statement shows how gross pay is calculated.

Social Security and Medicare **Social Security** (FICA) and Medicare taxes are based on a percentage of your earnings. FICA stands for Federal Insurance Contributions Act. It is a U.S. payroll tax on employees and employers to fund programs that provide benefits for retirees, the disabled, and children of deceased workers. Medicare provides hospital insurance benefits.

The W-4 Form Federal and state taxes are deducted based on an estimate of how much you will owe in yearly taxes. Most workers are required to fill out a W-4 form when they start a new job. It includes guidelines to help you do the calculations needed to estimate how much will be withheld from each paycheck. The W-4 gives you the option of taking certain personal allowances that will lower the amount of tax withheld from your income. For example, you may take an exemption for yourself and your spouse. You also can take an exemption for anyone who is dependent on your income, such as a child. Young people who are not married and have no children will generally claim a single exemption. The IRS offers an online withholding calculator (www.irs.gov/individuals) to help you avoid having too much or too little income tax withheld from your pay.

Taxes and You Welcome to the workforce! You have joined the ranks of taxpayers. But why do you have to pay taxes anyhow? Governments have expenses. They have to pay salaries for thousands of employees and provide services for millions of citizens. The biggest source of government revenue is taxes. And you are required by law to pay your share.

Don't Mess With the IRS Among taxes, the federal income tax is top dog. The Internal Revenue Service (IRS), an agency within the Treasury Department, applies federal income tax laws passed by Congress. The agency generates tax forms and collects taxes. The IRS will notice if you don't pay what you owe and impose hefty financial penalties for any misdeeds.

The federal income tax is a progressive tax, so people with the highest income have the highest tax rates. The system also includes hundreds of tax breaks for people with special financial burdens, such as people paying for college or starting a business, as well as rewards for actions like making a donation to charity.

Other Taxes Most state governments collect income tax, too. In addition, states and local communities levy other kinds of taxes, such as sales tax and property tax. Sales taxes vary from state to state, but they generally involve paying a fixed percentage on most items you buy. Essentials of life—such as food and medicine—are generally exempt from sales tax. Property taxes are based on the value of privately owned homes and land.

Taxes are also collected on income you didn't work for. If Aunt Bessie leaves you money in her will, you have to pay an inheritance tax. If you buy stock and you make a lot of money when you sell it, that's also taxed.

State Sales Tax

HIGHEST TAX RATE	LOWEST TAX RATE	NO SALES TAX
California 7.5%	Colorado 2.9%	Alaska Delaware Montana New Hampshire Oregon

<< Americans pay federal taxes no matter where they live. State taxes are another matter. Some states do not impose an income tax, but assess a sales tax. Alaska residents, who pay no sales or income tax, have the least per capita tax rates in the nation.

SOURCE: taxfoundation.org, Table 1: State and Local Sales Tax Rates, As of January 1, 2013

Forms, Forms, Forms Sometime during the "tax season," which runs from January to April 15, you need to fill out and file the appropriate tax forms. Filing is the only way to get a refund, or return of excess taxes paid. But whether you've got a refund coming or not, it's against the law not to file an income tax return.

The W-2 The most common federal tax form is the W-2, which reports wages paid to employees and taxes withheld from them. The form also reports FICA taxes to the Social Security Administration. Employers must complete and send out a W-2 to every employee by January 31. Save these documents! Your W-2's must be attached to your tax return when you file.

Form W-2 Wage and Tax Statement 2013

a Control number		Void X	c Employer's name, address, and ZIP code	Department of the Treasury - Internal Revenue Service OMB No. 1545-0008	
b Employer's identification number	d Employee's social security number			1 Wages, tips, other compensation	2 Federal income tax withheld
13 Statutory employee	Retirement plan	Third-party sick pay		3 Social security wages	4 Social security tax withheld
12 See Instrs. for Box 12	14 Other		e Employee's name, address, and ZIP code	5 Medicare wages and tips	6 Medicare tax withheld
				7 Social security tips	8 Allocated tips
				9 Advance EIC payment	10 Dependent care benefits
				11 Nonqualified plans	
15 State Employer's state ID No.		16 State wages, tips, etc.	17 State income tax	18 Local wages, tips, etc.	19 Local income tax	20 Locality name

>> People in the U.S. must pay federal taxes on their job earnings. Federal income tax forms are due to the IRS in April each year.

1040 and Beyond   When you file your income tax return, which is due by April 15, you'll use Form 1040, the Individual Income Tax Return. By filling it out properly, you will learn if you owe more money to the government or if the government owes you money.

To make life easier, the government introduced the Form 1040EZ, which is the simplest tax form. Its use is limited to taxpayers with taxable income below $100,000 who take the standard deduction instead of itemizing deductions, that is, listing them separately. Many unmarried people with no children also qualify to use this form.

If you have income other than wages, salaries, and tips, Form 1099 comes into play. It's a statement you receive from payers of interest income, such as banks and savings institutions, that summarizes your interest income for the year.

Don't Guess—Get Help!   You want to make sure you get all the tax deductions that the IRS allows. Each form has step-by-step instructions, but they might not answer all your questions. Here are some other places to get advice:

- The IRS has a user-friendly Web site, with lots of information. It can be found at www.irs.gov.
- Call the IRS at (800) 829-1040. You can talk to a tax specialist, or even schedule an appointment for help at IRS service centers. But don't delay. The closer you get to April 15, the harder it may be to get timely help.
- Tax-preparation services and tax accountants will prepare your tax return for a fee. Some will file your return for you.

If you prepare your return on paper, you must send it to the IRS Service Center listed in the instruction booklet and at the IRS Web site. There are ways you can prepare and "e-file" your return online. Filing in this way will get you a faster tax refund. But you usually will have to pay a fee, especially if you use a tax preparation firm.

Sequence

Sequence means "order," and placing things in the correct order is very important. What would happen if you tried to put toppings on a pizza before you put down the dough for the crust? When studying history, you need to analyze the information by sequencing significant events, individuals, and time periods in order to understand them. Practice this skill by using the reading on this page.

> **Two Crises for Banking** As a result of the many bank failures of the Great Depression, banks were closely regulated from 1933 through the 1960s. The government restricted the interest rates banks could pay depositors and the rates that banks could charge consumers for loans. By the 1970s, bankers were eager for relief from federal regulation.
>
> **The Savings and Loan Crisis** In the late 1970s and 1980s, Congress passed laws to deregulate, or remove some restrictions on, several industries. Unfortunately, this deregulation contributed to a crisis in a class of banks known as Savings and Loans (S&Ls). Government regulation had protected S&Ls from some of the stresses of the marketplace. Thus, they were unprepared for the intense competition they faced after deregulation.

[1.] Identify the topic and the main events that relate to the topic. Quickly skim titles and headings to determine the topic of the passage. As you read the passage, write a list of significant events, individuals, or time periods related to the topic.

[2.] Note any dates and time words such as "before" and "after" that indicate the chronological order of events. Look through your list of events, individuals, or time periods and write down the date for each. This will give you information to apply absolute chronology by sequencing the events, individuals, or time periods. Remember that some events may have taken place over a number of months or years. Is your date the time when the event started or ended? Make sure to note enough details that you can remember the importance of the information. If no date is given, look for words such as "before" or "after" that can tell you where to place this event, time period, or individual compared to others on your list. This will allow you to apply relative chronology by sequencing the events, individuals, or time periods.

[3.] Determine the time range of the events. Place the events in chronological order on a timeline. Look for the earliest and latest events, individuals, or time periods on your list. The span of time between the first and last entries gives you the time range. To apply absolute chronology, sequence the entries by writing the date of the first event on the left side of a piece of paper and the date of the last event on the right side. Draw a line connecting the two events. This will be your timeline. Once you have drawn your timeline, put the events in order by date along the line. Label their dates. To apply relative chronology, sequence the significant individuals, events, or time periods on an undated timeline, in the order that they happened. You now have a clear image of the important events related to this topic. You can organize and interpret information from visuals by analyzing the information and applying absolute or relative chronology to the events. This will help you understand the topic better when you can see how events caused or led to other events. You will also be able to analyze information by developing connections between historical events over time.

Categorize

When you analyze information by categorizing, you create a system that helps you sort items into categories, or groups with shared characteristics, so that you can understand the information. Categorizing helps you see what groups of items have in common. Practice this skill using the chart on this page. What categories are shown on this chart? Copy the chart on a sheet of paper and work with a partner to enter examples pertaining to the United States for each category.

Foreign Policy Challenge	Economic Challenge

[1.] Identify similarities and differences among items you need to understand. You need to pay careful attention and sometimes do research to find the similarities and differences among the facts, topics, or objects that you need to understand. Scientists find groups, or categories, of related animals by analyzing the details of the animals' bodies. For example, insects with similar wings, legs, and mouthparts probably belong in the same category. Gather similar information about all the things you need to understand. For example, if you know the location of one thing, try to find the locations of all the things you are studying. If you have different types of information about your topics, you will not be able to group them easily.

[2.] Create a system to group items with common characteristics. Once you have gathered similar kinds of information on the items you need to understand, look for items that share characteristics or features. Create categories based on a feature shared by all of the facts, topics, or objects you need to understand. For example, if you have gathered information on the population and political systems of several countries, you could categorize them by the size of their population or their type of political system.

[3.] Form the groupings. Put each of the items that you are studying into one of the categories that you have created. If some items do not fit, you may need to make a new category or modify your categories. Label each category for the characteristic shared by its members. Examples of labels for categories might include "Countries with more than 100 million people," "Countries with fewer than 1 million people," "Democracies," or "Dictatorships."

Analyze Cause and Effect

When you analyze information by identifying cause-and-effect relationships, you find how one event leads to the next. It is important to find evidence that one event caused another. If one event happened earlier than another, it did not necessarily cause the later event. Understanding causes and effects can help you solve problems. Practice this skill as you study the cause-and-effect chart on this page.

Agricultural Causes of the Depression of 1893

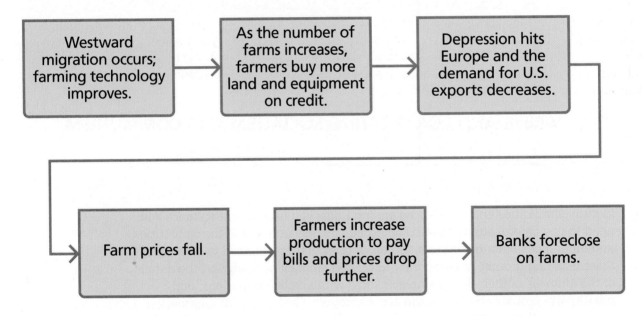

[1.] Choose a starting point of observation. When trying to understand a historical event, choose the time of that event. If you are trying to understand a current event, you can work backward from a starting point in the present.

[2.] Consider earlier events to try to find connections to your starting point, including any language that signals causes. Put the evidence together to identify true causes. When reading, look for events that come before your starting point. Analyze whether these earlier events caused later events. Identify words that signal cause, such as "reason," "because," and "led to." Analyze the information by developing connections between historical events. Make sure that there is evidence showing that the earlier events caused the later events and did not just happen earlier.

[3.] Consider later events to try to find connections to your starting point, including any language that signals effects. Put the evidence together to determine true effects. Look for events that come after your starting point. Analyze the information in order to determine whether these later events are effects of earlier events. Identify words that signal effect, such as "led to," "so," and "therefore." Make sure that there is evidence showing that these later events were caused by earlier events and did not just happen later.

[4.] Summarize the cause-and-effect relationship and draw conclusions. Once you have identified the cause-and-effect relationships between different events, describe these relationships. Draw a diagram that develops the connections between the two historical events. Draw conclusions about any relationships that you see.

Compare and Contrast

When you analyze information by comparing and contrasting two or more things, you look for similarities and differences between them. This skill helps you understand the things that you are comparing and contrasting. It is also a skill that you can use in making choices. Practice this skill as you study the Venn diagram comparing socialism and communism. What words would you use to describe how these two economic ideas compare and contrast?

COMPARING AND CONTRASTING SOCIALISM AND COMMUNISM

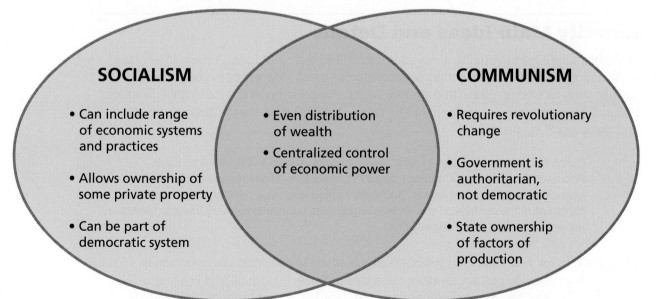

SOCIALISM
- Can include range of economic systems and practices
- Allows ownership of some private property
- Can be part of democratic system

- Even distribution of wealth
- Centralized control of economic power

COMMUNISM
- Requires revolutionary change
- Government is authoritarian, not democratic
- State ownership of factors of production

[**1.**] Look for related topics and characteristics that describe them. When you are looking for similarities and differences between two things, it can help to start by identifying relationships between them. What do the two things have in common? If two things have nothing in common, such as a dog and a piece of pie, it will be difficult to find similarities or differences. On the other hand, you can compare and contrast two countries or political systems. Look through the information you have on the things or topics you want to compare and contrast, and identify the characteristics, or features, that describe those things or topics.

[**2.**] Look for words that signal comparison ("both," "similar to," "also") or contrast ("unlike," "different," "instead"). Look for words that show comparison, or similarity, and those that show contrast, or difference. Take notes on these similarities and differences. This will make it possible to analyze information more quickly.

[**3.**] Identify similarities and differences in the topics, and draw conclusions about them. Look through your notes and analyze the ways in which your topics are similar and different. Usually, topics have both similarities and differences. Try to find patterns in these similarities and differences. For example, all the similarities between two countries might be related to climate, and all the differences might be related to economics. Draw conclusions based on these patterns. In this example, you might conclude that a country's economy does not depend on its climate. Identifying similarities and differences by comparing and contrasting two topics lets you draw conclusions that help you analyze both topics as well as other topics like them.

Identify Main Ideas and Details

You can analyze information in a selection by finding the main idea. A main idea is the most important point in a selection. Identifying the main idea will help you remember details, such as names, dates, and events, which should support the main idea. Practice this skill by reading the paragraph on this page. Find the main idea of this paragraph and the supporting details.

> During his first hundred days in office, which became known as the Hundred Days, Roosevelt proposed and Congress passed 15 major bills. These measures had three goals: relief, recovery, and reform. Roosevelt wanted to provide relief from the immediate hardships of the depression and achieve a long-term economic recovery. He also instituted reforms to prevent future depressions.

[**1.**] Scan titles, headings, and visuals before reading to see what the selection is about. Often, important ideas are included in titles, headings, and other special text. Special text may be primary sources, words that are highlighted, or ideas listed with bullet points. Also, take a look at visuals and captions. By analyzing these parts of the text, you should quickly get a sense of the main idea of the article.

[2.] Read the selection and then identify the main point of the selection, the point that the rest of the selection supports: this is the main idea. Read through the selection to identify the main idea. Sometimes, the main idea will be the first or second sentence of one of the first few paragraphs. Sometimes, it will be the last sentence of the first paragraph. Other times, no single sentence will tell you the main idea. You will have to come up with your own sentence answering the question, "What is the main point of this selection?"

[3.] Find details or statements within the selection that support or build on the main idea. Once you have identified the main idea, look for details that support the main idea. Many or most of the details should be related to the main idea. If you find that many of the details are not related to what you think is the main idea, you may not have identified the main idea correctly. Identify the main idea that the details in the selection support. Analyze the information in the text by finding the main idea and supporting details.

Summarize

When you analyze information by summarizing, you restate the main points of a passage in your own words. Using your own words helps you understand the information. Summarizing will help you understand a text and prepare for tests or assignments based on the text. Practice this skill by following the steps to summarize the excerpt on this page.

> Today, many countries are undergoing economic transition. Some are enjoying rapid growth, while others are changing their entire economic systems. Some places that are experiencing rapid economic change are Russia, China, India, and the countries of Africa and Latin America.
>
> For many nations, economic transition has meant moving from central planning to a market-based economy. In a command economy, the government owns and controls the factors of production. By contrast, in a market-based economy, the factors of production are owned and controlled by individuals. One of the first steps, then, in moving to a market economy is to sell or transfer government-owned businesses to individuals. This process is called privatization.

[1.] Identify and write down the main point of each paragraph in your own words. You may identify the main idea right at the beginning of each paragraph. In other cases, you will have to figure out the main idea. As you read each paragraph, ask yourself, "What is the point this paragraph makes?" The point the paragraph makes is the main idea. Write this idea down in your own words.

[2.] Use these main points to write a general statement of the overall main idea of the passage in your own words. Once you have written down the main idea for each paragraph, write down the main idea of the passage. Write the main idea in your own words. If you have trouble identifying the main idea of the passage, review the titles and headings in the passage. Often, titles and headings relate to the main idea. Also, the writer may state the main idea in the first paragraph of the passage. The main idea of a passage should answer the question, "What is the point this passage makes?"

[3.] Use this general statement as a topic sentence for your summary. Then, write a paragraph tying together the main points of the passage. Leave out unimportant details. Analyze the information in the passage by summarizing. Use the main idea of the passage as a topic sentence for your summary paragraph. Use the main ideas that you identified for each paragraph of the passage to write sentences supporting the main idea of the passage. Leave out details that are not needed to understand the main idea of the passage. Your summary should be in your own words, and it should be much shorter than the original passage. Once your summary is written, review it to make sure that it contains all the main points of the passage. If any are missing, revise your summary to include them. If the summary includes unimportant details, remove them.

Generalize

One good way to analyze materials about a particular subject is to make generalizations and predictions. What are the patterns and connections that link the different materials? What can you say about the different materials that is true of all them? Practice this skill by reading the following statements. What generalization can you make about the role of the government in the marketplace?

- The Federal Trade Commission Act says that advertisements cannot be deceptive.
- The Truth-in-Lending Act requires businesses offering loans to disclose certain information to consumers before they sign a loan agreement.
- The Federal Reserve System regulates banking and manages money supply.
- The Food and Drug Administration sets standards for food, drugs, and cosmetics.

[1.] Make a list. Listing all of the specific details and facts about a subject will help you find patterns and connections.

[2.] Generate a statement. From your list of facts and specific details, decide what most of the items listed have in common. Analyze your information by making generalizations and predictions.

[3.] Ensure your generalization is logical and well supported by facts. Generalizations can be valid or invalid. A generalization that is not logical or supported by facts is invalid.

Make Predictions

You can analyze information by making generalizations and predictions. Predictions are educated guesses about the future, based on clues you find in written material and information you already have. When you analyze information by making generalizations and predictions, you are thinking critically about the material you read. Practice this skill by analyzing the chart below and predicting the effect an economic downturn, with lower corporate and individual earnings, would have on government receipts.

Federal Receipts, 2014 (Estimated)

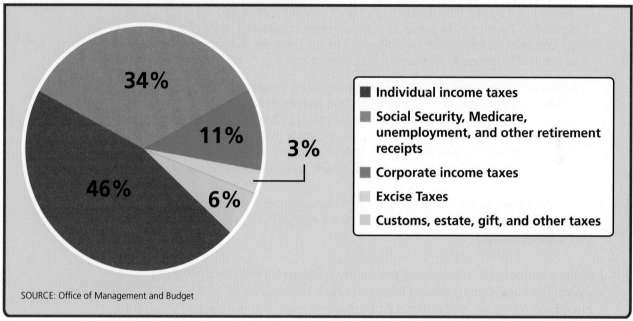

SOURCE: Office of Management and Budget

[1.] Review the content. Read your material carefully and research any terms or concepts that are new to you. It's important to understand the material before analyzing the information to make a prediction.

[2.] Look for clues. Gathering evidence is an important part of making predictions. Look for important words, statements, and evidence that seem to support the writer's point of view. Ask questions about what you are reading, including who, what, where, when, why, and how. Look for and analyze clues to help you generalize and predict.

[3.] Consider what you already know. Use related prior knowledge and/or connect to your own experiences to help you make an informed prediction. If you have experience with the subject matter, you have a much better chance of making an accurate prediction.

[4.] Generate a list of predictions. After studying the content, list the clues you've found. Then use these clues, plus your prior knowledge, to form your predictions. List as many possible outcomes as you can based on clues in the material and the questions you have considered.

Draw Inferences

What is the author trying to tell you? To make a determination about the author's message, you analyze information by drawing inferences and conclusions. You consider details and descriptions included in the text, compare and contrast the text to prior knowledge you have about the subject, and then form a conclusion about the author's intent. Practice this skill by analyzing the document below and drawing inferences about the author's view of the Soviet economy under communism in 1931.

> The fear of being exiled [banished, sent away] as a kulak [a landowner] has been a powerful factor in drawing workers into the collective farms. In the Stalin kolkhoz [collective farm] where I stayed, a sharp-eyed dark-haired peasant approached me in the Village Soviet hut. We were in the presence of the Communist president. He spoke to me of the successes of the kolkhoz, of the enthusiasm for the collective farm movement, and of the affection of the peasants for their young Bolshevist leader.
>
> Next morning, however, when far away from any of the Communist members of the kolkhoz, the same peasant . . . approached me and whispered, "It is terrible here in the kolkhoz. We cannot speak or we shall be sent away to Siberia. . . . We are afraid. I had three cows. They took them away and now I only get a crust of bread. It is a thousand times worse now than before the Revolution. . . . We have to keep quiet.
>
> —"The Real Russia: The Peasant on the Farm," Gareth Jones, *The Times*, October 14, 1931

[1.] Study the image or text. Consider all of the details and descriptions included. What is the author trying to tell you? Look for context clues that hint at the topic and subject matter.

[2.] Make a connection. Use related prior knowledge to connect to the text or image. Analyze information by asking questions such as who, what, where, when, and how. Look for cause-and-effect relationships; compare and contrast. This strategy will help you think beyond the available surface details to understand what the author is suggesting or implying.

[3.] Form a conclusion. When you draw an inference, you combine your own ideas with evidence and details you found within the text or image to form a new conclusion. This action leads you to a new understanding of the material.

Draw Conclusions

When you analyze information by drawing inferences and conclusions, you connect the ideas in a text with what you already know in order to understand a topic better. Using this skill, you can "fill in the blanks" to see the implications or larger meaning of the information in a text. Practice this skill by reading the excerpt. What conclusions can you draw based on the information in the paragraph?

Challenging Economic Times

From the Oval Office, Hoover worked hard to end the depression. But to many out-of-work Americans, the President became a symbol of failure. Some people blamed capitalism, while others questioned the responsiveness of democracy. Many believed the American system was due for an overhaul. Although some questioned the ability of America's capitalistic and democratic institutions to overcome the crisis, most Americans never lost faith in their country.

[1.] Identify the topic, main idea, and supporting details. Before reading, look at the titles and headings within a reading. This should give you a good idea of the topic, or the general subject, of a text. After reading, identify the main idea. The main idea falls within the topic and answers the question, "What is the main point of this text?" Find the details that the author presents to support the main idea.

[2.] Use what you know to make a judgment about the information. Think about what you know about this topic or a similar topic. For example, you may read that the English settlers of Jamestown suffered from starvation because many of them were not farmers and did not know how to grow food. Analyzing the information about their situation and what you know about people, you could draw the conclusion that these settlers must have had little idea, or the wrong idea, about the conditions that they would find in America.

[3.] Check and adjust your judgment until you can draw a well-supported conclusion. Look for details within the reading that support your judgment. Reading a little further, you find that these settlers thought that they would become rich after discovering gold or silver, or through trading with Native Americans for furs. You can use this information to support your conclusion that the settlers were mistaken about the conditions that they would find in America. By analyzing the information further, you might infer that the settlers had inaccurate information about America. To support your conclusions, you could look for reliable sources on what these settlers knew before they left England.

Interpret Sources

Outlines and reports are good sources of information. In order to interpret these sources, though, you'll need to identify the type of document you're reading, identify the main idea, organize the details of information, and evaluate the source for point of view and bias. Practice this skill by finding a newspaper or online report on U.S. unemployment. What steps will you take to interpret this report?

[1.] Identify the type of document. Is the document a primary or secondary source? Determine when, where, and why it was written.

[**2.**] Examine the source to identify the main idea. After identifying the main idea, identify details or sections of text that support the main idea. If the source is an outline or report, identify the topic and subtopics; review the supporting details under each subtopic. Organize the information from the outline or report and think about how it connects back to the overall topic listed at the top of the outline or report.

[**3.**] Evaluate the source for point of view and bias. Primary sources often have a strong point of view or bias; it is important to analyze primary sources critically to determine their validity. Evaluating each source will help you interpret the information they contain.

Create Databases

Databases are organized collections of information which can be analyzed and interpreted. You decide on a topic, organize data, use a spreadsheet, and then pose questions which will help you to analyze and interpret your data. Practice this skill by creating a database of features for five different smartphones. Analyze your database to decide which one would best meet your needs.

[**1.**] Decide on a topic. Identify the information that you will convert into a table. This information may come from various sources, including textbooks, reference works, and Internet sites.

[**2.**] Organize the data. Study the information and decide what to include in your table. Only include data that is pertinent and available. Based on the data you choose, organize your information. Identify how many columns there will be and what the column headings will be. Decide the order in which you are going to list the data in the rows.

[**3.**] Use a spreadsheet. A spreadsheet is a computer software tool that allows you to organize data so that it can be analyzed. Spreadsheets allow you to make calculations as well as input data. Use a spreadsheet to help you create summaries of your data. For instance, you can compute the sum, average, minimum, and maximum values of the data. Use the graphing features of your spreadsheet program to show the data visually.

[**4.**] Analyze the data. Once all of your data is entered and you have made any calculations you need, you are ready to pose questions to analyze and interpret your data. Organize the information from the database and use it to form conclusions. Be sure to draw conclusions that can be supported by the data available.

PEARSON
realize™

www.PearsonRealize.com
View Video Tutorials and other
21st Century Skills

Analyze Data and Models

Data and models can provide useful information about geographic distributions and patterns. To make sense of that information, though, you need to pose and answer questions about data and models. What does the data say? What does it mean? What patterns can you find? Practice this skill as you study the data below.

Top Remittance Destinations, 2012

COUNTRY	REMITTANCES
India	$67,258,000,000
China	$57,799,000,000
Philippines	$24,641,000,000
Mexico	$23,371,000,000
Nigeria	$20,633,000,000
Egypt	$19,236,000,000

SOURCE: World Bank

[**1.**] Read the title to learn the geographic distributions represented by the data set, graph, or model.

[**2.**] Read the data given. When reviewing a graph, read the labels and the key to help you comprehend the data provided. Pose and answer questions to further understand the material. For example, you might ask "Who could use this data?" or "How could this data be used?" or even "Why is this data presented in this particular format?" Thinking critically about the data presented will help you make predictions and comprehend the data.

[**3.**] Study the numbers, lines, and/or colors to find out what the graphs or data represent. Next, find similarities and differences between multiple models of the same data. Do any additional research to find out more about why the information in the models differs.

[**4.**] Interpret the graph, data set, or model. Look for interesting geographic distributions and patterns in the data. Look at changes over time or compare information from different categories. Draw conclusions.

Read Charts, Graphs, and Tables

If you pose and answer questions about charts, graphs, or tables you find in books or online, you can find out all sorts of information, such as how many calories are in your favorite foods or what the value of a used car is. Analyzing and interpreting the information you find in thematic charts, graphs, and tables can help you make decisions in your life. Practice this skill as you study the graph below.

U.S. Balance of Trade, 1965–2012

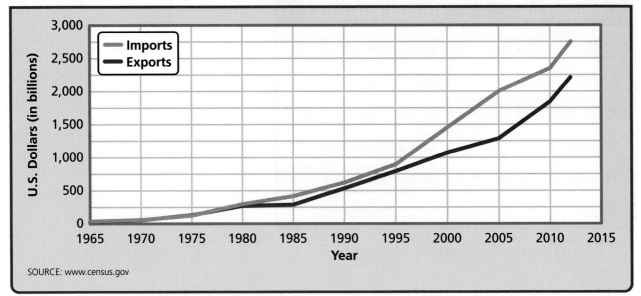

SOURCE: www.census.gov

[**1.**] Identify the title and labels of a chart, graph, or table, and read the key, if there is one, to understand the information presented. The title often tells you the topic of the chart, graph, or table, or the type of information you will find. Make sure you understand how the graph shows information. A key or legend often appears in a small box near the edge of the graph or chart. The key will tell you the meaning of lines, colors, or symbols used on the chart or graph. Notice also the column and row headings, and use your reading skills to figure out the meanings of any words you don't know.

[**2.**] Determine consistencies and inconsistencies, to see whether there is a trend in a graph, chart, or table. Organize information from visuals such as charts and graphs and decide whether or not there is a trend or pattern in the information that you see. Evaluate the data and determine whether the trend is consistent, or steady. Remember that there could be some inconsistencies, or exceptions to the pattern. Try not to miss the overall pattern because of a couple of exceptions.

[**3.**] Draw conclusions about the data in a chart, graph, or table. Once you understand the information, try to analyze and interpret the information and draw conclusions. If you see a pattern, does the pattern help you to understand the topic or predict future events?

[4.] Create a chart or graph to make the data more understandable or to view the data in a different way. Does the data in the chart or graph help you answer questions you have about the topic or see any causes or effects? For example, you could use your mathematical skills to create circle graphs or bar graphs that visually organize the data in a different way that allows you to interpret the data differently.

[5.] Use the data or information in charts and graphs to understand an issue or make decisions. Use your social studies skills to make inferences, draw conclusions, and take a stand on the issue.

Create Charts and Maps

Thematic charts, graphs, and maps are visual tools for representing information. When you create a thematic chart, graph, or map you will start by selecting the type of data you want to represent. Then you will find appropriate data to include, organize your data, and then create symbols and a key to help others understand your chart, graph, or map. Practice this skill by creating an economic activity map of your state. Use computer software to generate the state outline, then apply appropriate symbols to represent the major industries of the state.

[1.] To create a chart or map, first select a region or set of data. Use a map to represent data pertaining to a specific region or location; use a chart to represent trends reflected in a set of data.

[2.] Research and find the data you would like to present in the chart or map. Your choice of data will be based on the theme you wish to explore. For example, a chart or map that explores the theme of changing demographics in Texas might include data about the location of different ethnic groups in Texas in the nineteenth, twentieth, and twenty-first centuries.

[3.] Organize the data according to the specific format of your chart or map.

[4.] Create symbols, a key (as needed), and a title. Create symbols to represent each piece of data you would like to highlight. Keep each symbol simple and easy to understand. After you have created the symbols, place them in a key. Add a title to your map or chart that summarizes the information presented. Your symbols and key will make it easier for others to interpret your charts and maps.

Analyze Political Cartoons

Political cartoons are visual commentaries about events or people. As you learn to analyze political cartoons, you will learn to identify bias in cartoons and interpret their meaning. You can start by carefully examining the cartoon and considering its possible meanings. Then you can draw conclusions based on your analysis. Practice this skill as you study the political cartoon.

[1.] Fully examine the cartoon. Identify any symbols in the cartoon, read the text and title, and identify the main character or characters. Analyze the cartoon to identify bias and determine what each image or symbol represents. Conduct research if you need more information to decipher the cartoon.

[2.] Consider the meaning. Think about how the cartoonist uses the images and symbols in the cartoon to express his or her opinion about a subject. Try to interpret the artist's purpose in creating the image.

[3.] Draw conclusions. Use what you have gleaned from the image itself, plus any prior knowledge or research, to analyze, interpret, and form a conclusion about the artist's intentions.

Read Physical Maps

What mountain range is closest to where you live? What major rivers are closest to you? To find out, you would look at a physical map. You can use appropriate reading skills to interpret social studies information such as that found on different kinds of maps. Physical maps show physical features, such as elevation, mountains, valleys, oceans, rivers, deserts, and plains. Practice this skill as you study the map. Which economic activities do you think you would find in each geographic area? Why?

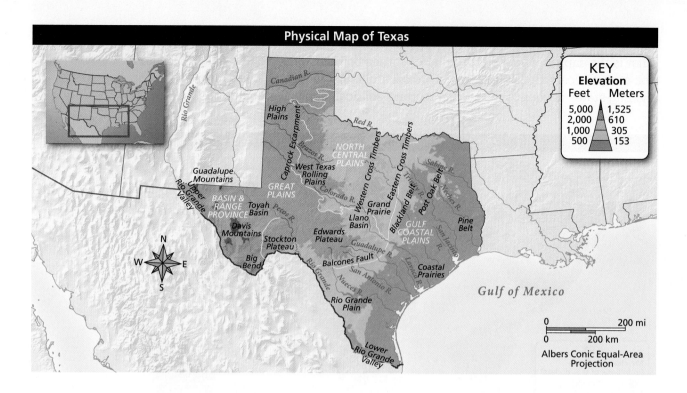

Physical Map of Texas

KEY
Elevation

Feet	Meters
5,000	1,525
2,000	610
1,000	305
500	153

Gulf of Mexico

0   200 mi
0   200 km

Albers Conic Equal-Area
Projection

[1.] Identify the title and region shown on a map. A map's title can help you to identify the region covered by the map. The title may also tell you the type of information you will find on the map. If the map has no title, you can identify the region by reading the labels on the map.

[2.] Use the map key to interpret symbols and colors on a map. A key or legend often appears in a small box near the edge of the map. The legend will tell you the meaning of colors, symbols, or other patterns on the map. On a physical map, colors from the key often show elevation, or height above sea level, on the map.

[3.] Identify physical features, such as mountains, valleys, oceans, and rivers. Using labels on the map and colors and symbols from the key, identify the physical features on the map. The information in the key allows you to interpret the information from visuals such as a map. Rivers, oceans, lakes, and other bodies of water are usually colored blue. Colors from the key may indicate higher and lower elevation, or there may be shading on the map that shows mountains.

[4.] Draw conclusions about the region based on natural resources and physical features. Once you understand all the symbols and colors on the map, try to interpret the information from the map. Is it very mountainous or mostly flat? Does it have a coastline? Does the region have lots of lakes and rivers that suggest a good water supply? Pose and answer questions about geographic distributions and patterns shown on the map. Physical maps can give you an idea of lifestyle and economic activities of people in the region.

Read Political Maps

What is the capital of your state? What countries border China? To find out, you could look at a political map. Political maps are colorful maps that show borders, or lines dividing states or countries. Practice reading political maps by studying the map below.

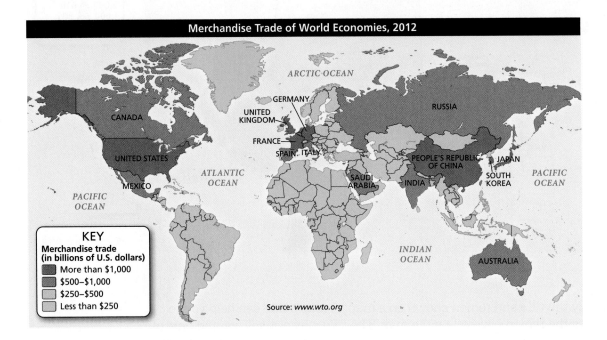

Merchandise Trade of World Economies, 2012

KEY
Merchandise trade (in billions of U.S. dollars)
- More than $1,000
- $500–$1,000
- $250–$500
- Less than $250

Source: *www.wto.org*

[**1.**] Identify the title of the political map and the region shown. A map's title can help you identify the region covered by the map. The title may also tell you the type of information you will find on the map. If the map has no title, you can identify the region by reading the labels on the map.

[**2.**] Use the map key to interpret symbols and colors on the map. A key or legend often appears in a small box near the edge of the map. The key will help you interpret information from visuals, including maps, by telling you the meaning of colors, symbols, or other patterns on the visual.

[**3.**] Identify boundaries between nations or states. Evaluate government data, such as borders, using the map. It is often easy to see borders, because each state or country will be a different color. If you cannot find the borders, check the key to find the lines used to mark borders on the map.

[**4.**] Locate capital cities. Look at the key to see whether capital cities are shown on the map. They are often marked with a special symbol, such as a star.

[**5.**] Draw conclusions about the region based on the map. Once you understand all the symbols and colors on the map, use appropriate reading and mathematical skills to interpret social studies information, such as that shown on the map, in order to draw conclusions about the region. For example, are some countries very large with many cities? These countries are likely to be powerful and influential.

Read Special-Purpose Maps

Some maps show specific kinds of information. These special-purpose maps may show features such as climate zones, ancient trade routes, economic and government data, geographic patterns, or population. Locating and interpreting information from visuals, including special-purpose maps, is an important research skill. Practice this skill as you study the map on this page.

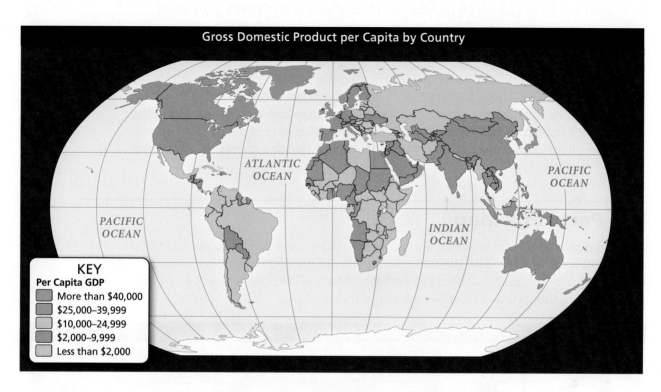

Gross Domestic Product per Capita by Country

KEY
Per Capita GDP
- More than $40,000
- $25,000–39,999
- $10,000–24,999
- $2,000–9,999
- Less than $2,000

[1.] Identify the title and determine the purpose of a map. A map's title can help you identify the region covered by the map. The title may also tell you the purpose of the map. If the map has no title, see what information the map shows to determine its purpose.

[2.] Use the map key to make sense of symbols and colors on a map. A key or legend often appears in a small box near the edge of the map. The key will tell you the meaning of colors, symbols, or other patterns on the map. Special-purpose maps use these colors and symbols to present information.

PEARSON
realize™

www.PearsonRealize.com
View Video Tutorials and other
21st Century Skills

[3.] Draw conclusions about the region shown on a map. Once you understand all the symbols and colors on the map, you can use appropriate skills, including reading and mathematical skills, to analyze and interpret social studies information such as maps. You can pose and answer questions about geographic patterns and distributions that are shown on maps. For example, a precipitation or climate map will show you which areas get lots of rainfall and which are very dry. You can evaluate government and economic data using maps. For example, a population map will show you which regions have lots of people and which have small, scattered populations. A historical map will show you the locations of ancient empires or trade routes. Thematic maps focus on a single theme or topic about a region. For example, you can interpret information from a thematic map representing various aspects of Texas during the nineteenth or twentieth century by studying the Great Military Map, which shows forts established in Texas during the nineteenth century, or by studying a map covering Texas during the Great Depression and World War II. By mapping this kind of detailed information, special-purpose maps can help you understand a region's history or geography.

Use Parts of a Map

If you understand how to organize and interpret information from visuals, including maps, you will be able to find the information you are looking for. Understanding how to use the parts of a map will help you better understand various types of economic data. Practice this skill as you study the map on this page.

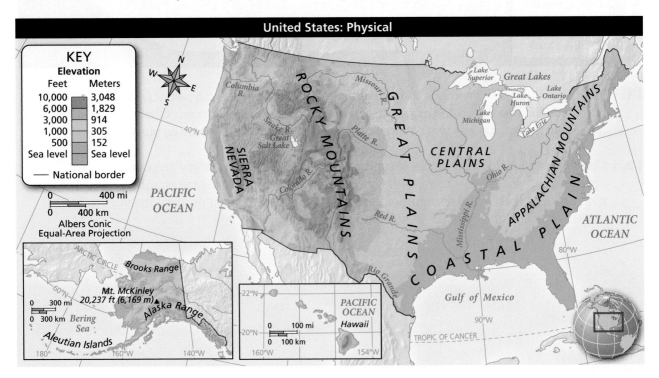

[**1.**] Identify the title and region of a map. Use appropriate reading skills to interpret social studies information such as map labels. A map's title can help you
to identify the region covered by the map. The title may also tell you the type of
information you will find on the map. If the map has no title, you can identify the
region by reading the labels on the map.

[**2.**] Use the compass rose to determine direction. Although on most maps north is at
the top of the map, you should always double check the compass rose. Often, on
the compass rose, the first letter of each direction represents that direction. For
example, "N" represents the direction "north." Some compass roses are as simple
as an arrow pointing north.

[**3.**] Use the scale to estimate the distance between places. Use appropriate
mathematical skills to interpret social studies information such as a map scale.
The scale on a map shows how a measurement on the map compares to the
distance on the ground. For example, if one inch on the map represents a mile,
the number of inches between two places on the map is the distance in miles.

[**4.**] Use the key or legend on a map to find information about colors or symbols on a
map. A key or legend often appears in a small box near the edge of the map. The
legend will tell you the meaning of colors, symbols, or other patterns on the map.

[**5.**] Use the latitude and longitude grid to determine absolute locations. An absolute
location is an exact description of a location on Earth's surface based on latitude
and longitude. You can use the latitude and longitude lines on a map to find the
absolute location of a place.

Analyze Primary and Secondary Sources

Primary sources are firsthand accounts of events. By contrast, secondary sources
are secondhand accounts of events. Both sources are useful, but it is important to
differentiate between valid primary and secondary sources. In this lesson, you'll learn
how to locate and use primary and secondary sources to acquire information about the
United States. Practice this skill by analyzing the two images below and distinguishing
between the primary and the secondary sources.

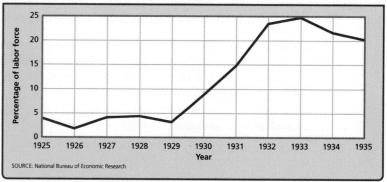

United States Unemployment Rate, 1925–1935

SOURCE: National Bureau of Economic Research

[1.] Determine who created the source as well as when and why it was created. Determine whether it is a primary or secondary source. Identify the author of the document. Next, look for the date the document was written or the date when the document was first published. Most primary sources are written close to the date of the events described. Secondary sources are often written well after the events described. Firsthand observers or participants in an event create primary sources. People who did not witness an event create secondary sources. Primary sources record an event. Secondary sources analyze or draw conclusions about events. Secondary sources rely on both primary and secondary sources. Good research requires you to analyze and evaluate the validity of information, arguments, and counterarguments from a primary or secondary source for frame of reference.

[2.] Identify the main idea and supporting details, and determine whether they are facts or opinions. Read the text carefully and ask yourself, "What point is this text making?" This point is the main idea. Then reread the text and list details that support this main idea. Decide whether these details are facts or opinions. If the details are facts, it should be possible to confirm them in other sources. If the author uses emotional language that shows feelings, the supporting details are probably opinions. Carefully analyze and evaluate the validity of information, arguments, and counterarguments from primary and secondary sources for point of view.

[3.] Decide whether the source's information is biased or if it is accurate and credible. Check statements in the text against reliable sources, such as encyclopedias or books written by experts on the topic. If reliable sources agree with the text, it is probably fairly accurate. If most of the text seems to be opinions rather than facts, it is not an accurate source of information. Still, these opinions can teach you about the author's world. A writer who observed an exciting or scary event may use emotional language to describe the event, but the source may still be a reliable account. An important part of research is analyzing and evaluating the validity of the information, arguments, and counterarguments from primary and secondary sources for bias or propaganda.

Compare Viewpoints

When people disagree about a topic, they have different viewpoints. Knowing how to analyze and evaluate the validity of information, arguments, and counterarguments from both primary and secondary sources for point of view can help you to learn more about a topic. Practice this skill by reading the following quotes and comparing the viewpoints.

> "A college degree is worth it. College graduates make an average of 84 percent more over the course of a lifetime than those who only attend high school. The unemployment rate for young college grads is under 5 percent compared to more than 13 percent for those with only a high school diploma."
>
> –Julie Margetta Morgan, Policy Analyst with the Postsecondary Education Program at the Center for American Progress

"For many students, the investment in college is not profitable. About 40 percent do not make it through a four-year bachelor's degree program in even six years. Others who major in subjects with low vocational demands often have trouble getting jobs."

–Richard Vedder, Director of Center for College Affordability and Productivity

[1.] Identify the authors of texts presenting different points of view and identify each author's frame of reference. Frame of reference is a term that describes the experiences, values, and ideas that influence a person's opinions and actions. It can also be referred to as *point of view*. First, identify the group or individual that wrote each text. Determine if the source is primary or secondary. As you read, take note of any information about the author's experiences or background. Also, look for any signs of what the author thinks is important. These types of statements can help you analyze and evaluate the validity of information, arguments, and counterarguments from both primary and secondary sources for point of view.

[2.] Recognize any similarities and differences between the authors' frames of reference and identify the opinion of each author. Pay attention to any similarities and differences between the two authors' experiences, values, and ideas. Read carefully to identify the opinion of each author. In an article about a rock band, an author who played guitar in a band for ten years argues that Band A is the best band today because of its great guitarist. In a second article, another author who sang for many years argues that Band B is the best because of its lead singer. Notice how authors' arguments and counterarguments are shaped by their frame of reference, or point of view.

[3.] Draw conclusions about similarities and differences between authors' points of view. With some information about the point of view of each author, you can understand why they have different opinions. This helps you to analyze and evaluate the validity of the information, arguments, and counterarguments. In the example of the two authors writing about rock bands, each author stresses his or her own areas of expertise. You might decide to listen to the band recommended by the singer if you share an interest in vocals. If you are more interested in instrumentals, you might choose the band recommended by the guitarist.

Identify Bias

Being able to analyze and evaluate the validity of information, arguments, and counterarguments for bias helps you to determine whether primary or secondary sources you find online, in books, or in the media are reliable. When you are able to identify bias in written, oral, and visual material, you can see when someone is presenting only one side of an issue or basing an argument on emotion instead of facts. Practice this skill whenever you read or hear a politician describing an economic policy.

[1.] Identify the author of a source and the author's purpose. First, identify the author of the source. The author may be a group or an organization rather than a single person. The author may state his or her purpose very clearly in the source. If not, the type of source may give you an idea of the purpose. For example, the writer of an encyclopedia aims to summarize information about a subject. The author of a political Web site may want you to vote for a candidate.

[2.] Identify the main idea, and check whether the main idea is supported with facts or opinions. Read the document carefully and ask yourself, "What is the main point of this selection?" Your answer to this question is the main idea. Reread the document and list details that support this main idea. Decide whether these details are facts or opinions. To find out whether they are facts, check whether other reliable sources include the same information. If your source uses statements that shows feelings, those statements are probably opinions.

[3.] Look for the use of emotional language or one-sided opinions. Look for words that can show opinions such as "good" and "bad." Be aware of statements that make you feel angry, scared, or excited. Also, watch out for statements that only express one side of an issue. These are all signs of bias.

[4.] Draw conclusions about the author's bias, if any. Is the author using mostly emotional language with few facts to support his or her ideas? Are there insults or other very negative language in the source? If so, the source is probably biased. Similarly, if you notice that the author is presenting only one side of an issue, the source is probably not reliable. It is important to analyze and evaluate the information, arguments, and counterarguments in both primary and secondary sources for bias.

Evaluate Existing Arguments

When you evaluate existing arguments, you must evaluate and analyze the point of view and biases of your sources and their authors. Who is the author and what is he or she trying to accomplish? How valid are the arguments in your primary and secondary sources? If you master these skills, you will be able to analyze and interpret social studies information such as speeches. Practice this skill as you read and evaluate the this excerpt.

> . . . Independence for the Gold Coast was my aim. It was a colony, and I have always regarded colonialism as the policy by which a foreign power binds territories to herself by political ties with the primary object of promoting her own economic advantage. . . .
>
> I saw that the whole solution to [our] problem lay in political freedom for our people, for it is only when a people are politically free that other races can give them the respect that is due to them. . . .

Once this freedom is gained, a greater task comes into view. All dependent territories are backward in education, in science, in agriculture, and in industry. The economic independence that should follow and maintain political independence demands every effort from the people, a total mobilization of brain and manpower resources. What other countries have taken three hundred years or more to achieve, a once dependent territory must try to accomplish in a generation if it is to survive. . . .

—Kwame Nkrumah, Ghana: *The Autobiography of Kwame Nkrumah*, 1957

[1.] Identify the claim or thesis. What is the author or source claiming? The claim or thesis is usually found in the introduction and/or conclusion of a written or spoken argument.

[2.] Identify the reasons (claims to truth or facts) the author offers in support of his or her claim. What evidence does the author or source provide to support their claims? Make a list of the evidence provided to support each claim.

[3.] Evaluate the argument. Analyze and evaluate the validity of the evidence presented to support each claim. Use the appropriate skills to analyze and interpret social studies information, such as speeches. Research each claim to be sure that the author's statements are accurate. Carefully check for evidence of bias or propaganda. Be sure you understand the author's point of view and his or her frame of reference. Finally, check to be sure that the author's conclusions follow logically from the evidence presented. If the evidence is accurate, the author is free from bias, and conclusions follow logically from the evidence, the claims are probably valid.

Consider and Counter Opposing Arguments

Before you can effectively counter opposing arguments, you'll need to analyze possible counterarguments for frame of reference, bias, point of view, and propaganda. You'll plan your response ahead of time, collecting research and data. Then, you'll make a point of acknowledging the opposing view before presenting your counterarguments. To practice this skill, suppose you are preparing for a debate about raising the minimum wage in your state. Choose a side of the debate to support. What arguments will you use to support your side of the debate? What counterarguments will you anticipate the other side using? Why is it useful to anticipate the other side's arguments?

[1.] Fully understand your argument and the potential counter points. Do research as needed to find out more about other opposing views. Analyze and evaluate the validity of possible counterarguments from primary and secondary sources for frame of reference, bias, point of view, and propaganda.

[2.] Make predictions and outline a response to several of the opposing views. Continue researching as needed. Researching, analyzing, and evaluating the validity of opposing arguments will help you support and strengthen your own. Opposing arguments can consist of any reasons, conclusions, or claims that oppose yours. Outline your response to each opposing reason, conclusion, or claim.

[3.] To counter an opposing argument, first acknowledge the opposing view. This strategy shows that you have heard the opposing argument and are responding accordingly. Consider using statements such as "I understand your point, but you should also consider the following..." You can also respond by refuting facts, logic, etc. Be sure to respond to each opposing argument. Ignoring or dismissing a counterargument shows that your response is weak and unsupported.

Participate in a Discussion or Debate

When you participate in a discussion or debate, your goal is to explain, analyze, and defend a point of view—often related to a current political or economic issue. To be a successful debater, you'll do your research, present your position, and defend your point of view in a courteous manner. Use the steps below to prepare for a discussion on this question: Overall, is the United States economy improving or not?

[1.] Research. Before participating in a discussion or debate, do research to gain knowledge of your subject so that you may be an informed and prepared participant. Take notes as needed to help you prepare. Jot down main points and any questions you may have. As you research, decide where you might stand on the issue. Be sure to gather research and sources that will allow you to explain, analyze, and defend your point of view.

[2.] Present your position. After you have organized your thoughts and decided where you stand, explain and defend your point of view. Be sure to stay focused on the topic and your line of argument. Ask questions that challenge the accuracy, logic, or relevance of opposing views.

[3.] During the discussion or debate, be patient and courteous. Listen attentively, be respectful and supportive of peers, and speak only when instructed to do so by the moderator. Be sure to allow others to express their views; do not monopolize the debate or discussion. Speak clearly and slowly.

Give an Effective Presentation

When you create a written, visual, and oral presentation, you teach, convince, or share information with an audience. Effective presentations use both words and visuals to engage audiences. Delivery is also important. For example, you can use the way you move, speak, and look at the audience to keep people interested. Use the steps below to prepare and deliver a presentation on key economic indicators.

[1.] Identify the purpose of your presentation and your audience. Think about the purpose of your written, visual, and oral presentation. If this is a research report, you will need facts and data to support your points. If you are trying to persuade your audience, look for powerful photos. Keep your audience in mind. Consider their interests and present your topic in a way that will engage them.

[2.] Write the text and find visual aids for your presentation. Look online and in books and magazines for information and images for your presentation. Organize the information and write it up carefully so that it is easy for your audience to understand. Diagrams can show complicated information in a clear way. Visuals also get people interested in the presentation. So choose large, colorful images that people in the back of the audience will be able to see.

[3.] Practice and work to improve your presentation. Keep practicing your oral presentation until you know the material well. Then, practice some more, focusing on improving your delivery.

[4.] Use body language, tone of voice, and eye contact to deliver an effective presentation. Answer questions if the audience has them. At the beginning of your oral presentation, take a breath, smile, and stand up tall. Speak more loudly and more clearly than you would in normal conversation. Also, try not to rush through the presentation. Glance at your notes but speak naturally, rather than reading. Look at people in the audience. If people are confused, pause to clarify. Finally, leave time for people in the audience to ask questions.

Write an Essay

There are four steps to writing an essay. You'll start by selecting a topic and research sources, then you'll write an outline and develop a thesis or point of view. After drafting your essay, you'll carefully proofread it to be sure you've used standard grammar, spelling, sentence structure, and punctuation. Finally, you'll revise and polish your work. To practice this skill, select a topic that interests you about the U.S. economy and develop a thesis. Then explain to a partner the steps you will take to write your essay.

[1.] Choose your topic and research sources. Check which types of sources you will need. Gather different types of reliable sources that support the argument you will be making.

[2.] Write an outline and generate a thesis. First write your topic at the top of the page then list all the points or arguments you want to make about the topic; also list the facts and examples that support these points. Your thesis statement will inform the reader of the point you are making and what question you will be answering about the topic. When writing your thesis, be as specific as possible and address one main idea.

[3.] Draft your essay. After finishing your research and outline, begin writing the body of your essay; start with the introduction then write a paragraph for each of your supporting points, followed by a conclusion. As you write, do your best to use standard grammar, spelling, sentence structure, and punctuation. Be sure any terminology is used correctly.

[4.] Revise. An important part of the writing process involves checking for areas in which information should be added, removed, or rewritten. Try to imagine that this paper belongs to someone else. Does the paper have a clear thesis? Do all of the ideas relate back to the thesis? Read your paper out loud and listen for awkward pauses and unclear ideas. Lastly, check for mistakes in standard grammar, spelling, sentence structure, punctuation, and usage.

Avoid Plagiarism

When you don't attribute ideas and information to source materials and authors, you are plagiarizing. Plagiarizing–claiming others' ideas and information as your own–is considered unethical. You can avoid plagiarizing by carefully noting down which authors and sources you'll be using, citing those authors and sources in your paper, and listing them in a bibliography. To practice this skill, suppose you have been assigned to write a research paper on the causes of the U.S. trade deficit. Name three types of sources you might use to help you gather information. Explain how you will avoid plagiarism when you use these sources.

[1.] Keep a careful log of your notes. As you read sources to gain background information on your topic, keep track of ideas and information and the sources and authors they come from. Write down the name of each source next to your notes from that particular source so you can remember to cite it later on. Create a separate section in your notes where you keep your own thoughts and ideas so you know which ideas are your own. Using someone else's words or paraphrasing their ideas does not make them yours.

[2.] Cite sources in your paper. You must identify the source materials and authors you use to support your ideas. Whenever you use statistics, facts, direct quotations, or paraphrases of others' views, you need to attribute them to your source. Cite your sources within the body of your paper. Check your assignment to find out how they should be formatted.

[3.] List your sources in a bibliography at the end of your paper. List your source materials and authors cited in alphabetical order by author, using accepted formats. As you work, be sure to check your list of sources from your notes so that none are left out of the bibliography.

Solve Problems

Problem solving is a skill that you use every day. It is a process that requires an open mind, clear thinking, and action. Suppose you found out that, compared to others in your company, you were being underpaid for the work you do. Practice this skill by using these steps to solve the problem of gaining a fair wage for yourself.

[1.] Understand the problem. Before trying to solve a problem, make sure that you gather as much information as possible in order to identify the problem. What are the causes and effects of the problem? Who is involved? You will want to make sure that you understand different perspectives on the problem. Try not to jump to conclusions or make assumptions. You might end up misunderstanding the problem.

[2.] Consider possible solutions and choose the best one. Once you have identified the problem and gathered some information, list and consider a number of possible options. Right away, one solution might seem like the right one, but try to think of other solutions. Be sure to consider carefully the advantages and disadvantages of each option. It can help to take notes listing benefits and drawbacks. Look for the solution whose benefits outweigh its drawbacks. After considering each option, choose the solution you think is best.

[3.] Make and implement a plan. Choose and implement a solution. Make a detailed, step-by-step plan to implement the solution that you choose. Write your plan down and assign yourself a deadline for each step. That will help you to stay on track toward completing your plan. Try to think of any problems that might come up and what you will do to address those problems. Of course, there are many things that you cannot predict. Stay flexible. Evaluate the effectiveness of the solution and adjust your plan as necessary.

Make Decisions

Everyone makes decisions. The trick is to learn how to make good decisions. How can you make good decisions? First, identify a situation that requires a decision and gather information. Then, identify possible options and predict the consequences of each option. Finally, choose the best option and take action to implement a decision. Consider the benefits of getting a job: you gain experience and earn money. The trade-off, or cost, is that you give up time that you could spend studying, playing sports, or just relaxing. Practice this skill by using these steps to decide how to spend your allowance or earnings from a part time job.

[1.] Determine the options between which you must decide. In some cases, like ordering from a menu at a restaurant, your options may be clear. In other cases, you will need to identify a situation that requires a decision, gather information, and identify the options that are available to you. Spend some time thinking about the situation and brainstorm a number of options. If necessary, do a little research to find more options. Make a list of options that you might choose.

[2.] Review the costs and benefits of each option. Carefully predict the consequences of each option. You may want to make a cost-benefit list for each option. To do this, write down the option and then draw two columns underneath it. One column will be the "pro" or benefit list. The other column will be the "con" or cost list. Note the pros and cons for each of your options. Try not to rush through this process. For a very important decision, you may even want to show your list to someone you trust. This person can help you think of costs and benefits that you had not considered.

[3.] Determine the best option and act on it. Look through your cost-benefit lists. Note any especially serious costs. If an option has the possibility of an extremely negative consequence, you might want to cross it off your list right away. Look closely at the options with the most benefits and the fewest costs, and choose the one that you think is best. Once you have made a choice, take action to implement a decision. If necessary, make a detailed plan with clear steps. Set a deadline to complete the steps to keep yourself moving toward your goal.

Being an Informed Citizen

Informed citizens understand the responsibilities, duties, and obligations of citizenship. They are well informed about civic affairs, involved with their communities, and politically active. When it comes to issues they personally care about, they take a stand and reach out to others.

[1.] Learn the issues. A great way to begin to understand the responsibilities of citizenship is to first find topics of interest to you. Next, become well informed about civic affairs in your town, city, or country. Read newspapers, magazines, and articles you find online about events happening in your area or around the world. Analyze the information you read to come to your own conclusions. Radio programs, podcasts, and social media are also great ways to keep up with current events and interact with others about issues.

[2.] Get involved. Attend community events to speak with others who know the issues. Become well informed about how policies are made and changed. Find out who to speak to if you would like to take part in civic affairs and policy creation. There are government websites that can help direct you to the right person. These websites will also provide his or her contact details.

[3.] Take a stand and reach out. Write, call, or meet with your elected officials to become a better informed, more responsible citizen. Do research about candidates who are running for office to be an informed voter. Start your own blog or website to explore issues, interact with others, and be part of the community or national dialogue.

Political Participation

Political participation starts with an understanding of the responsibilities, duties and obligations of citizenship, such as serving the public good. When you understand your role as a political participant, you can get involved through volunteering for a political campaign, running for office, or interacting with others in person or online.

[1.] Volunteer for a political campaign. Political campaigns offer a wide variety of opportunities to help you become involved in the political process and become a responsible citizen by serving the public good. As a political campaign volunteer you may have the opportunity to attend events, make calls to voters, and explore your community while getting to know how other voters think about the responsibilities, duties, and obligations of citizenship.

[2.] Run for office in your school or community. A good way to become involved in your school or community is to run for office. Student council or community positions offer a great opportunity for you to become familiar with the campaign and election process.

[3.] Reach out to others. Start or join an interest group. Interest groups enable people to work together on common goals related to the political process. Write a letter or email to a public official. By contacting an elected official from your area, you can either support or oppose laws or policies. You can also ask for help or support regarding certain issues.

[4.] Interact online. Social networking sites and blogs offer a great way for people of all ages to interact and write about political issues. As you connect with others, you'll become more confident in your role as a citizen working for the public good.

Voting

Voting is not only a right. It is also one of the primary responsibilities, duties, and obligations of citizenship. Before you can legally vote, however, you must understand the voter registration process and the criteria for voting in elections. You should also understand the issues and know where different candidates stand on those issues.

[1.] Check eligibility and residency requirements. In order to vote in the United States, you must be a United States citizen who is 18 years or older, and you must be a resident of the place where you plan to vote.

[2.] Register to vote. You cannot vote until you understand the voter registration process. You can register at city or town election offices, or when you get a driver's license. You can also register by mail or online. You may also have the option of registering at the polls on Election Day, but this does not apply in all states. Make sure to find out what you need to do to register in your state, as well as the deadline for registering. You may have the option of declaring a political party when registering.

[**3.**] Learn the issues. As the election approaches, research the candidates and issues in order to be an informed voter. Watch televised debates, if there are any. You can also review the candidates' websites. By doing these things and thinking critically about what you learn, you will be prepared to exercise your responsibility, duty and obligation as a United States citizen.

[**4.**] Vote. Make sure to arrive at the correct polling place on Election Day to cast your ballot. Research to find out when the polls will be open. Advance voting, absentee voting, and voting by mail are also options in certain states for those who qualify.

Serving on a Jury

As an American, you need to understand the duties, obligations and responsibilities of citizenship; among these is the expectation that you may be required to serve on a jury. You will receive a written notice when you are summoned to jury duty and you'll receive instruction on the special duties and obligations of a juror. You'll follow the American code of justice which assumes that a person is innocent until proven guilty, and you'll follow instructions about keeping trial information confidential.

[**1.**] Wait to receive notification. If you are summoned to serve as a juror, you will be first notified by mail. If you are chosen to move on to the jury selection phase, lawyers from both sides will ask you questions as they select the final jury members. It is an honor to serve as a juror, as it is a responsibility offered only to American citizens.

[**2.**] Follow the law and remain impartial. Your job is to determine whether or not someone broke the law. You may also be asked to sit on the jury for civil cases (as opposed to criminal cases); these cases involve lawsuits filed against individuals or businesses for any perceived wrong doing (such as broken contracts, trespassing, discrimination, etc.). Be sure to follow the law as it is explained to you, regardless of whether you approve of the law or not. Your decision about the trial should not be influenced by any personal bias or views you may have.

[**3.**] Remember that the defendant is presumed innocent. In a criminal trial, the defendant must be proven guilty "beyond a reasonable doubt" for the verdict to be guilty. If the trial team fails to prove the defendant to be guilty beyond a reasonable doubt, the jury verdict must be "not guilty."

[**4.**] During the trial, respect the court's right to privacy. As a juror, you have specific duties, obligations, and responsibilities under the law. Do not permit anyone to talk about the case with you or in your presence, except with the court's permission. Avoid media coverage once the trial has begun so as to prevent bias. Keep an open mind and do not form or state any opinions about the case until you have heard all of the evidence, the closing arguments from the lawyers, and the judge's instructions on the applicable law.

Paying Taxes

Paying taxes is one of the responsibilities of citizenship. How do you go about figuring out how much you've already paid in taxes and how much you still owe? It's your duty and obligation to find out, by determining how much has been deducted from your pay and filing your tax return.

[1.] Find out how taxes are deducted from your pay. In the United States, payroll taxes are imposed on employers and employees, and they are collected and paid by the employers. Check your pay stub to find out how much money was deducted for taxes. Be sure to also save the W-2 tax form your employer sends to you. You will need this form later on when filing your tax paperwork. Also save any interest income statements. All this information will help you fulfill your obligation as an American taxpayer.

[2.] Check the sales taxes in your state. All but five states impose sales and use taxes on retail sale, lease, and rental of many goods, as well as some services. Sales tax is calculated as the purchase price times the appropriate tax rate. Tax rates vary widely from less than one percent to over ten percent. Sales tax is collected by the seller at the time of sale.

[3.] File your tax return. Filing your tax return is more than an obligation: it's also a duty and responsibility of citizenship. You may receive tax forms in the mail, or pick them up at the local Post Office or library. Fill the forms in and then mail or electronically send completed tax forms and any necessary payments to the Internal Revenue Service (IRS) and your state's department of revenue. The IRS provides free resources to help people prepare and electronically file their tax returns; go to IRS.gov to learn more. Note: certain things such as charitable donations and business expenses are tax deductible.

PEARSON
realize™

www.PearsonRealize.com
View Video Tutorials and other
21st Century Skills

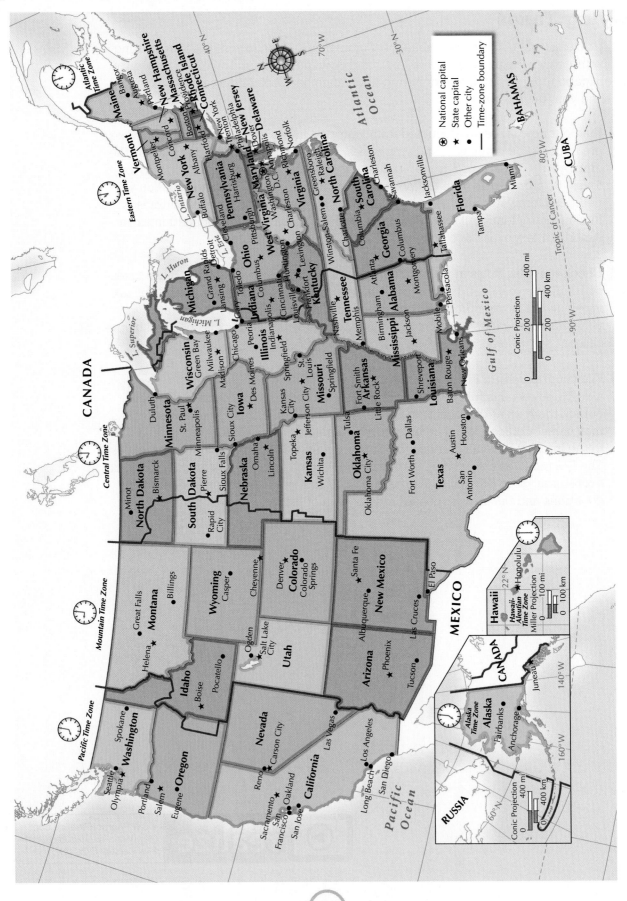

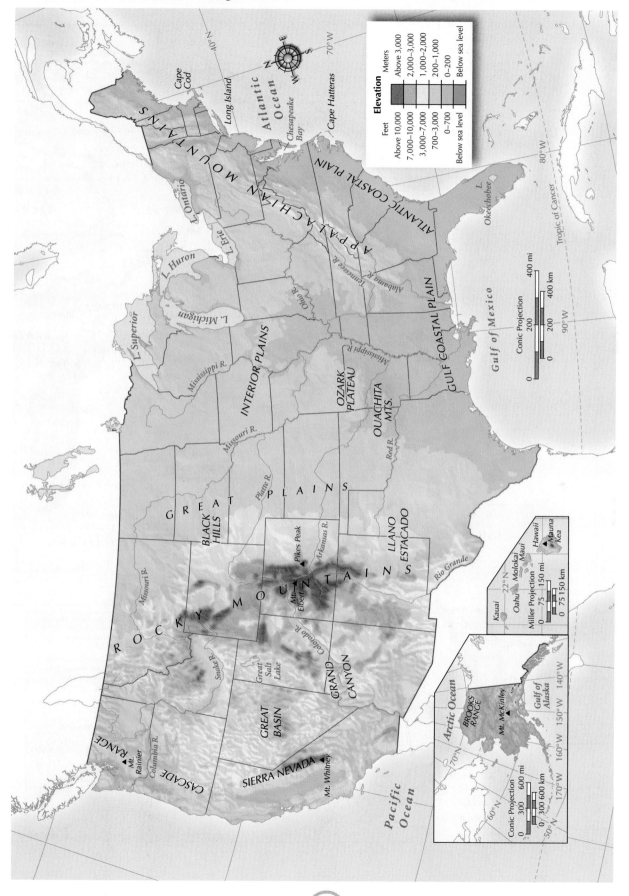

160°W 140°W 120°W 100°W 80°W 60°W

80°N

Alaska
(United States)

60°N

CANADA

**NORTH
AMERICA**

Toronto

Chicago   New York

40°N

UNITED STATES   Washington, D.C.

*Atlantic
Ocean*

Los Angeles

Houston

Hawaii
(United States)   Tropic of Cancer   **MEXICO**   see inset below

20°N

Mexico City

*Pacific
Ocean*

Galápagos
Islands   Bogotá   French Guiana
(Ecuador)   **COLOMBIA**   (France)

0°   Equator   Line Islands   **SURINAME**
(United States)   **ECUADOR**

PERU   **BRAZIL**
**SOUTH
AMERICA**

American Samoa
(United States)   **BOLIVIA**   Rio de
Janeiro

SAMOA

20°S   **PARAGUAY**   São Paulo
French Polynesia
(France)   Tropic of Capricorn   **CHILE**
TONGA   Pitcairn Islands   **ARGENTINA**
(U.K.)   **URUGUAY**
Buenos Aires

⊗ Capital
• Other city

40°S

160°W   140°W   120°W   100°W   80°W   60°W   40°

60°S

Antarctic Circle   *Southern Ocean*

80°S

90°W   85°W   80°W

Gulf of Mexico   **UNITED
STATES**   B
A
H
A
M
A
S   *Southern Ocean*

25°N   N
W   E
Tropic of Cancer   S

Turks and
Caicos Islands
(U.K.)   St. Martin (St. Maarten)
U.S. Virgin British Virgin   (France & Neth. Antilles)
20°N   **CUBA**   Islands Islands Anguilla   **ANTIGUA AND**
(U.S.)   (U.K.)   (U.K.)   **BARBUDA**
Cayman Islands   **HAITI**   Montserrat (U.K.)
(U.K.)   Puerto Rico   **ST. KITTS**   Guadeloupe (France)
MEXICO   **JAMAICA**   (U.S.)   **AND NEVIS**   **DOMINICA**
DOMINICAN
BELIZE   **REPUBLIC**   Martinique (France)
GUATEMALA   *Caribbean Sea*   **ST. LUCIA**   **BARBADOS**
15°N   **ST. VINCENT AND THE GRENADINES**
HONDURAS
EL SALVADOR   Conic Projection   **GRENADA**
0   200   400 mi   Aruba (Neth.)   Netherlands   **TRINIDAD**
NICARAGUA   Antilles   **AND TOBAGO**
0   200   400 km   75°W   (Neth.)
10°N   Caracas   60°W
*Pacific
Ocean*   **COSTA RICA**   **COLOMBIA**   *Lake
Maracaibo*   **VENEZUELA**
PANAMA   **SOUTH AMERICA**   **GUYANA**

90°W   85°W   80°W

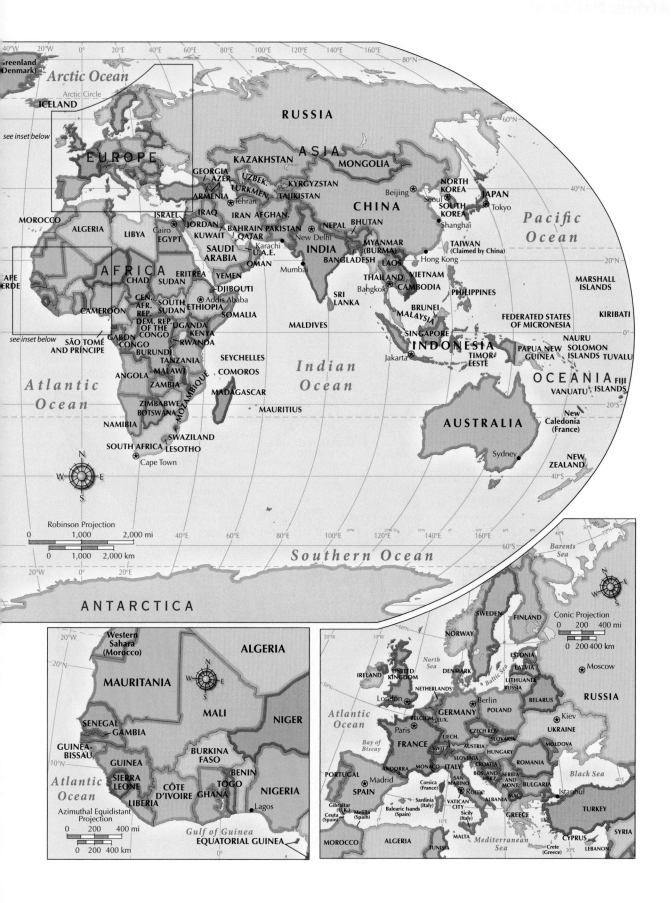

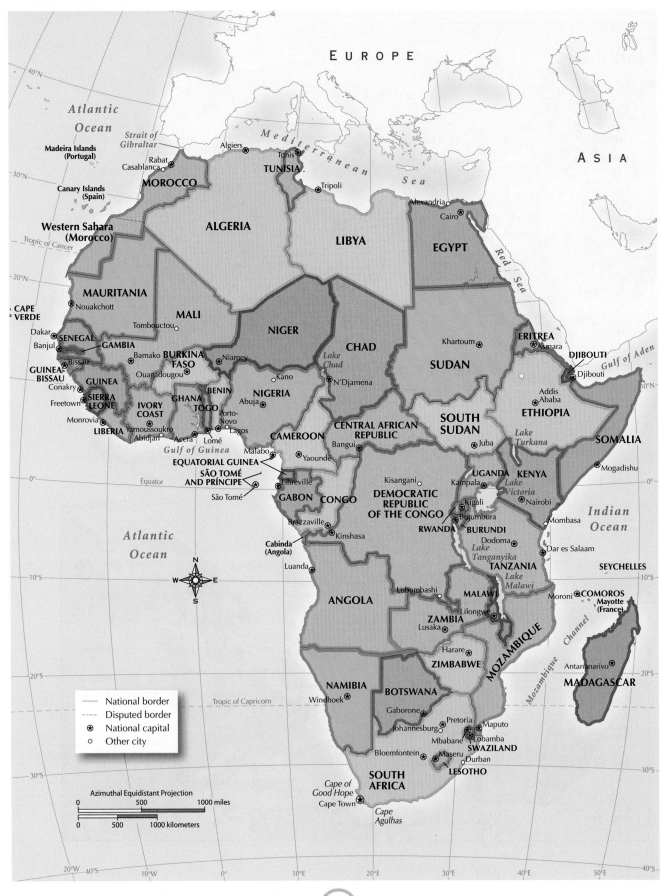

EUROPE

ASIA

Atlantic Ocean

Mediterranean Sea

Strait of Gibraltar

Madeira Islands (Portugal)

Algiers ⊛

Tunis ⊛

TUNISIA

Rabat ⊛
Casablanca ⊛

MOROCCO

Tripoli ⊛

Alexandria ○

Cairo ⊛

Red Sea

Canary Islands (Spain)

ALGERIA

LIBYA

EGYPT

Tropic of Cancer

Western Sahara (Morocco)

MAURITANIA

Nouakchott ⊛

MALI

Tombouctou ○

NIGER

CHAD

Khartoum ⊛

ERITREA

Asmara ⊛

DJIBOUTI

Gulf of Aden

⊛ CAPE VERDE

Dakar ⊛

SENEGAL

Banjul ⊛

GAMBIA

Bamako ○

BURKINA FASO

Ouagadougou ⊛

Niamey ⊛

Kano ○

Lake Chad

N'Djamena ⊛

SUDAN

Djibouti ⊛

GUINEA-BISSAU

Bissau ⊛

GUINEA

Conakry ⊛

SIERRA LEONE

Freetown ⊛

IVORY COAST

GHANA

TOGO

BENIN

NIGERIA

Abuja ⊛

Addis Ababa ⊛

ETHIOPIA

Monrovia ⊛

LIBERIA

Yamoussoukro ○

Abidjan ⊛

Accra ⊛

Lomé ⊛

Porto-Novo ⊛

Lagos ○

CAMEROON

CENTRAL AFRICAN REPUBLIC

Bangui ⊛

SOUTH SUDAN

Juba ⊛

Lake Turkana

SOMALIA

Mogadishu ⊛

Gulf of Guinea

Malabo ⊛

Yaoundé ⊛

EQUATORIAL GUINEA

SÃO TOMÉ AND PRÍNCIPE

Libreville ⊛

Kisangani ○

UGANDA

Kampala ⊛

Lake Victoria

KENYA

Nairobi ⊛

Equator

São Tomé ○

GABON

CONGO

DEMOCRATIC REPUBLIC OF THE CONGO

Kigali ⊛

Bujumbura ⊛

RWANDA

BURUNDI

Mombasa ○

Indian Ocean

Brazzaville ⊛

Kinshasa ⊛

Dodoma ⊛

Dar es Salaam ○

Atlantic Ocean

Cabinda (Angola)

Luanda ⊛

Lake Tanganyika

TANZANIA

Lake Malawi

SEYCHELLES

N
W ⊕ E
S

Lubumbashi ○

MALAWI

Moroni ⊛

COMOROS

Mayotte (France)

ANGOLA

Lilongwe ⊛

ZAMBIA

Lusaka ⊛

Mozambique Channel

Antananarivo ⊛

Harare ⊛

ZIMBABWE

MOZAMBIQUE

MADAGASCAR

NAMIBIA

BOTSWANA

Windhoek ⊛

Tropic of Capricorn

Gaborone ⊛

Pretoria ⊛

Maputo ⊛

Johannesburg ○

Mbabane ⊛

Lobamba ⊛

SWAZILAND

Bloemfontein ○

Maseru ⊛

Durban ○

LESOTHO

—— National border
------ Disputed border
⊛ National capital
○ Other city

SOUTH AFRICA

Cape of Good Hope

Cape Town ⊛

Cape Agulhas

Azimuthal Equidistant Projection

0   500   1000 miles

0   500   1000 kilometers

40°N 30°N 20°N 10°N 0° 10°S 20°S 30°S 40°S

20°W 10°W 0° 10°E 20°E 30°E 40°E 50°E

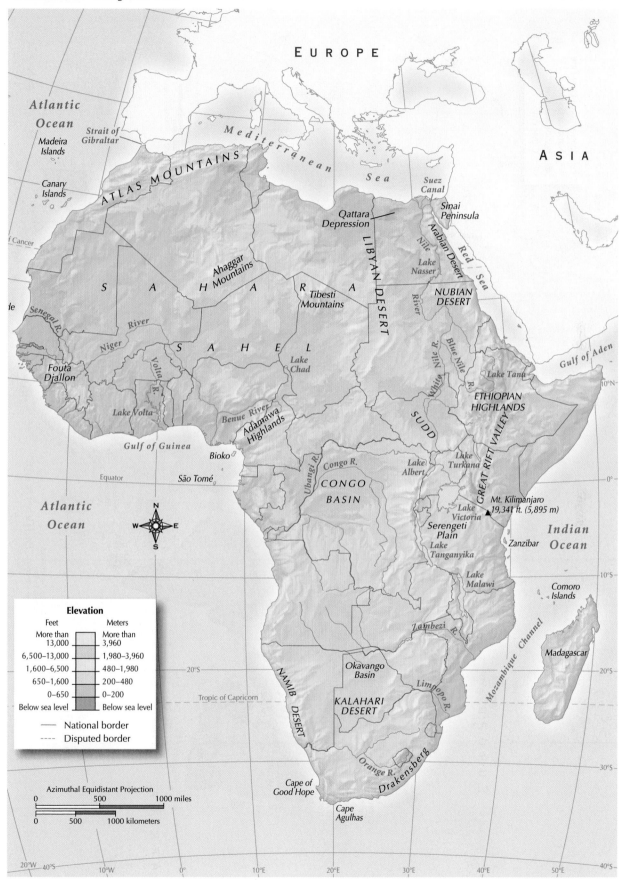

EUROPE

ASIA

Atlantic
Ocean

Madeira
Islands

Canary
Islands

Strait of
Gibraltar

Mediterranean
Sea

Suez
Canal

Sinai
Peninsula

Qattara
Depression

ATLAS MOUNTAINS

of Cancer

S A H

Ahaggar
Mountains

Tibesti
Mountains

LIBYAN DESERT

Nile

Arabian Desert

Red Sea

Lake
Nasser

NUBIAN
DESERT

Gulf of Aden

Senegal R.

River

Niger

River

S A H E L

Volta R.

Lake
Chad

Nile River

White Nile R.

Blue Nile R.

Lake Tana

10°N

ETHIOPIAN
HIGHLANDS

Fouta
Djallon

Lake Volta

Benue River

Adamawa
Highlands

SUDD

GREAT RIFT VALLEY

Gulf of Guinea

Bioko

Ubangi R.

Congo R.

Lake
Albert

Lake
Turkana

Equator

São Tomé

CONGO
BASIN

0°

Mt. Kilimanjaro
19,341 ft. (5,895 m)

Atlantic
Ocean

Lake
Victoria

Serengeti
Plain

Lake
Tanganyika

Zanzibar

Indian
Ocean

N
W   E
S

10°S

Lake
Malawi

Comoro
Islands

Mozambique Channel

Zambezi R.

Madagascar

Elevation

Feet		Meters
More than 13,000		More than 3,960
6,500–13,000		1,980–3,960
1,600–6,500		480–1,980
650–1,600		200–480
0–650		0–200
Below sea level		Below sea level

—— National border

------ Disputed border

20°S

Okavango
Basin

NAMIB DESERT

Limpopo R.

20°S

Tropic of Capricorn

KALAHARI
DESERT

Azimuthal Equidistant Projection

0   500   1000 miles

0   500   1000 kilometers

Orange R.

Drakensberg

30°S

Cape of
Good Hope

Cape
Agulhas

20°W   40°S   10°W   0°   10°E   20°E   30°E   40°E   50°E   40°S

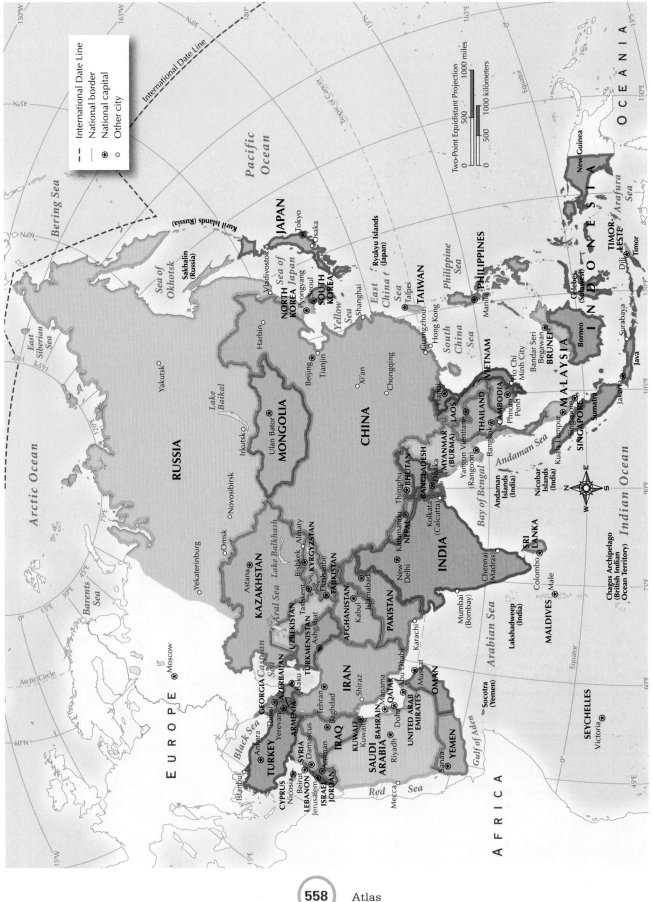

International Date Line
National border
National capital
Other city

Two-Point Equidistant Projection

Bering Sea

Pacific Ocean

Arctic Ocean

East Siberian Sea

Barents Sea

Sea of Okhotsk

Kuril Islands (Russia)

Sakhalin (Russia)

JAPAN
Tokyo
Osaka

Sea of Japan

NORTH KOREA
Pyongyang
Vladivostok

SOUTH KOREA
Seoul

Yellow Sea

East China Sea

Ryukyu Islands (Japan)

TAIWAN
Taipei

Philippine Sea

PHILIPPINES
Manila

OCEANIA

New Guinea

TIMOR-LESTE
Timor
Dili

Arafura Sea

INDONESIA

Celebes (Sulawesi)

Surabaya

Java

Jakarta

Borneo

BRUNEI
Bandar Seri Begawan

MALAYSIA
Kuala Lumpur
SINGAPORE
Singapore

Sumatra

RUSSIA

Yakutsk

Lake Baikal

Irkutsk

Harbin

Beijing
Tianjin

Shanghai

Xi'an
Chongqing

CHINA

Guangzhou
Hong Kong

South China Sea

VIETNAM
Hanoi
Ho Chi Minh City

Novosibirsk

Omsk

Ulan Bator

MONGOLIA

Yekaterinburg

Astana

KAZAKHSTAN

Aral Sea
Lake Balkhash

Bishkek
Almaty

KYRGYZSTAN

Tashkent
UZBEKISTAN

TAJIKISTAN
Dushanbe

Thimphu
BHUTAN

Kathmandu
NEPAL

Dhaka
BANGLADESH

MYANMAR (BURMA)
Yangon (Rangoon)

LAOS
Vientiane

THAILAND
Bangkok

CAMBODIA
Phnom Penh

Andaman Sea

Andaman Islands (India)

Nicobar Islands (India)

Kolkata (Calcutta)

New Delhi

INDIA

Chennai (Madras)

SRI LANKA
Colombo

Bay of Bengal

Turkmenistan
Ashgabat

AFGHANISTAN
Kabul

PAKISTAN
Islamabad

Karachi

Mumbai (Bombay)

Lakshadweep (India)

MALDIVES
Male

Chagos Archipelago (British Indian Ocean Territory)

Indian Ocean

SEYCHELLES
Victoria

Moscow

EUROPE

Arctic Circle

Baku
AZERBAIJAN

ARMENIA
Yerevan

GEORGIA
Tbilisi

Black Sea

Caspian Sea

IRAN
Tehran
Shiraz

Baghdad
IRAQ

KUWAIT
Kuwait

QATAR
Doha

BAHRAIN
Manama

Abu Dhabi

UNITED ARAB EMIRATES

OMAN
Muscat

Socotra (Yemen)

Arabian Sea

TURKEY
Ankara
Istanbul

CYPRUS
Nicosia

LEBANON
Beirut

SYRIA
Damascus

ISRAEL
Jerusalem

JORDAN
Amman

SAUDI ARABIA
Riyadh

Mecca

YEMEN
Sanaa

Red Sea

Gulf of Aden

AFRICA

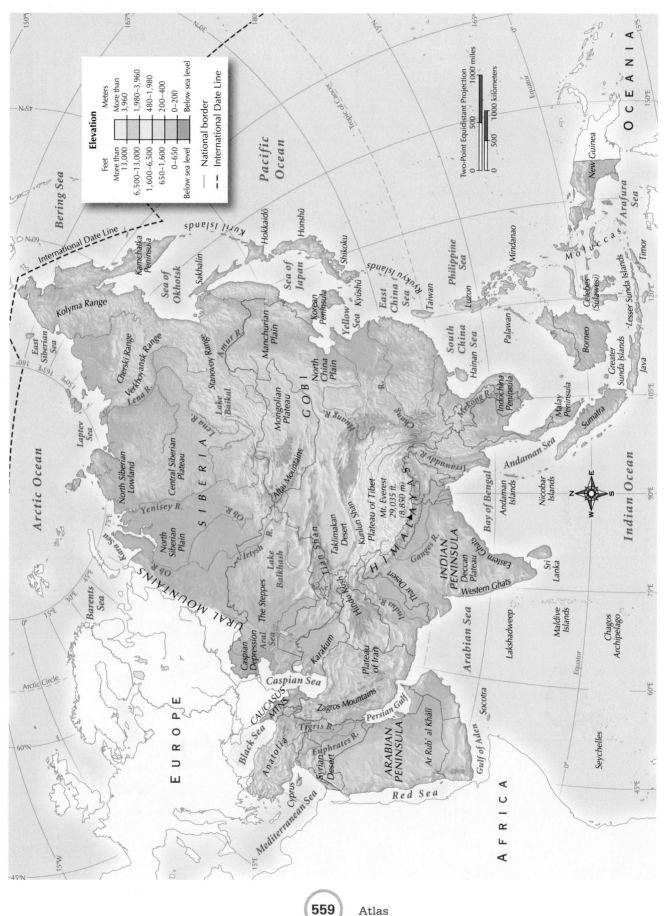

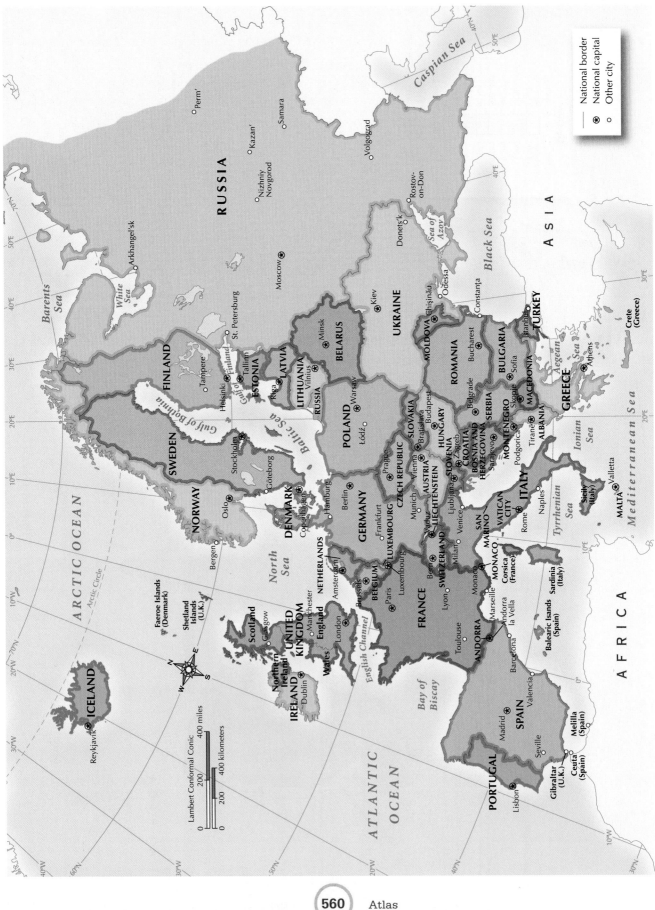

National border
National capital ⊛
Other city ○

Europe: Political

RUSSIA

Caspian Sea

Perm'

Kazan'

Samara

Nizhniy Novgorod

Volgograd

Rostov-on-Don

Arkhangel'sk

Barents Sea

White Sea

ASIA

Sea of Azov

Donets'k

Black Sea

Moscow ⊛

Kiev ⊛

UKRAINE

Odessa

Constanța

St. Petersburg

FINLAND

Gulf of Finland

Tampere

Helsinki ⊛

Tallinn ⊛

ESTONIA

LATVIA

Riga ⊛

Minsk ⊛

BELARUS

Chișinău ⊛

MOLDOVA

Bucharest ⊛

ROMANIA

Belgrade ⊛

BULGARIA

Sofia ⊛

Istanbul

TURKEY

GREECE

Athens ⊛

Aegean Sea

Crete (Greece)

LITHUANIA

Vilnius ⊛

RUSSIA

POLAND

Warsaw ⊛

Łódź

SLOVAKIA

Bratislava ⊛

HUNGARY

Budapest ⊛

SERBIA

CROATIA

Zagreb ⊛

BOSNIA AND HERZEGOVINA

Sarajevo ⊛

MONTENEGRO

Podgorica ⊛

Skopje ⊛

MACEDONIA

Tiranë ⊛

ALBANIA

Ionian Sea

Mediterranean Sea

SWEDEN

Stockholm ⊛

Göteborg

Gulf of Bothnia

Baltic Sea

NORWAY

Oslo ⊛

Bergen

DENMARK

Copenhagen ⊛

Hamburg

Berlin ⊛

GERMANY

Frankfurt

Prague ⊛

CZECH REPUBLIC

Munich

Vienna ⊛

AUSTRIA

LIECHTENSTEIN

Vaduz ⊛

SLOVENIA

Ljubljana ⊛

Venice

Milan

SAN MARINO

VATICAN CITY

Rome ⊛

ITALY

Naples

Tyrrhenian Sea

Sicily (Italy)

Valletta

MALTA

North Sea

NETHERLANDS

Amsterdam ⊛

Brussels ⊛

BELGIUM

LUXEMBOURG

Luxembourg ⊛

Paris ⊛

FRANCE

SWITZERLAND

Bern ⊛

Lyon

MONACO

Monaco ⊛

Marseille

Corsica (France)

Sardinia (Italy)

Balearic Islands (Spain)

Faeroe Islands (Denmark)

Shetland Islands (U.K.)

Scotland

Glasgow

Manchester

UNITED KINGDOM

England

London ⊛

English Channel

Wales

Northern Ireland

IRELAND

Dublin ⊛

Bay of Biscay

Toulouse

ANDORRA

Andorra la Vella ⊛

Barcelona

Valencia

SPAIN

Madrid ⊛

Seville

Melilla (Spain)

Ceuta (Spain)

Gibraltar (U.K.)

PORTUGAL

Lisbon ⊛

ICELAND

Reykjavik ⊛

ARCTIC OCEAN

Arctic Circle

ATLANTIC OCEAN

AFRICA

Lambert Conformal Conic

0   200   400 miles

0   200   400 kilometers

N
E
S
W

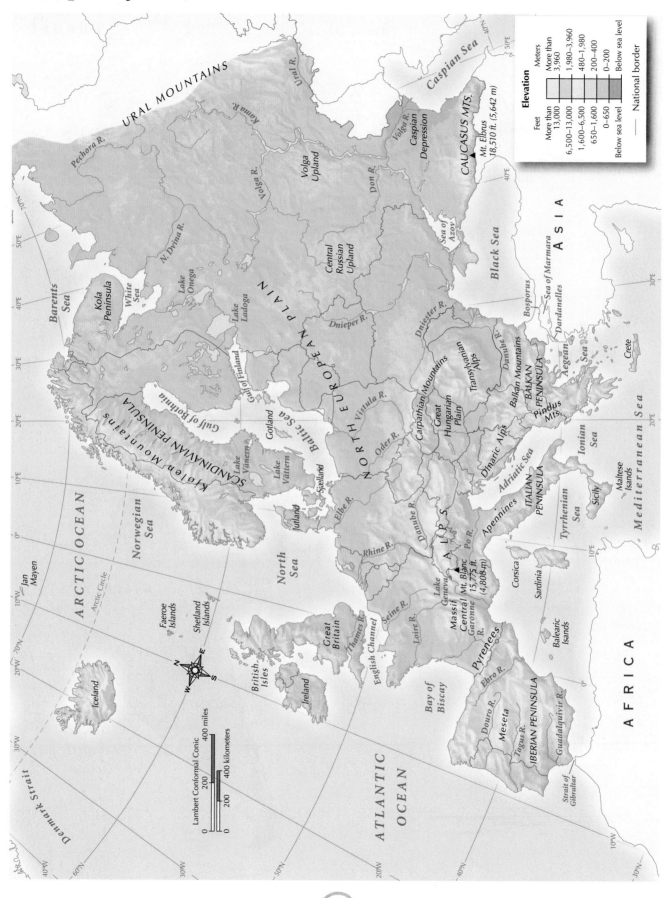

Elevation

Feet | Meters
More than 13,000 | More than 3,960
6,500–13,000 | 1,980–3,960
1,600–6,500 | 480–1,980
650–1,600 | 200–400
0–650 | 0–200
Below sea level | Below sea level

— National border

URAL MOUNTAINS

Pechora R.

Ural R.

Kama R.

Volga R.

Caspian Sea

Caspian Depression

CAUCASUS MTS.

▲ Mt. Elbrus
(18,510 ft. (5,642 m))

Volga Upland

Don R.

Sea of Azov

ASIA

Barents Sea

Kola Peninsula

White Sea

N. Dvina R.

Lake Onega

Central Russian Upland

Black Sea

Bosporus

Sea of Marmara

Dardanelles

Lake Ladoga

Dnieper R.

Dniester R.

Danube R.

Aegean Sea

Crete

Gulf of Finland

NORTH EUROPEAN PLAIN

Carpathian Mountains

Transylvanian Alps

Balkan Mountains

BALKAN PENINSULA

Pindus Mts.

SCANDINAVIAN PENINSULA

Kjölen Mountains

Baltic Sea

Gotland

Vistula R.

Great Hungarian Plain

Dinaric Alps

Adriatic Sea

Ionian Sea

Mediterranean Sea

Gulf of Bothnia

Lake Vänern

Lake Vättern

Sjælland

Oder R.

Elbe R.

Danube R.

A L P S

Apennines

ITALIAN PENINSULA

Tyrrhenian Sea

Sicily

Maltese Islands

ARCTIC OCEAN

Arctic Circle

Norwegian Sea

Jutland

Rhine R.

Lake Geneva

▲ Mt. Blanc
15,775 ft. (4,808 m)

Massif Central

Po R.

Corsica

Sardinia

Balearic Islands

Jan Mayen

Faeroe Islands

Shetland Islands

North Sea

Great Britain

Thames R.

Seine R.

Loire R.

Garonne R.

Pyrenees

Ebro R.

Iceland

British Isles

Ireland

English Channel

Bay of Biscay

Douro R.

Meseta

IBERIAN PENINSULA

Tagus R.

Guadalquivir R.

Strait of Gibraltar

AFRICA

Denmark Strait

ATLANTIC OCEAN

Lambert Conformal Conic

400 miles
200
0

400 kilometers
200
0

ASIA

Arctic Ocean

EUROPE

Bering Strait

180°

0°

International Date Line

Beaufort Sea

Baffin Bay

Greenland (Denmark)

Arctic Circle

60°N

Alaska (United States)

Bering Sea

Gulf of Alaska

Great Bear Lake

Great Slave Lake

Nuuk

Davis Strait

Labrador Sea

45°N

45°N

CANADA

Hudson Bay

Vancouver

Lake Winnipeg

Great Lakes

Ottawa

Toronto

Atlantic Ocean

Chicago

UNITED STATES

New York

Washington, D.C.

30°N

30°N

Los Angeles

Houston

Tropic of Cancer

Nassau

Gulf of Mexico

DOMINICAN REPUBLIC

MEXICO

Havana

BAHAMAS

CUBA

HAITI

Puerto Rico (United States)

Mexico City

JAMAICA

Santo Domingo

U.S. Virgin Islands (United States)

15°N

15°N

Belmopan

BELIZE

Kingston

Port-au-Prince

Guadeloupe (France)

Guatemala City

HONDURAS

Caribbean Sea

Martinique (France)

GUATEMALA

Tegucigalpa

NICARAGUA

DOMINICA

BARBADOS

San Salvador

Managua

TRINIDAD AND TOBAGO

EL SALVADOR

Caracas

GUYANA

San José

Panama

Georgetown

COSTA RICA

VENEZUELA

Paramaribo

PANAMA

Cayenne

French Guiana (France)

Bogotá

SURINAME

COLOMBIA

Equator

Quito

0°

0°

Galápagos Islands (Ecuador)

ECUADOR

Pacific Ocean

PERU

BRAZIL

Lima

Lake Titicaca

La Paz

Brasília

15°S

15°S

BOLIVIA

Sucre

Rio de Janiero

Tropic of Capricorn

PARAGUAY

São Paulo

CHILE

Asunción

ARGENTINA

National border

International Date Line

Santiago

URUGUAY

National capital

Montevideo

Buenos Aires

Río de la Plata

Other city

30°S

30°S

Atlantic Ocean

Lambert Azimuthal Equal-Area Projection

0   1000   2000 miles

0   1000   2000 kilometers

Falkland Islands (U.K.)

45°S

165°W   150°W   135°W   120°W   105°W   90°W   75°W   60°W   45°W   30°W   15°W

ASIA

Arctic Ocean

EUROPE

Bering Strait

Beaufort Sea

International Date Line

Bering Sea

Aleutian Islands

Gulf of Alaska

Mt. McKinley (Denali) 20,320 ft. (6,194 m)

Alaska Range

Yukon R.

Mackenzie R.

Ellesmere Island

Victoria Island

Great Bear Lake

Great Slave Lake

Baffin Island

Baffin Bay

Greenland

Davis Strait

Arctic Circle

CANADIAN SHIELD

Hudson Bay

Labrador Sea

Island of Newfoundland

ROCKY MOUNTAINS

Cascades

Sierra Nevada

Great Salt Lake

Colorado R.

Lake Winnipeg

Missouri R.

GREAT PLAINS

Great Lakes

St. Lawrence R.

APPALACHIAN MTS.

Mississippi R.

Ohio R.

Atlantic Ocean

Baja California

Gulf of California

Sierra Madre Occidental

Rio Grande

Sierra Madre Oriental

Tropic of Cancer

Gulf of Mexico

Cuba

Jamaica

Greater Antilles

Hispaniola

Lesser Antilles

Yucatán Peninsula

Caribbean Sea

Isthmus of Panama

Pacific Ocean

Galápagos Islands

Equator

N
W   E
S

Llanos

Orinoco R.

Guiana Highlands

AMAZON BASIN

Amazon R.

ANDES MOUNTAINS

Lake Titicaca

Gran Chaco

Paraguay R.

Paraná R.

São Francisco R.

Brazilian Highlands

Aconcagua 22,834 ft. (6,960 m)

Pampas

Rio de la Plata

Atlantic Ocean

Patagonia

Tierra del Fuego

Falkland Islands

Cape Horn

Elevation

Feet	Meters
More than 13,000	More than 3,960
6,500–13,000	1,980–3,960
1,600–6,500	480–1,980
650–1,600	200–400
0–650	0–200
Below sea level	Below sea level

—— National border

- - - International Date Line

Lambert Azimuthal Equal-Area Projection

0   1000   2000 miles

0   1000   2000 kilometers

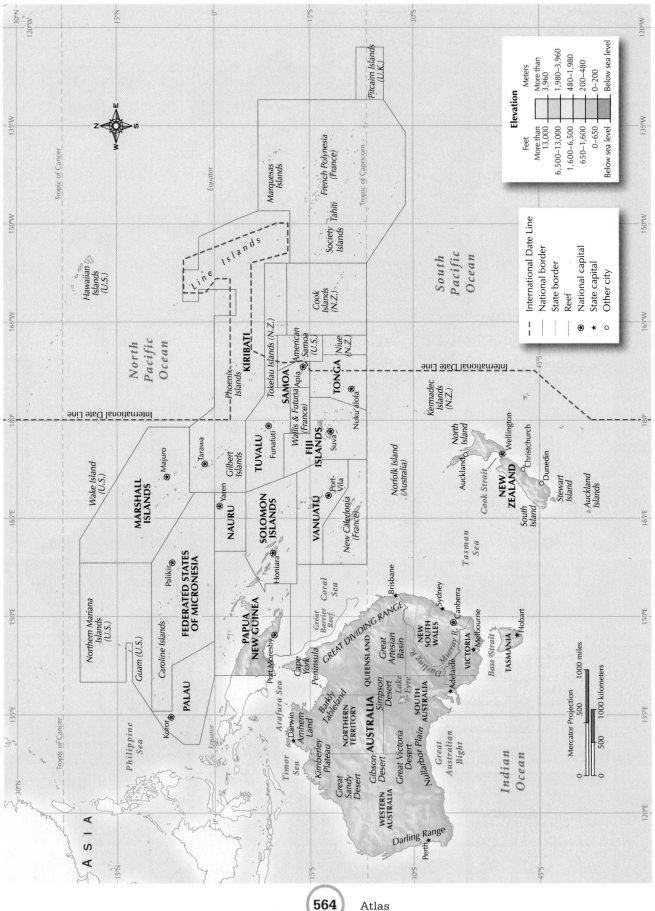

Elevation

Feet	Meters	
More than 13,000	More than 3,960	
6,500–13,000	1,980–3,960	
1,600–6,500	480–1,980	
650–1,600	200–480	
0–650	0–200	
Below sea level	Below sea level	

– – – International Date Line
——— National border
——— State border
Reef
⊛ National capital
★ State capital
○ Other city

Tropic of Cancer

Hawaiian Islands (U.S.)

Marquesas Islands

French Polynesia (France)

Society Islands · Tahiti

Tropic of Capricorn

Pitcairn Islands (U.K.)

South Pacific Ocean

Line Islands

North Pacific Ocean

Phoenix Islands

Cook Islands (N.Z.)

KIRIBATI

Tokelau Islands (N.Z.)

American Samoa (U.S.)

Niue (N.Z.)

SAMOA · Apia

Wake Island (U.S.)

Tarawa

Gilbert Islands

TUVALU · Funafuti

Wallis & Futuna Is. (France)

FIJI ISLANDS · Suva

TONGA · Nuku'alofa

International Date Line

Kermadec Islands (N.Z.)

Norfolk Island (Australia)

North Island · Auckland · Wellington

Christchurch

NEW ZEALAND

South Island · Dunedin

Stewart Island

Auckland Islands

Cook Strait

Majuro

MARSHALL ISLANDS

NAURU · Yaren

SOLOMON ISLANDS · Honiara

VANUATU · Port-Vila

New Caledonia (France)

Tasman Sea

FEDERATED STATES OF MICRONESIA · Palikir

Caroline Islands

Northern Mariana Islands (U.S.)

Guam (U.S.)

PALAU · Koror

PAPUA NEW GUINEA · Port Moresby

Cape York Peninsula

Coral Sea

Great Barrier Reef

Brisbane

Sydney

Canberra

NEW SOUTH WALES

QUEENSLAND

GREAT DIVIDING RANGE

Great Artesian Basin

Melbourne

VICTORIA

Murray R. · Darling R.

Adelaide

Hobart

TASMANIA

Bass Strait

Philippine Sea

ASIA

Equator

Timor Sea

Arafura Sea

Darwin · Arnhem Land

Kimberley Plateau

Barkly Tableland

NORTHERN TERRITORY

AUSTRALIA

SOUTH AUSTRALIA

Simpson Desert

Lake Eyre

Gibson Desert

Great Victoria Desert

Great Sandy Desert

WESTERN AUSTRALIA

Nullarbor Plain

Great Australian Bight

Indian Ocean

Perth

Darling Range

Mercator Projection

0   500   1000 miles

0   500   1000 kilometers

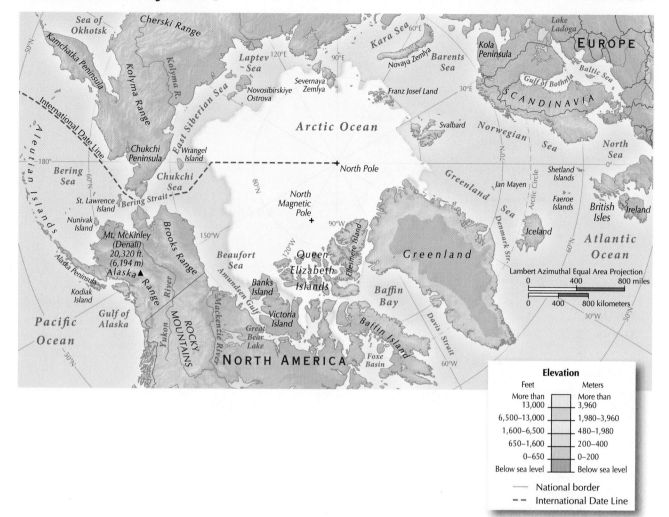

Sea of Okhotsk

Cherski Range

Kamchatka Peninsula

Kolyma Range

Kolyma R.

Laptev Sea

120°E

Novosibirskiye Ostrova

Severnaya Zemlya

90°E

Kara Sea

60°E

Novaya Zemlya

Barents Sea

Kola Peninsula

Lake Ladoga

EUROPE

Baltic Sea

Gulf of Bothnia

Franz Josef Land

30°E

S C A N D I N A V I A

International Date Line

Aleutian Islands

Bering Sea

60°N

St. Lawrence Island

Nunivak Island

Chukchi Peninsula

Wrangel Island

Chukchi Sea

Bering Strait

180°

East Siberian Sea

Arctic Ocean

80°N

North Magnetic Pole
+

90°W

Svalbard

Norwegian Sea

North Pole
+

Greenland Sea

Arctic Circle

Jan Mayen

70°N

Shetland Islands

Faeroe Islands

Iceland

Denmark Str.

North Sea

0°

British Isles

Ireland

Atlantic Ocean

Mt. McKinley (Denali) 20,320 ft. (6,194 m)
Alaska ▲ Range

Brooks Range

150°W

Beaufort Sea

Banks Island

Amundsen Gulf

Queen Elizabeth Islands

120°W

Ellesmere Island

Greenland

Lambert Azimuthal Equal Area Projection

0   400   800 miles

0   400   800 kilometers

30°W

Alaska Peninsula

Kodiak Island

Pacific Ocean

Gulf of Alaska

ROCKY MOUNTAINS

Yukon River

Mackenzie River

Great Bear Lake

Victoria Island

Baffin Bay

Baffin Island

Davis Strait

60°W

50°W

60°N

50°N

NORTH AMERICA

Foxe Basin

Elevation

Feet		Meters
More than 13,000		More than 3,960
6,500–13,000		1,980–3,960
1,600–6,500		480–1,980
650–1,600		200–400
0–650		0–200
Below sea level		Below sea level

—— National border

– – International Date Line

[Antarctica: Physical]

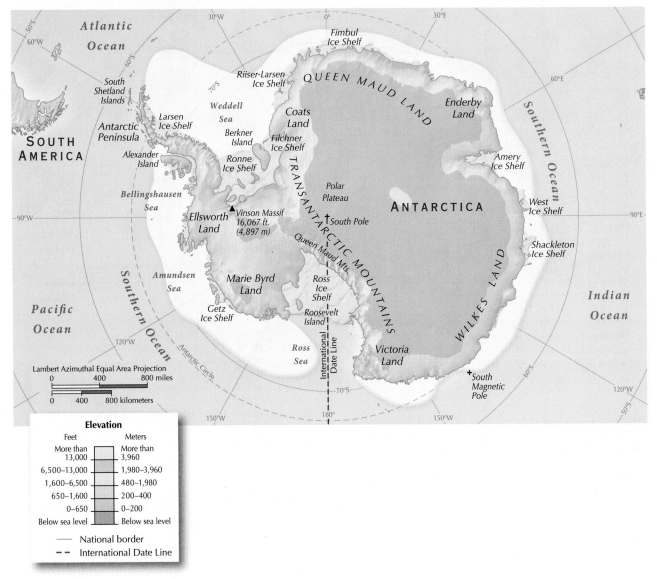

Atlantic Ocean

60°W

South Shetland Islands

Antarctic Peninsula

SOUTH AMERICA

Alexander Island

Bellingshausen Sea

90°W

Ellsworth Land

Amundsen Sea

Pacific Ocean

120°W

Southern Ocean

Antarctic Circle

30°W

70°S

Larsen Ice Shelf

Weddell Sea

Berkner Island

Ronne Ice Shelf

Riiser-Larsen Ice Shelf

Coats Land

Filchner Ice Shelf

Vinson Massif 16,067 ft. (4,897 m)

Marie Byrd Land

Getz Ice Shelf

Ross Sea

0°

Fimbul Ice Shelf

QUEEN MAUD LAND

Polar Plateau

TRANSANTARCTIC MOUNTAINS

Queen Maud Mts.

Ross Ice Shelf

Roosevelt Island

International Date Line

180°

150°W

70°S

South Pole

ANTARCTICA

Victoria Land

WILKES LAND

South Magnetic Pole

30°E

Enderby Land

Southern Ocean

60°E

Amery Ice Shelf

West Ice Shelf

Shackleton Ice Shelf

Indian Ocean

90°E

60°S

120°E

150°E

Lambert Azimuthal Equal Area Projection

0   400   800 miles

0   400   800 kilometers

Elevation

Feet		Meters
More than 13,000		More than 3,960
6,500–13,000		1,980–3,960
1,600–6,500		480–1,980
650–1,600		200–400
0–650		0–200
Below sea level		Below sea level

—— National border

-- -- International Date Line

Glossary

A

absolute advantage the ability to produce more of a given product using a given amount of resources

aggregate demand the amount of goods and services in the economy that will be purchased at all possible price levels

aggregate supply the total amount of goods and services in the economy available at all possible price levels

antitrust laws laws that encourage competition in the marketplace

appreciation an increase in the value of a currency

appropriations bill a bill that authorizes a specific amount of spending by the government

arbitration a settlement technique in which a neutral third party listens to both sides and then imposes a decision that is legally binding for both the company and the union

articles of partnership a partnership agreement that spells out each partner's rights and responsibilities

assets the money and other valuables belonging to an individual or business

authoritarian describes a form of government that limits individual freedoms and requires strict obedience from its citizens

automatic stabilizer tool of fiscal policy that increases or decreases automatically depending on changes in GDP and personal income

average cost total cost divided by quantity produced

B

balance of payments the value of all monetary transactions between a country's economy and the rest of the world

balance of trade the relationship between the value of a country's exports and the value of its imports

balanced budget a budget in which revenue and spending are equal

bank an institution for receiving, keeping, and lending money

bank holding company a company that owns more than one bank

bank runs widespread panics in which great numbers of people try to redeem their paper money at the same time

barrier to entry any factor that makes it difficult for a new firm to enter a market

barter the direct exchange of one set of goods or services for another

bear market a steady drop or stagnation in stock prices in general over a period of time

black market a market in which goods are sold illegally, without regard for government controls on price or quantity

block grants federal funds given to the states in lump sums

blue-collar worker someone who performs manual labor, often in a manufacturing job, and who earns an hourly wage

bond a formal contract issued by a corporation or other entity that includes a promise to repay borrowed money with interest at fixed intervals

brain drain the migration of the best-educated people of less developed countries to developed nations

brokerage firm a business that specializes in trading stocks

budget an estimate of future revenue and expenses

budget deficit a situation in which budget expenditures exceed revenues

budget surplus a situation in which budget revenues exceed expenditures

bull market a steady rise in stock prices in general over a period of time

business association a nonprofit group organized to promote the collective business interests of an area or a group of similar businesses

business cycle a period of macroeconomic expansion, or growth, followed by a period of contraction, or decline

business franchise a semi-independent business that pays fees to a parent company in return for the exclusive right to sell a certain product or service in a given area

business investment investment spending by businesses that creates additional output and jobs, helping to increase GDP and maintain the expansion

business license authorization to operate a business issued by a local government

business organization the ownership structure of a company or firm

C

call option a contract for buying stock at a particular price until a specified future date

capital any human-made resource that is used to produce other goods and services

capital budget a budget for spending on major investments

capital deepening the process of increasing the amount of capital per worker

capital formation the accumulation of savings made available for investment

capital gain the difference between the selling price and purchase price that results in a financial gain for the seller

capital loss the difference between the selling price and purchase price that results in a financial loss for the seller

capital market a market in which money is lent for periods longer than a year

cartel a formal organization of producers that agree to coordinate prices and production

cash transfers direct payments of money by the government to people who are poor, disabled, or retired

central bank a bank that can lend to other banks in times of need

centrally planned economy an economic system in which the government makes all decisions on the three key economic questions

certificate of incorporation a license to form a corporation issued by a state government

ceteris paribus a Latin phrase that means "all other things held constant"

check clearing the process by which banks record whose account gives up money and whose account receives money as a result of a customer writing a check

classical economics a school of thought based on the idea that free markets regulate themselves

closely held corporation a type of corporation that issues stock to only a few people, who are often family members

collective bargaining the process in which union and company management meet to negotiate a new labor contract

collusion an illegal agreement among firms to divide the market, set prices, or limit production

command economy another name for a centrally planned economy

Glossary

commodity a product, such as petroleum or milk, that is considered the same no matter who produces or sells it

commodity money consists of objects that have value in and of themselves and that are also used as money

communism a political system in which the government owns and controls all resources and means of production and makes all economic decisions

comparative advantage the ability to produce a product most efficiently given all the other products that could be produced

competition the struggle among producers for the dollars of consumers

complements two goods that are bought and used together

conglomerate a business combination merging more than three businesses that produce unrelated products or services

consumer cooperative a retail outlet owned and operated by consumers that sells merchandise to members at reduced prices

Consumer Price Index a price index determined by measuring the price of a standard group of goods meant to represent the "market basket" of a typical urban consumer

consumer sovereignty the power of consumers to decide what gets produced

contingent employment temporary and part-time jobs that are given to workers instead of full-time or permanent jobs

contraction an economic decline marked by falling real GDP

contractionary policy a fiscal policy used to reduce economic growth, often through decreased spending or higher taxes

cooperative a business organization owned and operated by a group of individuals for their shared benefit

copyright a government license that grants an author exclusive rights to publish and sell creative works

core inflation rate the rate of inflation excluding the effects of food and energy prices

corporate bond a bond issued by a corporation to help raise money for expansion

corporate income tax a tax based on a company's profits

corporation a legal entity, or being, owned by individual stockholders, each of whom has limited liability for the firm's debts

cost/benefit analysis a decision-making process in which you compare what you will sacrifice and gain by a specific action

coupon rate the interest rate that a bond issuer will pay to the bondholder

credit card a card entitling its owner to buy goods and services based on the owner's promise to pay for those goods and services

creditor a person or institution to whom money is owed

crowding-out effect the loss of funds for private investment caused by government borrowing

currency anything used as money; today we use coins and paper bills as money

cyclical unemployment unemployment that rises during economic downturns and falls when the economy improves

D

debit card a card used to withdraw money from a bank account

debt rescheduling an agreement between a lending nation and a debtor nation whereby the lending nation lengthens the time of debt repayment and forgives, or dismisses, part of the loan and, in return, the LDC agrees to accept a stabilization program

default to fail to pay back a loan

deficit spending the situation in which the government's expenditures exceed its revenues

deflation a sustained drop in the price level

deforestation the large-scale destruction of forests

demand the desire to own something and the ability to pay for it

demand curve a graphic representation of a demand schedule

demand deposits money in a checking account that can be paid "on demand," or at any time

demand schedule a table that lists the quantity of a good that a person will purchase at various prices in a market

demand-side economics a school of thought based on the idea that demand for goods drives the economy

demographics the statistical characteristics of populations and population segments, especially when used to identify consumer markets

depreciation the loss of the value of capital equipment that results from normal wear and tear

depression a deep recession with features such as high unemployment and low economic output

deregulation the removal of government controls over a market

derived demand a type of demand that is set by the demand for another good or service

developed nation a nation with a relatively high average level of material well-being

development the process by which a nation improves the economic, political, and social well-being of its people

differentiation making a product different from other, similar products

diminishing marginal returns the level of production in which the marginal product of labor decreases as the number of workers increases

discount rate the interest rate that the Federal Reserve charges commercial banks for loans

discouraged worker someone who wants a job but has given up looking

discretionary spending spending about which Congress is free to make choices

disequilibrium any price or quantity not at equilibrium; when quantity supplied is not equal to quantity demanded in a market

diversification the strategy of spreading out investments to reduce risk

dividend the portion of corporate profits paid out to stockholders

durable goods those goods that last for a relatively long time, such as refrigerators, cars, and DVD players

E

easy money policy a monetary policy that increases the money supply

economic growth a steady, long-term increase in real GDP

economic system the structure of methods and principles that a society uses to produce and distribute goods and services

economic transition a period of change in which a nation moves from one economic system to another

economics the study of how people seek to satisfy their needs and wants by making choices

economies of scale characteristics that cause a producer's average cost per unit to drop as production rises

efficiency the use of resources in such a way as to maximize the output of goods and services

elastic describes demand that is very sensitive to a change in price

elasticity of demand a measure of the way quantity supplied reacts to a change in price

elasticity of supply a measure of the way quantity supplied reacts to a change in price

embargo a ban on trade with a particular country

eminent domain the right of a government to take private property for public use

enterprise zone an area where businesses can locate free of certain local, state, and federal taxes and restrictions

entitlement social welfare program that people are "entitled to" benefit from if they meet certain eligibility requirements

entrepreneur a person who decides how to combine resources to create goods and services

equilibrium the point at which the demand for a product or service is equal to the supply of that product or service

equilibrium wage the wage rate, or price of labor services, that is set when the supply of workers meets the demand for workers in the labor market

estate tax a tax on the total value of the money and property of a person who has died

excess reserves bank reserves greater than the amount required by the Federal Reserve

exchange rate the value of a nation's currency in relation to a foreign currency

excise tax a tax on the production or sale of a good

expansion a period of economic growth as measured by a rise in real GDP

expansionary policy a fiscal policy used to encourage economic growth, often through increased spending or tax cuts

export a good or service sent to another country for sale

externality an economic side effect of a good or service that generates benefits or costs to someone other than the person deciding how much to produce or consume

F

factor market the arena of exchange in which firms purchase the factors of production from households

factor payments the income people receive in return for supplying factors of production

factors of production the resources that are used to make goods and services

fad a product that is popular for a short period of time

featherbedding the practice of negotiating labor contracts that keep unnecessary workers on the company's payroll

federal budget a written document estimating the federal government's revenue and authorizing its spending for the coming year

federal funds rate the interest rate that banks can charge each other for loans

Federal Reserve Banks The system created as many as 12 regional Federal Reserve Banks throughout the country. All banks chartered by the national government were required to become members of the Fed. The Federal Reserve Banks are the central banks for their districts.

Federal Reserve Board All of the Federal Reserve Banks were supervised by a Federal Reserve Board appointed by the President of the United States.

Federal Reserve Notes the national currency we use today in the United States

fiat money A fiat is an order or decree. Fiat money also called "legal tender," has value because a government has decreed that it is an acceptable means to pay debts.

financial asset a claim on the property or income of a borrower

financial intermediary an institution that helps channel funds from savers to borrowers

financial system the network of structures and mechanisms that allows the transfer of money between savers and borrowers

firm an organization that uses resources to produce a product or service, which it then sells

fiscal policy the use of government spending and revenue collection to influence the economy

fiscal year a 12-month period used for budgeting purposes

fixed cost a cost that does not change no matter how much of a good or service is produced

fixed exchange-rate system a system in which governments try to keep the values of their currencies somewhat constant against one another

fixed income income that does not increase even when prices go up

flexible exchange-rate system a system in which the exchange rate is determined by supply and demand

food stamp program a government program that helps low-income people buy food

foreclosures the seizure of property from borrowers who are unable to repay their loans

foreign direct investment this occurs when investors establish a business in another country

foreign exchange market system of financial institutions that facilitate the buying and selling of foreign currencies

foreign investment capital that originates in other countries, either by foreign direct investment or foreign portfolio investment

foreign portfolio investment foreign investors making purchases in another country's financial markets

fractional reserve banking a banking system that keeps only a fraction of its funds on hand and lends out the remainder

franchise a contract that gives a single firm the right to sell its good within an exclusive market

free contract the principle that people may decide what agreements they want to enter into

free enterprise system an economic system characterized by private or corporate ownership of capital goods

free market economy an economic system in which decisions on the three key economic questions are based on voluntary exchange in markets

free rider someone who would not be willing to pay for a certain good or service but who would get the benefits of it anyway if it were provided as a public good

free trade the lowering or elimination of protective tariffs and other trade barriers between two or more nations

free trade zone a region where a group of countries agrees to reduce or eliminate trade barriers

frictional unemployment type of unemployment that occurs when people take time to find a job

Friedman, Milton Milton Friedman (1912–2006) was an American economist who strongly supported free markets and believed in cutting government spending. He wrote several influential books describing his economic ideas, and with his wife, Rose, he produced a popular 10-part series for public television called "Free to Choose". Friedman won the Nobel Prize in Economics in 1976.

fringe benefits payments to employees other than wages or salary

full employment the level of employment reached when there is no cyclical unemployment

futures a contract to buy or sell commodities at a particular date in the future at a price specified today

G

Galbraith, John Kenneth John Kenneth Galbraith (1908–2006) was an American economist with sharply liberal views of economics and politics. He taught for many years at Harvard University, served in various government posts, and wrote 33 books. In his book "The Affluent Society" (1958), Galbraith criticized the "conventional wisdom" of U.S. economic policies, the rampant American consumer culture, and the lack of spending on government programs.

general partnership a type of partnership in which all partners share equally in both responsibility and liability

gift tax a tax on the money or property that one living person gives to another

glass ceiling an unofficial barrier that sometimes prevents some women and minorities from advancing to the top rank of organizations dominated by men

globalization the increasingly tight interconnection of producers, consumers, and financial systems around the world

gold standard a monetary system in which paper money and coins had the value of certain amounts of gold

goods the physical objects that someone produces

government monopoly a monopoly created by the government

grant a financial award given by a government agency to a private individual or group in order to carry out a specific task

greenbacks Printed in 1861 and so nicknamed because they were printed with green ink, these were the first paper currency issued by the U.S. Treasury since the Continental.

gross domestic product the total value of all final goods and services produced in a country in a given year

gross national product the annual income earned by a nation's companies and people

guest workers workers that are allowed to live and work in the United States only temporarily

guns or butter a phrase expressing the idea that a country that decides to produce more military goods ("guns") has fewer resources to produce consumer goods ("butter") and vice versa

H

Hayek, Friedrich Friedrich Hayek (1899–1992) was an Austrian economist who believed that economies function best without government interference. In his book "The Road to Serfdom", Hayek argued that free markets self-regulate and that government intervention distorts the price signals that allow self-regulation.

hedge fund a private investment organization that employs risky strategies that often make huge profits for investors

horizontal merger the combination of two or more firms competing in the same market with the same good or service

household a person or group of people living in a single residence

human capital the knowledge and skills a worker gains through education and experience

hyperinflation inflation that is out of control

I

imperfect competition a market structure that fails to meet the conditions of pure competition

import a good or service brought in from another country for sale

import quota a set limit on the amount of a good that can be imported

in-kind benefits goods and services provided for free or at greatly reduced prices

incentive the hope of reward or fear of penalty that encourages a person to behave in a certain way

incidence of a tax the final burden of a tax

income distribution the way in which a nation's total income is distributed among its population

income effect the change in consumption that results in response to changes in price

increasing marginal returns the level of production in which the marginal product of labor increases as the number of workers increases

individual income tax a tax based on a person's earnings

industrialization the organization of an economy for the purpose of manufacturing goods

inelastic describes demand that is not very sensitive to price changes

infant industry an industry in the early stages of development

infant mortality rate the number of deaths that occur in the first year of life per 1,000 live births

inferior good a good that consumers demand less of when their incomes increase

inflation a general increase in prices across an economy

inflation rate the percentage rate of change in price level over time

inflation-indexed bond a bond that protects the investor against inflation by its linkage to an index of inflation

infrastructure the basic facilities that are necessary for a society to function and grow

innovation the process of bringing new methods, products, or ideas into use

inside lag the time it takes to implement monetary policy

intellectual property creations, such as books, songs, or symbols, that consist of ideas rather than physical objects

interdependence the shared need of countries for resources, goods, services, labor, and knowledge supplied by other countries

interest the price paid for the use of borrowed money

interest group a private organization that tries to persuade public officials to act in ways that benefit its members

intermediate goods products used in the production of final goods

internal financing capital derived from the savings of a country's own citizens

inventory the quantity of goods that a firm has on hand

investment the act of redirecting resources from being consumed today so that they may create benefits in the future; the use of assets to earn income or profit

invisible hand a term coined by Adam Smith to describe the self-regulating nature of the marketplace

J

junk bond a bond with high risk and potentially high yield

K

Keynes, John Maynard John Maynard Keynes (1883–1946) was an British economist who greatly influenced how the United States and other countries used fiscal policy to battle recessions. In his book "The General Theory of Employment, Interest, and Money" (1935), Keynes theorized that a government-sponsored policy of full employment is the key to ending a recession. President Franklin Roosevelt adopted Keynesian spending policies during the Great Depression.

Keynesian economics a school of thought that uses demand-side theory as the basis for encouraging government action to help the economy

L

labor the effort people devote to tasks for which they are paid

labor force all nonmilitary people who are employed or unemployed

labor union an organization of workers that tries to improve working conditions, wages, and benefits for its members

Laffer, Arthur Arthur Laffer (1940–) is an American economist who contends that reducing federal tax rates can increase federal income. His line graph known as the Laffer curve, which supports supply-side economic theory, illustrates the effect that raising taxes has on tax revenue. Laffer was a member of President Ronald Reagan's Economic Policy Advisory Board.

laissez faire the doctrine that government generally should not intervene in the marketplace

land all natural resources used to produce goods and services

law of comparative advantage the principle that a nation is better off when it produces goods and services for which it has a comparative advantage

law of demand consumers will buy more of a good when its price is lower and less when its price is higher

law of increasing costs an economic principle which states that as production shifts from making one good or service to another, more resources are needed to increase production of the second good or service

law of supply producers offer more of a good or service as its price increases and less as its price falls

leading indicators a set of key economic variables that economists use to predict future trends in a business cycle

learning effect the theory that education increases efficiency of production and thus results in higher wages

legal equality the principle that everyone has the same legal rights

less developed country a nation with a relatively low average level of material well-being

liability the legal obligation to pay debts

license a government-issued right to operate a business

life expectancy the average expected life span of an individual

limited liability corporation a type of business with limited liability for the owners, with the advantage of not paying corporate income tax

limited liability partnership a type of partnership in which all partners are limited partners

limited partnership a type of partnership in which only one partner is required to be a general partner, while other partners have limited responsibilities

liquidity the ability to be used as, or directly converted into, cash

literacy rate the proportion of a nation's population over age 15 that can read and write

Lorenz Curve the curve that illustrates income distribution

M

macroeconomics the study of economic behavior and decision-making in a nation's whole economy

malnutrition consistently inadequate nutrition

mandatory spending spending that Congress is required by existing law to do

marginal benefit the extra benefit of adding one unit

marginal cost the extra cost of adding one unit

marginal product of labor the change in output that results from hiring one additional unit of labor

marginal revenue the additional income from selling one more unit of a good or service; sometimes equal to price

market any arrangement that allows buyers and sellers to exchange things

market basket a representative collection of goods and services

market demand schedule a table that lists the quantities demanded of a good at various prices by all consumers in the market

market failure a situation in which the free market, operating on its own, does not distribute resources efficiently

market power the ability of a company to control prices and total market output

market supply curve a graph of the total quantity supplied of a good or service by all suppliers at various prices

market supply schedule a chart that lists how much of a good or service all suppliers will offer at various prices

maturity the time at which payment to a bondholder is due

mediation a settlement technique in which a neutral person, the mediator, meets with each side to try to find a solution that both sides will accept

medical benefits health insurance provided by the government for children and people who are elderly, disabled, or poor

medium of exchange anything that is used to determine value during the exchange of goods and services

member banks banks that belong to the Fed

merger when two or more companies join to form a single firm

microeconomics the study of economic behavior and decision-making in small units, such as households and firms

minimum wage a minimum price that an employer can pay a worker for an hour of labor

mixed economy economic system that has some market-based elements and some level of government involvement

monetarism the belief that the money supply is the most important factor in macroeconomic performance

monetary policy the actions that the Federal Reserve System takes to influence the level of real GDP and the rate of inflation in the economy

money anything that serves as a medium of exchange, a unit of account, and a store of value

money creation the process by which money enters into circulation

money market a market in which money is lent for periods of one year or less

money market mutual funds funds that pool money from small savers to purchase short-term government and corporate securities

money multiplier formula a formula (initial cash deposit × 1 ÷ RRR) used to determine how much new money can be created with each demand deposit and added to the money supply

money supply all the money available in the United States economy

monopolistic competition a market structure in which many companies sell products that are similar but not identical

monopoly a market in which a single seller dominates

mortgage a specific type of loan that is used to buy real estate

multinational corporation a large corporation that produces and sells its goods and services in more than one country

multiplier effect the idea that every one-dollar change in fiscal policy creates a change greater than one dollar in the national income

municipal bond a bond issued by a state or local government or a municipality to finance a public project

mutual fund an organization that pools the savings of many individuals and invests this money in a variety of stocks, bonds, and other financial assets

N

national bank a bank chartered, or licensed, by the federal government

national debt the total amount of money the federal government owes to bondholders

national income accounting a system economists use to collect and organize macroeconomic statistics on production, income, investment, and savings

natural monopoly a market that runs most efficiently when one large firm provides all of the output

need something essential for survival, such as food or medical care

negative marginal return when the addition of a unit of labor actually reduces total output

net worth total assets minus total liabilities

newly industrialized country a less developed country that has made great progress toward developing its economy

nominal GDP GDP measured in current prices

non-price competition a way to attract customers through style, service, or location, rather than a lower price

non-price determinants factors other than price that can affect demand for a particular good or service

nondurable goods those goods that last a short period of time, such as food, light bulbs, and sneakers

nongovernmental organizations independent groups that raise money to fund aid and development programs

nonprofit organization an institution that functions much like a business but does not operate for the purpose of making a profit

normal good a good that consumers demand more of when their incomes increase

O

obsolescence situation in which older products and processes become out-of-date

offshoring the movement of some of a company's operations, or resources of production, to another country

oligopoly a market structure in which a few large firms dominate a market

open market operations the buying and selling of government securities in order to alter the supply of money

open opportunity the principle that anyone can compete in the marketplace

operating budget a budget for day-to-day spending needs

operating cost the cost of operating a facility, such as a factory or a store

opportunity cost the most desirable alternative given up as the result of a decision

options contracts that give investors the right to buy or sell stock and other financial assets at a particular price until a specified future date

outside lag the time it takes for monetary policy to have an effect

outsourcing the practice of contracting with another company to do a specific job that would otherwise be done by a company's own workers

P

par value a bond's stated value, to be paid to the bondholder at maturity

partnership business organization owned by two or more persons who agree on a specific division of responsibilities and profits

patent a government license that gives the inventor of a new product the exclusive right to produce and sell it

patriotism love of one's country

peak the height of an economic expansion

per capita GDP a nation's gross domestic product divided by its population

perfect competition a market structure in which a large number of firms all produce the same product and no single seller controls supply or prices

personal exemption a set amount that taxpayers may subtract from their gross income for themselves, their spouse, and any dependents

personal property movable possessions or assets

physical capital the human-made objects used to create other goods and services

population growth rate a measure of how rapidly a country's population increases in a given year

portfolio a collection of financial assets

poverty rate the percentage of people who live in households with income below the official poverty line

poverty threshold an income level below that which is needed to support families or households

predatory pricing selling a product below cost for a short period of time to drive competitors out of the market

price ceiling a maximum price that can legally be charged for a good or service

price discrimination the division of consumers into groups based on how much they will pay for a good

price fixing an agreement among firms to charge one price for the same good

price floor a minimum price for a good or service

price index a measurement that shows how the average price of a standard group of goods changes over time

price level the average of all prices in an economy

price war a series of competitive price cuts that lowers the market price below the cost of production

primary market a market for selling financial assets that can be redeemed only by the original holder

prime rate the interest rate banks charge on short-term loans to their best customers

principal the amount of money borrowed

private property property that is owned by individuals or companies, not by the government or the people as a whole

private property rights the principle that people have the right to control their possessions and use them as they wish

private sector the part of the economy that involves the transactions of individuals and businesses

privatization the process of selling businesses or services operated by the government to individual investors, and then allowing them to compete in the marketplace

producer cooperative an agricultural marketing cooperative that helps members sell their products

product market the arena of exchange in which households purchase goods and services from firms

production possibilities curve a graph that shows alternative ways to use a country's productive resources

production possibilities frontier a line on a production possibilities curve that shows the maximum possible output an economy can produce

productive capacity the maximum output that an economy can sustain over a period of time without increasing inflation

productivity of labor the quantity of output produced by a unit of labor

professional labor work that requires advanced skills and education

professional organization a nonprofit organization that works to improve the image, working conditions, and skill levels of people in particular occupations

profit the amount of money a business receives in excess of its expenses

profit motive the incentive that drives individuals and business owners to improve their material well-being

progressive tax a tax for which the percentage of income paid in taxes increases as income increases

property tax a tax based on real estate and other property

proportional tax a tax for which the percentage of income paid in taxes remains the same at all income levels

prospectus an investment report that provides information to potential investors

protectionism the use of trade barriers to shield domestic industries from foreign competition

public disclosure laws laws requiring companies to provide information to consumers about their products and services

public good a shared good or service for which it would be inefficient or impractical to make consumers pay individually and to exclude those who did not pay

public interest the concerns of society as a whole

public sector the part of the economy that involves the transactions of the government

publicly held corporation a type of corporation that sells stock on the open market

purchasing power the ability to purchase goods and services

pure competition a market structure in which a large number of firms all produce the same product and no single seller controls supply or prices; also called perfect competition

put option a contract for selling stock at a particular price until a specified future date

Q

quantity supplied the amount of a good or service that a producer is willing and able to supply at a specific price

quantity theory the theory that too much money in the economy causes inflation

R

rationing a system of allocating scarce goods and services using criteria other than price

real GDP GDP expressed in constant, or unchanging, prices

real GDP per capita real GDP divided by the total population of a country

real property land and any permanent structures on the land to which a person has legal title

recession a prolonged economic contraction

referendum a proposed law submitted directly to the public

regressive tax a tax for which the percentage of income paid in taxes decreases as income increases

regulation government intervention in a market that affects the production of a good

remittances cash payments sent by workers who have migrated to a new country to family members in their home country

rent control a price ceiling placed on apartment rent

representative money makes use of objects that have value solely because the holder can exchange them for something else of value

required reserve ratio the fraction of deposits that banks are required to keep in reserve

reserve requirements the amount of reserves that banks are required to keep on hand

reserves deposits that a bank keeps readily available as opposed to lending them out

return the money an investor receives above and beyond the sum of money initially invested

revenue the income received by a government from taxes and other nontax sources

right-to-work law a measure that bans mandatory union membership

royalties the share of earnings given by a franchisee as payment to the franchiser

S

safety net a set of government programs that protect people who face unfavorable economic conditions

sales tax a tax based on goods or services that are sold

sanctions actions a nation or group of nations takes in order to punish or put pressure on another nation

saving income not used for consumption

savings bond a low-denomination bond issued by the United States government

savings rate the proportion of disposable income that is saved

scarcity the principle that limited amounts of goods and services are available to meet unlimited wants

screening effect a theory that suggests that the completion of college signals to employers that a job applicant is intelligent and hard-working

search cost the financial and opportunity cost that consumers pay when searching for a good or service

seasonal unemployment type of unemployment that occurs as a result of harvest schedules, vacations, or when industries make seasonal shifts in their production schedules

secondary market a market for reselling financial assets

security a financial document, such as a stock certificate or bond, that represents ownership of corporate shares or the promise of repayment by a company or government

self-interest an individual's own personal gain

semi-skilled labor work that requires minimal specialized skills and education

service cooperative a type of cooperative that provides a service rather than a good

services the actions or activities that one person performs for another

share a portion of stock

short-term loans Each of the regional Federal Reserve Banks allowed member banks to borrow money to meet short-term demands. This helped prevent bank failures that occurred when large numbers of depositors withdrew funds during a panic.

shortage a situation in which consumers want more of a good or service than producers are willing to make available at a particular price

skilled labor work that requires specialized skills and training

Smith, Adam Adam Smith (1723–1790) was the first modern economist, whose book "The Wealth of Nations" describes how free markets function and self-regulate. In addition to economics, Smith published works on moral philosophy. His economic ideas have influenced many countries around the world, including the United States.

socialism a range of economic and political systems based on the belief that wealth should be distributed evenly throughout a society

sole proprietorship a business owned and managed by a single individual

special economic zones designated regions that operate under different economic laws from the rest of the country in order to attract foreign investment and promote exports

specialization the concentration of the productive efforts of individuals and businesses on a limited number of activities

specie coins made of gold or silver that one could be given in exchange for paper money

speculation the practice of making high-risk investments with borrowed money in hopes of getting a big return

stabilization program the changing of a nation's economic policies to meet IMF goals

stagflation a decline in real GDP (output) combined with a rise in the price level (inflation)

standard of living level of economic prosperity

start-up costs the expenses a new business must pay before it can begin to produce and sell goods

stock a certificate of ownership in a corporation

stock exchange a market for buying and selling stock

stock split the division of each single share of a company's stock into more than one share

stockbroker a person who links buyers and sellers of stock

store of value to keep value when held onto—or stored—it instead of spending

strike an organized work stoppage intended to force an employer to address union demands

structural unemployment type of unemployment that occurs when workers' skills do not match those needed for the jobs available

subsidy a government payment that supports a business or market

subsistence agriculture level of farming in which a person raises only enough food to feed his or her family

substitutes goods that are used in place of one another

substitution effect when a consumer reacts to a rise in the price of one good by consuming less of that good and more of a substitute good

supply the amount of a good or service that is available

supply curve a graph of the quantity supplied of a good or service at various prices

supply schedule a chart that lists how much of a good or service a supplier will offer at various prices

supply shock a sudden shortage of a good

supply-side economics a school of thought based on the idea that the supply of goods drives the economy

surplus when quantity supplied is more than quantity demanded

sustainable development the goal of meeting current development needs without using up resources needed by future generations

T

tariff a tax on imported goods

tariffs taxes on imported goods

tax a required payment to a local, state, or national government

tax assessor an official who determines the value of property

tax base the income, property, good, or service that is subject to a tax

tax credit a variable amount that taxpayers may subtract from the total amount of their income tax

tax deduction a variable amount that taxpayers may subtract from their gross income

tax exempt not subject to taxes

tax incentive the use of taxation to encourage or discourage certain types of behavior

tax return a form used to file income taxes

taxable income the earnings on which tax must be paid; total income minus exemptions and deductions

technological progress an increase in efficiency gained by producing more output without using more inputs

thinking at the margin the process of deciding whether to do or use one additional unit of some resource

tight money policy a monetary policy that reduces the money supply

total cost the sum of fixed costs and variable costs

total revenue the total amount of money a company receives by selling goods or services

trade association a nonprofit organization that promotes the interests of a particular industry

trade barrier a means of preventing a foreign product or service from freely entering a nation's territory

trade deficit a situation in which a nation imports more goods and services than it exports

trade surplus a situation in which a nation exports more goods and services than it imports

trade war a cycle of escalating trade barriers

trade-off the act of giving up one benefit in order to gain another, greater benefit

traditional economy an economic system that relies on habit, custom, or ritual to decide the three basic economic questions

Treasury bill a government bond with a maturity date of 26 weeks or less

Treasury bond a government bond that is issued with a term of 30 years

Treasury note a government bond with a term of 2 to 10 years

trough the lowest point in an economic contraction

trust an illegal grouping of companies that discourages competition, similar to a cartel

U

underemployed working at a job for which one is overqualified, or working part time when full-time work is desired

underutilization the use of fewer resources than an economy is capable of using

unemployment rate the percentage of a nation's labor force that is unemployed

Uniform Partnership Act a uniform law establishing rules for partnerships, which partnerships must follow if they have no partnership agreement.

unit of account a means for comparing the values of goods and services

unitary elastic describes demand whose elasticity is exactly equal to one

unskilled labor work that requires no specialized skills, education, or training

V

variable factor that can change

variable costs a cost that rises or falls depending on the quantity produced

vertical mergers the merger of two or more firms involved in different stages of producing the same good or service

voluntary exchange the principle that people may decide what, when, and how they want to buy and sell

W

wage-price spiral the process by which rising wages cause higher prices, and higher prices cause higher wages

want something that people desire but that is not necessary for survival

welfare government aid to the poor

white-collar worker someone who works in a professional or clerical job and who usually earns a weekly salary

withholding taking tax payments out of an employee's pay before he or she receives it

work ethic a commitment to the value of work

workfare a program requiring work in exchange for temporary government assistance

World Trade Organization international organization founded to make global trade more free

Y

yield the annual rate of return on a bond if the bond is held to maturity

Z

zoning laws laws in a city or town that designate certain areas, or zones, for residential and business use

A

absolute advantage > ventaja absoluta Capacidad para producir más de cierto producto usando una cantidad determinada de recursos.

aggregate demand > demanda agregada Cantidad de bienes y servicios que serán comprados a todos los niveles de precio posibles.

aggregate supply > oferta agregada Cantidad total de bienes y servicios disponibles a todos los niveles de precio posibles.

antitrust laws > leyes antimonopolio Leyes que promueven la competencia en el mercado.

appreciation > apreciación Incremento del valor de una moneda.

appropriations bill > ley de presupuesto Ley que autoriza una cantidad específica de gasto para el gobierno.

arbitration > arbitraje Tipo de acuerdo en el que un tercer grupo neutral escucha a ambos lados e impone una decisión con vínculo legal entre la compañía y el sindicato.

articles of partnership > estatutos de asociación Acuerdo de una sociedad que determina los derechos y responsabilidades de cada socio.

assets > activos Dinero y otros valores pertenecientes a un individuo o una empresa.

authoritarian > autoritario Tipo de gobierno que limita la libertad de los individuos y requiere obediencia estricta de sus ciudadanos.

automatic stabilizer > estabilizador automático Herramienta fiscal que se incrementa o disminuye dependiendo de cambios en el PIB y los ingresos personales.

average cost > costo total promedio Costo que surge al dividir el costo total por la cantidad producida.

B

balance of payments > balanza de pagos Valor de todas las transacciones monetarias entre la economía de un país y la del resto del mundo.

balance of trade > balanza comercial Relación entre el valor de las exportaciones de un país y el valor de sus importaciones.

balanced budget > presupuesto equilibrado Presupuesto en el que los ingresos y los gastos son equitativos.

bank > banco Institución que recibe, mantiene y presta dinero.

bank holding company > compañía tenedora de bancos Compañía dueña de más de un banco.

bank runs > pánicos bancarios Situaciones de pánico general en las cuales muchas personas retiran su dinero del banco.

barrier to entry > barrera comercial Factor que dificulta la entrada de una nueva entidad al mercado.

barter > trueque Intercambio directo de bienes o servicios.

bear market > mercado bajista Caída constante o estancamiento de la bolsa de inversiones por un período.

black market > mercado negro Mercado en el que se venden bienes ilegalmente, sin considerar los controles gubernamentales sobre precio y cantidad.

block grants > subvención de bloque Fondos federales otorgados a los estados en cantidades fijas.

blue-collar worker > obrero Persona que realiza trabajo manual, a menudo en el área industrial, y que recibe un salario por hora.

bond > bono Contrato formal expedido por una corporación u otra entidad que estipula pagar un préstamo con intereses a intervalos fijos.

brain drain > fuga de cerebros Emigración de individuos con alta capacitación de países menos desarrollados a naciones más desarrolladas.

brokerage firm > firma de corretaje Empresa de corredores de bolsa.

budget > presupuesto Estimación de ingresos y gastos a futuro.

budget deficit > déficit presupuestario Situación en la cual los gastos son mayores que los ingresos.

budget surplus > superávit presupuestario Situación en la cual los ingresos son mayores que los gastos.

bull market > mercado alcista Incremento constante en la bolsa de valores durante un período de tiempo.

business association > asociación de empresas Grupo que promueve los intereses colectivos de un área o grupo de empresas similares.

business cycle > ciclo económico Período de expansión o crecimiento macroeconómico, seguido por una contracción o declive.

business franchise > franquicia Negocio que paga honorarios a una empresa matriz a cambio del derecho exclusivo de venta de cierto producto o servicio en un área específica.

business investment > inversión empresarial Inversión llevada a cabo por empresas para generar producción y empleos adicionales, lo que contribuye a incrementar el PIB y mantener la expansión.

business license > licencia comercial Autorización emitida por un gobierno local para operar un negocio.

business organization > organización empresarial La estructura de propiedad de una compañía o entidad.

C

call option > opción de compra Contrato que permite la compra de acciones a un precio estipulado hasta una fecha determinada.

capital > capital Cualquier recurso fabricado por el hombre que se usa para producir otros bienes y servicios.

capital budget > presupuesto de capital Presupuesto destinado para inversiones de gran importancia.

capital deepening > desarrollo de capital Proceso en el cual se incrementa la cantidad de capital por trabajador.

capital formation > formación de capital La acumulación de ahorros disponibles para la inversión.

capital gain > plusvalía Diferencia entre el precio de venta y el precio de compra que resulta en una ganancia financiera para el vendedor.

capital loss > minusvalía Diferencia entre el precio de venta y el precio de compra que resulta en una pérdida financiera para el vendedor.

capital market > mercado de capitales Mercado en el cual se hacen préstamos por períodos de más de un año.

cartel > cartel Organización de productores que acuerdan la coordinación de precios y producción.

cash transfers > pensión Pagos de dinero hechos directamente por el gobierno a los infortunados, incapacitados y jubilados.

central bank > banco central Banco que puede hacer préstamos a otros bancos en momentos de necesidad.

centrally planned economy > economía centralizada Sistema económico en el cual el gobierno toma todas las decisiones sobre las tres preguntas económicas clave.

certificate of incorporation > acta constitutiva Licencia expedida por el gobierno estatal, que permite formar una corporación.

ceteris paribus > *ceteris paribus* Frase en latín que significa "lo demás permanece constante".

check clearing > compensación de cheques Proceso en el cual un banco lleva un registro de las cuentas que ceden dinero y las cuentas que reciben dinero cuando un cliente emite un cheque.

classical economics > economía clásica Corriente de pensamiento basada en la idea de que los mercados libres se regulan solos.

closely held corporation > sociedad cerrada Tipo de empresa que expide acciones a pocas personas, quienes por lo general son familiares.

collective bargaining > convenio colectivo de trabajo Proceso en el cual la administración del sindicato y de la compañía se reúnen con el fin de negociar un contrato de trabajo.

collusion > colusión Acuerdo ilegal entre entidades con el fin de dividir el mercado, ajustar precios o restringir la producción.

command economy > economía controlada Otro nombre para la economía centralizada.

commodity > bien de consumo Producto, tal como el petróleo o la leche, que se considera igual independientemente de quién lo produzca o lo venda.

commodity money > mercancía Objetos que tienen valor por sí mismos y que también se usan como dinero.

communism > comunismo Sistema político en el cual el gobierno posee y controla todos los recursos y medios de producción y toma todas las decisiones económicas.

comparative advantage > ventaja comparativa Habilidad para producir cierto producto de la manera más eficiente considerando todos los otros productos que se podrían producir.

competition > competencia Lucha entre productores por el dinero de los consumidores.

complements > bienes complementarios Dos bienes que se compran y se usan conjuntamente.

conglomerate > conglomerado Combinación de negocios donde se unen más de tres negocios que producen productos o servicios no relacionados entre sí.

consumer cooperative > cooperativa de consumidores Agrupación operada por consumidores que ofrece bienes y servicios para sus socios a precios reducidos.

Consumer Price Index > índice de precios al consumidor Índice de precios determinado al medir el precio de un grupo de bienes estándar que representa la "canasta familiar" del consumidor urbano común.

consumer sovereignty > soberanía del consumidor Poder del consumidor para decidir qué se produce.

contingent employment > trabajo eventual Trabajo temporal a tiempo parcial.

contraction > recesión Período de declive económico caracterizado por el descenso del PIB.

contractionary policy > política recesiva Política fiscal que reduce el crecimiento económico, usualmente por medio de la disminución de gastos o de impuestos más altos.

cooperative > cooperativa Organización comercial que pertenece y es operada por un grupo de individuos para un beneficio común.

copyright > derechos de autor Documento gubernamental que garantiza los derechos exclusivos a un autor para publicar y vender sus obras.

core inflation rate > tasa de inflación subyacente Tasa de inflación que excluye los efectos del precio de la comida y la energía.

corporate bond > bonos corporativos Bono expedido por una corporación para ayudar a recaudar dinero para su expansión.

corporate income tax > impuesto sobre sociedades Impuesto que se basa en las ganancias de la compañía.

corporation > corporación Entidad legal que pertenece a los accionistas, los cuales tienen responsabilidad limitada ante las deudas de la firma.

cost/benefit analysis > análisis del costo/beneficio Proceso de toma de decisiones en el cual se compara el costo y la ganancia de una operación en particular.

coupon rate > cupón de interés Tasa de interés que un emisor de bonos paga al titular del bono.

credit card > tarjeta de crédito Tarjeta que autoriza a su titular a comprar bienes y servicios partiendo de su promesa de pagar por esos bienes y servicios.

creditor > acreedor Persona o institución a la cual se le debe dinero.

crowding-out effect > efecto expulsión Pérdida de fondos destinados para inversiones privadas a causa de la deuda pública.

currency > moneda Monedas y billetes que se usan como dinero.

cyclical unemployment > desempleo cíclico Desempleo que incrementa al empeorar la economía y disminuye al mejorar la economía.

D

debit card > tarjeta de débito Tarjeta que se usa para retirar dinero de una cuenta bancaria.

debt rescheduling > renegociación de deudas Acuerdo entre la nación acreedora y la nación deudora que extiende el plazo de pago y perdona parte del préstamo. A cambio, el país en vías de desarrollo acepta implementar un programa de estabilización.

default > mora Situación que consiste en suspender el pago de una deuda.

deficit spending > gasto deficitario Situación en la que los gastos de un gobierno exceden sus ingresos.

deflation > deflación Descenso general de precios.

deforestation > deforestación Destrucción forestal masiva.

demand > demanda Deseo de poseer algo y la capacidad para pagar por ello.

demand curve > curva de demanda Representación gráfica de la tabla de demanda.

demand deposits > depósito a la vista Dinero en una cuenta corriente que se paga "a petición" o en cualquier momento.

demand schedule > tabla de demanda Tabla que representa la cantidad de bienes que un consumidor está dispuesto a adquirir a diferentes precios en el mercado.

demand-side economics > economía de demanda Corriente de pensamiento basada en la noción de que la demanda de bienes dirige la economía.

demographics > demografía Estudio estadístico de la población humana y sus segmentos, especialmente relacionados con el mercado de consumo.

depreciation > depreciación 1. Reducción del valor de los bienes de capital de equipo como resultado del uso. 2. Reducción en el valor de una moneda.

depression > depresión Recesión económica que se caracteriza por ser larga y grave.

deregulation > desregulación Supresión del control del gobierno sobre la actividad económica.

derived demand > demanda derivada Demanda que depende de la demanda de otro bien o servicio.

developed nation > país desarrollado País con un bienestar económico relativamente alto.

development > desarrollo País con un bienestar económico relativamente alto.

differentiation > diferenciación Hacer que un producto se distinga de otros productos similares.

diminishing marginal returns > rendimiento marginal decreciente Nivel de producción en el cual el producto laboral marginal disminuye al incrementar el número de trabajadores.

discount rate > tasa de descuento Interés que la Reserva Federal cobra sobre los préstamos a los bancos comerciales.

discouraged worker > trabajador desanimado Persona que quiere conseguir un trabajo pero ha desistido de la búsqueda.

discretionary spending > gastos discrecionales Gastos sobre los cuales el Congreso es libre de tomar decisiones.

disequilibrium > desequilibrio Estado de desigualdad económica; desigualdad entre la cantidad de oferta y la cantidad de demanda.

diversification > diversificación Estrategia en la que se distribuyen las inversiones para reducir el riesgo.

dividend > dividendo Porción de los beneficios corporativos que les pagan a los accionistas.

durable goods > bienes duraderos Bienes de consumo cuya durabilidad es relativamente larga, por ejemplo refrigeradores, automóviles y reproductores de DVD.

E

easy money policy > política de dinero Fácil política monetaria que incrementa la disponibilidad de dinero.

economic growth > crecimiento económico Aumento constante a largo plazo del PIB.

economic system > sistema económico Estructura de métodos y principios que una sociedad usa para producir y distribuir bienes y servicios.

economic transition > transición económica Período de cambio en el cual una nación pasa de un sistema económico a otro.

economics > economía Rama del saber que estudia cómo las personas buscan satisfacer sus necesidades y deseos al tomar decisiones.

economies of scale > economías de escala Factores que hacen que el costo promedio por unidad de un producto disminuya cuando la producción aumenta.

efficiency > eficiencia Uso de los recursos de manera que se alcance el máximo de producción de bienes y servicios.

elastic > elasticidad Describe la demanda que es muy susceptible a los cambios de precio.

elasticity of demand > elasticidad de la demanda Medida de cómo responden los consumidores a los cambios de precio.

elasticity of supply > elasticidad de la oferta Medida de la forma en que la cantidad ofrecida responde a un cambio de precio.

embargo > embargo Prohibición de comerciar con un país determinado.

eminent domain > dominio eminente Derecho de un gobierno de tomar la propiedad privada de alguien para darle un uso público.

enterprise zone > zona franca Área en la que se pueden establecer negocios exentos de ciertos impuestos y restricciones municipales, estatales y federales.

entitlement > derecho consuetudinario Programa de beneficencia social al que las personas tienen "derecho" si cumplen con ciertos requisitos.

entrepreneur > empresario Persona que decide cómo combinar recursos para crear bienes y servicios.

equilibrium > equilibrio Punto en el cual la demanda de un producto o servicio es igual a su oferta.

equilibrium wage > salario de equilibrio Tasa salarial, o precio de la mano de obra, que se establece cuando la disponibilidad de trabajadores cubre la demanda de trabajadores en el mercado laboral.

estate tax > impuesto de sucesión Impuesto sobre el valor total del dinero y las propiedades que deja una persona fallecida.

excess reserves > exceso de reservas Reservas bancarias que sobrepasan la cantidad que la Reserva Federal necesita.

exchange rate > tasa de cambio Valor de la moneda de una nación en relación con una moneda extranjera.

excise tax > impuesto sobre artículos de uso y consumo Impuesto sobre la producción o venta de un bien.

expansion > expansión Período de crecimiento económico determinado por un aumento del PIB real.

expansionary policy > política de expansión Política fiscal que se usa para estimular el crecimiento económico a través de un aumento del gasto o de una reducción de impuestos.

export > exportaciones Bien o servicio que se envía a otro país para la venta.

externality > externalidad Efecto económico de un bien o servicio que le genera beneficios o costos a alguien distinto a quien decide cuánto producir o consumir.

F

factor market > mercado de factores Área de intercambio en la cual hay compañías que compran los factores de producción de las economías domésticas.

factor payments > pago a los factores Ingreso que reciben las personas a cambio de proveer factores de producción.

factors of production > factores de producción Recursos que se usan para generar bienes y servicios.

fad > novedad Producto que está de moda por un corto período de tiempo.

featherbedding > sinecura Contratación retribuida de empleados innecesarios.

federal budget > presupuesto federal Documento escrito donde se estima el ingreso del gobierno federal y por medio del cual se autorizan los gastos del año siguiente.

federal funds rate > tasa de los fondos federales Tasa que se cobran entre sí los bancos por el préstamo de sus reservas.

Federal Reserve Banks > Bancos de la Reserva Federal El sistema creó hasta doce Bancos regionales de la Reserva Federal por todo el país. Se requirió a todos los bancos contratados por el gobierno hacerse miembros de la *Fed*. Los Bancos de la Reserva Federal son los bancos centrales para sus distritos.

Federal Reserve Board > Junta de Gobierno de la Reserva Federal Todos los Bancos de la Reserva Federal estaban supervisados por una Junta de Gobierno de la Reserva Federal nombrada por el Presidente de los Estado Unidos.

Federal Reserve Notes > Papel moneda de la Reserva Federal Moneda nacional utilizada actualmente en los Estados Unidos.

fiat money > dinero *fiat* Objetos que tienen valor sólo porque el gobierno ha decretado que son medios aceptables para pagar deudas.

financial asset > activo financiero Derecho que tiene una entidad sobre la propiedad o los ingresos de un prestatario.

financial intermediary > intermediario financiero Institución que ayuda a canalizar los fondos de los ahorristas a los prestatarios.

financial system > sistema financiero Red de estructuras y mecanismos que permiten la transferencia de dinero entre ahorristas y prestatarios.

firm > empresa Organización que usa recursos para crear un producto o servicio, que después vende.

fiscal policy > política fiscal Uso de los gastos y del ingreso del gobierno para causar una reacción en la economía.

fiscal year > año fiscal Período de doce meses con fines presupuestarios.

fixed cost > costo fijo Costo que no cambia, independientemente de la cantidad que se produzca de un bien.

fixed exchange-rate system > sistema de tasa cambiaria fija Sistema en el cual el gobierno trata de mantener constante el valor de su moneda con respecto a otra moneda.

fixed income > ingreso fijo Ingreso que no aumenta aunque los precios suban.

flexible exchange-rate system > sistema de tasa cambiaria flexible Sistema en el cual la tasa de cambio depende de la oferta y la demanda.

food stamp program > programa de cupones para alimentos Cupones que el gobierno distribuye entre personas de bajos ingresos y que se pueden cambiar por alimentos.

foreclosures > embargo Acción que consiste en tomar la propiedad de prestatarios que no pueden pagar sus préstamos.

foreign direct investment > inversión directa extranjera Establecimiento de un negocio de inversionistas de otro país.

foreign exchange market > mercado de divisas Sistema de instituciones financieras que facilitan la compra y venta de monedas extranjeras.

foreign investment > inversión extranjera Capital generado en otros países.

foreign portfolio investment > cartera de inversión extranjera Compras que los inversionistas de un país hacen en mercados financieros de otro país.

fractional reserve banking > sistema de reserva fraccionaria Sistema bancario en el cual el banco mantiene solamente una fracción de los fondos en reserva y presta el resto de los fondos.

franchise > franquicia Contrato que le otorga a una firma el derecho de vender sus bienes dentro de un mercado exclusivo.

free contract > principio de libre contrato Principio que establece que las personas pueden decidir qué acuerdos quieren hacer.

free enterprise system > sistema de libre empresa Sistema económico donde los bienes capitales están en manos privadas o corporativas.

free market economy > sistema de libre empresa Sistema económico en el cual los bienes capitales les pertenecen a compañías privadas o corporaciones.

free rider > polizón Persona que no está dispuesta a pagar por un bien o servicio determinado, pero quien se beneficiaría de él de todos modos si se le ofreciera como beneficio público.

free trade > libre comercio Disminución o eliminación de las tarifas y otras barreras comerciales entre dos o más naciones.

free trade zone > zona de libre comercio Región en la que un grupo de países acuerda reducir o eliminar las barreras comerciales.

frictional unemployment > desempleo friccional Tipo de desempleo que ocurre cuando a las personas les toma tiempo encontrar empleo.

Friedman, Milton > Friedman, Milton Milton Friedman (1912–2006) Economista estadounidense que apoyó fuertemente los mercados libres y creía en la reducción de los gastos gubernamentales. Escribió diversos libros de renombre que describían su pensamiento económico. Con su esposa, Rose, produjo una popular serie de diez episodios para la televisión pública, titulada *Free to Choose*. Friedman ganó el Premio Nobel de Economía en 1976.

fringe benefits > beneficio adicional Pago que los empleados reciben además de su sueldo o salario.

full employment > pleno empleo Nivel de empleo alcanzado cuando no hay desempleo cíclico.

futures > contrato de futuros Contratos que establece la compra o venta de bienes o valores en el futuro a un precio establecido con anticipación.

G

Galbraith, John Kenneth > Galbraith, John Kenneth John Kenneth Galbraith (1908–2006) Economista estadounidense con marcadas ideas liberales sobre la economía y la política. Dio clases por muchos años en la Universidad de Harvard, ocupó diversos cargos de gobierno y escribió 33 libros. En el libro *La sociedad opulenta* (1958), Galbraith criticaba la "sabiduría popular" de las políticas económicas estadounidenses, la cultura consumista rampante en los Estados Unidos y la falta de presupuesto para los programas gubernamentales.

general partnership > sociedad colectiva Tipo de sociedad en la cual todos los socios asumen la misma cantidad de responsabilidades y obligaciones.

gift tax > impuesto sobre donaciones Impuesto sobre el dinero o la propiedad que una persona viva le da a otra.

glass ceiling > techo de cristal Barrera no oficial que les impide a algunas mujeres y minorías avanzar a la cima de organizaciones dominadas por hombres blancos.

globalization > globalización Interconexión, cada vez más fuerte, entre productores, consumidores y sistemas financieros a nivel mundial.

gold standard > patrón oro Sistema monetario en el cual el papel moneda y las monedas tienen el mismo valor de una cantidad de oro determinada.

goods > bienes Objetos físicos que alguien produce.

government monopoly > monopolio gubernamental Monopolio creado por el gobierno.

grant > subvención Cantidad de dinero que otorga una organización gubernamental a una organización o grupo privado con el fin de utilizarlo en una actividad específica.

greenbacks > *greenback* Dinero creado durante la Guerra Civil estadounidense.

gross domestic product > producto interno bruto Valor en dólares de todos los bienes y servicios producidos en un país, en un año específico.

gross national product > producto nacional bruto Ingreso anual que obtienen las compañías y los habitantes de una nación.

guest workers > trabajadores invitados Miembros de la fuerza laboral que vienen de otro país y tienen permiso para vivir y trabajar en Estados Unidos temporalmente.

guns or butter > "pan o armas" Frase que expresa la idea de que un país que decide producir más objetos militares tiene menos recursos para producir bienes de consumo y viceversa.

H

Hayek, Friedrich > Hayek, Friedrich Friedrich Hayek (1899–1992) Economista austriaco que pensaba que la economía funciona mejor sin la interferencia del gobierno. En su libro *Camino de servidumbre,* Hayek sostenía que los mercados libres se autorregulan y que la intervención gubernamental distorsiona los indicadores de precios que permiten la autorregulación.

hedge fund > fondo de inversión libre Organización privada inversionista que emplea estrategias riesgosas para intentar obtener grandes ganancias para los inversionistas.

horizontal merger > fusión horizontal Combinación de dos o más empresas que compiten en el mismo mercado y ofrecen el mismo bien o servicio.

household > unidad familiar Persona o grupo de personas que viven bajo el mismo techo.

human capital > capital humano Conocimientos y destrezas que un trabajador obtiene a través de la educación y la experiencia.

hyperinflation > hiperinflación Inflación descontrolada.

I

imperfect competition > competencia imperfecta Estructura del mercado que no cumple con las condiciones de la competencia perfecta,

import > importaciones Bienes o servicios que se traen de otro país para la venta.

import quota > cuota de importación Límite establecido de la cantidad de un bien que se puede importar.

in-kind benefits > beneficios en especie Bienes y servicios que se ofrecen de forma gratuita o a un precio considerablemente bajo.

incentive > incentivo Esperanza de obtener una recompensa o temor de recibir un castigo que anima a una persona a comportarse de cierta manera.

incidence of a tax > incidencia fiscal Peso final de un impuesto.

income distribution > distribución de ingresos Forma en que se distribuye el ingreso total de una nación entre la población.

income effect > efecto ingreso Cambio en el consumo que ocurre cuando el aumento de un precio hace que el ingreso real disminuya.

increasing marginal returns > aumento del ingreso marginal Nivel de producción en el cual la productividad marginal aumenta a medida que el número de trabajadores aumenta.

individual income tax > impuesto sobre la renta individual Impuesto que se basa en los ingresos de una persona.

industrialization > industrialización Organización de una economía con el propósito de fabricar bienes.

inelastic > demanda inelástica Demanda que es poco sensible a las variaciones de precio.

infant industry > industria en período de arranque Industria en etapa temprana de desarrollo.

infant mortality rate > tasa de mortalidad infantil Número de muertes que ocurren en el primer año de vida por cada 1000 nacimientos.

inferior good > bien inferior Bien cuya demanda disminuye a medida que el ingreso de los consumidores aumenta.

inflation > inflación Aumento general de los precios en una economía.

inflation rate > tasa de inflación Porcentaje de cambio en los precios al transcurrir el tiempo.

inflation-indexed bond > bonos indexados por inflación Bono que protege al inversionista de la inflación porque se ajusta de acuerdo con un índice de inflación.

infrastructure > infraestructura Instalaciones básicas que una sociedad necesita para funcionar y desarrollarse.

innovation > innovación Proceso que consiste en usar nuevos métodos, productos o ideas.

inside lag > demora interna Tiempo que toma implementar una política monetaria.

intellectual property > propiedad intelectual Creaciones como libros, canciones o símbolos compuestos por ideas más que por objetos físicos.

interdependence > interdependencia Necesidad que comparten los países de obtener recursos, bienes, servicios, mano de obra y conocimiento provenientes de otros países.

interest > interés Precio que se paga por el uso de dinero prestado.

interest group > grupo de presión Organización privada que intenta persuadir a miembros de la administración pública de que actúen de una manera que beneficie a los miembros del grupo.

intermediate goods > bienes intermedios Productos usados en la producción de bienes finales.

internal financing > financiamiento interno Capital derivado de los ahorros de los ciudadanos de un país.

inventory > inventario Cantidad de bienes que una empresa tiene a su disposición.

investment > inversión Acto de redirigir recursos del presente para que puedan generar más beneficios en el futuro; uso de los bienes para obtener ingresos o ganancias.

invisible hand > mano invisible Término acuñado por Adam Smith para describir la capacidad del mercado para autorregularse.

J

junk bond > bono basura Bono que representa un gran riesgo y que podría tener un alto rendimiento.

K

Keynes, John Maynard > Keynes, John Maynard John Maynard Keynes (1883–1946) Economista británico de enorme influencia en la forma como los Estados Unidos y otros países emplearon las políticas fiscales para combatir la recesión. En su libro *Teoría general de la ocupación, el interés y el dinero* (1935), Keynes estipulaba que una política gubernamental de pleno empleo es la clave para terminar con la recesión. El presidente Franklin Roosevelt adoptó políticas de gastos keinesianas durante la Gran Depresión.

Keynesian economics > Economía keynesiana Escuela que usa la teoría de la demanda como base para provocar acciones gubernamentales que ayuden a la economía.

L

labor > trabajo Esfuerzo dedicado a tareas por las que se recibe compensación económica.

labor force > mano de obra Toda persona empleada o subempleada que no pertenece a las fuerzas armadas.

labor union > sindicato Organización de trabajadores que busca mejorar las condiciones de trabajo, los salarios y los beneficios laborales de sus miembros.

Laffer, Arthur > Laffer, Arthur Arthur Laffer (1940–) Economista estadounidense que sostiene que reducir las tasas de impuestos federales puede aumentar los ingresos de la federación. La representación gráfica de su teoría, conocida como Curva de Laffer, la cual sustenta la teoría de la economía de oferta, ilustra el efecto de elevar los impuestos en los ingresos fiscales. Laffer fue miembro del Consejo de Asesores en Política Económica del presidente Ronald Reagan.

laissez faire > liberalismo Doctrina que rechaza la intervención del gobierno en el mercado.

land > terreno Todo recurso natural que se utiliza para producir bienes y servicios.

law of comparative advantage > ley de la ventaja comparativa Principio que reconoce la ventaja que disfruta un país cuando puede producir un bien o servicio a menor costo que otro país.

law of demand > ley de la demanda Los consumidores compran más de un bien cuando su precio es bajo y menos cuando su precio es alto.

law of increasing costs > ley de los costos crecientes Principio económico según el cual al producirse un producto o bien adicional, éste requerirá cantidades cada vez mayores de recursos para aumentar su producción.

law of supply > ley de la oferta Los fabricantes proveen más de un bien cuando su precio sube y menos cuando su precio baja.

leading indicators > indicadores principales Conjunto de variables económicas clave que los economistas utilizan para predecir las futuras tendencias del ciclo económico.

learning effect > efecto aprendizaje Teoría que sostiene que la educación incrementa la productividad y por consiguiente genera mayores sueldos.

legal equality > igualdad legal Principio según el cual todas las personas tienen los mismos derechos legales.

less developed country > país en vías de desarrollo Nación con un bajo nivel de bienestar material.

liability > responsabilidad Obligación legal de pagar deudas.

license > licencia Permiso que el gobierno otorga a empresas para que puedan operar.

life expectancy > expectativa de vida Promedio de vida anticipado de una persona.

limited liability corporation > corporación de responsabilidad limitada Compañía que tiene propietarios con responsabilidad limitada y no paga el impuesto sobre sociedades.

limited liability partnership > sociedad de responsabilidad limitada Sociedad en la que la responsabilidad de los socios está limitada al capital aportado.

limited partnership > sociedad limitada Tipo de sociedad que solamente requiere un socio general.

liquidity > liquidez Capacidad para utilizar el dinero o para convertir algo en dinero fácilmente.

literacy rate > índice de alfabetización Proporción de la población mayor de 15 años de un país que sabe leer y escribir.

Lorenz Curve > Curva de Lorenz Curva que ilustra la distribución de los ingresos.

M

macroeconomics > Macroeconomía Estudio del comportamiento y la toma de decisiones de toda la economía nacional.

malnutrition > desnutrición Nutrición inadecuada continua.

mandatory spending > gasto obligatorio Gasto que el Congreso debe realizar de acuerdo con leyes vigentes.

marginal benefit > beneficio marginal Beneficio adicional que surge al añadirse una unidad.

marginal cost > costo marginal Costo que resulta al producirse una unidad adicional de un producto.

marginal product of labor > producto marginal del trabajo Producción adicional que se obtiene con una unidad adicional de trabajo.

marginal revenue > ingreso marginal Ingreso recibido al vender una unidad más de producto; en algunos casos similar al precio.

market > mercado Cualquier arreglo que les permite a compradores y vendedores intercambiar cosas.

market basket > canasta de mercado Conjunto representativo de bienes y servicios.

market demand schedule > tabla de demanda Tabla que muestra la cantidad de un producto determinado que los consumidores de un mercado estarían dispuestos a comprar a diferentes precios.

market failure > falla del mercado Situación en la que el mercado, operando de forma autónoma, asigna recursos ineficientemente.

market power > poder de mercado Capacidad de una empresa para influir en los precios y la producción del mercado.

market supply curve > curva de oferta Gráfico que ilustra la cantidad de un producto que las empresas proveerán a diferentes precios.

market supply schedule > tabla de oferta Tabla que muestra la cantidad de un producto determinado que las empresas proveerán a diferentes precios.

maturity > vencimiento Día en que se cumple el plazo dado para el pago de una deuda u obligación.

mediation > mediación Proceso de resolución en el que una persona neutral, el mediador, se reúne con las partes en conflicto para hallar una solución mutuamente aceptable.

medical benefits > beneficios médicos Seguro de salud otorgado por el gobierno para niños, ancianos y personas discapacitadas o pobres.

medium of exchange > medio de intercambio Estructura que se utiliza para asignar valor a algo durante un intercambio de bienes y servicios.

member banks > banco miembro Banco que pertenece al Sistema de la Reserva Federal.

merger > fusión Proceso mediante el cual dos o más compañías se unen para formar una sola.

microeconomics > Microeconomía Estudio del comportamiento económico de unidades individuales de decisión tales como familias y empresas.

minimum wage > salario mínimo Cantidad mínima que un empleador puede pagar a un empleado por la hora de trabajo.

mixed economy > economía mixta Sistema económico de mercado en el que el gobierno tiene cierto grado de intervención.

monetarism > monetarismo Doctrina que sostiene que el control del dinero en circulación es el factor más importante en el comportamiento macroeconómico de la economía.

monetary policy > política monetaria Medidas que el Sistema de la Reserva Federal utiliza para conseguir la estabilidad del PIB real y de la tasa de inflación de la economía.

money > dinero Todo lo que sirve como medio de cambio, unidad de cuenta y depósito de valor.

money creation > emisión de dinero Proceso que pone en circulación billetes y monedas.

money market > mercado monetario o de dinero Mercado que ofrece créditos por períodos de un año o menos.

money market mutual funds > fondos mutuales Fondo que reúne el dinero de pequeños ahorristas para comprar instrumentos de crédito a corto plazo emitidos por el gobierno o el sector privado.

money multiplier formula > fórmula del multiplicador monetario Fórmula que se utiliza para calcular la cantidad de dinero que cada depósito a la vista puede añadir a la oferta de dinero.

money supply > oferta monetaria Todo el dinero disponible en la economía de los Estados Unidos.

monopolistic competition > competencia monopolística Situación de mercado en la que muchas empresas venden bienes que son similares, pero no idénticos.

monopoly > monopolio Situación de mercado en la que un solo vendedor controla la oferta.

mortgage > hipoteca Tipo de préstamo que se utiliza para comprar bienes inmuebles.

multinational corporation > compañía multinacional Gran empresa que produce y vende sus bienes y servicios en más de un país.

multiplier effect > efecto multiplicador Concepto según el cual por cada dólar de cambio en una política fiscal, se producirá un cambio aún mayor en el ingreso nacional.

municipal bond > bono público Bono emitido por un estado, gobierno local o municipio para financiar obras públicas.

mutual fund > fondo de inversión Organización que reúne los ahorros de múltiples individuos e invierte el dinero en una cartera de acciones, bonos y otros activos financieros,

N

national bank > banco nacional Banco regulado por el gobierno federal.

national debt > deuda nacional Cantidad total de dinero que el gobierno federal debe a sus acreedores.

national income accounting > contabilidad nacional Sistema que los economistas utilizan para recopilar y organizar estadísticas macroeconómicas sobre producción, ingresos, inversión y ahorros.

natural monopoly > monopolio natural Mercado que funciona más eficientemente cuando una sola empresa produce un bien o servicio.

need > necesidad Algo considerado esencial para sobrevivir.

negative marginal return > rendimientos marginales negativos Cuando la adición de una unidad de trabajo ocasiona la reducción de la producción total.

net worth > patrimonio neto El total de los activos menos las deudas.

newly industrialized country > país recientemente industrializado País no completamente industrializado que ha logrado grandes avances en el desarrollo de su economía.

nominal GDP > PBI nominal Producto interno bruto medido en precios actuales.

non-price competition > competencia sin precios Estrategia para atraer consumidores enfocándose en el estilo, el servicio o la ubicación de un bien, sin tener que bajar su precio.

non-price determinants > factores distintos del precio Elementos distintos al precio que pueden afectar la demanda de un bien o servicio en particular.

nondurable goods > bienes perecederos Bienes que duran un corto período como comida, bombillas y zapatos deportivos.

nongovernmental organizations > organizaciones no gubernamentales Grupos independientes que recaudan dinero para financiar programas de ayuda y desarrollo.

nonprofit organization > organización sin fines de lucro Institución que funciona como una empresa, pero no opera con el propósito de generar ganancias.

normal good > bien normal Bien que el consumidor demanda más cuando sus ingresos aumentan.

O

obsolescence > obsolescencia Situación que ocurre cuando productos o procesos antiguos caen en desuso.

offshoring > deslocalización Traslado de las plantas productivas de una empresa a otro país.

oligopoly > oligopolio Estructura en la cual el mercado está dominado por unas pocas grandes empresas.

open market operations > operaciones de mercado abierto Compra y venta de valores del Estado para controlar la cantidad de dinero en circulación.

open opportunity > oportunidad abierta Principio que sostiene que cualquier persona puede competir en el mercado.

operating budget > presupuesto de operación Presupuesto para los gastos diarios.

operating cost > costo de operación Costo de operar instalaciones como fábricas y tiendas.

opportunity cost > costo de oportunidad Mejor alternativa que se desechó al tomarse una decisión.

options > opciones Contratos que le dan al inversionista el derecho de comprar o vender acciones u otros activos financieros a un determinado precio y dentro de un cierto período de tiempo.

outside lag > demora externa Cantidad de tiempo que demora en surtir efecto una política monetaria.

outsourcing > subcontratación Práctica que consiste en contratar a otra compañía para realizar una tarea específica que los trabajadores de la compañía original podrían haber hecho.

P

par value > valor nominal Valor original de un bono u obligación que debe pagarse a su vencimiento.

partnership > sociedad Dos o más personas organizadas para un fin comercial y con una división específica de responsabilidades y ganancias.

patent > patente Licencia que otorga al inventor de un nuevo producto el derecho exclusivo de venderlo por un determinado período de tiempo.

patriotism > patriotismo Amor por el país propio.

peak > punto máximo Máxima expansión económica, cuando el PIB cesa de crecer.

per capita GDP > PIB per cápita Producto interno bruto de un país dividido entre su población.

perfect competition > competencia perfecta Estructura del mercado en la que un gran número de negocios producen el mismo producto y ningún vendedor controla por sí solo la oferta o los precios.

personal exemption > deducción personal Cantidad fija que el contribuyente puede deducir de su ingreso bruto a cuenta de sí mismo, su cónyuge y otros dependientes.

personal property > propiedad personal Activos o bienes muebles.

physical capital > capital físico Objetos construidos que se utilizan para crear bienes y servicios.

population growth rate > tasa de crecimiento de la población Medida de cuán rápido crece la población de un país en un año.

portfolio > portafolio Conjunto de activos financieros.

poverty rate > tasa de pobreza Porcentaje de personas que viven en hogares con un ingreso por debajo de la línea de pobreza.

poverty threshold > nivel de pobreza Ingreso por debajo del nivel necesario para mantener a una familia o un hogar.

predatory pricing > precios depredatorios Vender un producto por debajo de su costo por un corto período de tiempo para sacar a los competidores del mercado.

price ceiling > precio tope Precio máximo que un vendedor puede cobrar legalmente por un bien o servicio.

price discrimination > discriminación de precios Práctica que consiste en dividir a los consumidores en grupos según la cantidad que están dispuestos a pagar por un bien.

price fixing > fijación de precios Acuerdo entre compañías para cobrar un determinado precio por el mismo bien.

price floor > precio mínimo Límite inferior al que puede llegar el precio de un bien o servicio.

price index > índice de precios Medida que muestra el cambio del precio promedio de un grupo de bienes estándar durante un tiempo determinado.

price level > nivel de precios Promedio de los precios en una economía.

price war > guerra de precios Serie de cortes de precio competitivos que reduce el precio de mercado por debajo de su costo de producción.

primary market > mercado primario Mercado para vender activos financieros que pueden ser cobrados sólo por el propietario original.

prime rate > tipo de interés preferencial Tipo de interés que un banco aplica a los préstamos de corto plazo de sus mejores clientes.

principal > capital Cantidad de dinero prestado.

private property > propiedad privada Propiedad que le pertenece a individuos o a compañías, no al gobierno o al público en general.

private property rights > derechos de propiedad privada Principio según el cual una persona tiene el derecho de controlar y usar sus pertenencias como quiera.

private sector > sector privado Parte de la economía que tiene que ver con los negocios de individuos y de compañías.

privatization > privatización Proceso de venta de compañías o servicios operados por el gobierno a inversionistas individuales para que compitan en el mercado.

producer cooperative > cooperativa de productores Cooperativa agraria que ayuda a sus miembros a vender sus productos.

product market > mercado de productos Lugar de intercambio comercial en el que un hogar compra bienes y servicios de empresas.

production possibilities curve > curva de posibilidades de producción Gráfico que muestra distintas maneras de utilizar los recursos de producción en una economía.

production possibilities frontier > frontera de posibilidades de producción Línea en una curva de posibilidad de producción que indica el límite máximo de lo que puede producir una economía.

productive capacity > capacidad de producción Volumen máximo de producción que una economía puede sostener por un período de tiempo sin que aumente la inflación.

productivity of labor > productividad Cantidad de rendimiento que genera una unidad de trabajo.

professional labor > trabajo profesional Trabajo que requiere habilidades y estudios avanzados.

professional organization > organización profesional Organización sin fines de lucro que busca mejorar la imagen, las condiciones de trabajo y la competencia técnica de individuos que ejercen una determinada profesión.

profit > ganancias Cantidad de dinero que una compañía recibe al deducirse sus gastos.

profit motive > motivación de ganancia Incentivo que conlleva al individuo o a la compañía a mejorar su bienestar material.

progressive tax > impuesto progresivo Impuesto cuyo porcentaje aumenta al aumentar el ingreso del contribuyente.

property tax > impuesto sobre la propiedad Impuesto basado en bienes inmuebles y otros tipos de propiedad.

proportional tax > impuesto proporcional Impuesto cuyo porcentaje permanece constante en cualquier nivel de ingreso.

prospectus > prospecto Documento que provee información pertinente a posibles inversionistas.

protectionism > proteccionismo Uso de barreras comerciales para proteger las industrias domésticas de los competidores extranjeros.

public disclosure laws > ley de divulgación pública Ley que exige que una compañía provea información acerca de sus productos o servicios.

public good > bien público Bien que satisface una necesidad pública o colectiva por lo que resulta ineficiente hacer pagar a los consumidores individualmente.

public interest > interés público Preocupaciones de la sociedad en conjunto.

public sector > sector público Parte de la economía que tiene que ver con los negocios del gobierno.

publicly held corporation > compañía pública Corporación que vende acciones en el mercado abierto.

purchasing power > poder adquisitivo Capacidad para comprar bienes y servicios.

pure competition > competencia pura Una estructura de mercado en la que muchas empresas elaboran el mismo producto y ningún vendedor individual controla la distribución ni el precio. También es llamada competencia perfecta.

put option > opción de venta Contrato para vender acciones a un determinado precio durante un período de tiempo preestablecido.

Q

quantity supplied > cantidad ofrecida Cantidad que un proveedor está dispuesto a ofrecer por un precio específico.

quantity theory > teoría de la cantidad Teoría de acuerdo con la cual la presencia de mucho dinero en la economía causa inflación.

R

rationing > racionamiento Sistema de distribución de los bienes y servicios escasos usando un criterio que no se basa en el precio.

real GDP > PIB real PIB expresado a precios constantes o invariables.

real GDP per capita > PIB real per cápita PIB real dividido por la población total de un país.

real property > inmueble Terreno y cualquier estructura permanente en el terreno que le pertenece a una persona según un título legal.

recession > recesión Contracción económica prolongada.

referendum > referendo Propuesta de ley que se somete directamente al público.

regressive tax > impuesto regresivo Impuesto para el cual el porcentaje de ingresos que se paga disminuye a medida que el ingreso aumenta.

regulation > regulación Intervención del gobierno en un mercado que afecta la producción de un bien.

remittances > remesas Pagos en efectivo que les envían los trabajadores inmigrantes a sus familiares en sus países de origen.

rent control > control de renta Precio tope del alquiler de apartamentos.

representative money > dinero representativo Objetos que tienen valor porque su dueño lo puede cambiar por otros objetos de valor.

required reserve ratio > tasa de encaje Fracción de los depósitos que los bancos tienen que guardar en reserva.

reserve requirements > encaje Cantidad de reservas que los bancos deben mantener disponibles.

reserves > reservas Depósitos que un banco tiene disponible, en vez de prestarlos.

return > rendimiento Dinero que un inversionista recibe por encima de la suma de dinero original que invirtió.

revenue > ingreso Dinero recibido por un gobierno que proviene de los impuestos y otras fuentes que no son fiscales.

right-to-work law > ley de derecho al trabajo Medida que establece que no es obligatorio ser miembro de un sindicato.

royalties > regalías Ganancias compartidas que otorga el dueño de una franquicia como pago a quien otorga la concesión.

S

safety net > programas de ayuda social Grupo de programas del gobierno que protegen a las personas con dificultades económicas.

sales tax > impuesto a las ventas Impuesto sobre los bienes y servicios que se venden.

sanctions > sanciones Acciones que una nación o un grupo de naciones toma para castigar o presionar a otra nación.

saving > ahorro Ingreso que no se consume.

savings bond > bono de ahorro Bono de baja denominación ofrecido por el gobierno de los Estados Unidos.

savings rate > tasa de ahorro Proporción de los ingresos disponibles que se ahorran.

scarcity > escasez Situación en la que existe una cantidad limitada de bienes y servicios disponibles para satisfacer deseos ilimitados.

screening effect > efecto de selección Teoría de que completar estudios universitarios indica que un candidato a un empleo es inteligente y trabaja duro.

search cost > costo de búsqueda Costos financieros y de oportunidad que los consumidores pagan mientras buscan un bien o servicio.

seasonal unemployment > desempleo estacional Tipo de desempleo que ocurre durante las cosechas y las vacaciones, o cuando las industrias establecen turnos durante ciertos períodos especiales de su calendario de producción.

secondary market > mercado secundario Mercado en el que se revenden bienes financieros.

security > valor Documento financiero, como una acción o un bono, que representa la posesión de acciones de una empresa o la promesa de pago por parte de una empresa o un gobierno.

self-interest > interés personal Beneficio de una persona.

semi-skilled labor > trabajo semicalificado Trabajo que requiere destrezas especializadas y educación mínimas.

service cooperative > cooperativa de servicios Tipo de cooperativa que ofrece un servicio en vez de un bien.

services > servicios Acciones o actividades que una persona ejecuta para otra persona.

share > acción Porción del capital de una empresa.

short-term loans > préstamos a corto plazo Cada uno de los Bancos regionales de la Reserva Federal permitía a los bancos miembros tomar préstamos para hacer frente a sus necesidades de corto plazo. Esto servía para evitar colapsos bancarios que ocurrían cuando grandes cantidades de depositantes retiraban su dinero durante situaciones de pánico.

shortage > escasez Situación en la que los consumidores quieren un bien o servicio en una cantidad mayor a la que los productores están dispuestos a producir a un precio determinado.

skilled labor > trabajo calificado Trabajo que requiere destrezas y capacitación profesional especializadas.

Smith, Adam > Smith, Adam Adam Smith (1723–1790) El primer economista moderno, cuyo libro *La riqueza de las naciones* describe la forma en que el mercado libre funciona y se autorregula. Además de su trabajo en economía, Smith publicó textos sobre filosofía moral. Su pensamiento económico influyó a muchos países del mundo entero, entre ellos los Estados Unidos.

socialism > socialismo Serie de sistemas económicos y políticos que se basan en la creencia de que la riqueza de una sociedad debe ser distribuida en partes iguales entre sus miembros.

sole proprietorship > empresa unipersonal Negocio que le pertenece y es administrado por un solo individuo.

special economic zones > zonas económicas especiales Regiones designadas que operan bajo leyes económicas distintas al resto del país con el fin de atraer la inversión extranjera y promover las exportaciones.

specialization > especialización Concentración del esfuerzo productivo de las personas y los negocios en un número limitado de actividades.

specie > metálico Dinero en monedas, generalmente de oro o plata, que se usa para respaldar el papel moneda.

speculation > especulación Práctica que consiste en hacer inversiones de alto riesgo con dinero prestado, con la esperanza de obtener una ganancia alta.

stabilization program > programa de estabilización Acuerdo entre una nación deudora y el Fondo Monetario Internacional mediante el cual la nación se compromete a cambiar su política económica para cumplir con los objetivos del FMI.

stagflation > estanflación Disminución del PIB real combinado con un aumento de precios.

standard of living > nivel de vida Nivel de prosperidad económica.

start-up costs > costos de inicio Gastos que un negocio nuevo debe hacer antes de que comience a producir y vender bienes.

stock > acción Certificado de propiedad de parte de una corporación.

stock exchange > bolsa de valores Mercado en el cual se compran y venden acciones.

stock split > desdoble División de cada acción de una compañía en más de una acción.

stockbroker > corredor de bolsa Persona que conecta a compradores y vendedores de la bolsa.

store of value > mantenimiento del valor Algo que mantiene su valor si se guarda, no cuando se gasta.

strike > huelga Suspensión organizada del trabajo, que se ejecuta para obligar a un empleador a cumplir con las peticiones de un sindicato.

structural unemployment > desempleo estructural Tipo de desempleo que ocurre cuando las destrezas de los trabajadores no cubren las necesidades de los empleos disponibles.

subsidy > subsidio Pago del gobierno que apoya un negocio o mercado.

subsistence agriculture > agricultura de subsistencia Tipo de agricultura en el que una persona cosecha sólo lo necesario para mantenerse a sí misma y a su familia.

substitutes > sustitutos Bienes que se usan para reemplazar otros bienes.

substitution effect > efecto de sustitución Reacción de los consumidores ante el aumento del precio de un bien, que consiste en disminuir el consumo de un producto y aumentar el consumo de un sustituto.

supply > oferta Cantidad disponible de bienes.

supply curve > curva de la oferta Gráfica que representa la cantidad ofrecida de un bien a varios precios.

supply schedule > tabla de la demanda Tabla que muestra la cantidad de un bien que un proveedor ofrecerá a diferentes precios.

supply shock > shock de la oferta Escasez repentina de un bien.

supply-side economics > economía por el lado de la oferta Escuela de pensamiento que se basa en la idea de que la oferta de bienes mueve la economía.

surplus > superávit Condición en la que la oferta es mayor que la demanda.

sustainable development > desarrollo sostenible Objetivo que consiste en cubrir las necesidades de desarrollo actuales sin gastar todos los recursos que necesitarán las generaciones futuras.

T

tariff > arancel Impuesto que se aplica a las importaciones.

tariffs > aranceles Impuestos que se aplican a las importaciones.

tax > impuesto Tributo o pago hecho al gobierno local, estatal o nacional.

tax assessor > tasador Especialista que determina el valor de una propiedad.

tax base > base gravable Ingreso, propiedad, bien o servicio bajo obligación tributaria.

tax credit > crédito fiscal Cantidad variable que los contribuyentes pueden restar del total de su deuda tributaria.

tax deduction > deducción fiscal Cantidad variable que los contribuyentes pueden restar de su ingreso bruto.

tax exempt > libre de impuestos Exento de impuestos.

tax incentive > incentivo fiscal Régimen tributario que tiene como objetivo estimular o no fomentar ciertas actividades económicas.

tax return > declaración de impuestos Formulario en el cual se reporta un impuesto, como la declaración de impuestos sobre la renta.

taxable income > ingreso gravable Entradas sobre las cuales se pagan impuestos; ingreso total menos exenciones y deducciones.

technological progress > progreso tecnológico Incremento en la eficiencia al producir más usando menos recursos.

thinking at the margin > pensar al margen Decidir si se debe hacer o usar una cantidad mayor de algún recurso.

tight money policy > política monetaria restrictiva Política monetaria que reduce la oferta de dinero.

total cost > costo total Suma de costos fijos y costos variables.

total revenue > ingreso total Cantidad total de dinero que recibe una compañía al vender bienes y servicios.

trade association > asociación mercantil Organizaciones sin fines de lucro que promueven los intereses de ciertas industrias en particular.

trade barrier > barreras comerciales Medida preventiva que reduce el flujo de bienes o servicios importados a un país.

trade deficit > déficit comercial Situación en la cual las importaciones de bienes y servicios de un país son más altas que sus exportaciones.

trade surplus > superávit comercial Situación en la cual las exportaciones de bienes y servicios de un país son más altas que las importaciones.

trade war > guerra comercial Ciclo en el cual las barreras comerciales escalan.

trade-off > compensación Acto de entregar un beneficio para obtener otro beneficio mayor.

traditional economy > economía tradicional Sistema económico que depende de hábitos, costumbres o rituales para decidir las tres preguntas económicas clave.

Treasury bill > Bono del Tesoro Documento emitido por el Estado con un vencimiento a 26 semanas o menos.

Treasury bond > Bono del Estado Documento emitido por el Estado con un vencimiento a 30 años.

Treasury note > Pagarés del Tesoro Documento emitido por el Estado con un vencimiento de 2 a 10 años.

trough > punto mínimo Punto más bajo en una contracción económica, cuando el PIB real deja de descender.

trust > *trust* Alianza sin fundamentación legal entre compañías para evitar la competencia.

U

underemployed > subempleado Estar calificado en exceso para un trabajo o trabajar a tiempo parcial cuando se desea trabajar a tiempo completo.

underutilization > subutilización Capacidad no utilizada de los recursos que una economía posee.

unemployment rate > tasa de desempleo Porcentaje de la población nacional sin empleo.

Uniform Partnership Act > Ley de Uniformidad de Sociedades Legislación que establece uniformidad en la regulación de las sociedades, y que toda sociedad debe seguir si no cuenta con un acuerdo de sociedad.

unit of account > unidad de cuenta Medida para comparar los valores de bienes y servicios.

unitary elastic > elasticidad unitaria Relación de demanda con un coeficiente igual a uno.

unskilled labor > trabajo no especializado Trabajo que no requiere habilidades, estudios o entrenamiento especializados.

V

variable > variable Factor que puede cambiar.

variable costs > costo variable Costo que aumenta o disminuye cuando la cantidad producida incrementa o disminuye.

vertical mergers > fusión vertical Agrupación de dos o más compañías involucradas en distintas fases de la producción de un bien o servicio.

voluntary exchange > intercambio voluntario Principio según el cual toda persona puede decidir cómo, cuándo y qué vender.

W

wage-price spiral > espiral salarios-precios Aumento de los precios, producido por el aumento de los salarios, que resulta en una nueva demanda de aumento de los salarios.

want > deseo Algo que una persona quiere, pero que no es necesario para sobrevivir.

welfare > asistencia social Ayuda que el gobierno presta a los pobres.

white-collar worker > empleado de oficina Persona que desempeña un trabajo de tipo profesional o administrativo y que generalmente gana un salario semanal.

withholding > retención Porcentaje que se descuenta del salario de un empleado a cuenta del pago de impuestos.

work ethic > ética profesional Respeto al valor del trabajo.

workfare > workfare Programa ofrecido por el gobierno mediante el cual las personas deben trabajar para poder recibir asistencia social temporal.

World Trade Organization > Organización Mundial del Comercio Organización internacional creada para hacer más libre el comercio mundial.

Y

yield > rendimiento Tasa anual de rendimiento que da un bono u obligación a su vencimiento.

Z

zoning laws > reglamentos de zonificación Leyes que designan ciertas áreas o zonas de una ciudad para uso residencial o comercial.

Index

disposable personal income, 274-275
distributed profits, 167, 204
diversification,
    risk, 244
    Spreading, 244
DJIA, 258
Do-it-yourself, 143
doing business as, 25, 120, 131, 162-
    163, 173-174, 189, 235, 258, 328, 340,
    408, 410, 424
dollar,
    bond, 369, 413
    currency, 408, 410
    Denomination, 218
    exchange rates, 408-410
    United States, 24, 40, 215, 220, 407,
      409-410
    weak, 409, 413
dollar value, 270-272, 433
Domestic industries,
    protectionist policies, 401
Dominican Republic, 404
double taxation, 173-174
Dow Jones Averages,
    trading, 173
Dow Jones Industrial Average, 173,
260
DPI, 270, 275
durable goods, 270

E

earned income, 28, 130, 241, 282,
    307-308
    tax rates, 327
Earned Income Tax Credit, 308, 313
Earnings,
    benefit, 188
Earnings gap, 193
economic,
    after recession, 278, 282-283
    benefit, 12, 25, 59
    boom, 371
    capital, 4
    challenges to, 355, 428
    condition, 227
    cost, 25, 59, 100, 298, 313
    crisis, 364
    decision making, 12, 389
    development, 415-416, 418, 424-426,
      434
    effect of, 53, 59, 123, 231, 273, 283,
      327, 377, 380
    efficiency, 16, 37, 58
    equilibrium, 418
    factor, 281
    force, 63
    franchising, 169
    freedom, 25, 44, 46-47, 63
    good, 59, 123, 165
    growth, 52, 352
    growth rate, 285

impact, 63, 313, 361, 385-386, 398
infrastructure, 17, 296
Keynesian, 363
labor, 4, 120, 193
leading indicators, 281
market, 28, 52, 145, 387
new, 6, 52, 100, 176, 201, 288, 357,
    428-429, 436
pressure, 442
price, 52, 69, 123, 162, 281
principle, 46
profit, 165, 241
stability, 51-52
trend, 281
economic activity,
    goods and services, 273, 351
    interest rates, 281, 302, 378, 386
economic benefit, 404
economic boom, 413
economic condition,
    stock market, 53
    unemployment rates, 53, 278, 291, 294
economic crisis, 83, 302, 430
    financial crisis, 378
    Great Depression, 217, 224
economic efficiency,
    in centrally planned economy, 37
economic equity, 24, 32, 331, 345
    in centrally planned economy, 34, 37
economic expansion,
    Business Cycle, 277, 351
    gross domestic product, 269
Economic fluctuations, 278
economic freedom,
    economies, 21
    in centrally planned economy, 21,
      36-38
    in United States, 24, 27, 38-39, 42, 63
    private property, 38-39, 42, 46-47, 65
    standard of living, 25, 38
    U.S. Constitution and, 65
economic growth,
    capital deepening, 284-288, 315
    government in, 51, 53, 55, 284, 360
    in centrally planned economy, 36-37
    in developing countries, 423, 426
    in free enterprise system, 32, 41, 45-
      46, 51, 63, 241-242, 361, 369, 423
    measure, 54, 277, 284, 289, 314
    political factors in, 423
    rate, 376, 421, 433
    sources of, 52, 54, 288-290
    standards of living, 25, 53-54, 284-285,
      287-288, 314, 389, 421
    technological progress, 54, 284, 288-
      290, 315
economic growth rate, 284
    income, 274
economic indicators, 314, 416
    economic activity, 387
    interest rates, 359, 379
economic institutions, 228, 420

economic integration, 430
economic interdependence,
    goods and services, 394
economic law, 85
economic performance, 268-276,
    278-283, 285-290, 292-296, 298-302,
    304-317, 353
economic power,
    goods and services, 405
economic principle, 61, 72
Economic recovery, 291, 364
economic sanctions, 399
economic security, 25, 47
economic stability,
    financial system, 378
economic system,
    centrally planned, 31, 33-38, 41-42, 45,
      63, 119, 428, 436
    centrally planned economy, 21, 33-38
    free market economy, 20, 28-29, 31-
      32, 37-38, 43, 65, 436
    goods and services, 22-25, 28-32, 37,
      40, 45-46, 49, 53, 58-59, 61, 63, 87,
      119
    market economy, 28, 33, 37, 54, 428
    mixed economy, 21, 37-43
    political system and, 34
    traditional economies, 22, 25-26, 38
Economic transition, 38, 41, 428
economic trend, 182
    economy, 381
economic trends, predicting, 381
Economic variables, 278, 280-281, 283
Economic well-being, 61, 396
economies of scale, 142, 175
    industry, 134, 145
    monopolies and, 133-134, 145
economist,
    inflation, 298, 300, 378
    supply and demand, 68, 357
economy,
    developed, 415
    goods and services, 13-14, 28, 32, 45-
      46, 53, 120, 211, 213, 231, 270-273,
      275, 279, 293, 298, 300, 351, 353,
      358-359, 367, 390, 394, 412, 416,
      424, 430
    knowledge, 295
    market, 262, 288, 355, 371, 382
    mixed, 39, 41
    new, 25, 184-185, 279, 354, 371, 381,
      418, 439, 441
    of scope, 230
    oil, 283, 390, 430, 433
    pricing, 24, 66, 118-120, 162, 211, 262,
      264, 273, 275, 283, 297-298, 300,
      302, 352, 359, 383, 403
    subsistence, 432
Edison, Thomas, 136
education,
    economic development and, 425
    Head Start, 313, 365

T

[Maps]

XNR Productions, Inc.

[Photography]

i, Oxford/Getty Images; **iv,** Dfikar/Fotolia; **v,** Goodluz/Shutterstock; **vii,** Fuse/Getty Images; **x,** Viktor Pravdica/Fotolia; **xi,** Image Source/Alamy; **xii,** ZUMA Press, Inc./Alamy; **xiii,** Pavel L Photo and Video/Shutterstock; **xiv,** Diego Cervo/Shutterstock; **xv,** Amazing Images/Alamy; **xvi,** Age fotostock/SuperStock; **xvii,** Joe Belanger/Alamy; **xviii,** Saul Loeb/AFP/Getty Images/Newscom; **xix,** Faraways/Shutterstock; **xxx,** Michael Flippo/Fotolia; **1,** Pat Benic/UPI/Newscom; **4,** Viktor Pravdica/Fotolia; **6,** Randy Faris/Corbis; **10,** Chew Chun Hian/AGE Fotostock; **11,** Chuck Savage/Corbis/Glow Images; **12,** David Grossman/Alamy; **15,** imageBROKER/Alamy; **18,** S Harris/CartoonStock; **24,** Image Source/Alamy; **26,** David Grossman/Alamy; **29T,** Tiffany L. Clark/Demotix/Corbis; **29B,** imageBROKER/Alamy; **31,** Jim West/Alamy; **37,** Jan Sochor/Demotix/Corbis; **41,** Imagebroker/SuperStock; **42,** Ian Dagnall/Alamy; **43T,** Horace Bristol/Corbis; **43B,** Bettmann/Corbis; **48,** Chuck Savage/AGE Fotostock; **50,** David Chapman/Age Fotostock; **51T,** NBC NewsWire/Contributor/Getty Images; **51B,** Blend Images/Shutterstock; **52,** Blend Images/SuperStock; **55,** Joe Raedle/Staff/Getty Images; **60,** John Gress/Corbis; **61,** Songquan Deng/Shutterstock; **63,** Swim Ink 2, LLC/Corbis; **65,** Marmaduke St. John/Alamy; **66,** Jack Corbett/CartoonStock; **72,** ZUMA Press, Inc./Alamy; **74,** Jacob Silberberg/Reuters; **79,** Jeff Greenberg/Age Fotostock; **83,** Ipatov/Shutterstock; **84,** LBarnwell/Alamy; **91,** Uwe Zucchi/dpa/Corbis; **93,** Ariel Skelley/Blend Images/Alamy; **97,** Shannon Faulk/DreamPictures/Blend Images/Corbis; **104,** Bloomberg/Contributor/Getty Images; **106T,** David R. Frazier Photolibrary, Inc./Alamy; **106B,** Ted Spiegel/Corbis; **107,** Jack Corbett/CartoonStock; **108,** Nicolaus Czarnecki/Metro US/ZUMA Press/Corbis; **110,** Bettmann/Corbis; **117,** Scott Audette/Reuters; **118,** American Spirit/Shutterstock; **123,** RosaIreneBetancourt 3/Alamy; **126,** Steve Lewis Stock/Getty Images; **127,** Rick Gomez/Corbis/Glow Images; **128,** S Harris/CartoonStock; **134,** Pavel L Photo and Video/Shutterstock; **136,** Greg Vaughn/Alamy; **138T,** Cavan Images/The Image Bank/Getty Images; **138B,** Robert Landau/Corbis; **141,** Ronald Martinez/Staff/Getty Images; **143,** Mario Tama/Staff/Getty Images; **148,** Kim Karpeles/Alamy; **149,** Patti McConville/Alamy; **151T,** Mark Lynch/Cartoonstock; **151B,** Neil Emmerson/Robert Harding World Imagery/Corbis; **156,** Stock Montage/Contributor/Getty Images; **159,** John-Marshall Mantel/Age Fotostock; **162,** Mia Song/Star Ledger/Corbis; **163,** Everett Collection Historical/Alamy; **168,** Diego Cervo/Shutterstock; **170,** KidStock/Age Fotostock; **172T,** RosaIreneBetancourt 1/Alamy; **172B,** Phelan M. Ebenhack/AP Images; **173T,** Arnie Levin The New Yorker Collection/The Cartoon Bank; **173B,** Jim Craigmyle/Corbis/Glow Images; **175,** John Lund/Drew Kelly/Glow Images; **181,** Jim West/AGE Fotostock; **184T,** Martha Campbell/Cartoonstock; **184B,** Doug Mills/AP Images; **186,** Chad Ehlers/Glow Images; **187,** Imagegallery2/Alamy; **189T,** ZUMA Press, Inc./Alamy; **189B,** John Moore/Staff/Getty Images; **190T,** Ted S. Warren/AP Images; **190B,** RosaIreneBetancourt 4/Alamy; **192,** Handout/Reuters; **199,** Forestpath/Shutterstock; **200,** Children's Healthcare of Atlanta/Reuters; **205T,** Robert Thompson/Cartoonstock; **205B,** Bettmann/Corbis; **206,** Jim West/Alamy; **207,** Everett Collection/SuperStock; **208T,** Randy Pench/ZUMA Press/Newscom; **208B,** North Wind Picture Archives/North Wind; **220,** Amazing Images/Alamy; **222,** 2/Ryan McVay/Ocean/Corbis; **223,** Ilene MacDonald/Alamy; **225,** GP Kidd/Blend Images/Alamy; **226,** Mark Lynch/CartoonStock; **227,** PhotoObjects.net/Getty Images; **228,** De Agostini Picture L/Age Fotostock; **230,** Herbert Orth/Contributor/Getty Images; **231,** Pics-xl/Shutterstock; **232,** Superstock/Glow images; **234,** Randy Faris/Corbis; **235,** Gary Cameron/Reuters/Landov; **240,** Daniel Bendjy/Getty Images; **245,** Robert Glenn/DK Stock/Corbis; **252,** Blue Images/Corbis; **253,** Bloomberg/Contributor/Getty Images; **257T,** Mike Flanagan/CartoonStock; **257B,** Robert Clay/Alamy; **260,** Yuriko Nakao/Reuters; **261,** akg images; **267,** Spencer Platt/Staff/Getty Images; **272,** John McPherson/CartoonStock; **273,** Science & Society Picture Library/Contributor/Getty Images; **275,** Sean Adair/Reuters; **277,** PhotoObjects.net/Getty Images; **282,** Age fotostock/SuperStock; **284,** Hill Street Studios/Blend Images/Corbis; **291,** Jim Urquhart/Reuters; **293,** Alfredo Martirena/Cartoonstock; **294,** DIZ Muenchen GmbH, Sueddeutsche Zeitung Photo/Alamy; **298,** Mike Segar/Reuters; **302,** Eduardo Verdugo/AP Images; **305,** Darrell Byers/Krt/Newscom; **306,** Larry Downing/Reuters; **307,** Bebeto Matthews/AP Images; **311,** Philimon Bulawayo/Reuters; **317,** Jim West/Age Fotostock; **322T,** Tim Larsen/AP Images; **322B,** Mike Stone/Reuters; **324,** Jim West/Alamy; **334,** Joe Belanger/Alamy; **336,** Marjorie Kamys Cotera/Bob Daemmrich Photography/Alamy; **337,** Art Resource, NY; **341,** Ed Fischer/CartoonStock; **342,** Mart of Images/Alamy; **346,** Andrew Evans/CartoonStock; **348,** Miguel Juarez Lugo/ZUMA Press/Newscom; **352,** Joe Raedle/Staff/Getty Images; **353,** Don Kohlbauer/ZUMA Press/Newscom; **364,** Saul Loeb/AFP/Getty Images/Newscom; **366,** Jonathan Ernst/Reuters; **374,** Dorothea Lange/Getty Images; **384,** Rudi Von Briel/Getty Images; **389,** Jeff Morgan 16/Alamy; **391,** Richard Ellis/Alamy; **396,** Mario Tama/Staff/Getty Images; **397,** Leslie Garland Picture Library/Alamy; **408,** Faraways/Shutterstock; **410,** Jim West/Alamy; **414,** Robert VAN DER HILST/Contributor/Getty Images; **416,** David Goldman/AP Images; **418,** Pongmanat Tasiri/EPA/Newscom; **421T,** Rebecca Cook/Reuters; **421B,** Bettmann/Corbis; **422T,** David Brown/Cartoonstock; **422B,** Bob Rowan/Progressive Image/Corbis; **424T,** Jack Corbett/CartoonStock; **424B,** Bloomberg/Contributor/Getty Images; **427,** JeffreyIsaacGreenberg/Alamy; **431,** Abe Fox/AP Images; **435,** Kristian Buus/In Pictures/Corbis; **440,** David Mercado/Reuters; **447,** Lutfallah Daher/AP Images; **448,** Fuyu Liu/Shutterstock; **452,** Kyodo/Newscom; **455,** Supri/Reuters; **457T,** Chung Sung-Jun/Staff/Getty Images; **457B,** Katsumi Kasahara/AP Images; **458,** Ricardo Bufolin/CON/Contributor/Getty Images; **459T,** Imagebroker/SuperStock; **459B,** JGI/Blend Images/Alamy; **461T,** Press Eye Ltd/Rex Features/AP Images; **461B,** Peter & Georgina Bowater Stock Connection Worldwide/Newscom; **468,** Stock Connection Blue/Alamy; **494,** ZUMA Press, Inc./Alamy; **498,** Patti McConville/Alamy; **501,** VStock/Alamy; **502,** Robert Glenn/DK Stock/Corbis; **509,** Mart of Images/Alamy; **511,** YinYang/Getty Images; **512,** Donald Higgs/Getty Images; **516,** Alfredo Martirena/Cartoonstock; **518,** Rob Marmion/Shutterstock; **520,** The Michigan collection/Alamy; **521,** Matt Detrich/AP Images; **523,** Blend Images/SuperStock; **527,** Q-Images/Alamy

[Text Acknowledgments]

60 Minutes, Excerpt from a Will Smith interview. Copyright © 60 Minutes.; **Alfred A. Knopf,** The Negro Speaks of Rivers," and "My People" from THE COLLECTED POEMS OF LANGSTON HUGHES by Langston Hughes, edited by Arnold Rampersad with David Roessel, Associate Editor, copyright © 1994 by the Estate of Langston Hughes. Used by permission of Alfred A. Knopf, an imprint of the Knopf Doubleday Publishing Group, a division of Random House LLC. All rights reserved; **Bloomberg News,** Goolsbee Expects 2012 Washington 'Gridlock' by Alex Kowalski and Tom Keene January 10, 2012. Copyright © 2012 Bloomberg.; **Bonus Books, Inc.,** Conservatives Betrayed: How George W. Bush and Other Big Government Republicans Hijacked the Conservative Cause. by Richard Viguerie. Copyright © 2006 Bonus Books.; **CBS News,** Fed Chairman Ben Bernankes Take on the Economy by Ben Bernankes from the Wall Street Journal, December 05, 2010. Copyright © CBS News.; **Cengage Learning/Global Rights and Permissions Administration,** Major Problems in American History, Volume II: Since 1865 edited by Hoffman, Blum and Gjerde. Copyright © Cengage.; **Center for Effective Government,** The Corporate Tax Rate Debate: Lower Taxes on Corporate Profits Not Linked to Job Creation by the Center for Effective Government. Copyright © the Center for Effective Government.; **CNN,** Owens, Christine. "To help jobs picture, raise the minimum wage." CNN. May 4, 2012.; **CPA Journal,** Bring Back Glass-Steagall, December 2009. Copyright © CPA Journal. Used by permission.; **Doubleday,** Excerpts from "Diary of a Young Girl: The Definitive Edition" by Anne Frank, edited by Otto H. Frank and Mirjam Pressler, translated by Susan Massotty, translation copyright © 1995 by Doubleday, a division of Random House LLC. Used by permission of Doubleday, an imprint of the Knopf Doubleday Publishing Group, a division of Random House LLC. All rights reserved.; **Dover Publications,** How the Other Half Lives by Jacob Riis. Copyright © Dover Publications.; **Earth Policy Institute,** J Matthew Roney, After Record 2012, Work Wind Power Set to Top 300,000 Megawatts in 2013. Economy Indicators, Wind Power. April 2, 2013 www.earth-policy.org; **Facts On File, Inc.,** The FDR Years by William D. Pederson. Copyright © 2009 Infobase Publishing.; **Federal Reserve Bank of Boston,** Putting it Simply—the Federal Reserve. Copyright © 1984 Public Services Department, Federal Reserve Bank of Boston.; **Federal Reserve Bank of Minneapolis,** Born of a Panic: Forming the Federal Reserve System from the Federal Reserve Board, Minneapolis. Copyright © Federal Reserve Bank of Minneapolis.; **Federal Reserve Bank of San Francisco,** "What Are Open Market Operations?" 2014. Copyright © Federal Reserve Bank of San Francisco.; **Forbes Magazine,** Financial Concepts: The Risk/Return Tradeoff from Forbes Magazine. Copyright © Forbes Magazine; **Forbes Media LLC,** Source: Laissez-Faire Capitalism Has